The Teachings of Modern Christianity
on Law, Politics, and Human Nature

{VOLUME 2}

The Teachings of Modern Christianity

❖ ON LAW, POLITICS, AND HUMAN NATURE ❖

{VOLUME 2}

EDITED BY

John Witte Jr. and Frank S. Alexander

For Laurie-Ann
LvR alumna
extraordinary
John

To Laurie-Ann,
with appreciation
for all of your
excellent assistance.
Frank

COLUMBIA UNIVERSITY PRESS   NEW YORK

Columbia University Press
Publishers Since 1893
New York, Chichester, West Sussex
Copyright © 2006 Columbia University Press
All rights Reserved

Library of Congress Cataloging-in-Publication Data

The teachings of modern Christianity on law, politics, and human nature / edited by John
Witte, Jr. and Frank S. Alexander.
     p. cm.
   Includes bibliographical references and index.
   ISBN 0–231–13718–4 (set) — ISBN 0–231–13360–X (v. 2 : cloth : alk. paper) — ISBN
0–231–50832–8 (v. 2 : electronic)
     1. Christian sociology. 2. Man (Christian theology) 3. Christianity and politics. 4.
Christianity and law. I. Witte, John, 1959– II. Alexander, Frank S., 1952–

BT738.T33 2006
261.8—dc22   2006045492

Columbia University Press books are printed on permanent and durable acid-free paper

Printed in the United States of America

c 10 9 8 7 6 5 4 3 2 1

References to Internet Web Sites (URLs) were accurate at the time of writing. Neither the
volume editors, the authors, nor Columbia University Press is responsible for Web Sites
that may have expired or changed since the articles in this book were prepared.

Contents

Acknowledgments   *vii*
Introduction   *ix*

Part I. The Roman Catholic Tradition

1. Pope Leo XIII (1810–1903)   3

2. Jacques Maritain (1882–1973)   34

3. John Courtney Murray (1904–1967)   68

4. Pope John XXIII (1881–1963)   94

5. Gustavo Gutiérrez (b. 1928)   116

6. Dorothy Day (1897–1980)   149

7. Pope John Paul II (1920–2005)   175

Part II. The Protestant Tradition

8. Abraham Kuyper (1837–1920)   219

9. Susan B. Anthony (1820–1906)   249

10. Karl Barth (1886–1968)   280

11. Dietrich Bonhoeffer (1906–1945)   307

12. Reinhold Niebuhr (1892–1971)   343

13. Martin Luther King Jr. (1929–1968)   369

14. William Stringfellow (1928–1985)   387

15. John Howard Yoder (1927–1997)   403

Part III. The Orthodox Tradition

16. Vladimir Soloviev (1853–1900)   425

17. Nicholas Berdyaev (1874–1948)   456

18. Vladimir Nikolaievich Lossky (1903–1958)   487

19. Mother Maria Skobtsova (1891–1945)   512

20. Dumitru Stăniloae (1903–1993)   537

Contributors   559
Copyright Information   561
Index   567

Acknowledgments

THIS VOLUME AND its companion are products of a three-year project of the Law and Religion Program at Emory University. Our project is part of a broader effort of The Pew Charitable Trusts and the University of Notre Dame to stimulate and support new scholarship on the place of Christianity in various fields of academic specialty. Armed with a major grant from The Pew Charitable Trusts, Notre Dame Provost Nathan O. Hatch and his colleagues have assembled ten groups of scholars in such fields as law, philosophy, literature, and economics, who have an interest in the scholarly place of Christianity in their particular discipline. Each of these ten groups of specialists has been asked to address the general theme of "Christianity and the Nature of the Person" from the perspective of its particular discipline. Each group has been asked to produce a major new study that speaks to this theme in a manner that is edifying both to scholars in other fields and to peers of all faiths in its own field.

We have been privileged to lead the team on law. We wish to thank the immensely talented group of contributors to this volume, with whom we have deliberated our project mandate and divided the work. From among this group, we give special thanks to Kent Greenawalt for his sage advice on the structure of these volumes; Russell Hittinger, Patrick Brennan, and Angela Carmella for helping us shape the Catholic materials; Milner Ball, Timothy Jackson, and Nicholas Wolterstorff for helping us shape the Protestant materials; and Vigen Guroian, Paul Valliere, and Mikhail Kulakov for helping us shape the Orthodox materials. We also wish to thank other scholars who offered us advice and criticism at the early stages of this project: James Billington, Librarian of Congress; Wolfgang Huber, Bishop of Berlin-Brandenburg; Judge Michael McConnell; as well as Kathy Caveny, John Erickson, Jon Gunnemann, Emily Hartigan, Jaroslav Pelikan, Jefferson

Powell, Steven Smith, Steven Tipton, Robert Tuttle, Johan van der Vyver, Joseph Vining, and Paul Zahl.

On behalf of our colleagues in the Law and Religion Program, we express our deep gratitude to our friends at The Pew Charitable Trusts for their generous support of this project, particularly Pew's president, Rebecca Rimel, and program officers Luis Lugo, Susan Billington Harper, and Diane Winston. We also express our gratitude to our friends at the University of Notre Dame, particularly Nathan Hatch, Kurt Berends, and Linda Bergling.

We wish to thank Craig Dykstra and his colleagues at the Lilly Endowment in Indianapolis for their generous grant in support of John Witte's project "Law, Religion, and the Protestant Tradition," which has provided him with release time to work on this and other book projects.

We wish also to recognize and thank several of our colleagues in the Law and Religion Program for their exceptional work on the administration of this project and the production of these two volumes. We are particularly grateful to Linda King for masterminding the administration of this project, for coordinating the three conferences that it occasioned, and for working so expertly and assiduously on the production of these manuscripts. We express our gratitude to Anita Mann, Amy Wheeler, Eliza Ellison, and Janice Wiggins for sharing so generously of their administrative expertise, and William J. Haines and Kelly Parker for their impeccable library services.

We owe a special word of thanks to Ms. Laurie-Ann Fallon, a joint degree student in the Law and Religion Program, for her excellent work in taking lead responsibility for assembling and verifying the selections in these chapters.

We thank Wendy Lochner and her colleagues at Columbia University Press for taking on these volumes and working so efficiently and effectively to ensure their timely production. We appreciate as well the very helpful criticisms and suggestions of the three anonymous outside reviewers of an earlier version of this manuscript.

Finally, we dedicate this volume to the students of the Law and Religion Program at Emory University, past, present, and future.

Introduction

UNTIL RECENTLY, MODERN Western Christian teachings on law, politics, and society have been lost on much of the modern academy. To be sure, the valuable contributions of a few modern Christian lights, such as Reinhold Niebuhr and Martin Luther King Jr., have long been closely studied. And, to be sure, medieval and early modern Christian influences on the later Western legal tradition have been recognized. But the prevailing view of most scholars has been that, for good or ill, the historical contributions of Christianity to our understanding of law, politics, and society have been gradually eclipsed in the modern period. Outside of specialist discussions of natural law and church-state relations, it has been widely assumed, modern Christianity has had little constructive or original to say.

The premise of this volume and its companion is that modern Christianity did have a great deal to say about law, politics, and society, and that its teachings can still have a salutary influence today, in the West and well beyond. To be sure, many quarters of modern Christianity did become theologically anemic, ethically compromised, and jurisprudentially barren. But in each generation, we submit, strong schools of Christian legal, political, and social teaching remained, each grounded in a rich and nuanced Christian theology, particularly a theology of human nature or, more technically, a theological anthropology. Most of the best such teaching emerged outside of the legal profession—in seminaries and church councils, among philosophers and ethicists, on soapboxes and in prison cells, in intellectual isolation if not outright exile. But by word, by deed, and by declaration, modern Christians addressed the cardinal issues of law, politics, and society drawing on a rich theology of human nature.

These two volumes sample these teachings and map their insights for the most pressing issues of our day. Such issues include topics that are familiar to scholars of law, politics, and society whatever their persuasion:

the nature and purpose of law and authority, the mandate and limits of rule and obedience, the rights and duties of officials and subjects, the care and nurture of the needy and innocent, the rights and wrongs of war and violence, the separation and cooperation of church and state, and the sources and sanctions of legal reasoning, among others. Such issues also include questions that are more specifically Christian in accent but no less important for our understanding of law, politics, and society: Are persons fundamentally good or evil? Is human dignity essentially rational or relational? Is law inherently coercive or liberating? Is law a stairway to heaven or a fence against hell? Did government predate or postdate the fall into sin? Should authorities only proscribe vices or also prescribe virtues? Is the state a divine or a popular sovereign? Are social institutions fundamentally hierarchical or egalitarian in internal structure and external relations? Are they rooted in creation or custom, covenant or contract? What is justice, and what must a Christian do in its absence?

We have prepared two companion volumes on twenty leading modern Catholic, Protestant, and Orthodox Christians who addressed these types of questions. This volume presents a convenient anthology of illustrative primary writings by modern theologians, philosophers, ethicists, jurists, statesmen, and clerics who spoke to many issues of law, politics, and society on the strength of their theological anthropology—or spoke to one or two issues with particular acuity and originality. The primary texts included herein are drawn from authoritative editions or are freshly translated, presented with critical notes and a brief introduction. (The notes at the end of each chapter are original to the primary sources unless they are identified by brackets; in some instances in text, however, the authors' original citations have been omitted silently. Endnotes in brackets have been added by the editors.) The companion volume provides a set of freshly commissioned analytical essays on these same twenty Christian figures, and it also provides introductory chapters on the Catholic, Protestant, and Orthodox traditions.

For reasons set out in our fuller introduction to the companion volume, these volumes focus on *modern* Christian teachings on law, politics, society, and human nature. *Modern, modernism,* and *modernity* are highly contested labels these days—not least within Christian churches, where the terms have often been associated with dangerous liberal tendencies. We are using the term *modern* nontechnically. We are focused principally on twentieth-century Christianity, reaching back into the later nineteenth century to understand movements that culminated in the twentieth century and that affected Christianity. The era under purview includes the Reconstruction era after the American Civil War, the later Industrial Revolution, the Bolshevik Revolution and the emergence of socialism, two world wars, the Holocaust and the Stalinist purges, the modern human rights revolution, the Great Depression and the rise of the Western welfare state, and the technological revolution and the emergence of globalization, among other movements. These modern moments and movements had monumental, and sometimes devastating, impacts on modern Christianity.

We have deliberately used the term *teachings*, rather than theories, theologies, or other formal labels to describe what modern Christianity has offered to law, politics, and society. In part, this is to underscore that the call to "teach" is what all Christians, despite their vast denominational differences, have in common. Christ's last words to his disciples, after all, were: "Go ye, therefore, and make disciples of all nations ... *teaching* them to observe all that I have commanded you" (Matt. 28:20). In part, this is to recognize that the terms "social teachings"—as well as "political teachings," "moral teachings" and "legal teachings"—have become terms of art in current scholarship. Particularly in the current Catholic and Protestant worlds, "social teaching" has now become shorthand for a fantastic range of speculation on issues of law, politics, society, and morality. And, in part, we use the term *teachings* to underscore that modern Christians have contributed to our understanding of law, politics, and society both by word and by deed, by books and by speeches, by brilliant writings and by sacrificial acts. It would be foolish to dismiss the novel teachings of Susan Anthony and Dorothy Day just because they had thin résumés. It would be equally foolish not to draw lessons from the martyrdom of Mother Maria and Dietrich Bonhoeffer just because they left their papers in disarray.

We have divided these twenty figures into Catholic, Protestant, and Orthodox Christian groups, even while recognizing that some of these figures were more ecumenically minded than others. We have arranged the chapters on these figures, in both volumes, more or less chronologically for each tradition. We have assigned varying word limits to the chapters and selections for each figure in accordance with their relative importance for the themes of these volumes.

With respect to the Catholic tradition, we have blended episcopal and lay voices from both sides of the Atlantic. Popes Leo XIII, John XXIII, and John Paul II offered the most original and enduring contributions among modern popes, though Pope Pius XII was critical as well. Leo XIII led the revival and reconstruction of the thought of thirteenth-century sage Thomas Aquinas. He applied this "neo-Thomism," as it was called, to the formulation of several of the church's core "social teachings," not least a theory of social institutions that would later ripen into subsidiarity doctrine, and a theory of labor that would later form the backbone of the church's stand for social, cultural, and economic rights. John XXIII was the architect of the Second Vatican Council (1962–1965) with its transforming vision of religious liberty, human dignity, and democracy and with its deliberate agenda to modernize the Catholic Church's political platforms and social teachings. John Paul II, who faced the ravages of both Nazi occupation and the Communist takeover of his native Poland, was a fierce champion of democratization and human rights in the first years of his pontificate, as well as an active sponsor of rapprochement among Catholics, Protestants, and Jews and of revitalization of canon law. In recent years before his death, he became an equally fierce critic of the growing secularization of society, liberalization of theology, and exploitation of human nature. These latter concerns have led the Catholic leadership to new (and sometimes controversial) interpretations of the church's earlier "social teachings."

The French philosopher Jacques Maritain and the American theologian John Courtney Murray were among the most original and influential of the many European and American Catholic writers in the mid-twentieth century. Maritain combined neo-Thomism and French existentialism into an intricate new theory of natural law, natural rights, human dignity, equality, and fraternity, which helped to inspire the Universal Declaration of Human Rights (1948). Murray combined neo-Thomism and American democratic theory into a powerful new argument for natural law, human dignity, religious liberty, church-state relations, and social organization. Both theories were initially controversial. Murray was censored for a time by the church; Maritain was blistered by his reviewers. But these two figures, and the many scholars whom they influenced, laid much of the foundation for the Second Vatican Council's declaration on human dignity and religious freedom, and the church's emerging global advocacy of human rights and democratization.

Both American political activist Dorothy Day and Latin American liberation theologian Gustavo Gutiérrez represent important new strains of social and political critique and activism within modern Catholicism. Day defied state and church authorities alike in her relentless crusade to protect the rights of workers and the poor, and to protest warfare, grounding her work in a robust theology of personalism. Gutiérrez combined some of the teachings of Vatican II and Marxism into a searing critique of global capitalism and its devastating impact on the poor and on the underdeveloped world. Both Day and Gutiérrez adduced scripture above all to press for a preferential option for the poor, the needy, and the vulnerable. Although both these figures have been controversial and drawn episcopal censure, they have helped to illustrate, if not inspire, many new forms of social and political activism among Catholics worldwide.

The Protestant tradition, with its hundreds of independent denominations that share only the Bible as their common authority, did not lend itself to easy illustration. We present Abraham Kuyper and Karl Barth as two strong and independent thinkers who addressed, and sometimes defined, many of the main themes of law, politics, society, and human nature that have occupied many modern Protestants. Kuyper, though not so well known today, was something of the Leo XIII of his day. He called for a return to the cardinal teachings of the sixteenth-century Protestant Reformation, and developed a comprehensive Reformed theory of human nature and human knowledge. He also developed an important new "sphere sovereignty" theory of liberty, democracy, and social institutions, which would become a Protestant analogue, if not answer, to Catholic subsidiarity theory. If Kuyper was the Leo of modern Protestantism, Barth was the Maritain. This brilliant Swiss theologian produced the most comprehensive Protestant dogmatic system of the twentieth century, centered on the Bible and on Christ. Many theories of law, politics, and society were embedded in his massive writings, not least Barth's famous critique of theories of natural law and natural rights, the source of a strong tendency against naturalism and rights among many later Protestants. Most memorable of all was Barth's leadership in crafting the Barmen Declaration of 1934 that denounced the emerging laws and policies of Adolf Hitler and the Nazi Party.

German theologian Dietrich Bonhoeffer knew firsthand about Nazi belligerence, for he was killed in a concentration camp for conspiring to assassinate Hitler. Bonhoeffer's decision to join this conspiracy had required a complex rethinking of his own Lutheran tradition of political ethics and Christian discipleship, and of the proper relations of the church and its members to a world that had abandoned reason and religion in pursuit of tribalism and totalitarianism. Bonhoeffer's American contemporary Reinhold Niebuhr saw some of these same lusts for power and self-interest in modern states and corporations alike. Building on the classic Protestant doctrine of total depravity, Niebuhr developed an applied theology of Christian realism that prized democratic government, but with strong checks and balances, that protected human rights but informed by moral duties, and that championed racial equality and economic justice.

We have included Susan B. Anthony, a freethinking Quaker, as an early exemplar of an important tendency of modern American Protestants to counsel both legal disobedience and legal reform at once on selected issues. Today, these Protestant political preoccupations include abortion, same-sex marriage, and religion in public schools. For Anthony, the cardinal issue was women's rights. Using basic biblical texts as her guide, Anthony worked relentlessly to affect many legal reforms in Congress and the states, not least passage of the Nineteenth Amendment to the United States Constitution, the world's first modern constitutional guarantee of a woman's right to vote.

Both Martin Luther King Jr. and William Stringfellow later led comparable movements for racial and economic justice, although they both grounded their advocacy more deeply in traditional biblical warrants and allied themselves more closely with the church. King, "America's Amos," used pulpit, pamphlet, and political platform alike to lead America to greater racial justice, including passage of the Civil Rights Act of 1964. When he faced political opposition and repression, King also developed a novel theology of nonviolent resistance to authority. William Stringfellow spent much of his career representing the interests of the poor and needy in Harlem as well as those who protested America's war policy, appearing in several sensational cases. He grounded his work in a novel Protestant theory of law and gospel. The Mennonite theologian John Howard Yoder likewise pressed for social and economic justice and democratic virtues on the strength of a classic Anabaptist biblicism and pacifism coupled with a new appreciation for natural law, human rights, and democratization.

We have thought it imperative to give ample time and space in the volumes to the Eastern Orthodox tradition. Many leading Orthodox lights dealt with fundamental questions of law, politics, society, and human nature with novel insight, often giving a distinct reading and rendering of the biblical, apostolic, and patristic sources. Moreover, the Orthodox Church has immense spiritual resources and experiences whose implications are only now beginning to be seen. These spiritual resources lie, in part, in Orthodox worship—the passion of the liturgy, the pathos of the icons, the power of spiritual silence. They lie, in part, in Orthodox church life—the distinct balancing between hierarchy and congregationalism through autocephaly, between uniform worship and liturgical freedom through alternative vernacular rites, between community and individuality through a trinitarian communalism, centered on the parish, on the extended family, on the wizened grandmother, the *babushka*. And these spiritual resources lie, in part, in the massive martyrdom of millions of Orthodox faithful in the last century.

To illustrate the potential of some of these Orthodox resources and the rich theological anthropologies that Orthodox has already produced, we have selected three key Russian Orthodox scholars—Soloviev, Berdyaev, and Lossky. Each of these figures interacted with several Western Christian thinkers. Each challenged the (increasingly compromised) Russian Orthodox authorities of their day, even while channeling the best theology and jurisprudence of the Russian Orthodox tradition into fundamentally new directions. Vladimir Soloviev, a philosopher, was the first modern Russian to work out an intricate Orthodox philosophy of law that grounded law and political order in morality, and that anchored morality directed in a Christian theology of salvation. Soloviev also challenged the traditional Orthodox theology of theocracy, which tied church, state, and nation into an organic whole and lay some of the foundations for a new theory of social pluralism. Nicholas Berdyaev, a theologian, worked out a complex new theology of human nature anchored in an ethic of creation, redemption, and law. He also crafted an original theory of human dignity and salvation that he tied to the Orthodox theology of theosis. Vladimir Lossky, a philosopher, drew from several earlier church fathers and mystics a brilliant new theory of human dignity, freedom, and discipline anchored in the Orthodox doctrine of the Trinity. He also challenged the politically compromised church and its socially anemic members to reclaim both their freedoms and their duties to discharge divinely appointed tasks. The Romanian theologian Dumitru Stăniloae drew from some of these same church fathers and mystics a comparable theory of the meaning of human freedom and sinfulness and the symphony of natural and supernatural sources of law and authority. Unlike Lossky, Stăniloae supported Romanian ethnic nationalism and had little say about the political compromises of the Romanian Orthodox Church during the period of Communism.

We have also included a chapter on the Russian nun and social reformer Mother Maria Skobtsova, whose thought and example evoke images of both Dorothy Day and Dietrich Bonhoeffer. Maria, who was exiled in Paris, worked tirelessly in the hostels feeding the poor and needy, even while developing a rich theology of incarnational living and sacramental care, and a harsh critique of some of the socially aversive tendencies of many monastics. Her work during the Nazi occupation of Paris brought her to the attention of the Gestapo, which condemned her to death in a concentration camp.

The biographies of some of these twenty figures are as edifying as their writings. (These biographies are summarized briefly in the introductions to each of the chapters that follow; fuller accounts are provided in the companion volume.) Fifteen of these figures served, at least for a time, as university professors of theology, philosophy, ethics, history, or law. Ten served in traditional church offices: three as popes (Leo XIII, John XXIII, and John Paul II), five as pastors (Gutiérrez, Barth, Bonhoeffer, Niebuhr, and King), two as monastics (Maria and Murray). Two served in political office—Kuyper as the prime minister of the Netherlands, Maritain as France's ambassador to the Vatican. One served as a lawyer (Stringfellow).

One was active as a political advisor (Niebuhr). Eight were stirred to radical social or political activism (Gutiérrez, Day, Barth, Bonhoeffer, Niebuhr, King, Stringfellow, and Maria). Four were censured by church authorities (Anthony, Day, Murray, and Gutiérrez). Three were exiled from their homeland (Berdyaev, Lossky, and Maria). Two were removed from their professorships (Bonhoeffer and Stăniloae). Nine were indicted or imprisoned by state authorities (Anthony, Day, Bonhoeffer, King, Stringfellow, Soloviev, Berdyaev, Maria, and Stăniloae). One faced brutal and lengthy political imprisonment (Stăniloae). Two were murdered in concentration camps (Bonhoeffer and Maria). One fell to an assassin's bullet (King).

The diversity of these biographies underscores an important criterion of selection that we have used in assembling these two volumes. The twenty figures included herein are intended to be points on a large canvas, not entries on an exhaustive roll of modern Christian teachers of law, society, and politics. We present them as illustrations of different venues, vectors, and visions of what a Christian understanding of law, politics, and society entails. Some of these figures were lone voices. Others attracted huge throngs of allies and disciples, many of whom make no appearance in these pages. Moreover, we have not included figures who are still alive and well today—including several authors in this volume—whose work will likely shape Christian teachings on law, politics, and society in the twenty-first century.

Many readers will thus look in vain in these volumes for some of their favorite authors. Missing from this collection are some of our favorites who did or do speak to some issues of law, politics, and society with a distinctly Christian understanding of human nature. These include Hans Urs von Balthasar, John Finnis, Joseph Fuchs, Mary Ann Glendon, Germain Grisez, Etienne Gilson, Bernard Longeran, Karl Rahner, Heinrich Rommen, Thomas Schaeffer, and Yves Simon, among Catholics; Emil Brunner, Herman Dooyeweerd, Johannes Heckel, Carl Henry, Karl Holl, Wolfgang Huber, Richard Niebuhr, Oliver O'Donovan, Wolfhart Pannenburg, Paul Ramsey, Walter Rauschenbusch, and Rudolph Sohm, among Protestants; John Erickson, Pavel Florensky, Georges Florovsky, John Meyendorff, and Christoph Yannoros, among Orthodox. Every reader will have a list of favorites beyond those included in these pages. The greatest compliment that could be made to this book is that it stimulates the production of many other and better studies of the scores of other modern Christian thinkers who deserve analysis.

PART 1

The Roman Catholic Tradition

{CHAPTER 1}

Pope Leo XIII (1810–1903)

SELECTED AND EDITED BY RUSSELL HITTINGER

Gioacchino Vincenzo Pecci was born on March 2, 1810, at Carpineto, in the south-central region of the Papal States. Just a few months earlier, Napoleon had kidnapped Pecci's temporal and spiritual sovereign, Pope Pius VII, and taken him to Savona on the Italian Riviera. The five-year-old Pecci witnessed the pope's return to Rome and his former dominions after the collapse of Napoleon's regime in 1815. Beginning in 1832 at the Accademia dei Nobili Ecclesiastici, and then at the Sapienza, Pecci received training in theology as well as in civil and canon law. Such training was typical for young men who sought careers in the prelatura, *a quasi-lay bureaucracy governing the Papal States, staffed mostly by the sons of Roman and Italian nobility. Some went on to become priests and bishops. Pecci did, spending forty years as an administrator, diplomat, and bishop in this system, fighting brigands, establishing banks and cooperatives for farmers, building hospitals, and supervising the construction of roads. In January 1843, Pope Gregory XVI made him nuncio to Brussels, where he was able to see firsthand the Industrial Revolution in northern Europe. Consecrated bishop of Perugia in 1846, Pecci's real passion was in the field of education. In Perugia he established the Accademia di S. Tommaso, the seedbed for his revival of Thomism more than thirty years later.*

When he was elected pope in February 1878, no one anticipated that Pecci would live until 1903, much less that he would have the energy and composure to write some 110 encyclicals and other teaching letters—by far the most prodigious output of teaching on the part of any modern pope. The Leonine letters are marked by a relentless drive to diagnose historical contingencies in the light of first principles. He did not invent the genre of encyclical letters, nor was he the first pope to make encyclical letters an ordinary means of communication with the universal church. His predecessor, Pius IX, wrote sixty-six letters during his turbulent pontificate. Rather, Leo so perfected the teaching letter that it became a new pedagogical art, best described as an amalgam of doctrine and public policy. His letters effect in the reader a speculative insight that is deeper and more synthetic than policy statements on issues of the day. In this respect, Leo was a public intellectual who took full advantage of the greatest bully pulpit in the world. His achievement is all the more remarkable in that he did not begin writing these letters until he was almost seventy years old. Each of his successors has tried, with varying degrees of success, to reduplicate the Leonine art of teaching.

The historical background can help us appreciate why Leo wrote so many letters. After the Congress of Vienna (1815), the papacy and most European states made a last bid to restore the alliance of throne and altar. To solidify the alliance, either Rome conceded or governments asserted rights to govern the church. As late as 1870, Rome nominated bishops in only five countries, four of them Protestant. The Restoration proved unworkable in the face of constant revolutions and civil wars in Europe as well as new states in Latin America. A token of the demise was the loss of the Papal States, the oldest standing monarchy in Europe, to the Kingdom of Italy (1870). Leo would be the first pope since the eighth century not to inherit the papal temporalities in Italy. The German Kulturkampf (1870–75) expelled religious orders and brought seminaries under state control, and five of eleven Prussian bishops were imprisoned for refusing to comply with state law on marriage. Germany's suppression of church liberty was done legally; elsewhere, suppression was more violent. From 1833 to 1876, Spain suffered three civil wars, replete with mass murder of clergy and destruction of churches. Ever volatile France, which suffered twelve different governments in Leo's lifetime, was always a rich source of trouble and disappointment for the church. In riots and revolutions and by assassination, three archbishops of Paris were murdered (in 1848, 1857, and 1871).

The First Vatican Council (1870) marked the beginning of a new era. Its most important act was to declare that the papacy enjoys a universal jurisdiction. Local churches and their hierarchies were no longer in the state but in the universal church. There would be no more national churches. Thus the council, not the states, ended Catholic political Christendom as it had been known and practiced for centuries. The papacy was now thrust into the position of preserving the unity of the church during an era that pulled in the opposite direction, toward nationalism and toward an ever greater control of society by the administrative law of the state. The outpouring of papal letters and directives reflects this profound change in the international situation of the Catholic Church.

When he was elected in 1878, Leo had the burden of teaching churchmen and statesmen how to understand the new situation. What ought to be the normal configuration of church, state, and society? How can we imagine a structured pluralism of diverse social forms and modes of authority without one trespassing or absorbing the rights of the others? If civil authority is no longer an "external bishop," does this mean that political authority stands completely outside the

sacred orbit? Is the tumult of the West due to excessive liberty or excessive
authority?

In these extracts, we see Leo's interest in what can be called the metaphysics
of jurisdiction. The issue is how liberty and authority are located within the
ordering wisdom of divine providence, which the human intellect participates
by nature and by grace. This was the problem that transcended all particular
questions of public policy. What is the origin of authority, and what are the
principled grounds for there being more than one kind of authority? What are
the titles and rights of the liberties of individuals, families, and voluntary asso-
ciations? Leo considers these questions according to a twofold divine pedagogy,
the natural law and the law of the gospel. Perhaps his greatest legacy is to have
developed this stereoscopic approach.[1]

A TWOFOLD PEDAGOGY

THE PERPETUAL AGREEMENT of the Catholic Church has maintained and
maintains that there is a twofold order of knowledge, distinct not only as
regards its source, but also as regards its object. With regard to the source,
we know at the one level by natural reason, at the other level by divine faith.
With regard to the object, besides those things to which natural reason can
attain, there are proposed for our belief mysteries hidden in God which,
unless they are divinely revealed, are incapable of being known. . . . Now
reason, if it is enlightened by faith, does indeed when it seeks persistently,
piously and soberly, achieve by God's gift some understanding, and that
most profitable, of the mysteries, whether by analogy from what is knows
naturally, or from the connexion of these mysteries with one another and
with the final end of humanity. . . . Even though faith is above reason, there
can never be any real disagreement between faith and reason, since it is
the same God who reveals the mysteries and infuses faith, and who has
endowed the human mind with the light of reason.[2]

We do not, indeed, attribute such force and authority to philosophy as
to esteem it equal to the task of combating and rooting out all errors; for,
when the Christian religion was first constituted, it came upon earth to restore it to its primeval dignity by the admirable light of faith, diffused "not
by persuasive words of human wisdom, but in the manifestation of spirit
and of power" [1 Cor. 2:4], so also at the present time we look above all
things to the powerful help of Almighty God to bring back to a right understanding the minds of man and dispel the darkness of error. But the natural
helps with which the grace of the divine wisdom, strongly and sweetly disposing all things,[3] has supplied the human race are neither to be despised
nor neglected, chief among which is evidently the right use of philosophy.

For, not in vain did God set the light of reason in the human mind; and so far is the super-added light of faith from extinguishing or lessening the power of the intelligence that it completes it rather, and by adding to its strength renders it capable of greater things.[4]

In the first place, philosophy, if rightly made use of by the wise, in a certain way tends to smooth and fortify the road to true faith, and to prepare the souls of its disciples for the fit reception of revelation; for which reason it is well called by ancient writers sometimes a steppingstone to the Christian faith,[5] sometimes the prelude and help of Christianity,[6] sometimes the Gospel teacher.[7] And, assuredly, the God of all goodness, in all that pertains to divine things, has not only manifested by the light of faith those truths which human intelligence could not attain of itself, but others, also, not altogether unattainable by reason, that by the help of divine authority they may be made known to all at once and without any admixture of error. Hence it is that certain truths which were either divinely proposed for belief, or were bound by the closest chains to the doctrine of faith, were discovered by pagan sages with nothing but their natural reason to guide them, were demonstrated and proved by becoming arguments. For, as the Apostle says, the invisible things of Him, from the creation of the world, are clearly seen, being understood by the things that are made: His eternal power also and divinity;[8] and the Gentiles who have not the Law show, nevertheless, the work of the Law written in their hearts.[9] But it is most fitting to turn these truths, which have been discovered by the pagan sages even, to the use and purposes of revealed doctrine, in order to show that both human wisdom and the very testimony of our adversaries serve to support the Christian faith—a method which is not of recent introduction, but of established use, and has often been adopted by the holy Fathers of the Church. What is more, those venerable men, the witnesses and guardians of religious traditions, recognize a certain form and figure of this in the action of the Hebrews, who, when about to depart out of Egypt, were commanded to take with them the gold and silver vessels and precious robes of the Egyptians, that by a change of use the things might be dedicated to the service of the true God which had formerly been the instruments of ignoble and superstitious rites.[10]

[St. Thomas] pushed his philosophic inquiry into the reasons and principles of things, which because they are most comprehensive and contain in their bosom, so to say, the seeds of almost infinite truths, were to be unfolded in good time by later masters and with a goodly yield. . . . Again, clearly distinguishing, as is fitting, reason from faith, while happily associating the one with the other, he both preserved the rights and had regard for the dignity of each; so much so, indeed, that reason, borne on the wings of Thomas to its human height, can scarcely rise higher, while faith could scarcely expect more or stronger aids from reason than those which she has already obtained through Thomas. . . . For, the teachings of Thomas on the true meaning of liberty, which at this time is running into license, on the divine origin of all authority, on laws and their force, on the paternal and just rule of princes, on obedience to the higher powers, on mutual charity one toward another—on all of these and kindred subjects—have very great and invincible force to overturn those principles of the new order [*ea iuris novi principia*][11] which are well known to be dangerous to the peaceful order of things and to public safety. In short, all studies ought to find hope of advancement and promise of assistance in this restoration of philosophic discipline which We have proposed.[12] By obeying Christ with his intellect man by no means acts in a servile manner, but in complete accordance with his reason and his natural dignity. For by his will he yields, not to the authority of any man, but to that of God, the author of his being, and the first principle to Whom he is subject by the very law of his nature. He does not suffer himself to be forced by the theories of any human teacher, but by the eternal and unchangeable truth. Hence he attains at one and the same time the natural good of the intellect and his own liberty. For the truth which proceeds from the teaching of Christ clearly demonstrates the real nature and value of every being; and man, being endowed with this knowledge, if he but obey the truth as perceived, will make all things subject to himself, not himself to them; his appetites to his reason, not his reason to his appetites. Thus the slavery of sin and falsehood will be shaken off, and the most perfect liberty attained: "You shall know the truth, and the truth shall make you free" (John viii., 32).[13]

LAW AND LIBERTY

It is with *moral* liberty, whether in individuals or in communities, that We proceed at once to deal. But, first of all, it will be well to speak briefly of *natural* liberty; for, though it is distinct and separate from moral liberty, natural freedom is the fountainhead from which liberty of whatsoever kind flows, *sua vi suaque sponte*. The unanimous consent and judgment of men ... recognizes this natural liberty in those only who are endowed with intelligence or reason; and it is by his use of this that man is rightly regarded as responsible for his actions. For, while other animate creatures follow their senses, seeking good and avoiding evil only by instinct, man has reason to guide him in each and every act of his life. Reason sees that whatever things that are held to be good upon earth may exist or may not, and discerning that none of them are of necessity for us, it leaves the will free to choose what it pleases. But man can judge of this contingency, as We say, only because he has a soul that is simple, spiritual, and intellectual—a soul, therefore, which is not produced by matter, and does not depend on matter for its existence. . . . In man's free will, therefore, or in the moral necessity of our voluntary acts being in accordance with reason, lies the very root of the necessity of law. Nothing more foolish can be uttered or conceived than the notion that, because man is free by nature, he is therefore exempt from law. Were this the case, it would follow that to become free we must be deprived of reason; whereas the truth is that we are bound to submit to law precisely because we are free by our very nature.[14]

All prescriptions of human reason can have force of law only inasmuch as they are the voice and the interpreters of some higher power on which our reason and liberty necessarily depend.[15] For, since the force of law consists in the imposing of obligations and the granting of rights, authority is the one and only foundation of all law—the power, that is, of fixing duties and defining rights, as also of assigning the necessary sanctions of reward and chastisement to each and all of its commands. But all this, clearly, cannot be found in man, if, as his own supreme legislator, he is to be the [supreme] rule of his own actions. It follows, therefore, that the law of nature is the same thing as the *eternal law*, implanted in rational creatures, and inclining them *to their right action and end*; and can be nothing else but the eternal reason of God, the Creator and Ruler of all the world. To this rule of action and restraint of evil God has vouchsafed to give special and most suitable aids for strengthening and ordering the human will. The first and most excellent of these is the power of His divine *grace*, whereby the mind can be enlightened and the will wholesomely invigorated and moved to the constant pursuit of moral good, so that the use of our inborn liberty becomes at once less difficult and less dangerous. Not that the divine assistance hinders in any way the free movement of our will; just the contrary, for grace works inwardly in man and in harmony with his natural inclinations, since it flows from the very Creator of his mind and will, by whom all things are moved in conformity with their nature. As the Angelic Doctor points out, it is because divine grace comes from the Author of nature that it is so admirably adapted to be the safeguard of all natures, and to maintain the character, efficiency, and operations of each.[16]

For, what reason and the natural law do for individuals, that *human law*, promulgated for their good, does for the citizens of States. Of the laws enacted by men, some are concerned with what is good or bad by its very nature; and they command men to follow after what is right and to shun what is wrong, adding at the same time a suitable sanction. But such laws by no means derive their origin from civil society, because, just as civil society did not create human nature, so neither can it be said to be the author of the good which befits human nature, or of the evil which is contrary to it. Laws come before men live together in society, and have their origin in the natural, and consequently in the eternal, law. The precepts, therefore, of the natural law, contained bodily in the laws of men, have not merely the force of human law, but they possess that higher and more august sanction which belongs to the law of nature and the eternal law.[17] And within the sphere of this kind of laws the duty of the civil legislator is, mainly, to keep the community in obedience by the adoption of a common discipline and by putting restraint upon refractory and viciously inclined men, so that, deterred from evil, they may turn to what is good, or at any rate may avoid causing trouble and disturbance to the State. Now, there are other enactments of the civil authority, which do not follow directly, but somewhat remotely, from the natural law, and decide many points which the law of nature treats only in a general and indefinite way.[18] For instance, though nature commands all to contribute to the public peace and prosperity, whatever belongs to the manner, and circumstances, and conditions under which such service is to be rendered must be determined by the wisdom of men and not by nature herself. It is in the constitution of these particular rules of life, suggested by reason and prudence, and put forth by competent authority, that human law, properly so called, consists, binding all citizens to work together for the attainment of the common end proposed to the community, and forbidding them to depart from this end, and, in so far as human law is in conformity with the dictates of nature, leading to what is good, and deterring from evil.[19] But no man has in himself or of himself the power of constraining the free will of others by fetters of authority of this kind.[20] This power resides solely in God, the Creator and Legislator of all things; and it is necessary that those who exercise it should do it as having received it from God. "There is one lawgiver and judge, who is able to destroy and deliver."[21] And this is clearly seen in every kind of power. That which resides in priests comes from God is so acknowledged that among all nations they are recognized as, and called, the ministers of God. In like manner, the authority of fathers of families preserves a certain impressed image and form of the authority which is in God, "of whom all paternity in heaven and earth is named."[22] But in this way different kinds of authority have between them wonderful resemblances, since, whatever there is of government and authority, its origin is derived from one and the same Creator and Lord of the world, who is God.[23] Law is of its very essence a mandate of right reason, proclaimed by a properly constituted authority, for the common good.[24] But true and legitimate authority is void of sanction, unless it proceed from God, the supreme Ruler and Lord of all. The Almighty alone can commit power to a man over his fellow men; nor may that be accounted as right reason which is in disaccord with truth and with divine reason; nor that held to be true good which is repugnant to the supreme and unchangeable good, or that wrests aside and draws away the wills of men from the charity of God.[25]

The only reason which men have for not obeying is when anything is demanded of them which is openly repugnant to the natural or the divine law, for it is equally unlawful to command to do anything in which the law of nature or the will of God is violated. If, therefore, it should happen to any one to be compelled to prefer one or the other, viz., to disregard either the commands of God or those of rulers, he must obey Jesus Christ, who commands us to "give to Caesar the things that are Caesar's, and to God the things that are God's,"[26] and must reply courageously after the example of the Apostles: "We ought to obey God rather than men."[27] And yet there is no reason why those who so behave themselves should be accused of refusing obedience; for, if the will of rulers is opposed to the will and the laws of God, they themselves exceed the bounds of their own power and pervert justice; nor can their authority then be valid, which, when there is no justice, is null.[28]

Those who believe civil society to have risen from the free consent of men, looking for the origin of its authority from the same source, say that each individual has given up something of his right, and that voluntarily every person has put himself into the power of the one man in whose person the whole of those rights has been centered. But it is a great error not to see, what is manifest, that men, as they are not a nomad race, have been created, without their own free will, for a natural community of life. It is plain, moreover, that the pact which they allege is openly a falsehood and a fiction,[29] and that it has no authority to confer on political power such great force, dignity, and firmness as the safety of the State and the common good of the citizens require. Then only will the government have all those ornaments and guarantees, when it is understood to emanate from God as its august and most sacred source.[30]

PLURAL SOCIETIES

Nevertheless, the naturalists, as well as all who profess that they worship above all things the divinity of the State, and strive to disturb whole communities with such wicked doctrines, cannot escape the charge of delusion. Marriage has God for its Author, and was from the very beginning a kind of foreshadowing of the Incarnation of His Son; and therefore there abides in it a something holy and religious; not extraneous, but innate; not derived from men, but implanted by nature. . . . So mighty, even in the souls ignorant of heavenly doctrine, was the force of nature, of the remembrance of their origin, and of the conscience of the human race. As, then, marriage is holy by its own power, in its own nature, and of itself [*sua vi, sua natura, sua sponte sacrum*[31]], it ought not to be regulated and administered by the will of civil rulers, but by the divine authority of the Church, which alone in sacred matters professes the office of teaching.[32]

It is surely undeniable that when a man engages in remunerative labor, the impelling reason and motive of his work is to obtain property, and thereafter to hold it as his very own. If one man hires out to another his strength or skill, he does so for the purpose of receiving in return what is necessary for the satisfaction of his needs; he therefore expressly intends to acquire a right full and real, not only to the remuneration, but also to the disposal of such remuneration, just as he pleases. Thus, if he lives sparingly, saves money, and, for greater security, invests his savings in land, the land, in such case, is only his wages under another form; and, consequently, a working man's little estate thus purchased should be as completely at his full disposal as are the wages he receives for his labor. But it is precisely in such power of disposal that ownership obtains, whether the property consist of land or chattels. Socialists, therefore, by endeavoring to transfer the possessions of individuals to the community at large, strike at the interests of every wage-earner, since they would deprive him of the liberty of disposing of his wages, and thereby of all hope and possibility of increasing his resources and of bettering his condition in life. . . . What is of far greater moment, however, is the fact that the remedy they propose is manifestly against justice. For, every man has by nature the right to possess property as his own.[33] This is one of the chief points of distinction between man and the animal creation, for the brute has no power of self-direction, but is governed by two main instincts, which keep his powers on the alert, impel him to develop them in a fitting manner, and stimulate and determine him to action without any power of choice. One of these instincts is self-preservation, the other the propagation of the species. Both can attain their purpose by means of things which lie within range; beyond their verge the brute creation cannot go, for they are moved to action by their senses only, and in the special direction which these suggest. But with man it is wholly different. He possesses, on the one hand, the full perfection of the animal being, and hence enjoys at least as much as the rest of the animal kind, the fruition of things material. But animal nature, however perfect, is far from representing the human being in its completeness, and is in truth but humanity's humble handmaid, made to serve and to obey. It is the mind, or reason, which is the predominant element in us who are human creatures; it is this which renders a human being human, and distinguishes him essentially from the brute. And on this very account—that man alone among the animal creation is endowed with reason—it must be within his right to possess things not merely for temporary and momentary use, as other living things do, but to have and to hold them in stable and permanent possession.[34]

This becomes still more clearly evident if man's nature be considered a little more deeply. For man, fathoming by his faculty of reason matters without number, linking the future with the present, and being master of his own acts, guides his ways under the eternal law and the power of God, whose providence governs all things. Wherefore, it is in his power to exercise his choice not only as to matters that regard his present welfare, but also about those which he deems may be for his advantage in time yet to come. Hence, man not only should possess the fruits of the earth, but also the very soil, inasmuch as from the produce of the earth he has to lay by provision for the future. Man's needs do not die out, but forever recur; although satisfied today, they demand fresh supplies for tomorrow. Nature accordingly must have given to man a source that is stable and remaining always with him, from which he might look to draw continual supplies. And this stable condition of things he finds solely in the earth and its fruits. There is no need to bring in the [*respublica*]. Man precedes the [*civitas*], and possesses, prior to the formation of any [*civitas*], the right of providing for the substance of his body.[35]

That right to property, therefore, which has been proved to belong naturally to individual persons, must in like wise belong to a man in his capacity of head of a family; nay, that right is all the stronger in proportion as the human person receives a wider extension in the family group. It is a most sacred law of nature that a father should provide food and all necessaries for those whom he has begotten; and, similarly, it is natural that he should wish that his children, who carry on, so to speak, and continue his personality, should be by him provided with all that is needful to enable them to keep themselves decently from want and misery amid the uncertainties of this mortal life. Now, in no other way can a father effect this except by the ownership of productive property, which he can transmit to his children by inheritance. A family [is] ... a true society, governed by an authority peculiar to itself, that is to say, by the authority of the father. Provided, therefore, the limits which are prescribed by the very purposes for which it exists be not transgressed, the family has at least equal rights with the [civil society] in the choice and pursuit of the things needful to its preservation and its just liberty. We say, "at least equal rights"; for, inasmuch as the domestic household is antecedent, as well in idea as in fact, to the gathering of men into a community, the family must necessarily have rights and duties which are prior to those of the community, and founded more immediately in nature.[36]

We have said that the [*respublica*][37] must not absorb the individual or the family; both should be allowed free and untrammeled action so far as is consistent with the common good and the interest of others.[38] Rulers should, nevertheless, anxiously safeguard the community and all its members; the community, because the conservation thereof is so emphatically the business of the supreme power [*principatus*], that the safety of the commonwealth is not only the first law, but it is a government's whole reason of existence; and the members, because both philosophy and the Gospel concur in laying down that the object of the government ... should be, not the advantage of the ruler, but the benefit of those over whom he is placed. As the power to rule comes from God, and is, as it were, a participation in His, the highest of all sovereignties, it should be exercised as the power of God is exercised—with a fatherly solicitude which not only guides the whole, but reaches also individuals.[39]

These lesser societies and the larger society differ in many respects, because their immediate purpose and aim are different. Civil society exists for the common good, and hence is concerned with the interests of all in general, albeit with individual interests also in their due place and degree. It is therefore called a public society, because by its agency, as St. Thomas of Aquinas says, "Men establish relations in common with one another in the setting up of a commonwealth."[40] But societies which are formed in the bosom of the commonwealth are styled *private*, and rightly so, since their immediate purpose is the private advantage of the associates. "Now, a private society," says St. Thomas again, "is one which is formed for the purpose of carrying out private objects; as when two or three enter into partnership with the view of trading in common."[41] Private societies, then, although they exist within the body politic, and are severally part of the commonwealth, cannot nevertheless be absolutely, and as such, prohibited by public authority. For, to enter into a "society" of this kind is the natural right of man; and the [*civitas*] has for its office to protect natural rights, not to destroy them; and, if it forbid its citizens to form associations, it contradicts the very principle of its own existence, for both they and it exist in virtue of the like principle, namely, the natural tendency of man to dwell in society. . . .[42] There are occasions, doubtless, when it is fitting that the law should intervene to prevent certain associations, as when men join together for purposes which are evidently bad, unlawful, or dangerous to the [*respublica*]. In such cases, public authority may justly forbid the formation of such associations, and may dissolve them if they already exist. But every precaution should be taken not to violate the rights of individuals and not to impose unreasonable regulations under pretense of public benefit. For laws only bind when they are in accordance with right reason, and, hence, with the eternal law of God. . . .[43] And here we are reminded of the confraternities, societies, and religious orders which have arisen by the Church's authority and the piety of Christian men. The annals of every nation down to our own days bear witness to what they have accomplished for the human race. It is indisputable that on grounds of reason alone such associations, being perfectly blameless in their objects, possess the sanction of the law of nature. In their religious aspect they claim rightly to be responsible to the Church alone. The [civil rulers] accordingly have no rights over them, nor can they claim any share in their control; on the contrary, it is the duty of the [*respublica*] to respect and cherish them, and, if need be, to defend them from attack. It is notorious that a very different course has been followed, more especially in our own times. In many places the [civil] authorities have laid violent hands on these communities, and committed manifold injustice against them; it has placed them under control of the civil law, taken away their rights as corporate bodies, and despoiled them of their property, in such property the Church had her rights, each member of the body had his or her rights, and there were also the rights of those who had founded or endowed these communities for a definite purpose, and, furthermore, of those for whose benefit and assistance they had their being.[44]

By the [*Respublica*] we here understand, not the particular form of government prevailing in this or that nation, but the [*respublica*] as rightly apprehended; that is to say, any government conformable in its institutions to right reason and natural law, and to those dictates of the divine wisdom which we have expounded in the encyclical *On the Christian Constitution of the* [*Civitas*].[45] The foremost duty, therefore, of the rulers of the [*civitas*] should be to make sure that the laws and institutions, the general character and administration of the commonwealth, shall be such as of themselves to realize public well-being and private prosperity. This is the proper scope of wise statesmanship and is the work of the rulers. Now a [*civitas*] chiefly prospers and thrives through moral rule, well-regulated family life, respect for religion and justice, the moderation and fair imposing of public taxes, the progress of the arts and of trade, the abundant yield of the land—through everything, in fact, which makes the citizens better and happier. Hereby, then, it lies in the power of a ruler to benefit every class in the [*civitas*], and amongst the rest to promote to the utmost the interests of the poor; and this in virtue of his office, and without being open to suspicion of undue interference—since it is the province of the commonwealth to serve the common good. And the more that is done for the benefit of the working classes by the general laws of the country, the less need will there be to seek for special means to relieve them. . . . There is another and deeper consideration which must not be lost sight of. As regards the [*civitas*], the interests of all, whether high or low, are equal. The members of the working classes are citizens by nature and by the same right as the rich; they are real parts, living the life which makes up, through the family, the body of the commonwealth; and it need hardly be said that they are in every city very largely in the majority. It would be irrational to neglect one portion of the citizens and favor another, and therefore the public administration must duly and solicitously provide for the welfare and the comfort of the working classes; otherwise, that law of justice will be violated which ordains that each man shall have his due. To cite the wise words of St. Thomas Aquinas: "As the part and the whole are in a certain sense identical, so that which belongs to the whole in a sense belongs to the part."[46] Among the many and grave duties of rulers who would do their best for the people, the first and chief is to act with strict justice—with that justice which is called *distributive*—toward each and every class alike.[47]

CHURCH AND CIVIL AUTHORITY

For, as there are on earth two principal societies, the one civil, the proximate end of which is the temporal and worldly good of the human race; the other religious, whose office it is to lead mankind to that true, heavenly, and everlasting happiness for which we are created; so these are twin powers [*gemina potestas est*], both subordinate to the eternal law of nature, and each working for its own ends in matters concerning its own order and domain. But when anything has to be settled which for different reasons and in a different way concerns both powers, necessity and public utility demand that an agreement [*concordia*] shall be effected between them, without which an uncertain and unstable condition of things will be the result, totally inconsistent with the peace either of Church or [*civitas*]. When, therefore, a solemn public compact has been made between the sacred and the civil power, then it is as much the interest of the [*respublica*] as it is just that the compact should remain inviolate; because, as each power has services to render to the other, a certain and reciprocal advantage is enjoyed and conferred by each.[48]

In very truth, Jesus Christ gave to His Apostles unrestrained authority in regard to things sacred, together with the genuine and most true power of making laws, as also with the twofold right of judging and of punishing, which flow from that power. "All power is given to Me in heaven and on earth: going therefore teach all nations ... teaching them to observe all things whatsoever I have commanded you."[49] And in another place: "If he will not hear them, tell the Church."[50] And again: "In readiness to revenge all disobedience."[51] And once more: "That ... I may not deal more severely according to the power which the Lord hath given me, unto edification and not unto destruction."[52] Hence, it is the Church, and not the State, that is to be man's guide to heaven. It is to the Church that God has assigned the charge [*munus*] of seeing to, and legislating for, all that concerns religion; of teaching all nations; of spreading the Christian faith as widely as possible; in short, of administering freely and without hindrance, in accordance with her own judgment, all matters that fall within its competence. . . . Now, this authority, perfect in itself, and plainly meant to be unfettered, so long assailed by a philosophy that truckles to the State, the Church, has never ceased to claim for herself and openly to exercise. The Apostles themselves were the first to uphold it, when, being forbidden by the rulers of the synagogue to preach the Gospel, they courageously answered: "We must obey God rather than men."[53] This same authority the holy Fathers of the Church were always careful to maintain by weighty arguments, according as occasion arose, and the Roman Pontiffs have never shrunk from defending it with unbending constancy. Nay, more, princes and all invested with power to rule have themselves approved it, in theory alike and in practice. It cannot be called in question that in the making of treaties, in the transaction of business matters, in the sending and receiving ambassadors, and in the interchange of other kinds of official dealings they have been wont to treat with the Church as with a supreme and legitimate power. And, assuredly, all ought to hold that it was not without a singular disposition of God's providence that this power of the Church was provided with a civil sovereignty as the surest safeguard of her independence. . . .[54] The Almighty, therefore, has given the charge of the human race to two powers, the ecclesiastical and the civil, the one being set over divine, and the other over human, things. Each in its kind is supreme, each has fixed limits within which it is contained, limits which are defined by the nature and special object of the province of each, so that there is, we may say, an orbit traced out within which the action of each is brought into play by its own native right. But, inasmuch as each of these two powers has authority over the same subjects, and as it might come to pass that one and the same thing—related differently, but still remaining one and the same thing—might belong to the jurisdiction and determination of both, therefore [the most provident] God, who foresees all things, and who is the author of these two powers, has marked out the course of each in right correlation to the other. "For the powers that are, are ordained of God."[55] Were this not so, deplorable contentions and conflicts would often arise, and, not infrequently, men, like travelers at the meeting of two roads, would hesitate in anxiety and doubt, not knowing what course to follow. Two powers would be commanding contrary things, and it would be a dereliction of duty to disobey either of the two. . . . But it would be most repugnant to them to think thus of the wisdom and goodness of God. Even in physical things, albeit of a lower order, the Almighty has so combined the forces and springs of nature with tempered action and wondrous harmony that no one of them clashes with any other, and all of them most fitly and aptly work together for the great purpose of the universe. There must, accordingly, exist between these two powers a certain orderly connection, which may be compared to the union of the soul and body in man. The nature and scope of that connection can be determined only, as We have laid down, by having regard to the nature of each power, and by taking account of the relative excellence and nobleness of their purpose. One of the two has for its proximate and chief object the well-being of this mortal life; the other, the everlasting joys of heaven. Whatever, therefore in things human is of a sacred character, whatever belongs either of its own nature or by reason of the end to which it is referred, to the salvation of souls, or to the worship of God, is subject to the power and judgment of the Church.[56] Whatever is to be ranged under the civil and political order is rightly subject to the civil authority. Jesus Christ has Himself given command that what is Caesar's is to be rendered to Caesar, and that what belongs to God is to be rendered to God.[57]

What judgment is to be formed of a Catholic state which throws overboard the sacred principles and the wise enactments of the Christian law on matrimony, and sets about the wretched job of creating a marital morality all its own, purely human in character, under forms and guarantees that are merely legal; and then with all its power goes on forcibly to impose this morality on the consciences of its subjects, substituting it for the religious and sacramental morality.

Full of solicitude for this union, we point out the dangers which threaten it arising from certain controversies concerning public law; a subject which, amongst you, engenders a strong difference of feeling. These controversies have for their object the necessity or opportuneness of conforming to the prescriptions of Catholic doctrine the existing forms of government, based on what is commonly called modern law [*iuris novi*]. Most assuredly we, more than any one, ought heartily to desire that human society should be governed in a Christian manner, and that the divine influence of Christ should penetrate and completely impregnate all orders of the [*civitas*]. From the commencement of our Pontificate we manifested, without delay, that such was our settled opinion; and that by public documents, and especially by the Encyclical Letters we published against the errors of Socialism, and, quite recently, upon the Civil Power [*de politico principatu*].[58] Nevertheless, all Catholics, if they wish to exert themselves profitably for the common good, should have before their eyes and faithfully imitate the prudent conduct which the Church herself adopts in matters of this nature: she maintains and defends in all their integrity the sacred doctrines and principles of right with inviolable firmness, and applies herself with all her power to regulating the institutions and the customs of public order, as well as the acts of private life, upon these same principles. Nevertheless, she observes in this the just measure of time and place; and, as commonly happens in human affairs, she is often constrained to tolerate at times evils that it would be almost impossible to prevent, without exposing herself to calamities and troubles still more disastrous.[59]

POLITICAL "FORMS"

There is, however, a difference between the political prudence that relates to the general good and that which concerns the good of individuals. This latter is shown forth in the case of private persons who obey the prompting of right reason in the direction of their own conduct; while the former is the characteristic of those who are set over others, and chiefly of rulers of the State, whose duty it is to exercise the power of command, so that the political prudence of private individuals would seem to consist wholly in carrying out faithfully the orders issued by lawful authority.[60]

Neither is it blameworthy in itself, in any manner, for the people to have a share greater or less, in the government: for at certain times, and under certain laws, such participation may not only be of benefit to the citizens, but may even be of obligation. Nor is there any reason why any one should accuse the Church of being wanting in gentleness of action or largeness of view, or of being opposed to real and lawful liberty. The Church, indeed, deems it unlawful to place the various forms of divine worship on the same footing as the true religion, but does not, on that account, condemn those rulers who, for the sake of securing some great good or of hindering some great evil, allow patiently custom or usage to be a kind of sanction for each kind of religion having its place in the [civitas]. And, in fact, the Church is wont to take earnest heed that no one shall be forced to embrace the Catholic faith against his will, for, as St. Augustine wisely reminds us, "Man cannot believe otherwise than of his own will."[61]

However, here it must be carefully observed that whatever be the form of civil power in a nation, it cannot be considered so definitive as to have the right to remain immutable, even though such were the intention of those who, in the beginning, determined it. . . . Only the Church of Jesus Christ has been able to preserve, and surely will preserve unto the consummation of time, her form of government. Founded by Him who *was*, who *is*, and who *will be forever*,[62] she has received from Him, since her very origin, all that she requires for the pursuing of her divine mission across the changeable ocean of human affairs. And, far from wishing to transform her essential constitution, she has not the power even to relinquish the conditions of true liberty and sovereign independence with which Providence has endowed her in the general interest of souls.... But, in regard to purely human societies, it is an oft-repeated historical fact that time, that great transformer of all things here below, operates great changes in their political institutions. On some occasions it limits itself to modifying something in the form of the established government; or, again, it will go so far as to substitute other forms for the primitive ones—forms totally different, even as regards the mode of transmitting sovereign power.[63]

For, once ascribe to human reason the only authority to decide what is true and what is good, and the real distinction between good and evil is destroyed; honor and dishonor differ not in their nature, but in the opinion and judgment of each one; pleasure is the measure of what is lawful; and, given a code of morality which can have little or no power to restrain or quiet the unruly propensities of man, a way is naturally opened to universal corruption. With reference also to public affairs: authority is severed from the true and natural principle whence it derives all its efficacy for the common good; and the law determining what it is right to do and avoid doing is at the mercy of a majority. Now, this is simply a road leading straight to tyranny. The empire of God over man and civil society once repudiated, it follows that religion, as a public institution, can have no claim to exist, and that everything that belongs to religion will be treated with complete indifference. Furthermore, with ambitious designs on sovereignty, tumult and sedition will be common amongst the people; and when duty and conscience cease to appeal to them, there will be nothing to hold them back but force, which of itself alone is powerless to keep their covetousness in check.[64]

The right to rule is not necessarily, however, bound up with any special mode of government. It may take this or that form, provided only that it be of a nature of the government, rulers must ever bear in mind that God is the paramount ruler of the world, and must set Him before themselves as their exemplar and law in the administration of the State. For, in things visible God has fashioned secondary causes, in which His divine action can in some wise be discerned, leading up to the end to which the course of the world is ever tending. In like manner, in civil society, God has always willed that there should be a ruling authority [*principatus*], and that they who are invested with it should reflect the divine power and providence in some measure over the human race.[65]

The fundamental doctrine of rationalism is the supremacy of the human reason, which, refusing due submission to the divine and eternal reason, proclaims its own independence, and constitutes itself the supreme principle and source and judge of truth. Hence, these followers of liberalism deny the existence of any divine authority to which obedience is due, and proclaim that every man is the law to himself; from which arises that ethical system which they style *independent* morality, and which, under the guise of liberty, exonerates man from any obedience to the commands of God, and substitutes a boundless license. The end of all this it is not difficult to foresee, especially when society is in question. For, when once man is firmly persuaded that he is subject to no one, it follows that the efficient cause of the unity of civil society is not to be sought in any principle external to man, or superior to him, but simply in the free will of individuals; that authority in the State comes from the people only; and that, just as every man's individual reason is his only rule of life, so the collective reason of the community should be the supreme guide in the management of all public affairs. Hence the doctrine of the supremacy of the greater number, and that all right and all duty reside in the majority. But, from what has been said, it is clear that all this is in contradiction to reason. To refuse any bond of union between man and civil society, on the one hand, and God the Creator and consequently the supreme Law-giver, on the other, is plainly repugnant to the nature, not only of man, but of all created things. . . .[66]

Indeed, very many men of more recent times, walking in the footsteps of those who in a former age assumed to themselves the name of philosophers, say that all power comes from the people; so that those who exercise it in the [*civitas*] do so not as their own, but as delegated to them by the people, and that, by this rule, it can be revoked by the will of the very people by whom it was delegated. But from these, Catholics dissent, who affirm that the right to rule is from God, as from a natural and necessary principle. . . . It is of importance, however, to remark in this place that those who may be placed over the [*respublica*] may in certain cases be chosen by the will and decision of the multitude, without opposition to or impugning of the Catholic doctrine. And by this choice, in truth, the ruler is designated [*princeps designatur*], but the rights of ruling [*iura principatus*] are not thereby conferred. Nor is the authority delegated to him, but the person by whom it is to be exercised is determined upon. . . . There is no question here respecting forms of government, for there is no reason why the Church should not approve of the chief power being held by one man or by more, provided only it be just, and that it tend to the common advantage. Wherefore, so long as justice be respected, the people are not hindered from choosing for themselves that form of government which suits best either their own disposition, or the institutions and customs of their ancestors.[67]

And how are these political changes of which We speak produced? They sometimes follow in the wake of violent crises, too often of a bloody character, in the midst of which preexisting governments totally disappear; then anarchy holds sway, and soon public order is shaken to its very foundations and finally overthrown. From that time onward a *social need* obtrudes itself upon the nation; it must provide for itself without delay. Is it not its privilege—or, better still, its duty—to defend itself against a state of affairs troubling it so deeply, and to re-establish public peace in the tranquility of order? Now, this social need justifies the creation and the existence of new governments, whatever form they take; since, in the hypothesis wherein we reason, these new governments are a requisite to public order, all public order being impossible without a government. Thence it follows that, in similar junctures, all the novelty is limited to the political form of civil power, or to its mode of transmission; it in no wise affects the power considered in itself. This continues to be immutable and worthy of respect, as, considered in its nature, it is constituted to provide for the common good, the supreme end which gives human society its origin. To put it otherwise, in all hypotheses, civil power, considered as such, is from God, always from God: "For there is no power but from God."[68]

A notable difference exists between every kind of civil rule and that of the kingdom of Christ. If this latter bear a certain likeness and character to a civil kingdom, it is distinguished from it by its origin, principle, and essence. The Church, therefore, possesses the right to exist and to protect herself by institutions and laws in accordance with her nature.[69] And since she not only is a perfect society in herself, but superior to every other society of human growth, she resolutely refuses, promoted alike by right and by duty, to link herself to any mere party and to subject herself to the fleeting exigencies of politics. On like grounds, the Church, the guardian always of her own right and most observant of that of others, holds that it is not her province to decide which is the best amongst many diverse forms of government and the civil institutions of Christian [peoples], and amid the various kinds of [*respublicae*] she does not disapprove of any, provided the respect due to religion and the observance of good morals be upheld.[70]

BELGIUM, FRANCE, AND THE UNITED STATES

The action undertaken by Catholics starting from the same points and traveling as far as possible along the same paths should be observed everywhere to be one and the same action.[71] Consequently this action should be honest, vigorous, and productive. To facilitate this, Catholics must urgently wish for and pursue only those goals which are seen quite truly to lead to the common good, in preference to their own personal opinions and interests. This would ensure: (1) that religion excels in its own function and spreads its power, a power which brings safety to civil, domestic, and economic affairs as well, in a wonderful way; (2) that by uniting public authority and freedom in a Christian manner, the kingdom remains unharmed by sedition and protected by tranquility; (3) that the good institutions of the state, especially the schools of the young, are promoted and improved; (4) that commerce and crafts are improved, especially by the help of those societies, each with its own particular purpose, which abound in your country and which it is desirable to develop further with religion as leader and support. Nor is it a matter of small importance to ensure that (5) the supreme counsels of God be accepted with the modesty which is obviously their due. Since God has ordered that different classes exist in the human race, but that among those classes an equality deriving from their friendly cooperation also exists, workers should in no way abandon their respect for and trust in their employers, and the employers should treat their workers with just kindness and prudent care.[72]

Various political governments have succeeded one another in France during the last century, each having its own distinctive form: the Empire, the Monarchy, and the Republic.[73] By giving one's self up to abstractions, one could at length conclude which is the best of these forms, considered in themselves; and in all truth it may be affirmed that each of them is good, provided it lead straight to its end—that is to say, to the common good for which social authority is constituted; and finally, it may be added that, from a relative point of view, such and such a form of government may be preferable because of being better adapted to the character and customs of such or such a nation. In this order of speculative ideas, Catholics, like all other citizens, are free to prefer one form of government to another precisely because no one of these social forms is, in itself, opposed to the principles of sound reason nor to the maxims of Christian doctrine. What amply justifies the wisdom of the Church is that in her relations with political powers she makes abstraction of the forms which differentiate them and treats with them concerning the great religious interests of nations."[74]

We shall not hold to the same language on another point, concerning the principle of the separation of the State [*l'État*] and Church, which is equivalent to the separation of human legislation from Christian and divine legislation. We do not care to interrupt Ourselves here in order to demonstrate the absurdity of such a separation; each one will understand for himself. As soon as the State refuses to give to God what belongs to God, by a necessary consequence it refuses to give to citizens that to which, as men, they have a right; as, whether agreeable or not to accept, it cannot be denied that man's rights spring from his duty toward God. Whence if follows that the State, by missing in this connection the principal object of its institution, finally becomes false to itself by denying that which is the reason of its own existence. These superior truths are so clearly proclaimed by the voice of even natural reason, that they force themselves upon all who are not blinded by the violence of passion; therefore, Catholics cannot be too careful in defending themselves against such a separation. In fact, to wish that the State would separate itself from the Church would be to wish, by a logical sequence, that the Church be reduced to the liberty of living according to the law common to all citizens. . . . It is true that in certain countries this state of affairs exists. It is a condition which, if it have numerous and serious inconveniences, also offers some advantages—above all when, by a fortunate inconsistency, the legislator is inspired by Christian principles—and, though these advantages cannot justify the false principle of separation nor authorize its defense, they nevertheless render worthy of toleration a situation which, practically, might be worse. . . . But in France, a nation Catholic in her traditions and by the present faith of the great majority of her sons, the Church should not be placed in the precarious position to which she must submit among other peoples; and the better that Catholics understand the aim of the enemies who desire this separation, the less will they favor it. To these enemies, and they say it clearly enough, this separation means that political legislation be entirely independent of religious legislation; nay, more, that Power be absolutely indifferent to the interests of Christian society, that is to say, of the Church; in fact, that it deny her very existence. But they make a reservation formulated thus: As soon as the Church, utilizing the resources which common law accords to the least among Frenchmen, will, by redoubling her native activity, cause her work to prosper, then the State intervening, can and will put French Catholics outside the common law itself. . . . In a word: the ideal of these men would be a return to paganism: the State would recognize the Church only when it would be pleased to persecute her.[75]

Precisely at the epoch when the American colonies, having, with Catholic aid, achieved liberty and independence, coalesced into a constitutional Republic the ecclesiastical hierarchy was happily established amongst you; and at the very time when the popular suffrage placed the great Washington at the helm of the Republic, the first bishop was set by apostolic authority over the American Church. The well-known friendship and familiar intercourse which subsisted between these two men seems to be an evidence that the United States ought to be conjoined in concord and amity with the Catholic Church. And not without cause; for without morality the State cannot endure––a truth which that illustrious citizen of yours, whom We have just mentioned, with a keenness of insight worthy of his genius and statesmanship perceived and proclaimed. . . . But, moreover (a fact which it gives pleasure to acknowledge), thanks are due to the equity of the laws which obtain in America and to the customs of the well-ordered Republic. For the Church amongst you, unopposed by the Constitution and government of your nation, fettered by no hostile legislation, protected against violence by the common laws and the impartiality of the tribunals, is free to live and act without hindrance.[76] Yet, though all this is true, it would be very erroneous to draw the conclusion that in America is to be sought the type of the most desirable status of the Church, or that it would be universally lawful or expedient for State and Church to be, as in America, dissevered and divorced. The fact that Catholicity with you is in good condition, nay, is even enjoying a prosperous growth, is by all means to be attributed to the fecundity with which God has endowed His Church, in virtue of which unless men or circumstances interfere, she spontaneously expands and propagates herself; but she would bring forth more abundant fruits if, in addition to liberty, she enjoyed the favor of the laws and the solicitude of the public authority.[77]

THE RULE OF CHRIST AND CHRISTIAN VIRTUE

But we should now give most special consideration to the declarations made by Jesus Christ, not through the Apostles or the Prophets but by His own words. To the Roman Governor who asked Him, "Art thou a king then?" He answered unhesitatingly, "Thou sayest that I am a king" (John xviii., 37). And the greatness of this power and the boundlessness of His kingdom is still more clearly declared in these words to the Apostles: "All power is given to me in heaven and on earth" (Matthew xxviii., 18). If then all power has been given to Christ it follows of necessity that His empire must be supreme, absolute and independent of the will of any other, so that none is either equal or like unto it: and since it has been given in heaven and on earth it ought to have heaven and earth obedient to it. And verily he has acted on this extraordinary and peculiar right when He commanded His Apostles to preach His doctrine over the earth, to gather all men together into the one body of the Church by the baptism of salvation, and to bind them by laws, which no one could reject without risking his eternal salvation. . . . But this is not all. Christ reigns not only by natural right as the Son of God, but also by a right that He has acquired.[78] For He it was who snatched us "from the power of darkness" (Colossians i., 13), and "gave Himself for the redemption of all" (I Timothy ii., 6). Therefore not only Catholics, and those who have duly received Christian baptism, but also all men, individually and collectively, have become to Him "a purchased people" (1 Peter ii., 9). St. Augustine's words are therefore to the point when he says: "You ask what price He paid? See what He gave and you will understand how much He paid. The price was the blood of Christ. What could cost so much but the whole world, and all its people? The great price He paid was paid for all" (T. 120 on St. John). . . . [79] How it comes about that infidels themselves are subject to the power and dominion of Jesus Christ is clearly shown by St. Thomas, who gives us the reason and its explanation. For having put the question whether His judicial power extends to all men, and having stated that judicial authority flows naturally from royal authority, he concludes decisively as follows: "All things are subject to Christ as far as His power is concerned, although they are not all subject to Him in the exercise of that power" (3a., p., q. 59, a.4).[80] This [imperium] of Christ over men is exercised by truth, justice, and above all, by charity.[81]

It is surely unnecessary to prove, what experience constantly shows and what each individual feels in himself, even in the very midst of all temporal prosperity—that in God alone can the human will find absolute and perfect peace. God is the only end of man. All our life on earth is the truthful and exact image of a pilgrimage. Now Christ is the "Way," for we can never reach God, the supreme and ultimate good, by this toilsome and doubtful road of mortal life, except with Christ as our leader and guide. ["No one comes to the Father, except through me" (Jn. 14:6).] How so? Firstly and chiefly by His grace; but this would remain "void" in man if the precepts of His law were neglected. For, as was necessarily the case after Jesus Christ had won our salvation, He left behind Him His Law for the protection and welfare of the human race, under the guidance of which men, converted from evil life, might safely tend towards God. "Going, teach ye all nations ... teaching them to observe all things whatsoever I have commanded you" (Matthew xxviii., 19–20). "Keep my commandments" (John xiv., 15). Hence it will be understood that in the Christian religion the first and most necessary condition is docility to the precepts of Jesus Christ, absolute loyalty of will towards Him as Lord and King. A serious duty, and one which oftentimes calls for strenuous labor, earnest endeavor, and perseverance! For although by Our Redeemer's grace human nature hath been regenerated, still there remains in each individual a certain debility and tendency to evil. Various natural appetites attract man on one side and the other; the allurements of the material world impel his soul to follow after what is pleasant rather than the law of Christ.[82] Still we must strive our best and resist our natural inclinations with all our strength "unto the obedience of Christ" [2 Cor. 10:5]. For unless they obey reason they become our masters, and carrying the whole man away from Christ, make him their slave. "Men of corrupt mind, who have made shipwreck of the faith, cannot help being slaves. . . . They are slaves to a threefold concupiscence: of will, of pride, or of outward show" (St. Augustine, De Vera Religione, 37).[83] In this contest every man must be prepared to undergo hard ships and troubles for Christ's sake. It is difficult to reject what so powerfully entices and delights. It is hard and painful to despise the supposed goods of the senses and of fortune for the will and precepts of Christ our Lord. But the Christian is absolutely obliged to be firm, and patient in suffering, if he wish to lead a Christian life. Have we forgotten of what Body and of what Head we are the members? "Having joy set before Him, He endured the Cross," and He bade us deny ourselves. The very dignity of human nature depends upon this disposition of mind. For, as even the ancient Pagan philosophy perceived, to be master of oneself and to make the lower part of the soul, obey the superior part, is so far from being a weakness of will that it is really a noble power, in consonance with right reason and most worthy of a man. Moreover, to bear and to suffer is the ordinary condition of man. Man can no more create for himself a life free from suffering and filled with all happiness that he can abrogate the decrees of his Divine Maker, who has willed that the consequences of original sin should be perpetual. It is reasonable, therefore, not to expect an end to troubles in this world, but rather to steel one's soul to bear troubles, by which we are taught to look forward with certainty to supreme happiness.[84]

The whole object of Christian doctrine and morality is that "we being dead to sin, should live to justice" (1 Peter ii., 24)—that is, to virtue and holiness. In this consists the moral life, with the certain hope of a happy eternity. This justice, in order to be advantageous to salvation, is nourished by Christian faith. "The just man liveth by faith" (Galatians iii., 11). "Without faith it is impossible to please God" (Hebrews xi., 6). Consequently Jesus Christ, the creator and preserver of faith, also preserves and nourishes our moral life. This He does chiefly by the ministry of His Church. To Her, in His wise and merciful counsel, He has entrusted certain agencies which engender the supernatural life, protect it, and revive it if it should fail. This generative and conservative power of the virtues that make for salvation is therefore lost, whenever morality is dissociated from divine faith. A system of morality based exclusively on human reason robs man of his highest dignity and lowers him from the supernatural to the merely natural life. Not but that man is able by the right use of reason to know and to obey certain principles of the natural law. But though he should know them all and keep them inviolate through life-and even this is impossible without the aid of the grace of our Redeemer—still it is vain for anyone without faith to promise himself eternal salvation. "If anyone abide not in Me, he shall be cast forth as a branch, and shall wither, and they shall gather him up and cast him into the fire, and he burneth" (John xv., 6). "He that believeth not shall be condemned" (Mark xvi., 16). We have but too much evidence of the value and result of a morality divorced from divine faith. How is it that, in spite of all the zeal for the welfare of the masses, nations are in such straits and even distress, and that the evil is daily on the increase? We are told that society is quite able to help itself; that it can flourish without the assistance of Christianity, and attain its end by its own unaided efforts. Public administrators prefer a purely secular system of government. All traces of the religion of our forefathers are daily disappearing from political life and administration. What blindness![85]

NOTES

1. [Unless otherwise noted, the translations that follow are from Claudia Carlen, ed., *The Papal Encyclicals*, 5 vols. (Wilmington, N.C.: McGrath, 1981). In some places I removed the word "state" because it is not the equivalent of *civitas* or *respublica*.]

2. [Vatican Council I, *Dogmatic Constitution of the Catholic Faith (Dei Filius)* (April 24, 1870), in *Decrees of the Ecumenical Councils*, ed. Norman P. Tanner (Washington, D.C.: Georgetown University Press, 1990), 2:808.]

3. [Paraphrasing Wisdom 8.1, Divine Wisdom "reacheth from end to end mightily and ordereth all things sweetly (*suaviter*)." It was one of Thomas's favorite scripture texts, identified with the eternal law and man's natural or supernatural participation in it. For Thomas, the natural law and the new law of grace are instances of *lex indita*—indicted or instilled law. God instills in the agent, by a kind of premotion, not only the knowledge of an end but also a kind of predeliberative thrust toward it. In the case of natural law, the agent is moved to naturally (*naturaliter*) know and approve of certain ends; in the case of the new law, grace is infused in the soul, inclining it to perform acts for the heavenly kingdom. God is said to govern *suaviter* (sweetly) because he gives the wherewithal to accomplish what is commanded. Positive law, on the other hand, does not dispose things *suaviter* because while it provides the directive term of action it does not confer the interior *modus*. On the natural and supernatural instances of *lex indita*, see *Summa theologiae* I, 103.8, and I–II, 100.2, and 106.1. Subsequent popes cited Wisdom 8.1 for the same purpose, indicating how the human soul is moved prior to and higher than the human positive law, indicating that God retains an original jurisdiction over the human soul.]

4. [*Aeterni Patris* §2 (1879), 18.]

5. Clement of Alexandria, *Stromata*, 1, 16 (PG 8, 795); 7, 3 (PG 9, 426).

6. Origen, *Epistola ad Gregorium* (PG 11, 87–91).

7. Clement of Alexandria, *Stromata*, 1, 5 (PG 8, 718–719)

8. Rom. 1:20.

9. Rom. 2:14–15.

10. [*Aeterni Patris* §4, 18.]

11. [Not to counter a new order in every respect; rather, "new principles of law" or jurisprudence.]

12. [*Aeterni Patris* §§18, 29: 23, 25.]

13. [*Tametsi futura prospicientibus* §9 (1900), 475.]

14. [*Libertas* §§3, 7 (1888), 169–170, 171. Law communicates a necessity of obligation, not the necessity of force. *De Veritate*, 17.3. Leo makes an additional point of some importance. Human law presupposes not only an intelligible good, but a range of goods such that no one of them is so absolutely good that, once apprehended, the will moves by necessity. With respect to finite goods, the intellect presents the will with a good under this or that aspect.]

15. [The intellect can measure action because it is first measured. As an interpreter of a higher power, see John Paul II for the idea "participated theonomy" and of human conscience as the "herald of a king." *Veritatis splendor* §§41, 58 (1993), AAS 85, 1166, 1179.]

16. [*Libertas* §8, 171.]

17. [In answer to the objection that it is unnecessary to have two laws, one eternal the other natural, Thomas responds that "this argument would hold if the natural law were something diverse from the eternal law, whereas it is nothing but a participation thereof." *Summa theologiae* I–II, 91.2.]

18. [Human jurisprudence has no authority and therefore no prudence with respect to the primordial rules and measures of the natural law. Its prudence pertains to *determinatio*, rendering precepts of natural law determinate with respect to the circumstances of the community. *Summa theologiae* I–II, 95.2. Leo follows Thomas's triadic conception of prudence (*Summa theologiae* II–II, 50.1–2): ordering judgments about one's own acts (individual), ordering judgments supplied to a household (domestic), and legislative prudence, which makes law for a political community (regnative). All three proceed from antecedent (natural or revealed) law, but only the latter issues commands called laws. The chief act of a political authority (*principatus regalis*) is directing by law a multitude to a political end. What makes his ordering judgment unique is that it remains totally within the genus of law.]

19. [*Libertas* §9, 171–172.]

20. [One of Leo's main theses: a "soul that is simple, spiritual, and intellectual" does not lose its ordering to God. Its dignity and equality forbids us to think that one man subjects another by natural right. Legal command and obedience, therefore, are rooted in this anthropology; at the same time, this anthropology does not suggest a merely anthropocentric ground of command and obedience to law. On *Diuturnum*'s implications for modern notions of liberty and equality, see Yves R. Simon, *Philosophy of Democratic Government* (Chicago: University of Chicago Press, 1951), 144–194.]

21. James 4:12.

22. Eph. 3:15.

23. [*Diuturnum* §11 (1881), 53.]

24. [Paraphrasing Thomas's well-known definition of law as an ordinance of reason promulgated by a competent authority for the common good, *Summa theologiae* I–II 90.1–4. Note, however, that command (*imperio*) for Thomas and Leo is essentially a work of the intellect, *Summa theologiae* I–II, 17.1. Law is not the

executive force of the will, for the execution presupposes a *ratio*, without which there is nothing to execute.]

25. [*Sapientiae Christianae* §8 (1890), 213.]

26. Matt. 22:21.

27. Acts 5:29. [Leo frequently used Acts 5.29 to trace the boundaries of Rom. 13.1 and Mt. 22.1. *Sapientiae Christianae* §7, 15 (duty of citizens not to be treasonous to God); *Immortale Dei* (1885), §12, Acta 5, 126 (liberty of the Church, but also in light of Rom. 13.1 at §3); *Officio sanctissimo* §9 (1887), Acta 7, 233 (Catholic resistance to the Bavarian *Kulturkampf*). Beginning with Leo, Acts 5:29 becomes a frequently quoted text in papal social teaching. Indeed, John Paul II cites it no less than eight times in *Evangelium vitae* (1995).]

28. [*Diuturnum* §15, 54.]

29. [Aimed at a social contract account of the *origin* of political society, not at republican government.]

30. [*Diuturnum* §12, 53.]

31. [Marriage is unlike the *civitas* in two important respects. First, human prudence may introduce or alter a political "form" (regime), but no human has legitimate authority, not even the spouses, to alter the form of the matrimonial institution. Divine providence retains an immediate jurisdiction over marriage. Second, unlike the *civitas*, marriage can be a sacrament. Divine grace thus impresses a new form, but by way of addition and elevation, not by derogating the natural form. Marriage and the rights flowing from it (such as education) was the fulcrum of the church-state jurisdictional battles of this era.]

32. [*Arcanum* §19 (1880), 33.]

33. [As "his own" for more than one reason. Because humans are rational animals, their dominion involves ordering things, an activity that presupposes that they rightfully have something to order. Inasmuch as humans are social, possessed of social obligations (chiefly, but not exclusively, in the family), they cannot give the gift of service and support to others without first possessing property. Against socialists, Leo argues that abolition of private property preempts the very activities that distinguish the human from the animal; the state, in effect, becomes the only agent entitled to make ordering judgments.]

34. [*Rerum novarum* §§5–6 (1891), 242.]

35. [Ibid. §7, 242–243.]

36. [Ibid. §13, 244.]

37. [Except where his letters in the vernacular require it, Leo does not use the term "state," which conjures the idea of an impersonal, power apparatus. His language is traditional: *regnum, regimen civile, potestas civilis, civitas, res publica, imperium,* and the word for political authority, *principatus*. The word *status* is used in the older sense of a condition, rank, or standing. In *Immortale*, for example, he uses the *status* in reference to the church's standing in the public order, *in hoc rerum publicarum* (§29, 136).]

38. [The principle of subsidiarity, developed later by Pius XI. Note, however, that "conservation" means something more than providing physical safety; it also entails preservation (nonabsorption) of distinct social forms. This, then, is the

germ of what will later be called "social justice," which positively entails help, and negatively, nonabsorption, of the sociality of society itself. According to Pius XI, social justice ensues "when each individual member is given what it needs for the exercise of its proper function … all that is necessary for the exercise of his social *munus* [role, gift of service, mission]." *Divini redemptoris* (1937) §51, AAS 29, 92.]

39. [*Rerum novarum* §35, 250.]

40. *Contra impugnantes Dei cultum et religionem*, part 2, chap. 8 (*Opera omnia*, ed. Vives, vol. 29, p. 16).

41. Ibid.

42. [Leo does not use the term "intermediate" associations, which would suggest that voluntary associations are buffers between the individual and the state. This idea does not adequately bring into view the inherent value of social activity. Men do not necessarily form societies to place a "check" upon the state. Leo is here citing Thomas's *Contra impugnantes*, which defends the right of Dominicans to associate freely with lay students and professors for the purpose of communicating knowledge. The multiplicity of vocations and avocations are grounded "primarily in Divine Providence, and, secondarily, in natural causes whereby certain men are disposed to the performance of certain functions in preference to others." *Contra impugnantes* I.5.]

43. ["Human law is law only by virtue of its accordance with right reason; and thus it is manifest that it flows from the eternal law. And in so far as it deviates from right reason it is called an unjust law; in such case it is no law at all, but rather a species of violence." Thomas Aquinas, *Summa theologiae*, I–II 93.3 ad 2.]

44. [*Rerum novarum* §§51–53, 254.]

45. [Referring to *Immortale Dei*.]

46. [Thomas Aquinas, *Summa theologiae* I–II, 61.1 ad 2.]

47. [*Rerum novarum* §§32–33, 249.]

48. [*Nobilissima Gallorum* §4 (1884), 87. The ancient Gelasian doctrine of the two powers, "twinned" because each, in its own order (*in suo ordine*), enjoys authority to rule. As he says in the next passage, the church has its own public law. Leo often uses the word *concordia* to characterize the relationship between the two powers. This word includes comity of jurisdictions, but much more than that.]

49. Matt. 28:18–20.

50. Matt. 18:12.

51. 2 Cor. 10:6.

52. 2 Cor. 13:10.

53. Acts 5:29.

54. [This is a reference to the Papal States. The Holy See still contested their appropriation by the Kingdom of Italy. The dispute was not settled until the Lateran Treaty of 1929.]

55. Rom. 13:1.

56. [He is referring chiefly to any institution or action sacramental in nature. Since this includes marriage, it is not an uncontroversial claim. He also says, "by reason of the end," which includes parental duty to educate children in the faith.]

57. [*Immortale Dei* §§11–14, 109–110.]

58. [Referring to *Quod Apostolici* (1878). Notice the two terms of art, *civitas* and *principatus*. Translators insist upon rendering *civitas* as "state." But when Leo says that Christianity should penetrate "all orders," he is not thinking of a power apparatus like a state; rather, he has in mind a public order embracing many different social spheres that are overseen by, but not reduced to, a *principatus*.]

59. [*Licet multa* § 3 (1881), 59–60.]

60. [*Sapientiae Christianae* §36, 219–220.] "Prudence proceeds from reason, and to reason it specially pertains to guide and govern. Whence it follows that, in so much as any one takes part in the control and government of affairs, in so far ought he to be gifted with reason and prudence. But it is evident that the subject, so far as subject, and the servant ought neither to control nor govern, but rather to be controlled and governed. Prudence, then, is not the special virtue of the servant, so far as servant, nor of the subject, so far as subject. But because any man, on account of his character of a reasonable being, may have some share in the government on account of the rational choice which he exercises, it is fitting that in such proportion he should possess the virtue of prudence. Whence it manifestly results that prudence exists in the ruler as the art of building exists in the architect, whereas prudence exists in the subject as the art of building exists in the hand of the workman employed in the construction." *Summa theologiae*, IIa–IIae, q xlvii, art. 12, Answer. St. Thomas Aquinas refers to Aristotle, *Ethic. Nic.*, Bk. VI, 8, 1141b 21–29.

61. [*Immortale* §36, 115. See Augustine, Tract. XXVI, *In Ioan*].

62. Heb. 13:8.

63. [*Au milieu des solicitudes* §17 (1892), 280.]

64. [*Libertas* §16, 174.]

65. [*Immortale* §4, 108. In these passages, Leo wrestles with a tricky issue much debated among Catholics at that time: Do human beings have power to create or abolish governments? Leo distinguishes between the institutional form and the binding power of government. Humans are free to designate (allocate) offices (*designatur principes*), and, in this sense, shape the form of a regime. Humans are not free to confer the binding or ruling power (*non conferuntur iura principatus*). From the premise that no one has by natural right the power to bind another, this power is always a participation in divine providence. However, Leo was concerned about more than the origin of the *principatus*. He also worried that social contract theories attempt to justify the absence of a *principatus*. The state is created to be the executive force of public opinion or the majority, in which case there might be (external) force but not the commands of a ruling power. Any legitimate "form" of government must in the first place be a real government.]

66. [*Libertas* §15, 173.]

67. [*Diuturnum* §§5–7, 52.]

68. [*Au milieu* §18, 280–81.] Rom. 13:1.

69. [Having defended the legitimacy of making or changing political regimes, Leo now cuts in the other direction. The form of the ecclesial polity is not subject

to human prudence. This issue was a flashpoint of Catholic political theology after the demise of political Christendom. In the old regime, it was believed that the regime of the prince and the priest proceeded, similarly, from the order of particular providence. The sacral narratives of kings and nations—of constitutions in the older sense of the term—were exploded by the revolutions, or, what was more troublesome, transposed into nationalism. The tendency to make the form of each power isomorphic is not easily overcome, for although modern societies subscribe to the idea of separation of the two powers, they also want the two regimes to reflect the principle of popular sovereignty. Indeed, the laicist spirit in matters political demanded that the constitution of the church follow suit. In Italy, Colombia, and above all France, efforts were made to transfer ecclesiastical property to associations of laity so that the church would mirror the principle of popular government in the civil sphere.]

70. [*Sapientiae Christianae* §28, 217–218.]

71. [Here follow Leo's addresses to Catholics in three different states: Belgium, France, and the United States. Belgian Catholics allied in 1830 with liberals against the absolutism of William I. Successfully completing their revolution against Holland, they put into place a constitution that was quite extraordinary for its time. The Constitution of 1831 forbade state exercise of the *ius praesentandi*, *placet*, and *exequatur* and provided for the liberty of public worship and speech. Yet the problem of public schools aggravated Catholic opinion. Leo wants them to steer a prudential course that resists splitting into either civil or ecclesial factions.]

72. [*Permoti nos* §6 (1895), 372.]

73. [Leo tirelessly endeavored to convince French Catholics to tone down their regime politics. In this first passage, he contends that church doctrine and tradition should not be wasted on the relative merits of monarchy versus republican forms of government. Catholics should rather attend to the mission of evangelizing society. In the next passage, he argues against the separationist principle that would prohibit the church from imprinting the gospel on society. Leo's efforts were unsuccessful on both counts. The Catholic right wing notched up its polemic and eventually was ensnared in the Dreyfus affair (1899). The Third Republic passed severe laws against Catholic institutions, culminating in the Law of Separation (1905).]

74. [*Au milieu* §14, 279–280.]

75. [Ibid. §§28–29, 282–283.]

76. [Leo was neither the first nor the last pope to appreciate the unique situation of Catholics in the United States. In an interview given to French journalists, published in *Petit Journal* (February 7, 1892), Leo praised the American regime, where the two powers "do not trespass on the rights of the other," and where each can be about its business without "barren quarrels." "The Church," he added, "claims liberty above all else." On the other hand, he worried that American separation of church and state was not a universal model. First, the same idea exported elsewhere meant suppression of church liberty. Second, Leo did not

believe that negative liberty represents the entirety of the *concordia* that ought to mark the relations of church and state.]

77. [*Longinqua oceani* §§4, 6 (1895), 364–365.]

78. [Only Christ, true God and true man, exercises the *principatus* over humans by natural right. Referring to Thomas's discussion of the judicial powers of Christ, *Summa theologiae* II–II, 67.2 ad 2.]

79. [Augustine, Tract 120, *In Ioan.*]

80. [Thomas Aquinas, *Summa theologiae* III, 59.4 ad 2.]

81. [*Annum sacrum* §§4–6 (1899), 452.]

82. [Adherence to the law is a necessary but not sufficient condition for the Christian life, which entails supernatural virtue. Such virtue is necessary even for faithfully abiding by the natural law.]

83. [Augustine, *De vera religione*, 37.]

84. [*Tametsi futura* §6, 473–474.]

85. [Ibid., §11, 476.]

[CHAPTER 2]

Jacques Maritain (1882–1973)

SELECTED AND EDITED BY PATRICK M. BRENNAN

The extraordinary life of Jacques Maritain began in Paris in 1882. His father was Catholic; his mother, Genevieve Favre (the daughter of Jules Favre, a founder of the Third Republic), was Protestant. His father and mother divorced when Jacques was a youth. The young Jacques was baptized in the French Reformed Church and received religious instruction from the liberal Protestant theologian Jean Reville. During his youth, however, Maritain considered himself an unbeliever. It was early in this barren period that Jacques met the seventeen-year-old Russian Jewish immigrant Raissa Oumansoff, whom he would marry in 1904. From the beginning Jacques and Raissa were united by a desire to search together untiringly for the truth. Raissa and Jacques Maritain's life together was structured, in important respects, according to a monastic ideal of prayer and work in the tradition of St. Benedict of Nursia. We do well to remember, encountering the sometimes strident and always passionate Jacques Maritain, that he was a convert, a "man God has turned inside out like a glove."[1]

Arrested by their friend Leon Bloy's uncompromising commitment to the call to sainthood, the Maritains began a tutorship in Catholicism under him and received the sacrament of baptism in 1906. From 1906 to 1908 the Maritains were in Germany, where Jacques studied biology at the University of Heidelberg. In 1912, following several years of editing and other independent intellectual work, Maritain accepted the offer of the chair of philosophy at the Institut Catholique of Paris. In 1914, he published his first book, Bergsonian Philosophy; *this scathing critique of his mentor's account of the mind's grasp of being promptly earned the young Maritain a reputation as a controversialist. Many other works followed, most notably* Art and Scholasticism *(1920),* The Degrees of Knowledge *(1932), and* A Preface to Metaphysics *(1934). These early speculative works revealed the young Maritain heeding Pope Leo XIII's call to take Thomas as the privileged starting point for meeting the challenges of the day.*

By working out the distinctions and unity among the philosophy of nature, experimental science, metaphysics, and mystical theology—in light of the un-

derlying unity and distinctions of being knowable by human intelligence—Maritain affirmed the unity of faith and reason. This unity and its consequences are a hallmark of all Maritain's work. When Maritain distinguished modes of human knowing, it was in order to call attention to the need for wisdom, both natural and supernatural. Jacques Maritain understood it to be his vocation, in sum, to work out a distinctly Christian and properly Thomist philosophy for the twentieth century, making way for wisdom to enter.

When Adolf Hitler came to power and war loomed, in the words of biographers Donald Gallagher and Idella Gallagher, "the circumstances of the time and their own zeal for justice obliged the Maritains to set aside some of their cherished projects in philosophy to devote more and more of their thought to social and political questions."[2] By 1936, when Jacques published his charter work in political philosophy, Integral Humanism, *he and Raissa had spent a decade involved in movements of many kinds, resisting totalitarianism both of the left and of the right.[3]*

The Maritains lived in exile in the United States until 1945. Then, from 1945 to 1948, Jacques was in Rome, serving at General de Gaulle's request as France's ambassador to the Vatican. Ambassadorial duties kept Maritain busy, but he continued to write and, during this period, published two works of great significance to his jurisprudence, Essence and the Existent *(1947) and* The Person and the Common Good *(1946).*

His work in Rome completed, Maritain accepted an appointment in philosophy at Princeton University. He taught for five years, retiring in 1953 at the age of seventy. Jacques and Raissa remained in the United States until they returned home to France in 1960. Later that year, Raissa died in Paris. In his dozen years in America, Maritain published fifteen books. He continued to publish until his death in 1973; even then, he was awaiting the proofs of a new book.

Maritain continued to be a philosopher, which to the end he insisted was his vocation. Yet, two complementary facets of the man and his life should be noted. First, relationships of all kinds, including deep friendships, were an integral part of this philosopher's life. Second, Maritain's life ended where he and Raissa began—in a passionate unwavering pursuit of the whole truth,[4] a truth sometimes found only on one's knees. The discovery, contemplation, and dissemination of the whole truth about man in unfolding Christian history: these are the sources and springs of Jacques Maritain's jurisprudence.

INAUGURAL ADDRESS TO THE SECOND INTERNATIONAL CONFERENCE OF UNESCO

OF THE TASKS assigned to the United Nations Organisation, one of those which could and should most nearly affect the conscience of the peoples is the drawing up of an *International Declaration of Human Rights*. The task was committed to the Economic and Social Council of the United Nations. UNESCO's part was to consult philosophers and assemble their replies. This volume is a collection of the most significant texts thus gathered in the course of UNESCO's enquiry into the philosophic bases of human rights.

This book then is devoted to the rational interpretation and justification of those rights of the individual which society must respect and which it is desirable for our age to strive to enumerate more fully. Many schools of thought are represented, each of which bring to the whole its particular view and justification of individual rights, leaning in various degrees towards the classical, or the revolutionary, interpretation: it is not the first time that expert witnesses have quarreled among themselves. The paradox is that such rational justifications are at once indispensable, and yet powerless to bring about agreement between minds. They are indispensable because each one of us believes instinctively in the truth, and will only assent to what he himself has recognised as true and based on reason. They are powerless to bring about a harmony of minds because they are fundamentally different, even antagonistic; and why should this surprise us? The questions they raise are difficult and the philosophic traditions to which they are related have long been divergent.

It is related that at one of the meetings of a UNESCO National Commission where human rights were being discussed, someone expressed astonishment that certain champions of violently opposed ideologies had agreed on a list of those rights. "Yes," they said, "we agree about the rights *but on condition that no one asks us why.*" That "why" is where the argument begins.

The question of human rights offers us an outstanding example of the situation I attempted to outline in an address at the Second General Conference of UNESCO, from which I venture to reproduce certain passages.

"How," I asked, "can we imagine an agreement of minds between men who are gathered together precisely in order to accomplish a common intellectual task, men who come from the four corners of the globe and who not only belong to different cultures and civilisations, but are of antagonistic spiritual associations and schools of thought?" ... Because, as I said at the beginning of my speech, the goal of UNESCO is a practical goal, agreement between minds can be reached spontaneously, not on the basis of common speculative ideas, but on common practical ideas, not on the affirmation of one and the same conception of the world, of man and of knowledge, but upon the affirmation of a single body of beliefs for guidance in action. No doubt, this is little enough, but it is the last resort to intellectual agreement. It is, nevertheless, enough to enable a great task to be undertaken, and it would do much to crystallise this body of common practical convictions.[5]

REDEEMING THE TIME

HUMAN EQUALITY

We arrive now at the third attitude to which I referred at the beginning of this chapter: the realist idea, the true idea of equality.

From a point of view that is neither nominalist nor idealist but realist, the unity or equality in nature among men is not a mere word nor a logical exigency of an abstract species fictitiously realized. It is ontological and concrete, just as much as the likenesses and affinities which in the external world serve as bases for that positive unity which the species has within our mind. For the universality of our ideas is grounded *in re*, in things, and it would be necessary to have angelic vision to measure the depth of the real relations and the real solidarity connoted by that maxim of the schools.

The equality in nature among men consists of their concrete communion in the mystery of the human species; it does not lie in an idea, it is hidden in the heart of the individual and of the concrete, in the roots of the substance of each man. Obscure because residing on the level of substance and its root energies, primordial because it is bound up with the very sources of being, human equality reveals itself, like the nearness of our neighbour, to every one who practices it; indeed it is identical with that proximity of all to each, and of each to all. If you treat a man as a man, that is to say if you respect and love the secret he carries within him and the good of which he is capable, to that extent do you make effective in yourself his closeness in nature to and his equality or unity in nature with yourself. It is the natural love of the human being for his own kind which reveals and makes real the unity of species among men. As long as love does not call it forth, that unity slumbers in a metaphysical retreat where we can perceive it only as an abstraction.

In the common experience of misery, in the common sorrow of great catastrophes, in humiliation and distress, under the blows of the executioner or the bombs of total war, in concentration camps, in the hovels of starving people in great cities, in any common *necessity*, the doors of solitude open and man recognizes man. Man also recognizes man when the sweetness of a great joy or of a great love for an instant clears his eyes. Whenever he does a service to his fellow men or is helped by them, whenever he shares the same elementary actions and the same elementary emotions, whenever he truly considers his neighbour, the simplest action discovers for him, both in others and in himself, the common resources and the common goodness—primitive, rudimentary, wounded, unconscious and repressed—of human nature. At once the realness of equality and community in nature is revealed to him as a very precious thing, an unknown marvel, a fundamental basis of existence, more important than all the differences and inequalities superimposed upon it. When he will have returned to his routine pleasures, he will have forgotten this discovery.

The authentic instinct of equality in nature, which naturally underlies and strengthens the fragile conception that our heedless intelligence can gain of this same equality when we retain that realist perspective which I have endeavoured to describe, is not secondary tendency like pride or envy, no matter how deep-seated it is within us; it is a primary instinct, the instinct of communication founded on a common membership in the same specific whole. The realist conception of equality in nature is an inheritance of the judeo-christian tradition; it is a natural prerequisite for Christian thought and life. Just as there is in every being a natural love for God above all else, without which charity would not serve to perfect nature but to destroy it,[6] so also, however it may be weakened by sin, there must be in man a natural love for his own kind without which the love of the gospel for men of every race and every condition would be contrary to nature rather than its exaltation. How should we all be called upon thus to love one another in god if we were not all equal in our condition and specific dignity as rational creatures?

Christianity confirms and emphasizes the concrete sense of equality in nature by affirming its historical and genealogical character, and by teaching that here we are concerned with a blood relationship, properly socalled, all men being descended from the same original parents, and being brothers in Adam before they are brothers in Christ. Heirs of the same sin and the same weaknesses, but heirs also of the same original greatness, all created in the image of God and all called to the same supernatural dignity as adopted sons of God, and to coheirship with Christ the Saviour, all redeemed by the same life-giving Blood, and thus destined to become equals of the angels in heaven,[7] what Christian can look upon man with the demented gaze of racist pride? The *unity of mankind* is at the basis of Christianity. . . .

It is because the Christian conception of life is based upon so concrete, broad, and fruitful a certainty of the equality and community in nature between men that it, at the same time, insists so forcefully on the orderings and hierarchies which spring and should spring from the very heart of this essential community, and on the particular inequalities which they necessarily involve. For in the world of man as in the world of creation, there can be no concourse or communication, no life or movement without differentiation, no differentiation without inequalities.[8]

Christianity fearlessly asserts the necessity of these inequalities; it respects them, furthers them, favours them, for it knows that as long as they remain normal—that is as long as the human will, by a kind of perversion, does not undertake to make them serve as means of exclusion rather than a communication and make them crush the essential equality and the primordial community which they presuppose—the inequalities, which lend variety to human life and intensify the richness of life's encounters, in no way injure the dignities which befit the unity of mankind and the rights which are grounded on this unity. On the contrary, these inequalities make such a unity all the more manifest. Every man is a man in his very essence, but no man is man in essence, that is, exhausts in himself all the riches of the various perfections of which human-kind is capable. In this sense all the diversity of perfections and virtues distributed through the generations of men in space and time is but a varied participation in the common and inexhaustible potentialities of man.[9]

MAN AND THE STATE

THE BODY POLITIC

In contradistinction to the *Nation*, both the *Body Politic* and the *State* pertain to the order of society, even society in its highest or "perfect" form. In our modern age the two terms are used synonymously, and the second tends to supersede the first. Yet if we are to avoid serious misunderstandings, we have to distinguish clearly between the State and the Body Politic. These do not belong to two diverse categories, but they differ from each other as a part differs from the whole. The *Body Politic* or the *Political Society* is the whole. The *State* is a part—the topmost part—of this whole.

Political Society, required by nature and achieved by reason, is the most perfect of temporal societies. It is a concretely wholly human reality, tending to a concretely and wholly human good—the common good. It is a work of reason, born out of the obscure efforts of reason disengaged from instinct, and implying essentially a rational order; but it is no more Pure Reason than man himself. The body politic has flesh and blood, instincts, passions, reflexes, unconscious psychological structures and dynamism—all of these subjected, if necessary by legal coercion, to the command of an Idea and rational decisions. Justice is a primary condition for the existence of the body politic, but Friendship is its very life-giving form. It tends toward a really human and freely achieved communion. It lives on the devotion of the human persons and their gift of themselves. They are ready to commit their own existence, their possessions and their honor for its sake. The civic sense is made up of this sense of devotion and mutual love as well as of the sense of justice and law.

The entire man—though not by reason of his entire self and of all that he is and has—is part of the political society; and thus all his community activities, as well as his personal activities, are of consequence to the political whole. As we have pointed out, a national community of a higher human degree spontaneously takes shape by virtue of the very existence of the body politic, and in turn becomes part of the substance of the latter. Nothing matters more, in the order of material causality, to the life and preservation of the body politic than the accumulated energy and historical continuity of that national community it has itself caused to exist. This means chiefly a heritage of accepted and unquestionable structures, fixed customs and deep-rooted common feelings which bring into social life itself something of the determined physical data of nature, and of the vital unconscious strength proper to vegetative organisms. It is, further, common inherited experience and the moral and intellectual instincts which constitute a kind of empirical, practical wisdom, much deeper and denser and much nearer the hidden complex dynamism of human life than any artificial construction of reason.

Not only is the national community, as well as all communities of the nation, thus comprised in the superior unity of the body politic. But the body politic also contains in its superior unity the family units, whose essential rights and freedoms are anterior to itself, and a multiplicity of other particular societies which proceed from the free initiative of citizens and should be as autonomous as possible. Such is the element of pluralism inherent in every truly political society. Family, economic, cultural, educational, religious life matter as much as does political life to the very existence and prosperity of the body politic. Every kind of law, from the spontaneous, unformulated group regulations to customary law and to law in the full sense of the term, contributes to the vital order of political society. Since in political society authority comes from below, through the people, it is normal that the whole dynamism of authority in the body politic should be made up of particular and partial authorities rising in tiers above one another, up to the top authority of the State. Finally, the public welfare and the general order of law are essential parts of the common good of the body politic, but this common good has far larger and richer, more concretely human implications, for it is by nature the good human life of the multitude and is common to both the *whole* and the *parts*, the persons into whom it flows back and who must benefit from it. The common good is not only the collection of public commodities and services which the organization of common life presupposes: a sound fiscal condition, a strong military force; the body of just laws, good customs, and wise institutions which provides the political society with its structure; the heritage of its great historical remembrances, its symbols and its glories, its living traditions and cultural treasures. The common good also includes the sociological integration of all the civic conscience, political virtues and sense of law and freedom, of all the activity, material prosperity and spiritual riches, of unconsciously operating hereditary wisdom, of moral rectitude, justice, friendship, happiness, virtue and heroism in the individual lives of the members of the body politic. To the extent to which all these things are, in a certain measure, *communicable* and revert to each member, helping him to perfect his life and liberty as a person, they all constitute the good human life of the multitude.

THE STATE

From this enumeration of the features of the body politic, it should be evident that the body politic differs from the State. The State is only that part of the body politic especially concerned with the maintenance of law, the promotion of the common welfare and public order, and the administration of public affairs. The State is a part which *specializes* in the interests of the *whole*. It is not a man or a body of men; it is a set of institutions combined into a topmost machine: this kind of work of art has been built by man and uses human brains and energies and is nothing without man, but it constitutes a superior embodiment of reason, an impersonal, lasting superstructure, the functioning of which may be said to be rational in the second degree, insofar as the reason's activity in it, bound by law and by a system of universal regulations, is more abstract, more sifted out from the contingencies of experience and individuality, more pitiless also, than our individual lives.

The State is not the supreme incarnation of the Idea, as Hegel believed; the State is not a kind of collective superman; the State is but an agency entitled to use power and coercion, and made up of experts or specialists in public order and welfare, an instrument in the service of man. Putting man at the service of that instrument is political perversion. The human person as an individual is for the body politic and the body politic is for the human person as a person. But man is by no means for the State. The State is for man.

When we say that the State is the superior part in the body politic, this means that it is superior to the other organs or collective parts of this body, but it does not mean that it is superior to the body politic itself. The part as such is inferior to the whole. The State is inferior to the body politic as a whole, and is at the service of the body politic as a whole. Is the State even the *head* of the body politic? Hardly, for in the human being the head is an instrument of such spiritual powers as the intellect and the will, which the whole body has to serve; whereas the functions exercised by the State are for the body politic, and not the body politic for them.

The theory which I have just summarized, and which regards the State as a part or an instrument of the body politic, subordinate to it and endowed with topmost authority not by its own right and for its own sake, but only by virtue and to the extent of the requirements of the common good, can be described as an "instrumentalist" theory, founding the genuinely *political* notion of the State. But we are confronted with quite another notion, the *despotic* notion of the State, based on a "substantialist" or "absolutist" theory. According to this theory the State is a subject of right, i.e., a moral person, and consequently a whole; as a result it is either superimposed on the body politic or made to absorb the body politic entirely, and it enjoys supreme power by virtue of its own natural, inalienable right and for its own final sake.

Of course there is for everything great and powerful an instinctive tendency—and a special temptation—to grow beyond its own limits. Power tends to increase power, the power machine tends ceaselessly to extend itself; the supreme legal and administrative machine tends toward bureaucratic self-sufficiency; it would like to consider itself an end, not a means. Those who specialize in the affairs of the whole have a propensity to take themselves for the whole; the general staffs to take themselves for the whole army, the Church authorities for the whole Church; the State for the whole body politic. By the same token, the State tends to ascribe to itself a peculiar common good—its own self-preservation and growth—distinct both from the public order and welfare which are its immediate end, and from the common good which is its final end. All these misfortunes are but instances of "natural" excess or abuse. . . .

[The absolutist] concept of the State, enforced in human history, has forced democracies into intolerable self-contradictions, in their domestic life and above all in international life. . . . For democracies today the most urgent endeavor is to develop social justice and improve world economic management, and to defend themselves against totalitarian threats from the outside and totalitarian expansion in the world; but the pursuit of these objectives will inevitably involve the risk of having too many functions of social life controlled by the State from above, and we shall be inevitably bound to accept this risk, as long as our notion of the State has not been restated on true and genuine democratic foundations, and as long as the body politic has not renewed its own structures and consciousness, so that the people become more effectively equipped for the exercise of freedom, and the State may be made an actual instrument for the common good of all. Then only will that very topmost agency, which is made by modern civilization more and more necessary to the human person in his political, social, moral, even intellectual and scientific progress, cease to be at the same time a threat to the freedoms of the human person as well as of intelligence and science. Then only will the highest functions of the State—to ensure the law and facilitate the free development of the body politic—be restored, and the sense of the State be regained by the citizens. Then only will the State achieve its true dignity, which comes not from power and prestige, but from the exercise of justice.[10]

CHURCH AND STATE

It should be pointed out ... first, that the subjects of rights are not abstract entities like "truth" or "error," but human persons, individually or collectively taken; second, that the equality of rights of all citizens is the basis tenet of modern democratic societies. Therefore the very fact (on which I have so often laid stress in this chapter) that the temporal society, become secular or strictly temporal, unites in its common task and common good men belonging to different religious lineages, has as its consequence that the principle of equality of rights is to be applied—not to "doctrines" or "creeds," this would have no meaning—but to the *citizens* who belong in these different religious lineages, which the body politic, from its own point of view, regards as parts of its own common moral heritage. Is it not, as I have previously remarked, through the citizens who are members of the Church that the Church, who is above the body politic, enters the sphere of the body politic and of its temporal common good? As a result it is from the point of view of the rights of the citizens who compose the body politic that the State will define its own positions with regard to the juridical status of the Church within the temporal sphere and in relation to the temporal common good.

Thus the Christian political society which I am discussing—supposing that the faith to which the majority of the people belonged were the Catholic faith—would know perfectly well that the Church herself was no part of it, but above it. And in this connection it would recognize the juridical personality of the Church as well as her spiritual authority in ruling her members in her spiritual realm, and it would deal with her as a perfect and perfectly independent society, with which it would conclude agreements and with the supreme authority of which it would maintain diplomatic relations. Yet, for all that, this Christian political society would have to hold that, in its own temporal sphere, and with regard to the rights they possess, Christian citizens (with the collective activities they and their multifarious institutions freely display in the national community) are no more legally privileged than any other citizens.

In other terms, this Christian political society would realize that there is only one temporal common good, that of the body politic, as there is only one supernatural common good, that of the Kingdom of God, which is supra-political. Once the political society had been fully differentiated in its secular type, the fact of inserting into the body politic a particular or partial common good, the temporal common good of the faithful of one religion (even though it were the true religion), and of claiming for them, accordingly, a privileged juridical position in the body politic, would be inserting into the latter a divisive principle and, to that extent, interfering with the temporal common good.

After these preliminary remarks, I come to the point under discussion, namely the specific forms of mutual help between the Church and the political society.

As I have observed ... man is a member both of the body politic and, if he adheres to the Church, of that supra-temporal society which is the Church. He would be cut in two if his temporal membership were cut off from his spiritual membership. They must be in actual contact and connection. And an actual contact and connection, if it is not a contact and connection of mutual antagonism, is a contact and connection of mutual help. Moreover the common good itself of the temporal society implies that human persons are indirectly assisted by the latter in their movement toward supra-temporal achievement, which is an essential part of the pursuit of happiness. Finally (not to speak even of the fact, defined by theology, that human nature in its existential condition needs divine grace in order to achieve its highest human ends, social as well as individual), the Christian political society which we are discussing would be aware of the fact that Christian truths and incentives and the inspiration of the Gospel, awakening common consciousness and passing into the sphere of temporal existence, are the very soul, inner strength, and spiritual stronghold of democracy. Just as democracy must, under penalty of disintegration, foster and defend the democratic charter; so a Christian democracy, that is, a democracy fully aware of its own sources, must, under penalty of disintegration, keep alive in itself the Christian sense of human dignity and human equality, of justice and freedom. For the political society really and vitally Christian which we are contemplating, the suppression of any actual contact and connection, that is, of any mutual help, between the Church and the body politic would simply spell suicide. . . .

Insuring to the Church her full liberty and the free exercise of her spiritual mission is fundamentally required by the God-given rights of the Church as well as by the basic rights of the human person. But it is also required by the common good of the body politic. For it is the condition for that spreading of the leaven of the Gospel throughout the whole social body which the temporal common good needs in its own sphere. The State acts simply in its own way, as providing the common good of the body politic, in guaranteeing the full freedom of the Church in her spiritual mission. And, as we have seen, it can insure that guarantee—in our historical age it ensures it in the best way—without granting any juridical privilege to the citizens who are members of the Church.

Finally there is a second specific form of mutual assistance which is also required. I mean not only a negative assistance, as is the insurance of freedom, but a positive one. This time I am not speaking of the State, but of the body politic with its free agencies and institutions. . . . They would positively facilitate the religious, social, and educational work by means of which she—as well as the other spiritual or cultural groups whose helpfulness for the common good would be recognized by them—freely cooperates in the common welfare. By removing obstacles and opening the doors, the body politic, its free agencies and institutions, would positively facilitate the effort of the apostles of the Gospel to go to the masses and share their life, to assist the social and moral work of the nation, to provide people with leisure worthy of human dignity, and to develop within them the sense of liberty and fraternity.[11]

GOD AND THE PERMISSION OF EVIL

MORAL EVIL AND THE ETERNAL PLAN

The leading idea of *Existence and the Existent* is very simple. It is a question of following through to the end that dissymmetry between the line of good and the line of evil on which I have already insisted so much; and consequently of recognizing all the bearing of this assertion that the first cause or the *inventor* of moral evil *in the existential reality of the world* is the liberty of the creature—I mean, this liberty *in the line of non-being*. All of this implies that at the very first origin of the evil act—and, above all, of the evil election, which takes place in the depths of the heart—there is not only the *fallibility* of the creature, but an *actual failure* of the creature, a created initiative which—since it is not caused by God—can only be an initiative of non-being, of deficiency in being, of lack, what I have called a nihilation.

At the bottom of the whole affair is contained in a Gospel saying: *Sine me nihil potestis facere*, it is said in Saint John, 15:5.

Well, this text can be read in two ways.

It can be read: *Without Me you can do nothing*—nothing *good*. This is the line of being or of good, where God has the first initiative.

And it can also be read: *Without Me you can do nothingness*, without me you can introduce into being that nothingness or that *non-being of the due good*, that *privation*, which is *evil*. And this even, this initiative of evil, you can have it only without Me (for with Me it is good only that you can do). Here we have the line of non-being or of evil, where created liberty has the first initiative. . . .

All right! It is indeed true that in this view the Creator of the world does not provide Himself with the absolutely safe spectacle of a game of marionettes which would but put into execution a program that He Himself has conceived for evil as well as for good. It is indeed true that in this view, if God wills that we engage ourselves headlong in the battle, it is because He Himself has first engaged in it the glory of His name, nay more, because He has engaged Himself in it completely, by sending us His Son, one with Him in nature.

In this view, the creature, each time that it does evil, introduces to this extent nothingness into being, and undoes for a part the work that God makes. The work of God runs risks, risks that are real because the drama is not merely portrayed, it is actually *lived*. There are abysses which open out, collapses, disasters. The gods from below that free agents are when they take the initiative of nothingness, cause evil and perversion to multiply, and invent forms of horror and of abomination which astonish the angels (and, if I may say so ... astonish the Author himself of the drama, in this sense that if He knows in His "science of simple intelligence" all *possible* evil, it is not He, it is the creature who invents *existing* evil, and in such an invention goes beyond all expectation).

But it is in all this, exactly, that the invincible wisdom and the dazzling power of the eternal purposes manifest themselves. He whose Name is above every name, the eternally Victorious is certain to win the game finally; He wins it at each instant, even when He seems to be losing it. Each time that a free creature undoes for its part the work that God makes, God remakes to that extent—for the better—this work and leads it to higher ends. Because of the presence of evil on earth, everything on earth, from the beginning to the end of time, is in perpetual recasting. However real the risks may be, much more real still is the strength of the arm which causes them to be surmounted by creation and repairs the damages incurred by the latter. However deep the abysses may be, however great the collapses and the disasters, sublimer are the heights and the goods to which created being will be transferred. And doubtless there will also be, finally, real losses—all too real—but themselves compensated by the manifestation of eternal justice in the creature when, in order to remain to itself its ultimate End, it prefers over love all the pains of Hell. And the more the gods from below cause horror and evil to multiply, the more the saints in their love, accomplishing in their flesh what is lacking to the sufferings of Christ, cause the magnificence of good to superabound. . . . And finally it is by having made good use of his liberty moved and activated from end to end by God, and by having from all eternity contributed for his part as free second cause to the very establishment of the eternal plan, that the creature saved—the one who in the end will not have said *No*—will enter into the glory that God has prepared for those who love Him, and which was His intention in creating the world, this world where evil is permitted. . . .

Let us hope (and let us do *all* that is humanly possible—in honesty of conscience—to attain this) that from social evils which revolt us, from slavery, from misery, from the power of great monsters which devour the individual person, from the barbarous conditions in which so many of God's creatures live, human history will emerge not only with the cessation of these evils, but with an increase of goods for humanity—so that the spirit may gain ascendancy, that the unification of the human race may come about under the sign of liberty, not of a herd conformism, and that all men may have access *free of charge* to the elementary goods of human life! But let us not forget that moreover all these advances themselves—we are in the history of this world—will be more or less spoiled (not *too* spoiled, may it please God!) by evil which progresses at the same time. And this kind of overlapping of good on evil, and of evil on good, and more still (with all the reservations I have just indicated) of good on evil—well, such is the history of the human race.[12]

NATURAL LAW AND MORAL LAW

In this chapter I should like to try to clarify certain basic concepts—basic for the theory of Natural Law—in the perspective of Thomistic philosophy.

NATURAL LAW (*LEX NATURALIS*)

Reason is "the measure of human actions." Thus reason—human reason—is a measuring measure (*mensura mensurans*). Yet reason is also a measured measure (*mensura mensurata*), for human reason is not the supreme rule of good and evil. In order to measure human conduct, practical reason has to be measured by something. What is it by which practical reason is measured? Natural Law (*lex naturalis*. In the expression "natural law" it is appropriate to understand "law" in the sense of *lex*, not of *jus*). Let us summarize as briefly as possible the fundamental characteristics of Natural Law.[13]

Two essential components must be recognized in the notion of Natural Law: the *ontological* and the *gnoseological*.

Considered in its ontological component, Natural Law is the normality of functioning of the human being. Every kind of being existing in nature, a plant, a dog, horse, has its own "natural law," that is, the proper way in which, by reason of its specific structure and ends, it "should" achieve fullness of being in its growth or in its behavior. Now this very word "should" begins to have a *moral* sense, that is, to imply moral obligation, when we pass the threshold of the world of free agents. Natural Law—strictly speaking, Natural Law for man—is moral law, because man obeys or disobeys it freely. We might compare natural law in general with an algebraic equation according to which a curve develops in space. But with man the curve must conform freely to the equation.

Let us say, then, that in its ontological aspect Natural Law is an ideal order or a *divide* between the suitable and the unsuitable, the proper and the improper, which depends on human nature and its essential ends. In this first consideration (ontological) Natural Law is co-extensive with the whole field of moral regulations which concern man as man—even if they are grounded on the most subtle and refined considerations—with the whole field of ethical philosophy, as universally valid.

But the second essential component of the notion of Natural Law, the gnoseological component, causes the extent of this notion to be greatly restricted. For Natural Law is natural not only in so far as it is the normality of functioning of human nature, but also in so far as it is *naturally known*: that is to say, known *through inclination*, by way of congeniality or connaturality, not through conceptual knowledge and by way of reasoning. Here we have a crucial point, which in my opinion has been too often disregarded. It deals with the manner in which Natural Law is made manifest to practical reason. Natural Law is made manifest to practical reason in certain judgments, but these very judgments do not proceed from any conceptual, discursive, rational exercise of reason. They proceed from *connaturality* or *congeniality* through which what is consonant with the essential inclinations of human nature is grasped by the intellect as good; what is dissonant, as bad. And they therefore remain always more or less immersed in the vital and experiential, conceptually inexpressible dynamism of inclinations and tendencies. The motive power on which they depend is not reason, demonstration, *logos*, but nature and nature's root inclinations. Thus it is that Natural Law is, in the fullest sense of this word, *unwritten* law. And, by the same token, it appears that Natural Law, considered not in its ontological component alone but also in its gnoseological component, only embraces those requirements of the human being's normality of functioning which are *known through inclination*—in other words, the principles "immediately" known (that is, without conceptual or rational medium) of human morality.

At this point two observations of the utmost importance should be made, which, to my regret, I cannot discuss here as fully as I should like. First, the inclinations to which I have just referred are not the animal instincts, qua animal, but the inclinations—ontological, animal and rational—of the human being *in so far as they are human,* or in so far as they are vitally rooted in the non-conceptual life of the mind, that is, in reason as "form" or entelechy of our psychological energies (a function of reason which is performed in a pre-conscious manner). Let us say, then, inclinations of nature as refracted through the crystal of reason in its unconscious or pre-conscious life. For what is consonant with reason spontaneously pleases the rational animal.

Second, these natural inclinations rooted in reason presuppose a primary, self-evident principle: "the good is to be done, the evil to be avoided," of which all men are aware. But as to further determinations, they are dependent upon historical progress which is characteristic of mankind. For man is an animal of culture, an historical animal. As a result, the essential inclinations of which we are speaking either developed or were released in the course of an historical progress which was constantly thwarted, moreover, by any kind of accidental process of regression or perversion. Thus it is that man's knowledge of the content of Natural Law was progressively formed and molded by the inclinations of human nature, starting with the most basic ones. The very history of human conscience distinguishes genuine human inclinations from spurious or perverted ones. The truly authentic inclinations were those which, in the long history of human conscience, led reason to an awareness of the regulations which, recognized more or less indeterminately from the time of the oldest social communities, have remained permanent in the human race, while assuming forms more definite and more clearly determined. At this point nothing appears more valuable to moral philosophy, especially to the theory of Natural Law, than the data of anthropology. . . .

We can understand, moreover, why there is a large measure of variability in the particular rules, customs, standards of life through which, among all of the earth's people, mankind has conveyed its knowledge of the most fundamental and deep-seated principles of Natural Law. This spontaneous knowledge does not bear upon conceptually discovered and rationally deduced moral regulations but upon regulations known through inclination, and in its ultimate source, upon general frameworks, which are tendential in nature, dynamic schemes of moral regulations still in a primitive state.

Within such tendential frameworks or dynamic schemes the content may be considerably varied and more or less deficient, not to mention those warped, perverted or devious inclinations which may be intermingled with authentic and fundamental inclinations.

ETERNAL LAW

These explanations, although summary, provide a sufficiently clear idea of what Natural Law is. It is necessary, however, to proceed further, for the concept of Natural Law is given its definitive meaning only when that of Eternal Law has been established.

This concept of Eternal Law is not solely theological. It is a philosophical truth as well, one which the philosopher with his means alone can reach and establish. God exists. He is the first cause of being, activating all beings. It is by His intellect and will that He acts: whence the notion of Providence. The entire community of the universe is governed by the divine reason. Hence, there is in God, as in One who governs the entirety of created beings, this very reality which is the judgment and command of the practical intellect applied to the governing of a unified community: in other words, this very reality which we call *law*. Eternal Law is one with the eternal wisdom of God and the divine essence itself. Saint Thomas defines this Eternal Law as "nothing other than the exemplar of divine wisdom insofar as this wisdom directs all the actions and movements of things."[14]

It is evidently to this Eternal Law that we must have recourse if we are in search of the first foundation of Natural Law. Because every law is a work of reason, at the source of Natural Law there must be reason: not human reason but Subsistent Reason, the intellect which is one with the First Truth itself. "Law is a measure and a rule," says Saint Thomas, "and hence is found in him who rules, and also in that which is measured and ruled, for a thing is ruled and measured insofar as it participates in the measure and rule existing in the one who rules. Now, since all things are ruled and measured by the Eternal Law, we must conclude that they participate in this Law insofar as they derive from it the inclinations through which they tend naturally toward their proper operations and ends. Now among all creatures, the rational creature is subject to divine providence in a particular and more excellent way, inasmuch as it has a share in providential government, by being provident both for itself and others. Thus the rational creature by its very rationality participates in the eternal reason, and because of this participation has a natural inclination to the actions and ends proper to it." (What is meant here are those inclinations "rooted in reason" of which we were just speaking.) "It is this participation in the Eternal Law enjoyed by the rational creature which is called the Natural Law."[15]

What emerges from this doctrine—and this is a fundamental point—is that the Natural Law is known by human reason, but that human reason, in its rational exercise, has no part in its establishment. The divine reason alone is the author of Natural Law. . . . The notion of law is essentially bound up with that of an ordering reason. Indeed, in the case of Natural Law, human reason has no share in the initiative and authority establishing the Law, either in making it exist or in making it known. How then does it know Natural Law? It knows it through inclination, by connaturality—through the inclinations of nature, which is the work of God, and not by its own rational effort. It knows the Law; it in no way makes it. According as human reason knows Natural Law through inclination, it is in a very precise sense "natural reason," *ratio naturalis*, and the light of this natural reason is "nothing other than a certain impression of the divine light upon us."[16] The author of Natural Law is exclusively the divine reason.

The fact that the divine reason is the only reason which is author of the Law enables us to understand better the meaning of Saint Thomas' expression: Natural Law is a participation in the Eternal Law. It is the divine reason which is involved. If human reason had a hand in it, the Law would, to that extent, have no more than the value of human authority.

The formal medium by which we advance in our knowledge of the regulations of Natural Law is not the conceptual work of reason, but rather those inclinations to which the practical intellect conforms in judging what is good and what is bad. Through the channel of natural inclinations the divine reason imprints its light upon human reason. This is why the notion of knowledge through inclination is basic to the understanding of Natural Law, for it brushes aside any intervention of human reason as a creative factor in Natural Law.

It is evident, then, how strongly and decisively Natural Law obliges *by virtue* of Eternal Law. It is from the divine reason that it possesses its rational character, and consequently, it is from the divine reason that it possesses its genuine nature as law and its obligatory character. . . .

I would like to remark further, concerning the concept of Eternal Law, that this concept enables us to realize the essentially analogical character of the notion of law. . . . For the definition of law: "A certain ordinance of reason for the common good, promulgated by him who has the care of the community,"[17] has its first realization—in itself, *secundum se*, and not with regard to us and our manner of knowing—in the Eternal Law. But God is not a legislator like the others. The community that He heads is the entire created universe. The Eternal Law is not written upon paper, it is promulgated in the divine intellect and is known in itself solely by God and by those who see Him in His essence. However, Saint Thomas writes that every rational creature knows a certain reflection of it insofar as this creature knows truth. "For all knowledge of truth is a sort of reflection of and participation in the Eternal Law, which is the unchangeable truth."[18] The Eternal Law is as infinitely distant from written or human law as the divine essence is from created being. Between the two there is only an analogical community. Likewise, the notion of law is only analogically common to the concepts of Natural Law and positive law, and so also to the concepts of Natural Law and Eternal Law. This analogicity of the notion of law will be even more readily grasped if we discuss the concept of "right" (*jus*) and compare it with that of "law" (*lex*).[19] What is the relation between law and right?

NATURAL RIGHT

When it is a question of positive law (written law), the relation between law and right is very simple—it is a relation of identity. Positive right and positive law are the same thing: they are synonyms, because the notion of right, or of juridical order, signifies a code of laws suited to a certain type of common life which men are not only obliged to obey in conscience, but can be constrained to obey by the coercive power of society. We are confronted, therefore, with the notion of *debitum legale*, of what is legally due or legally just, the neglect of which is punishable by the external sanctions established by law. Given this meaning of the word "right," it is clear that positive right and positive law are the same thing: positive right and positive law emanate from social authority and are sanctioned by the constraints of society. We have here the order of legality or the juridical order which supposes the moral order, but which adds something to it, namely, this possibility of constraint by society.

But let us consider now the domain of Natural Law, which is that of morality, and not of legality. As we have already remarked, although the notion of Natural Law in itself (*secundum se*) is prior to that of positive law, nevertheless, *as far as we ourselves* and our manner of knowing are concerned (*quoad nos*), it is from the idea of the positive law, which is first known, that we proceed to the idea of the Natural Law. Consequently, since we say positive law and positive right with equivalent meaning, it seems natural to say *right* and *law* equivalently when the question is one of Natural Law. Hence the use of the expression "natural right" (*Naturrecht, droit naturel*) in the habitual language of philosophers and jurists.

The application of the notion of right in such a domain, however, involves us in serious difficulties. Natural Law—which is not written, which concerns man as man, and a community which is neither the body politic nor the civilized community but simply the community of the human species, and which obliges us in conscience—Natural Law is promulgated in our reason as knowing (insofar as it knows through inclination), and not as legislating; and it concerns the moral, not the juridical order. What we have here is nothing other than the notion of *debitum morale*, of that which is morally due by virtue of right reason, or by virtue of Natural Law, but not by virtue of a juridical constraint. How, then, under these conditions, can we speak of natural *right*? Is there not a simple contradiction in terms here, and would it not be preferable to rid oneself of such an expression? This is a temptation for the philosopher, for it would be the most convenient thing to do. Nevertheless, I do not believe that we must yield to it. In considering things more closely, we see that, in spite of everything, we do have a solid basis for speaking of natural right, and not only in the sense that this or that precept of Natural Law may become an object of a prescription of the positive law. For in a considerably more profound and universal sense it is necessary to say that each man bears within himself the *judiciary authority* of humanity. (It is not a question here of the civilized community, as in the case of the law of nations, but of the human species.) This is true in an analogical but nonetheless real sense. Each member of the human species bears within him in a certain manner the judiciary authority of humanity, and consequently, the right of imposing constraint which derives from this authority. . . .

We have, then, the notion of a virtual juridical order which always remains virtual, and which never unfolds as a juridical order expressed in positive law and in the judiciary authority of human society, for we cannot conceive of a tribunal which would be charged with enforcing the Natural Law. As soon as a precept of Natural Law is expressed in written law, it becomes a precept of written law and by this token it is part of positive right, of the juridical positive order. But the *natural right* itself, insofar as it is natural *right*, remains *virtual*, enveloped in the Natural Law, and it is actualized in exceptional cases, for example, as we have seen, when a man or a State finds it necessary to exercise the judiciary authority of which the human species as such is depositary and which is derived from its Author, from the Divine Reason and Subsistent Justice.

Thus, natural right does not require, as a fulfillment which it should receive, formulation in positive law and in the juridical order in the full and formal sense of the word. It remains enveloped in the Natural Law.

JUS GENTIUM

With the *jus gentium* (the law of nations),[20] on the contrary, we enter a domain in which the notion of right (*jus*) no longer takes on merely a virtual but a formal and actual meaning as well. For the philosopher or jurist, there is no notion more fraught with difficulties than that of the law of nations. The different theories which have been advanced since the sixteenth century have succeeded in obscuring the concept rather than clarifying it. It is difficult to define the law of nations, because it is intermediary between the Natural Law and the positive law—although Saint Thomas does connect it rather with the positive law. Our thought on the subject would profit greatly if, as a result of the systematic elucidation to which we now proceed, we were able to determine clearly and exactly in what the law of nations consists.

Let us say, then, that in its most profound meaning, as we are able to disengage it from the thought of Saint Thomas, the law of nations (I would prefer to say the common law of civilization) differs from the Natural Law in the manner in which it is *known*, or in relation to the second essential component, the gnoseological component of the Natural Law. It is necessary to insist on the manner in which the law in question is known. The law of nations is known, not through inclination, but through the conceptual exercise of reason. This is the specific difference distinguishing the law of nations from the Natural Law. The Natural Law is known through inclination, the law of nations is known through the conceptual exercise of the human reason (considered not in such and such an individual, but in common civilized humanity). In this sense, it pertains to the positive law, and for this reason Saint Thomas relates it to positive law: since wherever human reason intervenes as author, we are in the general domain of the positive law. In this case, the human reason does not intervene as the author of the *existence of the law* (which is the case with positive law in the strict sense), but it does intervene as the author of the *knowledge of the law*. In consequence, with the law of nations, we have already a juridical order, no longer virtual as in the case of natural right but formal, although not necessarily written into a code. As to the manner in which the regulations of the law in question are known, it must be said that they are known through the rational, logical, conceptual exercise of the common reason, starting from more profound and more primary principles which are the principles of Natural Law.

Now it is necessary to make a distinction concerning the *content* of the law of nations. In the first place, the law of nations may include regulations pertaining also to the Natural Law (since the principle of distinction is not the content of the law, but the manner in which the knowledge of the law takes place). Hence, certain regulations which are based upon human nature, and which are connected necessarily with the first principle: "Do good and avoid evil," may be known on the one hand through inclination (in which sense they belong to Natural Law), and on the other hand through the conceptual exercise of reason (in which sense they belong to the law of nations). . . .

The same thing may belong to the Natural Law if it is known through inclination and if the divine reason is the only operative principle causing it to be known as well as to exist, and to the law of nations if it is known by human reason which, intervening between the Divine Reason, the cause of nature, and the knowledge of the precept, acts on its own account and thus introduces an element of positive law.

In the second place, and this is the most general and most interesting case, the content of the law of nations may concern things which, although universally obligatory since they are deduced from a principle of the Natural Law, and although necessarily connected with the first principle: "Do good and avoid evil," go beyond the Natural Law because they are not previously known through inclination but are known *only* as the result of the conceptual exercise of reason, a deduction made not by jurists or philosophers, but by the common reason of humanity. Take this example: "Do not condemn anyone without a hearing." I do not think that this rule is first known through inclination; it is known only as a conclusion logically deduced from what is due in justice to an accused man. In such a case we have a precept of the law of nations which is not a precept of the Natural Law. . . .

The law of nations or the common law of civilization has to do with duties which are necessarily bound up with the first principle: "Do good and avoid evil," but in cases like those I have just mentioned, this necessity is seen and established by human reason. And precisely because the regulations dealing with social life are *par excellence* the work of human reason, we have been gradually led to regard the law of nations as pertaining more to the social domain and especially to the international domain. But it is absurd to reduce the law of nations to the laws of international morality. According to what we have seen, every norm of conduct which is universally valid, but which is known to common consciousness because necessarily deduced by human reason, is a part of *jus gentium* or the common law of civilization.

The law of nations belongs at once to the moral order and to the juridical order; it presupposes a *debitum morale*, a moral obligation appealing to conscience, before the legal obligation, *debitum legale*. At the same time the law of nations is a formal juridical order, although not necessarily a written one. Hence it differs at once from natural right because it is not merely virtually contained in the order of natural morality, and from positive right because it is not necessarily promulgated by social authority and applied by judiciary authority. It may be formulated juridically; in fact, it seeks to be, but is not necessarily so formulated. Before it is at some future time formulated in the code of a supranational world society whose tribunals would be required to enforce it, the law of nations is first of all formulated in the common conscience by human reason in its legislative role, making the law known through its own conceptual means. In a word, it is based upon the natural order of morality, but it emanates necessarily from this order as the first formal juridical order.

POSITIVE RIGHT

We come finally to positive law. The positive law in force in any particular social group, whether it be a question of customary right or written right, has to do with the rights and duties which are bound up in a *contingent*, not a necessary, manner with the first principle of the practical intellect: "Do good and avoid evil." And it has as its author not the divine reason but the human reason.[21] By virtue of determined rules of conduct, established by the reason and will of men when they institute the laws or engender the customs of a particular social group, certain things will be good and permissible and certain things bad and not permissible, but it is the human reason which establishes this. Human reason intervenes here as a creative factor not only in that which concerns the knowledge of the law—as in the case of the law of nations—but in that which concerns the very existence of the law. It has the astounding power of laying it down that certain things will henceforth be good and others bad. Thus, for example, a police ordinance has decreed that it will henceforth be good for motorists to stop at the red light and to go when the light is green. There is no kind of natural structure which requires this; it depends uniquely upon the human reason. But once this regulation has been promulgated, it is evil not to stop at the red light. There is thus a moral good and a moral evil which depend upon the human reason because it takes into consideration the particular exigencies of the common good in these given circumstances, in conformity, however, with principles of the Natural Law, as for example: "Do not harm your fellow men." But the Natural Law itself does not prescribe the rules in question, it leaves them to the ultimate determination and initiative of the human reason. The Natural Law itself requires that what it leaves undetermined be ultimately determined by human reason.

Hence, the positive law obliges men in conscience—in other words the *debitum legale* that it institutes is also a *debitum morale*—because it obliges by virtue of the Natural Law. By the same token we see that an unjust law is not a law. This follows as a consequence from what I have just said, that is, from the fact that the positive law obliges by virtue of the Natural Law which is a participation in the Eternal Law. It is inconceivable that an unjust law should oblige by virtue of the Natural Law, by virtue of regulations which go back to the Eternal Law and which are in us a participation in that Law. It is essential to a philosophy such as that of Saint Thomas to regard an unjust law as not obligatory. It is the counterpart of this truth that the just law binds in conscience because it binds by virtue of the Natural Law. If we forget the one, we forget the other.[22]

THE RIGHTS OF MAN AND NATURAL LAW

RESUME OF THE RIGHTS ENUMERATED

We have not discussed in this study the rights concerned with the international order, whose consideration belongs to a special field, and among which the most important are the right of each State, large or small, to freedom and respect for its autonomy, the right to the respecting of solemn oaths and the sanctity of treaties, the right to peaceful development (a right which, being valid for all, requires for its own development the establishment of an international community having juridical power, and the development of federative forms of organization). It may not be altogether unnecessary at this point to make a summary list of those rights of which we have spoken.

Rights of the human person as such.—The right to existence.—The right to personal liberty or the right to conduct one's own life as master of oneself and of one's acts, responsible for them before God and the law of the community.—The right to the pursuit of the perfection of rational and moral human life.—The right to the pursuit of eternal life along the path which conscience has recognized as the path indicated by God.—The right of the Church and other religious families to the free exercise of their spiritual activity.—The right of pursuing a religious vocation; the freedom of religious orders and groups.—The right to marry according to one's choice and to raise a family, which will in its turn be assured of the liberties due it;—the right of the family society to respect for its constitution, which is based on natural law, not on the law of the State, and which fundamentally involves the morality of the human being.—The right to keep one's body whole.—The right to property.—Finally, the right of every human being to be treated as a person, not a thing.

Rights of the civic person.—The right of every citizen to participate actively in political life, and in particular the right of equal suffrage for all.—The right of the people to establish the Constitution of the State and to determine for themselves their form of government.—The right of association, limited only by the juridically recognized necessities of the common good, and in particular the right to form political parties or political schools.—The right of free investigation and discussion (free-dom of expression).[23]—Political equality, and the equal right of every cit-izen to his security and his liberties within the State.—The equal right of every one to the guarantees of an independent judiciary power.—Equal possibility of admission to public employment and free access to the vari-ous professions.

Rights of the social person, and more particularly of the working person.—The right freely to choose his work.—The right freely to form vocational groups or trade-unions.—The right of the worker to be considered socially as an adult.—The right of economic groups (trade-unions and working communities) and other social groups to freedom and autonomy.—The right to a just wage. The right to work. And wherever an associative system can be substituted for the wage system, the right to the joint ownership and joint management of the enterprise, and to the "worker's title."—The right to relief, unemployment insurance, sick benefits and social security.—The right to have a part, free of charge, depending on the possibilities of the community, in the elementary goods, both material and spiritual, of civi-lization.[24]

SCHOLASTICISM AND POLITICS

DEMOCRACY OF THE INDIVIDUAL AND DEMOCRACY OF THE PERSON

There is a common work to be accomplished by the social whole as such, by that whole of which human persons are parts, and which is not "neutral," which is itself engaged, held by a temporal calling. And thus the persons are *subordinated to this common work.* And yet, not only in the temporal order itself, is it essential for the common good to flow back to the persons; but in addition, with regard to an altogether different order, concerning what is deepest in the person, his eternal calling, with the goods attached to this calling,—there is in each human person a transcendent end, to which *soci-ety itself and its common work is subordinated.*

Do not forget that society's common work itself has its chief value in the freedom of personal expansion, with the guarantees it involves and with the diffusion of goodness which proceeds from it. Because the tem-poral common good is a common good of human persons, it happens, by the grace of justice and friendship, that through subordinating himself to the common work, each one still subordinates himself to the good of per-sons,—that is, to the accomplishment of the personal life of *others,*—and at the same time to the interior dignity of his own person. But this solution can acquire a practical value only if the real nature of common work is recognized, and if at the same time there is recognized, as Aristotle taught, the political value and importance of the virtue of *friendship*.

It is difficult not to think that the temporal advent of such a city of persons would come as a consequence and an earthly effectuation of this consciousness of the dignity of the human person and his eternal calling in every man whomsoever, which has for ever penetrated, through the Gospel, into the heart of humanity.

Democracy inspired by Rousseau, which is now threatened in the world, suffers from a philosophy of life which attempted an illusory naturalization or secularization of evangelical truths. Rather, is not human history, labouring to achieve another sort of democracy, which would be an *evangelization of nature*?

In his book on *Two Sources of Morality and Religion*, M. Bergson emphasized the originally religious character of the democratic ideal; in a formula charged with sense (and even with opposite senses), he writes that one must perceive "in the democratic state of mind a great effort whose direction is inverse to that of nature". . . .

Democracy of the individual and humanism of the individual arise from an anthropocentric inspiration. Materialism, atheism, dictatorship, are their fatalities. By saying to men, you are gods by your own essence and will, they have debased men. Practically they have left to men no other internal weight than flat egoism and longing for material possessions.

Democracy of the person and humanism of the person spring forth from a theocentric inspiration. Conquest of freedom in the social and political, as well as the spiritual order, is their aim,—I mean freedom of expansion, exultation and autonomy, so far as it conforms to the image of God. They say to men: you are gods by the gifts and the calling of God, gods in becoming and in suffering and in hope; gods by means of humility, virtue and grace. Their weight in men is the weight of love. They dignify the creature really—in God and as made by God and for God; not illusively—as a god itself. They know the grandeur of man, and they know his misery. They respect human dignity, not as something abstract, timeless and non-existent, ignoring historic conditions and historic diversities and devouring men pitilessly. They respect human dignity in each concrete and existing person, in its flesh and blood and in its historical context of life.

It is to the democracy of the person that one must apply, I think, and not without certain comments, the thought of M. Bergson when he writes that at the extreme limit one might say, "democracy is evangelic in its essence, and that its motive power is love."

I do not mean, in quoting this formula of M. Bergson, to link religion and the Gospel to any form of government whatsoever. The Christian religion is not enslaved to any temporal regime. It is compatible with all forms of legitimate government. It is not its business to determine which one of them must be adopted by men *hic et nunc*. It imposes none of them upon their preference. . . .

The relation which is noticed—I believe justly—by M. Bergson, between the Gospel and democracy, is not a relation of *right*, which would oblige us, in the name of Christian doctrine and of the Kingdom of God, to recognize a certain temporal conception and a certain social and political philosophy. It is a relation of *fact*, which concerns only,—as in the question of slavery,—the germinations naturally reduced in the depths of profane and temporal conscience itself under the influence of Christian leaven. It is from the historical and cultural point of view, from the point of view of the philosophy of history and culture, that things are here considered. Even under mixed and aberrant forms, and even in the Rousseauist tendency to naturize (and denaturize) the Gospel, is it not the Christian leaven that is still seen fermenting in the bosom of human history, while the unhappy adventure of the individualist democracy is unfolding itself? Under purer forms, and tending this time, as I have said before, to evangelize nature, is it not always, and more truly, the Christian leaven that is at work in history, preparing in it a personalist democracy? ...

These reflections induce me to think that the drama of modern democracies is to have sought, without knowing it, something good: the democracy of the person, disguised in an error, viz., the democracy of the individual, which leads by itself to serious failures. If democracies are still able to escape grave dangers, it is by turning themselves decisively in the direction of an essentially different type—the democracy of the person, discovered in its real significance. And this presupposes, truly speaking, something quite different from a simple weakening or a simple extenuation of the errors of the democracy of the individual; it means an internal transformation, a complete turn about toward spirit.

Is not the tragedy of our age to be found in the fact that modern democracies have lost all confidence in themselves? Their vital principle is justice, and they do not want to run the risks of justice. They do not want, it seems, to run any risks whatsoever. They invoke justice, but they pursue purely utilitarian politics, and they pursue them inefficiently and clumsily. . . .[25]

To the inhuman humanism of the individual would thus succeed a new humanism—the integral humanism of the person, open to that which surpasses it and leads it to achievement, and open to the common service of justice and friendship.[26]

THE INDIVIDUAL, THE PERSON, AND THE COMMON GOOD

We have noted ... that it is essential for personality to tend towards communion. We must insist on this point which is often forgotten: the person, by virtue of his dignity, as well as of his needs, requires to be a member of a society. Animal societies are improperly called societies or cities. Society, properly speaking—human society—is a society of persons. In so far as a city deserves this name, it is a city of human persons.

And why does the person demand for himself life in society? He demands this, first, by virtue of the very *perfections* which are inherent in him, and because of the fact of this being open to the communications of knowledge and of love, which I have spoken, and which require an entrance into relation with other persons.

Taken in the aspect of its radical generosity, the human person tends to super-abound in social communications, according to the law of super-abundance which is inscribed in the very depths of being, of life, of intelligence, of love.

And, secondly, it is because of his *needs* that the human person demands this life in society. Taken in the aspect of his indigences, he demands to be integrated to a body of social communications, without which it is impossible for him to attain to his full life and achievement.

Society thus appears as furnishing the person with the conditions of existence and development which he definitely needs. The human person cannot achieve his fullness alone, but only through receiving certain goods essential to him from society.

I do not mean only material needs, of bread, of clothes and lodging, for all of which man depends upon the aid of his fellows; but also, and first of all, the need of their aid in acting according to reason and virtue, which corresponds to the specific character of the human being. In order to attain to a certain degree of elevation in knowledge and perfection of moral life, man needs the education and the aid granted by his fellows. It is in this sense that one must give a very strict meaning to the words of Aristotle, that man is naturally a political animal. He is a political animal because he is a reasonable animal, because his reason seeks to develop with the help of education, through the teaching and the co-operation of other men, and because society is thus required to accomplish human dignity.

Yet we must not say that the aim of society is the individual good (or the mere collection of individual goods) of each person who constitutes it! ...

The end of society is its *common good*, the good of the body politic. But if one fails to grasp the fact that the good of the body politic is a common good of *human persons*—as the social body itself is a whole made up of human persons—this formula may lead in its turn to other errors of the collectivist or totalitarian type. The common good of society is neither a simple collection of private goods, nor a good belonging to a whole which (as in the case of the species in relation to its individual members) draws the parts to itself, as if they were pure means to serve itself alone. The common good is the *good human* life of the multitude, of a multitude of *persons*; it is their communion in the good life; it is therefore common *to the whole and to the parts*, on whom it flows back and who must all benefit from it. Under pain of being itself denatured, such a good implies and demands the recognition of the fundamental rights of the person (and of the rights of the family, in which the persons are engaged in a more primitive mode of communal living than in political society). It involves, as its chief value, the highest possible accession (an accession compatible with the good of the whole) of persons to their life as persons, and to their freedom of expansion, as well as to the communications of goodness which in turn proceed from it.

The end of the state is the common good, which is not only a collection of advantages and utilities, but also rectitude of life, an end good in itself, which the old philosophers called *bonum honestum*, the intrinsically worthy good. For, on one hand, it is a thing good in itself to insure the existence of the multitude. And, on the other hand, it is the just and morally good existence of the community which may thus be insured. It is only on this condition, of being in accordance with justice and with moral good, that the common good is what it is: the good of a people, the good of a city, and not the 'good' of an association of gangsters or of murderers. That is why perfidy, the contempt of treaties and of sworn faith, political murder or unjust war—all these can be *useful* to a government, and procure, if only for a time, *advantages* to the peoples who have recourse to them; but they debase and destroy, as far as in them lies, the *common good* of these peoples.

The common good is a thing ethically good. And this common good itself includes, as an essential element, the greatest possible development of human persons, of those persons who form the multitude, united, in order to constitute a community, according to relations not only of power, but also of justice. Historical conditions, and the present inferior state of humanity's development, make it difficult for social life fully to attain its end. But the end toward which it tends ... is to procure to the multitude the common good in such a fashion that the concrete person gains a real independence regarding nature, which is insured through the economic guaranties of labour and of property, through political rights, the civil virtues, and culture of the mind.

I have insisted upon the sociability of the person and on the properly human nature of the common good, which is a good according to justice, which must flow back to the persons, and whose chief value is the accession of persons to their freedom of expansion.

But I have not yet entered into what one might call the typical paradox of social life. Here we shall find once more the distinction between individual and person. For this paradox is linked to the fact that each of us is altogether an individual and altogether a person.

The person, as such, is a whole—a whole open and generous. Truly speaking, if human society were a society of *pure persons*, the good of society and the good of each person would be one and the same good. But man is very far from being a pure person. The human person is an unfortunate material individual, an animal who is born in an infinitely more depraved state than all the other animals. If the person, as such, is an independent whole, and that which is noblest in all of nature, yet the human person is placed at the lowest degree of personality. He is destitute and miserable—an indigent person, full of needs. Because of these profound indigences—deriving from the matter of which man is made and from material individuality—and because of the limitations of his perfection itself, which also, in another way, derive from material individuality, it so happens that, when such a person enters into the society of his fellows, he becomes a *part* of a whole, a whole which is larger and better than its parts, in so far as they are parts. According, not to his entire self, but to all the complements which he receives from society, and without which he would remain, so to speak, in a state of latent life, the human person is part of a larger whole, a whole which surpasses the person in so far as the latter is a *part*, and in so far as the common good is other than the good of each (and than the sum of the good of each). And yet, it is by reason of personality, as such, and of the perfections which it involves as an independent and open *whole*, that man must enter into society; so that it is necessary for the good of the social whole, as I have said, to flow back in a way to the person of each of its members. It is the *human person* which enters into society. And in so far as he is a *material individuality*, he enters into society as a part whose good is inferior to the good of the whole; nevertheless, this good itself of the whole, in order to be what it is,—that is to say, superior to the private good,—must necessarily profit individual persons and be redistributed to them, in respect of their rights and their dignity. Because, finally speaking, society, being a whole of persons, is a *whole of wholes*.

On the other hand, by reason of his destination to the absolute, and because he is called upon to fulfill a destiny superior to time,—in other words, according to the highest exigencies of personality as such,—the human person, as spiritual totality, referring to the transcendent Whole, *surpasses* all temporal societies and is superior to them. And from this point of view,—in other words, as regards the things *that are not Caesar's,*—it is to the perfect achievement of the person and of its supratemporal aspirations, that society itself and its common good are subordinated, as to the end of *another* order, which transcends them.

A single human soul is of more worth than the whole universe of bodies and material goods. There is nothing above the human soul,—except God. In regard to the eternal destiny of the soul, and its supra-temporal goods, society exists for each person and is subordinated to it.

It is thus in the nature of things that man sacrifices his temporal goods, and if necessary his life itself, for the sake of the community, and that social life imposes upon the life of the person, taken as part of the whole, many a constraint and many a sacrifice. But even as these sacrifices and constraints are demanded and accepted by justice and by friendship, even so they raise the spiritual level of the person. When man gives his life for the community's sake, he accomplishes, through an act of such great virtue, the moral perfection by which the person asserts his supreme independence as regards the world. By losing himself temporally for the city's sake, the person sacrifices himself in the truest and most complete fashion, and yet does not lose the stakes; the city serves him even then, for the soul of man is not mortal, and there is an eternal life.

In brief, while the person as such is a *totality*, the individual as such is a *part*; while the person, as person or as totality, demands that the common good of temporal society should flow back to him, and while through his ordination to the transcendent whole, he even surpasses the temporal society, the same person, as an individual or as part, is inferior to the social whole, and must serve the common cause as a member of the whole.

We thus perceive the state of tension and of conflict, which human society inevitably involves. Social life is naturally ordained—in the measure in which I have tried to define—to the good and to the freedom of the person. And yet there is in this very social life a natural tendency to enslave the person and to diminish him, in so far as this person is considered by society as a simple part and as a simple material individual. . . .

The person,—so far as a person,—wishes to serve the common good freely, by tending at the same time towards its own plenitude, by surpassing himself and by surpassing the community, in his proper movement towards the transcendent Whole. And, in so far as he is a material individuality, the person is obliged to serve the community and the common good by necessity, and even by constraint, being surpassed by them, as the part by the whole. . . .

Man is constituted as person, made for God and for eternal life, before being constituted part of a human community; and he is constituted part of familial society before being constituted part of political society. Hence, there are primordial rights, which the latter must respect, and which it dare not wrong when it demands for itself the aid of its members because they are its parts. . . .

We could also say that society,—its life, its peace,—cannot exist without the efficient causality of love, which is essentially personal, and yet the formal structure of society is constituted by justice, which is essentially measured according to things, and merits, without respect for persons.[27]

MORAL PHILOSOPHY

THE FIRST ACT OF FREEDOM AND GRACE

Up to this point we have talked as a philosopher, occupied only with the order of nature. That is why we focused our attention on the second of the two cases mentioned above, reducing the problem by isolating it in its purely natural conditions, disregarding what relates to the cultural conditions of education, tradition, religious formation, and considering only the natural energies at work in the first act of freedom. As we continue to meditate on this case, we now see that for the theologian it poses serious problems which we must be aware of if our ethics is an adequately considered moral philosophy, and if we bear in mind the concrete, existential state of human nature. What does the theologian tell us at this juncture? He tells us that to love God efficaciously above all else is, since the fall of Adam, impossible for human beings with only the forces of their nature. For this the grace which heals nature and which sanctifies is needed. Well, when the child makes his choice for the honorable good, this choice, as we have seen, implies that by the same act, even if unwittingly, he orders his life to God as to his ultimate End—and thus loves God above all else. From this it follows that the choice of the honorable good in the first act of freedom is only possible with sanctifying grace.

"When a man," Saint Thomas writes, "arrives at the age of discretion ... the first thing his thought should turn to is to ponder about himself. And if he directs himself to the end which is his true end, he is delivered from original sin by the sanctifying grace he then receives." In fact, the child we spoke of, who chooses to direct his activity toward the honorable good as universal Value, and by the same stroke, by virtue of a dynamism which he may be unconscious of, toward God as ultimate End, makes this choice by virtue of divine grace, and tends toward his ultimate end through divine charity. And thus, the first act of deliberate will, the first act of moral life in the strict sense of the word, is steeped in the mystery of grace and original sin. In whatever part of the world he is born, in whatever religion or cultural tradition he is raised, whether he knows or does not know Christ's name, a child of man cannot make a straightforward start in his moral life except in the grace of Christ. Here you have a new, outstanding example which illustrates our views on moral philosophy adequately considered. A moral philosophy which was ignorant of the theological data on the existential situation of humanity and which sought to constitute itself as a separate philosophy, would teach that the first moral choice on which the life of freedom hangs depends on the forces of nature and reason alone. Insufficiently informed, it would sin not only through ignorance, but through error.

We also see that, from the start, the moral life of humanity is inseparable from the hidden realities which are at the very origin of our religious life; knowledge of them develops in us on the religious plane. The first act of freedom is a moral act par excellence, and, at least implicitly, a religious act, since it can only be realized rightly if it is realized in divine charity, whether the subject knows it or not.[28]

NOTES

1. [Donald Gallagher and Idella Gallagher, *The Achievement of Jacques and Raissa Maritain: A Bibliography, 1906–1961* (New York: Doubleday, 1962), 12.]
2. [Ibid., 18.]
3. [See Bernard E. Doering, *Jacques Maritain and the French Catholic Intellectuals* (Notre Dame, Ind.: University of Notre Dame Press, 1983), 60–84.]
4. [Ibid., 217–241.]
5. [UNESCO, *Human Rights: Comments and Interpretations* (New York: Columbia University Press, 1949), 9–10.]
6. Cf. *Sum. Theol.* I, 60, 5.
7. Luke xx:36.
8. Cf. *Sum. Theol.* I, 47, 2.
9. [Jacques Maritain, *Redeeming the Time* (London: Geoffrey Bles, 1946), 15–18.]
10. [Jacques Maritain, *Man and the State* (Chicago: University of Chicago Press, 1951), 9–14, 18–19.]
11. [Ibid., 174–179.]
12. [Jacques Maritain, *God and the Permission of Evil*, trans. Joseph W. Evans (Milwaukee: Bruce Publishing, 1966), 33, 85–87, 89–90.]
13. Cf. my book *Man and the State* (The University of Chicago Press: 1951).
14. *Sum. Theol.*, 1–11, 93, 1.
15. *Sum. Theol.*, 1–11, 91, 2.
16. Saint Thomas Aquinas, *loc. cit.*

17. *Sum. Theol.*, 1–11, 90, 4.

18. Ibid., I–II, 93, 2.

19. In current language, these two concepts are expressed in English by the same word, "law." Hence a supplementary difficulty arises. For the sake of clarity, we may be permitted to use the word "right" to signify *jus* (*droit, Recht*), and the word "law" to signify solely *lex* (*loi, Gesetz*).

20. We use the expression "law of nations" as equivalent to *jus gentium* (*le droit des gens*), because the term is so well established in the language of political science and political philosophy, although the term "right of nations" would perhaps correspond better to our use of "positive right" and "natural right." (It is true that the *law* of nations is distinguished in this section from natural and positive *law*.)

21. We are speaking here of human positive law and passing over what concerns the divine positive law (which has God for its Author, but whose regulations are contingent with regard to what is required by the nature of the human being).

22. ["Natural Law and Moral Law," in *Moral Principles of Action: Man's Ethical Imperative*, ed. Ruth Nanda Anshen (New York: Harper and Brothers, 1952), 62–76.]

23. The right of association and the right of free investigation and discussion involve the human person considered simply as such, but they manifest themselves in an especially important manner in the sphere of political life.

24. [*The Rights of Man and Natural Law*, trans. Doris C. Anson (New York: Charles Scribner's Sons, 1945), 111–114.]

25. This was written before the second European war. In the face of catastrophe, the Western Democracies have been compelled by the force of things to choose finally, and courageously, to struggle for justice, at the risk of unheard of sacrifices.

26. [Jacques Maritain, *Scholasticism and Politics* (New York: Macmillan, 1940), 82–88.]

27. [Ibid., 67–74, 76–77.]

28. [Jacques Maritain, *An Introduction to the Basic Problems of Moral Philosophy* (New York: Magi Books, 1990), 139–141.]

[CHAPTER 3]

John Courtney Murray, S.J. (1904–1967)

SELECTED AND EDITED BY ANGELA CARMELLA

John Courtney Murray, S.J., was a Catholic theologian and public philosopher whose writings at mid-twentieth century helped shape the contemporary debate between Catholicism and liberalism and helped contribute a distinctly American voice to the Second Vatican Council. His best-known work, We Hold These Truths, *described deep connections between Catholic thought and American political principles. Together with numerous articles, that book articulated those connections in a way that helped a predominantly Protestant America better understand and accept Catholics as citizens and political leaders.*

Murray's public philosophy was based on the concept of civil conversation, in which the language of reason would govern the discourse. Thoroughly grounded in the natural law tradition, Murray considered this tradition superior to any other for social, political, and moral conversation within a pluralistic society. On legal matters, Murray focused on the coercive aspects (and therefore limited efficacy) of human law, and drew a clear distinction between the moral order of revealed and natural law on the one hand, and the legal order of human law, governed by prudential concerns, on the other. His theory of society and state revealed a limited state under the principle of subsidiarity, with the common good and spiritual life located in the society and its many nonstate communities.

Murray is mostly remembered, though, for his role as one of the primary architects of the Declaration on Religious Freedom, Dignitatis humanae, *at the Second Vatican Council. Influenced by the First Amendment to the U.S. Constitution and the religious freedom it ensured, Murray had long argued that the Catholic Church's embrace of religious freedom as a human right would represent its authentic doctrine and signify legitimate development of doctrine. He criticized the church's teachings on the ideal Catholic state and intolerance of non-Catholics, and argued from within the tradition (focusing his efforts at reinterpretation of the teachings of Pope Leo XIII) that the state had no sacral function. He recognized a historical consciousness, in which humankind had*

begun to grasp its profound dignity and the consequent need for civil and political
freedom, and he argued that the church must recognize this movement as well.

ON NATURAL LAW

FIRST, NATURAL-LAW THEORY does not pretend to do more than it can, which is to give a philosophical account of the moral experience of humanity and to lay down a charter of essential humanism. It does not show the individual the way to sainthood, but only to manhood. It does not promise to transform society into the City of God on earth, but only to prescribe, for the purposes of law and social custom, that minimum of morality which must be observed by the members of a society, if the social environment is to be human and habitable. At that, for a man to be reasonably human, and for a society to be essentially civil—these are no mean achievements. . . .

Second, beyond the fulfillment of the ideal of the reasonable man there lies the perennial question of youth, whatever its age. It is asked in the Gospel: "What do I still lack?" (Matthew 19:21). And there remains the Gospel's austere answer, put in the form of an invitation, but not cast in the categories of ethics, which are good and evil and the obligation to choose between them. The invitation opens the perspectives of a higher choice, to "be a follower of mine". . . .

Third, the mistake would be to imagine that the invitation, "Come, follow me," is a summons somehow to forsake the universe of human nature, somehow to vault above it, somehow to leave law and obligation behind, somehow to enter the half-world of an individualist subjectivist "freedom" which pretends to know no other norm save "love." In other words, the Gospel invitation, in so far as it is a summons to the moral life, is not a call to construct a "situation ethics" that knows no general principles of moral living but only particular instances of moral judgment, each one valid only for the instance; and that recognizes no order of moral law that is binding on freedom, but only a freedom that is free and moral singly in so far as it is sheer spontaneity.

Fourth, the law of nature, which prescribes humanity, still exists at the interior of the Gospel invitation, which summons to perfection. What the follower of Christ chooses to perfect is, and can only be, a humanity. And the lines of human perfection are already laid down in the structure of man's nature. Where else could they be found? The Christian call is to transcend nature, notably to transcend what is noblest in nature, the faculty of reason. But it is not a call to escape from nature, or to dismantle nature's own structure, and least of all to deny that man is intelligent, that nature is intelligible, and that nature's intelligibilities are laws for the mind that grasps them. In so far as they touch the moral life, the energies of grace, which are the action of the Holy Spirit, quicken to new and fuller life the dynamisms of nature, which are resident in reason. Were it otherwise, grace would not be supernatural but only miraculous.[1]

Man is regarded as a member of an order instituted by God, and subject to the laws that make the order an order—laws that derive from the nature of man, which is as essentially social as it is individual. In the natural-law climate of opinion (very different from that set by the "law of nature"), objective law has the primacy over subjective rights. Law is not simply the protection of rights but their source, because it is the foundation of duties.

The whole metaphysic involved in the idea of natural law may seem alarmingly complicated; in a sense it is. Natural law supposes a realist epistemology, that asserts the real to be the measure of knowledge, and also asserts the possibility of intelligence reaching the real, *i.e.*, the nature of things—in the case, the nature of man as a unitary and constant concept beneath all individual differences. Secondly, it supposes a metaphysic of nature, especially the idea that nature is a teleological concept, that the "form" of a thing is its "final cause," the goal of its becoming; in the case, that there is a natural inclination in man to become what in nature and destination he is—to achieve the fullness of his own being. Thirdly, it supposes a natural theology, asserting that there is a God, Who is eternal Reason, *Nous*, at the summit of the order of being, Who is the author of all nature, and Who wills that the order of nature be fulfilled in all its purposes, as these are inherent in the natures found in the order. Finally, it supposes a morality, especially the principle that for man, a rational being, the order of nature is not an order of necessity, to be fulfilled blindly, but an order of reason and therefore of freedom. The order of being that confronts his intelligence is an order of "oughtness" for his will; the moral order is a prolongation of the metaphysical order into the dimensions of human freedom.

This sounds frightfully abstract; but it is simply the elaboration by the reflective intelligence of a set of data that are at bottom empirical. Consider, for instance, the contents of the consciousness of a man who is protesting against injustice, let us say, in a case where his own interests are not touched and where the injustice is wrought by technically correct legislation. The contents of his consciously protesting mind would be something like these. He is asserting that there is an idea of justice; that this idea is transcendent to the actually expressed will of the legislator; that it is rooted somehow in the nature of things; that he really *knows* this idea; that it is not made by his judgment but is the measure of his judgment; that this idea is of the kind that ought to be realized in law and action; that its violation is injury, which his mind rejects as unreason; that this unreason is an offense not only against his own intelligence but against God, Who commands justice and forbids injustice.

Actually, this man, who may be no philosopher, is thinking in the categories of natural law and in the sequence of ideas that the natural-law mentality (which is the human mentality) follows. He has an objective idea of the "just" in contrast to the "legal." His theoretical reason perceives the idea as true; his practical reason accepts the truth as good, therefore as law; his will acknowledges the law as normative of action. Moreover, this man will doubtless seek to ally others in his protest, in the conviction that they will think the same as he does. In other words, this man, whether he be protesting against the Taft-Hartley Act or the Nazi genocidal laws, is making in his own way all the metaphysical affirmations that undergird the concept of natural law. In this matter philosophical reflection does not augment the data of common sense. It merely analyzes, penetrates, and organizes them in their full abstractness; this does not however, remove them from vital contact with their primitive source in experience.[2]

For the rest, I shall simply state the major contents of the political ideal as it emerges from natural law.

One set of principles is that which the Carlyles and others have pointed out as having ruled (amid whatever violations) the political life of the Middle Ages. First, there is the supremacy of law, and of law as reason, not will. With this is connected the idea of the ethical nature and function of the state (*regnum* or *imperium* in medieval terminology), and the educative character of its laws as directive of man to "the virtuous life" and not simply protective of particular interests. Secondly, there is the principle that the source of political authority is in the community. Political society as such is natural and necessary to man, but its form is the product of reason and free choice; no ruler has a right to govern that is inalienable and independent of human agency. Thirdly, there is the principle that the authority of the ruler is limited; its scope is only political, and the whole of human life is not absorbed in the polis. The power of the ruler is limited, as it were, from above by the law of justice, from below by systems of private right, and from the sides by the public right of the Church. Fourthly, there is the principle of the contractual nature of the relations between ruler and ruled. The latter are not simply material organized for rule by the *rex legibus solutus*, but human agents who agree to be ruled constitutionally, in accordance with law.

A second set of principles is of later development, as ideas and in their institutional form, although their roots are in the natural-law theories of the Middle Ages.

The first is the principle of subsidiarity. It asserts the organic character of the state—the right to existence and autonomous functioning of various sub-political groups, which unite in the organic unity of the state without losing their own identity or suffering infringement of their own ends or having their functions assumed by the state. These groups include the family, the local community, the professions, the occupational groups, the minority cultural or linguistic groups within the nation, etc. Here on the basis of natural law is the denial of the false French revolutionary antithesis, individual versus state, as the principle of political organization. Here too is the denial of all forms of state totalitarian monism, as well as of Liberalistic atomism that would remove all forms of social or economic life from any measure of political control. This principle is likewise the assertion of the fact that the freedom of the individual is secured at the interior of institutions intermediate between himself and the state (*e.g.*, trade unions) or beyond the state (the church).

The second principle is that of popular sharing in the formation of the collective will, as expressed in legislation or in executive policy. It is a natural-law principle inasmuch as it asserts the dignity of the human person as an active co-participant in the political decisions that concern him, and in the pursuit of the end of the state, the common good. It is also related to all the natural-law principles cited in the first group above. For instance, the idea that law is reason is fortified in legislative assemblies that discuss the reasons for laws.[3]

It is sometimes said that one cannot accept the doctrine of natural law unless one has antecedently accepted "its Roman Catholic presuppositions." This, of course, is quite wrong. The doctrine of natural law has no Roman Catholic presuppositions. Its only presupposition is threefold: that man is intelligent; that reality is intelligible; and that reality, as grasped by intelligence, imposes on the will the obligation that it be obeyed in its demands for action or abstention. Even these statements are not properly "presuppositions," since they are susceptible of verification.

The permeability of reality, especially moral reality, to intelligence is limited, as human intelligence itself is limited. But the limitations do not destroy the capacity of intelligence to do three things, in an order of diminishing ease and certainty. As these three things are done in orderly fashion, the structure of natural-law thought rises, and its style of argument appears.

First, intelligence can grasp the ethical a priori, the first principle of the moral consciousness, which does not originate by argument, but which dawns, as it were, as reason itself emerges from the darkness of infant animalism. Human reason that is conscious of itself is also conscious of the primary truths both of the intellectual and of the moral consciousness that what is true cannot at the same time and under the same respect be false, and that what is good is to be done and what is evil avoided. This latter truth is what I call the ethical a priori. Second, after some elementary experience of the basic situations of human life, and upon some simple reflection on the meaning of terms, intelligence can grasp the meaning of "good" and "evil" in these situations and therefore know what is to be done or avoided in them. For instance, to know the meaning of "parent" and of "disrespect" is to know a primary principle of the natural law, that disrespect to parents is evil, intrinsically and antecedent to any human prohibition. Third, as the experience of reality unfolds in the unfolding of the various relationships and situations that are the reality of human life, intelligence, with the aid of simple reasoning, can know, and know to be obligatory, a set of natural-law principles that are derivative. These, in general, are the Ten Commandments, the basic moral laws of human life, sanctioned by reason, and also sanctioned by their inclusion in the Jewish and Christian codes (the third, to "keep holy the Sabbath," is of course positive divine law).[4]

ON AMERICA

The first truth to which the American Proposition makes appeal is stated in that landmark of Western political theory, the Declaration of Independence. It is a truth that lies beyond politics; it imparts to politics a fundamental human meaning. I mean the sovereignty of God over nations as well as over individual men. This is the principle that radically distinguishes the conservative Christian tradition of America from the Jacobin laicist tradition of Continental Europe. The Jacobin tradition proclaimed the autonomous reason of man to be the first and the sole principle of political organization. In contrast, the first article of the American political faith is that the political community, as a form of free and ordered human life, looks to the sovereignty of God as to the first principle of its organization. In the Jacobin tradition religion is at best a purely private concern, a matter of personal devotion, quite irrelevant to public affairs. Society as such, and the state which gives it legal form, and the government which is its organ of action are by definition agnostic or atheist. The statesman as such cannot be a believer, and his actions as a statesman are immune from any imperative or judgment higher than the will of the people, in whom resides ultimate and total sovereignty (one must remember that in the Jacobin tradition "the people" means "the party"). This whole manner of thought is altogether alien to the authentic American tradition.

From the point of view of the problem of pluralism this radical distinction between the American and the Jacobin traditions is of cardinal importance. The United States has had, and still has, its share of agnostics and unbelievers. But it has never known organized militant atheism on the Jacobin, doctrinaire Socialist, or Communist model; it has rejected parties and theories which erect atheism into a political principle.[5]

The philosophy of the Bill of Rights was also tributary to the tradition of natural law, to the idea that man has certain original responsibilities precisely as man, antecedent to his status as citizen. These responsibilities are creative of rights which inhere in man antecedent to any act of government; therefore they are not granted by government and they cannot be surrendered to government. They are as inalienable as they are inherent. Their proximate source is in nature, and in history insofar as history bears witness to the nature of man; their ultimate source, as the Declaration of Independence states, is in God, the Creator of nature and the Master of history. The power of this doctrine, as it inspired both the Revolution and the form of the Republic, lay in the fact that it drew an effective line of demarcation around the exercise of political or social authority.[6]

ON SOCIAL CONVERSATION

Barbarism is not, I repeat, the forest primeval with all its relatively simple savageries. Barbarism has long had its definition, resumed by St. Thomas after Aristotle. It is the lack of reasonable conversation according to reasonable laws. Here the word "conversation" has its twofold Latin sense. It means living together and talking together.

Barbarism threatens when men cease to live together according to reason, embodied in law and custom, and incorporated in a web of institutions that sufficiently reveal rational influences, even though they are not, and cannot be, wholly rational. . . .

Barbarism likewise threatens when men cease to talk together according to reasonable laws. There are laws of argument, the observance of which is imperative if discourse is to be civilized. Argument ceases to be civil when it is dominated by passion and prejudice; when its vocabulary becomes solipsist, premised on the theory that my insight is mine alone and cannot be shared; when dialogue gives way to a series of monologues; when the parties to the conversation cease to listen to one another, or hear only what they want to hear, or see the other's argument only through the screen of their own categories; when defiance is flung to the basic ontological principle of all ordered discourse, which asserts that Reality is an analogical structure, within which there are variant modes of reality, to each of which there corresponds a distinctive method of thought that imposes on argument its own special rules. When things like this happen, men cannot be locked together in argument. Conversation becomes merely quarrelsome or querulous. Civility dies with the death of the dialogue.[7]

ON THE PUBLIC CONSENSUS

If therefore there is ... a public consensus constantly forming on the growing end of American life, its formation, I suggest, is a testimony to the slow and subtle operation of that rational dynamism, inherent in human nature, which is called natural law. This is the source from which human affairs acquire whatever quality of humanity may attach to them in any age of history. Again, the processes whereby the public consensus is formed are those characteristic of natural-law thinking. Finally, the social authority of the rules and standards that the consensus constantly develops is none other than the authority of natural law itself, that is, the high authority of right reason.[8]

And for the rest, there remains a secondary question in another and lower order of ideas and life; I mean that of the equal friendship of men of different faiths in the political order of society. Modern developments have revealed this is to be a political question separate from the theological question of the equality of religious faiths in the light of God's revealed law. The political question can be solved affirmatively, with that always limited measure of satisfaction that attends all human solutions. I know that the Catholic can give assurance that, whatever may have been historical situations of fact, there is nothing in any element of Catholic faith that requires the religious dissenter to be accounted a "second class citizen" in a society of Catholics. Reciprocally (to voice at the end a Catholic concern about today's Protestant "concern"), he would wish the assurance that the anti-Roman bias inherent in Protestantism should not issue in pro-secularist attitudes and policies in the civil order that will, he rightfully thinks, result in a society from which religion itself shall have been ruled as irrelevant.[9]

ON HISTORICAL CONSCIOUSNESS

It must be said that the contemporary difficulty with the classical conception is rooted in a truth—in an experience of the truth that the signs of the times reveal. What is really being said is that sheer submission to the will of the superior and mere execution of his orders do not satisfy the exigencies of the dignity of the person. They do not call into play the freedom of the person at its deepest point, where freedom appears as love. Still less do they exhaust the responsibilities of the person, which are to participate fully in community and to contribute actively to community. Thus stated, the contemporary difficulty is seen to be entirely valid. It is not to be solved by methods of repression. Nor will it yield to mere reiteration of the principle of authority: that authority is to be obeyed simply because it is authority.

There is need, therefore, to view the issue of freedom and authority in the new perspectives created by the signs of the times—that is, to view the issue within the context of the community, which is the milieu wherein the dignity of the person is realized.[10]

Man's sense of personal freedom is allied with a demand for political and social freedom, that is, freedom from social or legal restraint and constraint, except in so far as these are necessary, and freedom for responsible personal decision and action in society. Freedom, not force, is the dynamism of personal and social progress.

The common consciousness of men today considers the demand for personal, social, and political freedom to be an exigency that rises from the depths of the human person. It is the expression of a sense of right approved by reason. It is therefore a demand of natural law in the present moment of history. This demand for freedom is made especially in regard to the goods of the human spirit—the search for truth, the free expression and dissemination of opinion, the cultivation of the arts and sciences, free access to information about public events, adequate opportunities for the development of personal talents and for progress in knowledge and culture. In a particular way, freedom is felt to be man's right in the order of his most profound concern, which is the order of religion.[11]

However, this political phenomenon [of humanity's increased consciousness of dignity], it seems to me, has larger implications to which the Church herself surely must be alert. You see, here is the active self-conscious citizen within the civil community, [the citizen who] cannot be expected to be simply a passive subject within the community of the Church. This ancient symbolism of the Gospel retains all its validity of course. This symbolism, I mean, of the sheep. But this symbolism is not today to be pressed too far. We cannot consent to any schizophrenia. Between civic life and Christian life, we recognize direct differences between the civil and ecclesiastical community; but these differences must not be allowed to effect a schism within the soul of the Christian today. Here in society is the mature man or woman who cannot be considered in the Church to be an infant or an adolescent.

The problem is to harmonize an affirmation of this new spirit of self-consciousness, this new will to self-direction, to harmonize this new spirit with the altogether permanently necessary affirmation of the principle of authority in the Church and with the Christian spirit of obedience.[12]

ON THE DISTINCTION BETWEEN LAW AND MORALITY

There seems to be sufficient reason for thinking that the American mind has never been clear about the relation between morals and law. These two orders of reality are frequently confused, in either one of two ways.

First, there is a failure to understand the true meaning of the medieval adage: "Whatever is right ought to be law." The medieval man was not thinking of coercive statutes, backed by the state and its police that would compel the people to do whatever is right. He was merely saying that whatever is right ought to be a matter of custom; that is, the moral order ought to be reflected in the habitual order of everyday life and action. He could also, as he did, turn the adage around and say: "Whatever is law (custom) ought to be right." That is, the sanction of the mores, as we call them, is not in the sheer fact that they prevail, but in their rightness. In both cases the medieval man was expressing, quite exactly, a right concept of the distinction and relation that obtains between the order of moral law and the order of human law or custom. In American history, however, a perverted sense of the adage has been frequent. It chiefly appears in the reformer's constant shout: "There ought to be a law!" That is, whenever it appears that some good thing needs doing, or some evil thing needs to be done away with, the immediate cry is for the arm of the law. And there has often been no pause to ask, whether this is the sort of good or evil that law can, or ought to, cope with. The reformer's adage has been: "Whatever is moral ought to be legislated." The simplism of the adage reveals the failure to grasp the difference in order between moral precepts and civil statutes.

This confusion breeds another. If what is moral ought by that fact to be legal, it follows that what is legal is by that fact also moral. In common speech, if it's not against the law, it's all right; stay within the law and you can't go wrong. Here the chaos is complete. Law is deprived of all true sanction from the order of morals. Morality is invoked to sanction any sort of law. And as a result both law and morality lose all meaning.

Perhaps the heyday of reformist confusion of law and morals was the notorious "Comstock Era," the 1870's. And doubtless the most famous relic of the era is the Connecticut birth-control statute [providing for fines and/

or imprisonment for use of contraception]. It was passed in 1879 under Protestant pressure. . . .

The text reveals a characteristic Comstockian-Protestant ignorance of the rules of traditional jurisprudence. In general, the "free churches," so called, have never given attention to this subtle discipline, at once a science and an art, that mediates between the imperatives of the moral order and the commands or prohibitions of civil law. In fact, so far from understanding jurisprudence, these sects have never really understood law but only power, whether they wield the latter in the form of majority rule or of minority protest. In any case, the Connecticut statute confuses the moral and legal, in that it transposes without further ado a private sin into a public crime. The criminal act here is the private use of contraceptives. The real area where the coercions of law might, and ought to, be applied, at least to control an evil—namely, the contraceptive industry—is quite overlooked. As it stands, the statute is, of course, unenforceable without police invasion of the bedroom, and is therefore indefensible as a piece of legal draughtmanship. . . .

But what matters here is the mentality exhibited, and the menace in it. Protestant moral theory, as I shall later suggest seems never to have been able to grasp the distinction between private and public morality. But unless this distinction, like that between morality and law, is grasped, the result is a fiasco of all morality. From the foolish position that all sins ought to be made crimes, it is only a step to the knavish position that, since certain acts (like the private use of contraceptives) are obviously not crimes, they are not even sins. Upon a foolish disregard of the distinction between private and public morality there ensues a knavish denial that there is any such thing as public morality.[13]

ON THE LIMITED EFFICACY OF CENSORSHIP STATUTES

A preliminary answer is furnished by the principle, basic to jurisprudence, that morals and law are differentiated in character, and not coextensive in their functions. It is not the function of the legislator to forbid everything that the moral law forbids, or to enjoin everything that the moral law enjoins. The moral law governs the entire order of human conduct, personal and social; it extends even to motivations and interior acts. Law, on the other hand, looks only to the public order of human society; it touches only external acts, and regards only values that are formally social. For this reason the scope of law is limited. Moreover, though law is indeed a moral force, directive of human society to the common good, it relies ultimately for its observance on coercion. And men can be coerced only into a minimal amount of moral action. Again from this point of view the scope of law is limited.

Therefore the moral aspirations of law are minimal. Law seeks to establish and maintain only that minimum of actualized morality that is necessary for the healthy functioning of the social order. It does not look to what is morally desirable, or attempt to remove every moral taint from the atmosphere of society. It enforces only what is minimally acceptable, and in this sense socially necessary. Beyond this, society must look to other institutions for the elevation and maintenance of its moral standards—that is, to the church, the home, the school, and the whole network of voluntary associations that concern themselves with public morality in one or other aspect.

Law and morality are indeed related, even though differentiated. That is, the premises of law are ultimately found in the moral law. And human legislation does look to the moralization of society. But, mindful of its own nature and mode of action, it must not moralize excessively; otherwise it tends to defeat even its own more modest aims, by bringing itself into contempt.

Therefore the law, mindful of its nature, is required to be tolerant of many evils that morality condemns. A moral condemnation regards only the evil itself, in itself. A legal ban on an evil must consider what St. Thomas calls its own "possibility." That is, will the ban be obeyed, at least by the generality? Is it enforceable against the disobedient? Is it prudent to undertake the enforcement of this or that ban, in view of the possibility of harmful effects in other areas of social life? Is the instrumentality of coercive law a good means for the eradication of this or that social vice? And, since a means is not a good means if it fails to work in most cases, what are the lessons of experience in the matter? What is the prudent view of results—the long view or the short view? These are the questions that jurisprudence must answer, in order that legislation may be drawn with requisite craftsmanship.

It is, in fact, the differentiated character of law and morals that justifies the lawyer or judge when he insists that punitive censorship statutes should be clearly drawn, with the margin of uncertainty as narrow as possible.

The net of all this is that no society should expect very much in the way of moral uplift from its censorship statutes. Indeed the whole criminal code is only a minimal moral force. Particularly in the field of sexual morality the expectations are small; as I have suggested, they are smaller here than anywhere else. It is a sort of paradox, though an understandable one, that the greater the social evil, the less effective against it is the instrument of coercive law. Philip Wylie may have been right in saying that American society "is technically insane in the matter of sex." If so, it cannot be coerced into sanity by the force of law. In proportion as literary obscenity is a major social evil, the power of the police against it is severely limited.

This brings up the matter of consent. Law is indeed a coercive force; it compels obedience by the fear of penalty. However, a human society is inhumanly ruled when it is ruled only, or mostly, by fear. Good laws are obeyed by the generality because they are good laws; they merit and receive the consent of the community, as valid legal expressions of the community's own convictions as to what is just or unjust, good or evil. In the absence of this consent law either withers away or becomes tyrannical.

The problem of popular consent to the order of law and to its manifold coercions becomes critical in a pluralist society, such as ours. Basic religious divisions lead to conflict of moral views; certain asserted "rights" clash with other "rights" no less strongly asserted. And the divergences are often irreducible. Nevertheless, despite all the pluralism, some manner of consensus must support the order of law to which the whole community and all its groups are commonly subject. This consensus must include, in addition to other agreements, an agreement on certain rules which regulate the relations of the divergent groups among one another, and their common relation to the order of law. In what concerns our present subject of censorship, I suggest that there are four such rules. Before stating them, I would note that in the United States at present all the religious groups are—from the sociological, even if not from the statistical, point of view—minority groups.

First, within the larger pluralist society each minority group has the right to censor for its own members, if it so chooses, the content of the various media of communication, and to protect them, by means of its own choosing, from materials considered harmful according to its own standards.

Second, in a pluralist society no minority group has the right to demand that government should impose a general censorship, affecting all the citizenry, upon any medium of communication, with a view to punishing the communication of materials that are judged to be harmful according to the special standards held within one group.

Third, any minority group has the right to work toward the elevation of standards of public morality in the pluralist society, through the use of methods of persuasion and pacific argument.

Fourth, in a pluralist society no minority group has the right to impose its own religious or moral views on other groups, through the use of the methods of force, coercion, or violence.[14]

ON CIVIL UNITY

Both in fact and in law there is no public religion in America today. There is no common religious faith. The law—the First Amendment—that copes with the fact is a wise law. But once one has affirmed the fact and also affirmed the wisdom of the law that copes with it, one still is left with an unanswered question, namely: "Can a political society do without a public religion?" ...

You know very well, of course, that the Church is socially incomplete without a Christian society somehow surrounding it. It is indeed quite possible for man to live an integral Christian life amid the conditions of a concentration camp. But the conditions of a concentration camp have never been the civilizational ideal of the Catholic Church or of any other Christian church for that matter.

The Church does strive, as it were, to complete itself, not ecclesiastically, mind you, but socially, by creating an ambience, an environment that could be called a Christian society.

In the same way, a political society is normally incomplete without some spiritual bond of unity. Society—secular society—must have some spiritual substance that underlies the order of law, the order of public morality and all other orders and processes within society. And if there be no such spiritual substance to society, then society is founded on a vacuum; and society, like nature itself, abhors a vacuum and cannot tolerate it.

It may be possible, as pointed out by Hilaire Belloc and others, that an individual can live without religion, but a society cannot. All the evidence of history points in this direction. Arnold Toynbee and Christopher Dawson have commented on the fact that civilization rests upon the conception of spiritual and moral order, and secular civilization necessarily must base itself upon some concept of a higher law, some concept of a doctrine that is sacred.

Nowadays, in the modern world, traditional religion is outlawed as the public religion by the doctrine of separation of Church and State. What then remains to fill the vacuum that otherwise would result at the heart of society? ...

The only question is: what kind of unity and quality of unity shall we have? And on what will it be based, and what ends will it serve and pursue? And there is the related question, namely: What relation will be established between this national unity of ours and the religious pluralism and division that obtain among us? ...

I would suggest that the premises of any national unity that we want in this country are two: the first is the simple fact that there is no religious unity in this country. We exist in a state of religious division, a deplorable state, if you will, undoubtedly. Nevertheless, these religious divisions are not to be blurred, they are not to be transcended in the name of some common secular democratic faith and they are not to be reduced to some religious common denominator. This would, of course, be the end.

Secondly, regardless of our religious divisions, civil unity among us is necessary. Therefore, the only question that confronts us is this: What is civil unity in itself, and in its relation to religious pluralism in society? And secondly, how is it to be achieved?

Well, if this be the question, the outlines of the answer are not unclear. They are to be found quite readily in what we like to call the "liberal tradition of the West," the tradition that has dictated the norms for the creation of civil unity, the unity of a people. And it was said long ago by the Stoics, and even before them, that civil unity is based upon two things, first upon a constitutional consensus, and, secondly, upon a community of interests. . . .

Civil unity, therefore, is established by two things. First of all, by the rule of law, the rule of common law, and secondly, by the rule of law that serves as a framework for the orderly pursuit of a common good. And when you speak of civil unity, the enemy to it is not the stranger nor the religious heretic; the enemy of civil unity is the outlaw. . . .

If this be true, if civil unity is based upon the rule of law, a law that makes possible and regulates the orderly pursuits of the common good, then it follows, does it not, that civil unity is based on reason. I don't want to exaggerate, but I do maintain with all my strength and conviction that the forces of reason are basic in the creation of the civil community and its civil unity. If, and where, the forces of reason fail, civil unity becomes impossible.

I mean to speak of reason here in a multiple sense: there is moral reason and legal reason and political reason. It is, first of all, the moral reason to discern and to elect the ends and purposes of our national life: our domestic purposes and our purposes also within the wider community of nations. And a moral reason must discern and elect ends that are worthy, that are capable of calling forth the full energies of this still youthful people of ours.

Secondly, it is the legal reason to design and order a reasonable law which, because it is reasonable, will command the consents of the government, of the citizenry, and which, because it is a limited order of law—as the order of law must be—will leave room for all manner of legitimate freedom.

Thirdly, it is the political reason to master and to exercise the art of statesmanship and this art is forever architectonic. The art of statesmanship, the primary task of the statesman, is to organize; to organize the varying, the particular, the specific interests of the community into that community of interests that we call the common good [i.e., the good of the people, which is always redundant to the good] of the person. Political reason, to this end, must employ the canons of justice which are the canons of reason; political reason must observe the dictates of political prudence which are the dictates of reason; and political reason must utilize the high arts of persuasion.[15]

ON THE CHURCH-STATE DISTINCTION

Men might share the fear of Roger Williams, that the state would corrupt the church, or the fear of Thomas Jefferson, that the church would corrupt the state. In either case their thought converged to the one important conclusion, that an end had to be put to the current confusions of the religious and political orders. The ancient distinction between church and state had to be newly reaffirmed in a manner adapted to the American scene. Calvinist theocracy, Anglican Erastianism, Gallican absolutism—all were vitiated by the same taint: they violated in one way or another this traditional distinction.

The dualism of mankind's two hierarchically ordered forms of social life had been Christianity's cardinal contribution to the Western political tradition, as everyone knows who has looked into the monumental work of the two Carlyles, *Medieval Political Thought in the West.* Perhaps equally with the very idea of law itself it had been the most fecund force for freedom in society. The distinction had always been difficult to maintain in practice, even when it was affirmed in theory. But when it was formally denied the result was an infringement of man's freedom of religious faith or of his freedom as a citizen—an infringement of either or both. Hence the generalized American impulse toward freedom inevitably led to a new and specially emphatic affirmation of the traditional distinction.

The distinction lay readily within the reach of the early American lawyers and statesmen, for it was part of the English legal heritage, part of the patrimony of the common law.[16]

ON THE FIRST AMENDMENT RELIGION CLAUSES

On one hand, there are those who read into them certain ultimate beliefs, certain specifically sectarian tenets with regard to the nature of religion, religious truth, the church, faith, conscience, divine revelation, human freedom, etc. In this view these articles are invested with a genuine sanctity that derives from their supposed religious content. They are dogmas, norms of orthodoxy, to which one must conform on pain of some manner of excommunication. They are true articles of faith. Hence it is necessary to believe them, to give them a religiously motivated assent.

On the other hand, there are those who see in these articles only a law, not a dogma. These constitutional clauses have no religious content. They answer none of the eternal human questions with regard to the nature of truth and freedom or the manner in which the spiritual order of man's life is to be organized or not organized. Therefore they are not invested with the sanctity that attaches to dogma, but only with the rationality that attaches to law. Rationality is the highest value of law. In further consequence, it is not necessary to give them a religious assent but only a rational civil obedience. In a word, they are not articles of faith but articles of peace, that is to say, you may not act against them, because they are law and good law.[17]

ON COERCION OF CONSCIENCE

The theological argument is the tradition with regard to the necessary freedom of the act of faith which runs unbrokenly from the text of the New Testament to the Code of Canon Law (can. 1351). This tenet of Catholic doctrine is held no less firmly by all who bear the name of Christian. In fact, even the atheist holds it. It is part of the human patrimony of truth, embedded in the common consciousness of mankind. The ethical argument is the immunity of conscience from coercion in its internal religious decisions. Even the Church, which has authority to oblige conscience, has no power to coerce it. The political argument is the common conviction that the personal internal forum is immune from invasion by any powers resident in society and state. No external force may coerce the conscience of man to any form of belief or unbelief. The juridical argument enforces the same conclusion; it is contrary to the nature of civil law to compel assent to any manner of religious truth or ideology. The distinction between the sacred and the secular is binding on law and government; and the personal conscience is a sacred forum. Moreover, for the argument here, it does not matter whether the conscience be true or erroneous. It is not within the competence of society or state to judge whether conscience be true or erroneous. And jurisprudence declares the distinction to be irrelevant for the purposes of civil law.[18]

ON THE SCOPE OF THE RIGHT TO RELIGIOUS FREEDOM

First, freedom of conscience, freedom of religious association, and ecclesial freedom (in the sense of internal autonomy) are to be recognized as absolutely intangible by all legal or extralegal forces. (Obviously, when corporate religious bodies or voluntary associations perform civil acts, such as ownership of property, making contracts, etc., they are subject in these acts to the reasonable regulations of civil law.) Second, personal and corporate freedom of religious expression in worship, witness, teaching, and practice is likewise to be recognized, as inherently related to freedom of conscience and to internal ecclesial freedom. This freedom of religious expression, however, is not absolutely intangible, for the reasons given. Therefore the question arises, what is the criterion which makes limitation of this freedom legitimate.

First, the criterion cannot be theological, scil., the objective theological truth or error involved in some form of public worship, witness, teaching, observance, and practice. The public powers are not competent to make theological judgments. Nor may their action be instrumental in the public enforcement of theological judgments made by the Church. Second, the criterion cannot be ethical, scil., the rightness or wrongness of the personal or collective conscience that prompts particular forms of religious expression. The public powers are not competent to inquire into the norms whereby conscience is formed and to judge their truth or falsity. Third, the criterion is not social, scil., the common good of society. In the first place, the public powers are not the sole judge of what is or is not for the common good. This is a social judgment, to be made by the people, either through a constitutional consent (*consensu iuris*) or through the channels of public opinion. In the second place, in consequence of the distinction between society and state, not every element of the common good is instantly committed to the state to be protected and promoted. Under today's conditions of growth in the personal and political consciousness, this is particularly true of the spiritual goods of the human person, primary among which is religion. Therefore, fourth, the criterion can only be juridical, scil., the exigencies of public order in its threefold aspect—political, moral, and juridical.

This is the criterion which governs the action of law and the power of the state in regulating or limiting the exercise of the general civil rights of the citizenry, with which freedom of religious expression is cognate. Hence the public powers are authorized to intervene and to inhibit forms of religious expression (in public rites, teaching, observance, or behavior), only when such forms of public expression seriously violate either the public peace or commonly accepted standards of public morality, or the rights of other citizens. The public powers are competent to make judgments only with regard to the essential exigencies of the public order and with regard to the necessity of legal or police intervention in order to protect the public order.

Evidently, this juridical criterion is quite general in its manner of statement. The practical problem lies in its application in given cases. And the casuistry is endless. What chiefly matters is that the application should never be arbitrary. In what concerns religious freedom, the requirement is fourfold: that the violation of the public order be really serious; that legal or police intervention be really necessary; that regard be had for the privileged character of religious freedom, which is not simply to be equated with other civil rights; that the rule of jurisprudence of the free society be strictly observed, scil., as much freedom as possible, as much coercion as necessary.[19]

ON THE HUMAN RIGHT TO RELIGIOUS FREEDOM

The first thing to note is that the dignity and the freedom of the human person should receive primary attention since they pertain to the goods that are proper to the human spirit. As for these goods, the first of which is the good of religion, the most important and urgent demand is for freedom. For human dignity demands that in making this fundamental religious option and in carrying it out through every type of religious action, whether private or public, in all these aspects a person should act by his own deliberation and purpose, enjoying immunity from all external coercion so that in the presence of God he takes responsibility on himself alone for his religious decisions and acts. This demand of both freedom and responsibility is the ultimate ontological ground of religious freedom as it is likewise the ground of the other human freedoms.

Now, this demand is grounded upon the very existence of the human person, or, if one prefers, in the objective truth about the human person. Therefore it is revealed as a juridical value in society, so that it can impose upon the public power the duty to refrain from keeping the human person from acting in religious matters according to his dignity. For the public power is bound to acknowledge and to fulfill this duty by reason of its principal function, the protection of the dignity of the person. Once this duty is demonstrated and acknowledged, the immunity from coercion in religious matters demanded by human dignity becomes actually the object of a right. For the juridical actuality of a right is established wherever a corresponding duty is established and is acknowledged, once the validity of the ground for a right is assured and recognized.

Furthermore, the above mentioned principle of a free society—taken together with the principle of the juridical equality of all citizens—likewise sets the outer limits on just how far the public power must refrain from preventing someone from acting according to his conscience. The free exercise of religion in society ought not be restricted save insofar as it is necessary, that is, save when a public act ceases to be an exercise of religion because proven to be a crime against public order.

The following considerations will clarify this. The foundation of human society lies in the truth about the human person, or in its dignity, that is, in its demand for responsible freedom. That which in justice is preeminently owed to the person is freedom—as much freedom as possible—in order that society thus may be borne toward its goals, which are those of the human person itself, by the strength and energies of persons in society bound together with one another by love. Truth and justice, therefore, and love itself demand that the practice of freedom in society be kept vigorous, especially with respect to the goods belonging to the human spirit and so much the more with respect to religion. Now this demand for freedom, following as it does from the objective truth of the person in society and from justice itself, naturally engenders the juridical relationship between the person and the public power. The public power is duty-bound to acknowledge the truth about the person, to protect and advance the person, and to render the justice owed the person.

Again, from this follows the conclusion that no one is to be prevented in the matter of religion from acting according to the demands of his dignity or according to his inmost religious convictions. Nor does this immunity cease except where just demands of public order are proven to have the urgency of a higher force.[20]

ON THE CHURCH'S TEACHINGS ON RELIGIOUS FREEDOM

If therefore, using this theory [of Catholic establishment and legal intolerance of non-Catholics] as the criterion, you would find the ideal Catholic state, do not look at contemporary Brazil, Ireland, Portugal, Bavaria, or the Rhineland provinces; or at the Austria of 1855, or at Poland of 1925. In none of these Catholic countries are the abstract requirements of the Catholic ideal fulfilled. Look instead at the Kingdom of the Two Sicilies under Ferdinand I, at the Republic of Ecuador under Gabriel Garcia Moreno, at Italy under Mussolini, at Spain under Isabella II and under Generalissimo Franco. Only in these countries will you find the ultimate distinguishing work of the Catholic ideal—the legal establishment of Catholicism as the sole official religion of the state, and the legal exclusion of all other cults from public existence. Only in these countries, according to the theory under consideration, will you find the inherent and official intentions of the Church fulfilled to perfection. It is true that you may not find in these countries a Catholic people that intelligently and actively professes its public faith *animo et moribus*. You may even find a degree of religious dissension that erupts into assassination, as in the case of Moreno, or into a bloody civil war, as in the case of Spain. You certainly will fail to find the fulfillment of the Western Christian ideal of political life and government, which is certainly not dictatorship. No matter. You do find establishment and intolerance, and therefore you find the ideal Catholic state.[21]

ON LEO XIII

I would, however, emphasize the leading characteristic of Leo XIII's doctrine: he constantly presents the law of Christ as a principle that limits the scope of human law and government. His argument is always for constitutionalism, for limited government, against the *principatus sine modo, sine lege,* of the sectarian Liberals. His quarrel with the theory that separated the two laws was precisely on the ground that this separation left government unlimited in its power. With the law of Christ and His Church rejected as a limiting norm of political rule and legal enactment, there are no longer any sacrednesses left in society; everything is liable to profanation by the rough hand of government. A juridical monism which leaves government totalist in its scope is a form of tyranny, whether power is in the hands of a man, a party, or a majority. . . .

If one is to understand why Leo XIII condemned "separation of Church and state" in principle, it cannot be too strongly emphasized that this legal institution, which violently effected a juridical "union" of Church and state through a subordination of the Church to the state, was consciously intended to be the vehicle of a theological judgment on the nature of the Church. In sectarian Liberal theory government, as the political projection of the autonomy of reason, was fully entitled to be the supreme judge of religious truth. Theological judgments lay within its competence because it was omnicompetent. Like reason itself, government was "the highest principle and source and judge of truth" (*Libertas*).

Consequently, against this aspect of separationist theory—the juridical "union" of Church and state by the law which ruled that the Church is a voluntary religious association chartered by the state—Leo XIII emphasized two principles essential to the law of Christ. The first is that the Church exists as a society in her own right, a divine right; that the Church is a spiritual and supernatural community *sui generis*; that the Church is governed by an independent authority. From this premise Leo XIII consistently draws, as his first conclusion, what he calls "the principle of principles," that is, the freedom of the Church.

The principle includes the freedom of the Church as a spiritual authority, its independence in the exercise of its divinely given legislative, judicial, administrative, and disciplinary authority. The principle also includes the freedom of the Church as a spiritual community; this freedom is the prerogative of each of its members, of the Christian family, and of all the institutions within the Church, as, for instance, the religious orders and congregations. Moreover, the spiritual freedom of the Church as a community importantly includes a civil freedom, an empowerment in the face of civil society—the freedom "to follow the will of God and do His bidding within society, and not to have obstacles set in the way" (*Libertas*). This is, in Leo XIII's favorite phrase, the freedom to be "at once Christian and a citizen," a man subject to a dual allegiance, but undivided in the inner unity and integrity of his conscience by any conflict between the two authorities, ecclesiastical and civil, to which he owes obedience. . . .

It is therefore altogether in the line of Leo XIII's thought to say that the primary and indispensable care which government owes to religion is a care for the freedom of the Church. Religion, even as a social value, is not created by government but by the Church. The role of government is to see to it, by appropriate measures both positive and negative, that the Church is free to go about her creative mission; and likewise to see to it that such conditions of order obtain in society as will facilitate the fulfillment of the Church's high spiritual task. In the task itself, *cura animarum*, government has no share at all. But within limits it can make possible or impossible, easier or more difficult, the Church's exclusive task of caring for the needs of souls.

This care for the freedom of the Church means two things, in accord with what has been said above about the two senses of the formula. It means the assurance that the ministers of the Church as a spiritual authority will have the full freedom for their apostolic ministry in all its forms. It means also the assurance that the members of the Church as a spiritual community will have possession of their native freedom to live as Christians and citizens, to do the will of God within society without having obstacles put in their way. This latter freedom, as *Rerum novarum* makes particularly clear, creates a demand on government and on other social orders that they should provide proper conditions of social welfare and economic prosperity. Leo XIII struck a new note in his insistence on the economic and social conditions of spiritual freedom; the creation of these conditions is itself part of the care of religion.[22]

ON THE VATICAN II DECLARATION
OF RELIGIOUS FREEDOM

In the first place, in accordance with the world-wide outlook of the Council, the Declaration acknowledges the fact of the religiously pluralist society as the necessary historical context of the whole discussion. . . .

In the second place, the Declaration embraces the political doctrine of Pius XII on the juridical state (as it is called in Continental idiom), that is, on government as constitutional and as limited in function—its primary function being juridical, namely, the protection and promotion of the rights of man and the facilitation of the performance of man's native duties. The primacy of this function is based on Pius XII's personalist concept of society—on the premise that the "human person is the foundation, the goal, and the bearer of the whole social process," including the processes of government. . . .

In the present matter, the significance of the political doctrine of the Declaration (as also of the Constitution on the Church in the World Today) lies in its disavowal of the long-standing view of government as sacral in function, that is, as invested with the function of defending and promoting religious truth as such. This view of government is visible even in Leo XIII. Its disavowal by the Declaration follows on its intention to develop the doctrine of more recent popes on the constitutional order of society. In this development the function of government appears as the protection and promotion, not of religious truth, but of religious freedom as a fundamental right of the human person. This is a secular function, since freedom in society—notably religious freedom—is a secular value, as are the values of justice and love or civic friendship. All three of these values are rooted in the truth about the human person, which is the truth upon which the whole social and political order rests. Hence the tutelage of these values is proper to the notion of government as secular in the full range of its purposes. It is true that the final text of the Declaration is inadequate in its treatment of the limitations imposed on government by sound political doctrine. Nevertheless, the disavowal of the old notion of government as sacral in function is sufficiently clear, both from the firm statement of the essentially juridical function of government ... and also from the earlier statement that the proper purpose of government is to have a care for the common temporal good and that it would exceed its limits were it to presume to direct or impede religious acts. . . . These statements, jejune though they are, exclude the notion that government is to be the judge of religious truth, the defender of the true faith, or the guardian of religious unity. . . .

For the rest, it would seem to be in the sense of the Declaration to say that governmental favor of religion formally means favor of the freedom of religion. Similarly, conditions favorable to religious life should be understood to mean conditions favorable to the free profession and practice of religion. Government does not stand in the service of religious truth, as an instrument for its defense or propagation. Government, however, must somehow stand in the service of religion, as an indispensable element of the common temporal good. This duty of service is discharged by service rendered to the freedom of religion in society. It is religion itself, not government, which has the function of making society religious. The conditions favorable to the fulfilment of this function are conditions of freedom. In the way of sheer principle, it seems not possible to say more than this. And this much the Declaration says.[23]

ON CIVIL FREEDOM AND THE SECULARITY OF THE STATE

This progress reaches its inevitable term in the *Declaration on Religious Freedom*. The sacrality of society and state is now transcended as archaistic. Government is not *defensor fidei*. Its duty and rights do not extend to what had long been called *cura religionis*, a direct care of religion itself and of the unity of the Church within Christendom or the nation-state. The function of government is secular: that is, it is confined to a care of the free exercise of religion within society—a care therefore of the freedom of the Church and of the freedom of the human person in religious affairs. The function is secular because freedom in society, for all that it is most precious to religion and the Church, remains a secular value—the sort of value that government can protect and foster by the instrument of law. Moreover, to this conception of the state as secular, there corresponds a conception of society itself as secular. It is not only distinct from the Church in its origin and finality; it is also autonomous in its structures and processes. Its structural and dynamic principles are proper to itself and proper to the secular order—the truth about the human person, the justice due to the human person, the love that is the properly human bond among persons and, not least, the freedom that is the basic constituent and requirement of the dignity of the person.

This is the true Christian understanding of society and state in their genuine secularity which appears in *Pacem in terris*. The *Declaration on Religious Freedom* adds to it the final clarity in the essential detail, namely, that in the secular society, under the secular state, the highest value that both state and society are called upon to protect and foster is the personal and social value of the free exercise of religion. The values of religion itself for men and society are to be protected and fostered by the Church and by other religious communities availing themselves of their freedom. . . . Not nostalgic yearnings to restore ancient sacralizations, not futile efforts to find new forms of sacralizing the terrestrial and temporal order in its structures and processes, but the purification of these processes and structures and the sure direction of them to their inherently secular ends—this is the aim and object of the action of the Church in the world today. . . .

In the Pian and Joannine doctrine ... the primary function of govern-ment is juridical, namely, the protection and promotion of the exercise of human and civil rights, and the facilitation of the discharge of human and civil duties by the citizen who is fully citizen, that is, not merely subject to, but also participant in, the processes of government.[24]

ON THE DIFFICULTIES OF VATICAN II

I must say, with all due deference to the Fathers of the Council, that they were the victims of a defective ecclesiology, very Platonic in its implica-tions, as if somehow the Church were some supernal entity hovering *above* history and not involved at all *in* history or in the people who make up the Church.[25]

ON THE CHURCH'S TARDY RECOGNITION OF RELIGIOUS FREEDOM

The principle [of religious freedom] itself is accepted by the common consciousness of men and civilized nations. Hence the Church is in the unfortunate position of coming late, with the great guns of her authority, to a war that has already been won, however many rear-guard skirmishes remain to be fought.[26]

ON JOHN XXIII

The theologian's Pope, who listened while the theologians freely talked, had an even keener ear for the voice of the simple faithful, for whom alone the theologian undertakes to speak, and by whom, too he must be under-stood.

After John XXIII certain things are no longer possible. Chiefly, it is not possible abruptly to impose silence on any of the parties to the talk in the Church concerning old things and new. It is also not possible impatiently to turn away from the voices, within or without the Church, of whom it can now be said that a Pope once listened to them.[27]

NOTES

1. [John Courtney Murray, *We Hold These Truths: Catholic Reflections on the American Proposition* (New York: Sheed and Ward, 1960), 297–298.]
2. [Ibid., 327–329.]
3. [Ibid., 333–334.]

4. [Ibid., 109–110.]

5. [Ibid., 28–29.]

6. [Ibid., 37.]

7. [Ibid., 13–14.]

8. [Ibid., 121.]

9. [John Courtney Murray, "The Catholic Position: A Reply," in *Bridging the Sacred and the Secular: Selected Writings of John Courtney Murray, S.J.*, ed. J. Leon Hooper (Washington, D.C.: Georgetown University Press, 1994), 305.]

10. [John Courtney Murray, "Freedom, Authority, Community," in *Bridging the Sacred and the Secular*, 213.]

11. [John Courtney Murray, "The Problem of Religious Freedom," in *Religious Liberty: Catholic Struggles with Pluralism*, ed. J. Leon Hooper (Louisville, Ky.: Westminster John Knox Press, 1993), 138.]

12. [John Courtney Murray, "The Social Function of the Press," in *Bridging the Sacred and the Secular*, 206.]

13. [Murray, *We Hold These Truths*, 156–158.]

14. [Ibid., 165–168.]

15. [John Courtney Murray, "The Return to Tribalism," in *Bridging the Sacred and the Secular*, 151–154.]

16. [Murray, *We Hold These Truths*, 64.]

17. [Ibid., 48–49.]

18. [Murray, "The Problem of Religious Freedom," 147–148.]

19. [Ibid., 152–154.]

20. [John Courtney Murray, "The Human Right to Religious Freedom," in *Religious Liberty*, 240–241.]

21. [John Courtney Murray, "Leo XIII and Pius XII: Government and the Order of Religion," in *Religious Liberty*, 100.]

22. [Murray, "Government and the Order of Religion," 69–70, 79.]

23. [John Courtney Murray, "The Issue of Church and State at Vatican Council II, in *Religious Liberty*, 205–206, 217.]

24. [John Courtney Murray, "The Declaration on Religious Freedom," in *Bridging the Sacred and the Secular*, 192–193, 196.]

25. [John Courtney Murray, "The Unbelief of the Christian," in *Bridging the Sacred and the Secular*, 274.]

26. [John Courtney Murray, "This Matter of Religious Freedom," *America* 112 (January 9, 1965), 43.]

27. [John Courtney Murray, "Good Pope John: A Theologian's Tribute," in *Bridging the Sacred and Secular*, 313.]

[CHAPTER 4]

Pope John XXIII (1881–1963)

SELECTED AND EDITED BY LESLIE GRIFFIN

The future Pope John XXIII, Angelo Roncalli, was born on November 25, 1881, in Sotto il Monte, Italy, during the pontificate of Pope Leo XIII. The fourth of thirteen children in a family of sharecroppers, Roncalli left home to attend the Bergamo Seminary in 1893, when he was almost twelve years old. Thanks to a scholarship, in 1900 he began studies at the Pontifical Seminary in Rome, studies that were interrupted by a call to military service as a private in the Italian army. He returned to the seminary in 1902 and was ordained a priest in August 1904.

In 1905, Pope Pius X appointed Roncalli as secretary to the new bishop of Bergamo, Giacomo Radini-Tedeschi. On visits to Milan he gained access to the thirty-nine volumes recording Saint Charles Borromeo's visitation of the Bergamo diocese. Borromeo (1538–84), a leader of the sixteenth-century Catholic Reformation, had brought the reforms of the Council of Trent to Bergamo. Borromeo consumed Roncalli's attention and energy in ensuing years. He edited five volumes of the saint's work, which came out in 1936, 1937, 1938, 1946, and 1957.[1]

In 1921, Pope Benedict XV recalled Roncalli to Rome to direct the Congregation for the Propagation of the Faith, which coordinated the church's missionary activity throughout the world. Roncalli remained in Rome until Pope Pius XI sent him to Bulgaria in 1924.[2] Roncalli was apostolic visitor and apostolic delegate to Bulgaria from 1925 to 1935. In 1935 he went to Istanbul, where he served as apostolic delegate to Turkey and Greece until December 1944. After Charles de Gaulle refused to work with the papal nuncio and French bishops who had collaborated with the Vichy regime, Roncalli was hurriedly sent to Paris in December 1944. He served as papal nuncio to France from 1944 to 1953. He was the Vatican's first permanent observer at UNESCO (the United Nations Educational, Scientific, and Cultural Organization). In January 1953, Pope Pius XII appointed Roncalli the Cardinal and Patriarch of Venice, where he served until his election to the papacy in October 1958.

On the feast day of St. Charles, November 4, 1958, in his papal coronation address, Pope John asserted "vigorously and sincerely" that he intended to be a pastor. As he stated, "All other human gifts and accomplishments—learning, practical experience, diplomatic finesse—can broaden and enrich pastoral work, but they cannot replace it."[3]

On January 25, 1959, three months after his election, Roncalli, a student of the Council of Trent, announced an ecumenical council of Catholic bishops to a gathering of cardinals in Rome. In this context, ecumenical means general, not local or Roman; that is, it includes the bishops throughout the world who are in communion with Rome. The Second Vatican Council (Vatican II) would be the first ecumenical council in the Roman Church since 1870.

The first of Pope John's eight encyclical letters was Ad petri cathedram, *issued on June 29, 1959, on the subject of truth, unity, and peace. As the events of the council unfolded, John commissioned the two major encyclicals for which he is remembered:* Mater et magistra *(May 1961) and* Pacem in terris *(April 1963). Their optimistic voice about modernity marked a new emphasis in the tradition of Catholic social thought.*

The council remains John's greatest legacy. After John died on June 3, 1963, his successor, Pope Paul VI, led the council through three more sessions and sixteen promulgated documents to its conclusion in December 1965. John's ecumenical and optimistic influence is especially evident in four of those documents, namely the Decree on Ecumenism, *the* Declaration on the Relationship of the Church to non-Christian Religions, *the* Pastoral Constitution on the Church in the Modern World, *and the* Declaration on Religious Freedom.

ANNOUNCEMENT OF ECUMENICAL COUNCIL

VENERABLE BRETHREN and beloved sons! Trembling a little with emotion, but with humble firmness of purpose, We now tell you of a twofold celebration: We propose to call a diocesan synod for Rome, and an ecumenical council for the Universal Church.

To you, venerable brethren and beloved sons, We need hardly elaborate on the historical significance and juridical meaning of these two proposals. They will lead to the desired and long awaited modernization of the Code of Canon Law, which is expected to accompany and to crown these two efforts in the practical application of the rules of ecclesiastical discipline, applications the Spirit of the Lord will surely suggest to Us as We proceed. The coming promulgation of the Code of Oriental Law foreshadows these events.[4]

AD PETRI CATHEDRAM

TRUTH, UNITY, PEACE

All the evils which poison men and nations and trouble so many hearts have a single cause and a single source: ignorance of the truth—and at times even more than ignorance, a contempt for truth and a reckless rejection of it. Thus arise all manner of errors, which enter the recesses of men's hearts and the bloodstream of human society as would a plague. These errors turn everything upside down; they menace individuals and society itself.

And yet, God gave each of us an intellect capable of attaining natural truth. If we adhere to this truth, we adhere to God Himself, the author of truth, the lawgiver and ruler of our lives. But if we reject this truth, whether out of foolishness, neglect, or malice, we turn our backs on the highest good itself and on the very norm for right living.

REVEALED TRUTH

As We have said, it is possible for us to attain natural truth by virtue of our intellects. But all cannot do this easily; often their efforts will result in a mixture of truth and error. This is particularly the case in matters of religion and sound morals. Moreover, we cannot possibly attain those truths which exceed the capacity of nature and the grasp of reason, unless God enlightens and inspires us. This is why the word of God, "who dwells in light inaccessible,"[5] in His great love took pity on man's plight, "became flesh and dwelt among us,"[6] that He might "enlighten every man who cometh into the world"[7] and lead him not only to full and perfect truth, but to virtue and eternal happiness. All men, therefore, are bound to accept the teaching of the gospel. For if this is rejected, the very foundations of truth, goodness, and civilization are endangered. . . .

A SELF-EVIDENT TRUTH

There is one truth especially which We think is self-evident: when the sacred rights of God and religion are ignored or infringed upon, the foundations of human society will sooner or later crumble and give way.[8]

MATER ET MAGISTRA

THE POLITICAL FIELD

49. To turn to the political field, We observe many changes. In a number of countries all classes of citizens are taking a part in public life, and public

authorities are injecting themselves more each day into social and economic matters. We are witnessing the break-away from colonialism and the attainment of political independence by the peoples of Asia and Africa. Drawn together by their common needs nations are becoming daily more interdependent. There is, moreover, an ever-extending network of societies and organizations which set their sights beyond the aims and interests of individual countries and concentrate on the economic, social, cultural and political welfare of all nations throughout the world. . . .

AN INCREASE IN SOCIAL RELATIONSHIPS

59. Certainly one of the principal characteristics which seem to be typical of our age is an increase in social relationships, in those mutual ties, that is, which grow daily more numerous and which have led to the introduction of many and varied forms of associations in the lives and activities of citizens, and to their acceptance within our legal framework. Scientific and technical progress, greater productive efficiency and a higher standard of living are among the many present-day factors which would seem to have contributed to this trend.

60. This development in the social life of man is at once a symptom and a cause of the growing intervention of the State, even in matters which are of intimate concern to the individual, hence of great importance and not devoid of risk. We might cite as examples such matters as health and education, the choice of a career, and the care and rehabilitation of the physically and mentally handicapped.

It is also partly the result, partly the expression of a natural, well-nigh irresistible urge in man to combine with his fellows for the attainment of aims and objectives which are beyond the means or the capabilities of single individuals. In recent times, this tendency has given rise to the formation everywhere of both national and international movements, associations and institutions with economic, cultural, social, sporting, recreational, professional and political ends.

ADVANTAGES AND DISADVANTAGES

61. Clearly, this sort of development in social relationships brings many advantages in its train. It makes it possible for the individual to exercise many of his personal rights, especially those which we call economic and social and which pertain to the necessities of life, health care, education on a more extensive and improved basis, a more thorough professional training, housing, work, and suitable leisure and recreation. Furthermore, the progressive perfection of modern methods of thought-diffusion—the

press, cinema, radio, television—makes it possible for everyone to participate in human events the world over.

62. At the same time, however, this multiplication and daily extension of forms of association brings with it a multiplicity of restrictive laws and regulations in many departments of human life. As a consequence, it narrows the sphere of a person's freedom of action. The means often used, the methods followed, the atmosphere created, all conspire to make it difficult for a person to think independently of outside influences, to act on his own initiative, exercise his responsibility and express and fulfill his own personality. What then? Must we conclude that these increased social relationships necessarily reduce men to the condition of being mere automatons? By no means.

CREATION OF FREE MAN

63. For actually this growth in the social life of man is not a product of natural forces working, as it were, by blind impulse. It is, as we saw, the creation of men who are free and autonomous by nature—though they must, of course, recognize and, in a sense, obey the laws of economic development and social progress, and cannot altogether escape from the pressure of environment.

64. The development of these social relationships, therefore, can and ought to be realized in a way best calculated to promote its inherent advantages and to preclude, or at least diminish, its attendant disadvantages.

PROPER BALANCE NECESSARY

65. To this end, a sane view of the common good must be present and operative in men invested with public authority. They must take account of all those social conditions which favor the full development of human personality. Moreover, We consider it altogether vital that the numerous intermediary bodies and corporate enterprises—which are, so to say, the main vehicle of this social growth—be really autonomous, and loyally collaborate in pursuit of their own specific interests and those of the common good. For these groups must themselves necessarily present the form and substance of a true community, and this will only be the case if they treat their individual members as human persons and encourage them to take an active part in the ordering of their lives.

66. As these mutual ties binding the men of our age one to the other grow and develop, governments will the more easily achieve a right order the more they succeed in striking a balance between the autonomous and

active collaboration of individuals and groups, and the timely coordination and encouragement by the State of these private undertakings.

67. So long as social relationships do in fact adhere to these principles within the framework of the moral order, their extension does not necessarily mean that individual citizens will be gravely discriminated against or excessively burdened. . . .

OBLIGATION OF THE WEALTHY NATIONS

157. Probably the most difficult problem today concerns the relationship between political communities that are economically advanced and those in the process of development. Whereas the standard of living is high in the former, the latter are subject to extreme poverty. The solidarity which binds all men together as members of a common family makes it impossible for wealthy nations to look with indifference upon the hunger, misery and poverty of other nations whose citizens are unable to enjoy even elementary human rights. The nations of the world are becoming more and more dependent on one another and it will not be possible to preserve a lasting peace so long as glaring economic and social imbalances persist.

158. Mindful of Our position as the father of all peoples, We feel constrained to repeat here what We said on another occasion: "We are all equally responsible for the undernourished peoples."

FAILURE TO ACKNOWLEDGE THE MORAL ORDER

205. The root cause of so much mistrust is the presence of ideological differences between nations, and more especially between their rulers. There are some indeed who go so far as to deny the existence of a moral order which is transcendent, absolute, universal and equally binding upon all. And where the same law of justice is not adhered to by all, men cannot hope to come to open and full agreement on vital issues.

GOD, THE FOUNDATION OF MORAL ORDER

207. Mutual trust among rulers of States cannot begin nor increase except by recognition of, and respect for, the moral order.

208. But the moral order has no existence except in God; cut off from God it must necessarily disintegrate. Moreover, man is not just a material organism. He consists also of spirit; he is endowed with reason and freedom. He demands, therefore, a moral and religious order; and it is this order—and not considerations of a purely extraneous, material order—which

has the greatest validity in the solution of problems relating to his life as an individual and as a member of society, and problems concerning individual states and their inter-relations.

THE FUNDAMENTAL PRINCIPLE

219. This teaching rests on one basic principle: individual human beings are the foundation, the cause and the end of every social institution. That is necessarily so, for men are by nature social beings. This fact must be recognized, as also the fact that they are raised in the plan of Providence to an order of reality which is above nature.

220. On this basic principle, which guarantees the sacred dignity of the individual, the Church constructs her social teaching. She has formulated, particularly over the past hundred years, and through the efforts of a very well informed body of priests and laymen, a social doctrine which points out with clarity the sure way to social reconstruction. The principles she gives are of universal application, for they take human nature into account, and the varying conditions in which man's life is lived. They also take into account the principal characteristics of contemporary society, and are thus acceptable to all.

METHOD OF APPROACH

236. There are three stages which should normally be followed in the reduction of social principles into practice. First, one reviews the concrete situation; secondly, one forms a judgment on it in the light of these same principles; thirdly, one decides what in the circumstances can and should be done to implement these principles. These are the three stages that are usually expressed in the three terms: *look, judge, act.*[9]

OPENING ADDRESS TO THE COUNCIL

PESSIMISTIC VOICES

In the daily exercise of Our pastoral office, it sometimes happens that we hear certain opinions which disturb Us—opinions expressed by people who, though fired with a commendable zeal for religion, are lacking in sufficient prudence and judgment in their evaluation of events. They can see nothing but calamity and disaster in the present state of the world. They say over and over that this modern age of ours, in comparison with past ages, is definitely deteriorating. One would think from their attitude that history, that great teacher of life, had taught them nothing. They seem to imagine that in the days of the earlier councils everything was as it should be so far as doctrine and morality and the Church's rightful liberty were concerned.

We feel that We must disagree with these prophets of doom, who are always forecasting worse disasters, as though the end of the world were at hand.

A BASIS FOR OPTIMISM

Present indications are that the human family is on the threshold of a new era. We must recognize here the hand of God, who, as the years roll by, is ever directing men's efforts, whether they realize it or not, towards the fulfillment of the inscrutable designs of His providence, wisely arranging everything, even adverse human fortune, for the Church's good.[10]

PACEM IN TERRIS

Peace on Earth—which man throughout the ages has so longed for and sought after—can never be established, never guaranteed, except by the diligent observance of the divinely established order.

ORDER IN THE UNIVERSE

2. That a marvelous order predominates in the world of living beings and in the forces of nature, is the plain lesson which the progress of modern research and the discoveries of technology teach us. And it is part of the greatness of man that he can appreciate that order, and devise the means for harnessing those forces for his own benefit. . . .

ORDER IN HUMAN BEINGS

7. These laws clearly indicate how a man must behave toward his fellows in society, and how the mutual relationships between the members of a State and its officials are to be conducted. They show too what principles must govern the relations between States; and finally, what should be the relations between individuals or States on the one hand, and the world-wide community of nations on the other. Men's common interests make it imperative that at long last a world-wide community of nations be established.

EVERY MAN IS A PERSON WITH RIGHTS AND DUTIES

9. Any well-regulated and productive association of men in society demands the acceptance of one fundamental principle: that each individual man is truly a person. His is a nature, that is, endowed with intelligence and free will. As such he has rights and duties, which together flow as a direct consequence from his nature. These rights and duties are universal and inviolable, and therefore altogether inalienable.[11]

THE RIGHT TO LIFE AND TO A WORTHY STANDARD OF LIVING

11. But first We must speak of man's rights. Man has the right to live. He has the right to bodily integrity and to the means necessary for the proper development of life, particularly food, clothing, shelter, medical care, rest, and, finally, the necessary social services. In consequence, he has the right to be looked after in the event of ill health; disability stemming from his work; widowhood; old age; enforced unemployment; or whenever through no fault of his own he is deprived of the means of livelihood.[12]

RIGHTS PERTAINING TO MORAL AND CULTURAL VALUES

12. Moreover, man has a natural right to be respected. He has a right to his good name. He has a right to freedom in investigating the truth, and—within the limits of the moral order and the common good—to freedom of speech and publication, and to freedom to pursue whatever profession he may choose. He has the right, also, to be accurately informed about public events.

13. He has the natural right to share in the benefits of culture, and hence to receive a good general education, and a technical or professional training consistent with the degree of educational development in his own country. Furthermore, a system must be devised for affording gifted members of society the opportunity of engaging in more advanced studies, with a view to their occupying, as far as possible, positions of responsibility in society in keeping with their natural talent and acquired skill.[13]

THE RIGHT TO WORSHIP GOD ACCORDING TO ONE'S CONSCIENCE

14. Also among man's rights is that of being able to worship God in accordance with the right dictates of his own conscience, and to profess his religion both in private and in public. . . .

THE RIGHT TO CHOOSE FREELY ONE'S STATE IN LIFE

15. Human beings have also the right to choose for themselves the kind of life which appeals to them: whether it is to found a family—in the founding of which both the man and the woman enjoy equal rights and duties—or to embrace the priesthood or the religious life.[14]

16. The family, founded upon marriage freely contracted, one and indissoluble, must be regarded as the natural, primary cell of human society. The interests of the family, therefore, must be taken very specially into consideration in social and economic affairs, as well as in the spheres of faith and morals. For all of these have to do with strengthening the family and assisting it in the fulfillment of its mission.

17. Of course, the support and education of children is a right which belongs primarily to the parents.[15]

ECONOMIC RIGHTS

18. In the economic sphere, it is evident that a man has the inherent right not only to be given the opportunity to work, but also to be allowed the exercise of personal initiative in the work he does.[16]

19. The conditions in which a man works form a necessary corollary to these rights. They must not be such as to weaken his physical or moral fiber, or militate against the proper development of adolescents to manhood. Women must be accorded such conditions of work as are consistent with their needs and responsibilities as wives and mothers.[17]

20. A further consequence of man's personal dignity is his right to engage in economic activities suited to his degree of responsibility.[18] The worker is likewise entitled to a wage that is determined in accordance with the precepts of justice. This needs stressing. The amount a worker receives must be sufficient, in proportion to available funds, to allow him and his family a standard of living consistent with human dignity. Pope Pius XII expressed it in these terms:

"Nature imposes work upon man as a duty, and man has the corresponding natural right to demand that the work he does shall provide him with the means of livelihood for himself and his children. Such is nature's categorical imperative for the preservation of man."[19]

21. As a further consequence of man's nature, he has the right to the private ownership of property, including that of productive goods. This, as We have said elsewhere, is "a right which constitutes so efficacious a means of asserting one's personality and exercising responsibility in every field, and an element of solidity and security for family life, and of greater peace and prosperity in the State."[20]

22. Finally, it is opportune to point out that the right to own private property entails a social obligation as well.[21]

THE RIGHT OF MEETING AND ASSOCIATION

23. Men are by nature social, and consequently they have the right to meet together and to form associations with their fellows. They have the right to confer on such associations the type of organization which they consider best calculated to achieve their objectives. They have also the right to exercise their own initiative and act on their own responsibility within these associations for the attainment of the desired results.[22]

24. As We insisted in Our encyclical *Mater et Magistra*, the founding of a great many such intermediate groups or societies for the pursuit of aims which it is not within the competence of the individual to achieve efficiently, is a matter of great urgency. Such groups and societies must be considered absolutely essential for the safeguarding of man's personal freedom and dignity, while leaving intact a sense of responsibility.[23]

THE RIGHT TO EMIGRATE AND IMMIGRATE

25. Again, every human being has the right to freedom of movement and of residence within the confines of his own State. When there are just reasons in favor of it, he must be permitted to emigrate to other countries and take up residence there.[24] The fact that he is a citizen of a particular State does not deprive him of membership in the human family, nor of citizenship in that universal society, the common, world-wide fellowship of men.

POLITICAL RIGHTS

26. Finally, man's personal dignity involves his right to take an active part in public life, and to make his own contribution to the common welfare of his fellow citizens. . . .

27. As a human person he is entitled to the legal protection of his rights, and such protection must be effective, unbiased, and strictly just. . . .

RIGHTS AND DUTIES NECESSARILY LINKED IN THE ONE PERSON

28. The natural rights of which We have so far been speaking are inextricably bound up with as many duties, all applying to one and the same person. These rights and duties derive their origin, their sustenance, and

their indestructibility from the natural law, which in conferring the one imposes the other.

29. Thus, for example, the right to live involves the duty to preserve one's life; the right to a decent standard of living, the duty to live in a becoming fashion; the right to be free to seek out the truth, the duty to devote oneself to an ever deeper and wider search for it.

RECIPROCITY OF RIGHTS AND DUTIES BETWEEN PERSONS

30. Once this is admitted, it follows that in human society one man's natural right gives rise to a corresponding duty in other men; the duty, that is, of recognizing and respecting that right. Every basic human right draws its authoritative force from the natural law, which confers it and attaches to it its respective duty. Hence, to claim one's rights and ignore one's duties, or only half fulfill them, is like building a house with one hand and tearing it down with the other.

MUTUAL COLLABORATION

31. Since men are social by nature, they must live together and consult each other's interests. That men should recognize and perform their respective rights and duties is imperative to a well ordered society. But the result will be that each individual will make his whole-hearted contribution to the creation of a civic order in which rights and duties are ever more diligently and more effectively observed.

SOCIAL LIFE IN TRUTH, JUSTICE, CHARITY, AND FREEDOM

35. Hence, before a society can be considered well-ordered, creative, and consonant with human dignity, it must be based on truth. St. Paul expressed this as follows: "Putting away lying, speak ye the truth every man with his neighbor, for we are members one of another."[25] And so will it be, if each man acknowledges sincerely his own rights and his own duties toward others.

Human society, as We here picture it, demands that men be guided by justice, respect the rights of others and do their duty. It demands, too, that they be animated by such love as will make them feel the needs of others as their own, and induce them to share their goods with others, and to strive in the world to make all men alike heirs to the noblest of intellectual and spiritual values. Nor is this enough; for human society thrives on freedom, namely, on the use of means which are consistent with the dignity of its individual members, who, being endowed with reason, assume responsibility for their own actions.

36. And so, dearest sons and brothers, we must think of human society as being primarily a spiritual reality. By its means enlightened men can share their knowledge of the truth, can claim their rights and fulfill their duties, receive encouragement in their aspirations for the goods of the spirit, share their enjoyment of all the wholesome pleasures of the world, and strive continually to pass on to others all that is best in themselves and to make their own the spiritual riches of others. It is these spiritual values which exert a guiding influence on culture, economics, social institutions, political movements and forms, laws, and all the other components which go to make up the external community of men and its continual development.

GOD AND THE MORAL ORDER

37. Now the order which prevails in human society is wholly incorporeal in nature. Its foundation is truth, and it must be brought into effect by justice. It needs to be animated and perfected by men's love for one another, and, while preserving freedom intact, it must make for an equilibrium in society which is increasingly more human in character.

EQUALITY OF MEN

44. Today, on the contrary the conviction is widespread that all men are equal in natural dignity; and so, on the doctrinal and theoretical level, at least, no form of approval is being given to racial discrimination. All this is of supreme significance for the formation of a human society animated by the principles We have mentioned above, for man's awareness of his rights must inevitably lead him to the recognition of his duties. The possession of rights involves the duty of implementing those rights, for they are the expression of a man's personal dignity. And the possession of rights also involves their recognition and respect by other people.

45. When society is formed on a basis of rights and duties, men have an immediate grasp of spiritual and intellectual values, and have no difficulty in understanding what is meant by truth, justice, charity and freedom. They become, moreover, conscious of being members of such a society. And that is not all. Inspired by such principles, they attain to a better knowledge of the true God—a personal God transcending human nature. They recognize that their relationship with God forms the very foundation of their life—the interior life of the spirit, and the life which they live in the society of their fellows.

ATTAINMENT OF THE COMMON GOOD IS THE PURPOSE OF THE PUBLIC AUTHORITY

53. Men, both as individuals and as intermediate groups, are required to make their own specific contributions to the general welfare. The main consequence of this is that they must harmonize their own interests with the needs of others, and offer their goods and services as their rulers shall direct—assuming, of course, that justice is maintained and the authorities are acting within the limits of their competence. Those who have authority in the State must exercise that authority in a way which is not only morally irreproachable, but also best calculated to ensure or promote the State's welfare.

54. The attainment of the common good is the sole reason for the existence of civil authorities. In working for the common good, therefore, the authorities must obviously respect its nature, and at the same time adjust their legislation to meet the requirements of the given situation.

STRUCTURE AND OPERATION OF THE PUBLIC AUTHORITY

67. For the rest, it is not possible to give a general ruling on the most suitable form of government, or the ways in which civil authorities can most effectively fulfill their legislative, administrative, and judicial functions.

68. In determining what form a particular government shall take, and the way in which it shall function, a major consideration will be the prevailing circumstances and the condition of the people; and these are things which vary in different places and at different times.

We think, however, that it is in keeping with human nature for the State to be given a form which embodies a threefold division of public office properly corresponding to the three main functions of public authority. In such a State a precise legal framework is provided, not only for the official functions of government, but also for the mutual relations between citizens and public officials. This will obviously afford sure protection to citizens, both in the safeguarding of their rights and in the fulfillment of their duties.

LAW AND CONSCIENCE

70. There can be no doubt that a State juridical system which conforms to the principles of justice and rightness, and corresponds to the degree of civic maturity evinced by the State in question, is highly conducive to the attainment of the common good.

71. And yet social life is so complex, varied and active in this modern age, that even a juridical system which has been established with great prudence and foresight often seems inadequate to the need.

72. Moreover, the relations of citizens with each other, of citizens and intermediate groups with public authorities, and the relations between public authorities of the same State, are sometimes seen to be of so ambiguous and explosive a nature, that they are not susceptible of being regulated by any hard and fast system of laws.

In such cases, if the authorities want to preserve the State's juridical system intact—in itself and in its application to specific cases—and if they want to minister to the principal needs of society, adapt the laws to the conditions of modern life and seek solutions to new problems, then it is essential that they have a clear idea of the nature and limits of their own legitimate spheres of action. Their calmness, integrity, clear sightedness and perseverance must be such that they will recognize at once what is needed in a given situation, and act with promptness and efficiency.[26]

CHARACTERISTICS OF THE PRESENT DAY

75. There is every indication at the present time that these aims and ideals are giving rise to various demands concerning the juridical organization of States. The first is this: that a clear and precisely worded charter of fundamental human rights be formulated and incorporated into the State's general constitution.

76. Secondly, each State must have a public constitution, couched in juridical terms, laying down clear rules relating to the designation of public officials, their reciprocal relations, spheres of competence and prescribed methods of operation.

77. The final demand is that relations between citizens and public authorities be described in terms of rights and duties. It must be clearly laid down that the principal function of public authorities is to recognize, respect, co-ordinate, safeguard and promote citizens' rights and duties

78. We must, however, reject the view that the will of the individual or the group is the primary and only source of a citizen's rights and duties, and of the binding force of political constitutions and the government's authority.[27]

79. But the aspirations We have mentioned are a clear indication of the fact that men, increasingly aware nowadays of their personal dignity, have found the incentive to enter government service and demand constitutional recognition for their own inviolable rights. Not content with this, they are demanding, too, the observance of constitutional procedures in the

appointment of public authorities, and are insisting that they exercise their office within this constitutional framework.

SUBJECTS OF RIGHTS AND DUTIES

80. With respect to States themselves, Our predecessors have constantly taught, and We wish to lend the weight of Our own authority to their teaching, that nations are the subjects of reciprocal rights and duties. Their relationships, therefore, must likewise be harmonized in accordance with the dictates of truth, justice, willing cooperation, and freedom. The same law of nature that governs the life and conduct of individuals must also regulate the relations of political communities with one another.

SIGNS OF THE TIMES

129. Nevertheless, We are hopeful that, by establishing contact with one another and by a policy of negotiation, nations will come to a better recognition of the natural ties that bind them together as men. We are hopeful, too, that they will come to a fairer realization of one of the cardinal duties deriving from our common nature: namely, that love, not fear, must dominate the relationships between individuals and between nations. It is principally characteristic of love that it draws men together in all sorts of ways, sincerely united in the bonds of mind and matter; and this is a union from which countless blessings can flow. . . .

INADEQUACY OF MODERN STATES TO ENSURE THE UNIVERSAL COMMON GOOD

131. From this it is clear that no State can fittingly pursue its own interests in isolation from the rest, nor, under such circumstances, can it develop itself as it should. The prosperity and progress of any State is in part consequence, and in part cause, of the prosperity and progress of all other States.

132. No era will ever succeed in destroying the unity of the human family, for it consists of men who are all equal by virtue of their natural dignity. Hence there will always be an imperative need—born of man's very nature—to promote in sufficient measure the universal common good; the good, that is, of the whole human family. . . .

137. Today the universal common good presents us with problems which are world-wide in their dimensions; problems, therefore, which cannot be solved except by a public authority with power, organization and means

co-extensive with these problems, and with a world-wide sphere of activity. Consequently the moral order itself demands the establishment of some such general form of public authority.

RELATIONS BETWEEN CATHOLICS AND NON-CATHOLICS IN SOCIAL AND ECONOMIC AFFAIRS

157. The principles We have set out in this document take their rise from the very nature of things. They derive, for the most part, from the consideration of man's natural rights. Thus the putting of these principles into effect frequently involves extensive co-operation between Catholics and those Christians who are separated from this Apostolic See. It even involves the cooperation of Catholics with men who may not be Christians but who nevertheless are reasonable men, and men of natural moral integrity. "In such circumstances they must, of course, bear themselves as Catholics, and do nothing to compromise religion and morality. Yet at the same time they should show themselves animated by a spirit of understanding and unselfishness, ready to co-operate loyally in achieving objects which are good in themselves, or conducive to good."[28]

ERROR AND THE ERRANT

158. It is always perfectly justifiable to distinguish between error as such and the person who falls into error—even in the case of men who err regarding the truth or are led astray as a result of their inadequate knowledge, in matters either of religion or of the highest ethical standards. A man who has fallen into error does not cease to be a man. He never forfeits his personal dignity; and that is something that must always be taken into account. Besides, there exists in man's very nature an undying capacity to break through the barriers of error and seek the road to truth. God, in His great providence, is ever present with His aid. Today, maybe, a man lacks faith and turns aside into error; tomorrow, perhaps, illumined by God's light, he may indeed embrace the truth.

Catholics who, in order to achieve some external good, collaborate with unbelievers or with those who through error lack the fullness of faith in Christ, may possibly provide the occasion or even the incentive for their conversion to the truth.

PHILOSOPHIES AND HISTORICAL MOVEMENTS

159. Again it is perfectly legitimate to make a clear distinction between a false philosophy of the nature, origin and purpose of men and the world,

and economic, social, cultural, and political undertakings, even when such undertakings draw their origin and inspiration from that philosophy. True, the philosophic formula does not change once it has been set down in precise terms, but the undertakings clearly cannot avoid being influenced to a certain extent by the changing conditions in which they have to operate. Besides, who can deny the possible existence of good and commendable elements in these undertakings, elements which do indeed conform to the dictates of right reason, and are an expression of man's lawful aspirations?[29]

UNITATIS REDINTEGRATIO

1. The restoration of unity among all Christians is one of the principal concerns of the Second Vatican Council. Christ the Lord founded one Church and one Church only. However, many Christian communions present themselves to men as the true inheritors of Jesus Christ; all indeed profess to be followers of the Lord but they differ in mind and go their different ways, as if Christ himself were divided.[30] [Certainly, such] division openly contradicts the will of Christ, scandalizes the world, and damages that most holy cause, the preaching of the Gospel to every creature. . . .

4. Today, in many parts of the world, under the influence of the grace of the Holy Spirit, many efforts are being made in prayer, word and action to attain that fullness of unity which Jesus Christ desires. The sacred Council exhorts, therefore, all the Catholic faithful to recognize the signs of the times and to take an active and intelligent part in the work of ecumenism.

The term "ecumenical movement" indicates the initiatives and activities encouraged and organized, according to the various needs of the Church and as opportunities offer, to promote Christian unity. . . .

When such actions are undertaken prudently and patiently by the Catholic faithful, with the attentive guidance of their bishops, they promote justice and truth, concord and collaboration, as well as the spirit of brotherly love and unity. . . .

12. Before the whole world let all Christians confess their faith in the triune God, one and three in the incarnate Son of God, our Redeemer and Lord. United in their efforts, and with mutual respect, let them bear witness to our common hope which does not play us false. In these days when cooperation in social matters is so widespread today, all men without exception are called to work together; with much greater reason is this true of all who believe in God, but most of all, all Christians in that they bear the name of Christ. Cooperation among Christians vividly expresses the relationship which in fact already unites them, and it sets in clearer relief the features of Christ the Servant. This cooperation, which

has already begun in many countries, should be developed more and more, particularly in regions where social and technological evolution is taking place. . . . All believers in Christ can, through this cooperation, be led to acquire a better knowledge and appreciation of one another, and so pave the way to Christian unity.[31]

NOSTRA AETATE

1. In our time, when day by day mankind is being drawn closer together, and the ties between different peoples are becoming stronger, the Church examines more closely her relationship to non-Christian religions. In her task of promoting unity and love among men, indeed among nations, she considers above all in this declaration what men have in common and what draws them to fellowship. . . .

2. . . . The Catholic Church rejects nothing that is true and holy in these religions. She regards with sincere reverence those ways of conduct and of life, those precepts and teachings which, though differing in many aspects from the ones she holds and sets forth, nonetheless often reflect a ray of that Truth which enlightens all men. Indeed, she proclaims, and ever must proclaim Christ "the way, the truth, and the life" (John 14:6), in whom men may find the fullness of religious life, in whom God has reconciled all things to Himself.[32]

The Church, therefore, exhorts her sons, that through dialogue and collaboration with the followers of other religions, carried out with prudence and love and in witness to the Christian faith and life, they recognize, preserve and promote the good things, spiritual and moral, as well as the socio-cultural values found among these men.

4. As the sacred synod searches into the mystery of the Church, it remembers the bond that spiritually ties the people of the New Covenant to Abraham's stock. . . .

True, the Jewish authorities and those who followed their lead pressed for the death of Christ;[33] still, what happened in His passion cannot be charged against all the Jews, without distinction, then alive, nor against the Jews of today. Although the Church is the new people of God, the Jews should not be presented as rejected or accursed by God, as if this followed from the Holy Scriptures. All should see to it, then, that in catechetical work or in the preaching of the word of God they do not teach anything that does not conform to the truth of the Gospel and the spirit of Christ.

Furthermore, in her rejection of every persecution against any man, the Church, mindful of the patrimony she shares with the Jews and moved not by political reasons but by the Gospel's spiritual love, decries hatred, persecutions, displays of anti-Semitism, directed against Jews at any time and by anyone. . . .

5. . . . No foundation therefore remains for any theory or practice that leads to discrimination between man and man or people and people, so far as their human dignity and the rights flowing from it are concerned.

The Church reproves, as foreign to the mind of Christ, any discrimination against men or harassment of them because of their race, color, condition of life, or religion.[34]

GAUDIUM ET SPES

2. Hence this Second Vatican Council, having probed more profoundly into the mystery of the Church, now addresses itself without hesitation, not only to the sons of the Church and to all who invoke the name of Christ, but to the whole of humanity. For the council yearns to explain to everyone how it conceives of the presence and activity of the Church in the world of today. . . .

4. . . . The Church has always had the duty of scrutinizing the signs of the times and of interpreting them in the light of the Gospel. Thus, in language intelligible to each generation, she can respond to the perennial questions which men ask about this present life and the life to come, and about the relationship of the one to the other. We must therefore recognize and understand the world in which we live, its explanations, its longings, and its often dramatic characteristics.[35]

DIGNITATIS HUMANAE

2. The Vatican Council declares that the human person has a right to religious freedom. Freedom of this kind means that all men should be immune from coercion on the part of individuals, social groups and every human power, in such wise that no one is to be forced to act in a manner contrary to his own beliefs, whether privately or publicly, whether alone or in association with others, within due limits.

The Council further declares that the right to religious freedom has its foundation in the very dignity of the human person as this dignity is known through the revealed word of God and by reason itself. The right of the human person to religious freedom is to be recognized in the constitutional law whereby society is governed and thus it is to become a civil right.[36]

NOTES

1. [Thomas Cahill, *Pope John XXIII* (New York: Viking, 2002), 101.]
2. [Peter Hebblethwaite, *John XXIII: Pope of the Century* (London: Continuum, 2000), 54.]
3. [John XXIII, *The Encyclicals and Other Messages of John XXIII* (Washington, D.C.: TPS Press, 1964), 17.]

4. ["Address of Pope John XXIII to the Roman Cardinals (January 25, 1959)," in *The Encyclicals and Other Messages of John XXIII*, 22.]

5. I *Tim.* 6.16.

6. *John* 1.14.

7. *John* 1.9.

8. [*Ad Petri Cathedram*, in *The Encyclicals and Other Messages*, 25–26, 53.]

9. [*Mater et magistra*, in *The Encyclicals and Other Messages*, 262, 265–267, 290–291, 301–302, 305, and 308. *Mater et magistra* was issued in 1961 to commemorate Pope Leo XIII's *Rerum novarum*. Leo's encyclical had defended workers' rights and inaugurated modern Catholic social thought in 1891. John's encyclical reaffirmed the economic rights of workers and placed a new emphasis upon the state's responsibility to protect those rights. This highlighting of the state's obligation to protect workers, summarized in the word "socialization," (i.e., "an increase in social relationships" in §59), was the encyclical's primary contribution to international discussions of development and human rights.]

10. ["Opening Address to the Council," in *The Encyclicals and Other Messages*, 426–427. The Second Vatican Council convened in Rome in October 1962. Many Catholics, especially members of the Roman Curia, wanted the council to denounce the errors of the modern world and to reaffirm the church's traditional teaching. In his opening address to the council on October 11, the pope criticized such prophets of doom and gloom. He urged the church to see the hand of God at work in the modern world. The address confirmed that John's agenda for the Council was *aggiornamento*, that is, bringing the church up to date.]

11. Cf. Pius XII's broadcast message, Christmas 1942, AAS 35 (1943), 9–24; and John XXIII's sermon, Jan. 4, 1963, AAS 55 (1963), 89–91.

12. Cf. Pius XI's encyclical letter *Divini Redemptoris*, AAS 29 (1931), 78; and Pius XII's broadcast message, Pentecost, June 1, 1941, AAS 33 (1941), 195–205.

13. Cf. Pius XII's broadcast message, Christmas 1942, AAS 35 (1943), 9–24.

14. Ibid.

15. Cf. Pius XI's encyclical letter *Casti connubii*, AAS 22 (1930), 539–592, and Pius XII's broadcast message, Christmas 1942, AAS 35 (1943), 9–24.

16. Cf. Pius XII's broadcast message, Pentecost, June 1, 1941, AAS 33 (1941), 201.

17. Cf. Leo XIII's encyclical letter *Rerum novarum*, *Acta Leonis XIII*, XI, 1891, 128–129.

18. Cf. John XXIII's encyclical letter *Mater et magistra*, AAS 53 (1961) 422.

19. Cf. Pius XII's broadcast message, Pentecost, June 1, 1941, AAS 33 (1941) 201.

20. John XXIII's encyclical letter *Mater et Magistra*, AAS 53 (1961) 428. Cf. John XXIII's encyclical letter *Mater et Magistra*, AAS 53 (1961) 422.

21. Cf. *ibid.*, p. 430; TPS v. 7, no. 4, p. 318.

22. Cf. Leo XIII's encyclical letter *Rerum novarum*, *Acta Leonis XIII*, XI, 1891, pp. 134–142; Pius XI's encyclical letter *Quadregesimo anno*, AAS 23 (1931) 199–200; and Pius XII's encyclical letter *Sertum laetitiae*, AAS 31 (1939) 635–644.

23. Cf. AAS 53 (1961) 430.

24. Cf. Pius XII's broadcast message, Christmas 1952, AAS 45 (1953) 36–46.

25. *Eph.* 4:25.

26. Cf. Pius XII's broadcast message, Christmas 1944, AAS 37 (1945) 15–16.

27. Cf. Leo XIII's apostolic letter *Annum ingressi*, *Acta Leonis XIII*, XXII, 1902–1903, pp. 52–80.

28. Cf. John XXIII's encyclical letter *Mater et Magistra*, AAS 53 (1961) 456.

29. [*Pacem in terris*, in *The Encyclicals and Other Messages*, 327–336, 338–341, 345–348, 360–362, and 368–369. *Mater et magistra* had advocated a society of justice, truth and love. In *Pacem in terris*, Pope John added freedom to the list. Henceforth society must be ordered according to justice, truth, love, and freedom. The emphasis on freedom was another indication of the pope's acceptance of the circumstances of the modern world.]

30. Cf. 1 Cor. 1:13.

31. [*Unitatis Redintegratio* (1964), §§ 1, 4, 12; http://www.vatican.va/archive/hist_councils/ii_vatican_council/documents/vat-ii_decree_19641121_unitatis-redintegratio_en.html.]

32. Cf 2 Cor. 5:18–19.

33. Cf. *John.* 19:6.

34. [*Nostra Aetate* (1965), §§ 1–2, 4–5; http://www.vatican.va/archive/hist_councils/ii_vatican_council/documents/vat-ii_decl_19651028_nostra-aetate_en.html.]

35. [*Gaudium et spes* (1965), §§ 2, 4; http://www.vatican.va/archive/hist_councils/ii_vatican_council/documents/vat-ii_cons_19651207_gaudium-et-spes_en.html. John's influence and the method of his encyclicals *Mater et magistra* and *Pacem in terris* were evident in *Gaudium et spes*, the Pastoral Constitution on the Church in the Modern World, which was passed in the Fourth Session of the Council, in December 1965. *Gaudium et spes* followed the method of *Pacem in terris* in identifying the church's duty to read the "signs of the times" in §4.]

36. [*Dignitatis Humanae* (1965), §2; http://www.vatican.va/archive/hist_councils/ii_vatican_council/documents/vat-ii_decl_19651207_dignitatis-humanae_en.html.]

{CHAPTER 5}

Gustavo Gutiérrez (b. 1928)

SELECTED AND EDITED BY PAUL E. SIGMUND

In the first collection of his writings on liberation to appear in English, Gustavo Gutiérrez outlines the main features of his new approach to theology. First, he argues for a new theological method, "critical reflection on the present in the light of faith," a third kind of theology in addition to the spiritual wisdom of the church fathers, and the philosophical approach of St. Thomas Aquinas. Arguing against the developmentalist approach to Latin America taken by the Alliance for Progress and international aid agencies, he maintains that its emphasis on economic growth only benefits powerful foreign and domestic economic groups, and increases the dependency and underdevelopment of Latin America. Latin America cannot develop under the capitalist system, he says. Political and economic liberation requires a total break with the existing system, a break that is likely to take a "more or less Marxist approach" and "for many" will "sooner or later" involve the use of violence. The details of what will happen after the revolution "can only be written afterwards." The church has a duty to involve itself in the struggle against poverty, and for human emancipation.

A Theology of Liberation, *originally published in Spanish in 1971, is the book that gave liberation theology its name. It argues for the necessity of political and social commitment by the Christian. What made it controversial was its claim that in Latin America commitment must take the form of involvement in a political and social revolution, overthrowing, by force if necessary, the exploitation and oppression associated with dependent capitalism. Reflecting what he acknowledges as the influence of Marxist analysis, Gutiérrez rejects conciliatory and reformist approaches because they allow "the few to keep living off the poverty of the many," and he calls for the creation of a socialist society that may take diverse forms but will end the use of private property to exploit the labor of others. In support of his position, he quotes from the 1968 Conference of Latin American Bishops, quoting references to the "sinful situation" of "institutionalized violence" in Latin America from a document he helped to write. By the end of the book, the struggle against the class enemy has become an exercise in Christian love, and the mere existence of poverty has become an offense against God.*

In the early 1980s, as international attention turned to the revolutions in Nicaragua, El Salvador, and Guatemala, liberation theology that had played a role in encouraging cooperation between Marxists and Christians in revolutionary movements, provoked opposition in the Vatican and in conservative circles in the United States. The Power of the Poor in History, *which was published in English in 1983 but was made up of translations of articles by Gutiérrez written between 1969 and 1978, provided support to those who saw liberation theology as a kind of Christianized Marxism. They spoke of the proletariat and class conflict, and appeared to call on the church to support socialist revolution in Latin America. The option for the poor was interpreted to assign them a special position in the eyes of God, and to require the overthrow of dependent capitalism. Scripture was quoted to support a popular church, based on the poor, and a "militant reading of the Bible."*

The book also included Gutiérrez's attack on the preparatory document for the 1979 Latin American Bishops' Conference in Puebla, Mexico, published before the meeting by the conference secretariat, which had been reorganized under conservative auspices. Gutiérrez argued that the document never mentioned the torture, murder, and disappearances of the defenders of the poor currently taking place in Latin America, and that it ignored the oppression and exploitation suffered by the poor as a result of "dependent capitalism."

Speaking at the conference itself, the newly elected pope, John Paul II, attacked politicized versions of theology but endorsed a "Christian conception of liberation" theology. His criticisms of political, that is, Marxist, interpretations of theology, and of the popular church, were reflected in the final document of the conference, but it also denounced "capitalist liberalism" and supported "a preferential option for the poor, an option aimed at their liberation," thus incorporating central elements of liberation theology into the mainstream of Catholic social teaching in Latin America.

In the early 1980s, the Congregation for the Doctrine of the Faith, headed by Cardinal Joseph Ratzinger, began to question the orthodoxy of some aspects of liberation theology. In Peru, the Bishops' Conference conducted an investigation of Gutiérrez's writings. The selection that follows is taken from his ultimately successful response to their inquiry. It argues the tentative character of all the hypotheses of social science, including the theory of dependence that influenced the early liberation theologians, and maintains that the liberation theologians, as well as most social theorists, draw some analytical tools from Marxism but reject its dogmatic and all-embracing character. Gutiérrez opposes the deduction of political programs directly from theology, condemns the atheism of Marx, and denies that he ever attempted a synthesis of Marxism and Christianity. He rejects the economic determinism of Marxism and its theories of the class struggle but argues that social conflicts exist, caused not only by economic differences but also by race, culture, gender, and ethnicity. The Christian obligation of universal love still holds even in the midst of the struggle against oppression. By the end of the essay, Gutiérrez has successfully refuted the belief that liberation theology is a form of Christianized Marxism, and effectively reduced the central role of dependency theory in his social analysis.

Along with We Drink from Our Own Wells *(1984),* On Job *illustrates the increasing emphasis on the Bible (Gutiérrez's book contains more than five hundred biblical quotations or references) and the abandonment of Marxist themes in Gutiérrez's writings in the 1980s. It is a beautiful meditation, using the Book of Job as its text, on the relation of God to human suffering. It draws parallels between the experiences of Job and of the poor in Latin America, recognizes race, gender, political persecution, and terrorism as sources of oppression, and emphasizes the importance of prayer, contemplation, and active commitment as prior to abstract theologizing.*

In 1988, Orbis Books published a fifteenth anniversary edition of A Theology of Liberation. *In his introduction to the revised edition, Gutiérrez recognized race and gender, in addition to class, as important sources of oppression in Latin America. He also replaced a much-criticized section of the 1973 edition, "Christian Brotherhood and Class Struggle," with a new section, "Faith and Social Conflict," that gives more emphasis to race and gender as sources of conflict, but that also quotes from passages in papal encyclicals that recognize the importance of class conflict. Gutiérrez concludes that the Christian must work for a "fraternal society of equals" while maintaining an attitude of Christian love for all.*

NOTES FOR A THEOLOGY OF LIBERATION

DEFINITIONS

To GET AT the theological meaning of liberation, we first have to define our terms. That will make up the first part of this article. It will permit us to emphasize that in these pages we are particularly sensitive to the critical function of theory regarding the Church's presence and activity in the world. The principal fact about that presence today, especially in underdeveloped countries, is the participation by Christians in the struggle to construct a just and fraternal society in which men can live in dignity and be masters of their own destinies. We think that the word "development" does not well express those profound aspirations. "Liberation" seems more exact and richer in overtones; besides, it opens up a more fertile field for theological reflection. . . .

To approach this question properly, we should explain precisely what we mean by "theology" and by "liberation." Theological reflection is inherent in the life of faith and the life of the Church. However, the focus of theological study has varied down through the history of the Church. That evolution has been accelerated in recent years. Through the Church's history, theology has carried out various functions. Two stand out in particular. In the first centuries, what we today call theology was closely allied to the spiritual life. Primarily it dealt with a meditation on the Bible, geared toward spiritual progress. From the twelfth century on, theology began to be a science. The Aristotelian categories made it possible to speak of theology as a "subordinate science." This notion of science is ambiguous and does not satisfy the modern mind. But the essential in the work of St. Thomas is that theology is the fruit of the meeting between faith and reason. Perhaps we do better, then, to speak of a rational knowledge. In résumé, theology is necessarily spiritual and rational knowledge. These two elements are permanent and indispensable functions of all theological reflection.

Another function of theology has slowly developed and been accepted in recent years: theology as a critical reflection on the Church's pastoral action. The renewed stress on charity as the center of the Christian life has brought us to see faith more biblically, as a commitment to God and neighbor. In this perspective the understanding of faith is likewise seen to be the understanding of a commitment, an attitude, a posture toward life, in the light of the revealed Word. At the same time, the very life of the Church has become a *locus theologicus* [place where theology is done]. This was clear in the so-called "new theology," and has frequently been emphasized since then. God's word, which assembles us, is incarnated in the community of faith totally devoted to the service of all men.

Something similar happened with what has been called since Pope John and Vatican II a theology of the signs of the times. Let us not forget that the signs of the times are not only a call to intellectual analysis. They are, above all, a demand for action, for commitment, for service of others. "Scrutinizing" the signs of the times takes in both elements (*Gaudium et spes*, no. 44).

All these factors have brought us to rediscover and make explicit theology's function as a critical reflection on the Church's presence and activity in the world, in the light of revelation. By its preaching of the gospel message, by its sacraments, by the charity of its members, the Church announces and accepts the gift of the kingdom of God into the heart of human history. The Church is effective charity, it is action, it is commitment to the service of men.

Theology is reflection, a critical attitude. First comes the commitment to charity, to service. Theology comes "later." It is second. The Church's pastoral action is not arrived at as a conclusion from theological premises. Theology does not lead to pastoral activity, but is rather a reflection on it. Theology should find the Spirit present in it, inspiring the actions of the Christian community. The life of the Church will be for it a *locus theologicus*.

Reflecting on the Church's presence and activity in the world means being open to the world, listening to the questions asked in it, being attentive to the successive stages of its historical growth.[1] This task is indispensable. Reflection in the light of faith should always accompany the Church's pastoral efforts. Theology, by relativizing all its undertakings, keeps the Church from settling down into what is only provisory. Theology, by harking back to the sources of revelation, will guide action, setting it into a broader context, thus contributing to keep it from falling into activism and immediatism.

As reflection on the Church's activity, theology is a progressive and, in a certain sense, variable understanding. If the commitment of the Christian community takes on different forms down through history, the understanding that accompanies that commitment will constantly take a fresh look at it—and may then take surprising initiatives. Theology, therefore, as a critical reflection on the Church's presence and action in the world, in the light of faith, not only complements the other two functions of theology (wisdom and rational knowledge) but even presupposes them. . . .

In recent decades the term "development" has been used to express the aspirations of the poor nations. Of late, however, the term has seemed weak. In fact, today the term conveys a pejorative connotation, especially in Latin America. There has been much discussion recently of development, of aid to the poor countries; there has even been an effort to weave a mystique around those words. Attempts to produce development in the 1950's aroused hopes. But because they did not hit the roots of the evil, they failed, and have led to deception, confusion, and frustration.

One of the most important causes of this situation is the fact that development, in its strictly economic, modernizing sense, was advanced by international agencies backed by the groups that control the world economy. The changes proposed avoided sedulously, therefore, attacking the powerful international economic interests and those of their natural allies: the national oligarchies. What is more, in many cases the alleged changes were only new and concealed ways to increase the power of the mighty economic groups. Here is where conflict enters the picture. Development should attack the causes of our plight, and among the central ones is the economic, social, political, and cultural dependence of some peoples on others. The word "liberation," therefore, is more accurate and conveys better the human side of the problem.

Once we call the poor countries oppressed and dominated, the word "liberation" is appropriate. But there is also another, much more global and profound view of humanity's historical advance. Man begins to see himself as a creative subject; he seizes more and more the reins of his own destiny, directing it toward a society where he will be free of every kind of slavery.[2] Looking on history as the process of *man's emancipation* places the question of development in a broader context, a deeper and even a more radical one. This approach expresses better the aspiration of the poor peoples, who consider themselves primarily as oppressed. Thus the term "development" seems rather antiseptic, inaccurately applying to a tragic, tense reality. What is at stake, then, is a dynamic and historical concept of man as looking toward his future, doing things today to shape his tomorrow. . . .

Liberation, therefore, seems to express better both the hopes of oppressed peoples and the fullness of a view in which man is seen not as a passive element, but as an agent of history. More profoundly, to see history as a process of man's liberation places the issue of desired social changes in a dynamic context. It also permits us to understand better the age we live in. Finally, the term "development" clouds up somewhat the theological issues latent in the process. To speak of liberation, on the other hand, is to hint at the biblical sources that illuminate man's presence and actions in history: the liberation from sin by Christ our Redeemer and the bringing of new life. In résumé, then, there are three levels of meaning to the term "liberation": the political liberation of oppressed peoples and social classes; man's liberation in the course of history; and liberation from sin as condition of a life of communion of all men with the Lord. . . .

The developmental model has not produced the promised fruits. A pessimistic diagnostic has now replaced the former optimistic one. Today we see clearly that: the proposed model was an improper one. It was an abstract model, an ahistorical one, which kept us from seeing the complexity of the problem and the inevitably contradictory aspects of the proposed solution. The process of underdevelopment should be studied in historical perspective, i.e., contrasting it with the development of the great capitalist countries in whose sphere Latin America is situated.

Underdevelopment, as a global social fact, can be seen as the historical subproduct of the development of other countries. The dynamics of capitalistic economics lead simultaneously to the creation of greater wealth for fewer, and of greater poverty for more. Our national oligarchies, teamed up in complicity with these centers of power, perpetuate, for their own benefit and through various subterfuges, a situation of domination within each country, [and] the inequality between developed and underdeveloped countries is worse if we turn to the cultural point of view. The poor, dominated countries keep getting farther and farther behind. If things go on this way, we will soon be able to speak of two human groups, two kinds of men. All these studies lead us to conclude that Latin America cannot develop within the capitalistic system. Labeling Latin America an oppressed and dominated continent brings us naturally to speak of liberation and to start acting accordingly. Indeed, this is a word that reveals a new conviction of Latin Americans. The failure of the efforts at reform has accentuated this attitude. Today the most "conscientized" groups agree that there will be a true development for Latin America only through liberation from the domination by capitalist countries. That implies, of course, a showdown with their natural allies: our national oligarchies. Latin America will never get out of its plight except by a profound transformation, a social revolution that will radically change the conditions it lives in at present. Today, a more or less Marxist inspiration prevails among those groups and individuals who are raising the banner of the continent's liberation. And for many in our continent, this liberation will have to pass, sooner or later, through paths of violence. Indeed, we recognize that the armed struggle began some years ago. It is hard to weigh its possibilities in terms of political effectiveness. The reverses it has suffered have obliged it to rethink its program, but it would be naive to think that the armed struggle is over.

We must remember, however, that in this process of liberation there is, explicitly or implicitly, an added thrust. Achieving the liberation of the continent means more than just overcoming economic, social, and political dependence. It also means seeing that humanity is marching toward a society in which man will be free of every servitude and master of his own destiny.[3]

THE CHURCH IN THE LIBERATION PROCESS

The Latin American Church has lived, and still does, largely in a ghetto state. Thus the Church has had to seek support from the established powers and the economically powerful groups, in order to carry out its task and, at times, face its enemies. But for some time now, we have been witnessing a mighty effort to end that ghetto situation and shake off the ambiguous protection offered by the upholders of the unjust order our continent lives in.

The pastoral goal of setting up a "new Christianity" has brought about a political commitment by many Christians to create a more just society. The lay apostolic movements, in particular those of youth, have given their best leaders in years gone by to the political parties of Social Christian inspiration.[4] Today, however, the apostolic youth movements have gone more radical in their political stance. In most Latin American countries the militants no longer gravitate toward the Social Christian parties, or if they do, they become their more radical wing. The increasingly more revolutionary political postures of Christian groups frequently lead the lay apostolic movements into conflict with the hierarchy, open the question of where they fit into the Church, and cause serious conscience problems for them. In many cases the laymen's interest in social revolution is gradually displacing their interest in the kingdom. Clearer notions about the continent's tragic plight, sharp breaks provoked by the political polarization, the trend toward more active participation in the Church's life as urged by the Council and Medellín[5]—all of these have made the clergy (including religious) one of the most dynamic and restless segments of the Latin American Church. In many countries groups of priests have organized to channel and accentuate the growing restlessness. They call for radical changes in the Church's presence and activity. These activities, and other factors, have in a number of cases led to frictions with local bishops and [papal] nuncios. It seems probable that, unless radical changes take place, these conflicts will multiply and get even worse in coming years. Many priests, as well, feel bound in conscience to engage actively in the field of politics. And it happens frequently today in Latin America that priests are labeled "subversives." Many of them are watched or sought by the police. Others are in jail, are exiled, or are even assassinated by anticommunist terrorists. . . .

THE FAITH AND THE NEW MAN

The entire dynamism of human history, the struggle against all that depersonalizes man—social inequalities, misery, exploitation—have their origin, are sublimated, and reach their plentitude in the salvific work of Christ. . . . Political theology seeks to focus on the social dimensions of the biblical message. The Bible tells us not only of a *vocation* to communion with God but of a *convocation*. That fact ought to have an impact on the political behavior of Christians.

This conclusion is particularly appropriate in Latin America, where the Christian community is accepting more and more delicate and even radical political involvements. But some questions arise. Will political theology stop at analyzing the meaning of those involvements? Or will it go further and inspire a new political doctrine for the Church? In the latter case, how can we avoid a return to the familiar old problem of Christendom? Shall theology become a new "ideology"? The challenge will be to find a way between a Christian politics and an abstention. Very likely no solution can be found by hit-and-miss methods. Yet it is hard to work out in advance (as we used to believe we could) the precise norms that should govern the Church's conduct, which will probably have to be decided by the needs of the moment, with the lights the Church has at its disposition, and with a mighty effort to be true to the gospel. There are certain chapters of theology that can only be written afterwards. In any event, if we can recapture a historical vision focusing on the future and animated by hope that Christ will bring about the fullness we wait for, we shall see in a fresh light the *new man we* are trying to create by our activity in the present. If we hope in Christ, we will believe in the historical adventure—which opens a vast field of possibilities to the Christian's action. . . .

In Latin America the Church must realize that it exists in a continent undergoing revolution, where violence is present in different ways. The "world" in which the Christian community is called on to live and celebrate its eschatological hope is one in social revolution. Its mission must be achieved keeping that in account. The Church has no alternative. Only a total break with the unjust order to which it is bound in a thousand conscious or unconscious ways, and a forthright commitment to a new society, will make men in Latin America believe the message of love it bears. The Church's critico-political function becomes doubly important in Latin America, where the ecclesial institution carries so much prestige. In consideration, then, of the Church's mission, concrete circumstances should affect not only pastoral attitudes but theological thought itself.

POVERTY—IN SOLIDARITY AND IN PROTEST

For several years we have been hearing a growing call in the Church for an authentic witness of poverty. It is important, however, to grasp very precisely the point of this witness and to avoid sentimentalism (there has been trivial talk of the "eminent dignity of the poor in the Church"), as well as the fanciful project of making poverty into an ideal (which would be ironic indeed for those who undergo real misery).

In the Bible poverty, as deprivation of the basic needs for living, is considered an evil, something that degrades man and offends God; the words it uses in referring to the poor show this (cf. Is 10:2; Amos 2:6–7; 5:1–6; 2:1). On the other hand, spiritual poverty is not merely an interior indifference to the goods of this world, but an attitude of openness to God, of spiritual simplicity (Wis 2:3; Is 66:2; Ps 25, 34, 37,149; Prv 22:4; 15:33; 18:2; Mt 5:3).

Christian poverty makes no sense, then, except as a promise to be one with those suffering misery, in order to point out the evil that it represents. No one should "idealize" poverty, but rather hold it aloft as an evil, cry out against it, and strive to eliminate it. Through such a spirit of solidarity we can alert the poor to the injustice of their situation. When Christ assumed the condition of poverty, He did so not to idealize it, but to show love and solidarity with men and to redeem them from sin. Christian poverty, an expression of love, makes us one with those who are poor and protests against their poverty.

Yet we must watch the use of that word. The term "poor" can seem vague and churchy, sentimental, even antiseptic. The "poor" man today is the one who is oppressed, who is kept marginal to society, the proletarian or sub-proletarian struggling to get his most elemental rights. The solidarity and protest we are talking about have a real political overtone in today's world. Making oneself one with the poor today can entail personal risk, even of one's life. That is what many Christians—and non-Christians—who are dedicated to the revolutionary cause are finding out. Thus new forms of living poverty, different from the usual "giving up the goods of this world," are being found.

Only by repudiating poverty and making itself poor in protest against it can the Church preach "spiritual poverty," i.e., an openness of man and the history he lives in to the future promised by God. Only in that way can it fulfill honestly, and with a good chance of being heard, the critico-social function that political theology assigns. For the Church of today, this is the test of the authenticity of its mission.[6]

A THEOLOGY OF LIBERATION: HISTORY, POLITICS, AND SALVATION

THEOLOGY AS CRITICAL REFLECTION ON PRAXIS

Vatican Council II has strongly reaffirmed the idea of a Church of service and not of power. This is a Church which is not centered upon itself and which does not "find itself" except when it "loses itself", when it lives "the joys and the hopes, the griefs and the anxieties of men of this age" (*Gaudium et Spes* no. 1). All of these trends provide a new focus for seeing the presence and activity of the Church in the world as a starting point for theological reflection.

What since John XXIII and Vatican Council II began to be called a theology of the signs of the times can be characterized along the same lines, although this takes a step beyond narrow ecclesial limits. It must not be forgotten that the signs of the times are not only a call to intellectual analysis. They are above all a call to pastoral activity, to commitment, and to service. Studying the signs of the times includes both dimensions. Therefore *Gaudium et Spes*, no. 44, points out that discerning the signs of the times is the responsibility of every Christian, especially pastors and theologians, to hear, distinguish, and interpret the many voices of our age, and to judge them in the light of the divine Word. In this way, revealed truths can always be more deeply penetrated, better understood, and set forth to greater advantage. Attributing this role to every member of the People of God and singling out the pastors—charged with guiding the activity of the Church—highlights the call to commitment which the signs of the times imply. Necessarily connected with this consideration, the function of theologians will be to afford greater clarity regarding this commitment by means of intellectual analysis. . . .

To these factors can be added the influence of *Marxist thought*, focusing on praxis and geared to the transformation of the world.[7] ... Contemporary theology does in fact find itself in direct and fruitful confrontation with Marxism, and it is to a large extent due to Marxism's influence that theological thought, searching for its own sources, has begun to reflect on the meaning of the transformation of this world and the action of man in history. Further, this confrontation helps theology to perceive what its efforts at understanding the faith receive from the historical praxis of man in history as well as what its own reflection might mean for the transformation of the world.

Finally, the rediscovery of the *eschatological dimension* in theology has also led us to consider the central role of historical praxis. Indeed, if human history is above all else an opening to the future, then it is a task, a political occupation, through which man orients and opens himself to the gift which gives history its transcendent meaning: the full and definitive encounter with the Lord and with other men. "To do the truth," as the Gospel says,[8] thus acquires a precise and concrete meaning in terms of the importance of action in Christian life. Faith in a God who loves us and calls us to the gift of full communion with him and brotherhood among men not only is not foreign to the transformation of the world; it leads necessarily to the building up of that brotherhood and communion in history. Moreover, only by doing this truth will our faith be "verified," in the etymological sense of the word. From this notion has recently been derived the term *orthopraxis*, which still disturbs the sensitivities of some. The intention, however, is not to deny the meaning of *orthodoxy*, understood as a proclamation of, and reflection on statements considered to be true. Rather, the goal is to balance and even to reject the primacy and almost exclusiveness which doctrine has enjoyed in Christian life and above all to modify the emphasis, often obsessive, upon the attainment of an orthodoxy which is often nothing more than fidelity to an obsolete tradition or a debatable interpretation. In a more positive vein, the intention is to recognize the work and importance of concrete behavior, of deeds, of action, of praxis in the Christian life. . . .

Reflection in the light of faith must constantly accompany the pastoral action of the Church. By keeping historical events in their proper perspective, theology helps safeguard society and the Church from regarding as permanent what is only temporary. Critical reflection thus always plays the inverse role of an ideology which rationalizes and justifies a given social and ecclesial order. On the other hand, theology, by pointing to the sources of revelation, helps to orient pastoral activity; it puts it in a wider context and so helps it to avoid activism and immediatism. Theology as critical reflection thus fulfills a liberating function for man and the Christian community, preserving them from fetishism and idolatry, as well as from a pernicious and belittling narcissism. Understood in this way, theology has a necessary and permanent role in the liberation from every form of religious alienation—which is often fostered by the ecclesiastical institution itself when it impedes an authentic approach to the Word of the Lord.

As critical reflection on society and the Church, theology is an understanding which both grows and, in a certain sense, changes. If the commitment of the Christian community in fact takes different forms throughout history, the understanding which accompanies the vicissitudes of this commitment will be constantly renewed and will take untrodden paths. A theology which has as its points of reference only "truths" which have been established once and for all—and not the Truth which is also the Way—can be only static and, in the long run, sterile. . . .

Theology as a critical reflection on Christian praxis in the light of the Word does not replace the other functions of theology, such as wisdom and rational knowledge; rather it presupposes and needs them. But this is not all. We are not concerned here with a mere juxtaposition. The critical function of theology necessarily leads to redefinition of these other two tasks. Henceforth, wisdom and rational knowledge will more explicitly have ecclesial praxis as their point of departure and their context. It is in reference to this praxis that an understanding of spiritual growth based on Scripture should be developed, and it is through this same praxis that faith encounters the problems posed by human reason. Given the theme of the present work, we will be especially aware of this critical function of theology with the ramifications suggested above. This approach will lead us to pay special attention to the life of the Church and to commitments which Christians, impelled by the Spirit and in communion with other people, undertake in history. We will give special consideration to participation in the process of liberation, an outstanding phenomenon of our times, which takes on special meaning in the so-called Third World countries. . . .

THE PROCESS OF LIBERATION

The poor countries are becoming ever more clearly aware that their under-development is only the by-product of the development of other countries, because of the kind of relationship which exists between the rich and the poor countries. Moreover, they are realizing that their own development will come about only with a struggle to break the domination of the rich countries.

This perception sees the conflict implicit in the process. Development must attack the root causes of the problems and among them the deepest is economic, social, political and cultural dependence of some countries upon others—an expression of the domination of some social classes over others. Attempts to bring about changes within the existing order have proven futile. This analysis of the situation is at the level of scientific rationality. Only a radical break from the status quo, that is, a profound transformation of the private property system, access to power of the exploited class, and a social revolution that would break this dependence would allow for the change to a new society, a socialist society—or at least allow that such a society might be possible. . . .

We can distinguish three reciprocally interpenetrating levels of meaning of the term *liberation*, or in other words, three approaches to the process of liberation. In the first place, *liberation* expresses the aspirations of oppressed peoples and social classes, emphasizing the conflictual aspect of the economic, social, and political process which puts them at odds with wealthy nations and oppressive classes. In contrast, the word *development*, and above all the policies characterized as developmentalist [*desarrollista*] appear somewhat aseptic, giving a false picture of a tragic and conflictual reality. The issue of development does in fact find its true place in the more universal, profound, and radical perspective of liberation. It is only within this framework that *development* finds its true meaning and possibilities of accomplishing something worthwhile.

At a deeper level, *liberation* can be applied to an understanding of history. Man is seen as assuming conscious responsibility for his own destiny. This understanding provides a dynamic context and broadens the horizons of the desired social changes. In this perspective the unfolding of all of man's dimensions is demanded—a man who makes himself throughout his life and throughout history. The gradual conquest of true freedom leads to the creation of a new man and a qualitatively different society. This vision provides, therefore, a better understanding of what in fact is at stake in our times.

Finally, the word *development* to a certain extent limits and obscures the theological problems implied in the process designated by this term. On the contrary the word *liberation* allows for another approach leading to the Biblical sources which inspire the presence and action of man in history. In the Bible, Christ is presented as the one who brings us liberation. Christ the Savior liberates man from sin, which is the ultimate root of all disruption of friendship and of all injustice and oppression. Christ makes man truly free, that is to say, he enables man to live in communion with him; and this is the basis for all human brotherhood.

This is not a matter of three parallel or chronologically successive processes, however. There are three levels of meaning of a single, complex process, which finds its deepest sense and its full realization in the saving work of Christ. These levels of meaning, therefore, are interdependent. A comprehensive view of the matter presupposes that all three aspects can be considered together. In this way two pitfalls will be avoided: first, *idealist* or *spiritualist* approaches, which are nothing but ways of evading a harsh and demanding reality, and second, shallow analyses and programs of short-term effect initiated under the pretext of meeting immediate needs. . . .

THE LIBERATION MOVEMENT

To characterize Latin America as a dominated and oppressed continent naturally leads one to speak of liberation and above all to participate in the process. Indeed, *liberation* is a term which expresses a new posture of Latin Americans. The failure of reformist efforts has strengthened this attitude. Among more alert groups today, what we have called a new awareness of Latin American reality is making headway. They believe that there can be authentic development for Latin America only if there is liberation from the domination exercised by the great capitalist countries and especially by the most powerful, the United States of America. This liberation also implies a confrontation with these groups' natural allies, their compatriots who control the national power structure. It is becoming more evident that the Latin American peoples will not emerge from their present status except by means of a profound transformation, *a social revolution*, which will radically and qualitatively change the conditions in which they now live. The oppressed sectors within each country are becoming aware—slowly, it is true—of their class interests and of the painful road which must be followed to accomplish the breakup of the status quo. Even more slowly they are becoming aware of all that the building of a new society implies. . . .

In Latin America we are in the midst of a full-blown process of revolutionary ferment. This is a complex and changing situation which resists schematic interpretations and demands a continuous revision of the postures adopted. Be that as it may, the untenable circumstances of poverty, alienation, and exploitation in which the greater part of the people of Latin America live urgently demand that we find a path toward economic, social, and political liberation. This is the first step towards a new society.

These groups and individuals who have raised the banner of Latin American liberation are most frequently of socialist inspiration; socialism, moreover, represents the most fruitful and far-reaching approach. There is, however, no monolithic orientation. A theoretical and practical diversity is emerging. Strategies and tactics are different and in many cases even contrary. Theoretical approaches also vary. This can be a result both of different interpretations of reality and of conscious or unconscious imitation of others' approaches. Indeed, cultural dependence has a role to play even here. Nevertheless, the search for indigenous socialist paths continues. . . .

The liberation of our continent means more than overcoming economic, social, and political dependence. It means, in a deeper sense, to see the becoming of mankind as a process of the emancipation of man in history. It is to see man in search of a qualitatively different society in which he will be free from all servitude, in which he will be the artisan of his own destiny. It is to seek the building up of a *new man*. Ernesto Che Guevara wrote, "We revolutionaries often lack the knowledge and the intellectual audacity to face the task of the development of a new human being by methods different from the conventional ones, and the conventional methods suffer from the influence of the society that created them."[9]

This vision is what in the last instance sustains the liberation efforts of Latin Americans. But in order for this liberation to be authentic and complete, it has to be undertaken by the oppressed people themselves and so must stem from the values proper to these people. Only in this context can a true cultural revolution come about. . . .

THE CHURCH IN THE PROCESS OF LIBERATION

As for the bishops' vision of reality, they describe the misery and the exploitation of man by man in Latin America as "a situation of injustice that can be called institutionalized violence"; it is responsible for the death of thousands of innocent victims.[10] This view allows for a study of the complex problems of counterviolence without falling into the pitfalls of a double standard which assumes that violence is acceptable when the oppressor uses it to maintain "order" and is bad when the oppressed invoke it to change this "order." Institutionalized violence violates fundamental rights so patently that the Latin American bishops warn that "one should not abuse the patience of a people that for years has borne a situation that would not be acceptable to any one with any degree of awareness of human rights. . . ." Theologically, this situation of injustice and oppression is characterized as a "sinful situation" because "where this social peace does not exist, there we will find social, political, economic, and cultural inequalities, there we will find the rejection of the peace of the Lord, and a rejection of the Lord Himself. . . ." The reality so described is perceived ever more clearly as resulting from a situation of dependence, in which the centers of decision are to be found outside the continent; it follows that the Latin American countries are being kept in a condition of neo-colonialism. . . .

Old prejudices, inevitable ideological elements, and also the ambivalence of the term *socialism* require the use of cautious language and careful distinctions. There is always the risk that statements in this regard may be interpreted differently by different people. It is therefore important to link this subject to another which enables us at least under one aspect to clarify what we mean. We refer to the progressive radicalization of the debate concerning private property. The subordination of private property to the social good has been stressed often. But difficulties in reconciling justice and private ownership have led many to the conviction that "private ownership of capital leads to the dichotomy of capital and labor, to the superiority of the capitalist over the laborer, to the exploitation of man by man. . . . The history of the private ownership of the means of production makes evident the necessity of its reduction or suppression for the welfare of society. We must hence *opt for social ownership of the means of production . . . .*"[11]

However, existing structures block popular participation and marginate the great majorities, depriving them of channels for expression of their demands. Consequently, the Church feels compelled to address itself directly to the oppressed—instead of appealing to the oppressors—calling on them to assume control of their own destiny, committing itself to support their demands, giving them an opportunity to express these demands, and even articulating them itself. At Medellín a pastoral approach was approved which encourages and favors "the efforts of the people to create and develop their own grass-roots organizations for the redress and consolidation of their rights and the search for true justice."[12]

LIBERATION AND SALVATION

Creation ... is regarded in terms of the Exodus, a historical-salvific fact which structures the faith of Israel. And this fact is a political liberation through which Yahweh expresses his love for his people and the gift of total liberation is received. . . . Yahweh summons Israel not only to leave Egypt but also and above all to "bring them up out of that country into a fine, broad land; it is a land flowing with milk and honey" (3:8). The Exodus is the long march towards the promised land in which Israel can establish a society free from misery and alienation. . . .

When we assert that man fulfills himself by continuing the work of creation by means of his labor, we are saying that he places himself, by this very fact, within an all-embracing salvific process. To work, to transform this world, is to become a man and to build the human community; it is also to save. Likewise, to struggle against misery and exploitation and to build a just society is already to be part of the saving action, which is moving towards its complete fulfillment. . . .

CHRISTIAN BROTHERHOOD AND CLASS STRUGGLE

Those who speak of class struggle do not "advocate" it—as some would say—in the sense of creating it out of nothing by an act of (bad) will. What they do is to recognize a fact and contribute to an awareness of that fact. And there is nothing more certain than a fact. To ignore it is to deceive and to be deceived and moreover to deprive oneself of the necessary means of truly and radically eliminating this condition—that is, by moving towards a classless society. Paradoxically, what the groups in power call "advocating" class struggle is really an expression of a will to abolish its causes to abolish them, not cover them over, to eliminate the appropriation by a few of the wealth created by the work of the many and not to make lyrical calls to social harmony. It is a will to build a socialist society, more just, free, and human, and not a society of superficial and false reconciliation and equality. To "advocate" class struggle, therefore, is to reject a situation in which there are oppressed and oppressors. . . .

The class struggle is a fact and neutrality in this question is not possible. These two observations delimit the indicated problems, prevent us from getting lost in facile solutions, and provide a concrete context for our search. More exactly, the questions raised with regard to the universal character of love and the unity of the Church are real questions precisely because the class struggle confronts us as a fact and because it is impossible not to take part in it.

The Gospel announces the love of God for all people and calls us to love as he loves. But to accept class struggle means to decide for some people and against others. To live both realities without juxtapositions is a great challenge for the Christian committed to the totality of the process of liberation. This is a challenge that leads him to deepen his faith and to mature his love for others.

The universality of Christian love is only an abstraction unless it becomes concrete history, process, conflict; it is arrived at only through particularity. To love all men does not mean avoiding confrontations; it does not mean preserving a fictitious harmony. Universal love is that which in solidarity with the oppressed seeks also to liberate the oppressors from their own power, from their ambition, and from their selfishness. . . . One loves the oppressors by liberating them from their inhuman condition as oppressors, by liberating them from themselves. But this cannot be achieved except by resolutely opting for the oppressed, that is, by combating the oppressive class. It must be a real and effective combat, not hate. This is the challenge, as new as the Gospel: to love our enemies. This was never thought to be easy, but as long as it was only a question of showing a certain sweetness of character, it was preached without difficulty. The counsel was not followed, but it was heard without any uneasiness. In the context of class struggle today, to love one's enemies presupposes recognizing and accepting that one has class enemies and that it is necessary to combat them. It is not a question of having no enemies, but rather of not excluding them from our love. But love does not mean that the oppressors are no longer enemies, nor does it eliminate the radicalness of the combat against them. "Love of enemies" does not ease tensions; rather it challenges the whole system and becomes a subversive formula. . . .

POVERTY: SOLIDARITY AND PROTEST

Man is created in the image and likeness of God and is destined to dominate the earth. Man fulfills himself only by transforming nature and thus entering into relationships with other men. Only in this way does he come to a full consciousness of himself as the subject of creative freedom which is realized through work. The exploitation and injustice implicit in poverty make work into something servile and dehumanizing. Alienated work, instead of liberating man, enslaves him even more. And so it is that when just treatment is asked for the poor, the slaves, and the aliens, it is recalled that Israel also was alien and enslaved in Egypt (Exod. 22:21–23, 23:9; Deut. 10:19, Levc. 19:34).

And finally, man not only has been made in the image and likeness of God. He is also *the sacrament of God*. We have already recalled this profound and challenging Biblical theme. The other reasons for the Biblical rejection of poverty have their roots here: to oppress the poor is to offend God himself; to know God is to work justice among men. We meet God in our encounter with men; what is done for others is done for the Lord. In a word, the existence of poverty represents a sundering both of solidarity among men and also of communion with God. . . . [13]

THE POWER OF THE POOR IN HISTORY

LIBERATION PRAXIS AND CHRISTIAN FAITH

The poor, the oppressed, are members of one social class that is being subtly (or not so subtly) exploited by another social class. This exploited class, especially its most clear-sighted segment, the proletariat, is an active one. Hence, an option for the poor is an option for one social class over another. An option for the poor means a new awareness of class confrontation. It means taking sides with the dispossessed. It means entering into the world of the exploited social class, with its values, its cultural categories. It means entering into solidarity with its interests and its struggles. . . .

Latin American misery and injustice is too deep to be responsive to mere palliatives. Hence we speak of social revolution, not reform; of liberation, not development; of socialism, not modernization of the prevailing system. "Realists" call these statements romantic and utopian. And they should, for the rationality of these statements is of a kind quite unfamiliar to them. It is the rationalism of a concrete, historical undertaking that heralds a different society, one built in function of the poor and oppressed, and that denounces a society built for the benefit of a few. It is an undertaking "in progress," based on studies of the most rigorous scientific exactitude, from the point of departure of the exploitation of the Latin America's great majorities by the dominant classes—and the perception that we live on a continent that is economically, socially, politically, and culturally dependent on power centers outside it, in the affluent countries.

External dependency and internal domination are the marks of the social structures of Latin America. Hence only class analysis will show what is really at stake in the opposition between oppressed lands and dominant peoples. . . .

Only by overcoming a society divided into classes, only by installing a political power at the service of the great popular majorities, only by eliminating the private appropriation of the wealth created by human toil, can we build the foundation of a more just society. This is why the development of the concrete historical march forward of a new society is heading more and more in the direction of socialism in Latin America. But it is a socialism that is well aware of the deficiencies of many of its own concrete forms in the world today. It endeavors to break free of categories and clichés and creatively seek its own paths.

This effort to create a different society also includes the creation of a new human person, a human being that grows progressively free of all servitude preventing it from being the agent of its own lot in history. This leads us to question the dominant ideologies—in which certain religious elements are present—that today provide the model for the human being in our society. However, the construction of a different society, and a new human being, will be authentic only if it is taken on by the oppressed themselves. Hence the whole project must start out with their values. For it is from among the masses that this radical questioning of the prevailing social order, this effort for the abolition of the culture of oppressors, is arising. Only thus can a true social and cultural revolution be carried out.

Various political events that have profoundly modified history, the rapid development of science and the consequent mastery of nature, the use of new instrumentation for the understanding of social reality, as well as the cultural changes that all this has entailed, have hastened the maturation of political consciousness. Social praxis has become adult. Men and women are much more clear now about the conditions of their life in society, but also more conscious of being the active agents of their history.

This political awareness becomes acute when the contradiction is sharpened between growing aspirations for effective liberty and justice and a social order that recognizes them in law but denies them in fact, denies them in so many ways—to whole peoples, to social classes, to racial minorities. Hence the revolutionary, combative search for the genuine conditions for building a free and just society. Hence also a critical suspicion of any ideological justification of a cruel and conflictual situation. . . .

This option means taking a new position in the world of politics. It means, for many, taking a revolutionary, socialist option, and thus assuming a political task, in a global respective, that turns out to be both more scientific and more conflictual than it appeared in the first stages of political movement.

For a long time, the area of the political seemed an area apart, a sector of human existence subsisting alongside of, but distinct from one's family, professional, and recreational life. Political activity was something to be engaged in during the time left over from other occupations. Furthermore, it was thought politics belonged to a particular sector of society specially called to this responsibility. But today, those who have made the option for commitment to liberation look upon the political as a dimension that embraces, and demandingly conditions, the entirety of human endeavors. Politics is the global condition, and the collective field, of human accomplishment. Only from a standpoint of this perception of the global character of politics, in a revolutionary perspective, can one adequately understand the legitimate narrower meaning of the term—orientation to political power.

All human reality, then, has a political dimension. To speak in this way not only does not exclude, but positively implies, the multidimensionality of the human being. But this conception rejects all socially sterile sectarianism that diverts our attention from the concrete conditions in which human existence unfolds. For it is within the context of the political that the human existence unfolds. For it is within the context of the political that the human being rises up as a free and responsible being, as a truly human being, having a relationship with nature and with other human beings, as someone who takes up the reins of his or her destiny, and goes out and transforms history.

In the past, a stubbornly abstract and ahistorical education made Christians generally insensitive, and even hostile, to new ventures of scientific reason in the realm of the political. Nevertheless, Christians who were committed to the struggle for a different society did feel the urgency of as scientific an understanding as possible of the mechanisms of a capitalist society based on private profit and private ownership for profit. Without this understanding, their action would be ineffective. Vague, lyrical invitations to the "defense of the dignity of the human person," which ignored the in-depth causes of the prevailing social order and the concrete conditions for the construction of a just society, were totally effete and ineffectual. In fact in the long term they were but subtle forms of game-playing, rationalization.

THEOLOGY FROM THE UNDERSIDE OF HISTORY

An understanding of the faith from within the concrete, historical practice of liberation leads to a proclamation of the gospel at the very heart of this practice. It is a proclamation that is at once vigilant deed, active involvement, concrete solidarity with the interests and battles of the popular classes—and word which is rooted and verified in deed, which defines attitudes, and which is celebrated with thanksgiving.

Evangelization proclaims liberation in Jesus Christ. And the scope of this liberation is presented to us in the programmatic discourse recorded in the well-known text of Luke:

He came to Nazareth, where he had been brought up, and went into the synagogue on the Sabbath day as he usually did. He stood up to read, and they handed him the scroll of the prophet Isaiah. Unrolling the scroll, he found the place where it is written:

The spirit of the Lord has been given to me,
for he has anointed me.
He has sent me to bring the good news to the poor,
to proclaim liberty to captives

and to the blind new sight,
to set the downtrodden free,
to proclaim the Lord's year of favor

[ISAIAH 61:1–2]

He then rolled up the scroll, gave it back to the assistant and sat down. And all eyes in the synagogue were fixed on him. Then he began to speak to them. "This text is being fulfilled today, even as you listen" [Luke 4:16–21].

For Jesus, then, liberation is total liberation. And thereby he identifies the root of all injustice and exploitation: breach of friendship, breach of love. We are not presented with liberation open to a "spiritualistic" interpretation, still too tightly clung to in certain Christian circles. Hunger and justice are not just economic and social questions. They are global human questions, and they challenge our way of living the faith in its very roots.

We must radically revise our nations of matter and spirit. They are steeped in Greek thinking and idealistic philosophy, having little in common with the biblical mentality. . . . The proclamation of a God who loves all persons equally must take flesh in history, must become history.

The proclamation of this liberating love in a society scarred by injustice and the exploitation of one class by another will transform this "emergent history" into something challenging and conflictual. Within the heart of a society in which social classes, ethnic groups, and cultures are in conflict with one another, we verify God, we make God to be true, by taking the party of the poor, of the masses, of the despised ethnic groups, of the marginalized classes. It is from within them that we strive to live and proclaim the gospel. Its proclamation of the poor gives them to perceive that their situation is contrary to the will of God who makes himself known in events of liberation. This will contribute to the raising of their consciousness of the profound injustice of their situation—and a raising of their hope of liberation.

The gospel, read from the viewpoint of the poor, from the viewpoint of the militancy of their struggles for liberation, convokes a popular church—that is, a church born of the people, the "poor of the earth," the predilect of the kingdom, "God's favorites." It is a church rooted in a people that snatches the gospel from the hands of the great ones of this world. It prevents it from being utilized henceforward as an element in the justification of a situation contrary to the will of the Liberator-God.

Thus there comes into existence what for some time now has been called a "social appropriation of the gospel." It is one of the moments in what we also call a "militant reading of the Bible."[14]

THEOLOGY AND THE SOCIAL SCIENCES

In the contemporary intellectual world, including the world of theology, references are often made to Marx and various Marxists, and their contributions in the field of social and economic analysis are often taken into account. But these facts do not, by themselves, mean an acceptance of Marxism, especially insofar as Marxism embodies an all-embracing view of life and thus excludes the Christian faith and its requirements. The matter is a complex one and would require a close study of texts, a presentation of divergent interpretations in this area, and the resultant distinctions and critical observations. Without getting into details I shall state my views on some questions.

Let me begin by clarifying a first point. There is no question of a possible acceptance of an atheistic ideology. Were we to accept this possibility, we would already be separated from the Christian faith and no longer dealing with a properly theological issue. Nor is there any question of agreement with a totalitarian version of history that denies the freedom of the human person. These two options—an atheistic ideology and a totalitarian vision—are to be discarded and rejected, not only by our faith but by any truly humanistic outlook and even by a sound social analysis. . . .

At no time, either explicitly or implicitly, have I suggested a dialogue with Marxism with a view to a possible "synthesis" or to accepting one aspect while leaving others aside. Such undertakings were indeed frequent during those years in Europe (see the movement created by the Salzburg conversations in the late 1960s) and were beginning to be frequent in Latin American circles. Such was not my own intention, for my pastoral practice imposed pressing needs of a quite different kind.

As I have reminded the reader, once the situation of poverty and marginalization comes to play a part in theological reflection, an analysis of that situation from the sociological viewpoint becomes important, and thinkers are forced to look for help from the relevant disciplines. This means that if there is a meeting, it is between theology and the social sciences, and not between theology and Marxist analysis, except to the extent that elements of the latter are to be found in the contemporary social sciences, especially as these are practiced in the Latin American world.

Use of the social disciplines for a better understanding of the social situation implies great respect for the so-called human sciences and their proper spheres, and for the legitimate autonomy of the political order. The description that these sciences give of a situation, their analysis of its causes, the trends and searches for solutions that they propose—all these are important to us in theology to the extent that they involve human problems and challenges to evangelization. It is not possible, however, to deduce political programs or actions from the gospel or from reflection on the gospel. It is not possible, nor should we attempt it; the political sphere is something entirely different. . . .

In my view, the requirements and tasks I have outlined here are fundamental for theology. They are part of its proper sphere; what is unacceptable is to turn theological reflection into a premise in the service of a specific political choice. This statement does not suggest a lack of interest in the serious questions raised by the struggle for social justice; it signifies only that we must be clear regarding the scope and limits of every contribution to so vast and complex a subject.

CONFLICT IN HISTORY

When I speak of conflict in history I always mention different aspects of it. That is why I continually refer to races discriminated against, despised cultures, exploited classes, and the condition of women, especially in those sectors of society where women are "doubly oppressed and marginalized" (Puebla [Bishops' Conference] no. 1134, note). In this way, I take into account the noneconomic factors present in situations of conflict between social groups. The point of these constant references is to prevent any reduction of historical conflict to the fact of class struggle. I said earlier that in [A Theology of] Liberation, pp. 272–97 (of the first edition), I was discussing the class struggle aspect of the general problem because it is the one that poses the most acute problems for the universality of Christian love. If it is possible to clear that obstacle, then we have an answer to the questions raised by other, perhaps less thorny, kinds of conflict. For it is evident that history is marked by other forms of conflict and, unfortunately, of confrontation between persons. . . .

Marx thought that his own contribution was to have established the connection between class struggle and economic factors (as well as the dictatorship of the proletariat). These economic factors are often presented as operating historically in a deterministic manner. I am not concerned here with the important debate on this point or with the varying interpretations that the debate has produced within Marxism itself. The point I want to make is simply that an economically based determinist view of class struggle is completely alien to liberation theology.

THE REQUIREMENTS OF CHRISTIAN LOVE

There is obviously no question of identifying a preferential option for the poor with an ideology or specific political program that would serve as framework for reinterpreting the gospel or the task of the church. Nor is there any question of limiting oneself to one sector of the human race. . . . The universality of Christian love is incompatible with any exclusion of persons but not with a preference for some. I think it worth citing here a passage from Karl Lehmann, a theologian and presently archbishop of Mainz: "There can undoubtedly be situations in which the Christian message allows of only one course of action. In these cases, the church is under the obligation of decisively taking sides (see, for example, the experience of Nazi dictatorship in Germany). In these circumstances, an attitude of unconditional neutrality in political questions contradicts the command of the gospel and can have deadly consequences."[15]

There is no passage in my own writings that so incisively stresses specificity and points to one course of action as the only possible course. But, faced with so strong a statement, I cannot but ask: Does not what held for the experience of Nazism in Europe hold also for the Latin American experience of wretchedness and oppression? ...

All that has preceded brings me to a final, but fundamental, point. When we speak of taking social conflict (including the fact of class struggle) into account and of the necessity of overcoming the situation by getting at the causes that give rise to it, we are asserting a permanent demand of Christian love. We are thus recalling a basic injunction of the gospel: love of our enemies. In other words, a painful situation that may cause us to regard others as our adversaries does not dispense us from loving them; quite the contrary. When, therefore, I speak of social conflict, I am referring to social groups, classes, races, or cultures, and not to individuals.[16]

ON JOB, GOD-TALK, AND THE SUFFERING
OF THE INNOCENT

Theology is talk about God. . . . God is first contemplated when we do God's will and allow God to reign; only after that do we think about God. To use familiar categories, contemplation and practice make up a *first act*; theologizing is a *second act*. We must first establish our selves on the terrain of spirituality and practice; only subsequently is it possible to formulate discourse on God in an authentic and respectful way. Theologizing done without the mediation of contemplation and practice does not meet the requirements of the God of the Bible. The mystery of God comes to life in contemplation and in the practice of God's plan for human history; only in the second phase can this life inspire appropriate reasoning and relevant speech. (Given the two meanings of the Greek word *logos*—"reason" and "word"—theology is a reasoned word or reason put into words.) In view of this the first stage is *silence*, the second is *speech*.

Contemplation and practice feed each other; the two together make up the stage of silence before God. . . . Silence, the time of quiet, is first act; and the necessary mediation for the time of speaking about the Lord or doing theology which is second act. . . .

SPEAKING OF GOD IN LATIN AMERICA

How are we to speak about a God who is revealed as love in a situation characterized by poverty and oppression? How are we to proclaim the God of life to men and women who die prematurely and unjustly? How are we to acknowledge that God makes us a free gift of love and justice when we have before us the suffering of the innocent? What words are we to use in telling those who are not even regarded as persons that they are the daughters and sons of God? These are the key questions being asked in the theology that has been forming in Latin America and in other places throughout the world where the situation is the same.[17]

"I WILL NOT RESTRAIN MY TONGUE"

For us Latin Americans the question is not precisely "How are we to do theology after Auschwitz?" The reason is that in Latin America we are still experiencing every day the violation of human rights, murder, and the torture that we find so blameworthy in the Jewish holocaust of World War II. Our task here is to find the words with which to talk about God in the midst of the starvation of millions, the humiliation of races regarded as inferior, discrimination against women, especially women who are poor, systematic social injustice, a persistent high rate of infant mortality, those who simply "disappear" or are deprived of their freedom, the sufferings of peoples who are struggling for their right to live, the exiles and the refugees, terrorism of every kind. . . . What we must deal with is not the past but, unfortunately, a cruel present and a dark tunnel with no apparent end. . . .

These are our questions, and this is our challenge. Job shows us a way with his vigorous protest, his discovery of concrete commitment to the poor and all who suffer unjustly, his facing up to God, and his acknowledgment of the gratuitousness that characterizes God's plan for human history. It is for us to find our own route amid the present sufferings and hopes of the poor of Latin America, to analyze its course with the requisite historical effectiveness, and, above all, to compare it anew with the word of

God. This is what has been done by those, for example, who in recent years have been murdered for their witness of faith and solidarity with the poorest and most helpless, those now known as "the Latin American martyrs."

"That is why I cannot keep quiet: in my anguish of spirit I shall speak, in my bitterness of soul I shall complain" (Job 7:11). Nor can the poor and oppressed of Latin America remain silent. For them "day comes like a lamentation arising from the depths of the heart." What the poor and oppressed have to say may sound harsh and unpleasant to some. It is possible that they may be scandalized at hearing a frank avowal of the human and religious experience of the poor, and at seeing their clumsy attempts to relate their lives to the God in whom they have such deep faith. Perhaps those who live, and try to express, their faith and hope amid unjust suffering will some day have to say humbly with Job, "I spoke without understanding marvels that are beyond my grasp," and put aside their harsh language. Yet who knows but that the Lord may tell them, to the surprise of some: "You have spoken correctly about me."

The prophet Isaiah announces that "the Lord God will wipe away tears from all faces, and the reproach of his people he will take away from all the earth." Woe to those whom the Lord finds dry-eyed because they could not bring themselves to solidarity with the poor and suffering of this world! If we are to receive from God the tender consolation promised by the prophet, we must make our own the needs of the oppressed; our hearts must be moved at seeing a wounded person by the wayside, be attuned to the sufferings of others, and be more sensitive to persons in conflict and confusion than to "the order of the day.[18]

A THEOLOGY OF LIBERATION, REVISED EDITION

INTRODUCTION TO THE REVISED EDITION: EXPANDING THE VIEW

What we have called "the major fact" in the life of the Latin American church—the participation of Christians in the process of liberation—is simply an expression of a far-reaching historical event—*the irruption of the poor*. . . . Liberation theology is closely bound up with the new presence of those who in the past were always absent from our history. They have gradually been turning into the active agents of their own destiny and beginning a resolute process that is changing the condition of the poor and oppressed of this world. . . .

The fact that misery and oppression lead to a cruel, inhuman death, and are therefore contrary to the will of the God of Christian revelation who wants us to live, should not keep us from seeing the other aspects of poverty that I have mentioned. They reveal a human depth and a toughness that are a promise of life. This perception represents one of the most profound changes in our way of seeing the reality of poverty and consequently in the overall judgment we pass on it. . . .

One of our social lies has been the claim that there is no racism in Latin America. There may indeed be no racist laws as in some other countries, but there are very rigid racist customs that are no less serious for being hidden. The marginalization of Amerindian and black populations, and the contempt in which they are held, are situations we cannot accept as human beings, much less as Christians. These populations themselves are becoming increasingly aware of their situation and are beginning to claim their most basic human rights; this new attitude carries the promise of fruitful results.

The racial question represents a major challenge to the Christian community, and one to which we are only now beginning to respond. The approaching five-hundredth anniversary of the evangelization of Latin America should be the occasion for an examination of conscience regarding the immense human cost historically connected with that evangelization—I mean the destruction of individuals and cultures. Such an examination will help us define a commitment of the church to races that have for centuries been neglected and mistreated. The bold efforts of Bartolomé de Las Casas[19] and so many others past and present are there to point a way we must follow in accordance with our present historical situation.

I referred above to the conditions in which women live. We in Latin America are only now beginning to wake up to the unacceptable and inhuman character of their situation. One thing that makes it very difficult to grasp its true character is its hiddenness, for it has become something habitual, part of everyday life and cultural tradition. So true is this that when we point it out we sound a bit like foreigners bent on causing trouble. The issue was hardly raised at Medellín [the 1968 Bishops' Conference]. Puebla [the 1979 Bishops' Conference], however, did initiate reflection on it. . . . A growing number of persons are committed to the restoration of women's rights, even as we realize more and more clearly how intolerable the situation of women really is.

The situation of racial and cultural minorities and of women among us is a challenge to pastoral care and to commitment on the part of the Christian churches; it is therefore also a challenge to theological reflection. In this area ... racial and feminist themes are addressed more and more frequently in liberation theology. The most important part will have to be played by persons who themselves belong to these groups, despite the difficulties in the way of their doing so. It is not possible for others simply to stand up and effectively play the part of a protagonist. But the voices of these groups are beginning to be heard, and this development is promising. This will certainly be one of the richest veins to be mined by liberation theology in years ahead. . . .

The predominant characteristics of this complex and widespread world of the poor are, on the one hand, its unimportance in the eyes of the great powers that rule today's wider world and, on the other, its vast human, cultural, and religious wealth, and especially its capacity for creating new forms of solidarity in these areas. All this takes us far from the simplistic position we were perhaps in danger of initially adopting in analyzing the situation of poverty. A fundamental point has become clear: it is not enough to describe the situation; its *causes* must also be determined. Medellín, Puebla, and John Paul II in his encyclical on work and, more recently, on social concerns well as in other writings, have made a forceful analysis of these causes. Structural analysis has thus played an important part in building up the picture of the world to which liberation theology addresses itself. . . .

FAITH AND SOCIAL CONFLICT

Social conflict—including one of its most acute forms: the struggle between social classes—is a painful historical fact. We may not decide not to look at it in the light of faith and the demands of the kingdom. Faith in the God who is love is the source of light and energy for Christian commitment in this situation.

1. The claim that conflict is *a social fact* does not imply an unqualified acceptance of it as something beyond discussion. On the contrary, the claim is subject to scientific analysis, and science is in principle always critical of its own claims. The various social sciences, to say nothing of simple empirical observation, tell us that we are faced today with an unjust social situation in which racial groupings are discriminated against, classes exploited, cultures despised, and women, especially poor women, are "doubly oppressed and marginalized."

Situations such as the one in South Africa display a cruel and inhuman racism and an extreme form of conflictual confrontation that is also to be found, even if in less obvious forms, in other parts of the world. It raises difficult questions for Christians living in these countries. These and other situations, such as those in Northern Ireland, Poland, Guatemala, and Korea show us that in addition to economic factors others of a different character play a part in oppositions between social groups.

Acknowledgment of the facts of social conflict, and concretely of the class struggle, is to be seen in various documents of the church's magisterium. There are passages in the writings of Pius XI that are clear in this regard. He says, for example, in *Quadragesimo Anno*: "In fact, human society now, because it is founded on classes with divergent aims and hence opposed to one another and therefore inclined to enmity and strife, continues to be in a violent condition and is unstable and uncertain" (no. 82). A few lines later, he speaks of how far the struggle can go: "As the situation now stands, hiring and offering for hire in the so-called labor market separate persons into two divisions, as into battle lines, and the contest between these divisions turns the labor market itself almost into a battlefield where, face to face, the opposing lines struggle bitterly" (no. 83). The class struggle is a fact that Christians cannot dodge and in the face of which the demands of the gospel must be clearly stated. . . .

In his encyclical on human work [1988] John Paul II has dealt extensively and in depth with this difficult point. In the section "Conflict between Labor and Capital in the Present Phase of History" the pope writes:

> Throughout this period, which is by no means yet over, the issue of work has of course been posed on the basis of the *great conflict* that in the age of, and together with, industrial development emerged between "capital" and "labor"—that is to say, between the *small* but highly influential *group* of entrepreneurs, owners or holders of the means of production, and the *broader multitude* of persons who lacked these means and who shared in the process of production solely by their labor (*Laborem Exercens*, 11; emphasis added).

The conflict has its origin in exploitation of workers by "the entrepreneurs ... following the principle of maximum profit" (ibid.). A few pages later, the pope repeats his point that behind a seemingly abstract opposition there are concrete persons:

> It is obvious that, when we speak of opposition between labor and capital, we are not dealing only with abstract concepts or "impersonal forces" operating in economic production. Behind both concepts there are persons, *living, actual persons:* on the one side are those who do the work *without being the owners* of the means of production, and on the other side those who act as entrepreneurs and *who own these means* or represent the owners. (ibid., 14; emphasis added)

This fact enables him to conclude: "Thus *the issue of ownership or property* enters from the beginning into the whole of this historical process" (ibid.). What we have, then, is an opposition of *persons* and not a conflict between abstract concepts or impersonal forces. This is what makes the whole matter so thorny and challenging to a Christian conscience.

2. This harsh and painful situation cannot be ignored. Only if we acknowledge its existence can we give a *Christian evaluation* of it and find ways of resolving it. This second step should of course be the most important thing for us. These situations are caused, after all, by profound injustices that we cannot accept. Any real resolution requires, however, that we get to the causes that bring about these social conflicts and that we do away with the factors that produce a world divided in to the privileged and dispossessed, into superior and inferior racial groupings. The creation of a fraternal society of equals, in which there are no oppressors and no oppressed, requires that we not mislead others or ourselves about the real state of affairs.

Earlier in this book I said that awareness of the conflict going on in history does not mean acceptance of it and that the important thing is to struggle "for the establishment of peace and justice amid all humankind." The connection of peace with justice is an important theme in the Bible. Peace is promised along with the gift of the kingdom, and it requires the establishment of just social relationships. Drawing inspiration from some words of Paul VI, which it cites, Medellín begins its document on peace by saying: "'If development is the new name for peace,' Latin American underdevelopment, with its own characteristics in its different countries, is an unjust situation promoting tensions that conspire against peace" ("Peace," 1).

These tensions, which can develop into very sharp conflicts, are part of everyday life in Latin America. Moreover, they often place us in disconcerting situations in which theological reflection can advance only gropingly and in an exploratory way. But the trickiness of the subject does not justify an approach that forgets the universalist demands of Christian love and ecclesial communion. On the other hand, these demands must be shown to have a necessary connection with the concrete situations mentioned above if we are to give adequate and effective answers to the Christians who face them.

The gospel proclaims God's love for every human being and calls us to love as God loves. Yet recognition of the fact of class struggle means taking a position, opposing certain groups of persons, rejecting certain activities, and facing hostilities. For if we are convinced that peace indeed supposes the establishment of justice, we cannot remain passive or indifferent when the most basic human rights are at risk. That kind of behavior would not be ethical or Christian. Conversely, our active participation on the side of justice and in defense of the weakest members of society does not mean that we are encouraging conflict; it means rather that we are trying to eliminate its deepest root, which is the absence of love.

When we thus assert the universality of Christian love, we are not taking a stand at an abstract level, for this universality must become a vital energy at work in the concrete institutions within which we live. The social realities to which I have been referring in this section are difficult and much debated, but this does not dispense us from taking sides. It is not possible to remain neutral in the face of poverty and the resulting just claims of the poor; a posture of neutrality would, moreover, mean siding with the injustice and oppression in our midst. The position we take under the inspiration of the gospel must be real and effective. . . .

The universality of Christian love is, I repeat, incompatible with the exclusion of any persons, but it is not incompatible with a preferential option for the poorest and most oppressed. When I speak of taking into account social conflict, including the existence of the class struggle, I am not denying that God's love embraces all without exception. Nor is anyone excluded from our love, for the gospel requires that we love even our enemies; a situation that causes us to regard others as our adversaries does not excuse us from loving them. There are oppositions and social conflicts between diverse factions, classes, cultures, and racial groupings, but they do not exclude respect for persons, for as human beings they are loved by God and are constantly being called to conversion.

The conflict present in society cannot fail to have repercussions in the church, especially when, as is the case in Latin America, the church is, for all practical purposes, coextensive with society. Social tensions have effects within he church itself, which I understand here as the totality of its members—that is, as the people of God.[20]

NOTES

1. Y. Congar, *Situation et tâches présentes de la théologie* (Paris, 1967), p. 72.

2. This is the profound meaning of Hegel's dialectic Master-Slave.

3. Starting with this educational field, the most creative and fertile efforts along this line in Latin America are the experiences and works of P. Freire which attempt to build a "pedagogy of the oppressed."

4. [Gutierrez is referring to the Christian Democratic parties that emerged in many Latin American countries in the 1950s and 1960s and the radicalization of Catholic youth, students, and some clergy in mainly Latin American countries in the late 1960s.]

5. [The Second Vatican Council (1962–65) and the Second Conference of Latin American Bishops, Medellín, Colombia, 1968.]

6. ["Notes for a Theology of Liberation," in *Theological Studies* 31, no. 2 (1970): 243–251, 257–258, 260–261.]

7. The Marxian text is well-known: "The philosophers have only *interpreted* the world; the point is to *change* it" "*Theses on Feuerbach: no. 11*," in Karl Marx and Friedrich Engels, *On Religion* (New York: Schocken Books, 1964), p. 72. The exact role of the idea of praxis in Marxian thought is a controversial subject.

8. ["But be ye doers of the Word, and not hearers only." (James 1:22–25)]

9. "Man and Socialism in Cuba," in *Venceremos! The Speeches and Writings of Ernesto Che Guevara*, ed. John Gerassi (New York: The Macmillan Company, 1968), p. 396.

10. [All quotations are from the section on "Peace," probably written by Gutierrez, in the documents of the Second General Conference of Latin American Bishops, meeting at Medellin, Colombia, in August–September 1968, published in *The Church in the Present-day Transformation of Latin America* (Bogotá: General Secretariat of CELAM, 1970.)]

11. "Private Property", Statement of ONIS, IDOC-NA [Lima], no. 16, pp. 94–95. . . . All this recasts the interpretation of the social doctrine of the Church.

12. "Peace," no. 27, in *Medellín*. [See note 10.]

13. [*A Theology of Liberation: History, Politics, and Salvation*, ed. and trans. Sister Caridad Inda and John Eagleson (New York: Orbis Books, 1973), 8–10, 12–14, 26–27, 36–37, 88–91, 108–109, 111–112, 114, 156–157, 159, 274–276, 295.]

14. [*The Power of the Poor in History*, trans. Robert R. Barr (New York: Orbis Books, 1983), 45–47, 206–208.]

15. International Theological Commission, *Téologica de la Liberación* (Madrid: BAC, 1978), p. 37.

16. [*The Truth Shall Make You Free: Confrontations*, trans. Matthew McConnell (New York: Orbis Books, 1990), 61, 63–64, 66, 70–71, 77–79.]

17. I am thinking of theologies that spring from divergent racial and cultural situations—for example, those based on the situation of women. For the feminist perspective in theology, see the major work of Elizabeth Schüssler Fiorenza, *In Memory of Her: A Feminist Theological Reconstruction of Christian Origins* (New York: Crossroad, 1983).

18. [*On Job, God-talk and the Suffering of the Innocent* (New York: Orbis Books, 1990), xi–xiv, 101–103.]

19. [Bartolomé de las Casas, a sixteenth-century bishop who defended the rights of the Indians against the Spanish conquerors, condemning the enslavement and exploitation of the indigenous peoples. In 1993, Gutierrez published a book on Las Casas.]

20. [*A Theology of Liberation, History, Politics, and Salvation*, trans. Sister Caridad Inda and John Eagleson (New York: Orbis Books, 1988), xx–xxiii, 156–160.]

{CHAPTER 6}

Dorothy Day (1897–1980)

SELECTED AND EDITED BY DAVID GREGORY

Dorothy May Day was born on November 8, 1897, in Bath Beach, Brooklyn, New York. She died eighty-three years later, on November 29, 1980. Her family was not an easy one to be part of; Day and her family usually lived in poverty, primarily because of the inability of her father, John I. Day, to find regular work, a situation that forced the family to relocate a number of times. Dorothy Day and her father were never close, and only later in their lives were they able to treat each other civilly. In contrast, Day, especially during her early adulthood, was very close to her mother, Grace Satterlee Day. Neither Day's mother, an Episcopalian, nor her father, a Congregationalist, attended church services or took any steps to bring religion into their children's lives. Day and her siblings were not baptized as infants. Though she was eventually baptized and confirmed in the Episcopal Church, Dorothy Day's connection with Christianity was weak during her teenage years.

In the fall of 1914, Day matriculated into the University of Illinois at Urbana, where her grades reflected a student without distinction. When Day left the University of Illinois in June 1916, she was a different person from the impressionable, naive, and relatively apathetic young woman who had entered college two years before. She had developed a passion for a relatively new and radical movement, socialism. The nineteen-year-old Day headed to New York City. She received her first opportunity as a journalist with the socialist newspaper The Call. *Perhaps Day's first article offered an omen of future events, for in it she chronicled her attempt to live for a month on five dollars per week.*

Day resigned from The Call, *began working for another newspaper,* The Masses, *and in the summer of 1917 took up residence in Greenwich Village. In 1918, Day began working for* The Liberator, *which succeeded* The Masses *and became the American voice of the Russian Revolution. It was during this time that she met and became infatuated with Lionel Moise. Moise soon ended their brief romance, and the breakup threw Day into a massive depression that resulted in a suicide attempt; thereafter, though, she and Moise continued periodically to have romantic interludes, and Day became pregnant in 1919. When Moise refused to marry her, she decided to terminate the pregnancy.*

After a short-lived marriage to Barkeley Tobey, Day traveled to Chicago in an unsuccessful attempt to win Moise back. While there, she became a member of the International Workers of the World (the "Wobblies"), and was jailed, for the first time, in a Red Scare–era raid on the Wobbly rooming house where she had sought hospitality. Flush with royalties from the publication of her first book, The Eleventh Virgin *(1924), she left Chicago for New Orleans, where she did investigative reporting for* The Item *on the city's dancehalls.*

Upon her return to New York City in early April 1924, Day reunited with some old friends, who subsequently introduced her to Forster Batterham. A year later, the two were joined in a common-law marriage. The aloof and inarticulate Forster, an English anarchist and biologist, embodied none of the ideals that Day admired. During the winter of 1925, she spent much of her time socializing and indulging with her many friends. She bought a fishing shack on the shore of Staten Island, where the seclusion offered by this more rustic existence allowed her to focus upon her personal idea of God's handiwork, namely nature. It was at this time that Day began to pray informally.

In June 1926, Day discovered that she was again pregnant. The birth of Tamar Theresa Day in March 1927 simultaneously enhanced Day's working-class consciousness and brought her closer to the church. Day's determination to have Tamar baptized finalized her own commitment to established religion, and her choice of Catholicism reflected her desire to combine her passion for helping the less fortunate with her faith.

In December 1932, Day met Peter Maurin, one of twenty-two children of a strong family of Catholic peasants from southern France. He became Day's tutor in applied Catholic theology and in the hard, daily practice of personalism. With the entrance of Maurin and his belief in the dignity of labor and the worker into her life, Day began the task that would be the primary focus of her life: the creation and direction of the Catholic Worker movement.

That movement opened "houses of hospitality" throughout the United States, Canada, and Europe. These sites were established to provide shelter for the homeless and special care for the psychologically disabled. Throughout her life, Dorothy Day's primary witness took place through living out the precepts of the Gospel of St. Matthew, practicing corporal works of mercy for the poor and the homeless, standing in solidarity with workers, and, perhaps most important, working unfailingly for peace.

During the 1960s and 1970s, the natural consequences of age, combined with depression due to the deaths of so many of her early friends, began to limit Day's practice of advocacy; her physical condition particularly made it difficult for her to continue her work. Her last major action of political resistance and solidarity took place in August 1973, when she traveled to California to join Cesar Chavez's United Farm Workers' protest. There she was arrested during a peaceful march on behalf of workers' rights. After this protest, she returned to her Third Street apartment in the New York City Catholic Worker House, where she remained until her death, following a long illness, in 1980.

THE CATHOLIC WORKER COLLECTION

Ash Wednesday, 1936

DEAR FRIEND:

We wish to call to your attention the facts of the dispute between the Borden Milk Company and its employees which we feel is of vital concern to all Catholics seeking to further social justice.

The employees' union, which is strictly non-Communist and affiliated with A. F. of L., appealed to *The Catholic Worker* for help when the company refused to renew its union contract at the time of its expiration just before Christmas. We heard the Union's story; we interviewed numerous Borden employees, both union and non-union; we corresponded with the company; and finally had a conference, at the office of *The Catholic Worker*, with the high officials of the Borden Milk Company.

The company officials, speaking for the company, refused absolutely to consider a closed-shop agreement, which is the chief issue. They claimed that their men do not want it. When Father Paul H. Furfey, head of the Department of Sociology of the Catholic University who took part in the conference, pointed out to them that two of their shops where closed ballots had been taken the vote was overwhelmingly in favor of the A. F. of L. and against the company union, they did not deny this and offered no reply. The men tell us that in other shops a closed ballot had been denied them, although it has been requested at numerous company meetings.

The company officials could offer no explanation, either of the fact that an extra man (non-union) has been placed on many of their delivery wagons, for the purpose, it would seem, of intimidation, prior to the expiration of the old agreement. The issue is not primarily only of wages and hours, but of the right of workers to organize and the duty of employers to recognize and permit such organizations to bargain collectively with them.

In the current issue of *The Catholic Worker* we have called for a boycott, by Catholics, of all Borden products, and of retail stores dealing with the Borden Company. We feel that this is the only means left by which the dispute may be settled without a strike, and we believe that a strike in the milk business would be a great misfortune. A majority of the men are paying dues and approve of a boycott as a means of bringing union recognition.

If you believe, as we do, that we have a duty of charity to seek justice, not only for ourselves, but for others, will you join with us in making this boycott effective?

The office of *The Catholic Worker* will be glad to furnish any further information on the situation which you may desire, or to supply a speaker for any group desiring to learn further details.[1]

January 17, 1939

DEAR FATHER HASKINS:

Enclosed is a copy we made in the *Catholic Worker* in regard to sit-down strikes in Michigan. I suppose you have seen the statement made by Attorney General Murphy recently that accused the sit-down strike of being illegal. That does not necessarily mean that it is immoral. I was scandalized to find on my speaking trips throughout the country that many of our Catholic lay people think in terms of sin when they hear the word immoral. They picture men and women locked up in a factory, night and day, for weeks on end, dancing and carousing. It seems a shame that they should take so stupid an attitude.

Father John M. McGuire of St. Viator's College says that the sit-down strike is not morally wrong. Also Father Jerome Hannan, Assistant Chancellor of the Pittsburgh diocese in an article in Ecclesiastical Review in July, 1937. Both theologians indicated that its use can be justified. The sit-down strike can not be condemned in itself unless the circumstances justify condemnation. This is the statement quoted in the "Pittsburgh Catholic," provided that conditions for a just strike are present. There is noting in a sit-down strike that is immediately to be condemned, but property must not be damaged and unjust means must not be used. Of course, practically every strike is condemned as unjust by the employers and they use every means in their power, advertising in the daily papers, broadcasting over the radio, to convince the people that the strikes have violated the condition of a just strike. So it seems to me we must be very careful in judging. As St. Louis said, "We must always be on the side of the worker until he is proven wrong." And I should say that we must think of the credibility of witnesses and we must be convinced by our own knowledge, rather than by hearsay. This would presuppose that we had been with them and visited the strike headquarters, talked with the workers involved, and found out their point of view.

We have the greatest respect and admiration for Attorney General Murphy for his refusal to use force in connection with the sit-down strikes in Michigan. He has been bitterly attacked by many Catholics, both priests and laymen, and just as firmly defended. Governor Murphy himself, said in a speech before the graduating class of Duquesne University:

"Today the sit-down strike knocks at the door for recognition as another step in the procession. The employees' counterpart of the lockout, it is of doubtful legal justification for the reason that it lacks the relationship to property which characterizes the lockout.

"But here again we revert to the puzzling question of 'what is a man's legal right to his job?' for we are sure to be told that the workman has a property right to his job which is fully as real as that of the employer in the tangibles which make up his enterprise. The outcome of the debate over sit-downs will, of course, depend in large measure on the emphasis which the law will place on property right and their preservations."

I haven't a clipping handy which states his recent expression of opinion but doubtless you have seen it, or can get hold of it, since it was within the last week.

Peter Maurin will be in San Francisco shortly and I certainly hope that you will be in touch with him. Next fall I expect to start out again on another speaking trip and shall certainly hope to visit you. Thanking you for your interest in or work, and begging your prayers,

Sincerely yours in Christ,

DD:ACB[2]

March 4, 1949

DEAR CARDINAL SPELLMAN,

I am deeply grieved to see the reports in the papers last night and this morning, down here in Louisville, and doubtless the same story has appeared in every paper throughout the land, of your leading Dunwoodie seminarians into Calvary cemetery, past picket lines, to "break the strike," as all the papers say. Of course you know that a group of our associates at The Catholic Worker office in New York, have been helping the strikers, both in providing food for their families, and in picketing. We understand that from the very beginning of the strike, there had been Communist offers of help which the strikers rejected. Instead they came to us, knowing that we were Catholic that we were members of the Catholic Press Association, thinking that in some way we could aid them. They have come to our meetings and to our discussions, and we know them and know that there is no communist influence among them, that they are all Catholics. Their union is solidly Catholic. There may be communists in the Agricultural workers union you mention in one of the news stories, to which you say they are affiliated, but there is no trace of communism in their union. I know nothing of the other union. The fact that there may be Communists there proves nothing against their union, any more than the entire CIO is discredited because there are still some unions in the CIO which are tainted with communist leadership though the majority of unions have purged their unions. There is only your statement, which has certainly not been a fair statement to them, and has been aimed at alienating any sympathy from them. I am sure that you did not intend it in this way, but that you have been misinformed. I am writing to you, because this strike, though small, is a terribly significant one in a way. Instead of people being able to say of us "see how they love one another," and "behold, how good and how pleasant it is for brethren to dwell together in unity" now "we have become a reproach to our neighbors, as object of derision and mockery to those about us."

It is not just the issue of wages and hours as I can see from the conversations that our workers have had with the men. It is a question of their dignity as men, their dignity as workers, and the right to have a union of their own, and a right to talk over their grievances. It is no use going into the wages, or the offers that you have made for a higher wage (but the same work week). A wage such as the Holy Fathers have talked of which would enable the workers to raise and educate their families of six, seven and eight children, a wage which would enable them to buy homes, to save for such ownership, to put away for the education of the children,—certainly the wage which they have in these days of high prices and exorbitant rents, is not the wage for which they are working now. Regardless of what the board of trustees can afford to pay, the wage is small compared to the wealth of the men represented on the board of trustees. The way the workers live is in contrast to the way of living of the board of trustees. But I do not wish to compare "horizontally" as Xagr Betowsky used to warn us against in his conferences. Regardless of rich and poor, the class antagonisms which exist between the well-to-do, those who live on Park Avenue and Madison Avenue and those who dig the graves in the cemetery,—regardless of these contrasts which are most assuredly there,—the issue is always one of the dignity of the workers. It is a world issue.[3]

DIVIDING THE WORKERS

By addressing ourselves to "Catholic Workers" we are accused of dividing the workers. It is most assuredly not our intention to do this, and the fact that we emphasize the dogma of the Mystical Body of Christ, that we are members one of other, proves this point.

We do not feel that we are dividing the workers when we urge Catholics to learn more about the social teachings of Church. They are divided because they do not know these social teachings. The Holy Father in his great encyclical "Forty Years After" speaks of the organization of Christian Working Men in Catholic Action. In referring back to Pope Leo XIII he writes, "He attributed prime importance to societies consisting either of workmen alone, or of workmen and employers together." In the case of "certain established economic institutions" making the formation of truly Catholic unions difficult as in this country, then the Pope says that "side by side with these trade unions, there must always be associations which aim at giving their members a thorough religious and moral training, that these in turn may impart to the labor unions to which they belong the upright spirit which should direct their entire conduct."

There was an example of this in the industrial section Lille, France, when Catholic unions were set up side by side with Socialist unions which were much the stronger, and the two worked together for social justice. In this case the bishop, who headed the work, was condemned by the industrialists (even the Catholic industrialists) but approved by the Holy Father.

A more recent instance of it is the work of the Apostolate of the Sea in France where unions have been formed where only Communist unions existed before, for the education and recreation of seamen, and in addition to religious work there is much work done for social justice such as inquiries into such matters as wages and working conditions.

There is real need for work of this kind in America. Existing organizations such as the Holy Name Society or the Knights of Columbus, by taking up the study of social justice, forming groups within their own organizations, of men belonging to the same union or industry, would make a great impression on the depression, as Peter Maurin says.

THE DIGNITY OF LABOR

Another criticism directed at the paper is this: that we air too much the grievances of labor and do not point out its duties. Here is a letter, for instance, that came in this morning:

"I do wish you would stress a little more in your article the duties of the worker towards the employer. The guilt is not all on the side of the employer. But the attitude of the average Catholic worker is far from correct. Largely because he is always hearing of the exploiting of labor by the monied classes and never hearing of his duty as a worker. Your paper always impresses me as taking sides with labor regardless of conditions and always ranting against the employer. . . . "

We try to stress the duty of the workers towards God and himself first of all. And the Catholic neglects those duties when he does not work for social justice. There has been nothing but talk about duty to the employer.

I agree that the guilt is not all on the side of the employer. The Pope advises us to champion always the weaker side. The attitude, we will agree, of the Catholic worker is far from correct, not only in regard to social justice but in regard to his work. There is greed here, too. One of the difficulties of the labor movement in the United States is that there has been an aristocracy of labor, union men getting high wages in various trades, and ignoring their poorer comrades who have not had the benefits of unionization such as in the textile and mining fields. There is graft and racketeering in labor organizations which has justly prejudiced not only the employer but the poorer worker against them so that they are more willing very often to accept the radical trade unions than they are the old established ones. There is always a rank and file fight going on against existing trade unions and their technique.

I agree too that the attitude of the worker towards his labor is not correct. There is a loss of pride in craftsmanship which is due to the mechanization of industry. Pride in doing to the best of one's ability the work that God has given him to do, is a lesson which the American worker will have to relearn.

I saw a Communist movie over on Fourteenth Street last year which exemplifies what I mean. The name of the film was "The Return of Nathan Becker" and it was the story of a Russian Jew going back to Soviet Russia and working there at his trade of bricklaying. He has an intense pride in his work and there is a rivalry at once between him and a Russian worker as to the best way of laying bricks. So they have a contest to see whose work is the best. This is the entire theme of the picture, and the attitude towards the work of one's hands was a truly Catholic one. Without the captions and the lauding of the Soviet Union the picture could have been put on before any Catholic audience as a fine moral film exemplifying the nobility of attitude of the workers, who stressed the doctrine of the common good and took pride in their little part in working towards it.[4]

UNIONIZING THE UNEMPLOYED

Reading this morning the office of St. Peter Nolasco, who spent all his money ransoming the prisoners in Barcelona, I was struck by the lines, "he would sell himself to free them, or he would like to be fettered with their chains." And I thought gratefully of our readers, who were selling themselves in occupations they hated yet sending us portions of their hard-earned money to help those unemployed who come to our doors; of our workers here and in other cities, who were spending all their energies in the work, subsisting on just what God sends them, and all of them "fettered with their chains," of poverty, even of destitution. And I thought of the discouragement they must often feel, a mood which they share with those they are helping, which add to the weight of those claims which hinder them in their work.

LANDWARD

This month we are starting meetings for the unemployed, inviting those men who come to us on the bread line in the morning, to form themselves into an association of unemployed to discuss their abilities, their aptitudes, their chances of building up groups of workers ready to go on the land in farming communes, to find there a new way of life. We must do that as a first step even while we know that we have no place as yet to put them. We must try to infuse into their hearts some of the faith and hope that is in ours, so that they will be ready when God sends the opportunity to go out on the land. There is plenty of land, even around New York, which is not being used, land which belongs to private individuals, and to institutions. There are some we know who would be willing to turn over that land to groups such as ours. But ownership of that land must be assured.

Looked at in the light of history, the revolution which is going on today, springs from the inarticulate desire in the hearts of workers for ownership. We have neglected to emphasize the communal aspect of property so we have what we may term the heresy of communism which denies the right to private property. We have neglected to emphasize the dignity of the worker which has it roots in Christian teaching, so we have over one-sixth of the world's surface, a dictatorship of the proletariat.

MORE OWNERSHIP

Throughout the country union organizing goes on; we are still in the beginnings of forming those associations of workers which Pope Leo XIII said were necessary to better the condition of the workers. The fight is still for the right to form those associations, and then it goes on to the fight for better wages and conditions so that the men may have the leisure and the strength to take the next steps. And those next steps are toward ownership; ownership whether it comes in the form of cooperatives for producers and consumers, or ownership in land. No matter how many concessions the employer makes in regard to recognition of unions, better wages and hours, the fight will go on, on one pretext or another. Because often the workers themselves do not realize what that fight tends towards, getting rid of those chains of proletarian bondage which keep them from being recognized as free men, sons of God.

Meanwhile, in a land of plenty, there are around ten million unemployed. Union papers which come into our office through exchanges, are beginning to emphasize the problem and study it. There is beginning to be a discussion of the machine, and a discussion of means of finding work for the unemployed members of unions.

UNEMPLOYED

There is in this issue a letter from an unemployed reader of our paper in Regina. It is wrong to call him unemployed, when he finds so many ways of employing his time in indoctrination and the works of mercy. He is one small leader in a great movement which will spread over the country. Throughout the land industrial conferences and social action schools have been held for priests to study the condition of labor, but the problem of the unemployed has not yet been taken up except in isolated cases.

The Workers Alliance which numbers millions in membership throughout the country, has done much to get immediate relief for its clients. They have fought consistently for State and federal aid, and often their organized groups have had nuisance value in bringing immediate help to those in need. The leaders are Marxist in philosophy and work with the hope that come the revolution they will through the gratitude of the masses, be able to swing them to the left. Surely the children of this world are wiser in their generations than the children of the light.[5]

REASONS FOR CHILD LABOR LAW

Under a West Palm Beach dateline of November 24, 1935, the *Miami Herald* published the following:

"His right hand crushed between the spike-studded rollers, Neil Brant, 11, stood for twenty minutes without making a cry while fireman summoned from Central station, dismantled part of the machine to release him. Neil suffered the injury as he and another lad were feeding paper into a machine used for preparing cotton for stuffing mattresses. He was taken to Good Samaritan Hospital, his hand lacerated and some of his bones crushed."

The *Christian Science Monitor* says that the Massachusetts Consumers' League found "ridiculously low wages being offered to youngsters bearing work certificates" since the NRA was declared unconstitutional, citing the instance of one girl who "was offered $5 a week on a sewing job, working seven hours a day, provided she worked free for one week as an apprentice." The Secretary of the Massachusetts branch of the A. F. of L. according to the same paper, reports that firms "closed by NRA are reopening with the new opportunity of exploiting child labor," and mentions a slipper firm charged with reopening on a $4-a-week basis using child operatives.

And yet employer groups attended Congressional hearings on the Ellenbogen bill which would regulate conditions of labor to some extent to oppose it, claiming that to abolish child labor would violate the anti-trust laws and insisting that there was no need for regulation.[6]

VIGILANTES MOB SHARECROPPERS' MASS MEETING

The reign of terror continues for the sharecroppers who are daring to organize, for the betterment of their miserable lot, in the Southern Tenant Farmers' Union.

Some of the latest reports:

One hundred and five farmers and members of their families—including 28 children under six and four infants—have been evicted from their shacks on the plantation of C. H. Dibble near Earle, Arkansas. All were members of the Union.

Two churches in the same district were mobbed by vigilantes and police when Union members attempted to hold protest meetings there. Two sharecroppers were shot, men, women and children were beaten, Union leaders were driven from town, and Howard Kester, organizer of the Union, narrowly escaped lynching.

Pleas for help for the homeless, deprived not only of food and clothing, but of the most elementary shelter or fuel, are being made by the Emergency Committee for Strikers' Relief in New York City, with offices at 112 East 19th Street. Other planters in the district have refused assistance unless union membership is given up.

The lynch murder of Joseph Shoemaker in Florida recently for aiding sharecroppers is a horrible example of the tactics of the planters in combating the Union.

"In the South we've been having Fascism for a long time," said Organizer Howard Kester at a meeting in Washington. I appeal to the hearts and minds and imaginations of you to be aware of the forces of tyranny and terror operating not only the South but in all America. All we are trying to do is to maintain all those things that every loyal American citizen wants to maintain."[7]

THE CATHOLIC WORKER AND LABOR

In the last issue of *The Catholic Worker* we gave a summary of our work starting with Houses of Hospitality throughout the country and the History of the first Catholic Worker farming commune. We did not have room for a resume of our activities in the labor field. We have always pointed out *The Catholic Worker* as a labor paper and that the fundamental purpose of our indoctrination was to bring the worker back to Christ.

Frankly, we have always been on the side of the worker. We have tried not to take sides in factional disputes within unions but to repeat constantly to all workers, organized and unorganized, the teachings of the Church as expressed in the great labor encyclicals.

This means that we are not only urging the necessity for organization to all workers, combatting the "Red Herring" technique of keeping the worker out of unions but also stressing over and over again the dignity of labor, the dignity of the person—a creature composed of body and soul made in the image and likeness of God, and a Temple of the Holy Ghost. It is on these grounds that we fight the speed-up system in the factory, it is on these grounds that we work toward deproletarianizing the worker, working toward a share in the ownership and responsibility.

MAN'S DIGNITY

We pointed out again and again that the issue is not just one of wages and hours, but of ownership and of the dignity of man. It is not State ownership toward which we are working, although we believe that some industries should be run by the government for the common good, it is a more widespread ownership through cooperative ownership.

Again and again, we have participated in strikes regardless of all talk as to whether it was just or unjust, and this for two reasons: first, it is never wrong to perform the Works of Mercy, secondly, because a time of industrial warfare is best to get in touch with the workers by meetings and by widespread distribution of literature, it is the time when the workers are thinking and struggling, they are enduring hardships and making sacrifices, they are in a receptive frame of mind. To give a brief review of some of the issues we have dealt with. The first number of the paper came out in May, 1933. In that issue we featured a story of the Negro labor on the levees in the South which was being exploited by the War Department. We dealt with women and children in industry, widespread layoffs.

In the second issue we took up the farmers strike in the West as well as wages and hours of restaurant workers. In the third issue, child labor in the textile industry, as well as a two page synopsis of labor struggles during the month. In the 4th issue we had front page stories on the coal strike and the milk strike. As I go through the back issues of the paper there are stories on the race issue, the condition of the Negro in industry and professional workers. In the sixth issue of the paper we were already combating anti-Semitism. In the same issue we showed up some profit sharing plans of industrialists as a further move to exploit labor.

MANY NEW READERS

By the second year our circulation had jumped from 2,500 to 35,000 copies, and our readers were workers and students throughout the country. In the second year, 1934, the Seamen's strike on the West Coast, the strike of the rural workers in the onion fields, a silk workers' strike in New Jersey, the textile strike took up many columns in the paper. In New York City we helped the strike of Orbach's Department Store workers in their mass picketing, and called upon our readers not to patronize a store where such wages and long hours prevailed. We helped to defeat an injunction which was handed down against them which is one of the chief weapons of the employer to break strikes. Our participation in this strike and the National Biscuit Company strike cost us many readers. Our circulation was by now 65,000 but many Church groups and School groups cancelled their orders due to the pressure of the employer groups. There were 3,000 on strike in the National Biscuit Company factory on 14th St. and every day there were mass picket lines and scuffles with police.

In the March, 1935 issue of the paper there was printed a speech of Dorothy Weston, Associate Editor, made over the radio in regard to the child labor amendment. Our endorsement of the Child Labor amendment also cost us many subscribers as a majority of Catholics were opposed to it for fear of government interference in the education of our youth. But in spite of the consistent opposition which we have always pointed out as very good for the clarification of thought, our circulation rose to 100,000 at the beginning of the third year.

When the Borden Milk Company the next year attempted to foist a company union on their workers, the editors took up their cause and called public attention ... to the use of gangsters and thugs to intimidate Borden drivers, and urged our readers not to use Borden Milk while unfair conditions prevailed. As a result of the story we ran, the employers attached the Catholic Workers in paid advertisements in the *Brooklyn Tablet* and the *Catholic News*. This dispute also cost us some thousands of circulation.

SEAMEN SHELTERED

A few months later the Spring Strike of 1936 started among the seamen on the East Coast. Due to the fact that we had moved into our larger headquarters on Mott Street we were able to house about 50 of the seamen during the strike. In the fall strike, we not only housed them but also fed thousands of them daily in the store we opened on Tenth Avenue which we kept going for about four months. At that time we printed our "Stand on Strikes" which has been widely circulated in pamphlet form through labor unions throughout the country.

By publicity and our moral support we assisted the organization of the Steel industry when the CIO began its activities. The same year our workers assisted in the marble workers' strike in Vermont and the fishermen in Boston, the sharecroppers in Arkansas, the auto workers in Detroit, the sit-down strike in Michigan, the five and ten cent store strike in New York, and the steel strike in Chicago. We also helped in the organization drive of the stockyards in Chicago.

That was the tragic year when ten workers were killed and scores more wounded in the Memorial Day massacre. One of our staff had a friend killed in that tragic episode. Our workers in Chicago had been helping in the soup kitchens and marching on the picket lines as well as distributing literature.

Many of these strikes I covered personally in order to get a complete report to our readers, and also to speak to the workers at their meetings. I was one of the few newspaper reporters who was allowed in the Flint Fisher body plant to visit the hundreds of sit down strikers who had been in the plant for 40 days. By this time we had groups of Catholic Workers in many big industrial centers throughout the country.

In the labor field the Pittsburgh group was most prominent, headed as it was by Fathers Rice and Hensler. They were the first priests to go out on the picket line and on sound trucks on street corners. Their example led many others priests to become active in the labor field.

CONTRASTING CASES

The Lowell Textile strike was interesting from several angles. When our workers started distributing Catholic Workers to the strikers and the public, and started a food kitchen, the officials of the town telephoned the Chancery Office in Boston to find out if we were all right and were assured that we could go ahead. (On the other hand, we know of an occasion when a speaking engagement at a Church in Jersey City was cancelled because of Mayor Hague's opposition to the paper.) The local paper proclaimed in their headline that the entrance of *The Catholic Worker* in the Lowell strike marked the turning point in the conflict and lead to prompt negotiations with the employers.

Often the immediate work in the House of Hospitality in caring for the unemployed, many of whom are mentally as well as physically affected by their suffering, kept us from work further afield. It was of course impossible to answer all calls for help or to supply lay apostles where they were needed. We could only do the work which came to hand.

At the same time we covered a pretty wide field. I notice in looking back over the old issues that Eddie Priest put in some months in a machine shop in Brooklyn, John Cort in a brass factory in New York, Julia in a five and ten cent store where she did a good deal of indoctrinating and organizing by the distribution of literature, and attendance at union meetings. Stanley Vishnewski covered many picket lines with literature and Bill Callahan covered the Newspaper Guild Strike in Brooklyn and the auto worker strike in Michigan.

We tried to cover not only city industrial plants but also country. Certainly the Seabrook farm of four thousand acres in New Jersey, (sprayed by airplane) with their own canning plant, is an industrial set up. Some of the boys from the Catholic Worker Farm in Easton went down there and worked for a while, talking with union officials and workers and spreading literature. During the summer we plan to repeat this venture more intensively, giving almost the complete issue to discussing corporation farming as opposed to farming as a way of life, and upholding private property, the small land owner and cooperative owner against the State as well as against the industrialists. It is not only in California and in the South that horrible conditions exist for migratory workers and relief workers. We have them here in New Jersey just outside the door.[8]

CATHOLICS IN UNIONS

A worker from Borden's came to the *Catholic Worker* office the other night, a man who was typical of the point of view of all too many workers in that company and in others. He was an intelligent and well-informed Catholic, who saw clearly the issues at stake in the dispute with his company, and the need for a union to defend the rights of the men. He knew, too, that two Popes have issued encyclical letters upholding the right of the workers to bargain collectively through unions, and urging them to form unions. (He told us also that both the company men and some of the union men have us down for communists.)

But he didn't belong to the union—because he was afraid of losing his job or getting in trouble.

We met with the same attitude in other men with whom we talked. They criticized the union for not doing anything about the present dispute, but objected when the union suggested a boycott–because they would lose commissions if their sales were cut. They complained that the union hadn't benefited them much in the year it had a contract with the Borden Company, and that the delegates and leaders were too easy-going—and admitted that they themselves hadn't bothered to attend the union meetings or pay dues.

Briefly, they had been too shortsighted to realize that a union is what its members make it; that unless they stand firmly behind it in all its efforts, it cannot be effective; and that unless they, as individuals, are willing to sacrifice immediate gain—whether by the payment of dues or a decrease in commissions—for the long-range good of all the workers, they might as well have a Boy Scout Troop instead of a union. . . .

Pope Leo XIII has said that "these workingmen's associations should be organized and governed so as to furnish the best and most suitable means for attempting what is aimed at, that is to say, for helping each member to better his condition to the utmost in body, soul and property."

It seems obvious that a union instigated and controlled by the company, whose officers are paid for their "union" work by the company, is not likely to meet with success in gaining these benefits for the workers. Unless of course you believe, as the Borden Company tried to persuade us, that a large wealthy corporation, for which no one need assume personal responsibility, will voluntarily sacrifice profits to benefit its workers. We are forced to doubt the assurance of the Borden executives that their employees desire a company union, and that the requests for one have started from the men themselves. Common sense leads us to wonder why a man desiring a union to resist aggressions upon his rights would choose to have it controlled by the aggressor.

It should be obvious, too, that a union cannot function effectively in an "open shop"—a plant where the union represents only some of the men, and where the company is at liberty to hire non-union men. Such a condition means that the presence of men who will have no protection in the event of wage-cutting or any form of exploitation will act as an obstacle to union efforts and will tend to lower the general wage level. It means, too, that since any betterment in working conditions granted the union will normally apply to non-union employees as well, the union will be weakened by the murmurings of members who see others gaining, without paying dues, benefits for which they make sacrifices.

FOR THE COMMON GOOD

There must, then, be a sacrifice of individual freedom for the common good. We regret that, in the present instance of the Borden dispute, we have found some Catholics both too shortsighted to see the advantages of organization to the workers as a whole, and unwilling to make the sacrifices or take the risks involved in fulfilling their duty of charity.

We believe it is the duty of every Catholic worker to inform himself of the Church's teaching on labor, and to strive for the common good of himself and his fellow-workers by applying them to labor situations in which he may be involved. He should recognize these teachings as specifically Catholic, and not suspect any group defending workers or unions of Communist tendencies, or condemn a union or strike solely because it is supported by Communists; and at the same time should be aware of the dangers of any united front with Marxists.

We believe that strikes are a grave danger to the common good, and that we as Catholics have a duty to use every means in our power to prevent them. One of these means, arbitration, we have tried, as recounted in the news story on our front page dealing with the refusal of the Borden Company to renew its contract with the union.

NOW WE SUGGEST A BOYCOTT AS THE ONLY OTHER ALTERNATIVE TO A STRIKE.[9]

THE CATHOLIC WORKER: 25TH ANNIVERSARY ISSUE

Workers of the World United Under Christ, Light of the World—

Here is another May Day, our 25th anniversary and I have only today to get my copy ready for the paper which Bob Steed will have to make up alone, with Beth Rogers as general proof reader and editorial advisor. On makeup day I must be speaking in Holyoke, the last engagement of a week of speaking at Fordham, Swarthmore, Boston, and returning for a communion breakfast here in New York, and a talk at Iona College in New Rochelle. If today is a day like yesterday there will be people sick in the house to visit, letters, phone calls, the Puerto Rican and Negro neighbors for clothes, a priest from the Fiji Islands and another from Santa Fe, college students and others, and always the letters that don't get answered and the articles that don't get written.

Oh well, if the Lord wanted them done, I comfort myself, He would provide the time and the ability. But there is always the sneaking thought, I
am not efficient, I don't organize my time right. I should hide away and get
things done. But every one in St. Joseph's House of Hospitality is my family,
and those on Peter [Maurin's] farm too. I am "the barren woman that the
Lord makes joyful with many children." I am always thanking God that "my
lines have fallen in goodly places,"—and then falling from this happiness of
gratitude into the suffering that is inseparable from love. If we pray to grow
in love, burdens are bound to grow heavier on every side, our own burdens
and those of all the people in the CW around the country. It is a terrible
thing to see some of the suffering of our friends. Oh for the strength of the
apostles who came rejoicing from prisons and from beatings, "rejoicing
that they were accounted worthy to suffer for Christ."

Our main burden right now of course is that the subway down the street
is approaching ever closer and closer. Indeed it is a temptation not to leave
everything on a bright sunny day like this with the trees bursting into green
in the park, and lean against the fence that surrounds the big open pit at
the corner, and watch the work as the huge shovels eat inexorably towards
us. We are about to be devoured and we are fascinated by this process.
What is the sense of it all? Across the way there is an inadequate school for
the slum children around us. There is a playground understaffed. There are
derelicts sick and maimed on every park bench. There are so many ways to
spend money on people instead of on a little connecting link of subway, ex-
tending for five or six blocks and which is costing countless millions of dollars. And here is this Puerto Rican father, minus two fingers on one hand
recently lost in an accident at his machine in the factory, and an underfed
little boy with him, rooting around in a huge box of contributed shoes. No
compensation yet, he says, and the little boy and the little girl with him
look as though they have not had a decent meal in their lives. But unemployment brings one blessing with it. The father, or mother, can be at home
with their children! Among teen-agers throughout the five boroughs, the
mad and senseless violence continues. It is a guerrilla war against society
and against each other. Deane Mowrer said that the other night the gangs
of children on her block which is between Avenue C and Avenue D, went
rioting down the street knocking over every ash can and garbage can and
destroying property as they could.

But it is May Day. We cannot sorrow as though we have no hope. How
can one help but live in hope and the joy that faith and hope bring on such
a spring morning as this. A few weeks ago a deluge of rain and cold and
snow made us despair and the trees and shrubs in the park were dead ...
and now they are blooming. There is no one without such natural faith
and hope in such weather. So let us rejoice, as Fr. Roy was always telling

us. Let us rejoice in tribulations. Has there ever been a time when we were without them? We started out twenty five years ago thinking we were just going to get out a newspaper, small though it might be, which would allow us to exercise our journalistic talents. We were going to discuss the present problems, which began with depression and unemployment (and we have them again) and we would go on with all the problems which came with poverty, injustice, and the ever recurring wars, whether race wars, class wars, civil wars or international wars. We were always pacifists, many opinions to the contrary.

Peter Maurin exalted freedom as God's greatest gift to man, and he pointed to the gospels and Christ's teachings. We were to lead by example, by serving. We were not to seek leadership indeed, but to strive to be the least—to wash one another's feet in other words. "I have left you an example," Jesus said, when He washed the feet of His disciples. "As I have done, so do ye." "My little children, love one another," the beloved disciple kept repeating in his last days. "A new commandment I have given you, that you love one another as I have loved you." Jesus said. "The good shepherd lays down his life for the sheep."

Everything we knew in the Gospel was against the use of force. We were taught in the Gospel to work from the bottom up, not from the top down. Everything was personalist, we were our brothers' keepers, and we were not to pass by our neighbor who has fallen by the wayside and let the State, the all encroaching State, take over, but were to do all we could ourselves. These were the anarchist and pacifist teachings Peter Maurin, our founder, taught us. And he bolstered them up not only from all the religious sources we were familiar with, but from the writing of Kropotkin, Don Sturzo, Chesterton, Belloc, Eric Gill, Fr. Vincent McNabb, Fr. Tompkins, Fr. Coady.

When Fr. Dowling called Peter an anarchist, he admitted it, but he also said he would run for office on a proportional representation ticket in order to try to put his ideas across. He firmly believed in "the withering away of the state" which the Communists spoke of, but he did not believe it would happen under a dictatorship even of the Proletariat, and he always said that the only true communism was the voluntary communism of the Church.

He wanted farming communes, communities of families, though many people went to the land when they married, and there have been attempts at farming communes, we cannot point to any successful one. Peter was a personalist and a communitarian and he said that there could be a Christian capitalism and a Christian communism. We keep quoting from Peter, and keep repeating his writings because he was, to use his own words, "the theoretician of the green revolution" we were to promote.

Yes, we thought we were embarking on a career in journalism, the few of us who worked that first year getting out the paper, but like true revolutionary movements, we attracted all the cranks, the reformers, the theorists, the fools for Christ, who wander like wandering monks of St. Benedict's day, or like the pilgrims of Russia, or like the "lumpen proletariat," or the migrants of our own country.

Some who came to us were holy, some had not even begun to learn to "keep the commandments." In fact, to this very day, common sense in religion is rare and we are too often trying to be heroic instead of just ordinarily good and kind. Newman wrote how tragic if we come to the end of our lives and find that we have never even begun to do what God wanted of us. But I honestly do not think that can be said of us. I do sincerely think that we keep trying, that we keep beginning again, over and over, each day. And the fact that we were so soon involved, and are now so completely involved in the daily practice of the works of mercy and can't get out of them, nor ever can for all the rest of our lives, is some proof that we are continuing Peter Maurin's mission.

"It is good for us to be here," John Cort, in his article in this issue speaks of how I made the Catholic Worker sound like a "good time," like fun when he heard me speak in Boston. And it is true that there is a good deal of humor involved in The Catholic Worker movement. It is not only that we are fools for Christ. When we try to take literally the words of Christ He is always making us "put up, or shut up," as the vulgar saying is.

We wrote about houses of hospitality, and the poor came to the doors of the CW office and forced us to open one. "Why write about it otherwise," the first articulate homeless woman told us. "Peter Maurin wrote that we should not say, 'The Church or the State, doesn't do this or that.' 'We is a community; they is a crowd.' 'Be what you want the other fellow to be.' Why don't you have a house of hospitality?"

Maybe Peter Maurin was surprised at being taken at his word too. Anyway it was that woman who came in with a paper shopping bag, who had been sleeping on subways, who forced us to open the first house of hospitality. And there have been thirty or forty since—I cannot count them all, since each one is autonomous, and I am always finding new ones here and there around the country. Just this week we got a donation from D. Farnsworth, from Martin Joseph House, and I recognize the name and know that she was running a house in Stockton, California for some years. The Blanchet House of Hospitality in Portland, Oregon, is feeding almost two thousand men a day now, according to a priest who just visited us from there.

Once I asked Peter what he thought of our Baltimore House (which was finally closed not only because of overcrowding but also because we housed both Negro and white) and he looked rather doubtful, thinking of what he really wanted in a house, craftrooms, seminars, reading rooms, as well as a place to eat and sleep. "It at least arouses the conscience," he said. He always firmly held that the works of mercy were the means to show our love for God and our love for our brother.

It was the men in the house themselves that started our breadlines, by taking in one after another to share our meals. It seems we never do anything good by ourselves, we just get pushed into it. We are surely unprofitable servants. One time at Maryfarm I saw a man with a suitcase walking down the road towards our farmhouse, and since we were already filled to the door, and with problems too, I sighed deeply and remarked, "I suppose he is coming here." And a man sitting next to me said sternly, "Then you don't mean what you write in the paper?" Yes, we believe it. If "your brother is hungry feed him, if he is naked, cover him, if he is without shelter, [shelter] him, if he is sick comfort him, if he is in prison visit him, if he is dead bury him." The Lord Himself said it. And he was talking to each one of us, not to Holy Mother the State.

Of course there are some ideas which we change over the years. Personally I don't believe women should work out of the home if they can possibly help it. Personally I believe more in child labor than I used to. If the little boys who are running riot could be put to work and the mothers stay home, how much happier it would be. But we do not have a philosophy of work, as Peter Maurin said, and certainly the jobs open to most people in this mechanized age, are anything but attractive. I do believe however in the four hour day. And I do believe in manual labor for every one, everyone bearing their share of the hard work of the world.

Steve Hergenhan, God rest his soul, used to call me a pencil pusher when I did my writing and he dearly loved to see me in the kitchen working. There is always a war between worker and scholar and too often the scholar has it coming to him.

I'm afraid I believe in private property too, though St. Gertrude says that "property, the more common it is, the more holy it is." But when I speak of private property it is mostly personal property I am thinking of. A typewriter, for instance—a fountain pen, one's books, one's own bed. Of course if one is deprived of these things, one should thank the one who deprives, since they are lightening one's load on the journey to heaven. Once a policeman called up and said he had picked up a man who was bringing one of our typewriters to a Bowery hock shop. The man explained that all property was held in common around the Catholic Worker, so it was his as well as any one else's. The policeman restored our "property." We didn't press charges of course, and we thanked the policeman. Ammon would have refused the services of the police perhaps and gone to pick up the typewriter himself. He hangs on to his own pencil, book, clothes, so carefully indeed, that we sometimes call him "private-property-Hennacy." But it is really just Yankee thrift.

Once a passerby dropped into our store at Mott Street when Slim was being night watchman, and someone had brought us a turkey that night since it was the eve of thanksgiving. Slim wanted to take a little walk, so he left the stranger in charge and went out. When he came back the stranger and turkey were gone. There was great furore around the house, but we took the opportunity to explain that in the upside-down world of Christianity, Slim should have run after the thief and brought him the cranberries and celery and other fixings, so that he could have a really good meal. "If anyone takes your coat, give him your cloak too." Most of the family didn't see it that way. I have told this story before, but I did not tell the sequel. Only a year or so ago, but ten years after the incident, a man came in and handed us five dollars. "I was the one who stole your turkey," he said.

Sometimes perhaps we arouse a little fear in the hearts of our friends. For instance there had been a demonstration in England just after the war, when the needy moved into some of the uninhabited homes of the rich, and just took over. We expressed ourselves in the CW as pleased with this expropriation, and went on to say, that the Benedictine oblates amongst us would like to go to some of the Benedictine monasteries and become squatters on their vast tracts, and so induce them to start again and the guest houses which are part of the rule of the order. They don't need all the land the have, and we have plenty of landless folk. Not long after that (but we had forgotten our comments, thinking of them as casual illustrations of our point rather than plans for action) we went to visit a Benedictine monastery, Peter, Dwight Larrowe and I. (Dwight is now Brother Peter in the Trappist Monastery of our Lady of the Snows in Colorado.) We were fed a very good dinner rather hastily, and then the good monks pulled out bus schedules and rather hastily found a way of getting us off their premises. I thought the visit very short, there had been no time for any conversation, nor any dear-to-his-heart round table discussions for Peter, but it was only on the way home that it occurred to me that our dear friends the monks, had read the paper and had been afraid that in the parlance of the gangster, we were "casing the joint." In other words, that we were sizing up the place with the end in view of moving in some of our unemployed families.

Well, if they suffered from this misconception, we were made to suffer too. That month we had had a letter from one of our friends who was married and had two children and was dissatisfied with the farm his father had given for his use. He wanted to join one of our farm communities. We wrote and told him that he already had a home and that we were forced to say no. But he disregarded us and very soon after car and trailer arrived and little family with another baby imminent to move into our barn. We did not want them, but there they were; it was though God were teaching us a lesson, was having a little joke on us, making us eat our words.

Peter Maurin rejoiced in these situations. They made us think, he always said. There was nothing like a crisis for on-the-spot discussions. For clarification of thought. Everyone was an asset in a way. No need ever to eliminate anyone. They would eliminate themselves. It took a robust soul to live in a community. It was in fact a martyrdom.

There are so many stories that could be told about our communities, our houses of hospitality, and some of them grim and some of them so funny and so good, that one could laugh for joy.

TRIBULATION FOR AMMON

And speaking of tribulation,—one of them is Ammon. I used to say the same of Peter, of course, thinking of my quiet writing life before I met him in 1932 and became embroiled in what became a movement. But Ammon is such a fighting Irishman, such a belligerent pacifist! Take this last article of his on page two of the CW. Here he is carrying on a battle with the ushers of a church and a policeman rather than with the personnel of the guided missile base. He was all but tarred and feathered of course, and I am sure he inspired them with respect for his courage. But they needed more time to get acquainted. These guerrilla warfare tactics—descending on a town with pickets and leaflets and poster walks and radio talks and so on, may cause surprise and some thought but I liked the way things worked out in Phoenix, Arizona, where little by little Ammon got acquainted with all the priests and sisters in the town, and won their friendship and won, too, a very wide circulation for the ideas of the Catholic Worker. And now here he is threatening to fast for forty days. I wonder if this is truly a Gandhian technique—to fast at the government, if one can put it that way, Stop atomic tests, or else! What it practically amounts to is a fast to the death. Because I am sure the government out of plain stubbornness, even if they intended to stop would not give in to such pressure. It somehow does not seem the way. It is Ammon's recognition of course, that we are living in fearsome times and that only the most drastic, heroic remedies, much suffering, and self-inflicted sufferings, are going to serve as penance for our sins as a country. We do indeed need to fast and pray. And Ammon goes into these struggles with a joyful spirit, with a great courage, with the generosity of one who wishes to give all, even life itself, for Peace.

They used to say of Peter that he held up to us such lofty aims that we could only reach half way. And that if his aims were lower, we would still only be reaching half way, human nature being inclined to sloth. Certainly the State, love of country, demands and exacts and inspires and arouses the willingness, even the desire to die, to give up one's life for the ideal. Ammon is one of those people who have kept his ideal, and it is just as strong in him now as it was in his early youth. It has grown indeed with his daily communions since his baptism five years ago. He has been "putting on Christ" as St. Paul calls it, though for some people it is as hard to see Christ in Ammon Hennacy as it is to see Him in the derelict. Certainly he is not articulate about his faith, and philosophy and theology are not his forte. His actions are always better than his words when it comes to living his faith, putting in hours serving others, getting mail, answering it, giving up his bed, listening to the sick, the poor, and afflicted. Yes, we will stand by him, he is what God sent us as an apostle, an editor, and he is certainly an agitator par excellence.

PICKETING

And now he delights to call attention to the fact that we once picketed the Cardinal during the cemetery strike. It has gotten so now that some of the people at the CW deny that we ever did. The facts are that Michael Kovalak, Irene Mary Naughton and Helen Adler took signs and when all others were fearful of criticism, proceeded to the chancery office and after announcing their intention to one of the priests at the cathedral, who told them they of course had to follow their conscience, thereupon picketed for an hour, and then went into the cathedral and prayed, to make their picketing more effective.

It was so effective that Ammon Hennacy, not yet a Catholic, in far away Arizona, went into the Catholic Church for the first time and prayed joyfully for us all, and thanked God for companions of courage. Some time later, on another visit to the Church he said he began to be conscious that those praying, kneeling Catholics, no matter what their political opinions, "had something." And not to be outdone, now he has it too.

They are somewhat alike, Ammon and Peter, both close to the soil, both close to the people, both inspiring others to awake. On my last trip when I passed out some Catholic Worker papers in the bus which came from Mexico City to El Paso (fare eleven dollars) the insurance saleswoman who was reading the paper began to read Peter's essays out loud to her companion, a Canadian, and to laugh with startled amazement at his ideas. When people know Ammon they laugh at and with him, and because of him, and some of this laughter is that joyful laughter that the Christian ideal is so flaming, so alive, so burning still. "I have come to cast fire on the earth," Jesus said. And His fire is quite a different fire from that of the nuclear weapon, which is of hell.

THE ROLE OF WOMAN

I speak and write this way, of Peter and Ammon (and how often did I not have to speak so of Bob Ludlow!), because I feel that though they themselves do not feel they need to be interpreted, translated, explained, or justified—I am doing it to declare my own position. Sometimes some of our readers like to hold that I, Dorothy Day, editor of the Catholic Worker, do not go along with these ideas,—that others have seized control of the paper, that these ideas are somehow not in line with the works of mercy. They are all part and parcel of it. It all goes together! It is all for clarification of thought. Peter used to say that it was men who had the mission and that it was woman's place to follow the men who follow their mission. I believe that this is true. In the main, the Catholic Worker movement has been one of men throughout the country. There have been many great and generous men who have worked with it, Joe Zarrella, Gerry Griffin, Tom Sullivan, Bob Ludlow, Dwight Larrowe and Jack English (the last two now with the Trappists); Roger O'Neill and Charles McCormack, and now the present staff. And there are others still with us, too numerous to mention. Hank and John and Keith, and Larry and Roy and Joe and Red and John and Jim, and Pop and Tom and Mike, and then the men on the farm!

God be thanked for the work He as given us to do. And may we continue it another twenty-five years!

BULLETIN

Latest news is that the finances of the city are so embarrassed that they will not be able to purchase so large a block of property for the transit authorities who are building the subway, and consequently there will be a delay in the wrecking of our St. Joseph's House of Hospitality. We do not know how long this delay is, but our lawyer says that we are probably safe for the summer and fall. Deo gratias![10]

NOTES

1. [Catholic Worker Collection, Series W-6.2, Box 1. This collection is in the process of being archived at Marquette University Memorial Library.]

2. [Dorothy Day—Catholic Worker Collection, Series W-2, Box 1].

3. [Dorothy Day—Catholic Worker Collection, Series W-6.2, Box 1. The conclusion is missing from the original.]

4. [*The Catholic Worker* II, no. 6 (November 1934): 4.]

5. [*The Catholic Worker* V, no. 10 (February 1938): 2.]

6. [Source unknown.]

7. [Source unknown.]

8. [*The Catholic Worker* VI, no. 11 (June 1939): 1, 3.]

9. [*The Catholic Worker* III, no. 9 (February 1936): 4, 7.]

10. [*The Catholic Worker* XXIV, no. 10 (May 1958): 1, 11.]

{CHAPTER 7}

Pope John Paul II (1920–2005)

SELECTED AND EDITED BY ROBERT P. GEORGE

AND GERARD V. BRADLEY

On May 18, 1920, just months after Poland regained its independence, Karol Józef Wojtyla was born in Wadowice, a small city fifty kilometers from Krakow. He was the second of two sons born to Karol Wojtyla and Emilia Kaczorowska. His father was a tailor by trade, and he served as an administrative officer of the Austro-Hungarian army. He retired from the Polish army in 1927 with the rank of captain. Karol's mother died of kidney and heart disease in 1929, while he was in the third grade.

In the fall of 1930, Karol entered Marcin Wadowita, an all-boys state secondary school in Wadowice. There he achieved top grades in a classical curriculum: Latin, Greek, history, and mathematics, as well as Polish language and literature. After graduating in 1938, Karol spent his summer fulfilling his national service with a road construction crew. That fall he began his undergraduate studies at Krakow's Jagiellonian University. In 1939, the Nazi occupation forces closed the university. To remain in Krakow, every able-bodied male between fourteen and sixty had to carry a work card. Those without one were sent to a concentration camp or summarily executed. To forestall deportation and imprisonment, Karol found work as a restaurant store messenger, eventually moving to the Solvay chemical company, where he worked as a manual laborer.

After his father passed away, Karol entered the clandestine seminary of Krakow run by Cardinal Adam Stefan Sapieha. He continued his studies for the priesthood at the major seminary of Krakow, which reopened just after the war. He studied theology at the Jagiellonian University as well, until his priestly ordination on November 1, 1946. Immediately after ordination he attended Angelicum University in Rome, earning a licentiate in theology and eventually a doctorate. Successfully defending his second thesis, "The

Evaluation of the Possibility of Founding a Catholic Ethic on the Ethical System of Max Scheler," at Lublin Catholic University, and earning a second doctorate, Wojtyla accepted a professorship from the university in 1954 to teach moral theology and social ethics in the Faculty of Theology and in the major seminary of Krakow. Two years later he was appointed to the chair of ethics. Two years after that, on July 4, 1958, he became auxiliary bishop of Krakow.

On January 13, 1964, Wojtyla was named Archbishop of Krakow by Pope Paul VI. In 1966, Wojtyla was named president of the Episcopal Commission for the Apostolate of the Laity. Pope Paul VI made him a cardinal on June 26, 1967. On October 16, 1978, Cardinal Karol Wojtyla was elected the 264th pope and took the name John Paul II, becoming the first non-Italian pontiff in centuries. He has also become the most traveled and the most prolific writer of all the popes.

In his concise autobiography, Gift and Mystery: On the Fiftieth Anniversary of My Priestly Ordination, *the pope takes the reader through his youth all the way to his years as pope. In a moving description of the Nazi occupation of Poland and the conditions endured under the Soviet-backed Communist government, John Paul II barely mentioned the role he played in the downfall of Communism in Poland. Rather, he expressed "his conviction that the battle for human dignity [had] hardly [been] won. Consumerism [threatened] to undermine [human dignity] in a way Communism never could. He [asserted] that the answer to the corrosive philosophies of the modern world lies in priests fulfilling their ministry. His plea to his brother priests: celebrate the Eucharist with faith, hear confessions, be with young people, encourage married couples and above all, pray."*[1]

On April 3, 2005, John Paul II, after increasingly ailing health, died at the Vatican at the age of eighty-four; his pontificate, nearly twenty-seven years, was the third longest in history.

"*DOMINUS IESUS*": DECLARATION ON THE UNICITY AND SALVIFIC UNIVERSALITY OF JESUS CHRIST AND THE CHURCH

INTRODUCTION

1. THE *LORD JESUS*, before ascending into heaven, commanded his disciples to proclaim the Gospel to the whole world and to baptize all nations: "Go into the whole world and proclaim the Gospel to every creature. He who believes and is baptized will be saved; he who does not believe will be condemned" (*Mk* 16:15–16); "All power in heaven and on earth has been given to me. Go therefore and teach all nations, baptizing them in the name of

the Father, and of the Son, and of the Holy Spirit, teaching them to observe all that I have commanded you. And behold, I am with you always, until the end of the world" (*Mt* 28:18–20; cf. *Lk* 24:46–48; *Jn* 17:18, 20, 21; *Acts* 1:8).

The Church's universal mission is born from the command of Jesus Christ and is fulfilled in the course of the centuries in the proclamation of the mystery of God, Father, Son, and Holy Spirit, and the mystery of the incarnation of the Son, as saving event for all humanity. . . .

2. In the course of the centuries, the Church has proclaimed and witnessed with fidelity to the Gospel of Jesus. At the close of the second millennium, however, this mission is still far from complete.[2] For that reason, Saint Paul's words are now more relevant than ever: "Preaching the Gospel is not a reason for me to boast; it is a necessity laid on me: woe to me if I do not preach the Gospel!" (1 *Cor* 9:16). This explains the Magisterium's particular attention to giving reasons for and supporting the evangelizing mission of the Church, above all in connection with the religious traditions of the world. . . . [3]

I. The Fullness and Definitiveness of the Revelation of Jesus Christ

5. As a remedy for this relativistic mentality, which is becoming ever more common, it is necessary above all to reassert the definitive and complete character of the revelation of Jesus Christ. In fact, it must be *firmly believed* that, in the mystery of Jesus Christ, the Incarnate Son of God, who is "the way, the truth, and the life" (*Jn* 14:6), the full revelation of divine truth is given: "No one knows the Son except the Father, and no one knows the Father except the Son and anyone to whom the Son wishes to reveal him" (*Mt* 11:27); "No one has ever seen God; God the only Son, who is in the bosom of the Father, has revealed him" (*Jn* 1:18); "For in Christ the whole fullness of divinity dwells in bodily form" (*Col* 2:9–10).

Faithful to God's word, the Second Vatican Council teaches: "By this revelation then, the deepest truth about God and the salvation of man shines forth in Christ, who is at the same time the mediator and the fullness of all revelation."[4] Furthermore, "Jesus Christ, therefore, the Word made flesh, sent 'as a man to men,' 'speaks the words of God' (*Jn* 3:34), and completes the work of salvation which his Father gave him to do (cf. *Jn* 5:36; 17:4). To see Jesus is to see his Father (cf. *Jn* 14:9). For this reason, Jesus perfected revelation by fulfilling it through his whole work of making himself present and manifesting himself: through his words and deeds, his signs and wonders, but especially through his death and glorious resurrection from the dead and finally with the sending of the Spirit of truth, he completed and perfected revelation and confirmed it with divine testimony. . . . The Christian dispensation, therefore, as the new and definitive covenant, will never pass away, and we now await no further new public revelation before the glorious manifestation of our Lord Jesus Christ (cf. 1 *Tim* 6:14 and *Tit* 2:13). . . ."[5]

7. The proper response to God's revelation is *"the obedience of faith (Rom* 16:26; cf. *Rom* 1:5; 2 *Cor* 10:5–6) by which man freely entrusts his entire self to God, offering 'the full submission of intellect and will to God who reveals' and freely assenting to the revelation given by him."[6] Faith is a gift of grace: "in order to have faith, the grace of God must come first and give assistance; there must also be the interior helps of the Holy Spirit, who moves the heart and converts it to God, who opens the eyes of the mind and gives 'to everyone joy and ease in assenting to and believing in the truth.' "[7]

The obedience of faith implies acceptance of the truth of Christ's revelation, guaranteed by God, who is Truth itself:[8] "Faith is first of all a personal adherence of man to God. At the same time, and inseparably, it is a *free assent to the whole truth that God has revealed*."[9] Faith, therefore, as *"a gift of God"* and as *"a supernatural virtue infused by him*,"[10] involves a dual adherence: to God who reveals and to the truth which he reveals, out of the trust which one has in him who speaks. Thus, "we must believe in no one but God: the Father, the Son and the Holy Spirit."[11]

For this reason, the distinction between *theological faith* and *belief* in the other religions, must be *firmly held*. If faith is the acceptance in grace of revealed truth, which "makes it possible to penetrate the mystery in a way that allows us to understand it coherently,"[12]then belief, in the other religions, is that sum of experience and thought that constitutes the human treasury of wisdom and religious aspiration, which man in his search for truth has conceived and acted upon in his relationship to God and the Absolute. . . .[13]

V. The Church: Kingdom of God and Kingdom of Christ

18. The mission of the Church is "to proclaim and establish among all peoples the kingdom of Christ and of God, and she is on earth, the seed and the beginning of that kingdom."[14] On the one hand, the Church is "a sacrament—that is, sign and instrument of intimate union with God and of unity of the entire human race."[15] She is therefore the sign and instrument of the kingdom; she is called to announce and to establish the kingdom. On the other hand, the Church is the "people gathered by the unity of the Father, the Son and the Holy Spirit";[16] she is therefore "the kingdom of Christ already present in mystery"[17] and constitutes its *seed* and *beginning*. The kingdom of God, in fact, has an eschatological dimension: it is a reality present in time, but its full realization will arrive only with the completion or fulfillment of history.[18]

The meaning of the expressions *kingdom of heaven, kingdom of God*, and *kingdom of Christ* in Sacred Scripture and the Fathers of the Church, as well as in the documents of the Magisterium, is not always exactly the same, nor is their relationship to the Church, which is a mystery that cannot be totally contained by a human concept. Therefore, there can be various theological explanations of these terms. However, none of these possible explanations can deny or empty in any way the intimate connection between Christ, the kingdom, and the Church. In fact, the kingdom of God which we know from revelation, "cannot be detached either from Christ or from the Church. . . . If the kingdom is separated from Jesus, it is no longer the kingdom of God which he revealed. The result is a distortion of the meaning of the kingdom, which runs the risk of being transformed into a purely human or ideological goal and a distortion of the identity of Christ, who no longer appears as the Lord to whom everything must one day be subjected (cf. 1 *Cor* 15:27). Likewise, one may not separate the kingdom from the Church. It is true that the Church is not an end unto herself, since she is ordered toward the kingdom of God, of which she is the seed, sign and instrument. Yet, while remaining distinct from Christ and the kingdom, the Church is indissolubly united to both. . . ."[19]

VI. The Church and the Other Religions in Relation to Salvation

20. From what has been stated above, some points follow that are necessary for theological reflection as it explores the relationship of the Church and the other religions to salvation.

Above all else, it must be *firmly believed* that "the Church, a pilgrim now on earth, is necessary for salvation: the one Christ is the mediator and the way of salvation; he is present to us in his body which is the Church. He himself explicitly asserted the necessity of faith and baptism (cf. *Mk* 16:16; *Jn* 3:5), and thereby affirmed at the same time the necessity of the Church which men enter through baptism as through a door."[20] This doctrine must not be set against the universal salvific will of God (cf. 1 *Tim* 2:4); "it is necessary to keep these two truths together, namely, the real possibility of salvation in Christ for all mankind and the necessity of the Church for this salvation."[21]

INSTRUCTION ON CERTAIN ASPECTS OF THE "THEOLOGY OF LIBERATION"

INTRODUCTION

The Gospel of Jesus Christ is a message of freedom and a force for liberation. In recent years, this essential truth has become the object of reflection for theologians, with a new kind of attention which is itself full of promise.

Liberation is first and foremost liberation from the radical slavery of sin. Its end and its goal is the freedom of the children of God, which is the gift of grace. As a logical consequence, it calls for freedom from many different kinds of slavery in the cultural, economic, social, and political spheres, all of which derive ultimately from sin, and so often prevent people from living in a manner befitting their dignity. To discern clearly what is fundamental to this issue and what is a by-product of it, is an indispensable condition for any theological reflection on liberation.

Faced with the urgency of certain problems, some are tempted to emphasize, unilaterally, the liberation from servitude of an earthly and temporal kind. They do so in such a way that they seem to put liberation from sin in second place, and so fail to give it the primary importance it is due. Thus, their very presentation of the problems is confused and ambiguous. Others, in an effort to learn more precisely what are the causes of the slavery which they want to end, make use of different concepts without sufficient critical caution. It is difficult, and perhaps impossible, to purify these borrowed concepts of an ideological inspiration which is incompatible with Christian faith and the ethical requirements which flow from it. . . .

The present Instruction has a much more limited and precise purpose: to draw the attention of pastors, theologians, and all the faithful to the deviations, and risks of deviation, damaging to the faith and to Christian living, that are brought about by certain forms of liberation theology which use, in an insufficiently critical manner, concepts borrowed from various currents of marxist thought. . . .

VII—Marxist Analysis

10. A critical examination of the analytical methods borrowed from other disciplines must be carried out in a special way by theologians. It is the light of faith which provides theology with its principles. That is why the use of philosophical positions or of human sciences by the theologian has a value which might be called instrumental, but yet must undergo a critical study from a theological perspective. In other words, the ultimate and decisive criterion for truth can only be a criterion which is itself theological. It is only in the light of faith, and what faith teaches us about the truth of man and the ultimate meaning of his destiny, that one can judge the validity or degree of validity of what other disciplines propose, often rather conjecturally, as being the truth about man, his history and his destiny.

11. When modes of interpretation are applied to the economic, social, and political reality of today, which are themselves borrowed from marxist

thought, they can give the initial impression of a certain plausibility, to the degree that the present-day situation in certain countries is similar to what Marx described and interpreted in the middle of the last century. On the basis of these similarities, certain simplifications are made which, abstracting from specific essential factors, prevent any really rigorous examination of the causes of poverty and prolong the confusion.

12. In certain parts of Latin America, the seizure of the vast majority of the wealth by an oligarchy of owners bereft of social consciousness, the practical absence or the shortcomings of a rule of law, military dictators making a mockery of elementary human rights, the corruption of certain powerful officials, the savage practices of some foreign capital interests constitute factors which nourish a passion for revolt among those who thus consider themselves the powerless victims of a new colonialism in the technological, financial, monetary, or economic order. The recognition of injustice is accompanied by a *pathos* which borrows its language from marxism, wrongly presented as though it were scientific language.

13. The first condition for any analysis is a total openness to the reality to be described. That is why a critical consciousness has to accompany the use of any working hypotheses that are being adopted. One has to realize that these hypotheses correspond to a particular viewpoint which will inevitably highlight certain aspects of the reality while leaving others in the shade. This limitation which derives from the nature of human science is ignored by those who, under the guise of hypotheses recognized as such, have recourse to such an all-embracing conception of reality as the thought of Karl Marx.[22]

INSTRUCTION ON CHRISTIAN FREEDOM AND LIBERATION

I. PRELIMINARY APPROACHES TO FREEDOM

A Spontaneous Response

25. The spontaneous response to the question: "What does being free mean?" is this: a person is free when he is able to do whatever he wishes without being hindered by an exterior constraint and thus enjoys complete independence. The opposite of freedom would therefore be the dependence of our will upon the will of another.

But does man always know what he wants? Can he do everything he wants? Is closing in on oneself and cutting oneself off from the will of others in conformity with the nature of man? Often the desire of a particular moment is not what a person really wants. And in one and the same person there can exist contradictory wishes. But above all man comes up against the limits of his own nature: his desires are greater than his abilities. Thus the obstacle which opposes his will does not always come from outside, but from the limits of his own being. This is why, under pain of destroying himself, man must learn to harmonize his will with his nature.

Truth and Justice, Rules of Freedom

26. Furthermore, every individual is oriented toward other people and needs their company. It is only by learning to unite his will to the others for the sake of true good that he will learn rectitude of will. It is thus harmony with the exigencies of human nature which makes the will itself human. This in fact requires the criterion of truth and a right relationship to the will of others. Truth and justice are therefore the measure of true freedom. By discarding this foundation and taking himself for God, man falls into deception, and instead of realizing himself he destroys himself.

Far from being achieved in total self-sufficiency and an absence of relationships, freedom only truly exists where reciprocal bonds, governed by truth and justice, link people to one another. But for such bonds to be possible, each person must live in the truth.

Freedom is not the liberty to do anything whatsoever. It is the freedom to do good, and in this alone happiness is to be found. The good is thus the goal of freedom. In consequence man becomes free to the extent that he comes to a knowledge of the truth, and to the extent that this truth—and not any other forces—guides his will. Liberation for the sake of a knowledge of the truth which alone directs the will is the necessary condition for a freedom worthy of the name.

II. FREEDOM AND LIBERATION

Freedom for the Creature

27. In other words, freedom which is interior mastery of one's own acts and self-determination immediately entails a relationship with the ethical order. It finds its true meaning in the choice of moral good. It then manifests itself as emancipation from moral evil.

By his free action, man must tend toward the supreme good through lesser goods which conform to the exigencies of his nature and his divine vocation.

In exercising his freedom, he decides for himself and forms himself. In this sense man is *his own cause*. But he is this only as a creature and as God's image. This is the truth of his being which shows by contrast how profoundly erroneous are the theories which think they exalt the freedom of man or his "historical praxis" by making this freedom the absolute principle of his being and becoming. These theories are expressions of atheism or tend toward atheism by their own logic. Indifferentism and deliberate agnosticism go in the same direction. It is the image of God in man which underlies the freedom and dignity of the human person.[23]

The Call of the Creator

28. By creating man free, God imprinted on him his own image and likeness.[24] Man hears the call of his Creator in the inclination and aspiration of his own nature toward the Good, and still more in the word of Revelation, which was proclaimed in a perfect manner in the Christ. It is thus revealed to man that God created him free so that by grace man could enter into friendship with God and share his life.

A Shared Freedom

29. Man does not take his origin from his own individual or collective action, but from the gift of God who created him. This is the first confession of our faith, and it confirms the loftiest insights of human thought.

The freedom of man is a shared freedom. His capacity for self-realization is in no way suppressed by his dependence on God. It is precisely the characteristic of atheism to believe in an irreducible opposition between the causality of a divine freedom and that of man's freedom, as though the affirmation of God meant the negation of man, or as though God's intervention in history rendered vain the endeavors of man. In reality, it is from God and in relationship with him that human freedom takes its meaning and consistency.

Man's Free Choice

30. Man's history unfolds on the basis of the nature which he has received from God and in the free accomplishment of the purpose toward which the inclinations of this nature and of divine grace orient and direct him.

But man's freedom is finite and fallible. His desire may be drawn to an apparent good: in choosing a false good, he fails in his vocation to freedom. By his free will, man is master of his own life: he can act in a positive sense or in a destructive one.

By obeying the divine law inscribed in his conscience and received as an impulse of the Holy Spirit, man exercises true mastery over himself and thus realizes his royal vocation as a child of God. "By the service of God he reigns."[25] Authentic freedom is the "service of justice," while the choice of disobedience and evil is the "slavery of sin."[26]

Temporal Liberation and Freedom

31. This notion of freedom clarifies the scope of temporal liberation: it involves all the processes which aim at securing and guaranteeing the conditions needed for the exercise of an authentic human freedom.

Thus it is not liberation which in itself produces human freedom. Common sense, confirmed by Christian sense, knows that even when freedom is subject to forms of conditioning it is not thereby completely destroyed. People who undergo terrible constraints succeed in manifesting their freedom and taking steps to secure their own liberation. A process of liberation which has been achieved can only create better conditions for the effective exercise of freedom. Indeed a liberation which does not take into account the personal freedom of those who fight for it is condemned in advance to defeat.

III. FREEDOM AND HUMAN SOCIETY

The Rights of Man and his "Freedoms"

32. God did not create man as a "solitary being" but wished him to be a "social being."[27] Social life therefore is not exterior to man: he can only grow and realize his vocation in relation with others. Man belongs to different communities: the family and professional and political communities, and it is inside these communities that he must exercise his responsible freedom. A just social order offers man irreplaceable assistance in realizing his free personality. On the other hand, an unjust social order is a threat and an obstacle which can compromise his destiny.

In the social sphere, freedom is expressed and realized in actions, structures and institutions, thanks to which people communicate with one another and organize their common life. The blossoming of a free personality, which for every individual is a duty and a right, must be helped and not hindered by society.

Here we have an exigency of a moral nature which has found its expression in the formulation of the *Rights of Man*. Some of these have as their object what are usually called "*the freedoms*," that is to say, ways of recognizing every human being's character as a person responsible for himself and his transcendent destiny, as well as the inviolability of his conscience. . . . [28]

IV. HUMAN FREEDOM AND DOMINION OVER NATURE

Man's Call to Master Nature

34. As a consequence of his bodily dimension, man needs the resources of the material world for his personal and social fulfillment. In this vocation

to exercise dominion over the earth by putting it at his service through work, one can see an aspect of the image of God.[29] But human intervention is not "creative"; it encounters a material nature which like itself has its origin in God the Creator and of which man has been constituted the "noble and wise guardian."[30]

Man, the Master of his Works

35. Technical and economic transformations influence the organization of social life; they cannot help but affect to some extent cultural and even religious life.

However, by reason of his freedom man remains the master of his activity. The great and rapid transformations of the present age face him with a dramatic challenge: that of mastering and controlling by the use of his reason and freedom the forces which he puts to work in the service of the true purposes of human existence.

Scientific Discoveries and Moral Progress

36. It is the task of freedom then, when it is well ordered, to ensure that scientific and technical achievements, the quest for their effectiveness, and the products of work and the very structures of economic and social organization are not made to serve projects which would deprive them of their human purposes and turn them against man himself.

Scientific activity and technological activity each involve specific exigencies. But they only acquire their properly human meaning and value when they are subordinated to moral principles. These exigencies must be respected; but to wish to attribute to them an absolute and necessary autonomy, not in conformity with the nature of things, is to set out along a path which is ruinous for the authentic freedom of man.

V. SIN, THE SOURCE OF DIVISION AND OPPRESSION

Sin, Separation from God

37. God calls man to freedom. In each person there lives a desire to be free. And yet this desire almost always tends towards slavery and oppression. All commitment to liberation and freedom therefore presupposes that this tragic paradox has been faced.

Man's sin, that is to say his breaking away from God, is the radical reason for the tragedies which mark the history of freedom. In order to understand this, many of our contemporaries must first rediscover a sense of sin.

In man's desire for freedom there is hidden the temptation to deny his own nature. Insofar as he wishes to desire everything and to be able to do everything and thus forget that he is finite and a created being, he claims to be a god. "You will be like God" (*Gen* 3: 5). These words of the serpent reveal the essence of man's temptation; they imply the perversion of the meaning of his own freedom. Such is the profound nature of sin: man rejects the truth and places his own will above it. By wishing to free himself from God and be a god himself, he deceives himself and destroys himself. He becomes alienated from himself.

In this desire to be a god and to subject everything to his own good pleasure, there is hidden a perversion of the very idea of God. God is love and truth in the fullness of the mutual gift of the Divine Persons. It is true that man is called to be like God. But he becomes like God not in the arbitrariness of his own good pleasure but to the extent that he recognizes that truth and love are at the same time the principle and the purpose of his freedom.

Sin, the Root of Human Alienation

38. By sinning, man lies to himself and separates himself from his own truth. But seeking total autonomy and self-sufficiency, he denies God and denies himself. Alienation from the truth of his being as a creature loved by God is the root of all other forms of alienation.

By denying or trying to deny God, who is his Beginning and End, man profoundly disturbs his own order and interior balance and also those of society and even of visible creation.[31]

It is in their relationship to sin that Scripture regards all the different calamities which oppress man in his personal and social existence.

Scripture shows that the whole course of history has a mysterious link with the action of man who, from the beginning, has abused his freedom by setting himself up against God and by seeking to gain his ends without God.[32] Genesis indicates the consequences of this original sin in the painful nature of work and childbirth, in man's oppression of woman and in death. Human beings deprived of divine grace have thus inherited a common mortal nature, incapable of choosing what is good and inclined to covetousness. [33]

Idolatry and Disorder

39. Idolatry is an extreme form of disorder produced by sin. The replacement of adoration of the living God by worship of created things falsifies the relationships between individuals and brings with it various kinds of oppression.

Culpable ignorance of God unleashes the passions, which are causes of imbalance and conflicts in the human heart. From this there inevitably come disorders which affect the sphere of the family and society: sexual license, injustice and murder. It is thus that Saint Paul describes the pagan world, carried away by idolatry to the worst aberrations which ruin the individual and society.[34]

Even before Saint Paul, the Prophets and wise men of Israel saw in the misfortunes of the people a punishment for their sin of idolatry; and in the "heart full of evil" (*Eccles* 9: 3),[35] they saw the source of man's radical slavery and of the forms of oppression which he makes his fellowmen endure.

Contempt for God and a Turning Toward Creatures

40. The Christian tradition, found in the Fathers and Doctors of the Church, has made explicit this teaching of Scripture about sin. It sees sin as contempt for God (*contemptus Dei*). It is accompanied by a desire to escape from the dependent relationship of the servant to his Lord, or still more of the child to its Father. By sinning, man seeks to free himself from God. In reality he makes himself a slave. For by rejecting God he destroys the momentum of his aspiration to the infinite and of his vocation to share in the divine life. This is why his heart is a prey to disquiet.

Sinful man who refuses to accept God is necessarily led to become attached in a false and destructive way to creatures. In this turning toward creatures (*conversio ad creaturam*) he focuses on the latter his unsatisfied desire for the infinite. But created goods are limited; and so his heart rushes from one to another, always searching for an impossible peace.

In fact, when man attributes to creatures an infinite importance, he loses the meaning of his created being. He claims to find his center and his unity in himself. Disordered love of self is the other side of contempt for God. Man then tries to rely on himself alone; he wishes to achieve fulfillment by himself and to be self-sufficient in his own immanence.[36]

Atheism, a False Emancipation of Freedom

41. This becomes more particularly obvious when the sinner thinks that he can only assert his own freedom by explicitly denying God. Dependence of the creature upon the Creator, and the dependence of the moral conscience upon the divine law, are regarded by him as an intolerable slavery. Thus he sees atheism as the true form of emancipation and of man's liberation, whereas religion or even the recognition of a moral law constitute forms of alienation. Man then wishes to make independent decisions about what is good and what is evil, or decisions about values; and in a single step he rejects both the idea of God and the idea of sin. It is through the audacity of sin that he claims to become adult and free, and he claims this emancipation not only for himself but for the whole of humanity.

Sin and Unjust Structures

42. Having become his own center, sinful man tends to assert himself and to satisfy his desire for the infinite by the use of things: wealth, power and pleasure, despising other people and robbing them unjustly and treating them as objects or instruments. Thus he makes his own contribution to the creation of those very structures of exploitation and slavery which he claims to condemn.[37]

SOLLICITUDO REI SOCIALIS (ON SOCIAL CONCERN)

IV. AUTHENTIC HUMAN DEVELOPMENT

27. The examination which the Encyclical invites us to make of the contemporary world leads us to note in the first place that development *is not* a straightforward process, *as it were automatic and in itself limitless*, as though, given certain conditions, the human race were able to progress rapidly towards an undefined perfection of some kind.[38]

Such an idea—linked to a notion of "progress" with philosophical connotations deriving from the Enlightenment, rather than to the notion of "development"[39] which is used in a specifically economic and social sense—now seems to be seriously called into doubt, particularly since the tragic experience of the two world wars, the planned and partly achieved destruction of whole peoples, and the looming atomic peril. A naive *mechanistic optimism* has been replaced by a well founded anxiety for the fate of humanity.

28. At the same time, however, the *"economic"* concept itself, linked to the word development, has entered into crisis. In fact there is a better understanding today that the *mere accumulation* of goods and services, even for the benefit of the majority, is not enough for the realization of human happiness. Nor, in consequence, does the availability of the many *real benefits* provided in recent times by science and technology, including the computer sciences, bring freedom from every form of slavery. On the contrary, the experience of recent years shows that unless all the considerable body of resources and potential at man's disposal is guided by a *moral understanding* and by an orientation towards the true good of the human race, it easily turns against man to oppress him.

A *disconcerting conclusion* about the most recent period should serve to enlighten us: side-by-side with the miseries of underdevelopment, themselves unacceptable, we find ourselves up against a form of *superdevelopment*, equally inadmissible, because like the former it is contrary to what is good and to true happiness. This superdevelopment, which consists in an *excessive* availability of every kind of material goods for the benefit of certain social groups, easily makes people slaves of "possession" and of immediate gratification, with no other horizon than the multiplication or continual replacement of the things already owned with others still better. This is the so-called civilization of "consumption" or "consumerism," which involves so much "throwing-away" and "waste." An object already owned but now superseded by something better is discarded, with no thought of its possible lasting value in itself, nor of some other human being who is poorer.

All of us experience firsthand the sad effects of this blind submission to pure consumerism: in the first place a crass materialism, and at the same time a *radical dissatisfaction*, because one quickly learns—unless one is shielded from the flood of publicity and the ceaseless and tempting offers of products—that the more one possesses the more one wants, while deeper aspirations remain unsatisfied and perhaps even stifled.

The Encyclical of Pope Paul VI pointed out the difference, so often emphasized today, between "having" and "being,"[40] which had been expressed earlier in precise words by the Second Vatican Council.[41] To "have" objects and goods does not in itself perfect the human subject, unless it contributes to the maturing and enrichment of that subject's "being," that is to say unless it contributes to the realization of the human vocation as such.

Of course, the difference between "being" and "having," the danger inherent in a mere multiplication or replacement of things possessed compared to the value of "being," need not turn into a *contradiction*. One of the greatest injustices in the contemporary world consists precisely in this: that the ones who possess much are relatively *few* and those who possess almost nothing are *many*. It is the injustice of the poor distribution of the goods and services originally intended for all.

This then is the picture: there are some people—the few who possess much—who do not really succeed in "being" because, through a reversal of the hierarchy of values, they are hindered by the cult of "having"; and there are others—the many who have little or nothing—who do not succeed in realizing their basic human vocation because they are deprived of essential goods.

The evil does not consist in "having" as such, but in possessing without regard for the *quality* and the *ordered hierarchy* of the goods one has. *Quality and hierarchy* arise from the subordination of goods and their availability to man's "being" and his true vocation.

This shows that although *development* has *a necessary economic dimension*, since it must supply the greatest possible number of the world's inhabitants with an availability of goods essential for them "to be," it is not limited to that dimension. If it is limited to this, then it turns against those whom it is meant to benefit.

The characteristics of full development, one which is "more human" and able to sustain itself at the level of the true vocation of men and women without denying economic requirements, were described by Paul VI.[42]

29. Development which is not only economic must be measured and oriented according to the reality and vocation of man seen in his totality, namely, according to his *interior dimension*. There is no doubt that he needs created goods and the products of industry, which is constantly being enriched by scientific and technological progress. And the ever greater availability of material goods not only meets needs but also opens new horizons. The danger of the misuse of material goods and the appearance of artificial needs should in no way hinder the regard we have for the new goods and resources placed at our disposal and the use we make of them. On the contrary, we must see them as a gift from God and as a response to the human vocation, which is fully realized in Christ.

However, in trying to achieve true development we must never lose sight of that *dimension* which is in the *specific nature* of man, who has been created by God in his image and likeness (cf. *Gen* 1:26). It is a bodily and a spiritual nature, symbolized in the second creation account by the two elements: the *earth*, from which God forms man's body, and the *breath of life* which he breathes into man's nostrils (cf. *Gen* 2:7).

Thus man comes to have a certain affinity with other creatures: he is called to use them, and to be involved with them. As the Genesis account says (cf. *Gen* 2:15), he is placed in the garden with the duty of cultivating and watching over it, being superior to the other creatures placed by God under his dominion (cf. *Gen* 1:25–26). But at the same time man must remain subject to the will of God, who imposes limits upon his use and dominion over things (cf. *Gen* 2:16–17), just as he promises him immortality (cf. *Gen* 2:9; *Wis* 2:23). Thus man, being the image of God, has a true affinity with him too.

On the basis of this teaching, development cannot consist only in the use, dominion over and *indiscriminate* possession of created things and the products of human industry, but rather in *subordinating* the possession, dominion and use to man's divine likeness and to his vocation to immortality. This is the *transcendent reality* of the human being, a reality which is seen to be shared from the beginning by a couple, a man and a woman (cf. *Gen* 1:27), and is therefore fundamentally social.

30. According to Sacred Scripture therefore, the notion of development is not only "lay" or "profane," but it is also seen to be, while having

a socio-economic dimension of its own, the *modern expression* of an essential dimension of man's vocation. . . .

31. Furthermore, the concept of faith makes quite clear the reasons which impel the *Church* to concern herself with the problems of development, to consider them a *duty of her pastoral ministry*, and to urge all to think about the nature and characteristics of authentic human development. Through her commitment she desires, on the one hand, to place herself at the service of the divine plan which is meant to order all things to the fullness which dwells in Christ (cf. *Col* 1:19) and which he communicated to his body; and on the other hand she desires to respond to her fundamental vocation of being a "sacrament," that is to say "a sign and instrument of intimate union with God and of the unity of the whole human race."[43]

Some Fathers of the Church were inspired by this idea to develop in original ways a concept of the *meaning of history* and of *human work*, directed towards a goal which surpasses this meaning and which is always defined by its relationship to the work of Christ. In other words, one can find in the teaching of the Fathers an *optimistic vision* of history and work, that is to say of the *perennial value* of authentic human achievements, inasmuch as they are redeemed by Christ and destined for the promised Kingdom.[44]

Thus, part of the *teaching* and most ancient *practice* of the Church is her conviction that she is obliged by her vocation—she herself, her ministers and each of her members—to relieve the misery of the suffering, both far and near, not only out of her "abundance" but also out of her "necessities." Faced by cases of need, one cannot ignore them in favor of superfluous church ornaments and costly furnishings for divine worship; on the contrary it could be obligatory to sell these goods in order to provide food, drink, clothing and shelter for those who lack these things.[45] As has been already noted, here we are shown a *"hierarchy of values"*—in the framework of the right to property—between "having" and "being," especially when the "having" of a few can be to the detriment of the "being" of many others.

In his Encyclical Pope Paul VI stands in the line of this teaching, taking his inspiration from the Pastoral Constitution *Gaudium et Spes*.[46] For my own part, I wish to insist once more on the seriousness and urgency of that teaching, and I ask the Lord to give all Christians the strength to put it faithfully into practice.

32. The obligation to commit oneself to the development of peoples is not just an *individual* duty, and still less an *individualistic* one, as if it were possible to achieve this development through the isolated efforts of each individual. It is an imperative which obliges *each and every* man

and woman, as well as societies and nations. In particular, it obliges the Catholic Church and the other Churches and Ecclesial Communities, with which we are completely willing to collaborate in this field. In this sense, just as we Catholics invite our Christian brethren to share in our initiatives, so too we declare that we are ready to collaborate in theirs, and we welcome the invitations presented to us. In this pursuit of integral human development we can also do much with the members of other religions, as in fact is being done in various places.

Collaboration in the development of the whole person and of every human being is in fact a duty of *all towards all*, and must be shared by the four parts of the world: East and West, North and South; or, as we say today, by the different "worlds." If, on the contrary, people try to achieve it in only one part, or in only one world, they do so at the expense of the others; and, precisely because the others are ignored, their own development becomes exaggerated and misdirected.

Peoples or *nations* too have a right to their own full development, which while including—as already said—the economic and social aspects should also include individual cultural identity and openness to the transcendent. Not even the need for development can be used as an excuse for imposing on others one's own way of life or own religious belief.

33. Nor would a type of development which did not respect and promote *human rights*—personal and social, economic and political, including *the rights of nations and of peoples*—be really *worthy of man*.

Today, perhaps more than in the past, the *intrinsic contradiction* of a development limited *only* to its economic element is seen more clearly. Such development easily subjects the human person and his deepest needs to the demands of economic planning and selfish profit.

The *intrinsic connection* between authentic development and respect for human rights once again reveals the *moral* character of development: the true elevation of man, in conformity with the natural and historical vocation of each individual, is not attained *only* by exploiting the abundance of goods and services, or by having available perfect infrastructures.

When individuals and communities do not see a rigorous respect for the moral, cultural and spiritual requirements, based on the dignity of the person and on the proper identity of each community, beginning with the family and religious societies, then all the rest—availability of goods, abundance of technical resources applied to daily life, a certain level of material well-being—will prove unsatisfying and in the end contemptible. The Lord clearly says this in the Gospel, when he calls the attention of all to the true hierarchy of values: "For what will it profit a man, if he gains the whole world and forfeits his life?" (*Mt* 16:26).

True development, in keeping with the *specific* needs of the human being-man or woman, child, adult or old person—implies, especially for those who actively share in this process and are responsible for it, a lively *awareness* of the *value* of the rights of all and of each person. It likewise implies a lively awareness of the need to respect the right of every individual to the full use of the benefits offered by science and technology.

On the *internal level* of every nation, respect for all rights takes on great importance, especially: the right to life at every stage of its existence; the rights of the family, as the basic social community, or "cell of society"; justice in employment relationships; the rights inherent in the life of the political community as such; the rights based on the *transcendent vocation* of the human being, beginning with the right of freedom to profess and practice one's own religious belief.

On the *international level*, that is, the level of relations between States or, in present-day usage, between the different "worlds," there must be complete respect for the identity of each people, with its own historical and cultural characteristics. It is likewise essential, as the Encyclical *Populorum Progressio* already asked, to recognize each people's equal right "to be seated at the table of the common banquet,"[47] instead of lying outside the door like Lazarus, while "the dogs come and lick his sores" (cf. *Lk* 16:21). Both peoples and individuals must enjoy the *fundamental* equality[48] which is the basis, for example, of the Charter of the United Nations Organization: the equality which is the basis of the right of all to share in the process of full development.

In order to be genuine, development must be achieved within the framework of *solidarity* and *freedom*, without ever sacrificing either of them under whatever pretext. The moral character of development and its necessary promotion are emphasized when the most rigorous respect is given to all the demands deriving from the order of *truth* and *good* proper to the human person. Furthermore the Christian who is taught to see that man is the image of God, called to share in the truth and the good which is *God himself*, does not understand a commitment to development and its application which excludes regard and respect for the unique dignity of this "image." In other words, true development must be based on the *love of God and neighbor*, and must help to promote the relationships between individuals and society. This is the "civilization of love" of which Paul VI often spoke.[49]

ENCYCLICAL LETTER: *CENTESIMUS ANNUS*

VI. MAN IS THE WAY OF THE CHURCH

53. Faced with the poverty of the working class, Pope Leo XIII wrote: "We approach this subject with confidence, and in the exercise of the rights which manifestly pertain to us. . . . By keeping silence we would seem to neglect

the duty incumbent on us."[50] During the last hundred years the Church has repeatedly expressed her thinking, while closely following the continuing development of the social question. She has certainly not done this in order to recover former privileges or to impose her own vision. Her sole purpose has been *care and responsibility* for man, who has been entrusted to her by Christ himself: for *this man*, whom, as the Second Vatican Council recalls, is the only creature on earth which God willed for its own sake, and for which God has his plan, that is, a share in eternal salvation. We are not dealing here with man in the "abstract," but with the real, "concrete," "historical" man. We are dealing with *each individual*, since each one is included in the mystery of Redemption, and through this mystery Christ has united himself with each one forever.[51] It follows that the Church cannot abandon man, and that "*this man* is the primary route that the Church must travel in fulfilling her mission ... the way traced out by Christ himself, the way that leads invariably through the mystery of the Incarnation and the Redemption."[52]

This, and this alone, is the principle which inspires the Church's social doctrine. The Church has gradually developed that doctrine in a systematic way, above all in the century that has followed the date we are commemorating, precisely because the horizon of the Church's whole wealth of doctrine is man in his concrete reality as sinful and righteous.

54. Today, the Church's social doctrine focuses especially *on man* as he is involved in a complex network of relationships within modern societies. The human sciences and philosophy are helpful for interpreting *man's central place within society* and for enabling him to understand himself better as a "social being." However, man's true identity is only fully revealed to him through faith, and it is precisely from faith that the Church's social teaching begins. While drawing upon all the contributions made by the sciences and philosophy, her social teaching is aimed at helping everyone on the path of salvation.

The encyclical *Rerum novarum* can be read as a valid contribution to socio-economic analysis at the end of the nineteenth century, but its specific value derives from the fact that it is a document of the Magisterium and is fully a part of the Church's evangelizing mission, together with many other documents of this nature. Thus the Church's *social teaching* is itself a valid *instrument of evangelization*. As such, it proclaims God and his mystery of salvation in Christ to every human being, and for that very reason reveals man to himself. In this light, and only in this light, does it concern itself with everything else: the human rights of the individual, and in particular of the "working class," the family and education, the duties of the State, the ordering of national and international society, economic life, culture, war and peace, and respect for life from the moment of conception until death.

55. The Church receives "the meaning of man" from Divine Revelation. "In order to know man, authentic man, man in his fullness, one must know God," said Pope Paul VI, and he went on to quote Saint Catherine of Siena, who, in prayer, expressed the same idea: "In your nature, O eternal Godhead, I shall know my own nature."[53]

Christian anthropology therefore is really a chapter of theology, and for this reason, the Church's social doctrine, by its concern for man and by its interest in him and in the way he conducts himself in the world, "belongs to the field ... of theology and particularly of moral theology."[54] The theological dimension is needed both for interpreting and solving present-day problems in human society. It is worth noting that this is true in contrast both to the "atheistic" solution, which deprives man of one of his basic dimensions, namely the spiritual one, and to permissive and consumerist solutions, which under various pretexts seek to convince man that he is free from every law and from God himself, thus imprisoning him within a selfishness which ultimately harms both him and others. . . .

II. TOWARDS THE "NEW THINGS" OF TODAY

13. Continuing our reflections, and referring also to what has been said in the Encyclicals *Laborem exercens* and *Sollicitudo rei socialis*, we have to add that the fundamental error of socialism is anthropological in nature. Socialism considers the individual person simply as an element, a molecule within the social organism, so that the good of the individual is completely subordinated to the functioning of the socio-economic mechanism. Socialism likewise maintains that the good of the individual can be realized without reference to his free choice, to the unique and exclusive responsibility which he exercises in the face of good or evil. Man is thus reduced to a series of social relationships, and the concept of the person as the autonomous subject of moral decision disappears, the very subject whose decisions build the social order. From this mistaken conception of the person there arise both a distortion of law, which defines the sphere of the exercise of freedom, and an opposition to private property. A person who is deprived of something he can call "his own," and of the possibility of earning a living through his own initiative, comes to depend on the social machine and on those who control it. This makes it much more difficult for him to recognize his dignity as a person, and hinders progress towards the building up of an authentic human community.

In contrast, from the Christian vision of the human person there necessarily follows a correct picture of society. According to *Rerum novarum* and the whole social doctrine of the Church, the social nature of man is not completely fulfilled in the State, but is realized in various intermediary groups, beginning with the family and including economic, social, political and cultural groups which stem from human nature itself and have their own autonomy, always with a view to the common good. This is what I have called the "subjectivity" of society which, together with the subjectivity of the individual, was cancelled out by "Real Socialism."[55]

If we then inquire as to the source of this mistaken concept of the nature of the person and the "subjectivity" of society, we must reply that its first cause is atheism. It is by responding to the call of God contained in the being of things that man becomes aware of his transcendent dignity. Every individual must give this response, which constitutes the apex of his humanity, and no social mechanism or collective subject can substitute for it. The denial of God deprives the person of his foundation, and consequently leads to a reorganization of the social order without reference to the person's dignity and responsibility.

The atheism of which we are speaking is also closely connected with the rationalism of the Enlightenment, which views human and social reality in a mechanistic way. Thus there is a denial of the supreme insight concerning man's true greatness, his transcendence in respect to earthly realities, the contradiction in his heart between the desire for the fullness of what is good and his own inability to attain it and, above all, the need for salvation which results from this situation. . . .

15. *Rerum novarum* is opposed to state control of the means of production, which would reduce every citizen to being a "cog" in the State machine. It is no less forceful in criticizing a concept of the State which completely excludes the economic sector from the State's range of interest and action. There is certainly a legitimate sphere of autonomy in economic life which the State should not enter. The State, however, has the task of determining the juridical framework within which economic affairs are to be conducted, and thus of safeguarding the prerequisites of a free economy, which presumes a certain equality between the parties, such that one party would not be so powerful as practically to reduce the other to subservience.[56]

In this regard, *Rerum novarum* points the way to just reforms which can restore dignity to work as the free activity of man. These reforms imply that society and the State will both assume responsibility, especially for protecting the worker from the nightmare of unemployment. Historically, this has happened in two converging ways: either through economic policies aimed at ensuring balanced growth and full employment, or through unemployment insurance and retraining programs capable of ensuring a smooth transfer of workers from crisis sectors to those in expansion.

Furthermore, society and the State must ensure wage levels adequate for the maintenance of the worker and his family, including a certain amount for savings. This requires a continuous effort to improve workers' training and capability so that their work will be more skilled and productive, as well as careful controls and adequate legislative measures to block shameful forms of exploitation, especially to the disadvantage of the most vulnerable workers, of immigrants and of those on the margins of society. The role of trade unions in negotiating minimum salaries and working conditions is decisive in this area.

Finally, "humane" working hours and adequate free-time need to be guaranteed, as well as the right to express one's own personality at the work-place without suffering any affront to one's conscience or personal dignity. This is the place to mention once more the role of trade unions, not only in negotiating contracts, but also as "places" where workers can express themselves. They serve the development of an authentic culture of work and help workers to share in a fully human way in the life of their place of employment.[57]

The State must contribute to the achievement of these goals both directly and indirectly. Indirectly and according to the *principle of subsidiarity*, by creating favorable conditions for the free exercise of economic activity, which will lead to abundant opportunities for employment and sources of wealth. Directly and according to the *principle of solidarity*, by defending the weakest, by placing certain limits on the autonomy of the parties who determine working conditions, and by ensuring in every case the necessary minimum support for the unemployed worker.[58]

EVANGELIUM VITAE (THE GOSPEL OF LIFE)

CHAPTER III: YOU SHALL NOT KILL—GOD'S HOLY LAW

"If you would enter life, keep the commandments" (Mt 19:17): Gospel and commandment

52. "And behold, one came up to him, saying, 'Teacher, what good deed must I do, to have eternal life?' " (*Mt* 19:16). Jesus replied, "If you would enter life, keep the commandments" (*Mt* 19:17). The Teacher is speaking about eternal life, that is, a sharing in the life of God himself. This life is attained through the observance of the Lord's commandments, including the commandment "You shall not kill." This is the first precept from the

Decalogue which Jesus quotes to the young man who asks him what commandments he should observe: "Jesus said, 'You shall not kill, you shall not commit adultery, you shall not steal ...'" (*Mt* 19:18).

God's commandment is never detached from his love: it is always a gift meant for man's growth and joy. As such, it represents an essential and indispensable aspect of the Gospel, actually becoming "gospel" itself: joyful good news. The *Gospel of life* is both a great gift of God and an exacting task for humanity. It gives rise to amazement and gratitude in the person graced with freedom, and it asks to be welcomed, preserved and esteemed, with a deep sense of responsibility. In giving life to man, God *demands* that he love, respect and promote life. *The gift* thus *becomes a commandment, and the commandment is itself a gift. . . .*

53. "Human life is sacred because from its beginning it involves 'the creative action of God,' and it remains forever in a special relationship with the Creator, who is its sole end. God alone is the Lord of life from its beginning until its end: no one can, in any circumstance, claim for himself the right to destroy directly an innocent human being."[59] With these words the Instruction *Donum Vitae* sets forth the central content of God's revelation on the sacredness and inviolability of human life.

Sacred Scripture in fact presents the precept "You shall not kill" as a divine commandment (*Ex* 20:13; *Dt* 5:17). As I have already emphasized, this commandment is found in the Decalogue, at the heart of the Covenant which the Lord makes with his chosen people; but it was already contained in the original covenant between God and humanity after the purifying punishment of the Flood, caused by the spread of sin and violence (cf. *Gen* 9:5–6).

God proclaims that he is absolute Lord of the life of man, who is formed in his image and likeness (cf. *Gen* 1:26–28). Human life is thus given a sacred and inviolable character, which reflects the inviolability of the Creator himself. Precisely for this reason God will severely judge every violation of the commandment "You shall not kill," the commandment which is at the basis of all life together in society. He is the "*goel*," the defender of the innocent (cf. *Gen* 4:9–15; *Is* 41:14; *Jer* 50:34; *Ps* 19:14). God thus shows that he does not delight in the death of the living (cf. *Wis* 1:13). Only Satan can delight therein: for through his envy death entered the world (cf. *Wis* 2:24). He who is "a murderer from the beginning," is also "a liar and the father of lies" (*Jn* 8:44). By deceiving man he leads him to projects of sin and death, making them appear as goals and fruits of life.

54. As explicitly formulated, the precept "You shall not kill" is strongly negative: it indicates the extreme limit which can never be exceeded. Implicitly, however, it encourages a positive attitude of absolute respect for

life; it leads to the promotion of life and to progress along the way of a love which gives, receives and serves. The people of the Covenant, although slowly and with some contradictions, progressively matured in this way of thinking, and thus prepared for the great proclamation of Jesus that the commandment to love one's neighbor is like the commandment to love God; "on these two commandments depend all the law and the prophets" (cf. *Mt* 22:36–40). Saint Paul emphasizes that "the commandment ... you shall not kill ... and any other commandment, are summed up in this phrase: 'You shall love your neighbor as yourself'" (*Rom* 13:9; cf. *Gal* 5:14). Taken up and brought to fulfillment in the New Law, the commandment "You shall not kill" stands as an indispensable condition for being able "to enter life" (cf. *Mt* 19:16–19). In this same perspective, the words of the Apostle John have a categorical ring: "Anyone who hates his brother is a murderer, and you know that no murderer has eternal life abiding in him" (1 *Jn* 3:15).

From the beginning, the *living Tradition of the Church*—as shown by the *Didache*, the most ancient non-biblical Christian writing—categorically repeated the commandment "You shall not kill": "There are two ways, a way of life and a way of death; there is a great difference between them.... . In accordance with the precept of the teaching: you shall not kill ... you shall not put a child to death by abortion nor kill it once it is born.... . The way of death is this: ... they show no compassion for the poor, they do not suffer with the suffering, they do not acknowledge their Creator, they kill their children and by abortion cause God's creatures to perish; they drive away the needy, oppress the suffering, they are advocates of the rich and unjust judges of the poor; they are filled with every sin. May you be able to stay ever apart, O children, from all these sins!"[60]

As time passed, the Church's Tradition has always consistently taught the absolute and unchanging value of the commandment "You shall not kill." It is a known fact that in the first centuries, murder was put among the three most serious sins—along with apostasy and adultery—and required a particularly heavy and lengthy public penance before the repentant murderer could be granted forgiveness and readmission to the ecclesial community.

55. This should not cause surprise: to kill a human being, in whom the image of God is present, is a particularly serious sin. *Only God is the master of life!* Yet from the beginning, faced with the many and often tragic cases which occur in the life of individuals and society, Christian reflection has sought a fuller and deeper understanding of what God's commandment prohibits and prescribes.[61] There are in fact situations in which values proposed by God's Law seem to involve a genuine paradox. This happens

for example in the case of *legitimate defense*, in which the right to protect one's own life and the duty not to harm someone else's life are difficult to reconcile in practice. Certainly, the intrinsic value of life and the duty to love oneself no less than others are the basis of *a true right to self-defense.* The demanding commandment of love of neighbor, set forth in the Old Testament and confirmed by Jesus, itself presupposes love of oneself as the basis of comparison: "You shall love your neighbor *as yourself* " (*Mk* 12:31). Consequently, no one can renounce the right to self-defense out of lack of love for life or for self. This can only be done in virtue of a heroic love which deepens and transfigures the love of self into a radical self-offering, according to the spirit of the Gospel Beatitudes (cf. *Mt* 5:38–40). The sublime example of this self-offering is the Lord Jesus himself.

Moreover, "legitimate defense can be not only a right but a grave duty for someone responsible for another's life, the common good of the family or of the state."[62] Unfortunately it happens that the need to render the aggressor incapable of causing harm sometimes involves taking his life. In this case, the fatal outcome is attributable to the aggressor whose action brought it about, even though he may not be morally responsible because of a lack of the use of reason.[63]

56. This is the context in which to place the problem of the *death penalty*. On this matter there is a growing tendency, both in the Church and in civil society, to demand that it be applied in a very limited way or even that it be abolished completely. The problem must be viewed in the context of a system of penal justice ever more in line with human dignity and thus, in the end, with God's plan for man and society. The primary purpose of the punishment which society inflicts is "to redress the disorder caused by the offense."[64] Public authority must redress the violation of personal and social rights by imposing on the offender an adequate punishment for the crime, as a condition for the offender to regain the exercise of his or her freedom. In this way authority also fulfils the purpose of defending public order and ensuring people's safety, while at the same time offering the offender an incentive and help to change his or her behavior and be rehabilitated.[65]

It is clear that, for these purposes to be achieved, *the nature and extent of the punishment* must be carefully evaluated and decided upon, and ought not go to the extreme of executing the offender except in cases of absolute necessity: in other words, when it would not be possible otherwise to defend society. Today however, as a result of steady improvements in the organization of the penal system, such cases are very rare, if not practically non-existent.

In any event, t*he principle set forth in the new* Catechism of the Catholic Church remains valid: "If bloodless means are sufficient to defend human lives against an aggressor and to protect public order and the safety of persons, public authority must limit itself to such means, because they better correspond to the concrete conditions of the common good and are more in conformity to the dignity of the human person."[66]

57. If such great care must be taken to respect every life, even that of criminals and unjust aggressors, the commandment "You shall not kill" has absolute value when it refers to the *innocent person*. And all the more so in the case of weak and defenseless human beings, who find their ultimate defense against the arrogance and caprice of others only in the absolute binding force of God's commandment.

In effect, the absolute inviolability of innocent human life is a moral truth clearly taught by Sacred Scripture, constantly upheld in the Church's Tradition and consistently proposed by her Magisterium. This consistent teaching is the evident result of that "supernatural sense of the faith" which, inspired and sustained by the Holy Spirit, safeguards the People of God from error when "it shows universal agreement in matters of faith and morals."[67]

... The deliberate decision to deprive an innocent human being of his life is always morally evil and can never be licit either as an end in itself or as a means to a good end. It is in fact a grave act of disobedience to the moral law, and indeed to God himself, the author and guarantor of that law; it contradicts the fundamental virtues of justice and charity. "Nothing and no one can in any way permit the killing of an innocent human being, whether a fetus or an embryo, an infant or an adult, an old person, or one suffering from an incurable disease, or a person who is dying. Furthermore, no one is permitted to ask for this act of killing, either for himself or herself or for another person entrusted to his or her care, nor can he or she consent to it, either explicitly or implicitly. Nor can any authority legitimately recommend or permit such an action."[68]

As far as the right to life is concerned, every innocent human being is absolutely equal to all others. This equality is the basis of all authentic social relationships which, to be truly such, can only be founded on truth and justice, recognizing and protecting every man and woman as a person and not as an object to be used. Before the moral norm which prohibits the direct taking of the life of an innocent human being "there are no privileges or exceptions for anyone. It makes no difference whether one is the master of the world or the 'poorest of the poor' on the face of the earth. Before the demands of morality we are all absolutely equal."[69]

... 60. Some people try to justify abortion by claiming that the result of conception, at least up to a certain number of days, cannot yet be considered a personal human life. But in fact, "from the time that the ovum is fertilized, a life is begun which is neither that of the father nor the mother; it is rather the life of a new human being with his own growth. It would never be made human if it were not human already. This has always been clear, and ... modern genetic science offers clear confirmation. It has demonstrated that from the first instant there is established the program of what this living being will be: a person, this individual person with his characteristic aspects already well determined. Right from fertilization the adventure of a human life begins, and each of its capacities requires time—a rather lengthy time—to find its place and to be in a position to act."[70] Even if the presence of a spiritual soul cannot be ascertained by empirical data, the results themselves of scientific research on the human embryo provide "a valuable indication for discerning by the use of reason a personal presence at the moment of the first appearance of a human life: how could a human individual not be a human person?"[71]

Furthermore, what is at stake is so important that, from the standpoint of moral obligation, the mere probability that a human person is involved would suffice to justify an absolutely clear prohibition of any intervention aimed at killing a human embryo. Precisely for this reason, over and above all scientific debates and those philosophical affirmations to which the Magisterium has not expressly committed itself, the Church has always taught and continues to teach that the result of human procreation, from the first moment of its existence, must be guaranteed that unconditional respect which is morally due to the human being in his or her totality and unity as body and spirit: "*The human being is to be respected and treated as a person from the moment of conception*; and therefore from that same moment his rights as a person must be recognized, among which in the first place is the inviolable right of every innocent human being to life."[72]

... "*We must obey God rather than men*" (*Acts* 5:29): *civil law and the moral law*

68. One of the specific characteristics of present-day attacks on human life—as has already been said several times—consists in the trend to demand a *legal justification* for them, as if they were rights which the state, at least under certain conditions, must acknowledge as belonging to citizens. Consequently, there is a tendency to claim that it should be possible to exercise these rights with the safe and free assistance of doctors and medical personnel.

It is often claimed that the life of an unborn child or a seriously disabled person is only a relative good: according to a proportionalist approach, or one of sheer calculation, this good should be compared with and balanced against other goods. It is even maintained that only someone present and personally involved in a concrete situation can correctly judge the goods at stake: consequently, only that person would be able to decide on the morality of his choice. The state therefore, in the interest of civil coexistence and social harmony, should respect this choice, even to the point of permitting abortion and euthanasia.

At other times, it is claimed that civil law cannot demand that all citizens should live according to moral standards higher than what all citizens themselves acknowledge and share. Hence the law should always express the opinion and will of the majority of citizens and recognize that they have, at least in certain extreme cases, the right even to abortion and euthanasia. Moreover the prohibition and the punishment of abortion and euthanasia in these cases would inevitably lead—so it is said—to an increase of illegal practices: and these would not be subject to necessary control by society and would be carried out in a medically unsafe way. The question is also raised whether supporting a law which in practice cannot be enforced would not ultimately undermine the authority of all laws.

Finally, the more radical views go so far as to maintain that in a modern and pluralistic society people should be allowed complete freedom to dispose of their own lives as well as of the lives of the unborn: it is asserted that it is not the task of the law to choose between different moral opinions, and still less can the law claim to impose one particular opinion to the detriment of others.

69. In any case, in the democratic culture of our time it is commonly held that the legal system of any society should limit itself to taking account of and accepting the convictions of the majority. It should therefore be based solely upon what the majority itself considers moral and actually practices. Furthermore, if it is believed that an objective truth shared by all is *de facto* unattainable, then respect for the freedom of the citizens—who in a democratic system are considered the true rulers—would require that on the legislative level the autonomy of individual consciences be acknowledged. Consequently, when establishing those norms which are absolutely necessary for social coexistence, the only determining factor should be the will of the majority, whatever this may be. Hence every politician, in his or her activity, should clearly separate the realm of private conscience from that of public conduct.

As a result we have what appear to be two diametrically opposed tendencies. On the one hand, individuals claim for themselves in the moral sphere the most complete freedom of choice and demand that the State should not adopt or impose any ethical position but limit itself to guaranteeing maximum space for the freedom of each individual, with the sole limitation of not infringing on the freedom and rights of any other citizen. On the other hand, it is held that, in the exercise of public and professional duties, respect for other people's freedom of choice requires that each one should set aside his or her own convictions in order to satisfy every demand of the citizens which is recognized and guaranteed by law; in carrying out one's duties the only moral criterion should be what is laid down by the law itself. Individual responsibility is thus turned over to the civil law, with a renouncing of personal conscience, at least in the public sphere.

70. At the basis of all these tendencies lies the *ethical relativism* which characterizes much of present-day culture. There are those who consider such relativism an essential condition of democracy, inasmuch as it alone is held to guarantee tolerance, mutual respect between people and acceptance of the decisions of the majority, whereas moral norms considered to be objective and binding are held to lead to authoritarianism and intolerance.

But it is precisely the issue of respect for life which shows what misunderstandings and contradictions, accompanied by terrible practical consequences, are concealed in this position.

It is true that history has known cases where crimes have been committed in the name of "truth." But equally grave crimes and radical denials of freedom have also been committed and are still being committed in the name of "ethical relativism." When a parliamentary or social majority decrees that it is legal, at least under certain conditions, to kill unborn human life, is it not really making a "tyrannical" decision with regard to the weakest and most defenseless of human beings? Everyone's conscience rightly rejects those crimes against humanity of which our century has had such sad experience. But would these crimes cease to be crimes if, instead of being committed by unscrupulous tyrants, they were legitimated by popular consensus?

Democracy cannot be idolized to the point of making it a substitute for morality or a panacea for immorality. Fundamentally, democracy is a "system" and as such is a means and not an end. Its "moral" value is not automatic, but depends on conformity to the moral law to which it, like every other form of human behavior, must be subject: in other words, its morality depends on the morality of the ends which it pursues and of the means which it employs. If today we see an almost universal consensus with regard to the value of democracy, this is to be considered a positive "sign of the times," as the Church's Magisterium has frequently noted.[73] But the value of democracy stands or falls with the values which it embodies and promotes. Of course, values such as the dignity of every human person, respect for inviolable and inalienable human rights, and the adoption of the "common good" as the end and criterion regulating political life are certainly fundamental and not to be ignored.

The basis of these values cannot be provisional and changeable "majority" opinions, but only the acknowledgment of an objective moral law which, as the "natural law" written in the human heart, is the obligatory point of reference for civil law itself. If, as a result of a tragic obscuring of the collective conscience, an attitude of skepticism were to succeed in bringing into question even the fundamental principles of the moral law, the democratic system itself would be shaken in its foundations, and would be reduced to a mere mechanism for regulating different and opposing interests on a purely empirical basis.[74]

Some might think that even this function, in the absence of anything better, should be valued for the sake of peace in society. While one acknowledges some element of truth in this point of view, it is easy to see that without an objective moral grounding not even democracy is capable of ensuring a stable peace, especially since peace which is not built upon the values of the dignity of every individual and of solidarity between all people frequently proves to be illusory. Even in participatory systems of government, the regulation of interests often occurs to the advantage of the most powerful, since they are the ones most capable of maneuvering not only the levers of power but also of shaping the formation of consensus. In such a situation, democracy easily becomes an empty word.

71. It is therefore urgently necessary, for the future of society and the development of a sound democracy, to rediscover those essential and innate human and moral values which flow from the very truth of the human being and express and safeguard the dignity of the person: values which no individual, no majority and no state can ever create, modify or destroy, but must only acknowledge, respect and promote.

Consequently there is a need to recover the *basic elements of a vision of the relationship between civil law and moral law*, which are put forward by the Church, but which are also part of the patrimony of the great juridical traditions of humanity.

Certainly *the purpose of civil law* is different and more limited in scope than that of the moral law. But "in no sphere of life can the civil law take the place of conscience or dictate norms concerning things which are outside its competence,"[75] which is that of ensuring the common good of people through the recognition and defense of their fundamental rights, and the promotion of peace and of public morality.[76] The real purpose of civil law is to guarantee an ordered social coexistence in true justice, so that all may "lead a quiet and peaceable life, godly and respectful in every way" (1 *Tim* 2:2). Precisely for this reason, civil law must ensure that all members of society enjoy respect for certain fundamental rights which innately belong to the person, rights which every positive law must recognize and guarantee.

First and fundamental among these is the inviolable right to life of every innocent human being. While public authority can sometimes choose not to put a stop to something which—were it prohibited—would cause more serious harm,[77] it can never presume to legitimize as a right of individuals—even if they are the majority of the members of society—an offense against other persons caused by the disregard of so fundamental a right as the right to life. The legal toleration of abortion or of euthanasia can in no way claim to be based on respect for the conscience of others, precisely because society has the right and the duty to protect itself against the abuses which can occur in the name of conscience and under the pretext of freedom.[78]

In the Encyclical *Pacem in Terris,* John XXIII pointed out that "it is generally accepted today that the common good is best safeguarded when personal rights and duties are guaranteed. The chief concern of civil authorities must therefore be to ensure that these rights are recognized, respected, coordinated, defended and promoted, and that each individual is enabled to perform his duties more easily. For 'to safeguard the inviolable rights of the human person, and to facilitate the performance of his duties, is the principal duty of every public authority.' Thus any government which refused to recognize human rights or acted in violation of them, would not only fail in its duty; its decrees would be wholly lacking in binding force."[79]

72. The doctrine on the necessary *conformity of civil law with the moral law* is in continuity with the whole tradition of the Church. This is clear once more from John XXIII's Encyclical: "Authority is a postulate of the moral order and derives from God. Consequently, laws and decrees enacted in contravention of the moral order, and hence of the divine will, can have no binding force in conscience; … indeed, the passing of such laws undermines the very nature of authority and results in shameful abuse."[80] This is the clear teaching of Saint Thomas Aquinas, who writes that "human law is law inasmuch as it is in conformity with right reason and thus derives from the eternal law. But when a law is contrary to reason, it is called an unjust law; but in this case it ceases to be a law and becomes instead an act of violence."[81] And again: "Every law made by man can be called a law insofar as it derives from the natural law. But if it is somehow opposed to the natural law, then it is not really a law but rather a corruption of the law."[82]

Now the first and most immediate application of this teaching concerns a human law which disregards the fundamental right and source of all other rights which is the right to life, a right belonging to every individual. Consequently, laws which legitimize the direct killing of innocent human beings through abortion or euthanasia are in complete opposition to the inviolable right to life proper to every individual; they thus deny the equality of everyone before the law. It might be objected that such is not the case in euthanasia, when it is requested with full awareness by the person involved. But any state which made such a request legitimate and authorized it to be carried out would be legalizing a case of suicide-murder, contrary to the fundamental principles of absolute respect for life and of the protection of every innocent life. In this way the State contributes to lessening respect for life and opens the door to ways of acting which are destructive of trust in relations between people. Laws which authorize and promote abortion and euthanasia are therefore radically opposed not only to the good of the individual but also to the common good; as such they are completely lacking in authentic juridical validity. Disregard for the right to life, precisely because it leads to the killing of the person whom society exists to serve, is what most directly conflicts with the possibility of achieving the common good. Consequently, a civil law authorizing abortion or euthanasia ceases by that very fact to be a true, morally binding civil law.

73. Abortion and euthanasia are thus crimes which no human law can claim to legitimize. There is no obligation in conscience to obey such laws; instead there is a *grave and clear obligation to oppose them by conscientious objection.* From the very beginnings of the Church, the apostolic preaching reminded Christians of their duty to obey legitimately constituted public authorities (cf. *Rom* 13:7; 1 *Pet* 2:13–14), but at the same time it firmly warned that "we must obey God rather than men" (*Acts* 5:29). In the Old Testament, precisely in regard to threats against life, we find a significant example of resistance to the unjust command of those in authority. After Pharaoh ordered the killing of all newborn males, the Hebrew midwives refused. "They did not do as the king of Egypt commanded them, but let the male children live" (*Ex* 1:17). But the ultimate reason for their action should be noted: *"the midwives feared God"* (*ibid.*). It is precisely from obedience to God—to whom alone is due that fear which is acknowledgment of his absolute sovereignty—that the strength and the courage to resist unjust human laws are born. It is the strength and the courage of those prepared even to be imprisoned or put to the sword, in the certainty that this is what makes for "the endurance and faith of the saints" (*Rev* 13:10).

In the case of an intrinsically unjust law, such as a law permitting abortion or euthanasia, it is therefore never licit to obey it, or to "take part in a propaganda campaign in favor of such a law, or vote for it."[83]

A particular problem of conscience can arise in cases where a legislative vote would be decisive for the passage of a more restrictive law, aimed at limiting the number of authorized abortions, in place of a more permissive law already passed or ready to be voted on. Such cases are not infrequent. It is a fact that while in some parts of the world there continue to be campaigns to introduce laws favoring abortion, often supported by powerful international organizations, in other nations—particularly those which have already experienced the bitter fruits of such permissive legislation— there are growing signs of a rethinking in this matter. In a case like the one just mentioned, when it is not possible to overturn or completely abrogate a pro-abortion law, an elected official, whose absolute personal opposition to procured abortion was well known, could licitly support proposals aimed at limiting the harm done by such a law and at lessening its negative consequences at the level of general opinion and public morality. This does not in fact represent an illicit cooperation with an unjust law, but rather a legitimate and proper attempt to limit its evil aspects.

74. The passing of unjust laws often raises difficult problems of conscience for morally upright people with regard to the issue of cooperation, since they have a right to demand not to be forced to take part in morally evil actions. Sometimes the choices which have to be made are difficult; they may require the sacrifice of prestigious professional positions or the relinquishing of reasonable hopes of career advancement. In other cases, it can happen that carrying out certain actions, which are provided for by legislation that overall is unjust, but which in themselves are indifferent, or even positive, can serve to protect human lives under threat. There may be reason to fear, however, that willingness to carry out such actions will not only cause scandal and weaken the necessary opposition to attacks on life, but will gradually lead to further capitulation to a mentality of permissiveness.

In order to shed light on this difficult question, it is necessary to recall the general principles concerning *cooperation in evil actions*. Christians, like all people of good will, are called upon under grave obligation of conscience not to cooperate formally in practices which, even if permitted by civil legislation, are contrary to God's law. Indeed, from the moral standpoint, it is never licit to cooperate formally in evil. Such cooperation occurs when an action, either by its very nature or by the form it takes in a concrete situation, can be defined as a direct participation in an act against innocent human life or a sharing in the immoral intention of the person committing it. This cooperation can never be justified either by invoking respect for the freedom of others or by appealing to the fact that civil law permits it or requires it. Each individual in fact has moral responsibility for the acts which he personally performs; no one can be exempted from this responsibility, and on the basis of it everyone will be judged by God himself (cf. *Rom* 2:6; 14:12).

To refuse to take part in committing an injustice is not only a moral duty; it is also a basic human right. Were this not so, the human person would be forced to perform an action intrinsically incompatible with human dignity, and in this way human freedom itself, the authentic meaning and purpose of which are found in its orientation to the true and the good, would be radically compromised. What is at stake therefore is an essential right which, precisely as such, should be acknowledged and protected by civil law. In this sense, the opportunity to refuse to take part in the phases of consultation, preparation and execution of these acts against life should be guaranteed to physicians, health-care personnel, and directors of hospitals, clinics and convalescent facilities. Those who have recourse to conscientious objection must be protected not only from legal penalties but also from any negative effects on the legal, disciplinary, financial and professional plane.

"You shall love your neighbor as yourself" (*Lk* 10:27): *"promote"* life

75. God's commandments teach us the way of life. *The negative moral precepts*, which declare that the choice of certain actions is morally unacceptable, have an absolute value for human freedom: they are valid always and everywhere, without exception. They make it clear that the choice of certain ways of acting is radically incompatible with the love of God and with the dignity of the person created in his image. Such choices cannot be redeemed by the goodness of any intention or of any consequence; they are irrevocably opposed to the bond between persons; they contradict the fundamental decision to direct one's life to God.[84]

In this sense, the negative moral precepts have an extremely important positive function. The "no" which they unconditionally require makes clear the absolute limit beneath which free individuals cannot lower themselves. At the same time they indicate the minimum which they must respect and from which they must start out in order to say "yes" over and over again, a "yes" which will gradually embrace the *entire horizon of the good* (cf. *Mt* 5:48). The commandments, in particular the negative moral precepts, are the beginning and the first necessary stage of the journey towards freedom. As Saint Augustine writes, "the beginning of freedom is to be free from crimes ... like murder, adultery, fornication, theft, fraud, sacrilege and so forth. Only when one stops committing these crimes (and no Christian should commit them), one begins to lift up one's head towards freedom. But this is only the beginning of freedom, not perfect freedom."[85]

76. The commandment "You shall not kill" thus establishes the point of departure for the start of true freedom. It leads us to promote life actively, and to develop particular ways of thinking and acting which serve life. In this way we exercise our responsibility towards the persons entrusted to us

and we show, in deeds and in truth, our gratitude to God for the great gift of life (cf. *Ps* 139:13–14).

The Creator has entrusted man's life to his responsible concern, not to make arbitrary use of it, but to preserve it with wisdom and to care for it with loving fidelity. The God of the Covenant has entrusted the life of every individual to his or her fellow human beings, brothers and sisters, according to the law of reciprocity in giving and receiving, of self-giving and of the acceptance of others. In the fullness of time, by taking flesh and giving his life for us, the Son of God showed what heights and depths this law of reciprocity can reach. With the gift of his Spirit, Christ gives new content and meaning to the law of reciprocity, to our being entrusted to one another. The Spirit who builds up communion in love creates between us a new fraternity and solidarity, a true reflection of the mystery of mutual self-giving and receiving proper to the Most Holy Trinity. The Spirit becomes the new law which gives strength to believers and awakens in them a responsibility for sharing the gift of self and for accepting others, as a sharing in the boundless love of Jesus Christ himself.

77. This new law also gives spirit and shape to the commandment "You shall not kill." For the Christian it involves an absolute imperative to respect, love and promote the life of every brother and sister, in accordance with the requirements of God's bountiful love in Jesus Christ. "He laid down his life for us; and we ought to lay down our lives for the brethren" (1 *Jn* 3:16).

The commandment "You shall not kill," even in its more positive aspects of respecting, loving and promoting human life, is binding on every individual human being. It resounds in the moral conscience of everyone as an irrepressible echo of the original covenant of God the Creator with mankind. It can be recognized by everyone through the light of reason and it can be observed thanks to the mysterious working of the Spirit who, blowing where he wills (cf. *Jn* 3:8), comes to and involves every person living in this world.

It is therefore a service of love which we are all committed to ensure to our neighbor, that his or her life may be always defended and promoted, especially when it is weak or threatened. It is not only a personal but a social concern which we must all foster: a concern to make unconditional respect for human life the foundation of a renewed society.

We are asked to love and honor the life of every man and woman and to work with perseverance and courage so that our time, marked by all too many signs of death, may at last witness the establishment of a new culture of life, the fruit of the culture of truth and of love.[86]

NOTES

1. ["Books by and about John Paul II," LucidCafe Website, http://www.lucidcafe. com/library/96may/johnpaul.html.]

2. Cf. John Paul II., Encyclical Letter *Redemptoris missio*, 1: *AAS* 83 (1991), 249–340.

3. Cf. Second Vatican Council, Decree *Ad gentes* and Declaration *Nostra aetate*; cf. also Paul VI Apostolic Exhortation *Evangelii nuntiandi*: *AAS* 68 (1976), 5–76; John Paul II, Encyclical Letter *Redemptoris Missio*.

4. Second Vatican Council, Dogmatic Constitution *Dei verbum*, 2.

5. *Ibid.*, 4.

6. *Ibid.*, 5. [Referring to Second Vatican Council, *Dei verbum*, 4.]

7. *Ibid.*

8. Cf. *Catechism of the Catholic Church*, 144.

9. *Ibid.*, 150.

10. *Ibid.*, 153.

11. *Ibid.*, 178.

12. John Paul II, Encyclical Letter *Fides et ratio*, 13.

13. Cf. *ibid.*, 31–32.

14. Second Vatican Council, Dogmatic Constitution *Lumen gentium*, 5.

15. *Ibid.*, 1.

16. *Ibid.*, 4. Cf. St. Cyprian, *De Dominica oratione* 23: *CCSL* 3/A, 105.

17. Second Vatican Council, Dogmatic Constitution *Lumen gentium*, 3.

18. Cf. *ibid.*, 9; cf. also the prayer addressed to God found in the *Didache* 9,4: *SC* 248, 176: "May the Church be gathered from the ends of the earth into your kingdom" and *ibid.* 10, 5: *SC* 248, 180: "Remember, Lord, your Church ... and, made holy, gather her together from the four winds into your kingdom which you have prepared for her."

19. John Paul II, Encyclical Letter *Redemptoris missio*, 18; cf. Apostolic Exhortation *Ecclesia in Asia*, 17: *L'Osservatore Romano* (November 7, 1999). The kingdom is so inseparable from Christ that, in a certain sense, it is identified with him (cf. Origen, *In Mt. Hom.*, 14, 7: *PG* 13, 1197; Tertullian, *Adversus Marcionem*, IV, 33, 8: *CCSL* 1, 634.

20. Second Vatican Council, Dogmatic Constitution *Lumen gentium*, 14; cf. Decree *Ad gentes*, 7; Decree *Unitatis redintegratio*, 3.

21. John Paul II, Encyclical Letter *Redemptoris missio*, 9; cf. *Catechism of the Catholic Church*, 846–847. [*Dominus Iesus*: On the Unicity and Salvific Universality of Jesus Christ and the Church (2000), Official Vatican Website, http://www. vatican.va/roman_curia/congregations/cfaith/documents/rc_con_cfaith_doc_ 20000806_dominus-iesus_en.html.]

22. [*Instruction on Certain Aspects of the "Theology of Liberation"* (6 August 1984) (Pretoria, South Africa: Southern African Catholic Bishops' Conference, 1984), 3–4, 19–20.]

23. Cf. *Libertatis Nuntius*, VII, 9; VIII, 1–9: *AAS* 76 (1984), pp. 892 and 894–895.

24. Cf. *Gen* 1, 26.

25. John Paul II, Encyclical *Redemptor Hominis*, 21: *AAS* 71 (1979), p. 316.

26. Cf. *Rom* 6, 6; 7, 23.

27. Cf. *Gen* 2, 18. 23 [*sic*], "It is not good that man should be alone" … "This is flesh of my flesh and bone of my bones": in these words of Scripture, which refer directly to the relationship between man and woman, one can discern a more universal meaning. Cf. *Lev* 19, 18.

28. Cf. John XXIII, Encyclical *Pacem in Terris*, 5–15: *AAS* 55 (1963), pp. 259–265; John Paul II, *Letter to Dr Kurt Waldheim, Secretary General of the United Nations, on the occasion of the Thirtieth Anniversary of the Universal Declaration on Human Rights: AAS* 71 (1979), p. 122; *The Pope's Speech to the United Nations*, 9: *AAS* 71 (1979), p. 1149.

29. Cf. *Gen* 1, 27–28.

30. Cf. John Paul II, Encyclical *Redemptor Hominis*, 15: *AAS* 71 (1979), p. 286.

31. Cf. *Gaudium et Spes*, 13 §1.

32. Cf. John Paul II, Apostolic Exhortation *Reconciliatio et Paenitentia*, 13: *AAS* 77 (1985), pp. 208–211.

33. Cf. *Gen* 3, 16–19; *Rom* 5, 12; 7, 14–24; PAUL VI, *Sollemnis Professio Fidei*, 30 June 1968, 16: *AAS* 60.

34. Cf. *Rom* 1, 18–32.

35. Cf. *Jer* 5, 23; 7, 24; 17, 9; 18, 12.

36. Cf. St. Augustine, *De Civitate Dei*, XIV, 28 (*PL* 41, 435; *CSEL* 40/2, 56–57; *CCL* 14/2, 451–452).

37. [*Instruction on Christian Freedom and Liberation* (22 March 1986) (Washington, D.C.: United States Catholic Conference, 1986), 15–24.]

38. Cf. Apostolic Exhortation *Familiaris Consortio* (22 November 1981), 6: *AAS* 74 (1982), p. 88: "… history is not simply a fixed progression towards what is better, but rather an event of freedom, and even a struggle between freedoms. …"

39. For this reason the word "development" was used in the Encyclical rather than the word "progress," but with an attempt to give the word "development" its fullest meaning.

40. Encyclical Letter *Populorum Progressio*, 19, *loc. cit.*, pp. 266f.: "Increased possession is not the ultimate goal of nations or of individuals. All growth is ambivalent. . . . The exclusive pursuit of possessions thus becomes an obstacle to individual fulfillment and to man's true greatness … both for nations and for individual men, avarice is the most evident form of moral underdevelopment"; cf. also Paul VI, Apostolic Letter *Octogesima Adveniens* (14 May 1971), 9: *AAS* 63 (1971), pp. 407f.

41. Cf. Pastoral Constitution on the Church in the Modern World *Gaudium et Spes*, 35; Paul VI, Address to the Diplomatic Corps (7 January 1965): *AAS* 57 (1965), p. 232.

42. Cf. Encyclical Letter *Populorum Progressio*, 20–21: *loc. cit.*, pp. 267 f.

43. Second Vatican Ecumenical Council, Dogmatic Constitution on the Church *Lumen Gentium*, 1.

44. Cf. for example, St Basil the Great, *Regulae fusius tractatae, interrogatio* XXX-VII, 1–2: *PG* 31, 1009–1012; Theodoret of Cyr, *De Providentia, Oratio* VII: *PG* 83, 665–686; St Augustine, *De Civitate Dei*, XIX, 17: *CCL* 48, 683–685.

45. Cf. for example, St John Chrysostom, *In Evang. S. Matthaei, hom.* 50, 3–4: *PG* 58, 508–510; St Ambrose, *De Officiis Ministrorum*, lib. II, XXVIII, 136–140: *PL* 16, 139–141; St Possidius, *Vita s. Augustini Episcopi*, XXIV: *PL* 32, 53 f.

46. Encyclical Letter *Populorum Progressio*, 23: *loc. cit.*, p. 268: " 'If someone who has the riches of this world sees his brother in need and closes his heart to him, how does the love of God abide in him?' (1 Jn 3:17). It is well known how strong were the words used by the Fathers of the Church to describe the proper attitude of persons who possess anything towards persons in need." In the previous number, the Pope had cited No. 69 of the Pastoral Constitution *Gaudium et Spes* of the Second Vatican Ecumenical Council.

47. Cf. Encyclical Letter *Populorum Progressio*, 47: "... a world where freedom is not an empty word and where the poor man Lazarus can sit down at the same table with the rich man."

48. Cf. *ibid.*, 47: "It is a question, rather, of building a world where every man, no matter what his race, religion or nationality, can live a fully human life, freed from servitude imposed on him by other men ..."; cf. also Second Vatican Ecumenical Council, Pastoral Constitution on the Church in the Modern World *Gaudium et Spes*, 29. Such *fundamental equality* is one of the basic reasons why the Church has always been opposed to every form of racism.

49. [*Sollicitudo Rei Socialis* (1987) (Washington D.C.: United States Catholic Conference, 1988), 47–53, 57–64.]

50. Encyclical Letter *Rerum Novarum: loc. cit.*, 107.

51. Cf. Encyclical Letter *Redemptor Hominis*, 13: *loc. cit.*, 283.

52. *Ibid.*, 14: *loc. cit.*, 284f.

53. Paul VI, Homily at the Final Public Session of the Second Vatican Ecumenical Council (December 7, 1965): *AAS* 58 (1966), 58.

54. Encyclical Letter *Sollicitudo Rei Socialis*, 41: *loc cit.*, 571.

55. Cf. Encyclical Letter *Sollicitudo Rei Socialis*, 15, 28: *loc. cit.*, 530; 548ff.

56. Cf. Encyclical Letter *Rerum Novarum: loc. cit.*, 121–125.

57. Cf. Encyclical Letter *Laborem Exercens*, 20: *loc. cit.*, 629–632; Discourse to the International Labor Organization (I.L.O.) in Geneva (June 15, 1982): *Insegnamenti* V/2 (1982), 2250–2266; Paul VI, Discourse to the same Organization (June 10, 1969): *AAS* 61 (1969), 491–502.

58. Cf. Encyclical Letter *Laborem Exercens*, 8: *loc. cit.*, 594–598. [*Centesimus Annus* (1991), http://www.vatican.va/edocs/eng0214/_index.htm.]

59. Congregation for the Doctrine of the Faith, Instruction on Respect for Human Life in its Origin and on the Dignity of Procreation *Donum Vitae* (February 22, 1987), Introduction, no. 5: *AAS* 80 (1988), 76–77; cf. *Catechism of the Catholic Church*, no. 2258.

60. *Didache*, I, 1; II, 1–2; V, 1 and 3: *Patres Apostolici*, ed. F.X. Funk, I, 2–3, 6–9, 14–17; cf. *Letter of Pseudo-Barnabas*, XI, 5: *loc. cit.*, 90–93.

61. Cf. *Catechism of the Catholic Church*, nos. 2263–2269; cf. also *Catechism of the Council of Trent* III, 327–332.

62. *Catechism of the Catholic Church*, no. 2265.

63. Cf. Saint Thomas Aquinas, *Summa Theologiae*, II–II, q. 64, a. 7; Saint Alphonsus De'Liguori, *Theologia Moralis*, I, III, tr. 4, c.1, dub. 3.

64. *Catechism of the Catholic Church*, no. 2266.

65. Cf. *ibid.*

66. No. 2267.

67. Second Vatican Ecumenical Council, Dogmatic Constitution on the Church *Lumen Gentium*, 12.

68. Congregation for the Doctrine of the Faith, Declaration on Euthanasia *Iura et Bona* (May 5, 1980), II: *AAS* 72 (1980), 546.

69. John Paul II, Encyclical Letter *Veritatis Splendor* (August 6, 1993), 96: *AAS* 85 (1993), 1209.

70. Congregation for the Doctrine of the Faith, Declaration on Procured Abortion (18 November 1974), nos. 12–13: *AAS* 66 (1974), 738.

71. Congregation for the Doctrine of the Faith, Instruction on Respect for Human Life in its Origin and on the Dignity of Procreation *Donum Vitae* (February 22, 1987), I, no. 1: *AAS* 80 (1988), 78–79.

72. *Ibid., loc. cit.*, 79.

73. Cf. John Paul II, Encyclical Letter *Centesimus Annus* (May 1, 1991), 46: *AAS* 83 (1991), 850; Pius XII, Christmas Radio Message (December 24, 1944): *AAS* 37 (1945), 10–20.

74. Cf. John Paul II, Encyclical Letter *Veritatis Splendor* (August 6, 1993), 97 and 99: *AAS* 85 (1993), 1209–1211.

75. Congregation for the Doctrine of the Faith, Instruction on Respect for Life in its Origin and on the Dignity of Procreation *Donum Vitae* (February 22, 1987), III: *AAS* 80 (1988), 98.

76. Cf. Second Vatican Ecumenical Council, Declaration on Religious Freedom *Dignitatis Humanae*, 7.

77. Cf. Saint Thomas Aquinas, *Summa Theologiae* I–II, q. 96, a. 2.

78. Cf. Second Vatican Ecumenical Council, Declaration on Religious Freedom *Dignitatis Humanae*, 7.

79. Encyclical Letter *Pacem in Terris* (April 11, 1963), II: *AAS* 55 (1963), 273–274. The internal quote is from Pius XII Radio Message of Pentecost 1941 (June 1, 1941): *AAS* 33 (1941), 200. On this topic, the Encyclical cites: Pius XI, Encyclical Letter *Mit brennender Sorge* (March 14, 1937): *AAS* 29 (1937), 159; Encyclical Letter *Divini Redemptoris* (March 19, 1937), III: *AAS* 29 (1937), 79; Pius XII, Christmas Radio Message (December 24, 1942): *AAS* 35 (1943), 9–24.

80. Encyclical Letter *Pacem in Terris* (April 11, 1963), II: *loc. cit.*, 271.

81. *Summa Theologiae*, I–II, q. 93, a.3, ad 2um.

82. *Ibid.*, I–II, q. 95, a.2. Aquinas quotes Saint Augustine: "Non videtur esse lex, quae iusta non fuerit," *De Libero Arbitrrio*, I, 5, 11: PL 32, 1227.

83. Congregation for the Doctrine of the Faith, *Declaration on Procured Abortion* (November 18, 1974), no. 22: *AAS* 66 (1974), 744.

84. Cf. *Catechism of the Catholic Church,* nos. 1753–1755; John Paul II, Encyclical Letter *Veritatis Splendor* (August 6, 1993), 81–82: *AAS* 85 (1993), 1198–1199.

85. *In Iohannis Evangelium Tractatus*, 41, 10: *CCL* 36, 3 63; cf. John Paul II, Encyclical Letter *Veritatis Splendor* (August 6, 1993), 13: *AAS* 85 (1993), 1144.

86. [*Evangelium vitae* (1991) (Washington, D.C.: United States Catholic Conference, 1995), 57–103, 107–108, 124–140.]

The Protestant Tradition

[CHAPTER 8]

Abraham Kuyper (1837–1920)

SELECTED AND EDITED BY NICHOLAS P. WOLTERSTORFF

Abraham Kuyper was born in Maassluis near Rotterdam in 1837 to a Dutch Reformed minister and a former schoolteacher; he died at The Hague in 1920. He was an astonishing polymath and an organizational genius. He was origi- nally an ordained minister in the Dutch Reformed Church; in 1892, he became one of the founders of a new denomination, the Gereformeerde Kerken in Ned- erland. He was the founder of a nationwide society to promote the formation and funding of Calvinist day schools (1878), the founder of the Free University of Amsterdam (1880), a professor of theology in the Free University for some twenty years (1880–1901), and rector of the university on several occasions. He was the chief editor for almost fifty years of the daily newspaper De Standaard *and of its weekly supplement,* De Heraut. *He was the founder (1879) and ac- knowledged leader until his death of the first mass political party in the Neth- erlands, the Anti-Revolutionary Party. He served as a member of the Dutch Parliament on two occasions and as prime minister of the Netherlands from 1901 to 1905. In addition to all this he was, throughout his adult life, a writer of devotional literature, of theological treatises, of social and cultural analyses, and of an astonishing number of "tracts for the occasion," as well as being an extraordinarily gifted and busy platform speaker and lecturer.*

CONFIDENTIALLY (CONFIDENTIE)

I WAS ENTRUSTED with a congregation to which I came not primarily to give out of what I possessed but with the quiet prayer that my empty heart would be quickened and fed by the life of the church. For many days that hope was disappointed. The circles in which I moved were (with some ex- ceptions) characterized by a rigid conservatism, orthodox in appearance but without the genuine glow. . . . Everybody was content with the way things went. . . . I heard that there was a small group of malcontents in the flock, but the rumors about these know-it-alls were more for ill than good. They were a bunch of cantankerous, proud eccentrics who "make life miserable for every minister." Besides, most of them were of such low social status that it was deemed best not to worry about them but to ignore them, just as previous ministers had done.

But I found it impossible to do so. Thus, with a trembling heart that befits a young minister who has to face such fires, I knocked in the course of my visitations on the doors of these "fanatics" too. The reception that awaited me was far from cordial. . . . Nonetheless, these simple, if somewhat irritated, souls did not repel me. For here, I realized, was more than mere routine. Here was conviction. Here the topics of conversation went beyond the nice weather and who happened to be ill and who had dismissed his workman. Here was interest in spiritual matters. Moreover, here was knowledge. With the meager Bible knowledge I had picked up at the university I could not measure up to these simple folk. And not just knowledge of the Bible but also of a well-ordered worldview, be it of the old Reformed type. . . . All this made me come back, and that in turn won their welcome. And so the debate began.

It was soon over. Of course I did my best to maintain my ministerial honor but despite myself I felt more inclined to listen than to speak during these encounters. And somehow I noticed that, after such a meeting, the preaching on Sunday went better. Yet it annoyed me that these people were so inflexible. Having shown so much sensitivity myself, I felt I could rightfully claim a more flexible response. But no, never even a hint of budging. I observed that they were not intent on winning my sympathy but on the triumph of their cause. They knew of no compromise or concession, and more and more I found myself confronted with a painful choice: either sharply resist them or unconditionally join them in a principled recognition of "full sovereign grace"—as they called it. . . . Well, dear brother, I did not oppose them and I still thank God that I made that choice. Their unremitting perseverance has become the blessing of my heart, the rise of the morning star for my life. . . .

Yet, you can see, they didn't give me enough. . . . Their world of thought was literally still rooted in the days immediately following the Reformation. Where could I find help?[1]

LECTURES ON CALVINISM

CALVINISM AS A LIFE SYSTEM

Clearness of presentation demands that in this first lecture I begin by fixing the *conception* of Calvinism *historically*. [After dismissing a few conceptions as too narrow, Kuyper continues.] Historically, the name of Calvinism indicates the channel in which the Reformation moved, so far as it was neither Lutheran, nor Anabaptist nor Socinian. . . . Thus understood, Calvinism is rooted in a form of religion which was peculiarly its own, and from this specific religious consciousness there was developed first a peculiar theology, then a special church-order, and then a given form for political and social life, for the interpretation of the moral world-order, for the relation between nature and grace, between Christianity and the world, between church and state, and finally for art and science; and amid all these life-utterances it remained always the self-same Calvinism, in so far as simultaneously and spontaneously all these developments sprang from its deepest life-principle. Hence to this extent it stands in line with those other great *complexes* of human life, known as Paganism, Islamism and Romanism... .[2]

The supreme interest here at stake, however, forbids our accepting without more positive proof the fact that Calvinism really provides us with such an unity of life-system. . . . Hence we must first ask what are the required conditions for such general systems of life, as Paganism, Islamism, Romanism and Modernism, and then show that Calvinism really fulfils these conditions.

These conditions demand in the first place, that from a special principle a peculiar insight be obtained into the three fundamental relations of all human life, viz, 1. our relation *to God*, 2. our relation *to man*, and 3. our relation *to the world*.

Calvinism ... does not seek God *in* the creature, as Paganism, it does not *isolate* God *from* the creature, as Islamism; it posits no *mediate communion* between God and the creature, as does Romanism; but proclaims the exalted thought that, although standing in high majesty above the creature, God enters *into immediate fellowship with the creature*, as God the Holy Spirit. . . .

This brings us of itself to the second condition, with which, for the sake of creating a life system every profound movement has to comply: viz., a fundamental interpretation of its own touching *the relation of man to man.* . . . There is no uniformity among men, but endless multiformity. In creation itself the difference has been established between woman and man. Physical and spiritual gifts and talents cause one person to differ from the other. Past generations and our own personal life create distinctions. The social position of the rich and poor differs widely. Now, these differences are in a special way *weakened* or *accentuated* by every consistent life system. . . .

Modernism, which denies and abolishes every difference, cannot rest until it has made woman man and man woman, and, putting every distinction on a common level, kills life by placing it under the ban of uniformity. . . . In the same way Calvinism has derived from *its* fundamental relation to God a peculiar interpretation of man's relation to man. . . . If Calvinism places our entire human life immediately before God, then it follows that all men or women, rich or poor, weak or strong, dull or talented, as creatures of God, and as lost sinners, have no claim whatsoever to lord over one another, and that we stand as equals before God, and consequently equal as man to man. Hence we cannot recognize any distinction among men, save such as has been imposed by God Himself, in that He gave one authority over the other, or enriched one with more talents than the other, in order that the man of more talents should serve the man with less, and in him serve his God. Hence Calvinism condemns not merely all open slavery and systems of caste, but also all covert slavery of woman and of the poor; it is opposed to all hierarchy among men; it tolerates no aristocracy save such as is able, either in person or in family, by the grace of God, to exhibit superiority of character or talent, and to show that it does not claim this superiority for self-aggrandizement or ambitious pride, but for the sake of spending it in the service of God. So Calvinism was bound to find its utterance in the democratic interpretation of life; to proclaim the liberty of nations; and not to rest until both politically and socially every man, simply because he is man, should be recognized, respected and dealt with as a creature created after the Divine likeness. . . .

The third fundamental relation which decides the interpretation of life is the relation which you bear *to the world*. . . . Of Paganism it can be said in general, that it places *too high* an estimate upon the world, and therefore to some extent it both stands in fear of, and loses itself in it. On the other hand Islamism places *too low* an estimate upon the world, makes sport of it and triumphs over it in reaching after the visionary world of a sensual paradise. . . . Under the hierarchy of Rome the Church and the World were placed over against each other, the one as being sanctified and the other as being still under the curse. Everything outside the Church was under the influence of demons, and exorcism banished this demoniacal power from everything that came under the protection, influence and inspiration of the Church. Hence in a Christian country the entire social life was to be covered by the wings of the Church. . . . This was a gigantic effort to claim the entire world for Christ but one which of necessity brought with it the severest judgment upon every life-tendency which either as heretical or as demoniacal withdrew itself from the blessing of the Church. . . .

Thus making its appearance in a dualistic social state Calvinism has wrought an entire change in the world of thoughts and conceptions. In this also, placing itself before the face of God, it has not only honored *man* for the sake of his likeness to the Divine image, but also *the world* as a Divine creation, and has at once placed to the front the great principle that there is a *particular grace* which works Salvation, and also a *common grace* by which God, maintaining the life of the world, relaxes the curse which rests upon it, arrests its process of corruption, and thus allows the untrammeled development of our life in which to glorify Himself as Creator. Thus the Church receded in order to be neither more nor less than the congregation of believers, and in every department the life of the world was not emancipated from God, but from the dominion of the Church. . . . Henceforth the curse should no longer rest upon the *world* itself, but upon that which is *sinful* in it, and instead of monastic flight *from* the world the duty is now emphasized of serving God in the world, in every position in life. . . .

Thus it is shown that Calvinism has a sharply-defined starting-point of its own for the three fundamental relations of all human existence: viz., our relation to *God*, to *man* and to the *world*. . . . This justifies us fully in our statement that Calvinism duly answers the three above named conditions, and thus is incontestably entitled to take its stand by the side of Paganism, Islamism, Romanism and Modernism, and to claim for itself the glory of possessing a well-defined principle and an all-embracing life-system.[3]

CALVINISM AND RELIGION

Of course, religion, as such produces *also* a blessing for man, but it does not exist for the sake of man. It is not God who exists for the sake of His creation;—the creation exists for the sake of God. For, as the Scripture says, He has created all things for Himself. . . .

Just as the entire creation reaches its culminating point in man, so also religion finds its clear expression only in man who is made in the image of God, and this not because man seeks it, but because God Himself implanted in man's nature the real essential religious expression, by means of the "seed of religion" (*semen religionis*) as Calvin defines it, sown in our human heart.

God Himself *makes* man religious by means of the *sensus divinitatis*, i.e., the sense of the Divine, which He causes to strike the chords on the harp of his soul. A sound of need interrupts the pure harmony of this divine melody, but only in consequence of sin. In its original form, in its natural condition, religion is exclusively a sentiment of *admiration* and *adoration*, which elevates and unites, not a feeling of dependence which severs and depresses. . . . The starting-point of every motive in religion is God and not Man. Man is the instrument and means, God alone is here the goal, the point of departure and the point of arrival, the fountain from which the waters flow, and at the same time, the ocean into which they finally return. . . .

This leads me naturally, to the ... question: Is religion *partial*, or it is all-subduing, and comprehensive,—*universal* in the strict sense of the word? Now if the aim of religion be found in man himself and if its realization be made dependent on clerical mediators, religion cannot be but *partial*. In that case it follows logically that every man confines his religion to those occurrences of his life by which his religious needs are stirred, and to those cases in which he finds human intervention at his disposal. The partial character of this sort of religion shows itself in three particulars: in the religious *organ* through which, in the *sphere* in which, and in the *group of persons* among which, religion has to thrive and flourish.

Recent controversy affords a pertinent illustration of the first limitation. The wise men of our generation maintain that religion has to retire from the precinct of the human intellect. It must seek to express itself either by means of the mystical feelings, or else by means of the practical will. Mystical and ethical inclinations are hailed with enthusiasm, in the domain of religion, but in that same domain the intellect, as leading to metaphysical hallucinations, must be muzzled. Metaphysics and Dogmatics are increasingly tabooed. . . .

[Thus] religion is excluded from science, and its authority from the domain of public life; henceforth the inner chamber, the cell for prayer, and the secrecy of the heart should be its exclusive dwelling place. . . . And the result is that, in many different ways, religion, once the central force of human life, is now placed alongside of it. . . .

This brings us naturally to the third characteristic note of this partial view of religion;—religion as pertaining not to all, but only to *the group of pious people* among our generation. Thus the limitation of the *organ* of religion brings about the limitation of its *sphere*, and the limitation of its sphere consequently brings about the limitation of its group or *circle* among men. . . . It so happens that the great bulk of the people are almost devoid of mystical feeling, and energetic strength of will. . . .

Now this whole view of the matter is squarely antagonized by Calvinism, which vindicates for religion its full universal character, and its complete universal application. If everything that is, exists for the sake of God, then it follows that the whole creation must give glory to God. The sun, moon, and stars in the firmament, the birds of the air, the whole of Nature around us, but, above all, man himself, who, priestlike, must consecrate to God the whole of creation, and all life thriving in it. And although sin has deadened a large part of creation to the glory of God, the demand,—the ideal, remains unchangeable, that *every* creature must be immersed in the stream of religion, and end by lying as a religious offering on the altar of the Almighty. A religion confined to feeling or will is therefore unthinkable to the Calvinist.

The sacred anointing of the priest of creation must reach down to his beard and to the hem of his garment. His whole being, including all his abilities and powers, must be pervaded by the *sensus divinitatis*, and how then could he exclude his rational consciousness, —the *logos which* is in him, —the light of thought which comes from God Himself to irradiate him? ...

The same character of universality was claimed by the Calvinist for the *sphere* of religion and its *circle* of influence among men. Everything that has been created was, in its creation, furnished by God with an unchangeable law of its existence. And because God has fully ordained such laws and ordinances for all life, therefore the Calvinist demands that all life be consecrated to His service, in strict obedience. A religion confined to the closet, the cell, or the church, therefore, Calvin abhors. . . . No sphere of human life is conceivable in which religion does not maintain its demands that God shall be praised, that God's ordinances shall be observed, and that every *labora* shall be permeated with its *ora* in fervent and ceaseless prayer. . . . Consequently, it is impossible for a Calvinist to confine religion to a single group, or to some circles among men. Religion concerns the whole of our human race. . . . To be sure there is a concentration of religious light and life in the Church, but then in the walls of this church, there are wide open windows, and through these spacious windows the light of the Eternal has to radiate over the whole world. Here is a city, set upon a hill, which every man can see afar off. . . . And even he who does not yet imbibe the higher light, or maybe shuts his eyes to it, is nevertheless admonished, with equal emphasis, and in all things, to give glory to the name of the Lord. . . . [4]

This brings us, without any further transition, to our fourth main question, *viz.*, Must religion be *normal* or abnormal, i.e., *soteriological*? The distinction which I have in mind here is concerned with the question, whether in the matter of religion we must reckon *de facto* with man in his present condition as *normal* or as having fallen into sin, and having therefore become *abnormal*. In the latter case religion must necessarily assume a soteriological character. Now the prevailing idea, at present, favors the view that religion has to start from man as being *normal*. Not of course as though our race as a whole should conform already to the highest religious norm. This nobody affirms. . . . As a matter of fact, we meet with much irreligiousness, and imperfect religious development continues to be the rule. But precisely in this slow and gradual progress from the lowest forms to the highest ideals, the development demanded by this normal view of religion contends that it has found confirmation. . . .

Now, this whole theory is opposed by that other and entirely different theory, which, without denying the preformation of so much that is human,

in the animal ... nevertheless maintains that the first man was created in perfect relation to his God, *i.e.*, as imbued by a pure and genuine religion, and
consequently explains the many low, imperfect and absurd forms of religion
found in Paganism, not as the result of his creation but as the outcome of his
Fall. These low and imperfect forms of religion are not to be understood as a
process that leads from a lower to a higher, but as a lamentable degeneration.
. . . Now in the choice between these two theories Calvinism allows no hesitation. . . . Every attempt to explain sin, as an incomplete stage on the road to
perfection, aroused his wrath, as an insult to the majesty of God.

What now does the Calvinist mean by his faith in the ordinances of
God?[5] Nothing less than the firmly rooted conviction that all life has first
been in the *thoughts* of God, before it came to be realized in *Creation*.
Hence all created life necessarily bears in itself a law for its existence, instituted by God Himself. There is no life outside us in Nature, without such
divine ordinances,—ordinances which are called the laws of Nature; —a
term which we are willing to accept, provided we understand thereby, not
laws originating *from* Nature, but laws imposed *upon* Nature. So, there are
ordinances of God for the firmament above, and ordinances for the earth
below. . . . These ordinances are the servants of God. Consequently there
are ordinances of God for our bodies. . . . And even so are there ordinances
of God, in Logic, to regulate our thoughts; ordinances of God for our imagination, in the domain of aesthetics; and so, also, strict ordinances of God
for the whole of human life in the *domain of morals*. . . . And those ordinances of God, ruling both the mightiest problems and the smallest trifles,
are urged upon us, not like the statutes of a law-book, not like rules which
may be read from paper, not like a codification of life, which could even for
a single moment, exercise any authority of itself, —but they are urged upon
us as the constant will of the Omnipresent and Almighty God. . . .

Thence it follows that the true Calvinist adjusts himself to these ordinances not by force, as though they were a yoke of which he would like
to rid himself, but with the same readiness with which we follow a guide
through the desert, recognizing that *we* are ignorant of the path, which the
guide knows, and therefore acknowledging that there is no safety but in
closely following in his footsteps. When our respiration is disturbed, we try
irresistibly and immediately to remove the disturbance. . . . Just so, in every
disturbance of the moral life the believer has to strive as speedily as possible to restore his spiritual respiration, according to the moral commands
of his God, because only after this restoration can the inward life again
thrive freely in his soul, and renewed energetic action become possible.
Therefore every distinction between general moral ordinances, and more
special *Christian* commandments is unknown to him. Can we imagine that
at one time God willed to rule things in a certain moral order, but that now,

in Christ, He wills to rule it otherwise? ... Verily Christ has swept away the dust with which man's sinful limitations had covered up this world-order, and has made it glitter again in its original brilliancy. Verily Christ and He alone has disclosed to us the eternal love of God, which was, from the beginning, the moving principle of this world order. Above all, Christ has strengthened in us the ability to walk in this world-order with a firm, unfaltering step. But the world-order itself remains just what it was from the beginning. It lays full claim, not only to the believer (as though less were required from the unbeliever), but to every human being and to all human relationships. . . . [6]

ENCYCLOPEDIA OF SACRED THEOLOGY: ITS PRINCIPLES

SUBJECT AND OBJECT

In the conception of science the root-idea of *to know* must be sharply maintained. And the question arises: Who is the *subject* of this knowledge, and what is the *object*? Each of us knows innumerable things which lie entirely outside of the realm of science. . . . Science is not the sum-total of what A knows, neither is it the aggregate of what A, B and C know. The subject of science cannot be this man or that, but must be man*kind* at large, or, if you please, *the* human consciousness. And the content of knowledge already known by this human consciousness is so immeasurably great, that the most learned and the most richly endowed mind can never know but a very small part of it. Consequently you cannot attain unto a conception of "science" in the higher sense, until you take humanity as an organic whole. Science does not operate atomistically. . . . No, science works organically, i.e. in the sense that the thirst for knowledge lies in human nature; that within certain bounds human nature can obtain knowledge; that the impulse to devote oneself to this task, together with the gifts which enable one to work at it, become apparent of themselves; and that in the realm of intellectual pursuits these coryphaei of our race, without perceiving it and almost unconsciously, go to work according to a plan by which humanity at large advances. . . .

If the subject of science, i.e. the subject that wants to know and that acquires knowledge, lies in the consciousness of humanity, the *object* of science must be *all existing things*, as far as they have discovered their existence to our human consciousness, and will hereafter discover it or leave it to be inferred. . . . This object, as such, could never constitute the material of science for man, if it existed purely atomistically, or if it could only be atomistically known. . . . For the idea of science implies, that from the manifold things I know a *connected* knowledge is born, which would not be possible if there were no relation among the several parts of the object. The necessity of organic inter-relations, which was found to be indispensable in the subject, repeats itself in the object. . . . As long as something is merely *discovered*, it is taken up into our knowledge but not into our science. Only when the inference and the subsequent insight that the parts of the object are organically related prove themselves correct, is that distinction born between the special and the general which learns to recognize in the general the uniting factor of the special. . . .

Even yet enough has not been said. It is not sufficient that the subject of science, i.e. the human consciousness, lives organically in thinking individuals, and that the *object*, about which thinking man wants to know everything he can, exists organically in its parts; but there must also be an organic relation between this subject and this object. This follows already from what was said above, viz. that the subject itself, as well as the thinking of the subject, become objects of science. If there were no organic relation between everything that exists outside of us and ourselves, our consciousness included, the relation in the object would be wanting. But this organic relation between our person and the object of science is much more necessary, in order to render the *science* of the object possible for us. . . .

Thus for all science a threefold organic relation between subject and object is necessary. There must be an organic relation between that object and our *nature*, between that object and our *consciousness*, and between that object and our *world of thought*. . . .

By saying that our *consciousness* stands in the desired organic relation to the object of our science, we simply affirm that it is possible for man to have an apprehension, a perception, and an impression of the existence and of the method of existence of the object. . . . Perception and observation are simply impossible when all organic relation is wanting between any object and our consciousness. . . .

By this, however, this object has not yet been introduced into the world of our *thought*, and without further aid it would still lie outside of our "science. . . ."

[For] there are qualities belonging to the object which lie beyond the reach of the organs of sense, and therefore refuse all representation of themselves. . . . If science means that our human consciousness shall take up into itself what exists as an organic whole, it goes without saying that she makes no progress whatever by the simple presentation of the elements; and that she can achieve her purpose only when, in addition to a fairly complete presentation of the *elements*, she also comes to a fairly complete study of their *relations*. . . . That these relations can be grasped by thought alone and not by presentation lies in their nature. . . .

Thus understood, *science* presents itself to us *as a necessary and ever-continued impulse in the human mind to reflect within itself the cosmos, plastically as to its elements, and to think it through logically as to its relations; always with the understanding that the human mind is capable of this by reason of its organic affinity to its object. . . .*[7]

Suppose that no disturbance by sin had taken place in the subject or object, we should arrive by way of recapitulation at the following conclusion: The *subject* of science is the universal ego in the universal human consciousness; the *object* is the cosmos. This subject and object each exists *organically*, and an organic *relation* exists between the two. Because the *ego* exists dichotomically, i.e. psychically as well as somatically, our consciousness has two fundamental forms, which lead to *representations* and to *conceptions*; while in the object we find the corresponding distinction between *elements* and *relations*. And it is in virtue of this correspondence that science leads to an understanding of the cosmos, both as to its elements and relations. . . .

In this state of things, the *universality* and *necessity*, which are the indispensable characteristics of our knowledge of the cosmos if it is to bear the scientific stamp, would *not* have clashed with our subjectivism. Though it is inconceivable that in a sin*less* development of our race all individuals would have been uniform repetitions of the self-same model; ... yet in the absence of a disturbance, this multiformity would have been as *harmonious*, as now it works *unharmoniously*. With mutual supplementation there would have been no conflict. And there would have been no desire on the part of one individual subject to push other subjects aside, or to transform the object after itself. . . .

SCIENCE AND SIN

If there were no sin, nor any of its results, the subjectivity of A would merely be a variation of the subjectivity in B. In virtue of the organic affinity between the two, their subjectivity would not be mutually antagonistic, and the sense of one would harmoniously support and confirm the sense of the other. . . . But, alas, such is not the case in the domain of science. It is all too often evident, that in this domain the natural harmony of subjective expression is hopelessly broken; and for the feeding of skepticism this want of harmony has no equal. By an investigation of self and of the cosmos you have obtained a well-founded scientific conviction, but when you state it, it meets with no response from those who, in their way, have investigated with equally painstaking efforts; and not only is the unity of science broken, but you are shaken in the assurance of your conviction. For when you spoke your conviction, you did not mean simply to give expression to the insight of your own *ego*, but to the universal human insight; which, indeed, it ought to be, if it were wholly accurate.

But of necessity we must accept this hard reality, and in every theory of knowledge which is not to deceive itself, the fact of sin must henceforth claim a more serious consideration. . . .

It by no means follows, that you should skeptically doubt all science, but simply that it will not do to omit the fact of sin from your theory of knowledge. This would not be warranted if sin were only a thelematic conception and therefore purely ethic; how much less, now, since immediately as well as mediately, sin modifies so largely all those data with which you have to deal in the intellectual domain and in the building-up of your *science*. Ignorance wrought by sin is the most difficult obstacle in the way of all true science.[8]

CALVINISM AND POLITICS

In order that the influence of Calvinism on our political development may be felt, it must be shown, for what fundamental political conceptions Calvinism has opened the door, and how these political conceptions sprang from its root principle.

This dominating principle was not, soteriologically, justification by faith, but, in the widest sense cosmologically, *the Sovereignty of the Triune God over the whole Cosmos*, in all its spheres and kingdoms, visible and invisible. A *primordial* Sovereignty which eradiates in mankind in a threefold deduced supremacy, *viz.* 1. The Sovereignty in the *State*; 2. The Sovereignty in *Society*; and 3. The Sovereignty in the *Church*. . . .

First then a deduced Sovereignty in that political sphere, which is defined as *the State*. . . . The impulse to form states arises from man's social nature, which was expressed already by Aristotle, when he called man a *zoon politikon*. . . . Man is created from man, and by virtue of his birth he is organically united with the whole race. Together we form *one humanity*. . . . The conception of *States*, however, which subdivide the earth into continents, and each continent into morsels, does not harmonize with this idea. Then only would the organic unity of our race be realized politically, if *one State* could embrace all the world, and if the whole of humanity were associated in one world-empire. Had sin not intervened, no doubt, this would actually have been so. . . . The mistake of the Alexanders, and of the Augusti, and of the Napoleons was not, that they were charmed with the thought of the *One World-empire*, but it was this—that they endeavored to realize this idea notwithstanding that the force of sin had dissolved our unity. . . .

For indeed without sin there would have been neither magistrate nor state-order; but political life, in its entirety, would have evolved itself, after a patriarchal fashion, from the life of the family. Neither bar of justice, nor police nor army, nor navy is conceivable in a world without sin; and thus every rule and ordinance and law would drop away, even as all control and assertion of the power of the magistrate would disappear, were life to develop itself, normally and without hindrance, from its own organic impulse. Who binds up, where nothing is broken? Who uses crutches, where the limbs are sound?

Every State formation, every assertion of the power of the magistrate, every mechanical means of compelling order and of guaranteeing a safe course of life is therefore always something unnatural; something, against which the deeper aspirations of our nature rebel; and which, on this very account, may become the source both of a dreadful abuse of power, on the part of those who exercise it, and of a contumacious revolt on the part the multitude. . . . And thus all true conception of the nature of the State and of the assumption of authority by the magistrate, and on the other hand all true conception of the right and duty of the people to defend liberty, depend on what Calvinism has here placed in the foreground, as the primordial truth—*that God has instituted the magistrates, by reason of sin.*

In this one thought are hidden both the *light-side* and the *shady-side* of the life of the State. . . . These magistrates rule mechanically and do not harmonize with our nature. And this authority of government is exercised by sinful *men,* and is therefore subject to all manner of despotic ambitions. But the *light-side* also, for a sinful humanity, without division in states, without law and government, and without ruling authority, would be a veritable hell on earth. . . . Calvinism has therefore, by its deep conception of sin, laid bare the true root of state-life, and has taught us two things: First—that we have gratefully to receive, from the hand of God, the institution of the State with its magistrates, as a means of preservation, now indeed indispensable. And on the other hand also that, by virtue of our natural impulse, we must ever watch against the danger, which lurks, for our personal liberty, in the power of the State. . . .

No man has the right to rule over another man, otherwise such a right necessarily, and immediately becomes, *the right of the strongest.* . . .

Nor can a group of men, by contract, from their own right, compel you to obey a fellow-man. What binding force is there for me in the allegation, that ages ago one of my progenitors made a "Contrat Social," with other men of that time? As man I stand, free and bold, over against the most powerful of my fellow-men.

I do not speak of the family, for here organic, natural ties rule; but in the sphere of the State I do not yield or bow down to anyone, who is man, as I am.

Authority over men cannot arise from men. . . . And thus to the first Calvinistic thesis that *sin alone has necessitated the institution of governments*, this second and no less momentous thesis is added that: *all authority of governments on earth, originates from the Sovereignty of God alone.* When God says to me, "obey," then I humbly bow my head, without compromising in the least my personal dignity, as a man. For, in like proportion as you degrade yourself, by bowing low to a child of man, whose breath is in his nostrils; so, on the other hand do you raise yourself, if you submit to the authority of the Lord of heaven and earth.

Thus the word of Scripture stands: "By Me kings reign," or as the apostle has elsewhere declared: "The powers, that be, are ordained of God. Therefore he that resisteth the power, withstandeth the ordinance of God." The magistrate is an instrument of "common grace," to thwart all license and outrage and to shield the good against the evil. But he is more. Besides all this he is instituted by God as *His* Servant, in order that he may preserve the glorious work of God, in the creation of humanity, from total destruction. Sin attacks God's handiwork, God's plan, God's justice, God's honor, as the supreme Artificer and Builder. Thus God, ordaining the powers that be, in order that, through their instrumentality, He might maintain *His* justice against the strivings of sin, has given to the magistrate the terrible right of life and death. Therefore all the powers that be, whether in empires or in republics, in cities or in states, rule *"by the grace of God."* For the same reason justice bears a holy character. And from the same motive every citizen is bound to obey, not only from dread of punishment, but for the sake of conscience. . . .

Therefore in opposition both to the atheistic popular-sovereignty of the Encyclopedians, and the pantheistic state-sovereignty of German philosophers, the Calvinist maintains the sovereignty of God, as the source of all authority among men. . . . [Calvinism] teaches us to look upward from the existing law to the source of the eternal Right in God, and it creates in us the indomitable courage incessantly to protest against the unrighteousness of the law in the name of this highest Right. . . .

So much for the sovereignty of the State. We now come to *sovereignty in the sphere of Society.*[9]

In a Calvinistic sense we understand hereby, that the family, the business, science, art and so forth are all social spheres, which do not owe their existence to the State, and which do not derive the law of their life from the superiority of the state, but obey a high authority within their own bosom; an authority which rules, by the grace of God, just as the sovereignty of the State does. . . .

In this independent character a special *higher authority* is of necessity involved and this highest authority we intentionally call—*sovereignty in the individual social spheres*, in order that it may be sharply and decidedly expressed that these different developments of social life have *nothing above themselves but God*, and that the State cannot intrude here, and has nothing to command in their domain. As you feel at once, this is the deeply interesting question of our *civil liberties*.

It is here of the highest importance sharply to keep in mind the difference in grade between the *organic* life of society and the *mechanical* character of the government. Whatever among men originates directly from creation, is possessed of all the data for its development, in human nature as such. You see this at once in the family and in the connection of blood relations and other ties ... which dominate the whole of family-life. In all this there is nothing mechanical. The development is spontaneous, just as that of the stem and the branches of a plant. True, sin here also has exerted its disturbing influence and has distorted much which was intended for a blessing, into a curse. But this fatal efficiency of sin has been stopped by common grace. . . .

The same may be said of the other spheres of life.

Nature about us may have lost the glory of paradise ... [yet] the chief aim of all human effort remains, what it was by virtue of our creation and before the fall—namely *dominion over nature*. And this dominion cannot be acquired, except by the exercise of the powers, which, by virtue of the ordinances of creation, are innate in nature itself. Accordingly all Science is only the application to the cosmos of the powers of investigation and thought, created within us; and Art is nothing but the natural productivity of the potencies of our imagination. When we admit therefore that sin, though arrested by "common grace," has caused many modifications of these several expressions of life ... we still maintain that the fundamental character of these expressions remains as it was originally. All together they form the life of creation, in accord with the ordinances of creation, and therefore are *organically* developed.

But the case is wholly different with the assertion of the powers of government. For though it be admitted that even without sin the need would have asserted itself of combining the many families, in a higher unity; this unity would have *internally* been bound up in the Kingship of God, which would have ruled regularly; directly and harmoniously in the hearts of all men, and which would *externally* have incorporated itself in a patriarchal hierarchy. Thus no States would have existed, but only one organic world-empire, with God as its King; exactly what is prophesied for the future which awaits us, when all sin shall have disappeared.

But it is exactly this, which sin has now eliminated from our human life. This unity does no longer exist. . . . Thus peoples and nations originated. These peoples formed States. And over these States God appointed *governments*. And thus, if I may be allowed the expression, it is not a natural head, which organically grew from the body of the people, but a *mechanical* head, which from without has been placed upon the trunk of the nation. A mere remedy therefore, for a wrong condition supervening. A stick placed beside the plant to hold it up, since without it, by reason of its inherent weakness, it would fall to the ground. . . .

According to the apostolic testimony the magistrate bears the sword, and this sword has a threefold meaning. It is the sword of *justice*, to mete out corporeal punishment to the criminal. It is the sword of *war* to defend the honor and the rights and the interests of the State against its enemies. And it is the sword of *order*, to thwart at home all forcible rebellion. . . .

The highest duty of the government remains therefore unchangeably that of *justice*, and in the second place it has to care for the people as an unit, partly *at home*, in order that its unity may grow ever deeper and may not be disturbed, and partly *abroad*, lest the national existence suffer harm. The consequence of all this is that on the one hand, in a people, all sorts of *organic* phenomena of life arise, from its *social* spheres, but that, high above all these, the *mechanical* unifying force of the government is observable. From this arises all friction and clashing. For the government is always inclined, with its *mechanical* authority, to invade social life, to subject it and mechanically to arrange it. But on the other hand social life always endeavors to shake off the authority of the government. . . . It will be admitted that all healthy life of people or state has ever been the historical consequence of the struggle between these two powers. It was the so-called "constitutional government," which endeavored more firmly to regulate the mutual relation of these two. And in this struggle Calvinism was the first to take its stand. For just in proportion as it honored the authority of the magistrate, instituted by God, did it lift up that *second sovereignty*, which had been implanted by God in the social spheres, in accordance with the ordinances of creation.

It demanded for both independence in their own sphere and regulation of the relation between both, not by the executive, but *under the law*. And by this stern demand, Calvinism may be said to have generated constitutional public law, from its own fundamental idea. . . .

The idea is here fundamental therefore that the sovereignty of God, in its descent upon men, separates itself into two spheres. On the one hand the mechanical sphere of *State-authority*, and on the other hand the organic sphere of the authority of the *Social circles*. And in both these spheres the inherent authority is sovereign, that is to say, it has above itself nothing but God.

Now for the mechanically coercing authority of the government any further explanation is superfluous, not so, however, for the organic social authority.

Nowhere is the dominating character of this organic social authority more plainly discernable than in the sphere of Science. . . . The dominion of men like Aristotle and Plato, Lombard and Thomas, Luther and Calvin, Kant and Darwin, extends, for each of them, over a field of ages. Genius is a *sovereign* power; it forms schools; it lays hold on the spirits of men, with irresistible might; and it exercises an immeasurable influence on the whole condition of human life. This sovereignty of genius is a gift of God, possessed only by His grace. It is subject to no one and is responsible to Him alone Who has granted it this ascendancy. . . .

In relation herewith, and on entirely the same ground of organic superiority, there exists, side by side with this personal sovereignty, the sovereignty of *the sphere*. The University exercises scientific dominion; the Academy of fine arts is possessed of art-power; the guild exercised a technical dominion; the trades-union rules over labor; —and each of these spheres or corporations is conscious of the power of exclusive independent judgment and authoritative action, within its proper sphere of operation. Behind these organic spheres, with intellectual, aesthetical and technical sovereignty, the sphere of the family opens itself, with its right of marriage, domestic peace, education and possession; and in this sphere also the natural head is conscious of exercising an inherent authority, —not because the government allows it, but because God has imposed it. . . .

In all these [various] spheres the State-government cannot impose its laws, but must reverence the innate law of life. God rules in these spheres, just as supremely and sovereignly through his chosen *virtuosi*, as He exercises dominion in the sphere of the State itself, through his chosen *magistrates*.

Bound by its own mandate therefore the government may neither ignore nor modify nor disrupt the divine mandate, under which these social spheres stand. The sovereignty, by the grace of God, of the government is here set aside and limited, for God's sake, by another sovereignty, which is equally divine in origin. Neither the life of science nor of art, nor of agriculture, nor of industry, nor of commerce, nor of navigation, nor of the family, nor of human relationship may be coerced to suit itself to the grace of the government. The State may never become an octopus, which stifles the whole of life. It must occupy its own place, on its own root, among all the other trees of the forest, and thus it has to honor and maintain every form of life, which grows independently, in its own sacred autonomy.

Does this mean that the government has no right *whatever* of interference in these autonomous spheres of life? Not at all.

It possesses the threefold right and duty: 1. Whenever different spheres clash, to compel mutual regard for the boundary-lines of each; 2. To defend individuals and the weak ones, in those spheres, against the abuse of power of the rest; and 3. To coerce all together to bear *personal* and *financial* burdens for the maintenance of the natural unity of the State. The decision cannot, however, in these cases, *unilaterally* rest with the magistrate. The Law here has to indicate the rights of each, and the rights of the citizens over their own purses must remain the invincible bulwark against the abuse of power on the part of the government. . . .

Calvinism is to be praised for having built a dam across [state absolutism] not by appealing to popular force, nor to the hallucination of human greatness, but by deducing those rights and liberties of social life from the same source, from which the high authority of the government flows—even the *absolute sovereignty of God*. From this *one* source, in God, *sovereignty in the individual sphere*, in the family and in every social circle, is just as directly derived as the *supremacy of State-authority*. These two must therefore come to an understanding, and both have the same sacred obligation to maintain their God-given sovereign authority and to make it subservient to the majesty of God.

A people therefore which abandons to State Supremacy the right of the family, or a University which abandons to it the rights of science, is just as guilty before God, as a nation which lays its hands upon the rights of the magistrates. And thus the struggle for liberty is not only declared permissible, but is made a duty for each individual in his own sphere. . . .

Now let us put the theory itself to the test and look successively at the duty of the magistrate in things spiritual: 1. towards *God*, 2. towards the *Church*, and 3. towards *individuals*. As regards the first point, the magistrates are and remain—"God's servants." They have to recognize God as Supreme Ruler, from Whom they derive their power. They have to serve God, by ruling the people according to *His* ordinances. They have to restrain blasphemy, where it directly assumes the character of an affront to the Divine Majesty. And God's supremacy is to be recognized, by confessing His name in the Constitution as the Source of all political power, by maintaining the Sabbath, by proclaiming days of prayer and thanksgiving, and by invoking His Divine blessing.

Therefore in order that they may govern, according to His holy ordinances, every magistrate is in duty bound to investigate the rights of God, both in the natural life and in His Word. Not to subject himself to the decision of any church, but in order that he himself may catch the light which he needs for the knowledge of the Divine will. And as regards blasphemy, the *right* of the magistrate to restrain it rests in the God-consciousness innate in every man; and the *duty* to exercise this right flows from the fact that God is the Supreme and Sovereign Ruler over every State and over every Nation. But for this very reason the fact of blasphemy is only then to be deemed established, when the intention is apparent contumaciously to affront this majesty of God *as Supreme Ruler of the State*. What is then punished is not the religious offence, nor the impious sentiment, but the attack upon the foundation of public law, upon which both the State and its government are resting.

Meanwhile there is in this respect a noteworthy difference between States which are absolutely governed by a monarch and States which are governed constitutionally; or in a republic, in a still wider range, by an extensive assembly. . . .

But whether you are dealing with the will of a single individual, or with the will of many men, in a decision arrived at by a vote, the principal thing remains that the government has to judge and to decide independently. Not as an appendix to the Church, nor as its pupil. The sphere of State stands itself under the majesty of the Lord. In that sphere therefore an independent responsibility to God is to be maintained. The sphere of the State is not profane. But both Church and State must, each in their own sphere, obey God and serve His honor. And to that end in either sphere *God's Word* must rule, but in the sphere of the State only through the conscience of the persons invested with authority. The first thing of course is, and remains, that all nations shall be governed in a Christian way; that is to say, in accordance with the principle which, for all statecraft, flow from the Christ. But this can never be realized except through the subjective convictions of those in authority, according to their personal views of the demands of that Christian principle, as regards the public service.

Of an entirely different nature is the second question, what ought to be the relation between the government and the *visible Church*. . . . Nearly all nations begin with unity of religion. But it is equally natural that this unity is split up, where the individual life, in the process of development, gains in strength, and where multiformity asserts itself, as the undeniable demand of a richer development of life. And thus we are confronted with the fact that the visible church has been split up, and that in no country whatever the absolute unity of the visible church can be any longer maintained.

What then is the duty of the government?

Must it—for the question may be reduced to this—must it now form an individual judgment, as to which of those many churches is the true one? And must it maintain this one over against the others? Or is it the duty of the government to suspend its own judgment and to consider the multiform complex of all these denominations, as the totality of the manifestation of the Church of Christ on earth?

From a Calvinistic standpoint we must decide in favor of the latter suggestion. Not from a false idea of neutrality, nor as if Calvinism could ever be indifferent to what is true and what false, *but because the government lacks the data of judgment*, and because every magisterial judgment here infringes the *sovereignty of the Church*. . . .

Hence it is that the Calvinists have always struggled so proudly and courageously for the liberty, that is to say for the sovereignty, of the Church, within her own sphere, in distinction from the Lutheran theologians. In Christ, they contended, the Church has her own King. Her position in the State is not assigned her by the permission of the Government, but *jure divino*. She has her own organization. She possesses her own office-bearers. And in a similar way she has her own gifts to distinguish truth from the lie. It is therefore her privilege, and not that of the State, to determine her own characteristics as the true Church, and to proclaim her own confession, as the confession of the truth. . . .

But this can in no regard break the fundamental rule that the government must honor the complex of Christian churches, as the multiform manifestation of the Church of Christ on earth. That the magistrate has to respect the liberty, *i.e.*, the sovereignty of the Church of Christ in the individual sphere of these churches. That churches flourish most richly, when the government allows them to live from their own strength on the voluntary principle. . . . Only the system of a free Church, in a free State, may be honored from a Calvinistic standpoint. . . .

Of an entirely different nature, on the contrary, is the last question, to which I referred, namely the duty of the government, as regards the *sovereignty of the individual person*.

In the second part of this lecture I have already indicated that the developed man also possesses an individual sphere of life, with sovereignty in his own circle. . . .

(In some respect every man is a sovereign, for everybody must have and has, a sphere of life of his own, in which he has no one above him, but God alone.) I do not point to this to over-estimate the importance of conscience, for whosoever wishes to liberate conscience, where God and His Word are concerned, I meet as an opponent, not as an ally. This however does not prevent my maintaining the sovereignty of conscience, as the palladium of all personal liberty, in this sense—that conscience is never subject to man but always and ever to God Almighty.

This need of the personal liberty of conscience, however, does not immediately assert itself. It does not express itself with emphasis in the child, but only in the mature man; and in the same way it mostly slumbers among undeveloped peoples, and is irresistible only among highly developed nations. A man of ripe and rich development will rather become a voluntary exile, will rather suffer imprisonment, nay even sacrifice life itself, than tolerate constraint in the forum of his conscience. And the deeply rooted repugnance against the Inquisition, which for three long centuries would not be assuaged, grew up from the conviction that its practices violated and assaulted human life in man. This imposes on the government a twofold obligation. In the first place, it must cause this liberty of conscience to be respected by the Church; and in the second place, it must give way itself to the sovereign conscience.

As regards the first, the sovereignty of the Church find its natural limitation in the sovereignty of the free personality. Sovereign within her own domain, she has no power over those who live outside of that sphere. And wherever, in violation of this principle, transgression of power may occur, the government has to respect the claims on protection of every citizen. The Church may not be forced to tolerate as a member one whom she feels obliged to expel from her circle; but on the other hand no citizen of the State must be compelled to remain in a church which his conscience forces him to leave.

Meantime what the government in this respect demands of the churches, it must practice itself, by allowing to each and every citizen liberty of conscience, as the primordial and inalienable right of all men.

It has cost a heroic struggle to wrest this greatest of all human liberties from the grasp of despotism; and streams of human blood have been poured out before the object was attained. But for this very reason every son of the Reformation tramples upon the honor of the fathers, who does not assiduously and without retrenching, defend this palladium of our liberties. In order that it may be able to rule *men*, the government must respect this deepest ethical power of our human existence. A nation, consisting of citizens whose consciences are bruised, is itself broken in its national strength. . . .

In the French Revolution a civil liberty for every Christian *to agree with the unbelieving majority*; in Calvinism, a liberty of conscience, which enables every man to serve God, *according to his own conviction and the dictates of his own heart.*[10]

COMMON GRACE

There is neither doubt nor uncertainty about the situation that followed the fall. On the one hand, Scripture vividly pictures it to us; on the other, it continues in part to this day and can therefore be read from what we see and hear all around us. We have noted before that this newly inaugurated situation did not correspond to what had been predicted as the consequence of sin. Death, in its full effect, did not set in on that day, and Reformed theologians have consistently pointed out how in this non-arrival of what was prophesied for ill we see the emergence of a saving and long-suffering grace. Nor was this the first manifestation of grace, for human life in Paradise was inconceivable without an environing and invasive grace. To every rational creature grace is the air he breathes. But now for the first time this divine grace assumes its character as saving grace in which, inasmuch as we are sinners, we first and most naturally recognize the grace of God. . . .

This manifestation of grace served ultimately not to save us but to bring out the glory of the Divine Being, and only in the second place, as the consequence of this end, to snatch us from our self-sought ruin. This manifestation of grace consisted in restraining, blocking, or redirecting the consequences that would otherwise have resulted from sin. It intercepts the natural outworking of the poison of sin and either diverts and alters it or opposes and destroys it. For that reason we must distinguish two dimensions in this manifestation of grace: 1. a *saving* grace, which in the end abolishes sin and completely undoes its consequences; and 2. a *temporal restraining* grace, which holds back and blocks the effect of sin. The former, that is saving grace, is in the nature of the case *special* and restricted to God's elect. The second, *common* grace, is extended to the whole of our human life. The question then arises whether these two forms of grace, this *special* and this *common* grace, exist independently side-by-side or operate in connection with each other, and if so, how. . . . The connection is ... undeniable, but how are we to construe it? ...

Certainly; there is nothing wrong in saying that everything happens for Christ's sake, that therefore the *body of Christ* is the all-controlling and central element in history, and that on this basis the church of Christ is the pivot on which the life of humanity hinges. Those who overlook or deny this reality will never find any unity in the course of history. For them century follows century, and in the process development follows decline and regression progression, but the stream of life as a whole is not going anywhere, has no goal. This life lacks a center, a pivot on which it turns. . . . The Reformed confession—which maintains that all things, also in this world, aim at the Christ, that his Body is the key component, and that in this sense one can say the church of Christ forms the center of world history—offers a basis for a view of history far superior to the common one. So we will think twice before we will detract in any way from this confession. Not *common* grace but the order of *special grace* prevails.

But this thesis leads to a purer confession only if you respect the *order*. All things exist *for the sake of Christ* and only as a corollary for his *Body* and the *Church*—hence not for *you* and then for the *Church* and so also for the *Body* of Christ and finally for the *Christ*. No: Christ, by whom all things exist including ourselves, is before all things. He is the reflection of God's glory and bears the very stamp of his nature. We confess that all things are created by him—whether visible or invisible, in heaven and on earth—in whom all things now hold together. That is the Christ around whom all things revolve, since in him the fullness of God dwells bodily and before him every knee shall bow and every tongue confess that Christ is *Lord* to the glory of God the Father (Col. 1:16–19, Phil. 2: 10–11). Certainly the *Body* also shares in that honor. Something of his radiance is reflected by his church on earth, and every *elect* person catches some part of it. But surely that is very different from starting with myself as an elect person, putting myself in the foreground, and only from there ending up with Christ. In the only true system everything else is second, Christ is at the head and is made central not insofar as he became our brother but because he is the Son of God the Father, and because the Father loves the Son and glorifies him with everlasting honor. . . .

We have no right to conceptualize the image of the Mediator in ways other than Scripture presents it. People fall into one-sidedness ... if, reflecting on the Christ, they think exclusively of the blood shed in atonement and refuse to take account of the significance of Christ for the body, for the visible world, and for the outcome of world history. Consider carefully: by taking this tack you run the danger of isolating Christ for your soul and you view life in and for the world as something that exists *alongside* your Christian religion, not controlled by it. Then the word "Christian" seems appropriate to you only when it concerns certain matters of faith or things directly connected with the faith—your church, your school, missions and the like—but all the remaining spheres of life fall for you *outside the Christ*. In the world you conduct yourself as others do; that is less holy, almost unholy, territory which must somehow take care of itself. You only have to take a small step more before landing in the Anabaptist position which concentrated all sanctity in the human soul and dug a deep chasm between this inward-looking spirituality and life all around. Then scholarship becomes unholy; the development of art, trade, and business becomes unholy; unholy also the functions of government; in short, all that is not directly spiritual and aimed at the soul. This way of thinking results in your living in two distinct circles of thought: in the very circumscribed circle of your soul's salvation on the one hand, and in the spacious, life-encompassing sphere of the world on the other. Your Christ is at home in the former but not in the latter. . . .

. . . Scripture continually points out that the *Savior* of the world is also the *Creator* of the world, indeed that he could become its Savior only *because* he already was its *Creator*. . . .

Common grace opens a history, unlocks an enormous space of time, triggers a vast and long-lasting stream of events, in a word, precipitates a series of successive centuries. If that series of centuries is not directed toward an endless, unvarying repetition of the same things, then over the course of those centuries there has to be constant change, modification, transformation in human life. Though it pass through periods of deepening darkness, this change has to ignite ever more light, consistently enrich human life, and so bear the character of perpetual development from less to more, a progressively fuller unfolding of life. If one pictures the distance that exists even now between the life of a Hottentot in his kraal and the life of a highly refined family in European society, one can measure that progress in the blink of an eye. And though people imagine at the end of every century that its progress has been so astonishing that further progress can hardly be imagined, every century nevertheless teaches us that the new things added each time surpass all that has been imagined before. How has the nineteenth century not changed and enriched our human life and blessed it with new conveniences!

The tendency in devout circles to oppose that progress and perpetual development of human life was therefore quite misguided. It must undoubtedly be acknowledged that Christians, by refusing to participate in that development, were the reason why morally and religiously that development often took a wrong turn. Those who are in Christ must not oppose such development and progress, must not even distance themselves from it. Their calling also in this cultural realm is rather to be in the vanguard. . . .

Therefore, we must emphatically state that the interval of centuries that have passed since the fall is not a blank space in the plan of God. The ages lying behind us, by God's decree, must have a purpose and goal, and that purpose can be understood only if we understand that the ongoing development of humanity is *contained in the plan of God*. It follows that the history of our race resulting from this development is not from Satan nor from man *but from God* and that all those who reject and fail to appreciate this development deny the work of God in history. Scripture speaks of the "consummation of the ages" (Matt. 13:39–40), a term that does not mean the centuries will terminate at some point but that they are directed toward a final goal and that everything contained in those centuries is linked to that final goal. . . .

So then, we arrive at this clear insight. The ages must continue not solely for the sake of the elect, nor solely for God to disclose means to us in our struggle against suffering, but in the interest of developing the world itself to its consummation—for as long as is needed to take the world from its beginning and the earliest germination of our human life to the point where the whole process is complete and God has truly reached the final goal he had in mind for it. Thus not a half century, not even a quarter century, will be wasted. There is neither vacuity nor stagnation here. The things that do not yet grow above ground already grow underground in the germination of the seed or the strengthening of the root-system. Not a year, not a day, not an hour can be spared. For all those centuries God has restlessly continued his work in our human race, in the totality of the life of this world. Nothing in it is purposeless or redundant. Things had to go as they did, there was no other way, and the sign of the Son of man will appear in the clouds only when the whole magnificent work of God is complete and the consummation of the world has been inaugurated.

Therefore every view that would confine God's work to the small sector we might label "church life" must be set aside. There is beside the great work of God in *special* grace also that totally other work of God in the realm of *common* grace. That work encompasses the whole life of the world. . . . All of it was an indispensable part of the great work that God is doing to consummate the world's development. And though a great deal in all this *we* cannot connect with the Kingdom or the content of our faith, nevertheless it all has meaning. None of it can be spared because it pleases God, despite Satan's devices and human sin, to actualize everything he had put into this world at the time of creation, to insist on its realization, to develop it so completely that the full sum of its vital energies may enter the light of day at the consummation of the world.

The national church[11] preaches the principle that an entire people, an entire nation, must be incorporated into the church by baptism ... even though everybody knows that the real believers comprise no more than a painfully small number among the large masses of people. . . . Directly opposed to it is the system of the *church as organism*. . . . It maintains that the blessing of Christianity can only be truly effective in the wider circle [of human life] if the institutional church organizes itself in accordance with the demand of Scripture, if Baptism as an ecclesiastical sacrament is administered only to believers and their offspring, and if church discipline is consistently exercised to purify the church. Accordingly, they distinguish between the church as *organism* and the church as *institute* in order that *both* may come into their own: both the sanctity of the covenant among those who confess Christ *and* the influence that should impinge upon the world outside this circle.

This is impossible from the national-church standpoint, which recognizes only one circle, the circle of the church as institute. . . . But we believe there are two circles. First the circle of confessors, the objective church, the circle of the covenant. According to the Heidelberg Catechism, Baptism is extended solely to this first circle—that baptized children may be *"distinguished from the children of unbelievers"* (Q/A 74). The Lord's Supper is administered only within that circle, and solely within that circle can a "gathering of believers" be honored. Only the church that coincides with this circle can therefore possess the marks of the "true church" which are "the pure preaching of the gospel, the pure administration of the sacraments, and the exercise of church discipline both as to confession and the conduct of life" (Belgic Confession, art. XXIX).

But we cannot stop here. This institute does not cover everything that is Christian. Though the lamp of the Christian religion only burns within that institute's walls, its light shines out through its windows to areas far beyond, illumining all the sectors and associations that appear across the wide range of human life and activity. Justice, law, the home and family, business, vocation, public opinion and literature, art and science, and so much more are all illuminated by that light, and that illumination will be stronger and more penetrating as the lamp of the gospel is allowed to shine more brightly and clearly in the church institute.

Aside from this first circle of the institute and in necessary connection with it, we thus recognize another circle whose circumference is determined by the length of the ray that shines out from the church institute over the life of people and nation. Since this second circle is not attached to particular persons, is not circumscribed by a certain number of people listed in church directories, and does not have its own office-bearers but is interwoven with the very fabric of national life, this extra-institutional influence at work in society points us to the *church as organism*. That church, after all, exists before the institute; it lies behind the institute; it alone gives substance and value to that institute. The church as organism has its center in heaven, in Christ; it encompasses all ages from the beginning of the world to the end so as to fulfill all the ages coming after us. The church as organism may even manifest itself where all personal faith is missing but where nevertheless some of the golden glow of eternal life is reflected on the ordinary facades of the great edifice of human life. . . .

Precisely because the church, in Jesus' words, is a city set on a hill, its light must extend over a wide area. To put it in plain prose, a sanctifying and purifying influence must proceed from the church of the Lord to impact the whole society amid which it operates. That influence must begin by arousing a certain admiration for the heroic courage with which it has borne persecution and oppression. Next it must inspire respect for the earnestness and purity of life lived in church circles. It must further excite feelings of sympathy by the warm glow of love and compassion in the community of faith. And finally, as a result of all this, it must purify and ennoble the ideas in general circulation, elevate public opinion, introduce more solid principles, and so raise the view of life prevailing in state, society, and the family. In fact this has historically been the case. The church of Christ has almost nowhere established a lasting presence without also modifying the general outlook on life beyond its institutional walls. . . .

We can exert power for good, therefore, only if we are prepared to drum it into our heads that the church of Christ can never exert influence on civil society directly, only indirectly. Therefore its goal must remain (1) to assure the church full freedom of action and full authority to maintain its own unique character; (2) to avert any attempt to introduce pagan concepts and ideas into the country's laws, public institutions, and public opinion in place of Christian ones; and (3) to continually expand the dominance of nobler and purer ideas in civil society by the courageous action of its members in every area of life. In a nutshell: what we want is a strong confessional church but not a confessional civil society nor a confessional state.

This secularization of state and society is one of the most basic ideas of Calvinism, though it did not succeed in immediately and completely working out this idea in pure form. . . . Calvinism from its own roots produced the conviction that the church of Christ cannot be a national church because it had to be rigorously confessional and maintain Christian discipline, and that the Christian character of society therefore cannot be secured by the baptism of the whole citizenry but is to be found in the influence that the church of Christ exerts upon the whole organization of national life. By its influence on the state and civil society the church of Christ aims only at a *moral triumph*, not at the imposition of confessional bonds nor at the exercise of authoritarian control. The example of the United States of America, accordingly, demonstrates how the various divisions of the Christian church, the moment they unitedly adopt this position, not only give up fighting among themselves in order to contend together peacefully in matters of faith, but also that precisely these good mutual relations enable them to exert a much greater influence on civil and national conditions than the most powerful national church ever could. . . .

Terms such as "a Christian nation," "a Christian country," "a Christian society," "Christian art," and the like, do not mean that such a nation consists mainly of regenerate Christian persons or that such a society has already been transposed into the kingdom of heaven. This was never the case anywhere. Even in Israel the great majority was always apostate and idolatrous and the "faithful" always a rather small minority. No, it means that in such a country special grace in the church and among believers exerted so strong a formative influence on common grace that common grace thereby attained its highest development. The adjective "Christian" therefore says nothing about the spiritual state of the inhabitants of such a country but only witnesses to the fact that public opinion, the general mind-set, the ruling ideas, the moral norms, the laws and customs there clearly betoken the influence of the Christian faith. Though this is attributable to special grace, it is manifested on the terrain of common grace, i.e., in ordinary civil life. This influence leads to the abolition of slavery in the laws and life of a country, to the improved position of women, to the maintenance of public virtue, respect for the Sabbath, compassion for the poor, consistent regard for the ideal over the material, and—even in manners—the elevation of all that is human from its sunken state to a higher standpoint.[12]

NOTES

1. [Abraham Kuyper, "Confidentially," in *Abraham Kuyper: A Centennial Anthology*, ed. James D. Bratt (Grand Rapids, Mich.: Wm B. Eerdmans, 1988), 55–56. In 1863, having just received his doctorate in theology from the University of Leiden, where currents of theological liberalism were running strong, Kuyper took his first pastorate in the tiny village of Beesd in the southern part of the Netherlands (in the Brabant). His experience there with certain of his conservative parishioners proved formative for the rest of his life. He wrote about his experience in a small treatise that he published a few years later (1873), "Confidentially" ("Confidentie" in Dutch).]

2. [Kuyper then explains why he does not simply cite Christianity as the coordinate of paganism and Islam, but instead divides Christianity into Catholicism and Calvinism.]

3. [Abraham Kuyper, *Calvinism: Six Lectures Delivered in the Theological Seminary at Princeton* (New York: F. H. Revell, 1899), 5, 7, 12–13, 16, 18, 25–27, 29–33.]

4. [Kuyper moves on from this point to raise the question whether our condition as a whole, and religion along with it, should be seen as normal or abnormal. The terminology never became popular, but the meaning is clear enough.]

5. [Having argued that ours is the abnormal condition of creatures who have fallen from their state of religious and moral well-functioning, rather than normal creatures who are advancing to that state, Kuyper asks what is to guide us in this "abnormal" situation. His answer is: the ordinances of God. In his articulation of what he means by this, it becomes clear that he adheres to a version of natural law theory. This was of prime importance for his theory of politics in a pluralist society.]

6. [Kuyper, *Calvinism*, 52–53, 58–66. In the preceding discussion of paganism, Catholicism, Islam, modernism, and Calvinism, Kuyper was assuming that, unless they are in some way deformed, such religions, and others like them, orient a person's life in general. In this essay, the second of his Stone Lectures, Kuyper argues the case for this understanding of properly formed religion after first suggesting that religion is not an invention of human beings but the outcome of an impulse planted by God in all humankind, to the end that God's glory will be acknowledged and displayed.]

7. [Kuyper now goes on to argue that sin has introduced a "disturbance" into this picture: the human ego, which is the subject of science, has been broken up, especially at that third point of those worlds of thought whereby we try to grasp the relationships among elements; and the result of this, in turn, is that our diverse worlds of thought often obstruct rather than enable access to reality in its organic interrelationships.]

8. [Abraham Kuyper, *Encyclopedia of Sacred Theology: Its Principles*, trans. J. Hendrik De Vries (New York: Charles Scribner's Sons, 1898), 63–70, 72, 74–76, 83, 89–90, 106–107. In the preceding selections, Kuyper has argued that Calvinism in particular, and well-formed religion in general, incorporates not only a moral and an emotional component but an intellectual component as well. It comes as no surprise, then, to find him arguing that in a religiously pluralistic society, we must expect a pluralized academy as well, with some of the pluralism, though by no means all, grounded in religious disagreement. The point has its obvious analogue for politics. The Dutch word translated here as "science" is *wetenschap*, a synonym of the German *Wissenschaft*. A better translation would probably be "academic learning."]

9. [Having presented his account of state sovereignty, Kuyper now turns to his famous theory of "sphere sovereignty," without which one cannot fully understand his account of state sovereignty. Throughout his career Kuyper appealed to his theory of sphere sovereignty, most famously in his address at the opening of the Free University in 1880, titled "Sovereignty in its own Sphere" ("Souvereiniteit in eigen kring"). Probably the best statement of the theory, however, is the one that occurs here in the third of his Stone Lectures.]

10. [Kuyper, *Calvinism: Six Lectures*, 92–105, 115–127, 133–142.]

11. [Among the many uses Kuyper makes of his doctrine of common grace, prominent was his use of the doctrine to articulate his opposition to a national church.]

12. [Abraham Kuyper, "Common Grace," in *Abraham Kuyper: A Centennial Anthology*, 167–170, 172–176, 193–195, 197–199. One of the theological underpinnings of the account of human nature, law, justice, authority, civil society, and the state outlined in the preceding readings, was Kuyper's doctrine of common grace. He developed his thoughts on the matter in a long series of articles in the weekly paper he edited, *De Heraut*; these were later collected into a three-volume publication titled *Common Grace* (*De Gemeene Gratie*).]

[CHAPTER 9]

Susan B. Anthony (1820–1906)

SELECTED AND EDITED BY MARY D. PELLAUER

Susan B. Anthony was born in 1820 and brought up by an unconventional Quaker family in upstate New York. Her parents belonged to the abolition and suffrage causes before she did. They attended the first women's rights convention and signed its Declaration of Sentiments. Indeed, the Anthony family encouraged, supported, and often financed Susan's work throughout her life. For fifteen years, Anthony earned her living as a schoolteacher, leaving that career only for full-time devotion to struggling for justice, initially in the temperance movement and then for antislavery and women's rights.

At a temperance convention in 1853, Anthony met Elizabeth Cady Stanton, and they became fast friends. Stanton, the daughter of a judge, had been heartbroken in her youth when told that girls could not become lawyers. She was steeped in the American democratic tradition and adept at explicating legal precedents. Her husband, Henry Stanton, was a lawyer active in a less radical wing of the antislavery struggle than the one that held Anthony's allegiance. Stanton and Anthony became lifelong friends and collaborators, often working together to write speeches that one of them would deliver. Both agreed that they complemented each other's strengths.

In 1854, Anthony began her career as a full-time activist by systematizing a New York organization to work for women's property and custody rights. During the late 1850s, she was the general agent for the New York State Anti-Slavery Society and, along with many speakers whose campaigns she scheduled and assisted, met her trials by mob. To Anthony, the parallels between the struggles against slavery and for women's rights were vivid. In these antislavery days she absorbed principles such as "no union with slave-holders," "no compromise," "of two evils, choose neither," "do right and leave the consequences to God," and "resistance to tyranny is obedience to God."

In the late 1860s, Anthony published the stormy paper The Revolution, *with its slogan, "men, their rights and nothing more; women, their rights and nothing less." Stanton and Parker Pillsbury, a controversial "come-outer" from the antislavery ranks, wrote most of the copy for the paper.* The Revolution *did not hesitate to take sides on Victorian scandals, thus causing outrage among its readers and others. The paper's eventual failure committed Anthony to six years' work to repay its ten-thousand-dollar debt.*

For the next thirty years, Anthony dedicated herself to convincing the United States Congress to pass a Constitutional Amendment enfranchising women. The amendment became so identified with her that through its successive numerical designations (from XVI to XX), it was called "the Anthony Amendment."

In her sixties, Anthony—still very active in political work—turned her attention also to chronicling the movement of which she was a part. In the 1880s, Stanton and Anthony realized that no one else would write the history that they and their friends had made. The two women passed hundreds of hours with old letters and documents from women's rights conventions all over the country and by 1886 produced three large volumes (nine hundred or so pages each) of The History of Woman Suffrage.

Anthony spent fifty-odd years of her life agitating for reform, enticing others to join her, and doing the tedious "common work" of reform movements. She engaged speakers, laid out their itineraries in statewide or national campaigns, arranged publicity both before and after the fact, and herself gave innumerable lectures, frequently to hostile crowds. She recruited a whole generation of younger women to join the struggle. She was interminably busy at fund-raising. She went door-to-door with petitions. She arranged and gave testimony to congressional committees, both state and national. She buttonholed congressmen and more than one American president. And she demanded a suffrage plank on the platforms of political parties of all sorts. Everywhere, Anthony was the object of personal comments that Stanton's maternal status and respectable appearance did not provoke. As the two women grew older, these patterns did not change much.

Both Anthony and Stanton rejected original sin and the need for a uniquely redeeming savior figure. Both believed that human nature is basically good and that real strides of progress can be made. Both certainly believed that democratic principles are sacred. But Anthony's emphases, as we will see, were biblical and prophetic in character. According to Anthony, believers are especially commanded "to break every yoke and let the oppressed go free" (Isa. 58:6 RSV), "to love your neighbor as yourself " (Matt. 22:39 RSV), and to feed the hungry and clothe the naked in the awareness that as one performs these deeds for the

least among us, one does them for Jesus himself (Matt. 25:31–46). Though An-
thony called God "Father" or "All-Father," which strikes today's feminist ears
badly, her God was a God who loved freedom and helped to bring it about.

A TEMPERANCE SPEECH: THE CHURCH AND
THE LIQUOR TRAFFIC (1852)

I PROPOSE THIS evening, to speak to you upon the connection of the
Church with the Liquor Traffic. In attempting this, I am aware that I shall
tread upon what the world deems "Holy Ground," and that I thereby expose
myself to the anathema of Infidel, which is so universally bestowed upon
all who dare enter the sacred portals of that hoary institution, the Church,
and openly and fearlessly point out wherein it fails to live that blessed injunction, "Love thy neighbor as thyself," —that command on which hang
all the law and the Prophets (Mt 22: 39–40).

The ravages of intemperance are so fearful and wide spread, it needs no
argument to prove that the sale of rum is a violation of the Golden Rule,
"Do unto others as you would that others should do unto you" (Lk 6:31).
Since, according to the laws of God and man, he who is accessory to a
crime is equally guilty with the perpetrator, the man or institution that
sanctions or sustains the License System of our State... .

Now if the Church retain in its membership men who habitually use
intoxicating Liquors, those who traffic in them, and those who aid in elevating to the various offices of our government, Brandy drinking men
who license the sale of Liquor, does it not by so doing wink at the hideous
crimes of the Distiller, Rum Seller, and Drunkard? Does it not sanction the
Liquor Traffic?

Let us make enquiries into the week day occupations of the communi-
cants of any of our large, wealthy and popular Churches, and I might safely
add, most of our Churches, whether rich or poor, large or small, in country
or in city, and see if we do not find many of them, in some way connected
with the Liquor Traffic—see if we do not find a Deacon Distiller—a Church
Member rum seller or rum drinker—a Church Member who owns a tavern
stand or grocery which he rents to a Rum Seller—a Church Member who
continues a business partnership with a man whom he and the world know
to be engaged in the Liquor Traffic—a Church Member who will manufacture Cider and sell it to grocers, whom he knows will sell it as a bever-
age—a Church Member who will sell the contents of his granary, his corn,
rye, oats, wheat, and barley to the brewer and distiller—a Church Member,
who if elevated to the office of Justice of the Peace or Supervisor, Mayor or

Alderman, will sign petitions to license the sale of Rum—a church member Senator or Assemblyman who is in favor of the continuance of the present License System—or a Church Member, who from year to year deposits his vote for men to fill these various offices, whom he knows will sign petitions for license and do all in their power to defeat the efforts of the friends of Temperance, the lovers of God and man, to annihilate the Liquor Traffic.

I believe the discipline of no Church, no associated religious bodies except the Methodist, Free Will Baptist, Old Scotch Covenanters, prohibits its members from engaging in the Liquor Traffic. And none others that requires a man to pledge himself to total Abstention from drink that can intoxicate before accepting him as a member, acknowledging him as a follower of the meek and lowly Jesus. And even in those Churches we not infrequently find men who are guilty of one if not all of the serious connections with rum. It was not long ago that I visited a college in one of our western counties where there was a Methodist Distiller, who, not satisfied with the ill-gotten gains of six days of labor, kept his Still in operation the Seventh day also. This placing of a law upon the Statute Books, when there is not a public sentiment that will enforce it, is of no avail. So with a Church Discipline, be its restrictions ever so close, it affects nothing unless the moral sentiments of its members are sufficiently strong to require (enforcement). . . .

Is it not hypocrisy for Church members, Deacon and Clergymen, to pray from day to day and from week to week through each successive year, that God will bless the Temperance Cause—that he will banish drunkenness from our land—that he will protect and comfort the wretched wife and children of the drunkard—that he will be a Father to the fatherless, and the widow's God—and then, on election day, after these long and oft repeated prayers, for those same Church members, Deacons and Clergymen, to go to the Ballot Box and deposit their votes for Brandy drinking Presidents and Congressmen, Rum drinking, Rum selling Governors, Senators and Assemblymen, Mayors and Aldermen, Justices of the Peace and Supervisors, whom they know to be in favor of the License System?

. . . The Church in the present undeveloped state of the race, is the educator of the religious element in man—if then, the church gives its sanction to either national or individual sins, it becomes the great sustainer of those evils. While the Church, retaining its present power to influence public sentiment, fails to take a decided stand on the side of Total Abstinence from Rum making, vending, drinking and voting, difficult indeed will be the efforts of the temperance reformer to persuade the masses that to be in any way connected with the Liquor Traffic, is Unchristian. . . .

. . . While the Rum sellers' petition for license is signed by Church Members, Mayors and Justices of the Peace, Deacons, Alderman and Supervisors, vain are all our arguments to prove that the rum seller possesses no moral right to sell rum to his neighbor. While the Church Member farmer annually carries his abundant harvests of grain to the brewer and distiller, to be distorted into deadly poisons, it is in vain that the apostles of the Gospel of Temperance preach to these Brewers and Distillers. They hide themselves behind their refuge of lies, the Church. While the lady Church Member annually manufactures her gooseberry and currant wines, while she partakes freely of them herself, and serves them at her social parties, it is extremely difficult to persuade the lady of fashion to abandon the use of imported wines. . . .

The time may have been, but is not now, when a Church Member, Deacon and Clergyman who voted for Brandy drinking, Rum licensing men to fill the various offices of government, might have thought themselves Christians, might have thought that a man's religion was not to go with him to the ballot box.

The time may have been, but is not now, when a Church that fellowshipped rum drinking, rum selling, rum making and rum voting members, might have thought itself the Church of God—might have imagined itself the "light of the world, the city set on a hill" (Mt 5:14). Our present type of Christianity indeed is lamentably low, and be it woman's glory, now to accept her Heaven appointed mission to preach a risen Savior, to raise high the standards of Christianity. To fully take and live the great and immutable truth taught by Jesus, that a "good tree cannot bring forth evil fruit" (Mt 7:18). The only unmistakable evidence of a man's belief in the doctrines taught by Christ, is to be found in the every day acts of his life.

The simple act of voting involves a man's love of truth and right. A man's vote is the embodiment and exponent of his principles on all questions pertaining to the good of the race—and thus the ballot box is the medium, through which he gives effectual expression to those principles. The Liquor Traffic is a creation of law and can only be revoked through the legislation of the country. Moral suasion has done its work, those who still persist in trafficking in intoxicating liquors, are possessed of stony hearts, that can be touched only by the cold fingers of the law.

… Inasmuch as the All-Wise acts by great immutable laws, prayers unsustained by action rise no higher than the efforts of the soul that utters them. The act that decides whether God will answer a man's prayer, that intemperance may be banished from our midst, is the dropping of a slip of paper into the ballot box on election day. If that slip of paper have on it the name of a Distiller, Rum seller, Rum drinker, or one who is not an open and avowed friend of Total Abstinence, and the Maine Law, vain worse than vain are all his long prayers.

There is an instructive moral to be drawn from the following anecdote. . . .
On the morning of a cold winter day, surrounded as usual by his wife and
children, the pious man prayed God to "feed the hungry and clothe the naked." As they arose from their devotion, a gentle tap was heard at the door.
The stranger was bade to walk in, and there stood before them a little bare-
footed girl, shivering and pale, clad in the habiliments of extreme poverty,
and holding in one of her shrivelled hands a basket. She timidly raised her
eyes, and said to the man, "Please, Sir, will you let my mother have a half
bushel of potatoes. I have no money to pay you now, Sir, but my mother is
doing some sewing for Mr. Blank, and just so soon as she gets the job done,
she will get the money and send it to you. We are all very hungry." The
answer of that man fresh from communion with the God he worshipped
was, "No! I can't let you have any, I can sell my potatoes for cash down and
don't choose to let them go on trust." Thus did that praying man send away
the sorrow stricken little one to her home with an empty basket. The little
son went up to his father and with tears in his eyes said, "Father, I have
been thinking, why you couldn't answer the prayer you made this morning
yourself, and not wait for God to do it?"

Yes, friends, we ourselves are the instruments by means of which God
answers our prayers. Unphilosophical indeed are they who ask God to
banish from our land the three great national scourges of war, slavery and
intemperance, while they from year to year aid in elevating to the various
offices of government, wicked men, who know no love, either to God or
man, whose highest aim is to attain to a position, that will secure to them
the means of gratifying their own individual lusts after wealth, fame, power
and sensual enjoyments. . . .

My friends, the religion that cannot stand the test of an election day,
that dwells in the heart and governs the actions of men during 364 days of
the year and then forsakes them, as they rise from the bended knee on the
morning of the 365th day to repair to the polls, is not worth the possession.
Hollow hearted and hypocritical are all professions of sympathy for suffering, downtrodden humanity, unless they are sustained by the man's giving
his influence and his vote to elevate those only to the various governmental
offices who will ever bear in mind that it is the duty of the righteous legislator, to cast his vote on the side of right, of justice, of mercy, of humanity.
Is not the Christianity that sanctions the distiller, the rum seller, the rum
drinker, and the man who votes for the continuance of this abomination
of desolation, the Liquor Traffic—that allows the buying and selling as
chattels, human beings, and thereby licenses every sort of iniquity under
heaven, worse that the heathenism of the Sandwich Islands—worse than
the Hindu paganism, that compels the mother to throw her loved child

into the Ganges, and the widow to cast herself on the burning funeral pile of her husband. . . .

The term infidel has come to be an everyday "bugbear," which clergy thrust into the face of every one who ventures to give to the world a new view or new idea, which may chance to conflict with long established theories or practices. Its signification in the popular vocabulary is so vague that I shall not hazard any refutation in any attempt to define its exact meaning. Suffice it to say that very many of the truly great and good men and women of our day, who are loudly denounced as infidels are found doing the work of righteousness—feeding the hungry, clothing the naked, visiting the sick and in prison (Mt 25: 31–46), undoing the bonds of the slave and letting the oppressed go free (Is 58: 6), omitting the weightier matters of the Law, judgment, mercy and faith. What though they with their lips (Mk 7:6) declare the Bible a mere human production? Do not their every day acts, "the fruits by which we are to know them" (Mt 7:16), show that they believe the great and immutable truths contained therein to have emanated from none other than a Divine Source? On the other hand, do not the every day acts of very many of those who profess to believe the Bible, the "Word of God," the only infallible rule of faith and practice, plainly show disbelief. If these professors really felt every Bible declaration to be of God's revealing, think you they would knowingly fellowship in Church Communion those whom they know to be guilty of sins, upon which that Bible pronounces a woe? "No drunkard shall inherit the Kingdom of Heaven." "Woe unto him that putteth the cup to his neighbor's lips and maketh him drugged." "Woe unto those that devour widow's houses and for a pretense make long prayers" (Mt 23:14). Think you he who read the above denunciations and believe them to be of God's own handwriting will fail to cry out against the Liquor Traffickers?

If he really feels that no drunkard can inherit the kingdom of heaven, think you he can forget the mercy that God requires at his hands, the removing the temptations out of the way of his brothers? If he really believes that God's woe is upon those who devour widow's houses, will he not come out and be separate from those who make sell or vote for rum? Will he not see that his long prayers, his psalm singing, his observance of holy days, his rearing of gorgeous temples, are but the tithing of mint, anise and cumin (Mt 23:23)? "It is not all that cry Lord, Lord, but they that do work meet for repentance that shall be accepted of God" (Mt 7:21).

"A certain man had two sons, and he came to the first and said, "Son go work in my vineyard." He answered and said, 'I will not,' but afterward he repented and went. And he likewise said to the second, and he answered and said, 'I go' and went not. Whether of the twain did the will of his Father?

His disciples said unto him, 'the first' " (Mt 21:28–31). Friends, the time has fully come for us to cease to waste all our precious hours in discussing questions of mystical theology and speculative faith, and adopt the plain practical principles taught by Jesus of Nazareth, the Divine founder. . . . [1]

TWO ANTISLAVERY SPEECHES

WHAT IS AMERICAN SLAVERY? (1861)

The question of all questions that is now agitating our entire country: the one vexed question that intrudes itself upon our every thought—that is spoken of in all our news papers and magazines, that gives fertile theme to the moralist and novelist—that startles, nay, appalls, the Political Economist—that is discussed at the family fireside, at the public dinner, on the railroad car, at the corners of the streets, and wherever men and women most do congregate: What is American Slavery: the one disturbing question, that thrusts itself into every gathering of the people, that is the "apple of discord" in all our literary, political and religious organizations, that causes angry divisions and subdivisions in our churches, general assemblies, general conferences and associations, that has turned our American Congress into one great national debating club, and all our State Legislatures into schools, where declamations, both pro and con, are always in order.

What is this question of American slavery, that has thus the power to shake this mighty nation from center to circumference, and from circumference back to center again: The one blot on our nation's escutcheon, that shames the face of every true American, and astonishes the whole civilized world—the one "pet institution," that makes our professedly Christian, Democratic, Republican America, a lie—a hissing and a by-word in the mouth of all Europe, and an offense in the sight of High Heaven.

What is American slavery? It is the legalized systematized robbery of the bodies and souls of nearly four millions of men, women and children. It is the legalized traffic in God's image (Gen 1:27–28). It is the buying and selling Jesus Christ himself on the auction block as merchandise, as chattel property, in the person of the outraged slave. For the Divine Jesus said, "inasmuch as ye do it unto one of the least of these, my brethren, ye do it unto me" (Mt 25:40).

What is American slavery? It is the depriving four millions of native born citizens of these United States, of their inalienable right to life, liberty and the pursuit of happiness. It is the robbing of every sixth man, woman and child, of this glorious republic, of their God-given right to the ownership and control of their own persons, to the earnings of their own hands and brains, to the exercise of their own consciences and wills, to the possession and enjoyment of their own homes. It is the sundering of what God has joined together (Mt 19:06), the divorcing husbands and wives, parent and children, brothers and sisters. It is the robbery of every comfort, and every possession, sacred to a child of earth, and an heir of Heaven.

American slavery: It is a wholesale system of wrong and outrage perpetrated on the bodies and souls of these millions of God's children. It is the legalized prostitution of nearly two millions of the daughters of this proud republic. It is the blotting out from the soul of womanhood, the divine spark of purity, the god of her inheritance. It is the abomination of desolation spoken of by the Prophet Daniel (Dan 11:31), engrafted into the very heart of the American government. It is all and every villainy in crimes long back category, consolidated into one. It is theft, robbery, piracy, murder. It is avarice, covetousness, lust, licentiousness, concubinage, polygamy. It is atheism, blasphemy, sin against the Holy Ghost (Mt 12:31–32).

MAKE THE SLAVE'S CASE OUR OWN

We are assembled here this evening for the purpose of discussing the question of American Slavery. The startling fact that there are in these United States, under the sanction of this professedly Christian, Republican government, nearly four millions of human beings now clanking the chains of slavery. Four millions of men and women and children, who are owned like horses and cattle, and bought and sold in the market. Four millions of thinking, acting, conscious beings, like ourselves, driven to unpaid toil, from the rising to the setting of the sun, through the weary days and years of their wretched life times.

Let us, my friends, for the passing hour, make the slave's case our own. As much as in us lies, let us feel that it is ourselves, and our kith and our kin who are despoiled of our inalienable rights to life, liberty and the pursuit of happiness, that it is our own backs that are bared to the slave driver's lash. That it is our own flesh that is lacerated and torn. That it is our own life blood that is poured out.

Let us feel that it is our own children, that are ruthlessly torn from our yearning mother hearts, and driven in the "coffle gang," through burning suns, and drenching rains, to be sold on the auction block to the highest bidder, and worked up, body and soul, on the cotton, sugar and rice plantations of the more remote south.

That it is our own loved sister and daughter, who are shamelessly exposed to the public market, and whose beauty of face, delicacy of complexion, symmetry of form, and grace of motion, do but enhance their monied value, and the more surely victimize them to the unbridled passions and lusts of their proud purchasers.

Could we, my friends, but make the slave's case our own—could we but feel for the slave, as bound with him (Heb 13:3)—could we but make the slave our neighbor, and "love him as ourself" (Mt 22:39), and do unto him as we would that he should do unto us (Lk 6:31)—how very easy would be the task of converting us all to Abolitionism.

If, by some magic power, the color of our skins could be instantly changed and the slave's fate made really our own, then would there by no farther need of argument or persuasion, or rhetoric or eloquence. Then would we, every one, with heart and soul, and tone and action, respond to the truth and the justice of the glorious doctrine of "immediate and unconditional emancipation," as the right of the slave and the duty of the master. Were we, ourselves, the victims of this vilest oppression the sun ever shone upon—no appeal to Bible or Constitution, no regard for peace and harmony in our religious or political associations, no blind reverence for "Union" either in church or state, could for a moment quiet our consciences, silence our voices, or stay our action. Priests, Presidents, Bishops and Statesmen, laymen and voters, synods, general assemblies and conferences, congresses, supreme courts and legislatures, if standing between us and liberty, would all be swept away, without one thought or care of consequences. What to us would then be the venerated Books, idolized parchments, time worn creeds and musty statutes of the Fathers? All, all of them would sink into utter insignificance: Freedom, God's priceless boon to man, outweighs them all. "Liberty or Death" is now our watchword.

But we are wont to contemplate this question of slavery from quite another, and an opposite, standpoint. We look upon the slave, as a being all unlike ourselves. The sallow hue of his skin, the curl of his hair, the flattened features of his face, together with the fact that he has for so many generations been the victim of the white man, seem conclusive evidence to the masses, that a condition that would be torture worse than death to us, is quite endurable, nay, congenial to him.

Then, too, we quiet our consciences with the thought that these poor creatures, however wronged and outraged their condition here, are yet, infinitely better off than they would be in their African homes across the Atlantic. Their Fathers were wild beasts living in tents, on the hills of Congo, the arid plains of Soudan, or the coasts of Guinea. And there, in their own native land, were they hunted like beasts of prey, and made to drag out their lives in a hopeless bondage to their more powerful, warlike and treacherous neighbors.

Though slaves here, subject to the will of a master, with no hope of freedom but in death, their condition is still far better than it could be in their father land, where reigns the night of heathenism were all, all is shrouded in the thick gloom of ignorance, superstition. Here, the slave is surrounded by the elevating, refining influences of civilization. Here the blessed privileges of Christianity are extended to him. Here the Gospel of Jesus Christ is preached to him.

And here, though his life, on earth, shall be one of utter wretchedness, disgust and loathing, he may take to his crushed and bleeding spirit the Christian hope of eternal rest, of unfading glory—the Christian faith, that the white winged messenger of Death will but usher him into the immediate presence of the Father of all, where there will be no clanking of chains, no torturing "cat o nine tails," no red hot branding irons, where the wicked cease from troubling and the weary are at rest.

Just think of it, my friends, a civilization elevating and refining, that makes slaves and chattels of one sixth portion of its own children, and with iron heel, crushes out their every spark of manhood. A civilization that, by statute law, denies to every sixth man, woman and child, all its educational, industrial, social and political rights and privileges! Such is our boasted American civilization, that prates of elevating and refining the very victims it tramples in the dust. Heaven defend the benighted children of Africa from such a civilization!

Here, too, the slave enjoys the blessed privileges of Christianity. Think of it: A Christianity that traffics in human beings, that barters God's image for filthy lucre. And here is the Gospel of Jesus Christ preached to the poor slave. Think of it! A Gospel that transforms every sixth child of God into chattel. A Gospel that sells Jesus Christ himself in the person of the slave on the auction block. What a profanation. What blasphemy! Such a Gospel can be none other than that of the bottomless pit. And sooner will the true Christ take to his bosom the children of heathendom's midnight darkness than allow one of these slave-holding [illegible word in original text] to slip into the light of his presence.

Again, it is argued that we of the North are not responsible for the crime of slave holding, that the guilty ones dwell in the South and lord it over the rice swamps of Georgia, the tobacco fields of Virginia, and the sugar and cotton plantations of Louisiana and the Carolinas. Thus, do we put the slave's case far away from us, forgetting that he is a human being like ourselves, forgetting that we ourselves are bound up with the slave-holder, in his guilt, forgetting that we of the North stand pledged to the support of the Federal Government, the tenure of whose existence is vested in the one idea of protection to the slave-holder, in his slave-property, forgetting that by the terms of the unholy agreement of the Fathers of our union, the only property represented on the floor of Congress, is the slave-holders property in man, forgetting that every loyal citizen of the North, himself or through his representatives, swears to support the United States Constitution, by whose special provision, the slave holder is not only secured the right to own slaves, and give them a three-fifths representation in the legislation of the nation, but every such loyal citizen is solemnly bound to return fugitive slaves to their masters, to buckle on his armor and go down to Kentucky, Tennessee or any of the fifteen slave states and aid in putting down insurrections and in shooting down men and women, for no other crime save that of hating slavery and loving liberty. Nay! More than all, forgetting that we of the North, welcome slave-holding priests to our pulpits, and slave-holding laymen to our church conferences. Think of it, professing Christians—members of any and all of our popular churches here at the North—you talk about not being responsible for the crime of slave holding, while religiously you shake hands with the southern slave-holders, the perpetrators of every vile deed in crime's black category.

The Scotch Covenanters or Reformed Presbyterians is the only evangelical church in all the nominally free states of the North that can consistently claim freedom from all sanction of, or compromise with slavery, "the sum of all villainies." The Old Scotch Covenanters refuse church fellowship not only to slave-holders, but to churches that fellowship slave-holders. They also refuse to take the oath of allegiance to the United States Government, and thus are theoretically and practically Abolitionists and thus are the doers of the commands of Jesus: "Remember them in bonds, as bound with them" (Heb 13:3). "Break every yoke and let the oppressed go free" (Isa 58:6).

But as a nation, we do deny the manhood of the slave, both politically and religiously. And it is this failure to recognize the slave's humanity that keeps him in his chains.

From the very hour of the foundation of this government has slavery been considered a national curse. Able statesmen and shrewd politicians have denounced it in the halls of legislation and labored to defeat its merciless purpose. Pious divines have hurled at its monster head the thunderbolts of God's wrath, and prayed their Avenger to drive it from the land.

And yet after seventy years of such labors and such prayers, what do we see? Why, the number of slaves increased from a half a million to nearly four millions, the number of slave states from six to fifteen, one thousand millions of dollars pours out of the public treasury for the purchase and conquest of new slave territory—all the United States territories, at first, consecrated to freedom, then thrown open, every foot of them, to the desecrating tread of the slave-holders—the nominally free states, by the late decision of the Supreme Court, made the home of the slave-holder and his slave-property. And an entire nation, which at the beginning could but blush and hang its head that it held within its wide embrace so foul a thing as slavery, now glorying in its shame, crying "great is Diana of the Ephesians"[2] (Acts 19:28, 34).[3]

ANTHONY'S SPEECH AT HER TRIAL FOR VOTING (1873)

The Court: The prisoner will stand up. Has the prisoner anything to say why sentence shall not be pronounced?

Miss ANTHONY: Yes, your honor, I have many things to say; for in your ordered verdict of guilty, you have trampled underfoot every vital principle of our government. My natural rights, my civil rights, my political rights, are all alike ignored. Robbed of the fundamental privilege of citizenship, I am degraded from the status of a citizen to that of a subject; and not only myself individually, but all of my sex, are, by your honor's verdict, doomed to political subjection under this so-called Republican government.

Judge HUNT: The Court can not listen to a rehearsal of arguments the prisoner's counsel has already consumed three hours in presenting.

Miss ANTHONY: May it please your honor, I am not arguing the question, but simply stating the reasons why sentence can not, in justice, be pronounced against me. Your denial of my citizen's right to vote is the denial of my right of consent as one of the governed, the denial of my right of representation as one of the taxed, the denial of my right to a trial by a jury of my peers as an offender against law, therefore, the denial of my sacred rights to life, liberty, property, and—

Judge HUNT: The Court can not allow the prisoner to go on.

Miss ANTHONY: But your honor will not deny me this one and only poor privilege of protest against this high-handed outrage upon my citizen's rights. May it please the Court to remember that since the day of my arrest last November, this is the first time that either myself or any person of my disfranchised class has been allowed a word of defense before judge or jury.

Judge HUNT: The prisoner must sit down; the Court can not allow it.

Miss ANTHONY: All my prosecutors, from the 8th Ward corner grocery politician, who entered the complaint, to the United States Marshal, Commissioner, District Attorney, District Judge, your honor on the bench, not one is my peer, but each and all are my political sovereigns; and had your honor submitted my case to the jury, as was clearly your duty, even then I should have had just cause of protest, for not one of those men was my peer; but, native or foreign, white or black, rich or poor, educated or ignorant, awake or asleep, sober or drunk, each and every man of them was my political superior; hence, in no sense, my peer. Even, under such circumstances, a commoner of England, tried before a jury of lords, would have far less cause to complain than should I, a woman, tried before a jury of men. Even my counsel, the Hon. Henry R Selden, who has argued my cause so ably, so earnestly, so unanswerably before your honor, is my political sovereign. Precisely as no disfranchised person is entitled to sit upon a jury, and no woman is entitled to the franchise, so, none but a regularly admitted lawyer is allowed to practice in the courts, and no woman can gain admission to the bar—hence, jury, judge, counsel, must all be of the superior class.

Judge HUNT: The Court must insist—the prisoner has been tried according to the established forms of law.

Miss ANTHONY: Yes, your honor, but by forms of law all made by men, interpreted by men, administered by men, in favor of men, and against women; and hence, your honor's directed verdict of guilty, against a United States citizen for the exercise of "that citizen's right to vote," simply because that citizen was a woman and not a man. But, yesterday, the same man-made forms of law declared it a crime punishable with $1,000 fine and six months' imprisonment, for you, or me, or any of us, to give a cup of cold water, a crust of bread, or a night's shelter to a panting fugitive as he was tracking his way to Canada. And every man or woman in whose veins course a drop of human sympathy violated that wicked law, reckless of consequences, and was justified in so doing. As then the slaves who got their freedom must take it over, or under, or through the unjust forms of law, precisely so now much women, to get their right to a voice in this government, take it; and I have taken mine, and mean to take it at every possible opportunity.

Judge HUNT: The Court orders the prisoner to sit down. It will not allow another word.

Miss ANTHONY: When I was brought before your honor for trial, I hoped for a broad and liberal interpretation of the Constitution and its recent amendments, that should declare all United States citizens under its protecting aegis—that should declare equality of rights the national guarantee to all persons born or naturalized in the United States. But failing to get this justice—failing, even, to get a trial by a jury *not* of my peers—I ask not leniency at your hands—but rather the full rigors of the law.

Judge HUNT: The Court must insist—(Here the prisoner sat down.)

Judge HUNT: The prisoner will stand up. (Here Miss Anthony arose again.) The sentence of the Court is that you pay a fine of one hundred dollars and the costs of the prosecution.

Miss ANTHONY: May it please your honor, I shall never pay a dollar of your unjust penalty. All the stock in trade I possess is a $10,000 debt, incurred by publishing my paper—*The Revolution*—four years ago, the sole object of which was to educate all women to do precisely as I have done, rebel against your man-made, unjust, unconstitutional forms of law, that tax, fine, imprison, and hang women, while they deny them the right of representation in the Government; and I shall work on with might and main to pay every dollar of that honest debt, but not a penny shall go to this unjust claim. And I shall earnestly and persistently continue to urge all women to the practical recognition of the old revolutionary maxim, that "Resistance to tyranny is obedience to God."

Judge HUNT: Madam, the Court will not order you committed until the fine is paid.[4]

THE BREAD OF DEPENDENCE

My purpose tonight is to demonstrate the great historical fact that disfranchisement is not only political degradation, but also moral, social, educational and industrial degradation; and that it does not matter whether the disfranchised class live under a monarchial or a republican form of government, or whether it be white workingmen of England, negroes on our southern plantations, serfs of Russia, Chinamen on our Pacific coast, or native born, tax-paying women of this republic. Wherever, on the face of the globe or on the page of history, you show me a disfranchised class, I will show you a degraded class of labor. Disfranchisement means inability to make, shape or control one's own circumstances. The disfranchised must always do the work, accept the wages, occupy the position the enfranchised assign to them. The disfranchised are in the position of the pauper. You remember the old adage, "Beggars must not be choosers"; they must take what they can get or nothing! That is exactly the position of women in the world of work today; they can not choose. If they could, do you for a moment believe they would take the subordinate places and the inferior pay? Nor is it a "new thing under the sun" for the disfranchised, the inferior classes weighed down with wrongs, to declare they "do not want to vote." The rank and file are not philosophers, they are not educated to think for themselves, but simply to accept, unquestioned, whatever comes.

Years ago in England when the workingmen, starving in the mines and factories, gathered in mobs and took bread wherever they could get it, their friends tried to educate them into a knowledge of the causes of their poverty and degradation. At one of these "monster bread meetings," held in Manchester, John Bright said to them, "Workingmen, what you need to bring to you cheap bread and plenty of it, is the franchise;" but those ignorant men shouted back to Mr. Bright, precisely as the women of America do to us today, "It is not the vote we want, it is bread"; and they broke up the meeting, refusing to allow him, their best friend, to explain to them the powers of the franchise. The condition of those workingmen was very little above that of slavery. . . .

Sad as is the condition of the workingmen of England today, it is infinitely better than it was twenty years ago. . . . This is the way in which the ballot in the hands of the masses of wage-earners, even under a monarchial form of government, makes of them a tremendous balance of power whose wants and wishes the instinct of self-interest compels the political leaders to study and obey.

The great distinctive advantage possessed by the workingmen of this republic is that the son of the humblest citizen, black or white, has equal chances with the son of the richest in the land if he take advantage of the public schools, the colleges and the many opportunities freely offered. It is this equality of rights which makes our nation a home for the oppressed of all the monarchies of the old world.

And yet, notwithstanding the declaration of our Revolutionary fathers, "all men created equal," "governments derive their just powers from the consent of the governed," "taxation and representation inseparable"—notwithstanding all these grand enunciations, our government was founded upon the blood and bones of half a million human beings, bought and sold as chattels in the market. Nearly all the original thirteen states had property qualifications which disfranchised poor white men as well as women and negroes. Thomas Jefferson, at the head of the old Democratic party, took the lead in advocating the removal of all property qualifications, as so many violations of the fundamental principle of our government "the right of consent." In New York the qualification was $250. Martin Van Buren, the chief of the Democracy, was a member of the Constitutional Convention held in Buffalo in 1821, which wiped out that qualification so far as white men were concerned. He declared, "The poor man has as good a right to a voice in the government as the rich man, and a vastly greater need to possess it as a means of protection to himself and his family." It was because the Democracy enfranchised poor white men, both native and foreign, that that strong old party held absolute sway in this country for almost forty years, with only now and then a one-term Whig administration.

... The vast numbers of wage-earning men coming from Europe to this country, where manhood suffrage prevails with no limitations, find themselves invested at once with immense political power. They organize their trades unions, but not being able to use the franchise intelligently, they continue to strike and to fight their battles with the capitalists just as they did in the old countries. Neither press nor politicians dare to condemn these strikes or to demand their suppression because the workingmen hold the balance of power, and can use it for the success or defeat of either party.

(Miss Anthony here related various timely instances of strikes where force was used to prevent non-union men from taking the places of the strikers, and neither the newspapers nor political leaders ventured to sustain the officials in the necessary steps to preserve law and order, or if they did they were defeated at the next election.)

It is said women do not need the ballot for their protection because they are supported by men. Statistics show that there are 3,000,000 women in this nation supporting themselves. In the crowded cities of the East they are compelled to work in shops, stores and factories for the merest pittance. In New York alone, there are over 50,000 of these women receiving less than fifty cents a day. Women wage-earners in different occupations have organized themselves into trades unions, from time to time, and made their strikes to get justice at the hands of their employers just as men have done, but I have yet to learn of a successful strike of any body of women. The best organized one I ever knew was that of the collar laundry women of the city of Troy, N. Y., the great emporium for the manufacture of shirts, collars and cuffs. They formed a trades union of several hundred members and demanded an increase of wages. It was refused. So one May morning in 1867, each woman threw down her scissors and her needle, her starch-pan and flat-iron, and for three long months not one returned to the factories. At the end of that time they were literally starved out, and the majority of them were compelled to go back, but not at their old wages, for their employers cut them down to even a lower figure. . . .

The question with you, as men, is not whether you want your wives and daughters to vote, nor with you, as women, whether you yourselves want to vote; but whether you will help to put this power of the ballot into the hands of the 3,000,000 wage-earning women, so that they may be able to compel politicians to legislate in their favor and employers to grant them justice.

The law of capital is to extort the greatest amount of work for the least amount of money; the rule of labor is to do the smallest amount of work for the largest amount of money. Hence there is, and in the nature of things must continue to be, antagonism between the two classes; therefore, neither should be left wholly at the mercy of the other.

It was cruel, under the old regime, to give rich men the right to rule poor men. It was wicked to allow white men absolute power over black men. It is vastly more cruel, more wicked to give to all men—rich and poor, white and black, native and foreign, educated and ignorant, virtuous and vicious—this absolute control over women. Men talk of the injustice of monopolies. There never was, there never can be, a monopoly so fraught with injustice, tyranny and degradation as this monopoly of sex, of all men over all women. Therefore I not only agree with Abraham Lincoln that, "No man is good enough to govern another man without his consent;" but I say also that no man is good enough to govern a woman without her consent, and still further, that all men combined in government are not good enough to govern all women without their consent. There might have been some plausible excuse for the rich governing the poor, the educated governing the ignorant, the Saxon governing the African; but there can be none for making the husband the ruler of the wife, the brother of the sister, the man of the woman, his peer in birth, in education, in social position, in all that stands for the best and highest in humanity.

I believe that by nature men are no more unjust than women. If from the beginning women had maintained the right to rule not only themselves but men also, the latter today doubtless would be occupying the subordinate places with inferior pay in the world of work; women would be holding the higher positions with the big salaries; widowers would be doomed to a "life interest of one-third of the family estate;" husbands would "owe service" to their wives, so that every one of you men would be begging your good wives, "Please be so kind as to 'give me' ten cents for a cigar." The principle of self-government can not be violated with impunity. The individual's right to it is sacred—regardless of class, caste, race, color, sex or any other accident or incident of birth. What we ask is that you shall cease to imagine that women are outside this law, and that you shall come into the knowledge that disfranchisement means the same degradation to your daughters as to your sons.

Governments can not afford to ignore the rights of those holding the ballot, who make and unmake every law and law-maker. It is not because the members of Congress are tyrants that women receive only half pay and are admitted only to inferior positions in the departments. It is simply in obedience to a law of political economy which makes it impossible for a government to do as much for the disfranchised as for the enfranchised. Women are no exception to the general rule. As disfranchisement always has degraded men, socially, morally and industrially, so today it is disfranchisement that degrades women in the same spheres.

Again men say it is not votes, but the law of supply and demand which regulates wages. The law of gravity is that water shall run down hill, but when men build a dam across the stream, the force of gravity is stopped and the water held back. The law of supply and demand regulates free and enfranchised labor, but disfranchisement estops its operation. What we ask is the removal of the dam, that women, like men, may reap the benefit of the law. Did the law of supply and demand regulate work and wages in the olden days of slavery? This law can no more reach the disfranchised than it did the enslaved. There is scarcely a place where a woman can earn a single dollar without a man's consent.

There are many women equally well qualified with men for principals and superintendents of schools, and yet, while three-fourths of the teachers are women, nearly all of them are relegated to subordinate positions on half or at most two-thirds the salaries paid to men. The law of supply and demand is ignored, and that of sex alone settles the question. If a business man should advertise for a bookkeeper and ten young men, equally well qualified, should present themselves and, after looking them over, he should say, "To you who have red hair, we will pay full wages, while to you with black hair we will pay half the regular price;" that would not be a more flagrant violation of the law of supply and demand than is that now perpetrated upon women because of their sex.

And then again you say, "Capital, not the vote, regulates labor." Granted, for the sake of the argument, that capital does control the labor of women, Chinamen and slaves; but no one with eyes to see and ears to hear, will concede for a moment that capital absolutely dominates the work and wages of the free and enfranchised men of this republic. It is in order to lift the millions of our wage-earning women into a position of as much power over their own labor as men possess that they should be invested with the franchise. This ought to be done not only for the sake of justice to the women, but to the men with whom they compete; for, just so long as there is a degraded class of labor in the market, it always will be used by the capitalists to checkmate and undermine the superior classes.

Now that as a result of the agitation for equality of chances, and through the invention of machinery, there has come a great revolution in the world of economics, so that wherever a man may go to earn an honest dollar a woman may go also, there is no escape from the conclusion that she must be clothed with equal power to protect herself. That power is the ballot, the symbol of freedom and equality, without which no citizen is sure of keeping even that which he hath, much less of getting that which he hath not. Women are today the peers of men in education, in the arts and sciences, in the industries and professions, and there is no escape from the conclusion that the next step must be to make them the peers of men in the government—city, State and national—to give them an equal voice in the framing, interpreting and administering of the codes and constitutions.

We recognize that the ballot is a two-edged, nay, a many-edged sword, which may be made to cut in every direction. If wily politicians and sordid capitalists may wield it for mere party and personal greed; if oppressed wage-earners may invoke it to wring justice from legislators and extort material advantages from employers; if the lowest and most degraded classes of men may use it to open wide the sluice-ways of vice and crime; if it may be the instrumentality by which the narrow, selfish, corrupt and corrupting men and measures rule—it is quite as true that noble-minded statesmen, philanthropists and reformers may make it the weapon with which to reverse the above order of things, as soon as they can have added to their now small numbers the immensely larger ratio of what men so love to call "the better half of the people." When women vote, they will make a new balance of power that must be weighed and measured and calculated in its effect upon every social and moral question which goes to the arbitrament of the ballot box. Who can doubt that when the representative women of thought and culture, who are today the moral backbone of our nation, sit in counsel with the best men of the country, higher conditions will be the result?

Insurrectionary and revolutionary methods of righting wrongs, imaginary or real, are pardonable only in the enslaved and disfranchised. The moment any class of men possess the ballot, it is their weapon and their shield. Men with a vote have no valid excuse for resorting to the use of illegal means to fight their battles. When the masses of wage-earning men are educated into a knowledge of their own rights and of their duties to others, so that they are able to vote intelligently, they can carry their measures through the ballot-box and will have no need to resort to force. But so long as they remain in ignorance and are manipulated by the political bosses they will continue to vote against their own interests and turn again to violence to right their wrongs.

If men possessing the power of the ballot are driven to desperate means to gain their ends, what shall be done by disfranchised women? There are grave questions of moral, as well as of material interest in which women are most deeply concerned. Denied the ballot, the legitimate means with which to exert their influence, and, as a rule being lovers of peace, they have recourse to prayers and tears, those potent weapons of women and children, and, when they fail, must tamely submit to wrong or rise in rebellion against the powers that be. Women's crusades against saloons, brothels and gambling dens, emptying kegs and bottles into the streets, breaking doors and windows and burning houses, all go to prove that disfranchisement, the denial of lawful means to gain desired ends, may drive even women to violations of law and order. Hence to secure both national and "domestic tranquility," to "establish justice," to carry out the spirit of our Constitution, put into the hands of all women, as you have into those of all men, the ballot, that symbol of perfect equality, that right protective of all other rights.[5]

SOCIAL PURITY

Though women, as a class, are much less addicted to drunkenness and licentiousness than men, it is universally conceded that they are by far the greater sufferers from these evils. Compelled by their position in society to depend on men for subsistence, for food, clothes, shelter, for every chance even to earn a dollar, they have no way of escape from the besotted victims of appetite and passion with whom their lot is cast. They must endure, if not endorse, these twin vices, embodied, as they so often are, in the person of father, brother, husband, son, employer. No one can doubt that the sufferings of the sober, virtuous woman, in legal subjection to the mastership of a drunken, immoral husband and father over herself and children, not only from physical abuse, but from spiritual shame and humiliation, must be such as the man himself can not possibly comprehend.

It is not my purpose to harrow your feelings by any attempt at depicting the horrible agonies of mind and body that grow out of these monster social evils. They are already but too well known. Scarce a family throughout our broad land but has had its peace and happiness marred by one or the other, or both. That these evils exist, we all know; that something must be done, we as well know; that the old methods have failed, that man, alone, has proved himself incompetent to eradicate, or even regulate them, is equally evident. It shall be my endeavor, therefore, to prove to you that we must now adopt new measures and bring to our aid new forces to accomplish the desired end. . . .

The roots of the giant evil, intemperance, are not merely moral and social; they extend deep and wide into the financial and political structure of the government; and whenever women, or men, shall intelligently and seriously set themselves about the work of uprooting the liquor traffic, they will find something more than tears and prayers needful to the task. Financial and political power must be combined with moral and social influence, all bound together in one earnest, energetic, persistent force.

(Statistics given of pauperism, lunacy, idiocy and crime growing out of intemperance.)

The prosecutions in our courts for breach of promise, divorce, adultery, bigamy, seduction, rape; the newspaper reports every day of every year of scandals and outrages, of wife murders and paramour shootings, of abortions and infanticides, are perpetual reminders of men's incapacity to cope successfully with this monster evil of society.

The statistics of New York show the number of professional prostitutes in that city to be over twenty thousand. Add to these the thousands and tens of thousands of Boston, Philadelphia, Washington, New Orleans, St. Louis, Chicago, San Francisco, and all our cities, great and small, from ocean to ocean, and what a holocaust of the womanhood of this nation is sacrificed to the insatiate Moloch of lust. And yet more: those myriads of wretched women, publicly known as prostitutes, constitute but a small portion of the numbers who actually tread the paths of vice and crime. For, as the oft broken ranks of the vast army of common drunkards are steadily filled by the boasted moderate drinkers, so are the ranks of professional prostitution continually replenished by discouraged, seduced, deserted unfortunates, who can no longer hide the terrible secret of their lives.

The Albany Law Journal, of December, 1876, says: "The laws of infanticide must be a dead letter in the District of Columbia. According to the reports of the local officials, the dead bodies of infants, still-born and murdered, which have been found during the past year, scattered over parks and vacant lots in the city of Washington, are to be numbered by hundreds."

In 1869 the Catholics established a Foundling Hospital in New York City. At the close of the first six months Sister Irene reported thirteen hundred little waifs laid in the basket at her door. That meant thirteen hundred of the daughters of New York, with trembling hands and breaking hearts, trying to bury their sorrow and their shame from the world's cruel gaze. That meant thirteen hundred mothers' hopes blighted and blasted. Thirteen hundred Rachels weeping for their children because they were not!

Nor is it womanhood alone that is thus fearfully sacrificed. For every betrayed woman, there is always the betrayer, man. For every abandoned woman, there is always *one* abandoned man and oftener many more. It is estimated that there are 50,000 professional prostitutes in London, and Dr. Ryan calculates that there are 400,000 men in that city directly or indirectly connected with them, and that this vice causes the city an annual expenditure of $40,000,000.

All attempts to describe the loathsome and contagious disease which it engenders defy human language. The Rev. Wm. G. Eliot, of St. Louis, says of it: "Few know of the terrible nature of the disease in question and its fearful ravages, not only among the guilty, but the innocent. Since its first recognized appearance in Europe in the fifteenth century, it has been a desolation and a scourge. In its worst forms it is so subtle, that its course can with difficulty be traced. It poisons the constitution, and may be imparted to others by those who have no outward or distinguishable marks of it themselves. It may be propagated months and years after it seems to have been cured. The purity of womanhood and the helplessness of infancy afford no certainty of escape.

(Medical testimony given from cities in Europe.)

Man's legislative attempts to set back this fearful tide of social corruption have proved even more futile and disastrous than have those for the suppression of intemperance—as witness the Contagious Diseases Acts of England and the St. Louis experiment. And yet efforts to establish similar laws are constantly made in our large cities, New York and Washington barely escaping last winter.

To license certain persons to keep brothels and saloons is but to throw around them and their traffic the shield of law, and thereby to blunt the edge of all moral and social efforts against them. Nevertheless, in every large city, brothels are virtually licensed. When "Maggie Smith" is made to appear before the police court at the close of each quarter, to pay her fine of $10, $25 or $100, as an inmate or a keeper of a brothel, and allowed to continue her vocation, so long as she pays her fine, *that is license*. When a grand jury fails to find cause for indictment against a well-known keeper of a house of ill-fame, that, too, is *permission* for her and all of her class to follow their trade, against the statute laws of the State, and that with impunity.

The work of woman is not to lessen the severity or the certainty of the penalty for the violation of the moral law, but to prevent this violation by the removal of the causes which lead to it. These causes are said to be wholly different with the sexes. The acknowledged incentive to this vice on the part of man is his own abnormal passion; while on the part of woman, in the great majority of cases, it is conceded to be destitution—absolute want of the necessaries of life. Lecky, the famous historian of European morals, says: "The statistics of prostitution show that a great proportion of those women who have fallen into it have been impelled by the most extreme poverty, in many instances verging on starvation." All other conscientious students of this terrible problem, on both continents, agree with Mr. Lecky. Hence, there is no escape from the conclusion that, while woman's want of bread induces her to pursue this vice, man's love of the vice itself leads him into it and holds him there. While statistics show no lessening of the passional demand on the part of man, they reveal a most frightful increase of the temptations, the necessities, on the part of woman.

In the olden times, when the daughters of the family, as well as the wife, were occupied with useful and profitable work in the household, getting the meals and washing the dishes three times in every day of every year, doing the baking, the brewing, the washing and the ironing, the whitewashing, the butter and cheese and soap making, the mending and the making of clothes for the entire family, the carding, spinning and weaving of the cloth—when everything to eat, to drink and to wear was manufactured in the home, almost no young women "went out to work." But now, when nearly all these handicrafts are turned over to men and to machinery, tens of thousands, nay, millions, of the women of both hemispheres are thrust into the world's outer market of work to earn their own subsistence. Society, ever slow to change its conditions, presents to these millions but few and meager chances. Only the barest necessaries, and oftentimes not even those, can be purchased with the proceeds of the most excessive and exhausting labor.

Hence, the reward of virtue for the homeless, friendless, penniless woman is ever a scanty larder, a pinched, patched, faded wardrobe, a dank basement or rickety garret, with the colder, shabbier scorn and neglect of the more fortunate of her sex. Nightly, as weary and worn from her day's toil she wends her way through the dark alleys toward her still darker abode, where only cold and hunger await her, she sees on every side and at every turn the gilded hand of vice and crime outstretched, beckoning her to food and clothes and shelter; hears the whisper in softest accents, "Come with me and I will give you all the comforts, pleasures and luxuries that love and wealth can bestow." Since the vast multitudes of human beings, women like men, are not born to the courage or conscience of the martyr, can we wonder that so many poor girls fall, that so many accept material ease and comfort at the expense of spiritual purity and peace? Should we not wonder, rather, that so many escape the sad fate?

Clearly, then, the first step toward solving this problem is to lift this vast army of poverty-stricken women who now crowd our cities, above the temptation, the necessity, to sell themselves, in marriage or out, for bread and shelter. To do that, girls, like boys, must be educated to some lucrative employment; women, like men, must have equal chances to earn a living. If the plea that poverty is the cause of woman's prostitution be not true, perfect equality of chances to earn honest bread will demonstrate the falsehood by removing that pretext and placing her on the same plane with man. Then, if she is found in the ranks of vice and crime, she will be there for the same reason that man is and, from an object of pity, she, like him, will become a fit, subject of contempt. From being the party sinned against, she will become an equal sinner, if not the greater of the two. Women, like men, must not only have "fair play" in the world of work and self-support, but, like men, must be eligible to all the honors and emoluments of society and government. Marriage, to women as to men, must be a luxury, not a necessity; an incident of life, not all of it. And the only possible way to accomplish this great change is to accord to women equal power in the making, shaping and controlling of the circumstances of life. That equality of rights and privileges is vested in the ballot, the symbol of power in a republic. Hence, our first and most urgent demand-that women shall be protected in the exercise of their inherent, personal, citizen's right to a voice in the government, municipal, state, national.

Alexander Hamilton said one hundred years ago, "Give to a man the right over my subsistence, and he has power over my whole moral being." No one doubts the truth of this assertion as between man and man; while, as between man and woman, not only does almost no one believe it, but the masses of people deny it. And yet it is the fact of man's possession of this right over woman's subsistence which gives to him the power to dictate to her a moral code vastly higher and purer than the one he chooses for himself. Not less true is it, that the fact of woman's dependence on man for her subsistence renders her utterly powerless to exact from him the same high moral code she chooses for herself.

Of the 8,000,000 women over twenty-one years of age in the United States, 800,000, one out of every ten, are unmarried, and fully one-half of the entire number, or 4,000,000, support themselves wholly or in part by the industry of their own hands and brains. All of these, married or single, have to ask man, as an individual, a corporation, or a government, to grant to them even the privilege of hard work and small pay. The tens of thousands of poor but respectable working girls soliciting copying, clerkships, shop work, teaching, must ask of men, and not seldom receive in response, "Why work for a living? There are other ways!"

Whoever controls work and wages, controls morals. Therefore, we must have women employers, superintendents, committees, legislators; wherever girls go to seek the means of subsistence, there must be some woman. Nay, more; we must have women preachers, lawyers, doctors—that—wherever women go to seek counsel—spiritual, legal, physical—there, too, they will be sure to find the best and noblest of their own sex to minister to them.

Independence is happiness. "No man should depend upon another; not even upon his own father. By depend I mean, obey without examination-yield to the will of any one whomsoever." This is the conclusion to which Pierre, the hero of Madame Sand's "Monsieur Sylvestre," arrives, after running away from the uncle who had determined to marry him to a woman he did not choose to wed. In freedom he discovers that, though deprived of all the luxuries to which he had been accustomed, he is happy, and writes his friend that "without having realized it, he had been unhappy all his life; had suffered from his dependent condition; that nothing in his life, his pleasures, his occupations, had been of his own choice." And is not this the precise condition of what men call the "better half" of the human family? ...

In a western city the wives conspired to burn down a house of ill-fame in which their husbands had placed a half-dozen of the demi-monde. Would

it not have shown much more womanly wisdom and virtue for those legal wives to have refused to recognize their husbands, instead of wreaking
their vengeance on the heads of those wretched women? But how could
they without finding themselves, as a result, penniless and homeless? The
person, the services, the children, the subsistence, of each and every one
of those women belonged by law, not to herself, but to her unfaithful husband.

Now, why is it that man can hold woman to this high code of morals,
like Caesar's wife-not only pure but above suspicion-and so surely and severely punish her for every departure, while she is so helpless, so powerless
to check him in his license, or to extricate herself from his presence and
control? His power grows out of his right over her subsistence. Her lack of
power grows out of her dependence on him for her food, her clothes, her
shelter.

Marriage never will cease to be a wholly unequal partnership until the
law recognizes the equal ownership in the joint earnings and possessions.
The true relation of the sexes never can be attained until woman is free and
equal with man. Neither in the making nor executing of the laws regulating these relations has woman ever had the slightest voice. The statutes
for marriage and divorce, for adultery, breach of promise, seduction, rape,
bigamy, abortion, infanticide—all were made by men. They, alone, decide
who are guilty of violating these laws and what shall be their punishment,
with judge, jury and advocate all men, with no woman's voice heard in our
courts, save as accused or witness, and in many cases the married woman
is denied the poor privilege of testifying as to her own guilt or innocence
of the crime charged against her. . . .

It is worse than folly, it is madness, for women to delude themselves with
the idea that their children will escape the terrible penalty of the law. The
taint of their birth will surely follow them. For pure women to continue
to devote themselves to their man-appointed mission of visiting the dark
purlieus of society and struggling to reclaim the myriads of badly-born human beings swarming there, is as hopeless as would be an attempt to ladle
the ocean with a teaspoon; as unphilosophical as was the undertaking of
the old American Colonization Society, which, with great labor and pains
and money, redeemed from slavery and transported to Liberia annually
400 negroes; or the Fugitive Slave Societies, which succeeded in running
off to Canada, on their "under-ground railroads," some 40,000 in a whole
quarter of a century. While those good men were thus toiling to rescue the
400 or the 40,000 individual victims of slavery, each day saw hundreds
and each year thousands of human beings born into the terrible condition
of chattelism. All see and admit now what none but the Abolitionists saw

then, that the only effectual work was the entire overthrow of the system of slavery; the abrogation of the law which sanctioned the right of property in man. . . .

Thus, wherever you go, you find the best women, in and out of the churches, all absorbed in establishing or maintaining benevolent or reform institutions; charitable societies, soup-houses, ragged schools, industrial schools, mite societies, mission schools—at home and abroad—homes and hospitals for the sick, the aged, the friendless, the foundling, the fallen; asylums for the orphans, the blind, the deaf and dumb, the insane, the inebriate, the idiot. The women of this century are neither idle nor indifferent. They are working with might and main to mitigate the evils which stare them in the face on every side, but much of their work is without knowledge. It is aimed at the effects, not the cause; it is plucking the spoiled fruit; it is lopping off the poisonous branches of the deadly upas tree, which but makes the root more vigorous in sending out new shoots in every direction. A right understanding of physiological law teaches us that the cause must be removed; the tree must be girdled; the tap-root must be severed.

The tap-root of our social upas lies deep down at the very foundations of society. It is woman's dependence. It is woman's subjection. Hence, the first and only efficient work must be to emancipate woman from her enslavement. The wife must no longer echo the poet Milton's ideal Eve, when she adoringly said to Adam, "God, thy law; thou, mine!" She must feel herself accountable to God alone for every act, fearing and obeying no man, save where his will is in line with her own highest idea of divine law. . . .

If the divine law visits the sins of the fathers upon the children, equally so does it transmit to them their virtues. Therefore, if it is through woman's ignorant subjection to the tyranny of man's appetites and passions that the life current of the race is corrupted, then must it be through her intelligent emancipation that the race shall be redeemed from the curse, and her children and children's children rise up to call her blessed. When the mother of Christ shall be made the true model of womanhood and motherhood, when the office of maternity shall be held sacred and the mother shall consecrate herself, as did Mary, to the one idea of bringing forth the Christ-child, then, and not till then, will this earth see a new order of men and women, prone to good rather than evil.

I am a full and firm believer in the revelation that it is through woman that the race is to be redeemed. And it is because of this faith that I ask for her immediate and unconditional emancipation from all political, industrial, social and religious subjection. . . .

A minister of Chicago sums up the infamies of that great metropolis of the West as follows: 3,000 licensed dram-shops and myriad patrons;

300 gambling houses and countless frequenters, many of them young men from the best families of the city; 79 obscene theatres, with their thousands of degraded men and boys nightly in attendance; 500 brothels, with their thousands of poor girls, bodies and souls sacrificed to the 20,000 or 30,000 depraved men—young and old, married and single—who visit them. While all the participants in all these forms of iniquity, victims and victimizers alike—the women excepted-may go to the polls on every election day and vote for the mayor and members of the common council, who will either continue to license these places, or fail to enforce the laws which would practically close them—not a single woman in that city may record her vote against those wretched blots on civilization. The profane, tobacco-chewing, whiskey-drinking, gambling libertines may vote, but not their virtuous, intelligent, sober, law-abiding wives and mothers! ...

As the fountain can rise no higher than the spring that feeds it, so a legislative body will enact or enforce no law above the average sentiment of the people who created it. Any and every reform work is sure to lead women to the ballot-box. It is idle for them to hope to battle successfully against the monster evils of society until they shall be armed with weapons equal to those of the enemy—votes and money. Archimedes said, "Give to me a fulcrum on which to plant my lever, and I will move the world." And I say, give to woman the ballot, the political fulcrum, on which to plant her moral lever, and she will lift the world into a nobler and purer atmosphere.

Two great necessities forced this nation to extend justice and equality to the negro:

First, Military necessity, which compelled the abolition of the crime and curse of slavery, before the rebellion could be overcome.

Second, Political necessity, which required the enfranchisement of the newly-freed men, before the work of reconstruction could begin.

The third is now pressing, Moral necessity—to emancipate woman, before Social Purity, the nation's safeguard, ever can be established.[6]

ANTHONY AND THE SPIRITUALISTS (1890s)

After the Berlin meeting Miss Anthony and I were invited to spend a weekend at the home of Mrs. Jacob Bright, that "Aunt Susan" might renew her acquaintance with Annie Besant. . . . Now she could not conceal her disapproval of the "other-worldliness" of Mrs. Besant, Mrs. Bright, and her daughter. . . .

"Annie," demanded Aunt Susan, "why don't you make that aura of yours do its gallivanting in this world, looking up the needs of the oppressed, and investigating the causes of present wrongs? Then you could reveal to us workers just what we should do to put things right, and we could be about it."

Mrs. Besant sighed and said that life was short and aeons were long, and that while every one would be perfected some time, it was useless to deal with individuals here.

"But, Annie!" exclaimed Miss Anthony, pathetically, "We *are* here! Our business is here! It's our duty to do what we can here."

Mrs. Besant seemed not to hear her. She was in a trance, gazing into the aeons. . . . It was plain that she could not bring herself back from the other world, so Miss Anthony, perforce, accompanied her to it.

"When your aura goes visiting in the other world," she asked, curiously, "does it ever meet your old friend Charles Bradlaugh?"

... Mrs. Besant heaved a deeper sigh. "I am very much discouraged over Mr. Bradlaugh," she admitted, wanly. "He is hovering too near this world. He cannot seem to get away from his mundane interests. He is as much concerned with parliamentary affairs now as when he was on this plane."

"Humph!" said Miss Anthony; "that's the most sensible thing I've heard yet about the other world. It encourages me. I've always felt sure that if I entered the other life before women were enfranchised nothing in the glories of heaven would interest me so much as the work for women's freedom on earth."[7]

SPEECH IN THE WOMAN'S BIBLE CONTROVERSY (1896)

The one distinct feature of our association has been the right of individual opinion for every member. We have been beset at each step with the cry that somebody was injuring the cause by the expression of sentiments which differed from those held by the majority. The religious persecution of the ages has been carried on under what was claimed to be the command of God. I distrust those people who know so well what God wants them to do, because I notice it always coincides with their own desires. All the way along the history of our movement there has been this same contest on account of religious theories. Forty years ago one of our noblest men said to me, "You would better never hold another convention than allow Ernestine L. Rose on your platform"; because that eloquent woman, who ever stood for justice and freedom, did not believe in the plenary inspiration of the Bible. Did we banish Mrs. Rose? No, indeed!

Every new generation of converts threshes over the same old straw. The point is whether you will sit in judgment on one who questions the divine inspiration of certain passages in the Bible derogatory to women. If Mrs. Stanton had written approvingly of these passages you would not have brought in this resolution for fear the case might be injured among the *liberals* in religion. In other words, if she had written *your* views, you would not have considered a resolution necessary. To pass this one is to set back the hands on the dial of reform.

What you should say to outsiders is that a Christian has neither more nor less rights in our association than an atheist. When our platform becomes too narrow for people of all creeds and of no creeds, I myself can not stand upon it. Many things have been said and done by our *orthodox* friends which I have felt to be extremely harmful to our case; but I should no more consent to a resolution denouncing them than I shall consent to this. Who is to draw the line? Who can tell now whether these commentaries may not prove a great help to woman's emancipation from old superstitions which have barred its way?

Lucretia Mott at first thought Mrs. Stanton had injured the cause of all woman's other rights by insisting upon the demand for suffrage, but she had sense enough not to bring in a resolution against it. In 1860 when Mrs. Stanton made a speech before the New York Legislature in favor of a bill making drunkenness a ground for divorce, there was a general cry among the friends that she had killed the woman's cause. I shall be pained beyond expression if the delegates here are so narrow and illiberal as to adopt this resolution. You would better not begin resolving against individual action or you will find no limit. This year it is Mrs. Stanton; next year it may be I or one of yourselves, who will be the victim.

If we do not inspire in women a broad and catholic spirit, they will fail, when enfranchised, to constitute that power for better government which we have always claimed for them. Ten women educated into the practice of liberal principles would be a stronger force than 10,000 organized on a platform of intolerance and bigotry. I pray you vote for religious liberty, without censorship or inquisition. This resolution adopted will be a vote of censure upon a woman who is without a peer in intellectual and statesmanlike ability; one who has stood for half a century the acknowledged leader of progressive thought and demand in regard to all matters pertaining to the absolute freedom of women.[8]

NOTES

1. [This is the first known speech by Susan B. Anthony, published for the first time here, I believe. Its major point—that any church member who supports any aspect of the liquor trade is guilty of its sins—is reminiscent of arguments of the antislavery people that the North, too, was implicated in the guilt of slavery, or

the refusal of Quaker abolitionists to wear clothing made of cotton, since cotton was grown by slaveholders. It is studded with biblical quotations, and I have added chapter and verse for those who may not be aware of this material.]

2. [This was the cry from a crowd that believed its profit from the sale of statues of Diana was threatened by the preaching of Christians.]

3. [These unpublished speeches are from the Library of Congress; there is no date on the manuscript of the second, but it is most likely from roughly the same time as the first. The manuscript may also be missing some pages, since it simply ends in the middle of a thought. Anthony's commitment to antislavery was deep and long. After the Civil War she was incensed that abolitionists had given up agitation, since racism in the North was still strong.]

4. [Elizabeth Cady Stanton, Susan B. Anthony, et al., eds., *The History of Woman Suffrage*, 6 vols., repr. ed. (New York: Arno Press, 1969), 2:687–689. After sitting through days with lawyers expounding at the judge and jury without being able to say a word on her own behalf, Anthony was probably simmering when the judge pulled his written verdict from his pocket, instructed to jurors to find her guilty without deliberating, and then dismissed them.]

5. [Ida Husted Harper, *The Life and Work of Susan B. Anthony*, 3 vols. (Indianapolis: Hollenbeck Press, 1898–1908), 2:996–1003. In the 1870s, Anthony put her thoughts together into a speech she delivered regularly. This version was assembled and edited by Ida Husted Harper from newspaper accounts. (In complete contradistinction to its contents, the published version called it "woman wants bread, not the ballot.")]

6. [Harper, *The Life and Work of Susan B. Anthony*, 2:1004-1012. For its time, it was relatively fearless, mentioning prostitution, infanticide, and venereal disease (though the last earned a euphemism). Its major point, that enfranchisement was necessary to regulate these evils, may seem quaint and outdated to those of us who have been through both a so-called sexual revolution and the movement to end violence against women and children. But it was important for her attempt to talk about a systemic issue that required a systemic solution.]

7. [Anna Howard Shaw with Elizabeth Jordan, *The Story of a Pioneer* (New York: Harper, 1915), 214–216. Many suffragists were involved with the spiritualist movement of the late nineteenth century, including Elizabeth Stanton. Though many of them sought to win Anthony over, she had little patience with them, as we can see in this excerpt.]

8. [*The History of Woman Suffrage*, 4:263–264. After the publication of the first volume of *The Woman's Bible*, more religiously conservative members of the NAWSA were offended. They proposed a resolution at the annual convention disavowing any connection to that work. Anthony, who had begged off from being a part of this project of Stanton's, nonetheless was distressed when the rank and file of the suffrage organization in effect disowned her old friend. She left the chair to deliver this exhortation.]

[CHAPTER 10]

Karl Barth (1886–1968)

SELECTED AND EDITED BY GEORGE HUNSINGER

Karl Barth was born in Basel, Switzerland on May 10, 1886. Inspired by his father, a professor of New Testament at Bern, Barth resolved to study theology. He matriculated at the University of Bern and studied Reformed theology, as well as the thought of German philosophers Immanuel Kant and Friedrich Schleiermacher, who left a deep impression on him. He also studied at the University of Berlin with the great church historian Adolf von Harnack, and at the University of Marburg with the neo-Kantian theologian Wilhelm Hermann. He was ordained, and in 1911 took a pastorate in Safenwil, Switzerland.

It was during this first pastorate that Barth came to an acute rethinking of his theology, as well as his views of law, politics, and society. As his biographer James B. Torrance puts it: "On the one hand, when World War I broke out, he was deeply disturbed by the 'Manifesto of the Intellectuals,' 'the black day,' as he called it, when ninety-three scholars and artists, including his own teachers Harnack and Hermann, supported the war policy of Kaiser Wilhelm II, which seemed to him to call into question his colleagues' understanding of the Bible, history, and dogmatics. Was this where the synthesis of (German) culture and religion was leading the Christian church? On the other hand, in his industrial parish, he became acutely aware of the issues of social justice, poor wages, factory legislation, and true union affairs."[1]

Never having studied for a doctorate, Barth did more than anyone to revitalize theology in the twentieth century. His massive Church Dogmatics *remained unfinished—like the cathedral in Strasbourg, he once quipped, with its missing tower. Thoroughly modern, he rejected modernism in theology. Deeply traditional, he left no stone of tradition unturned. Without deterring easy classifications from critics, he has defied easy classification. Not since Luther and Calvin has there been a Protestant theologian so prodigious in written output and so active in worldly affairs, both ecclesiastical and political. Though Barth was reputed for sharp polemic, his infectious childlike joy, his self-deprecating humor, his love for Mozart, and his profound understanding of Holy Scripture have endeared him to many whose lives he has immeasurably enriched.*

Dietrich Bonhoeffer once suggested that in Barth we find the same hilaritas *that we do in Mozart. The good cheer which knows how to incorporate all that is negative within itself without losing its basic gladness was surely one of Barth's most appealing characteristics. It was a* hilaritas *that was informed by* gravitas *but never succumbed to it. For all his greatness, or perhaps just because of it, Barth did not take himself too seriously. Along with* hilaritas *and* gravitas, *an element of* humilitas *pervaded his work. Barth had no higher aspiration than to place his intellect in the service of God's grace. Grace inspires the cheerfulness, gravity, and humility he saw as proper to the theologian's task.*

JESUS CHRIST AND THE MOVEMENT FOR SOCIAL JUSTICE

I AM HAPPY to be able to speak to you about *Jesus,* especially because the initiative for it has come from your side. The best and greatest thing that I can bring to you as a pastor will always be Jesus Christ and a portion of the powers which have gone out from his person into history and life. I take it as a sign of the mutual understanding between us that you for your part have come to me with a request for this best and greatest thing. I can say to you, however, that the other half of our theme lies just as much on my heart: *the movement for social justice.* A well-known theologian and author has recently argued that these two ought not to be joined together as they are in our topic: "Jesus Christ *and* the movement for social justice," for that makes it sound as if they are really two different realities which must first be connected more or less artificially. Both are seen as one and the same: Jesus *is* the movement for social justice, and the movement for social justice *is* Jesus in the present. I can adopt this view in good conscience if I reserve the right to show more precisely in what sense I do so. The real contents of the person of Jesus can in fact be summed up by the words: "movement for social justice."

And now, in conclusion, allow me a few personal words which I would like to say to you as a pastor of this community.

First, to those friends present who up to now have related themselves to socialism in an indifferent, reserved, or *hostile* way: At this moment you are perhaps feeling somewhat disappointed and upset, so that it would not be inconceivable that one or another might go out from here and report: "He said that the socialists are right." I would be sorry if anyone said that. I repeat once again: I have spoken about what socialists *want,* not about the manner in which they *act* to attain it. *About what they want, I say: That is what Jesus wanted, too.* About the manner in which they *act* to attain it, I could not say the same thing. It would be easy for me to come up with a broad critique about the manner in which the socialists act to attain it. But I fail to see what good such an easy exercise would accomplish. Therefore, I have not said that the socialists are right! Nonetheless, I do not want to say that you nonsocialists should now go home comforted and reassured. If you feel upset, then that is good. If you have the feeling that "Oh, no, Christianity is a hard and dangerous matter if one gets to the roots of it," then you have rightly understood me—or, rather, not me, but *Jesus*. For I did not want to tell you my view, but the view of Jesus as I have found it in the Gospels. Consider, then, whether as followers of Jesus you ought not to bring more understanding, more goodwill, more *participation* in the movement for social justice in our time than you have up to now.

And now to my *socialist* friends who are present: I have said that Jesus wanted what you want, that he wanted to help those who are least, that he wanted to establish the kingdom of God upon this earth, that he wanted to abolish self-seeking property, that he wanted to make persons into comrades. Your concerns are in line with the concerns of Jesus. *Real* socialism is real Christianity in our time. That may fill you with pride and satisfaction about your concerns. But I hope you have also heard the rebuke implied in the distinction I have made between Jesus and yourselves! He wanted what you want—as you *act* to attain it. There you have the difference between Jesus and yourselves. He wanted what you want, but he *acted* in the way you have heard. That is generally the difference between Jesus and the rest of us, that among us the greatest part is program, whereas for Jesus program and performance were one. Therefore, Jesus says to you quite simply that you should carry out your program, that you should *enact* what you *want*. Then you will be Christians and true human beings. Leave the superficiality and the hatred, the spirit of mammon and the self-seeking, which also exists among your ranks, behind: They do *not* belong to your concerns. Let the faithfulness and energy, the sense of community and the courage for sacrifice found in Jesus be effective among you, in your whole life; then you will be true socialists.

However, the unrest and the sharpening of conscience which Jesus in this hour has hopefully brought to us all should not be the last word in this beautiful Christmas season. I think we all have the impression that Jesus was someone quite different than we are. His image stands strangely great and high above us all, socialists and nonsocialists. Precisely for that reason he has something to say to us. Precisely for that reason he can be something for us. Precisely for that reason we touch the living God himself when we touch the hem of his garment. And if we now let our gaze rest upon him, as he goes from century to century in ever-new revelations of his glory, then something is fulfilled in us of the ancient word of promise which could also be written of the movement for social justice in our day: "*The people who walked in darkness have seen a great light.*"[2]

COMMENTARY ON ROM. 13.1

Let every man be in subjection to the existing ruling power. Though subjection may assume from time to time many various concrete forms, as an ethical conception it is here pure negative. It means to withdraw and make way; it means to have no resentment, and not to overthrow. Why, then, does not the rebel turn back and become no more a rebel? Simply because the conflict in which he is immersed cannot be represented as a conflict between him and the *existing ruling powers*; it is, rather a conflict of evil with evil. Even the most radical revolution can do no more than set what *exists* against what *exists*. Even the most radical revolution—and this is so even when it is called a "spiritual" or "peaceful" revolution—can be no more than a revolt; that is to say, it is in itself simply a justification and confirmation of what already exists. For the whole relative right of what exists is established only by the relative wrong of revolution in its victory; whereas the relative right of revolution in its victory is in no way established by the relative wrong of the existing order. Similarly also, the power of resistance in the existing order is in no way broken by the victorious attack of revolution; it is merely driven backwards, embarrassed, and compelled to adopt different forms, and thus rendered the more dangerous; whereas the energy of revolution is dissipated and rendered innocuous—simply by its victory. And so the whole conduct of the rebel in no way constitutes a judgement upon the existing order, however much his act of revolution may do so. The rebel has thoughtlessly undertaken the conflict between God's Order and the existing order. Should he allow himself to appeal directly to the ordinance of God, "should he boldly and confidently storm the heavens and bring down thence his own eternal rights which hang aloft inalienable, unbroken as the stars themselves" (Schiller), he betrays thereby perception of the true "limit to the tyrant's power," but his bold storming of the heavens in no way brings about this limitation. He may be justified at the bar of history; but he is not justified before the judgement-seat of God. The sequel shows "the return of the old natural order where men oppose their fellow men." When men undertake to substitute themselves for God, the problem of God, His mind and His judgement, still remain, but they are rendered ineffective. And so, in his rebellion, the rebel stands on the side of the existing order.

Let the existing order—State, Church, Law, Society, &c., &c.—in their totality be:

(a b c d)

Let their dissolution by the Primal Order of God, by which their totality is contradicted, be expressed by a minus sign outside the bracket:

-(+a+b+c+d)

It is then clear that no revolution, however radical, which takes place within the realm of history, can ever be identical with the divine minus sign outside the bracket, by which the totality of human ordinances is dissolved. Revolution can do no more than change the plus sign within the bracket—the plus, that is to say, which existing ordinances possess within the bracket because they exist—into a minus sign. The result of a successful revolution is therefore:

-(-a-b-c-d)

And now we see that for the first time the great divine minus sign outside the bracket has transformed the anticipatory, revolutionary minus sign into a genuine plus sign. Revolution has, therefore, the effect of restoring the old after its downfall in a new and more powerful form. (Equally false, however, is the reckoning of the legitimists: false, because they consciously and as a matter of principle—in their consciousness and in their appeal to principle lies the arrogant and titanic element in Legitimism—add a positive sign to the terms within the bracket. But the divine minus sign outside the bracket means that all human consciousness, all human principles and axioms and orthodoxies and—isms, all *principality and power and dominion*, are AS SUCH subjected to the destructive judgement of God. *Let every man be in subjection* means, therefore, that every man should consider the falsity of all human reckoning as such. We are not competent to place the decisive minus sign before the bracket; we are only competent to perceive how completely it damages our plus and our minus. Accordingly, the subjection here recommended must not be allowed to develop into a new and subtle manner of reckoning, whereby we reintroduce once more an absolute right. It is evident that there can be no more devastating undermining of the existing order than the recognition of it which is here recommended, a recognition rid of all illusion and devoid of all the joy of triumph. State, Church, Society, Positive Right, Family, Organized Research, &c, &c, live of the credulity of those who have been nurtured upon vigorous sermons-delivered-on-the-field-of-battle and upon other suchlike solemn humbug. Deprive them of their PATHOS, and they will be starved out; but stir up revolution against them, and their PATHOS is provided with fresh fodder. No-revolution is the best preparation for the true Revolution; but even no-revolution is no safe recipe. *To be in subjection* is, when it is rightly understood, an action void of purpose, an action, that is to say, which can spring only from obedience to God. Its meaning is that men have encountered God, and are thereby compelled to leave the judgement to Him. The actual occurrence of this judgement cannot be identified with the purpose or with the secret reckoning of the man of this world.)[3]

ETHICS

THESES ON CHURCH AND STATE

I. Church

1. The humility required of us, as repentance before God, means concretely that our action takes place in the order of the church and confirms the order of the church. The correlation between repentance and the church rests on the incarnation of the Christ who summons us to repentance; in this the church has its basis.

2. The church is not an order of creation. It is an order of grace relating to sin. It is not to be confused with the "barest, purest, and simplest religion" (Luther, EA, o.e. 1.1, 133) of the lost state of innocence. Nor, according to Revelation 21:22, will there any longer be a church in the consummation.

3. The church is the order, sanctified by the actual presence of the Word and Spirit of God, in which, by the grace of God, the message of man's reconciliation with God through Christ is proclaimed, where, by the grace of God, the right answer is given to this by man, i.e., the act of repentance, and where, again by the grace of God, the fellowship of men takes place in this hearing and answering, the only possible and real fellowship.

4. In virtue of the actual presence of God and to his glory, the church is the one order, holy and infallible, which is binding on all men, outside which there is no salvation, and which is the legitimate bearer and recipient of the prophetic and apostolic witness. But this actual presence of God as the ontic and noetic ground of these qualities has to be continually given to it, and therefore believed in it and acknowledged as grace in the act of repentance before God.

5. As a human work, and therefore in all its reality apart from the grace of God, the church has a share in the folly and wickedness of man, whose sin has been forgiven but has not ceased to be sin. It cannot ignore, then, the improper nature of that which is actively or passively done by men in

it. It will not be led astray by the opposition of the rest of the world to its task and promise, but it will also be constantly reminded by this of its own worldliness and therefore of its starting-point, allowing itself to be referred back to the grace of God. It cannot abandon its fundamental and concrete attitude of humility before the World and Spirit of God that constitute it, in favor of a disposable plenitude of truth and power inherent either in its offices or in the whole community. Even as the bride of Christ, it cannot for a single moment or in any respect cease to be his handmaid. It knows that it can only be *led* into all truth [cf. John 16:13].

6. The human work of the church is thus the service of God in the broadest sense, because it can never act effectively except under the proviso of the grace of God. It is the setting up of the symbol of proclamation and repentance whose reality is God's work alone. The symbol of this symbol is divine service in the narrower sense of the word (worship). This is the characteristic function of the church as such (in distinction from other human orders and societies which are not intrinsically the church).

7. The decisive elements of divine service in the narrower sense are as follows:

a. personal, commissioned, and responsible transmission of the biblical witness to Christ in preaching and the administration of the sacraments as necessary recollection of the givenness of this witness which is not tied to human speech and hearing.

b. all the other cultic possibilities which have their inner and outer criterion in whether or not they are commanded and responsible as expressions of repentance before God and to that extent as means of edification.

8. With the task of divine service in the broader and narrower senses the following special tasks are assigned to the church:

a. individual pastoral care, which is not possible without energetic physical care of every type;

b. the acts of individual members of the church as such, as these are characterized by repentance before God, namely, their participation and cooperation in the word of preaching oriented to the biblical witness;

c. Christian education of youth, whose Christian nature can be basically only a human question and a divine answer;

d. evangelization and missions as a necessary expression of the church's life and its responsible proclamation to the rest of the world, which is alien to it but with which it must reckon in humility before God;

e. theology, i.e., the never unnecessary critical self-reflection of the church on its origin, on the promises and warnings of its history, on its nature, and on its central and also its peripheral task.

9. The task and promise of this human work is fundamentally given to the church as such, i.e., to all its members. The holders of its special offices (the offices of pastor, deacon, theologian, and administrator) are no less servants of Christ, if God gives them grace, because they are also and as such separated servants of the community. The exalting of a special episcopal office above that of the pastor, being a disruption of the created balance of leadership and equality, is a poor symbol of the fact that in the community, as all serve the sovereign God, so each can only serve the other.

II. The State

1. As service of the neighbor the humility required of us means concretely that our action takes place in the order of the state and confirms the order of the state. The correlation between service and the state also rests on the incarnation of Christ, which is the basis of the possibility of people being for one another—not merely living with one another before God, but also living for one another among one another. This living for one another among one another is the purpose of the state.

2. The state, too, is not an order of creation. Even more palpably than the church, it is an order of grace relating to sin. It is particularly an order of the patience of God which finds its limit and end in the eternal consummation. It is "a necessary remedy for corrupt nature" [Luther, EA, o.e. 1.1, 130].

3. The state, too, is the order, sanctified by the actual presence of the Word and Spirit of God, in which, by the grace of God, the rules are set up and upheld for common life, all being also made responsible for each and each for all, i.e., placed in mutual service. Thus the final and true purpose of the state can only be the Christian one, that on the basis of mutual forgiveness we should be not only with one another but also for one another.

4. Insofar as the state, too, is established and upheld by the actual presence of God, it is in every possible form a minister in God's place [cf. Rom. 13:4], and it is Christian obedience to render to Caesar what is Caesar's [cf. Matt. 22:21]. The divine dignity of the state, too, is ultimately a matter of revelation and faith, so that in the age of the Reformation it was rightly made an object of church confession. This means, of course, that where the actual presence of God in the reality of the state cannot possibly be believed, i.e., where it is not at all visible, God is to be obeyed rather than men [cf. Acts 5:29] to the extent that even the service of others, which is the purpose of its reality, can sometimes be turned into its opposite.

5. As a human work, and therefore in all its reality, the state too, and even more palpably than the church, has a share in the corruption in which man, far from forgiving sin, with cunning and force pursues his own ends in the struggle for existence. The dignity of the individual state, and the

respect that is owed and paid it, can for the following reasons be called service of the neighbor only in an improper sense:

a. because each individual state (contrary to its true nature) orders the common life of man and man on the assumption that the right of each must be protected and on the other hand each must be charged with his sins;

b. because the decisive means of existence of each individual state in relation to its members (contrary to its true nature) is brute force;

c. because each individual state (contrary to its true nature) is only one among others in relation to which it relies more or less on the right of might to maintain its existence. All this shows that the existing order of the state, more palpably than that of the church, is a relative order whose establishment and maintenance is service of the neighbor only insofar as it takes place in repentance before God, i.e., in the belief that God will make good what we cannot help but do badly.

6. The human work of the state is thus service of the neighbor because it, too, can act effectively only under the proviso of the grace of God. It is the setting up of the symbol of fellowship whose reality is God's work alone. The symbol of this symbol is the setting up and upholding of this rule of law in an ethnographically and geographically defined territory by which a particular state is distinguished from other states and from other entities (economic, cultural, and ecclesiastical) in and outside its sphere of sovereignty.

7. The decisive functions of the state are:

a. legislation, whose fundamental purpose is the creation of fundamentally equal rights in all questions of social life;

b. government, i.e., provision for the sure, complete, impartial, and objective observance of all existing laws;

c. justice as a system of applying the laws fairly in cases of dispute.

8. The tasks of legislation and government always include:

a. a concern to provide and protect national labor;

b. protection of all who temporarily or permanently have a part in the organization of labor;

c. promotion of free learning;

d. concern for popular education and culture;

e. concern for the freedom of action and expression of individuals, groups, and parties to the extent that this can be understood as an affirmation of the purpose of the state;

f. public acknowledgement and support of the church in particular as the society in which recollection of the ultimate purpose of the state particularly resides.

9. The task and promise of this work are fundamentally for all, and in particular they are fundamentally for men and women equally. Christians especially realize that they are personally responsible for the life of the state and its activity. Here, too, leadership and office have to be, and can only be, a commission and ministry and not an intrinsic distinction of individuals or of certain families, ranks, or classes. Insofar as office is held by fallible people on the basis of fallible laws, it is open to criticism, and insofar as its exercise rests on force, one cannot rule out, as a last resort, in opposition to it, violent revolution on the part of the rest of the citizens.

III. Church and State

1. As Boniface VIII (bull *Unam Sanctam*, 1302) rightly presupposed, church and state, as two expressions of one and the same temporally though not eternally valid divine order, are the two swords of the one power of Jesus Christ. The dualism of this order is conditioned and demanded by the dualism of man reconciled to God as a sinner saved by grace. Christian humility will in the same way recognize the relativity of the distinction and the necessity of the relative distinction. It will not reckon, then, either with an absolutizing of the distinction (the metaphysical differentiation of a religious and a secular sphere of life) or a one-sided removal of it (caesaropapism or "theocracy").

2. There is no equality of rank between church and state but a superiority in favor of the church. "The one sword then should be subject to the other, and temporal authority subject to spiritual" (Boniface VIII). The temple is prior to the home and above it (Luther EA o.c. 1.1, 130). State and church coinhere. Yet the church is not first in the state, but the state in the church, for repentance before God establishes but does not presuppose service of the neighbor, whereas service of the neighbor presupposes but does not establish repentance before God. In all circumstances, then, the Christian is first of all a member of the church and only then and as such a citizen.

3. If the responsible representatives of the church are not to lose their humility, the church can assert its principial superiority to the state only to the glory of God as Lord of both church and state, and not to its own glory, and it can do so only with the means that have been given to it, the proclamation of the Word and repentance, and not, with Boniface VIII, by the direct or indirect uniting of the two swords in its hands, or by the exercise of quasi-political authority in competition with that of the state.

4. The church, to the extent that it acts as such, renounces not only the appeal to the individual instinct of self-preservation and the assertion of the distinction between right and wrong, and not only the use of external compulsion within or force without, but fundamentally also the setting up and upholding of any rigid rule of law. Canons and dogmas are not legal

but spiritual norms, and are to be applied only as such. Church law in the strict sense can be only the church-recognized law of the state that exists even in the church. As an inevitable change into another genre the formation of special church law can be understood only as an incidental and doubly improper function of the church, and it comes under the rule: "The less of it, the better!"

5. As one society among others, the church in practice adjusts and subordinates itself to the state as the guardian of the rule of law. In relation to the national differentiation of states, things being as they are the church will accept as nonessential its necessary distinction and characterization over against other parts of the church. The freedom and superiority which it maintains precisely in so doing are not tied to the amount of independence of leadership and organization in relation to the state, nor to the presence of a visible supernational church unity, but to the measure of certainty with which, as a fellowship of the proclamation of the Word and repentance, it maintains itself over against the justifiable and unjustifiable claims of the state as the bearer of its materially transcendent, and in fact united and therefore international, task. A state church that knows and is true to its cause, and to the unity of this cause, is to be preferred to even the freest of churches as a symbol of the ultimate unity of church and state.

6. The church acknowledges and promotes the state insofar as service of the neighbor, which is the purpose of the state, is necessarily included in its own message of reconciliation and is thus its own concern. In relation to the activity of the state, it will adopt a restrained attitude to the extent that the state diverges from this purpose or that it cannot accept co-responsibility for it as the church. Finally, with the means at its disposal, it will move on to protest against the state if the latter's activity becomes a denial of its purpose and it is no longer visible or credible as the order of God. Either way it will always confess positively the purpose of the state and therefore the national state itself.

7. If the representatives of the state are not to lose their humility, the state can assert its practical superiority over the church only to the glory of God as Lord of both church and state and not to its own glory—and it can do so only in its own field as the guardian of the rule of law, not as the herald of a philosophy or morality conformable to its own *raison d'etre*, nor with the desire for a special civil Christianity. It gives the church freedom to fashion its own worship, dogma, and constitution and to practice its own preaching and theology.

8. The state for its part cannot be tied in principle to any specific form of the church. It recognizes and supports the church insofar as its own purpose is grounded and included in that of the church. Thus far it is neither

nonreligious nor nonconfessional. But it is supraconfessional insofar as it is tolerant in face of the confessional division of the church, in principle assuring the same freedom to all church bodies within the framework of law.

9. In practice, however, without intolerance to others, and as an expression of the specificity with which it is conscious of its own purpose, the state may address and claim a specific form of the church in a special way as *the* form of the church in accordance with the recognition of the specific national state which the church does not withhold. As a symbol of the ultimate unity of church and state, the qualified recognition and support of the church is, even from the state's point of view, more appropriate than the system of a real organizational separation of church and state.[4]

THE KNOWLEDGE OF GOD AND THE SERVICE OF GOD

There is a particular passage in Article 14 of the Confession, in its exposition of the sixth Commandment, to which we must now return and which compels us to go one step further in this connection. It is explicitly stated there that to the fulfillment of the commandment "Thou shalt not kill" belongs also the command "to represse tyrannie" and not to allow the shedding of innocent blood when we can prevent it. What does this mean? It means that, according to the Scottish Confession, under certain conditions there may be a *resistance* to the political power, which is not merely allowed but enjoined by God. John Knox and his friends have supplied the unambiguous commentary to this by their words and deeds. This may be not only a passive resistance but an *active* one, a resistance which can in certain circumstances be a matter of opposing *force* by force, as did occur in Scotland in the sixteenth century. It may be that the repressing of tyranny and the prevention of the shedding of innocent blood can be carried out in no other way.

What are we to say to this? I think, all things being considered, we must agree with the Confession here. We certainly cannot escape obedience to God and to the political order. Nor can we evade praying in accordance with I Timothy 2, 1–4 for those who administer that order, whoever they may be and however they may do it. This prayer and this obedience may not cease, no matter whether the significance of the political order be clear or obscure. But in certain circumstances the form which this obedience and prayer take as regards the actual administrators and representatives of the political power, may be not that of the active or passive position mentioned above but a third alternative. Obedience not to the political order, but to its actual representatives can become impossible for us, if we wish at the same time to hold fast to faith and love. It could well be that we could obey specific rulers only by being disobedient to God, and by being thus in fact disobedient to the political order ordained of God as well. It could well be that we had to do with a Government of liars, murderers and incendiaries, with a Government which wished to usurp the place of God, to fetter the conscience, to suppress the church and become itself the Church of Antichrist. It would be clear in such a case that we could only choose either to obey this Government by disobeying God or to obey God by disobeying this Government. In such a case must not God be obeyed rather than men? Must it not be forbidden us then to desire merely to endure? In such a case must not faith in Jesus Christ active in love necessitate our active resistance in just the same way as it necessitates passive resistance or our positive cooperation, when we are not faced with this choice? Must it not necessitate this in precisely the same way as in corresponding circumstances it necessitates reformation and therefore a breach in the church, the breach between the true and the false church? Must not the prayer for this Government, without ceasing to be intercession for them personally before God, for their conversion and their eternal salvation become quite plainly the prayer that as political rulers they may be set aside? And in such a case would we not have to act in accordance with our prayer? Against this it may be asked, can we and have we the right as Christians to take part in the use of force in certain circumstances? This question recalls once again the position with which we began the whole subject in this chapter. We are here as we deal with church and State, so to speak, on the edge of the church in the sphere of the world not yet redeemed. To live in this world and to obey God in it is to take part in the use of force directly or indirectly. It is not first of all in connection with this last case of active resistance to definite powers that the question of force arises.

Let us be quite clear; by obeying the political order in accordance with God's command, we have in any case directly or indirectly a share in the exercise of force. We have a share in this even when we feel it is our duty to choose that middle way of passive participation. And whether the repressing of tyranny will be a matter of forcible resistance or not, is not something which can be decided in advance. But active resistance as such cannot and may not be excluded out of fear of the ultima ratio of forcible resistance. And the possible consequence of forcible resistance may certainly not be excluded in advance.

We may and should pray to be spared that choice, or, if that be not possible, at least to be spared the ultima ratio of forcible resistance. And we should and must examine our responsibilities here, indeed, if possible, even more carefully than in the decisions previously mentioned. But there is one thing which must not happen. We may neither pray nor wish to be spared obedience to God in this worldly sphere either, to be spared the political service of God as such. And since we now have been claimed for it we may not take flight from any of its consequences demanded of us. The world needs men and it would be sad if it were just the Christians who did not wish to be men.[5]

CHURCH DOGMATICS

THE MERCY AND RIGHTEOUSNESS OF GOD

The people to whom God in His righteousness turns as helper and Savior is everywhere in the Old Testament harassed and oppressed people of Israel, which, powerless in itself, has no rights, and is delivered over to the superior force of its enemies; and in Israel it is especially the poor, the widows and orphans, the weak and defenseless. The branch out of the root of Jesse "will have his delight in the fear of the Lord. He shall not judge after the sight of his eyes, neither reprove after the hearing of his ears," which means obviously that he will not vindicate him who in the common opinion is already in the right, "but with righteousness he shall judge the poor, and reprove with equity for the meek of the earth: and he shall smite the earth with the rod of his mouth, and with the breath of his life shall he slay the wicked." And so "righteousness shall be the girdle of his loins and faithfulness the girdle of his reins" (Is. 11 3f). For this reason the human righteousness required by God and established in obedience—the righteousness which according to Amos 5:24 should pour down as a mighty stream—has necessarily the character of a vindication of right in favour of the threatened innocent, the oppressed poor, widows, orphans and aliens. For this reason, in the relations and events in the life of His people, God always takes His stand unconditionally and passionately on this side and on this side alone: against the lofty and on behalf of the lowly; against those who already enjoy right and privilege and on behalf of those who are denied it and deprived of it. What does all this mean? It is not really to be explained by talking *in abstracto* of the political tendency and especially the forensic character of the Old Testament and the biblical message generally. It does in fact have this character and we cannot hear it and believe it without feeling a sense of responsibility in the direction indicated.

As a matter of fact, from the belief in God's righteousness there follows logically a very definite political problem and task. But seen and understood *in abstracto*, the latter—i.e., the connexion between justification and law in all its relevance for that between Church and state—cannot really be evident and necessary of itself. It becomes so when we appreciate the fact that God's righteousness, the faithfulness in which He is true to Himself, is disclosed as help and salvation, as a saving divine intervention for man directly only to the poor, the wretched and the helpless as such, while with the rich and the full and the secure as such, according to His very nature He can have nothing to do. God's righteousness triumphs when man has no means of triumphing. It is light when man in himself lies in darkness, and life when man walks in the shadow of death. When we encounter divine righteousness we are all like the people of Israel, menaced and altogether lost according to its own strength. We are all widows and orphans who cannot procure right for themselves. It is obviously in the light of this confrontation that we have all those sayings in the Psalms about God's righteousness and the believer and his righteousness before God. The connexion between God's righteousness and mercy now becomes clear. The righteousness of the believer consists in the fact that God acts for him—utterly, because he cannot plead his own case and no one else can represent him. Faith grasps this full intervention on the part of God and it is therefore *eo ipso* faith in God's mercy, the faith of those who are poor and wretched before God. According to the Gospel of Luke and the Epistle of James, as also according to the message of the prophets, there follows from this character of faith a political attitude, decisively determined by the fact that man is made responsible to all those who are poor and wretched in his eyes, that he is summoned on his part to espouse the cause of those who suffer wrong. Why? Because in them it is manifested to him what he himself is in the sight of God; because the living, gracious, merciful action of God towards him consists in the fact that God Himself in His own righteousness procures right for him, the poor and wretched; because he and all men stand in the presence of God as those for whom right can be procured only by God Himself. The man who lives by the faith that this is true stands under a political responsibility. He knows that the right, that every real claim which one man has against another or others, enjoys the special protection of the God of grace. As surely as he himself lives by the grace of God he cannot evade this claim. He cannot avoid the question of human rights. He can only will and affirm a state which is based on justice. By any other political attitude he rejects the divine justification.[6]

THE CHRISTIAN COMMUNITY AND THE CIVIL COMMUNITY

The direction of Christian judgments, purposes and ideals in political affairs is based on the analogical capacities and needs of political organization.

A simple and absolute heterogeneity between State and Church on the one hand and State and Kingdom of God on the other is therefore just as much out of the question as a simple and absolute equating. The only possibility that remains—and it suggests itself compellingly—is to regard the existence of the State as an allegory, as a correspondence and an analogue to the Kingdom of God which the Church preaches and believes in. Since the State forms the outer circle, within which the Church, with the mystery of its faith and gospel, is the inner circle, since it shares a common centre with the Church, it is inevitable that, although its presuppositions and its tasks are its own and different, it is nevertheless capable of reflecting indirectly the truth and reality which constitute the Christian community.

Among the political possibilities open at any particular moment it will choose those which most suggest a correspondence to, an analogy and a reflection of, the content of its own faith and gospel.

In the decisions of the State the Church will always support the side which clarifies rather than obscures the Lordship of Jesus Christ over the whole, which includes this political sphere outside the Church. The Church desires that the shape and reality of the State in this fleeting world should point towards the Kingdom of God, not away from it. Its desire is not that human politics should cross the politics of God, but that they should proceed, however distantly, on parallel lines.

Even its political activity is therefore a profession of its Christian faith. By its political activity it calls the State from neutrality, ignorance and paganism into co-responsibility before God, thereby remaining faithful to its own particular mission. It sets in motion the historical process whose aim and content is the moulding of the State into the likeness of the Kingdom of God and hence the fulfillment of the State's own righteous purposes.

The Church is witness of the divine justification, that is, of the act in which God in Jesus Christ established and confirmed His original claim to man and hence man's claim against sin and death. The future for which the Church waits is the definitive revelation of this divine justification. This means that the Church will always be found where the order of the State is based on a commonly acknowledged law, from submission to which no one is exempt, and which also provides equal protection for all. The Church will be found where all political activity is in all circumstances regulated by this law. The Church always stands for the constitutional State, for the maximum validity and application of that twofold rule (no exemption from and full protection by the law), and therefore it will always be against any degeneration of the constitutional State into tyranny or anarchy. The Church will never be found on the side of anarchy or tyranny. In its politics it will always be urging the civil community to treat this fundamental purpose of its existence with the utmost seriousness: the limiting and the preserving of man by the quest for and the establishment of law.

The Church is witness of the fact that the Son of man came to seek and to save the lost. And this implies that—casting all false impartiality aside—the Church most concentrate first on the lower and lowest levels of human society. The poor, the socially and economically weak and threatened, will always be the object of its primary and particular concern, and it will always insist on the State's special responsibility for these weaker members of society. That it will bestow its love on them—within the framework of its own task (as part of its service), is one thing and the most important thing; but it must not concentrate on this and neglect the other thing to which it is committed by its political responsibility: the effort to achieve such a fashioning of the law as will make it impossible for "equality before the law" to become a cloak under which strong and weak, independent and dependent, rich and poor, employers and employees, in fact receive different treatment at its hands: the weak being unduly restricted, the strong unduly protected. The Church must stand for social justice in the political sphere. And in choosing between the various socialistic possibilities (social–liberalism? co-operativism? syndicalism? free trade? moderate or radical Marxism?) it will always choose the movement from which it can expect the greatest measure of social justice (leaving all other considerations on one side).[7]

CHURCH DOGMATICS

THE PROTECTION OF LIFE

A first essential is that war should not on any account be recognized as a normal, fixed and in some sense necessary part of what on the Christian view constitutes the just state, or the political order demanded by God. Certainly the state as such possesses power and must be able to exercise it. But it does this in any case, and it is no primary concern of Christian ethics to say that it should do so, or to maintain that the exercise of power constitutes the essence of the state, i.e., its *opus proprium*, or even a part of it. What Christian ethics must insist is that it is an *opus alienum* for the state to have to exercise power. It cannot assure the state that in the exercise of power either the state or its organs may do gaily and confidently whatever they think is right. In such cases it must always confront them with the question whether there is really any necessity for this exercise. Especially the state must not be given *carte blanche* to grasp the *ultima ratio* of organizing mass slaughter in its dealings with other states. Christian ethics cannot insist too loudly that such mass slaughter might well be mass murder, and therefore that this final possibility should not be seized like any other, but only at the very last hour in the darkest of days. The Church and theology have first and supremely to make this detached and delaying movement. If they do not first and for a long time make this the burden of their message, if they do not throw in their weight decisively on this side of the scales, they have become savourless salt, and must not be surprised if they are freely trampled underfoot on every side. It is also to be noted that, if the Church and theology think otherwise, if they do not say this first, if they do not throw in their weight on this side, if they speak tediously and tritely of war as a political *opus proprium*, then at the striking of the last hour in the darkest of days they will be in no position to say authentically and authoritatively what they may say at such a time. That is to say, they will be in no position authentically and authoritatively to issue a call to arms, to the political *opus alienum*. For they can do this only if they have previously held aloof, calling for peace right up the very last moment.

What Christian ethics has to emphasize is that neither inwardly nor outwardly does the normal task of the state, which is at issue even in time of war, consist in a process of annihilating rather than maintaining and fostering life. Nor should it be rashly maintained that annihilating life is also part of the process of maintaining and fostering it. Biological wisdom of this kind cannot serve as the norm or rule in ethics. The state which Christian ethics can and must affirm, which it has to proclaim as the political order willed and established by God, is not in itself and as such the mythological beast of the jungle, the monster with the Janus head, which by its very nature is prepared at any moment to turn thousands into killers and thousands more into killed. The Church does the state no honour, nor does it help it, if in relation to it it acts on this assumption concerning its nature. According to the Christian understanding, it is no part of the normal task of the state to wage war; its normal task is to fashion peace in such a way that life is served and war kept at bay. If there is a mistake in pacifism, apart from the inadvisable ethical absolutism of its thesis, it consists in its abstract negation of war, as if war could be understood and negated in isolation and not in relation to the so-called peace which precedes it. Our attention should be directed to this relation. It is when a state does not rightly pursue its normal task that sooner or later it is compelled to take up the abnormal one of war, and therefore to inflict this abnormal task on other states. It is when the power of the state is insufficient to meet the inner needs of the country that it will seek an outer safety-valve for the consequent unrest and think it is found in war. It is when interest-bearing capital rather than man is the object whose maintenance and increase are the meaning and goal of the political order that the mechanism is already set going which one day will send men to kill and be killed. Against such a perversion of peace neither the supposed, though already undermined and no longer steadfast, love of the masses for peace, nor the well-meant and vocal declaiming of idealists against war, is of any avail. For the point is that when war does break out it is usually the masses who march, and even the clearest words spoken against war, and the most painful recollections of previous wars, are rendered stale and impotent. A peace which is no real peace can make war inevitable. Hence the first, basic and decisive point which Christian ethics must make in this matter is that the state, the totality of responsible citizens, and each individual in his own conduct should so fashion peace while there is still time that it will not lead to this explosion but make war superfluous and unnecessary instead of inevitable. Relatively speaking, it requires no great faith, insight nor courage to condemn war radically and absolutely, for no one apart from leaders of the armaments industry and a few high-ranking officers really believes that war is preferable to peace. Again, it requires no faith, insight nor courage at all to howl with the wolves that unfortunately war belongs no less to the present world order, historical life and the nature of the state than does peace, so that from the very outset we must regard it as an emergency for which preparation must be made. What does require Christian faith, insight and courage—and the Christian Church and Christian ethics are there to show them—is to tell nations and governments that peace is the real emergency to which all our time, powers and ability must be devoted from the very outset in order that men may live and live properly, so that no refuge need be sought in war, nor need there be expected from it what peace has denied. Pacifists and militarists are usually agreed in the fact that for them the fashioning of peace as the fashioning of the state for democracy, and of democracy for social democracy, is a secondary concern as compared with rearmament or disarmament. It is for this reason that Christian ethics must be opposed to both. Neither rearmament nor disarmament can be a first concern, but the restoration of an order of life which is meaningful and just. When this is so, the two slogans will not disappear. They will have their proper place. They will come up for discussion at the proper time. But they will necessarily lose their fanatical tone, since far more urgent concerns will be up for discussion. And there can always be the hope that some day both will prove to be irrelevant.

It is only against the background of this first concern, and only as the Church has a good conscience that it is doing its best for a just peace among states and nations, that it can and should plead for the preservation of peace among states and nations, for fidelity and faith in their mutual dealings as the reasonable presupposition of a true foreign policy, for solid agreements and alliances and their honest observance, for international courts and conventions, and above all, and in all nations, for openness, understanding and patience towards others and for such education of young people as will lead them to prefer peace to war. The Church and should raise its voice against the institution of standing armies in which the officers constitute *per se* a permanent danger to peace. It can and should resist all kinds of hysterical or premature war scares. It exists in this aeon. Hence it is not commissioned to proclaim that war is absolutely avoidable. But it is certainly commissioned to oppose the satanic doctrine that war is inevitable and therefore justified, that it is unavoidable and therefore right when it occurs, so that Christians have to participate in it. Even in a world in which states and nations are still in the early stages and never at the end of the long road in respect of that first concern, there is never in practice an absolute necessity of war, and the Church certainly has neither right nor obligation to affirm this necessity either in general or in detail as the occasion may arise. We do not need optimism but simply a modicum of sane intelligence to recognize that relatively if not absolutely, in practice if not in principle, war can be avoided to a very large extent. The Church must not preach pacifism, but it must see to it that this sane intelligence is voiced and heard so long as this is possible, and that the many ways of avoiding war which now exist in practice should be honestly applied until they are all exhausted. It is better in this respect that the Church should stick to it post too long and become a forlorn hope than that it should leave it too soon and then have to realize that it has become unfaithful by yielding to the general excitement, and that it is thus the accessory to an avoidable war which can only be described as mass murder. In excitement and propaganda there lurks already the mass killing which can only be mass murder. On no account, not even *in extremis*, should the Church be found among the agitators or use their language. Deliberate agitators, and those deceived by them, must always be firmly and quietly resisted, whether they like it or not. And this is what the Church can do with its word. Hence its word must never be a howling with the pack.

If only the Church had learned the two lessons *(a)* of Christian concern for the fashioning of true peace among nations to keep war at bay, and *(b)* of Christian concern for peaceful measures and solutions among states to avert war; if only these two requirements and their unconditional primacy were the assured possession of all Christian ethics, we might feel better assured both against misunderstandings and also against threatened relapses into the post-Constantinian theology of war, and we might therefore be confident to say that we cannot accept the absolutism of the pacifist thesis, and that Christian support for war and in war is not entirely beyond the bounds of possibility.

It might be argued that it is inopportune to say this today. But surely it is always most opportune to keep to the truth. And the truth in this matter surely includes this further point. Even the cogent element of truth in the pacifist position—more cogent perhaps today than ever before—will surely benefit rather than suffer if it is not presented as the exclusive and total truth, but is deliberately qualified, perhaps at the expense of logical consistency, by this further point. After all, the consistency of ethics, or at any rate of theological ethics, may for once differ from that of logic.

This further point rests on the assumption that the conduct of one state or nation can throw another into the wholly abnormal situation of emergency in which not merely its greater or lesser prosperity but its very existence and autonomy are menaced and attacked. In consequence of the attitude of this other state, a nation can find itself faced by the question whether it must surrender or assert itself as such in face of the claims of the other. Nothing less than this final question must be at issue if a war is to be just and necessary.

Perhaps a state desires to expand politically, geographically or economically, and therefore to extend its frontiers and dominion. Perhaps it thinks it necessary to rectify its internal conditions, e.g., to bring about political unity, by external adventure. Perhaps it considers that its honour and prestige are violated by the attitude of another state. Perhaps it feels that it is threatened by a shift in the balance of power among other states. Perhaps it thinks it sees in the internal conditions of another state, whether revolutionary or reactionary, a reason for displeasure or anxiety. Perhaps it believes it can and should ascribe to itself a historical mission, e.g., a call to lead and rule other nations. All this may well be so. Yet it certainly does not constitute a valid reason for setting one's own great or little war machine in motion, for sending out one's troops to the battlefield to kill and be killed. Such aims may be well worth striving for. But they are too paltry to be worth the terrible price involved in their realization by war. War for such reasons could always have been avoided. War for such reasons is an act of murder. When such reasons lie on one side of the scale, and the knowledge of war and its necessary terrors on the other, we should have to be either incorrigible romanticists or malevolent sophists even to doubt which side ought to rise and which to fall. The Christian Church has to testify unambiguously that wars waged for such reasons are not just, and therefore ought not to be undertaken.

If the state makes participation in war obligatory upon all, the individual must face the question whether as a citizen he can approve and cooperate in war, i.e., every war as such, or whether as a citizen he must resist and evade it.

The state is not God, nor can it command as He does. No compulsory duty which it imposes on the individual, nor urgency with which it presses for its fulfillment, can alter the fact that the attitude of the individual to all its decisions and measures, and therefore to this too, is limited and defined by his relationship to God, so that, although as a citizen he is committed to what is thought right and therefore resolved by the government or the majority, he is not bound by it finally or absolutely. Hence it cannot be denied that in virtue of his relationship to God the individual may sometimes find himself compelled, even with a full sense of his loyalty as a citizen, to contradict and oppose what is thought right and resolved by the government or the majority. He will be aware of the exceptional character of this action. Such insubordination cannot be ventured too easily or frequently. He will also be aware of the risk entailed. He cannot but realize that by offering resistance he renders himself liable to prosecution. He cannot deny to the government or the majority the right to take legal and constitutional proceedings against him. He must not be surprised or aggrieved if he has to bear the consequences of his resistance. He must be content in obedience to God to accept his responsibility as a citizen in this particular way. The contradiction and resistance to compulsory military service can indeed take the form of the actual refusal of individuals to submit to conscription as legally and constitutionally imposed by the government or the majority, and therefore of their refusal to participate directly either in war itself or preparation for it. Such refusal means that these individuals think they must give a negative answer to the question posed by conscription, even though it is put to them in the form of a compulsory duty calling urgently for fulfillment.[8]

PETITION OF THE BRUDERSCHAFTEN ON NUCLEAR WEAPONS

I. The Evangelical Church confesses that in Jesus Christ she finds "joyous liberation from the Godless bonds of the world unto free, thankful service to His creatures." (Barmen Thesis 2.) This forbids to her not only any approval of or collaboration in an atomic war and its preparation, but also her tacitly letting it happen. This awareness demands that in the obedience of faith ... here as in every issue ... we ourselves must take the first step to hold back the threatening destruction and to trust more in the reality of the Word of God than in the "realism" of political calculation. The first step is the act of *diakonia* which we, as Christians, owe to the menaced and anxious world of today. Let the faithless hesitate ... we as Christians may and must dare it in trust in God, who created this World and every living creature in East and West for the sake of the suffering and victorious Jesus Christ, and will preserve the same through Christ and the preaching of His Gospel until His Day.

II. If the Synod finds itself unable to assent to this confession, we must ask how the Synod can refute it on the grounds of Scripture, the Confessions, and reason.

For the sake of the men and women for whom we are responsible, and for our own sakes, we must insist upon receiving an answer to this question. We owe it to the Synod to remind it of its spiritual responsibility, since it is in the shouldering of this responsibility that it shows itself to be the legitimate authority in the Church. It is our conviction that in the face of this issue the Church finds herself in the *status confessionis*.

If the Synod agrees with us, than an unreserved *No* is demanded of Christians facing the problem of the new weapons, must she not also say promptly and clearly to the State, that the true proclamation of the Gospel, also in the Chaplaincy, includes the testimony that the Christian may not and cannot participate in the design, testing, manufacture, stocking and use of atomic weapons, nor in training with these weapons?

III. We, therefore, ask the Synod whether she can affirm together with us the following ten propositions, for the instruction of consciences concerning Christian behavior with regard to atomic weapons:

1. War is the ultimate means, but always, in every form a questionable means, of resolving political tensions between nations.

2. For various reasons, good and less good, churches in all lands and all ages have hitherto not considered the preparation and the application of this ultimate means to be impossible.

3. The prospect of a future war to be waged with the use of modern means of annihilation has created a new situation, in the face of which the Church *cannot* remain *neutral*.

4. War, in the form of *atomic war*, means the mutual annihilation of the participating peoples as well as of countless human beings of other peoples, which are not involved in the combat between the two adversaries.

5. War, in the form of atomic war, is therefore seen to be an *instrument incapable of being used* for the resolution of political conflicts, because it destroys every presupposition of political resolution.

6. Therefore, the Church and the individual Christian can say nothing but an *a priori No* to a war with atomic weapons.

7. Even preparation for such a war is under all circumstances *sin against God and the neighbor,* for which no Church and no Christian can accept responsibility.

8. We therefore demand in the Name of the Gospel that an *immediate end be made* to preparations for such a war within our land and nation regardless of all other considerations.

9. We challenge all those who seriously want to be Christians to *renounce*, without reserve and under all circumstances, any participation in preparations for atomic war.

10. In the face of this question, the opposing point of view, or neutrality, *cannot be advocated* Christianly. Both mean the denial of all three articles of the Christian faith.[9]

THE CHRISTIAN LIFE

FIAT IUSTITA

... Christians are claimed for action in the effort and struggle for human righteousness. At issue is human, not divine righteousness. That the latter should come, intervene, assert itself, reign, and triumph can never be the affair of any human action. Those who know the reality of the kingdom, Christians, can never have anything to do with the arrogant and foolhardy enterprise of trying to bring in and build up by human hands a religious, cultic, moral, or political kingdom of God on earth. God's righteousness is the affair of God's own act, which has already been accomplished and is still awaited. God's righteousness took place in the history of Jesus Christ, and it will take place again, comprehensively and definitively, in his final manifestation. The time between that beginning and that end, our time as the time of the presence of Jesus Christ in the Holy Spirit, is for Christians the space for gratitude, hope, and prayer, and also the time of responsibility for the occurrence of human righteousness. They have to be concerned about the doing of this righteousness. On no pretext can they escape responsibility for it: not on that of the gratitude and hope with which they look to God and wait for his action; not on that of their prayer for the coming of his kingdom. For if they are really grateful and really hope, if their prayer is a brave prayer, then they are claimed for a corresponding inner and outer action which is also brave. If they draw back here, or even want to, then there is serious reason to ask whether and how far their gratitude, hope, and prayer are to be taken seriously.

Human righteousness! We shall not develop at length here the self-evident point that, measured by God's righteousness and in unconquerable distinction from it, this will always be, even at best, an imperfect, fragile and highly problematical righteousness. Others may deceive themselves in this regard, but to those who have the prayer for the kingdom in their hearts and on their lips it is indeed self-evident. Nevertheless, it is not so important that they can refrain from doing what they have to do in this relativity. We Protestants have always had a certain inclination to find it too important. We should break free from this. Those who pray that prayer start off with the thesis that the perfect righteousness of God's kingdom is not their own doing, that they can only seek it (Mt. 6:33), as is appropriate, in gratitude for its reality, in hope of its manifestation, in prayer that it may come. This means, however, that any concern for the imperfection of all human action, their own included, is taken from them as idle and pointless. They are also forbidden the lazy excuse of all lazy servants that since all they can do will always be imperfect anyway it is not worth exerting themselves and growing weary in the causes of petty human righteousness. No, precisely because perfect righteousness stands before them as God's work, precisely because they are duly forbidden to attempt the impossible, precisely because all experiments in this direction are prevented and prohibited, they are with great strictness required and with great kindness freed and empowered to do what they can do in the sphere of the relative possibilities assigned to them, to do it very imperfectly yet heartily, quietly, and cheerfully. They are absolved from wasting time and energy sighing over the impassable limits of their sphere of action and thus missing the opportunities that present themselves in this sphere. They may and can and should rise up and accept responsibility to the utmost of their power for the doing of the little righteousness. The only concern should be their awareness of how far they fall short in this sphere of what is not only commanded but also possible for them. But they can quickly rid themselves of this concern by setting to work to snatch the available possibilities of doing what is commanded and thus catching up in God's name where they are in arrears. A little righteousness and holiness of works—there will certainly never be a great deal!—does not have to be an illusion or a danger here. The only danger arising out of the (ill-founded) anxiety that one might become too righteous and too holy, a man of works, is the temptation to remain passive where what is required, with a full sense of one's limitations, is to become active.

It is not self-evident, of course, that in the sphere of human activity, alongside and far below divine righteousness, there should be in all seriousness a human righteousness which Christians are freed to do and for whose occurrence they are made responsible. It is not self-evident that the same lofty concept of righteousness, denoting on the one hand perfect divine action and on the other most imperfect human action, should be appropriate or necessary in this context. In relation to human action as such and in general, the analogy is in truth an impossible one. Here, however, we are referring to the obedience of the action of those whom God has freed and summoned to call upon him for the coming of his kingdom and the doing of righteousness. In relation to the action of these people, it cannot be denied that in all its imperfection this action stands related to the kingdom of God, and therefore to the perfect righteousness of God, inasmuch as it derives from the event of the kingdom in Jesus Christ and hastens toward its manifestation in Jesus Christ. Obviously, this whence and whither mean that it cannot be alien to it but is given a determination which it does not have in itself and cannot give itself but which it acquires, which it cannot escape as it takes place in that relation, and which cannot be denied to it. The determination that it acquires and has in that relation is that it can take place only in correspondence with its whence and whither and therefore with God's kingdom and righteousness. If it never can or will be like this, and should not try to aim at equality with it, neither can it be or remain totally unlike it. There is a third possibility. The action of those who pray for the coming of God's kingdom and therefore for the taking place of his righteousness will be *kingdom-like*, and therefore on a lower level and within its impassable limits it will be *righteous* action. Certainly we should not say too much here, yet we should not say too little either. Done in that relation, under that determination, and therefore in that correspondence, the action of Christians may in its own way and within the limits of its own sphere be called and be a righteous action. This is the one talent that is entrusted to Christians, who are neither angels nor archangels but only people, and they must not wrap it in a cloth or bury it anywhere, as did the stupid fellow in Luke 19:20 and Matthew 25:25. Following their prayer, their action can and should be kingdom-like, righteous in its own place and manner. There is not the shadow of a serious reason to contest this.[10]

NOTES

1. [James B. Torrance, "Barth, Karl," in *The Encyclopedia of Religion*, ed. Mircea Eliade, 16 vols. (New York: Macmillan, 1987), 2:69. See also Eberhard Busch, *Karl Barth: His Life from Letters and Autobiographical Texts*, trans. John Bowden (Philadelphia: Fortress Press, 1976).]

2. [Karl Barth, "Jesus Christ and the Movement for Social Justice," in *Karl Barth and Radical Politics*, ed. George Hunsinger (Philadelphia: Westminster Press, 1976), 19, 36–37.]

3. [Commentary on Romans 13:1 in *The Epistle to the Romans*, trans. Edwyn C. Hoskyns (London: Oxford University Press, 1957), 481–484.]

4. [Karl Barth, "Theses on Church and State," appendix to *Ethics*, ed. Dietrich Braun, trans. Geoffrey W. Bromiley (New York: Seabury Press, 1981), 517–521.]

5. [Karl Barth, "The State's Service of God," in *The Knowledge of God and the Service of God* (New York: Charles Scribner's Sons, 1939), 229–232.]

6. [Karl Barth, "The Mercy and Righteousness of God," in *Church Dogmatics*, 4 vols. (Edinburgh: T & T Clark, 1936–1961), vol. 2, part 1, 386–387.

7. [Karl Barth, "The Christian Community and the Civil Community," in *Against the Stream: Shorter Post-War Writings, 1946–1952*, ed. Ronald Gregor Smith (New York: Philosophical Library, 1954), 32–36.]

8. [Karl Barth, "The Protection of Life," in *Church Dogmatics*, vol. 3, part 4, 456–467.]

9. [Karl Barth, "The Continuing Church Struggle" (petition of the Bruderschaften on nuclear weapons, addressed to the Synod of the Evangelical Church in Germany in March, 1958), in John H. Yoder, *Karl Barth and the Problem of War* (Nashville, Tenn.: Abingdon Press, 1970), 134–136.]

10. [Karl Barth, "The Struggle for Human Righteousness," in *The Christian Life: Church Dogmatics IV, 4: Lecture Fragments*, trans. Geoffrey Bromiley (Grand Rapids, Mich.: Eerdmans, 1981), 264–267.]

{CHAPTER 11}

Dietrich Bonhoeffer (1906–1945)

SELECTED AND EDITED BY MILNER BALL

Dietrich Bonhoeffer was one of the twentieth century's Christian martyrs, executed on the orders of Adolf Hitler just as World War II drew to a close. Born in 1906, one of eight children in a cultivated, well-connected German family, he was no stranger to war. He lost an elder brother in World War I, lived with the deprivations that marked postwar Germany, and would soon enough be caught up in the turmoil produced by the Nazis.

He started out to be a Lutheran theologian and pastor. He was an exceptional student and received a doctorate from the University of Berlin at the age of twenty-one. He then served several congregations, became active in the ecumenical movement, made a study trip to Union Theological seminary in New York in 1930–31, and on his return was appointed lecturer in theology at Berlin.

A brilliant academic career lay ahead of him, but then Hitler became chancellor of Germany in 1933. The majority of church members—the "German Christians"—would pledge loyalty to him. A minority of Protestants formed the resistant Confessing Church. Bonhoeffer took a leading role in the latter and directed a clandestine seminary for pastors. He made a second trip to America in 1939 for what was planned as a year of lecturing. Within a few, agonizing weeks, he cut the visit short. He felt compelled to trade his security abroad for the difficult and dangerous, but faithful, responsibility of the Christian at home.

Soon after his return, Bonhoeffer joined the active conspiracy against Hitler and became a double agent in the employ of the Abwehr, the military's counterintelligence agency. He was arrested and jailed in April 1943. The extent of his involvement in the conspiracy came to light after an attempt to assassinate Hitler failed on July 20, 1944. Bonhoeffer was convicted of treason. He was hanged on April 9, 1945.

Bonhoeffer's professional education began with an introduction to his teachers' liberal theology in the tradition of nineteenth-century German Lutheranism, but he was soon deeply affected by Karl Barth and to some extent by his exposure to Reinhold Niebuhr at Union Theological Seminary in New York. But his post-1939 life and thought are distinctively his own, and it is they which have drawn the most attention, proved the most influential, and provided the most inspiration.

His late theology is challenging in part because of its physical condition: his Letters and Papers from Prison *is composed of fragments that survived the war, and his* Ethics *was left incomplete, its pages in disarray. But it is challenging primarily because of its substance. Bonhoeffer was exploring new territory. He was critical of religion, including Christian religion, on Christian theological grounds. He thought that religion's worship of an imagined god beyond what we know and see is a flight from the world and therefore a diversion from the God of the Bible who is in the midst of the world, embracing all things human. This God frees us to take responsibility for others. This God calls us to bold action and promises forgiveness to those who become sinners in the process.*

Bonhoeffer therefore sought to address people in their worldliness, strength, and responsibility rather than in their weakness and guilt. This did not make him an advocate of Christian triumphalism. It made him an advocate of solidarity with outcasts—in the form of Christ's solidarity with sinners. God's power, he said, is manifest in the world as powerlessness. It is manifest in the Crucifixion.

Bonhoeffer also sought to exercise the freedom to take responsibility. It is a freedom, he believed, that comes with obedience to Christ. He joined the military conspiracy against Hitler. He made no self-justifying claim for his action. He accepted the guilt of it and was hanged.

Bonhoeffer's closest friend, Eberhard Bethge, says that his life and theology achieved a breakthrough that reveals "the future normality: 'Being for others' as sharing in the suffering of Jesus." His life and work lose their exceptional character and become, as Bethge says, "an example of being Christian today."

THE NATURE OF THE CHURCH: SUMMER 1932

CONFESSION OF FAITH is not be confused with professing a religion. Such profession uses the confession as propaganda and ammunition against the Godless. The confession of faith belongs rather to the "Discipline of the Secret" (*Arkanum*) in the Christian gathering of those who believe. Nowhere else is it tenable. It is, for example, untenable in the new "Confession sessions" now coming into vogue in which one dialogues with those antagonistic to faith. The primary confession of the Christian before the world is the deed that interprets itself. If this deed is to have become a force, then the world itself will long to confess the Word. This is not the same as loudly shrieking out propaganda. This Word must be preserved as the most sacred possession of the community. This is a matter between God and the community, not between the community and the world. It is the Word of recognition between friends, not a word to use against enemies. This attitude was first learned at baptism. The deed alone is our confession of faith before the world.[1]

THY KINGDOM COME: THE PRAYER OF THE CHURCH FOR THE KINGDOM OF GOD ON EARTH

We are otherworldly—ever since we hit upon the devious trick of being religious, yes even "Christian," at the expense of the earth. Otherworldliness affords a splendid environment in which to live. Whenever life begins to become oppressive and troublesome a person just leaps into the air with a bold kick and soars relieved and unencumbered into so-called eternal fields. He leaps over the present. He disdains the earth; he is better than it. After all, besides the temporal defeats he still has his eternal victories, and they are so easily achieved. Other-worldliness also makes it easy to preach and to speak words of comfort. An other-worldly church can be certain that it will in no time win over all the weaklings, all who are only too glad to be deceived and deluded, all utopianists, all disloyal sons of the earth. When an explosion seems imminent, who would not be so human as to quickly mount the chariot that comes down from the skies with the promise of taking him to a better world beyond? What church would be so merciless, so inhuman, as not to deal compassionately with this weakness of suffering humans thereby save souls for the kingdom of heaven? Humans are weak; they cannot bear having the earth so near, the earth that bears them. They cannot stand it, because the earth is stronger than they and because they want to be better than the evil earth. So people extricate themselves from it; they refuse to take it seriously. Who could blame them for that—who but the have-nots in their envy? Humans are weak, that's just the way they are; and these weaklings are open to the religion of otherworldliness. "Should it be denied them? Should the weaklings remain without help? Would that be in the spirit of Jesus Christ? No, the weak should receive help. They do in fact receive help, from Christ. However, Christ does not will or intend this weakness; instead, he makes humans strong. He does not lead them in a religious flight from this world to other worlds beyond; rather, he gives them back to the earth as its loyal children. . . .

The kingdom of God is not found in some other world beyond, but in the midst of this world. Our obedience is demanded in terms of its contradictory appearance, and then, through our obedience, the miracle, like lightning, is allowed to flash up again and again from the perfect, blessed new world of the final promise. God wants us to honor him on earth; he wants us to honor him in our fellow man and woman—and nowhere else. He sinks his kingdom down into the cursed ground. Let us open our eyes, become sober, and obey him here. "Come, O blessed of my Father, inherit the kingdom!" This the Lord will say to no other than the one to whom he says, "I was hungry and you gave me food, I was thirsty and you gave me drink. . . . As you did it to one of the least of my brethren, you did it to me" (Matt. 25:34, 35, 40).[2]

CREATION AND FALL: THE IMAGE OF GOD ON EARTH

... In the language of the Bible, freedom is not something persons have for themselves but something they have for others. No one enjoys freedom "in itself," that is, in a vacuum, the same way that one may be musical, intelligent, or blind as such. Freedom is not a quality of the human person. Nor is it an ability, a disposition, a kind of being that somehow deeply germinates in a person. Whoever scrutinizes the human to discover freedom will find nothing of it. Why? Because freedom is not a quality that can be discovered. It is not a possession, a presence, or an object. Nor is it a pattern for existence. Rather, it is a relationship; otherwise, it is nothing. Indeed it is a relationship between two persons. Being free means "being free for the other," because the other has bound me to himself or herself. Only in relationship with the other am I free. . . .

Those who are created are free in that they are in relationship with other creatures; the human person is free for others. And he created them a man and a woman. The man is not alone; he exists in duality and it is in this dependence on the other that his creatureliness consists. The creatureliness of humans, no more than their freedom, is neither a quality, nor a disposition to be encountered, nor is it a mode of being. It is to be defined, rather, as absolutely nothing other than the relations of human beings with one another, over against one another, in dependence on one another. The "image ... after God's likeness" is, consequently, not an *analogia entis* (analogy of being) by which humans, in their existence in and for themselves, would in their being live in the likeness to God's being. Indeed, there is no such analogy between God and the human. . . . The likeness, the analogy, of the human to God, is not *analogia entis* but *analogia relationis* (analogy of relationship).[3]

DISCIPLESHIP

When holy scripture speaks of following Jesus, it proclaims that people are free from all human rules, from everything which pressures, burdens, or causes worry and torment of conscience. In following Jesus, people are released from the hard yoke of their own laws to be under the gentle yoke of Jesus Christ. Does this disparage the seriousness of Jesus' commandments? No. Instead, only where Jesus' entire commandment and the call to unlimited discipleship remain intact are persons fully free to enter into Jesus' community. Those who follow Jesus' commandment entirely, who let Jesus' yoke rest on them without resistance, will find the burdens they must bear to be light. In the gentle pressure of this yoke they will receive the strength to walk the right path without becoming weary. . . .

Cheap grace is the deadly enemy of our Church. We are fighting today for costly grace.

Cheap grace means grace sold on the market like cheapjack's wares. The sacraments, the forgiveness of sin, and the consolations of religion are thrown away at cut prices. . . . Grace without price; grace without cost! The essence of grace, we suppose, is that the account has been paid in advance; and, because it has been paid, everything can be had for nothing. . . .

Cheap grace means grace as a doctrine, a principle, a system. It means forgiveness of sins proclaimed as a general truth; it means God's love as merely a Christian idea of God. Those who affirm it have already had their sins forgiven. . . .

Cheap grace means the justification of sin without the justification of the sinner. Because grace alone does everything, everything can stay in its old ways. . . .

Cheap grace is the preaching of forgiveness without repentance; it is baptism without the discipline of community; it is the Lord's Supper without confession of sin; it is absolution without personal confession. Cheap grace is grace without discipleship, grace without the cross, grace without the living, incarnate Jesus Christ.

Costly grace is the treasure hidden in the field; for the sake of which people go and sell with joy everything they have. It is the costly pearl, for whose price the merchant sells all that he has. . . . It is the call of Jesus Christ which causes a disciple to leave his nets and to follow him. . . .

Above all, grace is costly because it was costly to God, because it costs God the life of God's son. . . .

It comes to us as a gracious call to follow Jesus; it comes as a forgiving word to the fearful spirit and the broken heart. Grace is costly, because it forces people under the yoke of following Jesus Christ; it is grace when Jesus says: "My yoke is easy and my burden is light."[4]

TEMPTATION

Lead us not into temptation. Natural humans and moral humans cannot understand this prayer. Natural humans want to prove their strength in adventure, in struggle, in encounter with the enemy. That is life. "If you do not stake your life you will never win it." Only the life which has run the risk of death is life which has been won. That is what natural humans know. Moral humans also know that their knowledge is true and convincing only when it is tried out and proved, they know that the good can live only from evil, and that it would not be good but for evil. So moral humans call out evil, their daily prayer is—Lead us into temptation, that we may test out the power of the good in us.

If temptation were really what natural humans and moral humans understand by it, namely, testing of their own strength—whether their vital or their moral or even their Christian strength—in resistance, on the enemy, then it is true that Christ's prayer would be incomprehensible. . . . The temptation of which the whole bible speaks does not have to do with the testing of my strength—to my horror, and without my being able to do anything about it—is turned against me; really all my powers, including my good and pious powers (the strength of my faith), fall into the hands of the enemy power and are now led into the field against me. . . .

A defeat shows the physical and the moral humans that their powers have to increase before they can withstand the trial. So their defeat is never irrevocable. Christians know that in every hour of temptation all their strength will leave them. For them temptation means a dark hour which can be irrevocable. They do not seek for their strength to be proved, but they pray, "Lead us not into temptation." So the biblical meaning of temptation is not a testing of strength, but the loss of all strength, defenseless deliverance into Satan's hands. . . .

So Christians live from the times of God, and not from their own ideas of life. They do not say that they live in constant temptation and constant testing, but in the time when they are preserved from temptation they pray that God may not let the time of temptation come over them.[5]

LETTERS AND PAPERS FROM PRISON

PROLOGUE: AFTER TEN YEARS

Ten years is a long time in anyone's life. As time is the most valuable thing that we have, because it is the most irrevocable, the thought of any lost time troubles us whenever we look back. Time lost is time in which we have failed to live a full human life, gain experience, learn, create, enjoy, and suffer; it is time that has not been filled up, but left empty. These last years have certainly not been like that. Our losses have been great and immeasurable, but time has not been lost. . . . In the following pages I should like to try to give some account of what we have experienced and learnt in common during these years—not personal experiences, or anything systematically arranged, or arguments and theories, but conclusions reached more or less in common by a circle of like-minded people, and related to the business of human life, put down one after the other, the only connection between them being that of concrete experience. . . . One cannot write about these things without a constant sense of gratitude for the fellowship of spirit and community of life that have been proved and preserved throughout these years.

NO GROUND UNDER OUR FEET

One may ask whether there have ever before in human history been people with so little ground under their feet—people to whom every available alternative seemed equally intolerable, repugnant, and futile, who looked beyond all these existing alternatives for the source of their strength so entirely in the past or in the future, and who yet, without being dreamers, were able to await the success of their cause so quietly and confidently. Or perhaps one should rather ask whether the responsible thinking people of any generation that stood at a turning-point in history did not feel much as we do, simply because something new was emerging that could not be seen in the existing alternatives.

WHO STANDS FAST?

The great masquerade of evil has played havoc with all our ethical concepts. For evil to appear disguised as light, charity, historical necessity, or social justice is quite bewildering to anyone brought up on our traditional ethical concepts, while for Christians who base their lives on the Bible it merely confirms the fundamental wickedness of evil.

The "reasonable" people's failure is obvious. With the best intentions and a naive lack of realism, they think that with a little reason they can bend back into position the framework that has got out of joint. In their lack of vision they want to do justice to all sides, and so the conflicting forces wear them down with nothing achieved. Disappointed by the work's unreasonableness, they see themselves condemned to ineffectiveness; they step aside in resignation or collapse before the stronger party.

Still more pathetic is the total collapse of moral *fanaticism*. Fanatics think that their single-minded principles qualify them to do battle with the powers of evil; but like a bull they rush at the red cloak instead of the person who is holding it; they exhaust themselves and are beaten. They get tangled in non-essentials and fall into the trap set by cleverer people.

Then there are the people with a *conscience*, who fight single-handed against heavy odds in situations that call for a decision. But the scale of the conflicts in which they have to choose—with no advice or support except from their own consciences—tears them to pieces. Evil approaches them in so many respectable and seductive disguises that their conscience becomes nervous and vacillating, till at last they content themselves with a salved instead of a clear conscience. . . .

Who stands fast? Only those whose final standard is not their reason, their principles, their conscience, their freedom, or their virtue, but who are ready to sacrifice all this when they are called to obedient and responsible action in faith and in exclusive allegiance to God—responsible people, who try to make their whole life an answer to the question and call of God. Where are these responsible people?

CIVIL COURAGE?

What lies behind the complaint about the dearth of civil courage? In recent years we have seen a great deal of bravery and self-sacrifice, but civil courage hardly anywhere, even among ourselves. To attribute this simply to personal cowardice would be too facile a psychology. . . . Civil courage, in fact, can grow only out of the free responsibility of free people. Only now are the Germans beginning to discover the meaning of free responsibility. It depends on a God who demands responsible action in a bold venture of faith, and who promises forgiveness and consolation to the person who becomes a sinner in that venture.

OF SUCCESS

Although it is certainly not true that success justifies an evil deed and shady means, it is impossible to regard success as something that is ethically quite neutral. The fact is that historical success creates a basis for the continuance of life, and it is still a moot point whether it is ethically more responsible to take the field like a Don Quixote against a new age, or to admit one's defeat, accept the new age, and agree to serve it. In the last resort success makes history; and the ruler of history repeatedly brings good out of evil over the heads of the history-makers. . . . As long as goodness is successful, we can afford the luxury of regarding it as having no ethical significance; it is when success is achieved by evil means that the problem arises. . . . We ... must take our share of responsibility for the molding of history in every situation and at every moment, whether we are the victors or the vanquished. . . .

CONTEMPT FOR HUMANITY?

There is a very real danger of our drifting into an attitude of contempt for humanity. We know quite well that we have no right to do so, and that it would lead us into the most sterile relation to our fellow humans. The following thoughts may keep us from such a temptation. It means that we at once fall into the worst blunders of our opponents. The people who despise others will never be able to make anything of them. Nothing that we despise in the other is entirely absent from ourselves. We often expect from others more than we are willing to do ourselves. Why have we hitherto thought so intemperately about humans and their frailty and temptability? We must learn to regard people less in the light of what they do or omit to do, and more in the light of what they suffer. The only profitable relationship to others—and especially to our weaker brothers and sisters—is one of love, and that means the will to hold fellowship with them. God himself did not despise humanity, but became human for human's sake. . . .

A FEW ARTICLES OF FAITH ON THE SOVEREIGNTY OF GOD IN HISTORY

I believe that God can and will bring good out of evil, even out of the greatest evil. For that purpose he needs people who make the best use of everything. I believe that God will give us all the strength we need to help us resist in all time of distress. But he never gives it in advance, lest we should rely on ourselves and not on him alone. A faith such as this should allay our fears for the future. I believe that even our mistakes and shortcomings are turned to good account, and that it is no harder for God to deal with them than with our supposedly good deeds. I believe that God is no timeless fate, but that he waits for and answers sincere prayers and responsible actions. . . .

ARE WE STILL OF ANY USE?

We have been silent witnesses of evil deeds; we have been drenched by many storms; we have learnt the arts of equivocation and pretense; experience has made us suspicious of others and kept us from being truthful and open; intolerable conflicts have worn us down and even made us cynical. Are we still of any use? What we shall need is not geniuses, or cynics, or misanthropes, or clever tacticians, but plain, honest, straightforward people. Will our inward power of resistance be strong enough, and our honesty with ourselves remorseless enough, for us to find our way back to simplicity and straightforwardness?

THE VIEW FROM BELOW

There remains an experience of incomparable value. We have for once learnt to see the great events of world history from below, from the perspective of the outcast, the suspects, the maltreated, the powerless, the oppressed, the reviled—in short, from the perspective of those who suffer. The important thing is that neither bitterness nor envy should have gnawed at the heart during this time, that we should have come to look with new eyes at matters great and small, sorrow and joy, strength and weakness, that our perception of generosity, humanity, justice and mercy should have become clearer, freer, less corruptible. We have to learn that personal suffering is a more effective key, a more rewarding principle for exploring the world in thought and action than personal good fortune. This perspective from below must not become the partisan possession of those who are eternally dissatisfied; rather, we must do justice to life in all its dimensions from a higher satisfaction, whose foundation is beyond any talk of "from below" or "from above." This is the way in which we may affirm it. . . . [6]

LETTERS TO EBERHARD BETHGE

DECEMBER 5, 1943

My thoughts and feelings seem to be getting more and more like those of the Old Testament, and in recent months I have been reading the Old Testament much more than the New. It is only when one knows the unutterability of the name of God that one can utter the name of Jesus Christ; it is only when one loves life and the earth so much that without them everything seems to be over that one may believe in the resurrection and a new world; it is only when one submits to God's law that one may speak of grace; and it is only when God's wrath and vengeance are hanging as grim realities over the heads of one's enemies that something of what it means to love and forgive them can touch our hearts. In my opinion it is not Christian to want to take our thoughts and feelings too quickly and too directly from the New Testament. We have already talked about this several times, and every day confirms my opinion. One cannot and must not speak the last word before the last but one. We live in the last but one and believe the last, don't we? Lutherans (so-called!) and pietists would shudder at the thought, but it is true all the same. In *The Cost of Discipleship* (ch. I) I just hinted at this, but did not follow it up; I must do so later. But the logical conclusions are far-reaching, e.g. for the problem of Catholicism, for the concept of the ministry, for the use of the Bible, etc., and above all for ethics. Why is it that in the Old Testament people tell lies vigorously and often to the glory of God (I've now collected the passages), kill, deceive, rob, divorce, and even fornicate (see the genealogy of Jesus), doubt, blaspheme, and curse, whereas in the New Testament there is nothing of all this? "An earlier stage" of religion? That is a very naive way out; it is one and the same God. But more of this later when we meet. . . .

I've been thinking again over what I wrote to you recently about our own fear. I think that here, under the guise of honesty, something is being passed off as "natural" that is at bottom a symptom of sin; it is really quite analogous to talking openly about sexual matters. After all, "truthfulness" does not mean uncovering everything that exists. God himself made clothes for humans; and that means that *in statu corruptionis* many things in human life ought to remain covered, and that evil, even though it cannot be eradicated, ought at least to be concealed. Exposure is cynical, and although cynics pride themselves on their exceptional honesty, or claim to want truth at all costs, they miss the crucial fact that since the fall there must be reticence and secrecy. . . . I believe we Germans have never properly grasped the meaning of "concealment," i.e., what is in the end the *status corruptionis* of the world. Kant says quite rightly in his *Anthropologie* that anyone who misunderstands or questions the significance of outward appearance in the world is a traitor to humanity.[7]

DECEMBER 18, 1943

... I believe that we ought so to love and trust God in our *lives,* and in all the good things that he sends us, that when the time comes (but not before!) we may go to him with love, trust, and joy. But, to put it plainly, for a husband in his wife's arms to be hankering after the other world is, in mild terms, a piece of bad taste, and not God's will. We ought to find and love God in what he actually gives us; if it pleases him to allow us to enjoy some overwhelming earthly happiness, we mustn't try to be more pious than God himself and allow our happiness to be corrupted by presumption and arrogance, and by unbridled religious fantasy which is never satisfied with what God gives.[8]

APRIL 30, 1944

... You would be surprised, and perhaps even worried, by my theological thoughts and the conclusions that they lead to; and this is where I miss you most of all, because I don't know anyone else with whom I could so well discuss them to have my thinking clarified. What is bothering me incessantly is the question what Christianity really is, or indeed who Christ really is, for us today. The time when people could be told everything by means of words, whether theological or pious, is over, and so is the time of inwardness and conscience—and that means the time of religion in general. We are moving towards a completely religionless time; people as they are now simply cannot be religious any more. Even those who honestly describe themselves as "religious" do not in the least act up to it, and so they presumably mean something quite different by "religious."

Our whole nineteen-hundred-year-old Christian preaching and theology rest on the "religious *a priori*" of humankind. "Christianity" has always been a form—perhaps the true form—of "religion." But if one day it becomes clear that this *a priori* does not exist at all, but was a historically conditioned and transient form of human self-expression, and if therefore people become radically religionless—and I think that that is already more or less the case (else how is it, for example, that this war, in contrast to all previous ones, is not calling forth any "religious" reaction?)—what does that mean for "Christianity"? It means that the foundation is taken away from the whole of what has up to now been our "Christianity," and that there remain only a few "last survivors of the age of chivalry," or a few intellectually dishonest people, on whom we can descend as "religious." Are they to be the chosen few? Is it on this dubious group of people that we are to pounce in fervour, pique, or indignation, in order to sell them our goods? Are we to fall upon a few unfortunate people in their hour of need and exercise a sort of religious compulsion on them? If we don't want to do all that, if our final judgment must be that the western form of Christianity, too, was only a preliminary stage to a complete absence of religion, what kind of situation emerges for us, for the church? How can Christ become the Lord of the religionless as well? Are there religionless Christians? If religion is only a garment of Christianity—and even this garment has looked very different at different times—then what is a religionless Christianity?

Barth, who is the only one to have started along this line of thought, did not carry it to completion, but arrived at a positivism of revelation, which in the last analysis is essentially a restoration. For the religionless working person (or any other person) nothing decisive is gained here. The questions to be answered would surely be: What do a church, a community, a sermon, a liturgy, a Christian life mean in a religionless world? How do we speak of God—without religion, i.e. without the temporally conditioned presuppositions of metaphysics, inwardness, and so on? How do we speak (or perhaps we cannot now even "speak" as we used to) in a "secular" way about "God"? In what way are we "religionless—secular" Christians, in what way are we the *ek-klesia*, those who are called forth, not regarding ourselves from a religious point of view as specially favoured, but rather as belonging wholly to the world? In that case Christ is no longer an object of religion, but something quite different, really the Lord of the world. But what does that mean? What is the place of worship and prayer in a religionless situation? Does the secret discipline, or alternatively the difference (which I have suggested to you before) between penultimate and ultimate, take on a new importance here? ...

... The Pauline question whether [circumcision] is a condition of justification seems to me in present-day terms to be whether religion is a condition of salvation. Freedom from [circumcision] is also freedom from religion. I often ask myself why a "Christian instinct" often draws me more to the religionless people than to the religious, by which I don't in the least mean with any evangelizing intention, but, I might almost say, "in brotherhood." While I'm often reluctant to mention God by name to religious people—because that name somehow seems to me here not to ring true, and I feel myself to be slightly dishonest (it's particularly bad when others start to talk in religious jargon; I then dry up almost completely and feel awkward and uncomfortable)—to people with no religion I can on occasion mention him by name quite calmly and as a matter of course. Religious people speak of God when human knowledge (perhaps simply because they are too lazy to think) has come to an end, or when human resources fail—in fact it is always the *deus ex machina* that they bring on to the scene, either for the apparent solution of insoluble problems, or as strength in human failure—always, that is to say, exploiting human weakness or human boundaries. Of necessity, that can go on only till people can by their own strength push these boundaries somewhat further out, so that God becomes superfluous as a *deus ex machina*. I've come to be doubtful of talking about any human boundaries (is even death, which people now hardly fear, and is sin, which they now hardly understand, still a genuine boundary today?). It always seems to me that we are trying anxiously in this way to reserve some space for God; I should like to speak of God not on the boundaries but at the centre, not in weaknesses but in strength; and therefore not in death and guilt but in a person's life and goodness. As to the boundaries, it seems to me better to be silent and leave the insoluble unsolved. Belief in the resurrection is *not* the "solution" of the problem of death. God's "beyond" is not the beyond of our cognitive faculties. The transcendence of epistemological theory has nothing to do with the transcendence of God. God is beyond in the midst of our life. The church stands, not at the boundaries where human powers give out, but in the middle of the village. That is how it is in the Old Testament, and in this sense we still read the New Testament far too little in the light of the Old. How this religionless Christianity looks, what form it takes, is something that I'm thinking about a great deal, and I shall be writing to you again about it soon. It may be that on us in particular, midway between East and West, there will fall a heavy responsibility.[9]

MAY 5, 1944

... A few more words about "religionlessness." I expect you remember Bultmann's essay on the "demythologizing" of the New Testament? My view of it today would be, not that he went "too far," as most people thought, but that he didn't go far enough. It's not only the "mythological" concepts, such as miracle, ascension, and so on (which are not in principle separable from the concepts of God, faith, etc.), but "religious" concepts generally, which are problematic. You can't, as Bultmann supposes, separate God and miracle, but you must be able to interpret and proclaim *both* in a "non-religious" sense. Bultmann's approach is fundamentally still a liberal one (i.e. abridging the gospel), whereas I'm trying to think theologically.

What does it mean to "interpret in a religious sense"? I think it means to speak on the one hand metaphysically, and on the other hand individualistically. Neither of these is relevant to the biblical message or to the person of today. Hasn't the individualistic question about personal salvation almost completely left us all? Aren't we really under the impression that there are more important things than that question (perhaps not more important than the *matter* itself, but more important than the *question*!)? I know it sounds pretty monstrous to say that. But, fundamentally, isn't this in fact biblical? Does the question about saving one's soul appear in the Old Testament at all? Aren't righteousness and the Kingdom of God on earth the focus of everything, and isn't it true that Rom. 3.24ff. is not an individualistic doctrine of salvation, but the culmination of the view that God alone is righteous? It is not with the beyond that we are concerned, but with this world as created and preserved, subjected to laws, reconciled, and restored. What is above this world is, in the gospel, intended to exist *for* this world; I mean that, not in the anthropocentric sense of liberal, mystic pietistic, ethical theology, but in the biblical sense of the creation and of the incarnation, crucifixion, and resurrection of Jesus Christ. . . .

I'm thinking about how we can reinterpret in a "worldly" sense—in the sense of the Old Testament and of John 1.14—the concepts of repentance, faith, justification, rebirth, and sanctification. I shall be writing to you about it again. . . . [10]

THOUGHTS ON THE DAY OF THE BAPTISM OF DIETRICH WILHELM RÜDIGER BETHGE

... Our church, which has been fighting in these years only for its self-preservation, as though that were an end in itself, is incapable of taking the word of reconciliation and redemption to humankind and the world. Our earlier words are therefore bound to lose their force and cease, and our being Christians today will be limited to two things: prayer and righteous action among people. All Christian thinking, speaking, and organizing must be born anew out of this prayer and action. By the time you have grown up, the church's form will have changed greatly. We are not yet out of the melting-pot, and any attempt to help the church prematurely to a new expansion of its organization will merely delay its conversion and purification. It is not for us to prophesy the day (though the day will come) when people will once more be called so to utter the word of God that the world will be changed and renewed by it. It will be a new language, perhaps quite non-religious, but liberating and redeeming—as was Jesus' language; it will shock people and yet overcome them by its power; it will be the language of a new righteousness and truth, proclaiming God's peace with humans and the coming of his kingdom. . . . [11]

FURTHER LETTERS TO EBERHARD BETHGE

MAY 29, 1944

Weizsäcker's book *The World-View of Physics* ... has again brought home to me quite clearly how wrong it is to use God as a stop-gap for the incompleteness of our knowledge. If in fact the frontiers of knowledge are being pushed further and further back (and that is bound to be the case), then God is being pushed back with them, and is therefore continually in retreat. We are to find God in what we know, not in what we don't know; God wants us to realize his presence, not in unsolved problems but in those that are solved. That is true of the relationship between God and scientific knowledge, but it is also true of the wider human problems of death, suffering, and guilt. It is now possible to find, even for these questions, human answers that take no account whatever of God. In point of fact, people deal with these questions without God (it has always been so), and it is simply not true to say that only Christianity has the answers to them. As to the idea of "solving" problems, it may be that the Christian answers are just as unconvincing—or convincing—as any others. Here again, God is no stop-gap; he must be recognized at the centre of life, not when we are at the end of our resources; it is his will to be recognized in life, and not only when death comes; in health and vigour, and not only in suffering; in our activities, and not only in sin. The ground for this lies in the revelation of God in Jesus Christ. He is the centre of life, and he certainly didn't "come" to answer our unsolved problems. From the centre of life certain questions, and their answers, are seen to be wholly irrelevant (I'm thinking of the judgment pronounced on Job's friends). In Christ there are no "Christian problems." Enough of this; I've just been disturbed again.[12]

JUNE 8, 1944

You now ask so many important questions on the subjects that have been occupying me lately, that I should be happy if I could answer them myself. But it's all very much in the early stages; and, as usual, I'm being led on more by an instinctive feeling for questions that will arise later than by any conclusions that I've already reached about them. I'll try to define my position from the historical angle.

The movement that began about the thirteenth century (I'm not going to get involved in any argument about the exact date) towards the autonomy of humans (in which I should include the discovery of the laws by which the world lives and deals with itself in science, social and political matters, art, ethics, and religion) has in our time reached an undoubted completion. People have learned to deal with themselves in all questions of importance without recourse to the "working hypothesis" called "God." In questions of science, art, and ethics this has become an understood thing at which one now hardly dares to tilt. But for the last hundred years or so it has also become increasingly true of religious questions; it is becoming evident that everything gets along without "God"—and, in fact, just as well as before. As in the scientific field, so in human affairs generally, "God" is being pushed more and more out of life, losing more and more ground.

Roman Catholic and Protestant historians agree that it is in this development that the great defection from God, from Christ, is to be seen; and the more they claim and playoff God and Christ against it, the more the development considers itself to be anti-Christian. The world that has become conscious of itself and the laws that govern its own existence has grown self-confident in what seems to us to be an uncanny way. False developments and failures do not make the world doubt the necessity of the course that it is taking, or of its development; they are accepted with fortitude and detachment as part of the bargain, and even an event like the present war is no exception. Christian apologetic has taken the most varied forms of opposition to this self-assurance. Efforts are made to prove to a world thus come of age that it cannot live without the tutelage of "God." Even though there has been surrender on all secular problems, there still remain the so-called "ultimate questions"—death, guilt—to which only "God" can give an answer, and because of which we need God and the church and the pastor. So we live, in some degree, on these so-called ultimate questions of humanity. But what if one day they no longer exist as such, if they too can be answered "without God"? Of course, we now have the secularized offshoots of Christian theology, namely existentialist philosophy and the psychotherapists, who demonstrate to secure, contented, and happy humankind that it is really unhappy and desperate and simply unwilling to admit that it is in a predicament about which it knows nothing, and from which only they can rescue it. Wherever there is health, strength, security, simplicity, they scent luscious fruit to gnaw at or to lay their pernicious eggs in. They set themselves to drive people to inward despair, and then the game is in their hands. That is secularized methodism. And whom does it touch? A small number of intellectuals, of degenerates, of people who regard themselves as the most important thing in the world, and who therefore like to busy themselves with themselves. Ordinary people, who spend their everyday lives at work and with their families, and of course with all kinds of diversions, are not affected. They have neither the time nor the inclination to concern themselves with their existential despair, or to regard their perhaps modest share of happiness as a trial, a trouble, or a calamity.

The attack by Christian apologetic on the adulthood of the world I consider to be in the first place pointless, in the second place ignoble, and in the third place unchristian. Pointless, because it seems to me like an attempt to put grown-ups back into adolescence, i.e. to make them dependent on things on which they are, in fact, no longer dependent, and thrusting them into problems that are, in fact, no longer problems to them. Ignoble, because it amounts to an attempt to exploit people's weakness for purposes that are alien to them and to which they have not freely assented. Unchristian, because it confuses Christ with one particular stage in human's religiousness, i.e. with a human law. More about this later.

But first, a little more about the historical position. The question is: Christ and the world that has come of age. The weakness of liberal theology was that it conceded to the world the right to determine Christ's place in the world; in the conflict between the church and the world it accepted the comparatively easy terms of peace that the world dictated. Its strength was that it did not try to put the clock back, and that it genuinely accepted the battle (Troeltsch), even though this ended with its defeat.

Defeat was followed by surrender, and by an attempt to make a completely fresh start based on the fundamentals of the Bible and the Reformation. . . .

Barth was the first to realize the mistake that all these attempts (which were all, in fact, still sailing, though unintentionally, in the channel of liberal theology) were making in leaving clear a space for religion in the world or against the world. He brought in against religion the God of Jesus Christ, "*pneuma* against *sarx*." That remains his greatest service. . . . [13]

JUNE 27, 1944

The decisive factor is said to be that in Christianity the hope of resurrection is proclaimed, and that that means the emergence of a genuine religion of redemption, the main emphasis now being on the far side of the boundary drawn by death. But it seems to me that this is just where the mistake and the danger lie. Redemption now means redemption from cares, distress, fears, and longings, from sin and death, in a better world beyond the grave. But is this really the essential character of the proclamation of Christ in the gospels and by Paul? I should say it is not. The difference between the Christian hope of resurrection and the mythological hope is that the former sends a person back to life on earth in a wholly new way which is even more sharply defined than it is in the Old Testament. Christians, unlike the devotees of the redemption myths, have no last line of escape available from earthly tasks and difficulties into the eternal, but, like Christ himself ("My God, why hast thou forsaken me?"), they must drink the earthly cup to the dregs, and only in their doing so is the crucified and risen Lord with them, and they crucified and risen with Christ. This world must not be permanently written off; in this the Old and New Testaments are at one. Redemption myths arise from human boundary-experiences, but Christ takes hold of persons at the centre of their life.[14]

JUNE 30, 1944

Now I will try to go on with the theological reflections that I broke off not long since. I had been saying that God is being increasingly pushed out of a world that has come of age, out of the spheres of our knowledge and life, and that since Kant he has been relegated to a realm beyond the world of experience. Theology has on the one hand resisted this development with apologetics, and has taken up arms—in vain—against Darwinism, etc. On the other hand, it has accommodated itself to the development by restricting God to the so-called ultimate questions as a *deus ex machina*; that means that he becomes the answer to life's problems, and the solution of its needs and conflicts. So if people have no such difficulties, or if they refuses to go into these things, to allow others to pity them, then either they cannot be open to God; or else they must be shown that they are, in fact, deeply involved in such problems, needs, and conflicts, without admitting or knowing it. If that can be done—and existentialist philosophy and psychotherapy have worked out some quite ingenious methods in that direction—then these people can now be claimed for God, and methodism can celebrate its triumph. But if they cannot be brought to see and admit that their happiness is really an evil, their health sickness, and their vigour despair, theologians are at their wits' end. It's a case of having to do either with a hardened sinner of a particularly ugly type, or with a person of "bourgeois complacency," and the one is as far from salvation as the other.

You see, that is the attitude that I am contending against. When Jesus blessed sinners, they were real sinners, but Jesus did not make everyone a sinner first. He called them away from their sin, not into their sin. It is true that encounter with Jesus meant the reversal of all human values. So it was in the conversion of Paul, though in his case the encounter with Jesus preceded the realization of sin. It is true that Jesus cared about people on the fringe of human society, such as harlots and tax-collectors, but never about them alone, for he sought to care about the person as such. Never did he question a person's health, vigour, or happiness, regarded in themselves, or regard them as evil fruits; else why should he heal the sick and restore strength to the weak? Jesus claims for himself and the Kingdom of God the whole of human life in all its manifestations.

Of course I have to be interrupted just now! Let me just summarize briefly what I'm concerned about—How to claim for Jesus Christ a world that has come of age.

I can't write any more today, or else the letter will be kept here another week, and I don't want that to happen. So: To be continued![15]

JULY 8, 1944

Now for a few more thoughts on our theme. Marshalling the biblical evidence needs more lucidity and concentration than I can command at present. Wait a few more days, till it gets cooler! I haven't forgotten, either, that I owe you something about the nonreligious interpretation of biblical concepts. But for today, here are a few preliminary remarks:

The displacement of God from the world, and from the public part of human life, led to the attempt to keep his place secure at least in the sphere of the "personal," the "inner," and the "private." And all individuals still have a private sphere somewhere, that is where they were thought to be the most vulnerable. The secrets known to a person's servant—that is, to put it crudely, the range of one's intimate life, from prayer to one's sexual life—have become the hunting-ground of modern pastoral workers. In that way they resemble (though with quite different intentions) the dirtiest gutter journalists. . . . In the one case it's social, financial, or political blackmail and in the other, religious blackmail.

Regarded theologically, the error is twofold. First, it is thought that people can be addressed as sinners only after their weaknesses and meannesses have been spied out. Secondly, it is thought that people's essential nature consists of their inmost and most intimate background; that is defined as their "inner life," and it is precisely in those secret human places that God is to have his domain!

On the first point it is to be said that humans are certainly sinners, but they are far from being mean or common on that account. To put it rather tritely, were Goethe and Napoleon sinners because they weren't always faithful husbands? It's not the sins of weakness, but the sins of strength, which matter here. It's not in the least necessary to spy out things; the Bible never does so. . . .

On the second point: the Bible does not recognize our distinction between the outward and the inward. Why should it? It is always concerned with *anthropôs teleios*, the *whole* person, even where, as in the Sermon on the Mount, the decalogue is pressed home to refer to "inward disposition." That a good "disposition" can take the place of total goodness is quite unbiblical. The discovery of the so-called inner life dates from the Renaissance, probably from Petrarch. The "heart" in the biblical sense is not the inner life, but the whole person in relation to God. But as people live just as much from "outwards" to "inwards" as from "inwards" to "outwards," the view that their essential nature can be understood only from their intimate spiritual background is wholly erroneous.

I therefore want to start from the premise that God shouldn't be smuggled into some last secret place, but that we should frankly recognize that the world, and people, have come of age, that we shouldn't run people down in their worldliness, but confront them with God at their strongest point, that we should give up all our clerical tricks, and not regard psychotherapy and existentialist philosophy as God's pioneers. The importunity of all these people is far too unaristocratic for the Word of God to ally itself with them. The Word of God is far removed from this revolt of mistrust, this revolt from below. On the contrary, it reigns.[16]

JULY 16, 1944

In politics Machiavelli detaches politics from morality in general and founds the doctrine of "reasons of state." Later, and very differently from Machiavelli, but tending like him towards the autonomy of human society, comes Grotius, setting up his natural law as international law, which is valid *etsi deus non daretur*, "even if there were no God. . . . "

And we cannot be honest unless we recognize that we have to live in the world *etsi deus non daretur*. And this is just what we do recognize—before God! God himself compels us to recognize it. So our coming of age leads us to a true recognition of our situation before God. God would have us know that we must live as humans who manage our lives without him.

The God who is with us is the God who forsakes us (Mark 15.34). The God who lets us live in the world without the working hypothesis of God is the God before whom we stand continually. Before God and with God we live without God. God lets himself be pushed out of the world on to the cross. He is weak and powerless in the world, and that is precisely the way, the only way, in which he is with us and helps us. Matt. 8.17 makes it quite clear that Christ helps us, not by virtue of his omnipotence, but by virtue of his weakness and suffering.

Here is the decisive difference between Christianity and all religions. Humans' religiosity makes them look in their distress to the power of God in the world: God is the *deus ex machina.* The Bible directs people to God's powerlessness and suffering; only the suffering God can help. To that extent we may say that the development towards the world's coming of age outlined above, which has done away with a false conception of God, opens up a way of seeing the God of the Bible, who wins power and space in the world by his weakness. This will probably be the starting-point for our "secular interpretation."[17]

JULY 18, 1944

... Jesus asked in Gethsemane, "Could you not watch with me one hour?" That is a reversal of what the religious people expect from God. People are summoned to share in God's sufferings at the hands of a godless world.

They must therefore really live in the godless world, without attempting to gloss over or explain its ungodliness in some religious way or other. They must live a "secular" life, and thereby share in God's sufferings. They *may* live a "secular" life (as those one who have been freed from false religious obligations and inhibitions). To be a Christian does not mean to be religious in a particular way, to make something of oneself (a sinner, a penitent, or a saint) on the basis of some method or other, but to be a human—not a type of human, but the human that Christ creates in us. It is not the religious act that makes the Christian, but participation in the sufferings of God in the secular life. That is *metanoia:* not in the first place thinking about one's own needs, problems, sins, and fears, but allowing oneself to be caught up into the way of Jesus Christ, into the messianic event, thus fulfilling Isa. 53. Therefore "believe in the gospel," or, in the words of John the Baptist, "Behold, the Lamb of God, who takes away the sin of the world" (John 1.29). (By the way, Jeremias has recently asserted that the Aramaic word for "lamb" may also be translated "servant"; very appropriate in view of Isa. 53!)

This being caught up into the messianic sufferings of God in Jesus Christ takes a variety of forms in the New Testament. . . . The only thing that is common to all these is their sharing in the suffering of God in Christ. That is their "faith." There is nothing of religious method here. The "religious act" is always something partial; "faith" is something whole, involving the whole of one's life. Jesus calls people, not to a new religion, but to life.

But what does this life look like, this participation in the powerlessness of God in the world? I will write about that next time, I hope. Just one more point for today. When we speak of God in a "non-religious" way, we must speak of him in such a way that the godlessness of the world is not in some way concealed, but revealed, and thus exposed to an unexpected light. The world that has come of age is more godless, and perhaps for that very reason nearer to God, than the world before its coming of age. Forgive me for still putting it all so terribly clumsily and badly, as I really feel I am. But perhaps you will help me again to make things clearer and simpler, even if only by my being able to talk about them with you and to hear you, so to speak, keep asking and answering.[18]

JULY 21, 1944

During the last year or so I've come to know and understand more and more the profound this-worldliness of Christianity. The Christian is not a *homo religiosus,* but simply a human, as Jesus was a human—in contrast, shall we say, to John the Baptist. I don't mean the shallow and banal this-worldliness of the enlightened, the busy, the comfortable, or the lascivious, but the profound this-worldliness, characterized by discipline and the constant knowledge of death and resurrection. I think Luther lived a this-worldly life in this sense.

I remember a conversation that I had in America thirteen years ago with a young French pastor. We were asking ourselves quite simply what we wanted to do with our lives. He said he would like to become a saint (and I think it's quite likely that he did become one). At the time I was very impressed, but I disagreed with him, and said, in effect, that I should like to learn to have faith. For a long time I didn't realize the depth of the contrast. I thought I could acquire faith by trying to live a holy life, or something like it. I suppose I wrote *The Cost of Discipleship* as the end of that path. Today I can see the dangers of that book, though I still stand by what I wrote.

I discovered later, and I'm still discovering right up to this moment, that is it only by living completely in this world that one learns to have faith. One must completely abandon any attempt to make something of oneself, whether it be a saint, or a converted sinner, or a churchman (a so-called priestly type!), a righteous person or an unrighteous one, a sick person or a healthy one. By this-worldliness I mean living unreservedly in life's duties, problems, successes and failures, experiences and perplexities. In so doing so we throw ourselves completely into the arms of God, taking seriously not our own sufferings, but those of God in the world—watching with Christ in Gethsemane. That, I think, is faith; that is *metanoia;* and that is how one becomes a human and a Christian (cf. Jer. 45!) How can success make us arrogant, or failure lead us astray, when we share in God's sufferings through a life of this kind?

I think you see what I mean, even though I put it so briefly. I'm glad to have been able to learn this, and I know I've been able to do so only along the road that I've traveled. So I'm grateful for the past and present, and content with them. . . . [19]

ETHICS

THE LOVE OF GOD AND THE DECAY OF THE WORLD

The World of Conflicts

The knowledge of good and evil seems to be the aim of all ethical reflection. The first task of Christian ethics is to invalidate this knowledge. In launching this attack on the underlying assumptions of all other ethics, Christian ethics stands so completely alone that it becomes questionable whether there is any purpose in speaking of Christian ethics at all. But if one does so notwithstanding, that can only mean that Christian ethics claims to discuss the origin of the whole problem of ethics, and thus professes to be a critique of all ethics simply as ethics.

Already in the possibility of the knowledge of good and evil Christian ethics discerns a falling away from the origin. Humans at their origin know only one thing: God. It is only in the unity of their knowledge of God that individuals know of other individuals, of things, and of themselves. They know all things only in God, and God in all things. The knowledge of good and evil shows that they are no longer at one with this origin. . . .

The overcoming of the knowledge of good and evil is accomplished in Jesus. . . .

Proving

... The will of God is not a system of rules which is established from the outset; it is something new and different in each different situation in life, and for this reason a person must ever anew examine what the will of God may be. The heart, the understanding, observation and experience must all collaborate in this task. It is no longer a matter of a person's own knowledge of good and evil, but solely of the living will of God; our knowledge of God's will is not something over which we ourselves dispose, but it depends solely upon the grace of God, and this grace is and requires to be new every morning. . . .

ETHICS AS FORMATION

The Idolization of Death

The person whom God has taken to Himself, sentenced and awakened to a new life, this is Jesus Christ. In Him it is all humankind. It is ourselves. Only the form of Jesus Christ confronts the world and defeats it. And it is from this form alone that there comes the formation of a new world, a world which is reconciled with God.

Conformation

The word "formation" arouses our suspicion. We are sick and tired of Christian programmes and of the thoughtless and superficial slogan of what is called "practical" Christianity as distinct from "dogmatic" Christianity. . . . Whenever [the scriptures] speak of forming they are concerned only with the one form which has overcome the world, the form of Jesus Christ. Formation can come only from this form. But here again it is not a question of applying directly to the world the teaching of Christ or what are referred to as Christian principles, so that the world might be formed in accordance with these. On the contrary, formation comes only by being drawn in into the form of Jesus Christ. It comes only as formation in His likeness, as *conformation*, with the unique form of Him who was made a man, was crucified, and rose again.

This is not achieved by dint of efforts "to become like Jesus," which is the way in which we usually interpret it. It is achieved only when the form of Jesus Christ itself works upon us in such a manner that it molds our form in its own likeness (Gal. 4.19). . . .

. . . The longing of the Incarnate to take form in all humans is as yet still unsatisfied. He bore the form of humans as a whole, and yet He can take form only in a small band. These are His Church.

"Formation" consequently means in the first place Jesus' taking form in His Church. What takes form here is the form of Jesus Christ Himself. The New Testament states the case profoundly and clearly when it calls the Church the Body of Christ. The body is the form. So the Church is not a religious community of worshipers of Christ but is Christ Himself who has taken form among humans. . . .

The form of Christ is one and the same at all times and in all places. . . . And yet Christ is not a principle in accordance with which the whole world must be shaped. Christ is not the proclaimer of a system of what would be good today, here and at all times. Christ teaches no abstract ethics such as must at all costs be put into practice. Christ was not essentially a teacher and legislator, but a person, a real person like ourselves. And it is not therefore His will that we should in our time be the adherents, exponents and advocates of a definite doctrine, but that we should be humans, real humans before God.

The Concrete Place

This leads us away from any kind of abstract ethic and towards an ethic which is entirely concrete. What can and must be said is not what is good once and for all, but the way in which Christ takes form among us here and now. The attempt to define that which is good once and for all has, in the nature of the case, always ended in failure. Either the proposition was asserted in such general and formal terms that it retained no significance as regards its contents, or else one tried to include in it and elaborate the whole immense range of conceivable contents, and thus to say in advance what would be good in every single conceivable case; this led to a casuistic system so unmanageable that it could satisfy the demands neither of general validity nor of concreteness. The concretely Christian ethic is beyond formalism and casuistry. Formalism and casuistry set out from the conflict between the good and the real, but the Christian ethic can take for its point of departure the reconciliation, already accomplished, of the world with God and the human Jesus Christ and the acceptance of the real human by God.

THE LAST THINGS AND THE THINGS BEFORE THE LAST

The Penultimate

Justification by grace and faith alone remains in every respect the final word and for this reason, when we speak of the things before the last, we must not speak of them as having any value of their own, but we must bring to light their relation to the ultimate. It is for the sake of the ultimate that we must now speak of the penultimate. This must now be made clearly intelligible. . . . Radicalism always springs from a conscious or unconscious hatred of what is established. Christian radicalism, no matter whether it consists in withdrawing from the world or in improving the world, arises from the hatred of creation. The radical cannot forgive God His creation. . . .

Compromise always springs from hatred of the ultimate. The Christian spirit of compromise arises from hatred of the justification of the sinner by grace alone. . . .

To contrast the two attitudes in this way is to make it sufficiently clear that both alike are opposed to Christ. For in Jesus Christ those things which are here ranged in mutual hostility are one. The question of the Christian life will not, therefore, be decided and answered either by radicalism or by compromise, but only by reference to Jesus Christ Himself. In Him alone lies the solution for the problem of the relation between the ultimate and the penultimate.

The Preparing of the Way

What is this penultimate? It is everything that precedes the ultimate, everything that precedes the justification of the sinner by grace alone, everything which is to be regarded as leading up to the last thing when the last thing has been found. It is the same time everything which follows the ultimate and yet again precedes it. There is, therefore, no penultimate in itself; as though a thing could justify itself in itself as being a thing before the last thing; a thing becomes penultimate only through the ultimate, that is to say, at the moment when it has already lost its own validity. The penultimate, then, does not determine the ultimate; it is the ultimate which determines the penultimate. . . .

. . . For the sake of the ultimate the penultimate must be preserved. Any arbitrary destruction of the penultimate will do serious injury to the ultimate. . . .

Preparing the way for the word: this is the purpose of everything that has been said about the things before the last. . . .

But all this does not exclude the task of preparing the way. This task is, on the contrary, a charge of immense responsibility for all those who know of the coming of Christ. The hungry person needs bread and the homeless person needs a roof; the dispossessed need justice and the lonely need fellowship; the undisciplined need order and the slave needs freedom. To allow the hungry to remain hungry would be blasphemy against God and one's neighbor, for what is the nearest to God is precisely the need of one's neighbor. To provide the neighbor with bread is to prepare the way for the coming of grace.

The Natural

The concept of the natural has fallen into discredit in Protestant ethics. For some it was completely lost to sight in the darkness of general sinfulness, while for others, conversely, it was lighted up by the brilliance of absolute historicity. In both cases this was a disastrous mistake, for its consequence was that the concept of the natural no longer had a place in Protestant thought but was entirely abandoned to Catholic ethics. Now this meant a serious and substantial loss to Protestant thought, for it was now more or less deprived of the means of orientation in dealing with the practical questions of natural life. . . .

The concept of the natural must, therefore, be recovered on the basis of the gospel. We speak of the natural, as distinct from the creaturely, in order to take into account the fact of the Fall; and we speak of the natural rather than of the sinful so that we may include in it the creaturely. The natural is that which, after the Fall, is directed towards the coming of Christ. The unnatural is that which, after the Fall, closes its doors against the coming of Christ. . . .

Natural Life

To idealistic thinkers it may seem out of place for a Christian ethic to speak first of rights and only later of duties. But our authority is not Kant; it is the Holy Scripture, and it is precisely for that reason that we must speak first of the rights of natural life, in other words of what is given to life, and only later of what is demanded of life. God gives before He demands. . . . The rights of natural life are in the midst of the fallen world the reflected splendour of the glory of God's creation. They are not primarily something that a person can sue for his own interest, but they are something that is guaranteed by God Himself. The duties, on the other hand, derive from the rights themselves, as tasks are implied by gifts. They are implicit in the rights. Within the framework of the natural life, therefore, we in every case speak first of the rights and then of the duties, for by so doing, in the natural life too, we are allowing the gospel to have its way.

CHRIST, REALITY, AND GOOD

Thinking in Terms of Two Spheres

... Since the beginnings of Christian ethics after the times of the New Testament the main underlying conception in ethical thought, and the one which consciously or unconsciously has determined its whole course, has been the conception of a juxtaposition and conflict of two spheres, the one divine, holy, supernatural and Christian, and the other worldly, profane, natural and un-Christian. . . .

It may be difficult to break the spell of this thinking in terms of two spheres, but it is nevertheless quite certain that it is in profound contradiction to the thought of the Bible and to the thought of the Reformation, and that consequently it aims wide of reality. There are not two realities, but only one reality, and this is the reality of God, which has become manifest in Christ in the reality of the world. . . . Thus the theme of the two spheres, which has repeatedly become the dominant factor in the history of the Church, is foreign to the New Testament. The New Testament is concerned solely with the manner in which the reality of Christ assumes reality in the present world, which it has already encompassed, seized and possessed. . . .

Ethical thinking in terms of spheres, then, is invalidated by faith in the revelation of the ultimate reality in Jesus Christ, and this means that there is no real possibility of being a Christian outside the reality of the world and that there is no real worldly existence outside the reality of Jesus Christ. There is no place to which the Christian can withdraw from the world, whether it be outwardly or in the sphere of the inner life. Any attempt to escape from the world must sooner or later be paid for with a sinful surrender to the world. . . .

The Four Mandates

The world, like all created things, is created through Christ and with Christ as its end, and consists in Christ alone (John 1.10; Col. 1.16). To speak of the world without speaking of Christ is empty and abstract. The world is relative to Christ, no matter whether it knows it or not. This relativeness of the world to Christ assumes concrete form in certain mandates of God in the world. The Scriptures name four such mandates: labour, marriage, government and the Church. We speak of divine mandates rather than of divine orders because the word "mandate" refers more clearly to a divinely imposed task rather than to a determination of being. It is God's will that there shall be labour, marriage, government and church in the world; and it is His will that all these, each in its own way, shall be through Christ, directed towards Christ, and in Christ. . . . It is not because labour, marriage, government and church *are* that they commanded by God, but it is because they are commanded by God that they *are*. And they are divine mandates only in so far as their being consciously or unconsciously subordinated to the divinely imposed task. If a concrete form of labour, marriage, government or church persistently and arbitrarily violates the assigned task, then the divine mandate lapses in this particular concrete instance.

The mandate of labour confronts us, according to the Bible, already with the first human. Adam is "to dress and to keep" the Garden of Eden (Gen. 2.15). Even after the Fall labour remains a mandate of divine discipline and grace (Gen. 3.17–19). In the sweat of their brow humans wrest their nourishment from the soil, and the range of human labour soon embraces everything from agriculture and economy to science and art (Gen. 4.17ff.). The labour which is instituted in Paradise is a participation by humans in the action of creation. . . .

Like the mandate of labour, the mandate of marriage also confronts us after the creation already with the first human. In marriage man and woman become one in the sight of God, just as Christ becomes one with His Church. "This is a great mystery" (Eph. 5.32f). God bestows on this union the blessing of fruitfulness, the generation of new life. Humans enter into the will of the Creator in sharing in the process of creation. . . .

The divine mandate of government presupposes the divine mandates of labour and marriage. In the world which it rules, the governing authority finds already present the two mandates through which God the Creator exercises his creative power, and is therefore dependent on these. Government cannot itself produce life or values. It is not creative. It preserves what has been created, maintaining it in the order which is assigned to it through the task which is imposed by God. It protects it by making law to consist in the acknowledgement of the divine mandates and by securing respect for this law by the force of the sword. . . . By the establishment of law and by the force of the sword the governing authority preserves the world for the reality of Jesus Christ. Everyone owes obedience to this governing authority—for Christ's sake.

The divine mandate of the Church is different from these three. This mandate is the task of enabling the reality of Jesus Christ to become real in the preaching and organization of the Church and the Christian life. It is concerned, therefore, with the eternal salvation of the whole world. The mandate of the Church extends to all humankind, and it does so within all the other mandates. The person is at the same time a labourer, a partner in marriage, and the subject of a government, so that there is an overlapping of the three mandates in the person and all three must be fulfilled simultaneously; and the mandate of the Church impinges on all these mandates, for now it is the Christian who is at once labourer, partner in marriage, and subject of a government. No division into separate spheres or spaces is permissible here. The whole person stands before the whole earthly and eternal reality, the reality which God has prepared for the person in Jesus Christ. . . .

HISTORY AND GOOD

Correspondence with Reality
Action which is in accordance with Christ is in accordance with reality because it allows the world to be the world; it reckons with the world as the world; and yet it never forgets that in Jesus Christ the world is loved, condemned and reconciled by God. . . . It is the essence of Greek tragedy that a

person's downfall is brought about by the conflict of incompatible laws. Creon and Antigone, Jason and Medea, Agamemnon and Clytemnestra, all are subject to the claim of these eternal laws which cannot be reconciled in one and the same life; obedience is rendered to the one law at the price of guilt in respect of the other law. The meaning of all genuine tragedies is not that one person is right and the other wrong, but that both incur guilt towards life itself; the structure of their life is an incurring of guilt in respect of the laws of the gods. This is the most profound experience of classical antiquity. Especially since the Renaissance it has exercised a decisive influence over western thought; … but in modern times it has only very rarely been perceived that this tragic experience has been overcome by the message of Christ. Even the modern Protestant ethic invokes the pathos of tragedy in its representation of the irreconcilable conflict of the Christian in the world, and claims that in this it is expressing an ultimate reality. All this unconsciously lies entirely under the spell of the heritage of antiquity; it is not Luther, but it is Aeschylus, Sophocles and Euripides who have invested human life with this tragic aspect. The seriousness of Luther is quite different from the seriousness of the classical tragedians. For the Bible and for Luther what ultimately requires to be considered in earnest is not the disunion of the gods in the form of their laws, but it is the unity of God and the reconciliation of the world with God in Jesus Christ; it is not the inescapability of guilt, but it is the simplicity of the life which follows from the reconciliation; it is not to fate, but the gospel as the ultimate reality of life; it is not the cruel triumph of the gods over falling humanity, but it is the election of the human to be human as the child of God in the world which is reconciled through grace. . . .

The Acceptance of Guilt
From what has just been said it emerges that the structure of responsible action includes both readiness to accept guilt and freedom. . . .

When people take guilt upon themselves in responsibility, and no responsible person can avoid this, they impute this guilt to themselves and to no one else; they answer for it; they accept responsibility for it. They do not do this in the insolent presumptuousness of their own power, but they do it in the knowledge that this liberty is forced upon them and that in this liberty they are dependent on grace. Before other people the people of free responsibility are justified by necessity; before themselves they are acquitted by their conscience; but before God they hope only for mercy.

Freedom
We must therefore conclude our analysis of the structure of responsible action by speaking of freedom.

Responsibility and freedom are corresponding concepts. Factually, though not chronologically, responsibility presupposes freedom and freedom can consist only in responsibility. Responsibility is the freedom of humans which is given only in the obligation to god and to our neighbor. . . .

... What is the place and what are the limits of my responsibility?

THE PLACE OF RESPONSIBILITY

Vocation

... It is not in the loyal discharge of the earthly obligations of their calling as citizens, workers and parents that a people fulfill the responsibility which is imposed on them, but is in hearing the call of Jesus Christ. This call does indeed summon them to earthly duties, but that is never the whole of the call, for it lies always beyond these duties, before them and behind them. The calling, in the New Testament sense, is never a sanctioning of worldly institutions as such; its "yes" to them always includes at the same time an extremely emphatic "no," an extremely sharp protest against the world.

THE "ETHICAL" AND THE "CHRISTIAN" AS A THEME

The Commandment of God

This brings us to the only possible object of a "Christian ethic," an object which lies beyond the "ethical," namely, the "commandment of God."

... God's commandment is the speech of God to humans. Both in its contents and in its form it is concrete speech to the concrete human. God's commandment leaves the human no room for application or interpretation. It leaves room only for obedience or disobedience. God's commandment cannot be found and known in detachment from time and place; it can only be heard in a local and temporal context. If God's commandment is not clear, definite and concrete to the last detail, then it is not God's commandment.

... Does this mean that at every moment of our lives we may be informed of the commandment of God by some special direct divine inspiration? ... No, it does not mean that, for the concreteness of the divine commandment consists in its historicity; it confronts us in a historical form. Does this mean, then, that we are utterly lacking in certainty in the face of the extremely varying claims of the historical powers, and that, so far as the commandment of God is concerned, we are groping in the darkness? No, the reason why it does not mean this is that God makes His commandment heard in a definite historical form. We cannot now escape the question where and in what historical form God makes His commandment known. For the sake of simplicity and clarity, and even at the risk of a direct misunderstanding, we will begin by answering this question in the form of a thesis. God's commandment, which is manifested in Jesus Christ, comes to us in the Church, in the family, in labour and in government. . . .

. . . The commandment of God becomes the element in which one lives without always being conscious of it, and, thus it implies freedom of movement and of action, freedom from the fear of decision, freedom from fear to act, it implies certainty, quietude, confidence, balance and peace. I honour my parents, I am faithful in marriage, I respect the lives and property of others, not because at the frontiers of my life there is a threatening "thou shalt not," but because I accept as holy institutions of God these realities, parents, marriage, life and property, which confront me in the midst and in the fulness of life. It is only when the commandment no longer merely threatens me as a transgressor of the limits, it is only when it convinces and subdues me with its real contents, that it sets me free from the anxiety and the uncertainty of decision. If I love my wife, if I accept marriage as an institution of God, then there comes an inner freedom and certainty of life and action in marriage; I no longer watch with suspicion every step that I take; I no longer call into question every deed that I perform. The divine prohibition of adultery is then no longer the centre around which all my thought and action in marriage revolves. (As though the meaning and purpose of marriage consisted of nothing except the avoidance of adultery!) But it is the honouring and the free acceptance of marriage, the leaving behind of the prohibition of adultery, which is now the precondition for the fulfilment of the divine commission of marriage. The divine commandment has here become the permission to live in marriage in freedom and certainty.

The commandment of God is the permission to live as human before God.

The commandment of God is permission. It differs from all human laws in that it commands freedom. It is by overcoming this contradiction that it shows itself to be God's commandment; the impossible becomes possible, and that which lies beyond the range of what can be commanded, liberty, is the true object of this commandment. . . .

Before the commandment of God people do not permanently stand like Hercules at the crossroads. They are not everlastingly striving for the right decision. They are not always wearing themselves out in a conflict of duties. They are not continually failing and beginning again. Nor does the commandment of God itself make its appearance only in these great, agitated and intensely conscious moments of crisis in life. On the contrary, before the commandment of God humans may at last really move forward along the road and no longer stand endlessly at the crossroads. They can now have the right decision really behind them, and not always before them. Entirely without inner conflict they can do one thing and leave undone another thing which, according to theoretical ethics, is perhaps equally urgent. They can already have made a beginning and they can allow themselves to be guided, escorted and protected on their way by prayers as though by a good angel. And God's commandment itself can give life unity of direction and personal guidance only in the form of seemingly small and insignificant everyday words, sayings, hints and help.

The purpose of the commandment lies not in the avoidance of transgression, and not in the torment of ethical conflict and decision, but in freely accepted, self-evident life in the Church, in marriage, in the family, in work and in the state. . . .

STATE AND CHURCH

The Basis of Government

A. In the Nature of Humanity. The ancients, especially Aristotle, base the state on the character of humans. The state is the supreme consummation of the rational character of humans, and to serve it is the supreme purpose of human life. All ethics is political ethics. Virtues are political virtues. This theory of the state was taken over in principle by Catholic theology. The state is a product of human nature. Human's ability to live in society derives from the Creation, as does also the relation of rulers and ruled. . . .

B. In Sin. The Reformation, by taking up ideas of St. Augustine, broke away from the ancient Greek concept of the state. The Reformation does not represent the state as a community arising from the created nature of humanity, although traces of this idea, too, can be found in the writings of some of the Reformers; it places the origin of the state, as government, in the Fall. It was sin that made necessary the divine institution of government. The sword which God has given to government is to be used by it in order to protect humans against the chaos which is caused by sin. Government is to punish the criminal and to safeguard life. . . .

C. In Christ. It becomes clear from these last remarks, and indeed from everything that we have said so far on this subject, that the basing of the state on sin or on the nature of humanity leads to a conception of the state as a self-contained entity, a conception which fails to take account of the relation of the state to Jesus Christ. . . . It is through Jesus Christ and for Jesus Christ that all things are created (John 1.2; I Cor. 8.6; Heb. 1.2), and in particular "thrones, dominions, principalities and powers" (Col. 1.16). It is only in Jesus Christ that all these things "consist" (Col. 1.17). And it is He who is "the head of the church" (Col. 1.1). A theological proposition with regard to government, with regard, that is to say, to the government which is instituted by God and not to some general philosophical idea of government, is therefore in no circumstances possible without reference to Jesus Christ, and to Jesus Christ as the head of His Church; no such proposition is possible without reference to the Church of Jesus Christ. The true basis of government is therefore Jesus Christ Himself. . . .

The Divine Character of Government

A. In Its Being. Government is given to us not as an idea or a task to be fulfilled but as a reality and as something which "is" (. . . Rom. 13.1c). It is in its being that it is a divine office. . . . The being of government is independent of the manner of its coming into being. No matter if human's path to governmental office repeatedly passes through guilt (cf. Shakespeare's histories), the being of government lies beyond its earthly coming into being; for government is an institution of God, not in its coming into being but in its being. . . . This is that historical relationship of one actual entity to another which is found again in the relationship between father and child. . . . There can be no ethical isolation of the son from his father, and indeed, on the basis of actual being, there is a necessity of sharing in the assuming and carrying of the guilt of a father or a brother. There is no glory in standing amid the ruins of one's native town in the consciousness that at least one has not oneself incurred any guilt. . . .

B. In Its Task. The being of government is linked with a divine commission. Its being is fulfilled only in the fulfilment of the commission. A total apostasy from its commission would jeopardize its being. But by God's providence this total apostasy is possible only as an eschatological event, and as such it leads amidst grievous torments to a total separation of the congregation from the government as the embodiment of Antichrist. The mission of government consists in serving the dominion of Christ on earth by the exercise of the worldly power of the sword and of justice. Government serves Christ by establishing and maintaining an outward justice by means of the sword which is given to it, and to it alone, in deputyship for God. And it has not only the negative task of punishing the wicked; but also the positive task of praising the good or "them that do well" (I Pet. 2.14). It is therefore endowed, on the one hand, with a judicial authority, and on the other hand, with a right to educate for goodness, i.e., for outward justice or righteousness. . . .

C. In Its Claim. ... In the exercise of the mission of government the demand for obedience is unconditional and qualitatively total; it extends both to conscience and to bodily life. Belief, conscience and bodily life are subject to an obligation of obedience with respect to the divine commission of government. A doubt can arise only when the contents and the extent of the commission of government become questionable. Christians are neither obliged nor able to examine the rightfulness of the demand of government in each particular case. Their duty of obedience is binding on them until government directly compels them to offend against the divine commandment, that is to say, until government openly denies its divine commission and thereby forfeits it claim. . . . The refusal of obedience in the case of a particular historical and political decision of government must, therefore, like this decision itself, be a venture undertaken on one's own responsibility. A historical decision cannot be entirely resolved into ethical terms; there remains a residuum, the venture of action. That is true both of the government and of its subjects.[20]

NOTES

1. [Dietrich Bonhoeffer, "The Nature of the Church," in *A Testament to Freedom: The Essential Writings of Dietrich Bonhoeffer*, ed. Geffrey B. Kelly and F. Burton Nelson (San Francisco: HarperSanFrancisco, 1990), 91.]

2. [Dietrich Bonhoeffer, "Thy Kingdom Come: The Prayer of the Church for the Kingdom of God on Earth," in *A Testament to Freedom*, 94, 97.]

3. [Dietrich Bonhoeffer, "Creation and Fall: The Image of God on Earth," in *A Testament to Freedom*, 113–115.]

4. [Dietrich Bonhoeffer, *Discipleship*, trans. Martin Kaske and Ilse Tödt, in *Dietrich Bonhoeffer Works* (Minneapolis: Fortress Press, 1996–), 4:39, 43–45.]

5. [Dietrich Bonhoeffer, *Temptation*, ed. Eberhard Bethge, trans. Kathleen Downham (London: SCM Press Ltd, 1955), 9–11. The Confessing Church seminary held a reunion in 1937. Bonhoeffer began each day with a Bible study for the group. The manuscript for his presentations was found and was published as *Temptation*.]

6. [Dietrich Bonhoeffer, *Letters and Papers from Prison*, ed. Eberhard Bethge, trans. Reginald Fuller, enlarged edition (New York: Simon & Schuster, 1997), 3–7, 9–11, 16–17. Eberhard Bethge was able to save letters and papers that Bonhoeffer had sent him from prison. In 1950 he overcame his reluctance to make them public and began making extracts of them into a small volume to share with friends and others who might be interested. He was surprised at the response that would ultimately make it a best seller and stimulate intense interest and debate. Bonhoeffer wrote this essay, 'Prologue: After Ten Years," as a 1943 Christmas gift for his fellow conspirators, friends, and family. The final, unfinished paragraph may have been intended for inclusion with this essay.]

7. [*Letters from Prison*, 156–158. Bethge had been Bonhoeffer's student, then colleague, then closest friend. And after Bonhoeffer's imprisonment he became the person with whom Bonhoeffer could frankly explore his new theological approaches. The correspondence—in spite of delays, interruptions and other difficulties—allowed Bethge to raise questions and make suggestions about the developments in Bonhoeffer's thinking. It must have been a great, influential help to Bonhoeffer.]

8. [Ibid., 168.]

9. [Ibid., 279–282.]

10. [Ibid., 285–287.]

11. [Ibid., 300.]

12. [Ibid., 311–312.]

13. [Ibid., 325–328.]

14. [Ibid., 336–337.]

15. [Ibid., 341–342.]

16. [Ibid., 344–346.]

17. [Ibid., 359–361.]

18. [Ibid., 361–362.]

19. [Ibid., 369–370.]

20. [Dietrich Bonhoeffer, *Ethics*, trans. Neville Horton Smith (New York: Simon & Schuster, 1995), 21, 40, 41, 81–82, 84, 86, 87, 125, 128–130, 133–136, 142–143, 150, 193–198, 204–208, 227–228, 236, 244, 250, 251, 272–280, 328–332, 335, 334–339. Bonhoeffer regarded his *Ethics* as the great task of his life, and he deeply regretted not having the chance to complete it. He worked on a manuscript from 1940–43. During this period, his theology was changing, his life was subject to ongoing disruption and the extraordinary demands of the conspiracy against Hitler, and he had no opportunity to develop his thoughts into a whole. Eberhard Bethge retrieved the existing pieces of the manuscript from their hiding places and published them in 1949. The various sections carried no definitive proposal for their proper sequence. In writing earlier books, Bonhoeffer never followed a set plan. He allowed his work to grow organically, subject to constant change. Bethge had no easy task in settling on a fit ordering of the pages. He revised the 1949 sequence for a 1963 edition, and the *Dietrich Bonhoeffer Werke* edition of 1992 has established yet a third sequence. The following excerpts follow the 1949 ordering. What Bonhoeffer was able to set down is creatively and intriguingly challenging. "Ethics" did not mean for him establishing a system or set of principles but a way of describing specific, relational conformation to the living presence of Christ in the world. Because Christ is the person who exists for others, and because the Church is the body of Christ in the world, she, too, exists for others. The "others" are all those with whom Christ identifies, and in Bonhoeffer's circumstance this meant those, especially Jews, who were Nazi victims. In solidarity with them, members of the Church are in conscience free to take bold, responsible action and to accept guilt in the process.]

{CHAPTER 12}

Reinhold Niebuhr (1892–1971)

SELECTED AND EDITED BY DAVISON M. DOUGLAS

Reinhold Niebuhr was the most influential American theologian of the twentieth century. He was raised and educated in the German Evangelical Synod of North America, a church in the tradition of the Union Church of Prussia, with both Lutheran and Reformed roots, that later joined the United Church of Christ. Niebuhr began his professional work as a parish minister in Detroit in 1915, where he remained for thirteen years. In 1928, Niebuhr joined the faculty of Union Theological Seminary in New York City as a professor of applied Christianity. He would remain on the Union faculty until his retirement in 1960.

An extraordinarily prolific writer, Niebuhr wrote more than twenty books and hundreds of articles in which he articulated a "Christian realist" approach to theology and human society. Pursuant to Niebuhr's Christian realist perspective, humans should strive to create a just society but should also recognize that the depths of human sinfulness and self-interest will make the achievement of such a society extraordinarily difficult. Niebuhr's emphasis on human sinfulness placed him in the tradition of Augustine and the Protestant reformers. In his passion for justice, Niebuhr drew on the social justice emphasis of the Hebrew prophets. Niebuhr claimed that "all theology really begins with Amos," the biblical prophet who constantly urged the Hebrew people to do justice.

THE NATURE AND DESTINY OF MAN:
A CHRISTIAN INTERPRETATION

OUR PRESENT INTEREST is to relate the Biblical and distinctively Christian conception of sin as pride and self-love to the observable behaviour of men. It will be convenient in this analysis to distinguish between three types of pride, which are, however, never completely distinct in actual life:

pride of power, pride of knowledge and pride of virtue. The third type, the pride of self-righteousness, rises to a form of spiritual pride, which is at once a fourth type and yet not a specific form of pride at all but pride and self-glorification in its inclusive and quintessential form.

... "Of the infinite desires of man," declares Bertrand Russell, "the chief are the desires for power and glory. . . ."[1] Mr. Russell is not quite clear about the relation of the two to each other, and the relation is, as a matter of fact, rather complex. There is a pride of power in which the human ego assumes its self-sufficiency and self-mastery and imagines itself secure against all vicissitudes. It does not recognize the contingent and dependent character of its life and believes itself to be the author of its own existence, the judge of its own values and the master of its own destiny. This proud pretension is present in an inchoate form in all human life but it rises to greater heights among those individuals and classes who have a more than ordinary degree of social power. Closely related to the pride which seems to rest upon the possession of either the ordinary or some extraordinary measure of human freedom and self-mastery, is the lust for power which has pride as its end. The ego does not feel secure and therefore grasps for more power in order to make itself secure. It does not regard itself as sufficiently significant or respected or feared and therefore seeks to enhance its position in nature and in society. . . .

The second form of the pride of power is more obviously prompted by the sense of insecurity. It is the sin of those, who knowing themselves to be insecure, seek sufficient power to guarantee their security, inevitably of course at the expense of other life. . . .

Greed as a form of the will-to-power has been a particularly flagrant sin in the modern era because modern technology has tempted contemporary man to overestimate the possibility and the value of eliminating his insecurity in nature. Greed has thus become the besetting sin of a bourgeois culture. . . .

Since man's insecurity arises not merely from the vicissitudes of nature but from the uncertainties of society and history, it is natural that the ego should seek to overcome social as well as natural insecurity and should express the impulse of "power over men" as well as "power over matter." The peril of a competing human will is overcome by subordinating that will to the ego and by using the power of many subordinated wills to ward off the enmity which such subordination creates. The will-to-power is thus inevitably involved in the vicious circle of accentuating the insecurity which it intends to eliminate. . . . The will-to-power in short involves the ego in injustice. It seeks a security beyond the limits of human finiteness and this inordinate ambition arouses fears and enmities which the world of pure nature, with its competing impulses of survival, does not know. . . .

The truth is that man is tempted by the basic insecurity of human existence to make himself doubly secure and by the insignificance of his place in the total scheme of life to prove his significance. The will-to-power is in short both a direct form and an indirect instrument of the pride which Christianity regards as sin in its quintessential form. . . .

... The egotism of man has been defined and illustrated thus far without a careful discrimination between group pride and the pride and egotism of individuals. This lack of discrimination is provisionally justified by the fact that, strictly speaking, only individuals are moral agents, and group pride is therefore merely an aspect of the pride and arrogance of individuals. It is the fruit of the undue claims which they make for their various social groups. Nevertheless some distinctions must be made between the collective behaviour of men and their individual attitudes. This is necessary in part because group pride, though having its source in individual attitudes, actually achieves a certain authority over the individual and results in unconditioned demands by the group upon the individual. Whenever the group develops organs of will, as in the apparatus of the state, it seems to the individual to have become an independent centre of moral life. He will be inclined to bow to its pretensions and to acquiesce in its claims of authority, even when these do not coincide with his moral scruples or inclinations.

A distinction between group pride and the egotism of individuals is necessary, furthermore, because the pretensions and claims of a collective or social self exceed those of the individual ego. The group is more arrogant, hypocritical, self-centered and more ruthless in the pursuit of its ends than the individual. An inevitable moral tension between individual and group morality is therefore created. "If," said the great Italian statesman, Cavour, "we did for ourselves what we do for our country, what rascals we would be." This tension is naturally most apparent in the conscience of responsible statesmen, who are bound to feel the disparity between the canons of ordinary morality and the accepted habits of collective and political behaviour. Frederick the Great was not, as statesmen go, a man of unique moral sensitivity. His confession of a sense of this tension is therefore the more significant. "I hope," said he, "that posterity will distinguish the philosopher from the monarch in me and the decent man from the politician. I must admit that when drawn into the vortex of European politics it is difficult to preserve decency and integrity. One feels oneself in constant danger of being betrayed by one's allies and abandoned by one's friends, of being suffocated by envy and jealousy, and is thus finally driven to the terrible alternative of being false either to one's country or to one's word."[2]

The egotism of racial, national and socio-economic groups is most consistently expressed by the national state because the state gives the collective impulses of the nation such instruments of power and presents the imagination of individuals with such obvious symbols of its discrete collective identity that the national state is most able to make absolute claims for itself, to enforce those claims by power and to give them plausibility and credibility by the majesty and panoply of its apparatus. In the life of every political group, whether nation or empire, which articulates itself through the instrument of a state, obedience is prompted by the fear of power on the one hand and by reverence for majesty on the other. The temptation to idolatry is implicit in the state's majesty. Rationalists, with their simple ideas of government resting purely upon the consent of the governed, have never appreciated to what degree religious reverence for majesty is implicit in this consent. The political history of man begins with tribal polytheism, can be traced through the religious pretensions of empires with their inevitable concomitants of imperial religions and their priest-kings and god-kings, and ends with the immoderate and idolatrous claims of the modern fascist state. No politically crystallized social group has, therefore, ever existed without entertaining, or succumbing to, the temptation of making idolatrous claims for itself. Frequently the organs of this group pride, the state and the ruling oligarchy which bears the authority of the state, seek to detach themselves from the group pride of which their majesty is a symbol and to become independent sources of majesty. But this inversion is possible only because the original source of their majesty lies in something which transcends their individual power and prestige, namely the pride and greatness of the group itself.

Sinful pride and idolatrous pretension are thus an inevitable concomitant of the cohesion of large political groups. This is why it is impossible to regard the lower morality of groups, in comparison with individuals, as the consequence of the inertia of "nature" against the higher demands of individual reason. It is true of course that the group possesses only an inchoate "mind" and that its organs of self-transcendence and self-criticism are very unstable and ephemeral compared to its organs of will. A shifting and unstable "prophetic minority" is the instrument of this self-transcendence, while the state is the organ of the group's will. For this reason the immorality of nations is frequently regarded as in effect their unmorality, as the consequence of their existence in the realm of "nature" rather than the realm of reason. "I treat government not as a conscious contrivance," wrote Professor Seeley in a sentiment which expresses the conviction of many modern political scientists, "but as an half-instinctive product of the effort of human beings to ward off from themselves certain evils to which they are exposed."[3]

Such an interpretation has a measure of validity but it certainly does not do justice to the "spiritual" character of national pride, nor to the contribution which individuals, with all their rational and spiritual faculties, make to pride of groups and the self-deification of nations. The most conducive proof that the egotism of nations is a characteristic of the spiritual life, and not merely an expression of the natural impulse of survival, is the fact that its most typical expressions are the lust-for-power, pride (comprising considerations of prestige and "honour"), contempt toward the other (the reverse side of pride and its necessary concomitant in a world in which self-esteem is constantly challenged by the achievements of others); hypocrisy (the inevitable pretension of conforming to a higher norm than self-interest); and finally the claim of moral autonomy by which the self-deification of the social group is made explicit by its presentation of itself as the source and end of existence.

It cannot be denied that the instinct of survival is involved in all these spiritual manifestations of egotism; but that is equally true of individual life. We have previously noted that the fear of death is a basic motive of all human pretensions. Every human self-assertion, whether individual or collective, is therefore involved in the inconsistency of claiming, on the one hand, that it is justified by the primary right of survival and, on the other hand, that it is the bearer of interests and values larger than its own and that these more inclusive values are the justification of its conflict with competing social wills. No modern nation can ever quite make up its mind whether to insist that its struggle is a fight for survival or a selfless effort to maintain transcendent and universal values. In the World War both claims were constantly made; and it is significant that even modern Germany, though it has constructed a primitive tribal religion which makes the power and pride of the nation a self-justifying end, nevertheless feels constrained to pretend that its expected victory in Europe is desired as a triumph of a high type of (Aryan) culture over an allegedly inferior and decadent form of (Jewish or liberal) culture. The nation claims (or the claim is made for it) that it is the instrument of a value more universal than its contingent self, because, like the individual, the determinateness of its life is too obvious to be denied, at least by modern man. But the claim that it is itself the final and ultimate value, the cause which gives human existence meaning, is one which no individual can plausibly make for himself. It is plausible, though hardly credible, only because the social unit, particularly the nation, to which the individual belongs, transcends the individual life to such a degree in power, majesty, and pseudo-immortality that the claim of unconditioned value can be made for it with a degree of plausibility.

The significance of this claim is that through it human pride and self-assertion reach their ultimate form and seek to break all bounds of finiteness. The nation pretends to be God. A certain ambiguity which envelops this claim has already been noted. It is on the one hand a demand of a collective will and mind upon the individual. The social group asks for the individual's unconditioned loyalty, asserting that its necessities are the ultimate law of the individual's existence. But on the other hand it is a pretension which the individual makes for himself, not as an individual but as a member of his group. Collective egotism does indeed offer the individual an opportunity to lose himself in a larger whole; but it also offers him possibilities of self-aggrandizement beside which mere individual pretensions are implausible and incredible. Individuals "join to set up a god whom each then severally and tacitly identifies with himself, to swell the chorus of praise which each then severally and tacitly arrogates to himself."[4] It may be that such group pride represents a particular temptation to individuals who suffer from specific forms of the sense of inferiority. The relation of modern fascist nationalism to the insecurity and sense of inferiority of the lower middle classes is therefore significant. But it hardly can be denied that extravagant forms of modern nationalism only accentuate a general character of group life and collective egotism; and that specific forms of inferiority feeling for which this pride compensates only accentuate the general sense of inferiority from which all men suffer. Collective pride is thus man's last, and in some respects most pathetic, effort to deny the determinate and contingent character of his existence. The very essence of human sin is in it. It can hardly be surprising that this form of human sin is also most fruitful of human guilt, that is of objective social and historical evil. In its whole range from pride of family to pride of nation, collective egotism and group pride are a more pregnant source of injustice and conflict than purely individual pride.

The pride of nations is, of course, not wholly spurious. Their claim to embody values which transcend their mere existence has foundations in fact. It is the very character of human life, whether individual or collective, that it incarnates values which transcend its immediate interests. A particular nation or group of nations may actually be the bearers of a "democratic civilization" or of a communist one. Men are not animals and never fight merely for existence, because they do not have a mere animal existence. Their physical life is always the base for a superstructure of values which transcends physical life.

The pride of nations consists in the tendency to make unconditioned claims for their conditioned values. The unconditioned character of these claims has two aspects. The nation claims a more absolute devotion to values which transcend its life than the facts warrant; and it regards the values to which it is loyal as more absolute than they really are. Nations, may fight for "liberty" and "democracy" but they do not do so until their vital interests are imperiled. They may refuse to fight and claim that their refusal is prompted by their desire to "preserve civilization." Neutral nations are not less sinful than belligerent ones in their effort to hide their partial interests behind their devotion to "civilization." Furthermore the civilization to which they claim loyalty does not deserve such absolute devotion as the nation asks for it. . . .

The pride of nations and the arrogance of self-deification of collective man are the more extravagant for being expressed in and against a Christian culture in which it must consciously negate and defy the highest insights of the faith which formed the culture of the western world.

The most daemonic form of nationalism today is expressed against rather than in a Christian culture. The German Nazis were quite right in regarding the Christian faith as incompatible with their boundless national egoism. While Christianity may itself be made the tool of nationalism, the Christian faith, if it retains any vitality, is bound to mediate some word of divine judgment upon the nation, which the Nazis find intolerable. No nation is free of the sin of pride, just as no individual is free of it. Nevertheless it is important to recognize that there are "Christian" nations, who prove themselves so because they are still receptive to prophetic words of judgment spoken against the nation. It may be that only a prophetic minority feels this judgment keenly. But there is a genuine difference between nations which do not officially destroy the religious-prophetic judgment against the nation and those which do. While all modern nations, and indeed all nations of history, have been involved in the sin of pride, one must realize, in this as in other estimates of human sinfulness, that it is just as important to recognize differences in the degree of pride and self-will expressed by men and nations, as it is to know that all men and nations are sinful in the sight of God. Here, as in individual life, the final sin is the unwillingness to hear the word of judgment spoken against our sin. By that criterion, the modern fascist nations have achieved a daemonic form of national self-assertion which is more dangerous even than that of the ancient religious empires because it is expressed within and against the insights of a Christian culture.[5]

CHRISTIANITY AND POWER POLITICS: WHY THE CHRISTIAN CHURCH IS NOT PACIFIST

The pacifists do not know human nature well enough to be concerned about the contradictions between the law of love and the sin of man, until sin has conceived and brought forth death. They do not see that sin introduces an element of conflict into the world and that even the most loving relations are not free of it. They are, consequently, unable to appreciate the complexity of the problem of justice. They merely assert that if only men loved one another, all the complex, and sometimes horrible, realities of the political order could be dispensed with. They do not see that their "if" begs the most basic problem of human history. It is because men are sinners that justice can be achieved only by a certain degree of coercion on the one hand, and by resistance to coercion and tyranny on the other hand. The political life of man must constantly steer between the Scylla of anarchy and the Charybdis of tyranny.

Human egotism makes large-scale co-operation upon a purely voluntary basis impossible. Governments must coerce. Yet there is an element of evil in this coercion. It is always in danger of serving the purposes of the coercing power rather than the general weal. We cannot fully trust the motives of any ruling class or power. That is why it is important to maintain democratic checks upon the centers of power. It may also be necessary to resist a ruling class, nation or race, if it violates the standards of relative justice which have been set up for it. Such resistance means war. It need not mean overt conflict or violence. But if those who resist tyranny publish their scruples against violence too publicly the tyrannical power need only threaten the use of violence against non-violent pressure to persuade the resisters to quiescence. (The relation of pacifism to the abortive effort to apply non-violent sanctions against Italy in the Ethiopian dispute is instructive at this point.) ...

The gospel is something more than the law of love. The gospel deals with the fact that men violate the law of love. The gospel presents Christ as the pledge and revelation of God's mercy which finds man in his rebellion and overcomes his sin.

The question is whether the grace of Christ is primarily a power of righteousness which so heals the sinful heart that henceforth it is able to fulfil the law of love; or whether it is primarily the assurance of divine mercy for a persistent sinfulness which man never overcomes completely. When St. Paul declared: "I am crucified with Christ; nevertheless I live, yet it is no more I that live but Christ that dwelleth in me," did he mean that the new life in Christ was not his own by reason of the fact that grace, rather than his own power, enabled him to live on the new level of righteousness? Or did he mean that the new life was his only in intention and by reason of God's willingness to accept intention for achievement? Was the emphasis upon sanctification or justification?

This is the issue upon which the Protestant Reformation separated itself from classical Catholicism, believing that Thomistic interpretations of grace lent themselves to new forms of self-righteousness in place of the Judaistic-legalistic self-righteousness which St. Paul condemned. If one studies the whole thought of St. Paul, one is almost forced to the conclusion that he was not himself quite certain whether the peace which he had found in Christ was a moral peace, the peace of having become what man truly is; or whether it was primarily a religious peace, the peace of being "completely known and all forgiven," of being accepted by God despite the continued sinfulness of the heart. Perhaps St. Paul could not be quite sure about where the emphasis was to be placed, for the simple reason that no one can be quite certain about the character of this ultimate peace. There must be, and there is, moral content in it, a fact which Reformation theology tends to deny and which Catholic and sectarian theology emphasizes. But there is never such perfect moral content in it that any man could find perfect peace through his moral achievements, not even the achievements which he attributes to grace rather than the power of his own will. This is the truth which the Reformation emphasized and which modern Protestant Christianity has almost completely forgotten.

We are, therefore, living in a state of sorry moral and religious confusion. In the very moment of world history in which every contemporary historical event justifies the Reformation emphasis upon the persistence of sin on every level of moral achievement, we not only identify Protestant faith with a moralistic sentimentality which neglects and obscures truths in the Christian gospel (which it was the mission of the Reformation to rescue from obscurity), but we even neglect those reservations and qualifications upon the theory of sanctification upon which classical Catholicism wisely insisted.

We have, in other words, reinterpreted the Christian gospel in terms of the Renaissance faith in man. Modern pacifism is merely a final fruit of this Renaissance spirit, which has pervaded the whole of modern Protestantism. We have interpreted world history as a gradual ascent to the Kingdom of God which waits for final triumph only upon the willingness of Christians to "take Christ seriously." There is nothing in Christ's own teachings, except dubious interpretations of the parable of the leaven and the mustard seed, to justify this interpretation of world history. In the whole of the New Testament, Gospels and Epistles alike, there is only one interpretation of world history. That pictures history as moving toward a climax in which both Christ and anti-Christ are revealed.

The New Testament does not, in other words, envisage a simple triumph of good over evil in history. It sees human history involved in the contradictions of sin to the end. That is why it sees no simple resolution of the problem of history. It believes that the Kingdom of God will finally resolve the contradictions of history; but for it the Kingdom of God is no simple historical possibility. The grace of God for man and the Kingdom of God for history are both divine realities and not human possibilities.

The Christian faith believes that the Atonement reveals God's mercy as an ultimate resource by which God alone overcomes the judgment which sin deserves. If this final truth of the Christian religion has no meaning to modern men, including modern Christians, that is because even the tragic character of contemporary history has not yet persuaded them to take the fact of human sinfulness seriously.

The contradiction between the law of love and the sinfulness of man raises not only the ultimate religious problem how men are to have peace if they do not overcome the contradiction, and how history will culminate if the contradiction remains on every level of historic achievement; it also raises the immediate problem how men are to achieve a tolerable harmony of life with life, if human pride and selfishness prevent the realization of the law of love.

The pacifists are quite right in one emphasis. They are right in asserting that love is really the law of life. It is not some ultimate possibility which has nothing to do with human history. The freedom of man, his transcendence over the limitations of nature and over all historic and traditional social situations, makes any form of human community which falls short of the law of love less than the best. Only by a voluntary giving of life to life and a free interpenetration of personalities could man do justice both to the freedom of other personalities and the necessity of community between personalities. The law of love therefore remains a principle of criticism over all forms of community in which elements of coercion and conflict destroy the highest type of fellowship.

To look at human communities from the perspective of the Kingdom of God is to know that there is a sinful element in all the expedients which the political order uses to establish justice. That is why even the seemingly most stable justice degenerates periodically into either tyranny or anarchy. But it must also be recognized that it is not possible to eliminate the sinful element in the political expedients. They are, in the words of St. Augustine, both the consequence of, and the remedy for, sin. If they are the remedy for sin, the ideal of love is not merely a principle of indiscriminate criticism upon all approximations of justice. It is also a principle of discriminate criticism between forms of justice.

As a principle of indiscriminate criticism upon all forms of justice, the law of love reminds us that the injustice and tyranny against which we contend in the foe is partially the consequence of our own injustice, that the pathology of modern Germans is partially a consequence of the vindictiveness of the peace of Versailles, and that the ambition of a tyrannical imperialism is different only in degree and not in kind from the imperial impulse which characterizes all of human life.

The Christian faith ought to persuade us that political controversies are always conflicts between sinners and not between righteous men and sinners. It ought to mitigate the self-righteousness which is an inevitable concomitant of all human conflict. The spirit of contrition is an important ingredient in the sense of justice. If it is powerful enough it may be able to restrain the impulse of vengeance sufficiently to allow a decent justice to emerge. This is an important issue facing Europe in anticipation of the conclusion of the present war. It cannot be denied that the Christian conscience failed terribly in restraining vengeance after the last war. It is also quite obvious that the natural inclination to self-righteousness was the primary force of this vengeance (expressed particularly in the war guilt clause of the peace treaty). The pacifists draw the conclusion from the fact that justice is never free from vindictiveness, that we ought not for this reason ever to contend against a foe. This argument leaves out of account that capitulation to the foe might well subject us to a worse vindictiveness. It is as foolish to imagine that the foe is free of the sin which we deplore in ourselves as it is to regard ourselves as free of the sin which we deplore in the foe.

The fact that our own sin is always partly the cause of the sins against which we must contend is regarded by simple moral purists as proof that we have no right to contend against the foe. They regard the injunction "Let him who is without sin cast the first stone" as a simple alternative to the schemes of justice which society has devised and whereby it prevents the worst forms of anti-social conduct. This injunction of Christ ought to remind every judge and every juridical tribunal that the crime of the criminal is partly the consequence of the sins of society. But if pacifists are to be consistent they ought to advocate the abolition of the whole judicial process in society. It is perfectly true that national societies have more impartial instruments of justice than international society possesses to date. Nevertheless, no impartial court is as impartial as it pretends to be, and there is no judicial process which is completely free of vindictiveness. Yet we cannot dispense with it; and we will have to continue to put criminals into jail. There is a point where the final cause of the criminal's anti-social conduct becomes a fairly irrelevant issue in comparison with the task of preventing his conduct from injuring innocent fellows.

The ultimate principles of the Kingdom of God are never irrelevant to any problem of justice, and they hover over every social situation as an ideal possibility; but that does not mean that they can be made into simple alternatives for the present schemes of relative justice. The thesis that the so-called democratic nations have no right to resist overt forms of tyranny, because their own history betrays imperialistic motives, would have meaning only if it were possible to achieve a perfect form of justice in any nation and to free national life completely of the imperialistic motive. This is impossible; for imperialism is the collective expression of the sinful will-to power which characterizes all human existence. The pacifist argument on this issue betrays how completely pacifism gives itself to illusions about the stuff with which it is dealing in human nature. These illusions deserve particular censure, because no one who knows his own heart very well ought to be given to such illusions.

The recognition of the law of love as an indiscriminate principle of criticism over all attempts at social and international justice is actually a resource of justice, for it prevents the pride, self-righteousness and vindictiveness of men from corrupting their efforts at justice. But it must be recognized that love is also a principle of discriminate criticism between various forms of community and various attempts at justice. The closest approximation to a love in which life supports life in voluntary community is a justice in which life is prevented from destroying life and the interests of the one are guarded against unjust claims by the other. Such justice is achieved when impartial tribunals of society prevent men "from being judges in their own cases," in the words of John Locke. But the tribunals of justice merely codify certain equilibria of power. Justice is basically dependent upon a balance of power. Whenever an individual or a group or a nation possesses undue power, and whenever this power is not checked by the possibility of criticizing and resisting it, it grows inordinate. The equilibrium of power upon which every structure of justice rests would degenerate into anarchy but for the organizing center which controls it. One reason why the balances of power, which prevent injustice in international relations, periodically degenerate into overt anarchy is because no way has yet been found to establish an adequate organizing center, a stable international judicatory, for this balance of power.[6]

THE CHILDREN OF LIGHT AND THE CHILDREN OF DARKNESS: A VINDICATION OF DEMOCRACY AND A CRITIQUE OF ITS TRADITIONAL DEFENCE

Democracy has a more compelling justification and requires a more realistic vindication than is given it by the liberal culture with which it has been associated in modern history. The excessively optimistic estimates of human nature and of human history with which the democratic credo has been historically associated are a source of peril to democratic society;

for contemporary experience is refuting this optimism and there is danger that it will seem to refute the democratic ideal as well.

A free society requires some confidence in the ability of men to reach tentative and tolerable adjustments between their competing interests and to arrive at some common notions of justice which transcend all partial interests. A consistent pessimism in regard to man's rational capacity for justice invariably leads to absolutistic political theories; for they prompt the conviction that only preponderant power can coerce the various vitalities of a community into a working harmony. But a too consistent optimism in regard to man's ability and inclination to grant justice to his fellows obscures the perils of chaos which perennially confront every society, including a free society. In one sense a democratic society is particularly exposed to the dangers of confusion. If these perils are not appreciated they may overtake a free society and invite the alternative evil of tyranny.

But modern democracy requires a more realistic philosophical and religious basis, not only in order to anticipate and understand the perils to which it is exposed; but also to give it a more persuasive justification. Man's capacity for justice makes democracy possible; but man's inclination to injustice makes democracy necessary. In all nondemocratic political theories the state or the ruler is invested with uncontrolled power for the sake of achieving order and unity in the community. But the pessimism which prompts and justifies this policy is not consistent; for it is not applied, as it should be, to the ruler. If men are inclined to deal unjustly with their fellows, the possession of power aggravates this inclination. That is why irresponsible and uncontrolled power is the greatest source of injustice.

The democratic techniques of a free society place checks upon the power of the ruler and administrator and thus prevent it from becoming vexatious. The perils of uncontrolled power are perennial reminders of the virtues of a democratic society; particularly if a society should become inclined to impatience with the dangers of freedom and should be tempted to choose the advantages of coerced unity at the price of freedom.

The consistent optimism of our liberal culture has prevented modern democratic societies both from gauging the perils of freedom accurately and from appreciating democracy fully as the only alternative to injustice and oppression. When this optimism is not qualified to accord with the real and complex facts of human nature and history, there is always a danger that sentimentality will give way to despair and that a too consistent optimism will alternate with a too consistent pessimism.

I have not sought to elaborate the religious and theological convictions upon which the political philosophy of the following pages rests. It will be apparent, however, that they are informed by the belief that a Christian view of human nature is more adequate for the development of a democratic society than either the optimism with which democracy has become historically associated or the moral cynicism which inclines human communities to tyrannical political strategies. . . .

In illumining this important distinction more fully, we may well designate the moral cynics, who know no law beyond their will and interest, with a scriptural designation of "children of this world" or "children of darkness." Those who believe that self-interest should be brought under the discipline of a higher law could then be termed "the children of light." This is no mere arbitrary device; for evil is always the assertion of some self-interest without regard to the whole, whether the whole be conceived as the immediate community, or the total community of mankind, or the total order of the world. The good is, on the other hand, always the harmony of the whole on various levels. Devotion to a subordinate and premature "whole" such as the nation, may of course become evil, viewed from the perspective of a larger whole, such as the community of mankind. The "children of light" may thus be defined as those who seek to bring self-interest under the discipline of a more universal law and in harmony with a more universal good.

According to the scripture "the children of this world are in their generation wiser than the children of light." This observation fits the modern situation. Our democratic civilization has been built, not by children of darkness but by foolish children of light. It has been under attack by the children of darkness, by the moral cynics, who declare that a strong nation need acknowledge no law beyond its strength. It has come close to complete disaster under this attack, not because it accepted the same creed as the cynics; but because it underestimated the power of self-interest, both individual and collective, in modern society. The children of light have not been as wise as the children of darkness.

The children of darkness are evil because they know no law beyond the self. They are wise, though evil, because they understand the power of self-interest. The children of light are virtuous because they have some conception of a higher law than their own will. They are usually foolish because they do not know the power of self-will. They underestimate the peril of anarchy in both the national and the international community. Modern democratic civilization is, in short, sentimental rather than cynical. It has an easy solution for the problem of anarchy and chaos on both the national and international level of community, because of its fatuous and superficial view of man. It does not know that the same man who is ostensibly devoted to the "common good" may have desires and ambitions, hopes and fears, which set him at variance with his neighbor.

It must be understood that the children of light are foolish not merely because they underestimate the power of self-interest among the children of darkness. They underestimate this power among themselves. The democratic world came so close to disaster not merely because it never believed that Nazism possessed the demonic fury which it avowed. Civilization refused to recognize the power of class interest in its own communities. It also spoke glibly of an international conscience; but the children of darkness meanwhile skilfully set nation against nation. They were thereby enabled to despoil one nation after another, without every civilized nation coming to the defence of each. Moral cynicism had a provisional advantage over moral sentimentality. Its advantage lay not merely in its own lack of moral scruple but also in its shrewd assessment of the power of self-interest, individual and national, among the children of light, despite their moral protestations. . . .

The confidence of modern secular idealism in the possibility of an easy resolution of the tension between individual and community, or between classes, races and nations is derived from a too optimistic view of human nature. This too generous estimate of human virtue is intimately related to an erroneous estimate of the dimensions of the human stature. The conception of human nature which underlies the social and political attitudes of a liberal democratic culture is that of an essentially harmless individual. The survival impulse, which man shares with the animals, is regarded as the normative form of his egoistic drive. If this were a true picture of the human situation man might be, or might become, as harmless as seventeenth- and eighteenth-century thought assumed. Unfortunately for the validity of this picture of man, the most significant distinction between the human and the animal world is that the impulses of the former are "spiritualized" in the human world. Human capacities for evil as well as for good are derived from this spiritualization. There is of course always a natural survival impulse at the core of all human ambition. But this survival impulse cannot be neatly disentangled from two forms of its spiritualization. The one form is the desire to fulfill the potentialities of life and not merely to maintain its existence. Man is the kind of animal who cannot merely live. If he lives at all he is bound to seek the realization of his true nature; and to his true nature belongs his fulfillment in the lives of others. The will to live is thus transmuted into the will to self-realization; and self-realization involves self-giving in relations to others. When this desire for self-realization is fully explored it becomes apparent that it is subject to the paradox that the highest form of self-realization is the consequence of self-giving, but that it cannot be the intended consequence without being prematurely limited. Thus the will to live is finally transmuted into its opposite in the sense that only in self-giving can the self be fulfilled, for: "He that findeth his life shall lose it: and he that loseth his life for my sake shall find it" (Matthew 10:39).

On the other hand the will-to-live is also spiritually transmuted into the will-to-power or into the desire for "power and glory." Man, being more than a natural creature, is not interested merely in physical survival but in prestige and social approval. Having the intelligence to anticipate the perils in which he stands in nature and history, he invariably seeks to gain security against these perils by enhancing his power, individually and collectively. Possessing a darkly unconscious sense of his insignificance in the total scheme of things, he seeks to compensate for his insignificance by pretensions of pride. The conflicts between men are thus never simple conflicts between competing survival impulses. They are conflicts in which each man or group seeks to guard its power and prestige against the peril of competing expressions of power and pride. Since the very possession of power and prestige always involves some encroachment upon the prestige and power of others, this conflict is by its very nature a more stubborn and difficult one than the mere competition between various survival impulses in nature. It remains to be added that this conflict expresses itself even more cruelly in collective than in individual terms. Human behaviour being less individualistic than secular liberalism assumed, the struggle between classes, races and other groups in human society is not as easily resolved by the expedient of dissolving the groups as liberal democratic idealists assumed.

Since the survival impulse in nature is transmuted into two different and contradictory spiritualized forms, which we may briefly designate as the will-to-live-truly and the will-to-power, man is at variance with himself. The power of the second impulse places him more fundamentally in conflict with his fellowman than democratic liberalism realizes. The fact he cannot realize himself, except in organic relation with his fellows, makes the community more important than bourgeois individualism understands. The fact that the two impulses, though standing in contradiction to each other, are also mixed and compounded with each other on every level of human life, makes the simple distinctions between good and evil, between selfishness and altruism, with which liberal idealism has tried to estimate moral and political facts, invalid. The fact that the will-to-power inevitably justifies itself in terms of the morally more acceptable will to realize man's true nature means that the egoistic corruption of universal ideals is a much more persistent fact in human conduct than any moralistic creed is inclined to admit. . . .

But the question arises, how the strategies of coercion of the community are judged and prevented from becoming inordinate. If it is granted that both the rulers and the community as such are also centers of vitality and expansive impulse, would not their use of restrictive power be purely arbitrary if it were not informed by some general principles of justice, which define the right order of life in a community? The fact is that there are no living communities which do not have some notions of justice, beyond their historic laws, by which they seek to gauge the justice of their legislative enactments. Such general principles are known as natural law in both Catholic and earlier liberal thought. Even when, as in the present stage of liberal democratic thought, moral theory has become too relativistic to make appeal to natural law as plausible as in other centuries, every human society does have something like a natural-law concept; for it assumes that there are more immutable and purer principles of justice than those actually embodied in its obviously relative laws.

The final question to confront the proponent of a democratic and free society is whether the freedom of a society should extend to the point of allowing these principles to be called into question. Should they not stand above criticism or amendment? If they are themselves subjected to the democratic process and if they are made dependent upon the moods and vagaries of various communities and epochs, have we not sacrificed the final criterion of justice and order, by which we might set bounds to what is inordinate in both individual and collective impulses?

It is on this question that Catholic Christianity has its final difficulties with the presuppositions of a democratic society in the modern, liberal sense, fearing, in the words of a recent pronouncement of the American bishops, that questions of "right and wrong" may be subjected to the caprice of majority decisions. For Catholicism believes that the principles of natural law are fixed and immutable, a faith which the secular physiocrats of the eighteenth century shared.[7] It believes that the freedom of a democratic society must stop short of calling these principles of natural law into question.

The liberal democratic tradition of our era gave a different answer to this question. It did not have very plausible reasons for its answer; but history has provided better ones. The truth is that the bourgeois democratic theory held to the idea of absolute and unrestricted liberty, partly because it assumed the unlimited right of private judgment to be one of the "inalienable" rights which were guaranteed by the liberal version of the natural law.[8] Its adherence to the principle of complete liberty of private judgment was also partly derived from its simple confidence in human reason. It was certain that reason would, when properly enlightened, affirm the "self-evident" truths of the natural law. Both the Catholic and the liberal confidence in the dictates of the natural law, thus rest upon a "non-existential" description of human reason. Both fail to appreciate the perennial corruptions of interest and passion which are introduced into any historical definition of even the most ideal and abstract moral principles. The Catholic confidence in the reason of common men was rightly less complete than that of the Enlightenment. Yet it wrongly sought to preserve some realm of institutional religious authority which would protect the uncorrupted truths of the natural law. The Enlightenment erroneously hoped for a general diffusion of intelligence which would make the truths of the natural law universally acceptable. Yet it rightly refused to reserve any area of authority which would not be subject to democratic criticism.

The reason this final democratic freedom is right, though the reasons given for it in the modern period are wrong, is that there is no historical reality, whether it be church or government, whether it be the reason of wise men or specialists, which is not involved in the flux and relativity of human existence; which is not subject to error and sin, and which is not tempted to exaggerate its errors and sins when they are made immune to criticism.

Every society needs working principles of justice, as criteria for its positive law and system of restraints. The profoundest of these actually transcend reason and lie rooted in religious conceptions of the meaning of existence. But every historical statement of them is subject to amendment. If it becomes fixed it will destroy some of the potentialities of a higher justice, which the mind of one generation is unable to anticipate in the life of subsequent eras.

Alfred Whitehead has distinguished between the "speculative" reason which "Plato shared with God" and the "pragmatic" reason which "Ulysses shared with the foxes."[9] The distinction is valid, provided it is understood that no sharp line can be drawn between the two. For man's spirit is a unity; and the most perfect vantage point of impartiality and disinterestedness in human reason remains in organic relation to a particular center of life, individual or collective, seeking to maintain its precarious existence against competing forms of life and vitality. Even if a particular age should arrive at a "disinterested" vision of justice, in which individual interests and passions were completely transcended, it could not achieve a height of disinterestedness from which it could judge new emergents in history. It would use its apparatus of "self-evident truths" and "inalienable rights" as instruments of self-defence against the threat of the new vitality.

Because reason is something more than a weapon of self-interest it can be an instrument of justice; but since reason is never dissociated from the vitalities of life, individual and collective, it cannot be a pure instrument of the justice. Natural-law theories which derive absolutely valid principles of morals and politics from reason, invariably introduce contingent practical applications into the definition of the principle.[10]

LOVE AND LAW IN PROTESTANTISM AND CATHOLICISM

The whole question about the relation of love to law in Christian thought is really contained in the question how love is the fulfillment of the law. The analysis of this issue may well begin with a definition of the nature of law. Subjectively considered, law is distinguished by some form of restraint or coercion, or, as Aquinas puts it, it is the direction to "perform virtuous acts by reason of some outward cause." The compulsion may be the force and prestige of the mores and customs of a community, persuading or compelling an individual to act contrary to his inclinations. But there is also an inner compulsion of law. It is the compulsion of conscience, the force of the sense of obligation, operating against other impulses in the personality. If there is no friction or tension between duty and inclination law is, at least in one sense, dissolved into love.

Materially, law usually represents detailed prescriptions of duties and obligations which the self owes to itself, to God, and to its neighbors. There may of course be general principles of law which gather together the logic of detailed prescriptions, as for instance the proposition, defined in Catholic thought as the "preamble" of the natural law, "that we ought to do good and avoid evil"; or Jesus' own summary of the law and the prophets. But that summary is, significantly, the "law of love" and therefore no longer purely law, but a law transcending law. Some degree of detail is characteristic of pure law. The "positive law" of historic communities gains its force primarily from its specificity. Many a law has been annulled by our Supreme Court on the ground that "vagueness" invalidated it. Even if we do not accept the Catholic theory of a highly specific "natural law" we all do accept principles of justice which transcend the positive enactments of historic states and which are less specific and not so sharply defined as positive law, and yet more specific than the law of love. These are generated in the customs and mores of communities; and they may rise to universal norms which seem to have their source not in particular communities but in the common experience of mankind.

The question of how love is related to law must be considered in terms of both the subjective and the material dimensions of both love and law. Subjectively, the question is how the experience of love, in which the "ought" is transcended, nevertheless contains a "thou shalt." Materially, the question is how the indeterminate possibilities of love are related to the determinate and specified obligations defined by law. The dialectical relation of love to law as both its fulfillment and its end (*pleroma* and *telos*), as fulfilling all possibilities of law and yet as standing in contradiction to it ("The law was given by Moses, but grace and truth came by Jesus Christ," John 1:17), is the basis and the problem of all Catholic and Protestant speculations on the relation of love to law.

In this debate Catholic thought, both in its classical version and in such a modem treatise as D'Arcy's *Mind and Heart of Love*, is more inclined than the Reformation to interpret love as *pleroma* of everything intended in nature and in law. But it is also inclined to interpret love as yet a more rigorous law, thus obscuring the elements of ecstasy and spontaneity, which are the marks of "grace." Reformation thought (or at least Lutheran thought, for Calvin does not deviate essentially from the Catholic version), on the other hand, is much nearer in its apprehension of a dimension of love which transcends law and even contradicts it; but it usually fails to do justice to love as the fulfillment of law and therefore tends to obscure the intimate relation between love and justice. Modern liberal Protestantism is inclined to equate law and love by its effort to comprehend all law within the love commandment. It does not deny the higher dimensions of love which express themselves in sacrifice, forgiveness, individual sympathy, and universal love, but it regards them as simple possibilities and thereby obscures the tensions between love and law, both on the subjective and the objective side. . . .

In terms of the subjective dimension of the problem of love and law is the problem of the "push" of duty and the "pull" of grace. If the law of love comes to us as a "thou shalt" it is obviously a law. We can have a sense of obligation toward the interests of others without a definition of specific obligations. In this case love is simply the summary of all our obligations. This is why Thomas Aquinas includes love in the "old law" though this inclusion is inconsistent with his definition of the "old law" as the "law of fear" and his confining it to the restraint of actions rather than attitudes, to "restraining the hand rather than the will." On the other hand, love means a perfect accord between duty and inclination in such a way that duty is not felt as duty and "we love the things that thou commandest." This second aspect of love is disregarded in Kant's interpretation of love, for instance. For him the sense of obligation in its most universal and least specific form is identical with the law of love.

In Luther's exposition of the life of grace, "law" and "conscience" are left behind with sin and self. This freedom from the sense of "ought" is described by him as an ecstatic experience in which the self calculates no advantages, rises above every form of prudence, and feels itself at one with Christ, being motivated purely by a sense of gratitude for the divine forgiveness. Brunner stands in the Lutheran tradition when he also emphasizes this transcendence over the "ought" and declares that "if we feel we ought it is a proof that we cannot." It is a question whether this point of "grace" is understood by Calvin at all. For his ethic is one of obedience to the divine law. Love is a summary of this law, but he is also careful to spell it out in specific detail. The detail is as specific as Catholic "natural law" except that he draws the details not from the intuitions of reason but from "various portions of Scripture." He is convinced that we need this law in specific form to guide our conscience, corrupted by sin; and there is no suggestion that law and conscience do not operate in the state of grace.

This contrast between the conception of an identity of love and the sense of obligation, on the one hand, and a contradiction between them, on the other, is the proof of a complicated relationship between love and law in both the subjective and the objective sphere. What is described by Luther as freedom from law may well conform to momentary heights of spiritual experience in which there is such a "pull" of grace (which may include everything from ecstatic religious experience to the "common grace" of family love) that we are not conscious of any "ought" or any sense of obligation. But it may be questioned whether it can describe anything more than such moments. It certainly does not describe the ongoing experience of even the most consecrated Christian, particularly not if it is true about him, as Luther asserts, that he is *"justus et peccator simul."* For if he remains a sinner it must be true of him that he feels the tension between his self-interest, his anxieties and insecurities and the obligation to forget himself for the sake of his concern for others. It may well be that everything defined as the "sense of justice" is an expression of the law of love within the limits of law. There are some aspects of the law of love, objectively considered, which are more clearly in the realm of duty than in the realm of grace. The injunction "If ye love them that love you what thanks have ye?" for instance, points to the universalistic tendencies in the law of love. It expresses our obligations beyond the boundaries of the natural communities of family, tribe, and nation. But paradoxically the love within the family may be by "grace" rather than law, while the love of "mankind" must be by law. That is, there may be such conjugal or paternal or filial affection as disposes us to seek the good of wife, husband, or child without any sense of duty, "common grace" or "habitual grace" having drawn the self beyond itself and out of itself into the lives of others. But our concern for those beyond our circle, our obligation to the peoples of the world and the community of mankind, comes to us very much with the push of the "ought" against the force of our more parochial habits of grace.

Yet on the other hand, pure obligation, while not so impotent as Brunner suggests, is more impotent than generally recognized, which is why purely moralistic sermons, which always tell us what we ought to do, tend to be boring. The best modern psychiatry, when dealing with the problem of delinquency in children, significantly does not preach to them what they ought to do, not even that they "ought to accept themselves." It insists that they must be accepted, must find security in the love of others, out of which security they gain sufficient freedom from self to "let go" and love others. Common grace, in short, rather than law is offered as a cure for their ills. It might be added that a good deal of modern Christian teaching about Christian love may be by comparison very loveless. For the preacher chides his congregation endlessly for not meeting the most ultimate possibilities of the law of love, such as sacrifice, forgiveness, and uncalculated freedom from self, as if these were simple possibilities of the will. Thus the law of love becomes the occasion for loveless castigation because it is not recognized that, on the subjective side, love is a curious compound of willing through the strength of the sense of obligation and of willing not by the strength of our will but by the strength which enters the will through grace. This defect in the liberal Protestant attitude toward love is the subjective aspect of its lack of a doctrine of grace. The objective aspect, which must be considered subsequently, is revealed in its lack of distinction between love and justice. In both aspects the basis of the defect lies in the failure to appreciate the force of self-love in life. The consequence of this failure creates the belief that love is a law which can be easily fulfilled if only the preacher will establish its validity and present it persuasively. Grace, whether "common" or "saving," has meaning only when life is measured at the limits of human possibilities and it is recognized that there are things we ought to do which we cannot do merely by the strength of our willing but which may become possible because we are assisted by the help which others give us by their love, by the strength which accrues to our will in moments of crisis, and by the saving grace of the Spirit of God indwelling our spirit. . . .

This analysis of love as law and love as transcending law is incomplete without consideration of one further problem: the relation of love to law as such. Law as such is composed of norms of conduct prescribed by custom, legal enactment, scriptural injunction, or rational intuition, in which duties and obligations are prescribed without seeming reference to the ultimate spirit of law, namely, love. What is the standing of such law in a Christian scheme of ethics and how is love related to it? In Catholic thought this law is drawn from the intuitions or logical deductions of reason, so that even the Decalogue is regarded as normative by Aquinas only in so far as it corresponds to the natural law. In Reformation thought, systematically in Calvin and less systematically in Luther, this law is drawn from Scripture, either from explicit law, such as the Decalogue, or from moral admonitions in various portions of Scripture which are raised to the authority of explicit norms for the Christian life.

All such law will be found to have two characteristics: a) It states our obligations to our neighbor is minimal and usually in negative terms. "Thou shalt not kill." "Thou shalt not steal." b) It states our obligations to our neighbors in terms which presuppose the fact of sin and self-interest and the complexity of claims and counterclaims which are arbitrated by some "rule of reason" rather than by the ultimate scruples of the law of love.

Thus the law, however conceived, accepts and regulates self-interest and prohibits only the most excessive forms of it. It does not command that we love the neighbor but only that we do not take his life or property. It does not command that we seek our neighbor's good but that we respect his rights. Broadly speaking, the end of the law is justice. But we have already seen that justice is related to love. Thus there is a dialectical relation between love and law even as there is between love beyond law and love as law. It might be stated as follows: The law seeks for a tolerable harmony of life with life, sin presupposed. It is, therefore, an approximation of the law of love on the one hand and an instrument of love on the other hand. Consequently the distinction between law and love is less absolute and more dialectical than conceived in either Catholic or Reformation thought.

If this conclusion be correct, it follows that law, however conceived, whether drawn from Scripture (as in Reformation thought) or from rational intuitions (as in Catholicism) or from historical tradition, is less fixed and absolute than all these theories assume. The scriptural authority, below the level of love, is less valid in the realm of law than the Reformation assumes because there is always an element of historical contingency in the allegedly absolute norms of Scriptures which makes its authority questionable in a different historical context. (St. Paul's attitude toward women in the Church is a case in point.) The authority of rational "natural" law is less valid than Catholicism supposes. The whole concept of natural law rests upon a Stoic-Aristotelian rationalism which assumes fixed historical structures and norms which do not in fact exist. Furthermore, it assumes a human participation in a universal reason in which there is no ideological taint. The moral certainties of natural law in Catholic thought are all dubious. Sometimes they rest upon deductive reason. It is assumed that it is impossible to draw logical conclusions in the field of material ethics, from the formal ethical principle that good is to be done and evil avoided. But there is no guide in the formal principle of ethics about the norms of good and evil. Sometimes they rest upon the "intuitions" of reason. While there are some seemingly universal moral judgments such as the prohibition of murder, it must be noted that they are the most universal if they are the most minimal and most negative expressions of the law of love. The more specific they become the more they are suspect as "self-evident" propositions of the natural law.

Sometimes Catholic natural theory sinks to the level of eighteenth-century rationalism, which it ostensibly abhors. It regards the propositions of natural law as propositions of analytic reason. This reason analyzes the structures of nature, including human nature, and arrives at certain conclusions about what nature "intends," as, for instance, that nature intends procreation in sexual union. In this case it forgets that human nature is characterized not only by an indeterminate freedom but by an intimate and organic relation between the impulses of nature and human freedom which permits endless elaborations of human vital capacities for which it is not easy to find a simple descriptive norm.

In short, both Catholic and Reformation theory are too certain about the fixities of the norms of law. All law, whether historical, positive, scriptural, or rational, is more tentative and less independent in its authority than orthodox Christianity, whether Catholic or Protestant, supposes, even as it is more necessary than liberal Protestantism assumes. The final dyke against relativism is to be found, not in these alleged fixities, but in the law of love itself. This is the only final law, and every other law is an expression of the law of love in minimal or in proximate terms or in terms appropriate to given historical occasions.[11]

NOTES

1. Power, *A New Social Analysis*, p. 11.

2. Quoted by F. Meinecke, *Die Idee der Staatsraison*, p. 377.

3. *Political Science*, p. 129. . . .

4. Philip Leon, *The Ethics of Power*, p. 140.

5. [*Nature and Destiny of Man: A Christian Interpretation* (New York: Charles Scribner's Sons, 1941, 1943), 1:188–192, 208–213, 218–220. In 1939, Niebuhr delivered the prestigious Gifford Lectures at the University of Edinburgh. Niebuhr actually delivered two series of lectures in Edinburgh—one on human nature (published in 1941) and the second on human destiny (published in 1943). In his lectures on human nature, Niebuhr surveyed classical, biblical, and modern views on the issue. Niebuhr concluded that modern thinkers were too optimistic in their assessment of human nature, uncomfortable with Christian conceptions of human sinfulness. By contrast, Niebuhr articulated an Augustinian notion of human sin that manifests itself as pride. Niebuhr identified three types of pride that humans exhibit as a means of dealing with the anxieties and inse-

curities of life: pride of power, pride of knowledge, and pride of virtue. Expanding on certain ideas that he had first introduced in his 1932 book *Moral Man and Immoral Society*, Niebuhr argued that this tendency toward human pride is particularly nefarious when exhibited by social groups and nations. Niebuhr delivered the lectures against the backdrop of the rise of Nazism. As he notes in his preface to the two volumes, the "first of these lectures was given in April and May of 1939 when the clouds of war were already hovering ominously over Europe; dark forebodings had become a dreadful reality before the second series was given in October, 1939." As Niebuhr speaks of the perils of the "pride of nations," he clearly has Nazi Germany in mind. Ironically, during one of Niebuhr's lectures, his audience could literally hear the bombs of the German Luftwaffe exploding at a nearby naval base.]

6. ["Why the Christian Church Is Not Pacifist," in *Christianity and Power Politics* (Hamden, Conn.: Archon Books, 1940), 14–15, 18–26. During the 1920s and early 1930s, Niebuhr was a pacifist and served as national chair of the Fellowship of Reconciliation. In time, however, influenced in part by the expansionism of Nazi Germany, Niebuhr rejected pacifism, believing that in a sinful world, evil must be resisted. On the eve of America's entry into World War II, many Christian groups in the United States opposed American participation in the war. Niebuhr did not. He believed that America should enter the war to restrain the expansionism of Nazi Germany. Niebuhr resigned in 1940 from the editorial board of the *Christian Century*, to which he had contributed for many years, because of the journal's advocacy of a policy of American neutrality. Niebuhr founded another journal instead, *Christianity and Crisis*, which he used to articulate his "Christian realist" theology—a theology grounded in the reality of human sinfulness and the need to develop political and legal institutions to corral the manifestations of that sinfulness. Niebuhr's Christian realism also encompassed a rejection of pacifism.

In 1940, Niebuhr published an essay "Why the Christian Church is Not Pacifist" in his book *Christianity and Power Politics*. This essay was one of Niebuhr's clearest expressions of his Christian realist theology and its implications for public life.]

7. Catholic theory regards natural law as prescriptive and as derived from "right reason," whereas modern naturalism frequently defines it as merely descriptive, that is, as the law, which men may observe by analyzing the facts of nature. Jacques Maritain defines the natural law as "an order or a disposition which human reason can discover and according to which the human will must act in order to attune itself to the necessary ends of the human being." *The Rights of Man and Natural Law*, p. 61.

8. The fact that the content of the natural law as Catholicism conceives it differs so widely from the content of the natural law as the eighteenth century conceived it, though the contents of both are supposed to represent "self-evident" truths of reason, must make the critical student skeptical.

9. *The Function of Reason*, pp. 23–30.

10. [*The Children of Light and the Children of Darkness: A Vindication of Democracy and a Critique of its Traditional Defense* (New York: Charles Scribner's Sons, 1944), xii–xv, 9–12, 18–22, 67–72. During the early 1940s, Niebuhr continued to engage the question of the political and social implications of his view of human nature that he had articulated in earlier works such as *The Nature and Destiny of Man*. At the height of the struggle between western democracies and totalitarian states, Niebuhr reconsidered the traditional justifications for democracy. Niebuhr presented the results of his reflections in a series of lectures at Stanford University in 1944 that he subsequently published as a book, *The Children of Light and the Children of Darkness*, which provided an intellectual blueprint for the postwar Americans for Democratic Action, founded in 1947.

   In these lectures, Niebuhr argued that the "excessively optimistic estimates of human nature and of human history with which the democratic credo has been historically associated are a source of peril to democratic society" (xii) and sought to explain why. Niebuhr observed that some people, whom he labeled "children of light," do not understand the power of human self-interest while others, whom he labeled "children of darkness," understand all too well the power of self-interest and how both to pursue and to harness it for their own purposes. For Niebuhr, the children of light must come to appreciate the depths of human self-interest and then establish and retain political institutions designed to control this self-interest. In Niebuhr's view, the "democratic techniques of a free society place checks upon the power of the ruler and administrator and thus prevent it from becoming vexatious" (xiv).]

11. ["Love and Law in Protestantism and Catholicism," in *Christian Realism and Political Problems* (New York: Charles Scribner's Sons, 1953), 147–154, 170–173. Throughout his writings, Niebuhr addressed the relationship between the "law of love," which was Niebuhr's fundamental ethical principle, and ethical norms found in the natural law or the positive law of particular communities. In his 1952 essay, "Love and Law in Protestantism and Catholicism," Niebuhr revisited this question of the relationship between the law of love and natural law and positive law from the perspective of both the Catholic and Protestant traditions. For Niebuhr, all laws should be "an approximation of" or "an instrument of" the law of love. Every legal norm, whether derived from natural law, historical tradition, or even scripture, must ultimately be assessed against the law of love. Niebuhr concludes that "both Catholic and Reformation theory are too certain about the fixities of the norms of law" and have not sufficiently appreciated the preeminence of the law of love as the lodestone against which all law must be measured.]

[CHAPTER 13]

Martin Luther King Jr. (1929–1968)

SELECTED AND EDITED BY TIMOTHY P. JACKSON

Martin Luther King Jr. was born on January 15, 1929, into an upper-middle-class home on Auburn Avenue in Atlanta, Georgia. Martin Luther King Sr. was a Baptist preacher and active in the NAACP, while Mrs. King was a home-maker and church organist. Young Martin, called "M.L.," was shaped by three basic factors: his family's emphasis on spiritual and cultural values, such as biblical piety, secular education, and social service; his family's social and fi-nancial standing in a comparatively prosperous (though largely segregated) black neighborhood; and the racism of the South, including the Jim Crow laws that enforced white supremacy and racial separatism. Growing up on "Sweet Auburn," just a few hundred yards up the road from Ebenezer Baptist Church, where his father was pastor, allowed King to see three worlds at once: a vibrant black church, a thriving black community, and an unjust wider society. This vantage point clearly influenced how he would eventually understand justice, law, and human nature. He was given a moral education and sense of self that allowed him both to perceive social problems and to address them without de-spair, both to see the importance and power of human laws and to appreciate their limit and fallibility.

During King's time at Morehouse College, his worldview developed under the influence of his professors. Professor George D. Kelsey helped him to see that Daddy King's fundamentalism was not the only form of Christianity. By 1946 the once skeptical King felt called to the ministry, and in 1947 he was licensed to preach and became assistant to his father at Ebenezer Baptist Church. On February 25, 1948, King was ordained to the Baptist clergy. While still at Morehouse, he read Thoreau's "Civil Disobedience" and for the first time was exposed to the idea of nonviolent resistance. In June of 1948, King graduated from Morehouse College with a B.A. in sociology, and in September he entered Crozer Theological Seminary in Pennsylvania.

At Crozer, King became a disciple of Walter Rauschenbusch and the Christian activism of the Social Gospel Movement. King graduated in 1951 from Crozer with a bachelor of divinity degree; in June 1953 he married Coretta Scott in Marion, Alabama; and in June 1955, he received his doctorate in systematic theology from Boston University. Shortly after he embraced Mahatma Gandhi's teachings on nonviolence at Crozer, King had to come to grips with Reinhold Niebuhr and his critique of Protestant liberalism's optimism about human nature and tendency toward a vapid pacifism. This King did at Boston University. King concluded that, for all of Niebuhr's insight, he failed to appreciate the difference between nonresistance to evil and nonviolent resistance to evil, and he had not balanced his pessimism about human nature with an optimism about divine nature. Part of what contributed to King's own optimism was his study at Boston University of personalist philosophy with Edgar S. Brightman and L. Harold DeWolf. Personalism, the view that only personality is ultimately real, provided King a metaphysical foundation for his faith in a theistic God as well as for his affirmation of the dignity of all human persons.

In September 1954, King was appointed pastor at the Dexter Avenue Baptist Church in Montgomery, Alabama. In December 1955, he was unanimously elected president of the Montgomery Improvement Association (MIA), which was organizing the boycott of city buses in protest of segregation laws. At biweekly meetings of the MIA, King related his philosophy of nonviolent love and redemptive suffering. The vision of an interracial society governed by the "liberal" values of freedom and equality continued, in part, to define the balance of King's career.

Even as King and others attempted to put a just vision into practice in Montgomery, hate mail and crank calls flowed in. In the face of death threats and legal obstructionism, anxiety and frustration grew among members of the MIA and in King's own soul. Late on the night of January 27, 1956, yet another phone caller crudely threatened his life, leaving him frightened and near despair. Unable to sleep, King made a pot of coffee and considered how he might withdraw from his position of leadership without seeming to be a coward. Ready to give up, he nonetheless prayed to God for assistance. And then came the kitchen table epiphany in which he felt the presence of the Divine as he never had before. An inner voice assured him with the words: "Stand up for righteousness, stand up for truth. God will be at your side forever."

Thus unfolded the most memorable moment of King's life, one to which King returned again and again for inspiration. Three nights later, an unknown assailant threw a bomb onto the porch of King's Montgomery home. Though wife Coretta, daughter Yolanda, and a family friend were in the house, no one was injured. Three days after that, on February 2, a suit was filed in federal district court asking that Montgomery's travel segregation laws be declared unconstitutional.

On June 4, the federal district court ruled that racial segregation on city bus lines was unconstitutional. On November 13, the Supreme Court affirmed the lower court, thus voiding Alabama's state and local segregation laws. And on December 21, 1956, one year and twenty days after Rosa Parks's refusal to give up her seat to a white person, the Montgomery buses were integrated.

King's leadership of the MIA inaugurated a dozen years of crusading for social justice. Elected to the leadership of the Southern Christian Leadership Conference (SCLC) in Atlanta on January 10–11, 1957, he was assassinated on a balcony of the Lorraine Motel in Memphis on April 4, 1968.

King and his associates were strikingly effective in bringing about legal reforms in America, often using federal courts to challenge state practices and regulations. Being first and foremost a Baptist minister, however, King was well aware that salvation, in its full religious sense, comes through faith and grace, rather than through works and law. Whatever his political successes or setbacks, his abiding mandate was to champion those things that undergird positive law—righteousness and truth—even as his abiding assurance was of the loving presence of God. The distinction between political efficacy and biblical principles, between temporal goods and an eternal God, lay at the heart of King's thought and action.

LETTER FROM BIRMINGHAM JAIL

April 16, 1963

MY DEAR FELLOW CLERGYMEN:

While confined here in the Birmingham city jail,[1] I came across your recent statement calling my present activities "unwise and untimely." Seldom do I pause to answer criticism of my work and ideas. If I sought to answer all the criticisms that cross my desk, my secretaries would have little time for anything other than such correspondence in the course of the day, and I would have no time for constructive work. But since I feel that you are men of genuine good will and that your criticisms are sincerely set forth, I want to try to answer your statement in what I hope will be patient and reasonable terms.

I think I should indicate why I am here in Birmingham, since you have been influenced by the view which argues against "outsiders coming in." I have the honor of serving as president of the Southern Christian Leadership Conference, an organization operating in every southern state, with headquarters in Atlanta, Georgia. We have some eighty-five affiliated organizations across the South, and one of them is the Alabama Christian Movement for Human Rights. Frequently we share staff, educational and financial resources with our affiliates. Several months ago the affiliate here in Birmingham asked us to be on call to engage in a nonviolent direct-action program if such were deemed necessary. We readily consented, and when the hour came we lived up to our promise. So I, along with several members of my staff, am here because I was invited here; I am here because I have organizational ties here.

But more basically, I am in Birmingham because injustice is here. Just as the prophets of the eighth century B.C. left their villages and carried their "thus saith the Lord" far beyond the boundaries of their home towns, and just as the Apostle Paul left his village of Tarsus and carried the gospel of Jesus Christ to the far corners of the Greco-Roman world, so am I compelled to carry the gospel of freedom beyond my own home town. Like Paul, I must constantly respond to the Macedonian call for aid.

Moreover, I am cognizant of the interrelatedness of all communities and states. I cannot sit idly by in Atlanta and not be concerned about what happens in Birmingham. Injustice anywhere is a threat to justice everywhere. We are caught in an inescapable network of mutuality, tied in a single garment of destiny. Whatever affects one directly, affects all indirectly. Never again can we afford to live with the narrow, provincial "outside agitator" idea. Anyone who lives inside the United States can never be considered an outsider anywhere within its bounds.

You deplore the demonstrations taking place in Birmingham. But your statement, I am sorry to say, fails to express a similar concern for the conditions that brought about the demonstrations. I am sure that none of you would want to rest content with the superficial kind of social analysis that deals merely with effects and does not grapple with underlying causes. It is unfortunate that demonstrations are taking place in Birmingham, but it is even more unfortunate that the city's white power structure left the Negro community with no alternative.

In any nonviolent campaign there are four basic steps: collection of the facts to determine whether injustices exist; negotiation; self-purification; and direct action. We have gone through all these steps in Birmingham. There can be no gainsaying the fact that racial injustice engulfs this community. Birmingham is probably the most thoroughly segregated city in the United States. Its ugly record of brutality is widely known. Negroes have experienced grossly unjust treatment in the courts. There have been more unsolved bombings of Negro homes and churches in Birmingham than in any other city in the nation. These are the hard, brutal facts of the case. On the basis of these conditions, Negro leaders sought to negotiate with the city fathers. But the latter consistently refused to engage in good-faith negotiation.

Then, last September, came the opportunity to talk with leaders of Birmingham's economic community. In the course of the negotiations, certain promises were made by the merchants—for example, to remove the stores' humiliating racial signs. On the basis of these promises, the Reverend Fred Shuttlesworth and the leaders of the Alabama Christian Movement for Human Rights agreed to a moratorium on all demonstrations. As the weeks and months went by, we realized that we were the victims of a broken promise. A few signs, briefly removed, returned; the others remained.

As in so many past experiences, our hopes bad been blasted, and the shadow of deep disappointment settled upon us. We had no alternative except to prepare for direct action, whereby we would present our very bodies as a means of laying our case before the conscience of the local and the national community. Mindful of the difficulties involved, we decided to undertake a process of self-purification. We began a series of workshops on nonviolence, and we repeatedly asked ourselves: "Are you able to accept blows without retaliating?" "Are you able to endure the ordeal of jail?" We decided to schedule our direct-action program for the Easter season, realizing that except for Christmas, this is the main shopping period of the year. Knowing that a strong economic-withdrawal program would be the by-product of direct action, we felt that this would be the best time to bring pressure to bear on the merchants for the needed change.

Then it occurred to us that Birmingham's mayoral election was coming up in March, and we speedily decided to postpone action until after election day. When we discovered that the Commissioner of Public Safety, Eugene "Bull" Connor, had piled up enough votes to be in the run-off we decided again to postpone action until the day after the run-off so that the demonstrations could not be used to cloud the issues. Like many others, we waited to see Mr. Connor defeated, and to this end we endured postponement after postponement. Having aided in this community need, we felt that our direct-action program could be delayed no longer.

You may well ask: "Why direct action? Why sit-ins, marches and so forth? Isn't negotiation a better path?" You are quite right in calling for negotiation. Indeed, this is the very purpose of direct action. Nonviolent direct action seeks to create such a crisis and foster such a tension that a community which has constantly refused to negotiate is forced to confront the issue. It seeks so to dramatize the issue that it can no longer be ignored. My citing the creation of tension as part of the work of the nonviolent-resister may sound rather shocking. But I must confess that I am not afraid of the word "tension." I have earnestly opposed violent tension, but there is a type of constructive, nonviolent tension which is necessary for growth. Just as Socrates felt that it was necessary to create a tension in the mind so that individuals could rise from the bondage of myths and half-truths to the unfettered realm of creative analysis and objective appraisal, so must we see the need for nonviolent gadflies to create the kind of tension in society that will help men rise from the dark depths of prejudice and racism to the majestic heights of understanding and brotherhood.

The purpose of our direct-action program is to create a situation so crisis-packed that it will inevitably open the door to negotiation. I therefore concur with you in your call for negotiation. Too long has our beloved Southland been bogged down in a tragic effort to live in monologue rather than dialogue.

One of the basic points in your statement is that the action that I and my associates have taken in Birmingham is untimely. Some have asked: "Why didn't you give the new city administration time to act?" The only answer that I can give to this query is that the new Birmingham administration must be prodded about as much as the outgoing one, before it will act. We are sadly mistaken if we feel that the election of Albert Boutwell as mayor will bring the millennium to Birmingham. While Mr. Boutwell is a much more gentle person than Mr. Connor, they are both segregationists, dedicated to maintenance of the status quo. I have hope that Mr. Boutwell will be reasonable enough to see the futility of massive resistance to desegregation. But he will not see this without pressure from devotees of civil rights. My friends, I must say to you that we have not made a single gain in civil rights without determined legal and nonviolent pressure. Lamentably, it is an historical fact that privileged groups seldom give up their privileges voluntarily. Individuals may see the moral light and voluntarily give up their unjust posture; but, as Reinhold Niebuhr has reminded us, groups tend to be more immoral than individuals.

We know through painful experience that freedom is never voluntarily given by the oppressor; it must be demanded by the oppressed. Frankly, I have yet to engage in a direct-action campaign that was "well timed" in the view of those who have not suffered unduly from the disease of segregation. For years now I have heard the word "Wait!" It rings in the ear of every Negro with piercing familiarity. This "Wait" has almost always meant "Never." We must come to see, with one of our distinguished jurists, that "justice too long delayed is justice denied."

We have waited for more than 340 years for our constitutional and God-given rights. The nations of Asia and Africa are moving with jetlike speed toward gaining political independence, but we still creep at horse-and-buggy pace toward gaining a cup of coffee at a lunch counter. Perhaps it is easy for those who have never felt the stinging darts of segregation to say, "Wait." But when you have seen vicious mobs lynch your mothers and fathers at will and drown your sisters and brothers at whim; when you have seen hate-filled policemen curse, kick and even kill your black brothers and sisters; when you see the vast majority of your twenty million Negro brothers smothering in an airtight cage of poverty in the midst of an affluent society; when you suddenly find your tongue twisted and your speech stammering as you seek to explain to your six-year-old daughter why she can't go to the public amusement park that has just been advertised on television, and see tears welling up in her eyes when she is told that Funtown is closed to colored children, and see ominous clouds of inferiority beginning to form in her little mental sky, and see her beginning to distort her personality by developing an unconscious bitterness toward white people; when you have to concoct an answer for a five-year-old son who is asking: "Daddy, why do white people treat colored people so mean?"; when you take a cross-county drive and find it necessary to sleep night after night in the uncomfortable corners of your automobile because no motel will accept you; when you are humiliated day in and day out by nagging signs reading "white" and "colored"; when your first name becomes "nigger," your middle name becomes "boy" (however old you are) and your last name becomes "John," and your wife and mother are never given the respected title "Mrs."; when you are harried by day and haunted by night by the fact that you are a Negro, living constantly at tiptoe stance, never quite knowing what to expect next, and are plagued with inner fears and outer resentments; when you are forever fighting a degenerating sense of "nobodiness"—then you will understand why we find it difficult to wait. There comes a time when the cup of endurance runs over, and men are no longer willing to be plunged into the abyss of despair. I hope, sirs, you can understand our legitimate and unavoidable impatience.

You express a great deal of anxiety over our willingness to break laws. This is certainly a legitimate concern. Since we so diligently urge people to obey the Supreme Court's decision of 1954 outlawing segregation in the public schools, at first glance it may seem rather paradoxical for us consciously to break laws. One may well ask: "How can you advocate breaking some laws and obeying others?" The answer lies in the fact that there are two types of laws: just and unjust. I would be the first to advocate obeying just laws. One has not only a legal but a moral responsibility to obey just laws. Conversely, one has a moral responsibility to disobey unjust laws. I would agree with St. Augustine that "an unjust law is no law at all."

Now, what is the difference between the two? How does one determine whether a law is just or unjust? A just law is a man-made code that squares with the moral law or the law of God. An unjust law is a code that is out of harmony with the moral law. To put it in the terms of St. Thomas Aquinas: An unjust law is a human law that is not rooted in eternal law and natural law. Any law that uplifts human personality is just. Any law that degrades human personality is unjust. All segregation statutes are unjust because segregation distorts the soul and damages the personality. It gives the segregator a false sense of superiority and the segregated a false sense of inferiority. Segregation, to use the terminology of the Jewish philosopher Martin Buber, substitutes an "I-it" relationship for an "I-thou" relationship and ends up relegating persons to the status of things. Hence segregation is not only politically, economically and sociologically unsound, it is morally wrong and sinful. Paul Tillich has said that sin is separation. Is not segregation an existential expression of man's tragic separation, his awful estrangement, his terrible sinfulness? Thus it is that I can urge men to obey the 1954 decision of the Supreme Court, for it is morally right; and I can urge them to disobey segregation ordinances, for they are morally wrong.

Let us consider a more concrete example of just and unjust laws. An unjust law is a code that a numerical or power majority group compels a minority group to obey but does not make binding on itself. This is *difference* made legal. By the same token, a just law is a code that a majority compels a minority to follow and that it is willing to follow itself. This is *sameness* made legal.

Let me give another explanation. A law is unjust if it is inflicted on a minority that, as a result of being denied the right to vote, had no part in enacting or devising the law. Who can say that the legislature of Alabama which set up that state's segregation laws was democratically elected? Throughout Alabama all sorts of devious methods are used to prevent Negroes from becoming registered voters, and there are some counties in which, even though Negroes constitute a majority of the population, not a single Negro is registered. Can any law enacted under such circumstances be considered democratically structured?

Sometimes a law is just on its face and unjust in its application. For instance, I have been arrested on a charge of parading without a permit. Now, there is nothing wrong in having an ordinance which requires a permit for a parade. But such an ordinance becomes unjust when it is used to maintain segregation and to deny citizens the First-Amendment privilege of peaceful assembly and protest.

I hope you are able to see the distinction I am trying to point out. In no sense do I advocate evading or defying the law, as would the rabid segregationist. That would lead to anarchy. One who breaks an unjust law must do so openly, lovingly, and with a willingness to accept the penalty. I submit that an individual who breaks a law that conscience tells him is unjust, and who willingly accepts the penalty of imprisonment in order to arouse the conscience of the community over its injustice, is in reality expressing the highest respect for law.

Of course, there is nothing new about this kind of civil disobedience. It was evidenced sublimely in the refusal of Shadrach, Meshach and Abednego to obey the laws of Nebuchadnezzar, on the ground that a higher moral law was at stake. It was practiced superbly by the early Christians, who were willing to face hungry lions and the excruciating pain of chopping blocks rather than submit to certain unjust laws of the Roman Empire. To a degree, academic freedom is a reality today because Socrates practiced civil disobedience. In our own nation, the Boston Tea Party represented a massive act of civil disobedience.

We should never forget that everything Adolf Hitler did in Germany was "legal" and everything the Hungarian freedom fighters did in Hungary was "illegal." It was "illegal" to aid and comfort a Jew in Hitler's Germany. Even so, I am sure that, had I lived in Germany at the time, I would have aided and comforted my Jewish brothers. If today I lived in a Communist country where certain principles dear to the Christian faith are suppressed, I would openly advocate disobeying that country's antireligious laws.

I must make two honest confessions to you, my Christian and Jewish brothers. First, I must confess that over the past few years I have been gravely disappointed with the white moderate. I have almost reached the regrettable conclusion that the Negro's great stumbling block in his stride toward freedom is not the White Citizen's Counciler or the Ku Klux Klanner, but the white moderate, who is more devoted to "order" than to justice; who prefers a negative peace which is the absence of tension to a positive peace which is the presence of justice; who constantly says: "I agree with you in the goal you seek, but I cannot agree with your methods of direct action"; who paternalistically believes he can set the timetable for another man's freedom; who lives by a mythical concept of time and who constantly advises the Negro to wait for a "more convenient season." Shallow understanding from people of good will is more frustrating than absolute misunderstanding from people of ill will. Lukewarm acceptance is much more bewildering than outright rejection.

I had hoped that the white moderate would understand that law and order exist for the purpose of establishing justice and that when they fail in this purpose they become the dangerously structured dams that block the flow of social progress. I had hoped that the white moderate would understand that the present tension in the South is a necessary phase of the transition from an obnoxious negative peace, in which the Negro passively accepted his unjust plight, to a substantive and positive peace, in which all men will respect the dignity and worth of human personality. Actually, we who engage in nonviolent direct action are not the creators of tension. We merely bring to the surface the hidden tension that is already alive. We bring it out in the open, where it can be seen and dealt with. Like a boil that can never be cured so long as it is covered up but must be opened with all its ugliness to the natural medicines of air and light, injustice must be exposed, with all the tension its exposure creates, to the light of human conscience and the air of national opinion before it can be cured.

In your statement you assert that our actions, even though peaceful, must be condemned because they precipitate violence. But is this a logical assertion? Isn't this like condemning a robbed man because his possession of money precipitated the evil act of robbery? Isn't this like condemning Socrates because his unswerving commitment to truth and his philosophical inquiries precipitated the act by the misguided populace in which they made him drink hemlock? Isn't this like condemning Jesus because his unique God-consciousness and never-ceasing devotion to God's will precipitated the evil act of crucifixion? We must come to see that, as the federal courts have consistently affirmed, it is wrong to urge an individual to cease his efforts to gain his basic constitutional rights because the quest may precipitate violence. Society must protect the robbed and punish the robber.

I had also hoped that the white moderate would reject the myth concerning time in relation to the struggle for freedom. I have just received a letter from a white brother in Texas. He writes: "All Christians know that the colored people will receive equal rights eventually, but it is possible that you are in too great a religious hurry. It has taken Christianity almost two thousand years to accomplish what it has. The teachings of Christ take time to come to earth." Such an attitude stems from a tragic misconception of time, from the strangely irrational notion that there is something in the very flow of time that will inevitably cure all ills. Actually, time itself is neutral; it can be used either destructively or constructively. More and more I feel that the people of ill will have used time much more effectively than have the people of good will. We will have to repent in this generation not merely for the hateful words and actions of the bad people but for the appalling silence of the good people. Human progress never rolls in on wheels of inevitability; it comes through the tireless efforts of men willing to be co-workers with God, and without this hard work, time itself becomes an ally of the forces of social stagnation. We must use time creatively, in the knowledge that the time is always ripe to do right. Now is the time to make real the promise of democracy and transform our pending national elegy into a creative psalm of brotherhood. Now is the time to lift our national policy from the quicksand of racial injustice to the solid rock of human dignity.

You speak of our activity in Birmingham as extreme. At fist I was rather disappointed that fellow clergymen would see my nonviolent efforts as those of an extremist. I began thinking about the fact that I stand in the middle of two opposing forces in the Negro community. One is a force of complacency, made up in part of Negroes who, as a result of long years of oppression, are so drained of self-respect and a sense of "somebodiness" that they have adjusted to segregation; and in part of a few middle-class Negroes who, because of a degree of academic and economic security and because in some ways they profit by segregation, have become insensitive to the problems of the masses. The other force is one of bitterness and ha-tred, and it comes perilously close to advocating violence. It is expressed in the various black nationalist groups that are springing up across the nation, the largest and best-known being Elijah Muhammad's Muslim movement. Nourished by the Negro's frustration over the continued ex-istence of racial discrimination, this movement is made up of people who have lost faith in America, who have absolutely repudiated Christianity, and who have concluded that the white man is an incorrigible "devil."

I have tried to stand between these two forces, saying that we need emulate neither the "do-nothingism" of the complacent nor the hatred and despair of the black nationalist. For there is the more excellent way of love and nonviolent protest. I am grateful to God that, through the influ-ence of the Negro church, the way of nonviolence became an integral part of our struggle.

If this philosophy had not emerged, by now many streets of the South would, I am convinced, be flowing with blood. And I am further con-vinced that if our white brothers dismiss as "rabble-rousers" and "outside agitators" those of us who employ nonviolent direct action, and if they refuse to support our nonviolent efforts, millions of Negroes will, out of frustration and despair, seek solace and security in black-nationalist ide-ologies—a development that would inevitably lead to a frightening racial nightmare.

Oppressed people cannot remain oppressed forever. The yearning for freedom eventually manifests itself, and that is what has happened to the American Negro. Something within has reminded him of his birthright of freedom, and something without has reminded him that it can be gained. Consciously or unconsciously, he has been caught up by the *Zeitgeist*, and with his black brothers of Africa and his brown and yellow brothers of Asia, South America and the Caribbean, the United States Negro is moving with a sense of great urgency toward the promised land of racial justice. If one recognizes this vital urge that has engulfed the Negro community, one should readily understand why public demonstrations are taking place. The Negro has many pent-up resentments and latent frustrations, and he must release them. So let him march; let him make prayer pilgrimages to the city hall; let him go on freedom rides—and try to understand why he must do so. If his repressed emotions are not released in nonviolent ways, they will seek expression through violence; this is not a threat but a fact of history. So I have not said to my people: "Get rid of your discontent." Rather, I have tried to say that this normal and healthy discontent can be channeled into the creative outlet of nonviolent direct action. And now this approach is being termed extremist.

But though I was initially disappointed at being categorized as an extremist, as I continued to think about the matter I gradually gained a measure of satisfaction from the label. Was not Jesus an extremist for love: "Love your enemies, bless them that curse you, do good to them that hate you, and pray for them which despitefully use you, and persecute you." Was not Amos an extremist for justice: "Let justice roll down like waters and righteousness like an ever-flowing stream." Was not Paul an extremist for the Christian gospel: "I bear in my body the marks of the Lord Jesus." Was not Martin Luther an extremist: "Here I stand; I cannot do otherwise, so help me God." And John Bunyan: "I will stay in jail to the end of my days before I make a butchery of my conscience." And Abraham Lincoln: "This nation cannot survive half slave and half free." And Thomas Jefferson: "We hold these truths to be self-evident, that all men are created equal ... " So the question is not whether we will be extremists, but what kind of extremists we will be. Will we be extremists for hate or for love? Will we be extremists for the preservation of injustice or for the extension of justice? In that dramatic scene on Calvary's hill three men were crucified. We must never forget that all three were crucified for the same crime—the crime of extremism. Two were extremists for immorality, and thus fell below their environment. The other, Jesus Christ, was an extremist for love, truth and goodness, and thereby rose above his environment. Perhaps the South, the nation and the world are in dire need of creative extremists.

I had hoped that the white moderate would see this need. Perhaps I was too optimistic; perhaps I expected too much. I suppose I should have realized that few members of the oppressor race can understand the deep groans and passionate yearnings of the oppressed race, and still fewer have the vision to see that injustice must be rooted out by strong, persistent and determined action. I am thankful, however, that some of our white brothers in the South have grasped the meaning of this social revolution and committed themselves to it. They are still all too few in quantity, but they are big in quality. Some—such as Ralph McGill, Lillian Smith, Harry Golden, James McBride Dabbs, Ann Braden and Sarah Patton Boyle—have written about our struggle in eloquent and prophetic terms. Others have marched with us down nameless streets of the South. They have languished in filthy, roach-infested jails, suffering the abuse and brutality of policemen who view them as "dirty nigger-lovers." Unlike so many of their moderate brothers and sisters, they have recognized the urgency of the moment and sensed the need for powerful "action" antidotes to combat the disease of segregation.

Let me take note of my other major disappointment. I have been so greatly disappointed with the white church and its leadership. Of course, there are some notable exceptions. I am not unmindful of the fact that each of you has taken some significant stands on this issue. I commend you, Reverend Stallings, for your Christian stand on this past Sunday, in welcoming Negroes to your worship service on a non-segregated basis. I commend the Catholic leaders of this state for integrating Spring Hill College several years ago.

But despite these notable exceptions, I must honestly reiterate that I have been disappointed with the church. I do not say this as one of those negative critics who can always find something wrong with the church. I say this as a minister of the gospel, who loves the church; who was nurtured in its bosom; who has been sustained by its spiritual blessings and who will remain true to it as long as the cord of life shall lengthen.

When I was suddenly catapulted into the leadership of the bus protest in Montgomery, Alabama, a few years ago, I felt we would be supported by the white church. I felt that the white ministers, priests and rabbis of the South would be among our strongest allies. Instead, some have been outright opponents, refusing to understand the freedom movement and misrepresenting its leaders; all too many others have been more cautious than courageous and have remained silent behind the anesthetizing security of stained-glass windows.

In spite of my shattered dreams, I came to Birmingham with the hope that the white religious leadership of this community would see the justice of our cause and, with deep moral concern, would serve as the channel through which our just grievances could reach the power structure. I had hoped that each of you would understand. But again I have been disappointed.

I have heard numerous southern religious leaders admonish their worshipers to comply with a desegregation decision because it is the law, but I have longed to hear white ministers declare: "Follow this decree because integration is morally right and because the Negro is your brother." In the midst of blatant injustices inflicted upon the Negro, I have watched white churchmen stand on the sideline and mouth pious irrelevancies and sanctimonious trivialities. In the midst of a mighty struggle to rid our nation of racial and economic injustice, I have heard many ministers say: "Those are social issues, with which the gospel has no real concern." And I have watched many churches commit themselves to a completely otherworldly religion which makes a strange, un-Biblical distinction between body and soul, between the sacred and the secular.

I have traveled the length and breadth of Alabama, Mississippi and all the other southern states. On sweltering summer days and crisp autumn mornings I have looked at the South's beautiful churches with their lofty spires pointing heavenward. I have beheld the impressive outlines of her massive religious-education buildings. Over and over I have found myself asking: "What kind of people worship here? Who is their God? Where were their voices when the lips of Governor Barnett dripped with words of interposition and nullification? Where were they when Governor Wallace gave a clarion call for defiance and hatred? Where were their voices of support when bruised and weary Negro men and women decided to rise from the dark dungeons of complacency to the bright hills of creative protest?"

Yes, these questions are still in my mind. In deep disappointment I have wept over the laxity of the church. But be assured that my tears have been tears of love. There can be no deep disappointment where there is not deep love. Yes, I love the church. How could I do otherwise? I am in the rather unique position of being the son, the grandson and the great-grandson of preachers. Yes, I see the church as the body of Christ. But, oh! How we have blemished and scarred that body through social neglect and through fear of being nonconformists.

There was a time when the church was very powerful—in the time when the early Christians rejoiced at being deemed worthy to suffer for what they believed. In those days the church was not merely a thermometer that recorded the ideas and principles of popular opinion; it was a thermostat that transformed the mores of society. Whenever the early

Christians entered a town, the people in power became disturbed and immediately sought to convict the Christians for being "disturbers of the peace" and "outside agitators." But the Christians pressed on, in the conviction that they were "a colony of heaven," called to obey God rather than man. Small in number, they were big in commitment. They were too God-intoxicated to be "astronomically intimidated." By their effort and example they brought an end to such ancient evils as infanticide and gladiatorial contests.

Things are different now. So often the contemporary church is a weak, ineffectual voice with an uncertain sound. So often it is an archdefender of the status quo. Far from being disturbed by the presence of the church, the power structure of the average community is consoled by the church's silent—and often even vocal—sanction of things as they are.

But the judgment of God is upon the church as never before. If today's church does not recapture the sacrificial spirit of the early church, it will lose its authenticity, forfeit the loyalty of millions, and be dismissed as an irrelevant social club with no meaning for the twentieth century. Every day I meet young people whose disappointment with the church has turned into outright disgust.

Perhaps I have once again been too optimistic. Is organized religion too inextricably bound to the status quo to save our nation and the world? Perhaps I must turn my faith to the inner spiritual church, the church within the church, as the true *ekklesia* and the hope of the world. But again I am thankful to God that some noble souls from the ranks of organized religion have broken loose from the paralyzing chains of conformity and joined us as active partners in the struggle for freedom. They have left their secure congregations and walked the streets of Albany, Georgia, with us. They have gone down the highways of the South on tortuous rides for freedom. Yes, they have gone to jail with us. Some have been dismissed from their churches, have lost the support of their bishops and fellow ministers. But they have acted in the faith that right defeated is stronger than evil triumphant. Their witness has been the spiritual salt that has preserved the true meaning of the gospel in these troubled times. They have carved a tunnel of hope through the dark mountain of disappointment.

I hope the church as a whole will meet the challenge of this decisive hour. But even if the church does not come to the aid of justice, I have no despair about the future. I have no fear about the outcome of our struggle in Birmingham, even if our motives are at present misunderstood. We will reach the goal of freedom in Birmingham and all over the nation, because the goal of America is freedom. Abused and scorned though we may be, our destiny is tied up with America's destiny. Before the pilgrims landed at Plymouth, we were here. Before the pen of Jefferson etched the majestic words of the Declaration of Independence across the pages of history, we were here. For more than two centuries our forebears labored in this country without wages; they made cotton king; they built the homes of their masters while suffering gross injustice and shameful humiliation—and yet out of a bottomless vitality they continued to thrive and develop. If the inexpressible cruelties of slavery could not stop us, the opposition we now face will surely fail. We will win our freedom because the sacred heritage of our nation and the eternal will of God are embodied in our echoing demands.

Before closing I feel impelled to mention one other point in your statement that has troubled me profoundly. You warmly commended the Birmingham police force for keeping "order" and "preventing violence." I doubt that you would have so warmly commended the police force if you had seen its dogs sinking their teeth into unarmed, nonviolent Negroes. I doubt that you would so quickly commend the policemen if you were to observe their ugly and inhumane treatment of Negroes here in the city jail; if you were to watch them push and curse old Negro women and young Negro girls; if you were to see them slap and kick old Negro men and young boys; if you were to observe them, as they did on two occasions, refuse to give us food because we wanted to sing our grace together. I cannot join you in your praise of the Birmingham police department.

It is true that the police have exercised a degree of discipline in handling the demonstrators. In this sense they have conducted themselves rather "nonviolently" in public. But for what purpose? To preserve the evil system of segregation. Over the past few years I have consistently preached that nonviolence demands that the means we use must be as pure as the ends we seek. I have tried to make clear that it is wrong to use immoral means to attain moral ends. But now I must affirm that it is just as wrong, or perhaps even more so, to use moral means to preserve immoral ends. Perhaps Mr. Connor and his policemen have been rather nonviolent in public, as was Chief Pritchett in Albany, Georgia, but they have used the moral means of nonviolence to maintain the immoral end of racial injustice. As T. S. Eliot has said: "The last temptation is the greatest treason: To do the right deed for the wrong reason."

I wish you had commended the Negro sit-inners and demonstrators of Birmingham for their sublime courage, their willingness to suffer and their amazing discipline in the midst of great provocation. One day the

South will recognize its real heroes. They will be the James Merediths, with the noble sense of purpose that enables them to face jeering and hostile mobs, and with the agonizing loneliness that characterizes the life of the pioneer. They will be old, oppressed, battered Negro women, symbolized in a seventy-two-year-old woman in Montgomery, Alabama, who rose up with a sense of dignity and with her people decided not to ride segregated buses, and who responded with ungrammatical profundity to one who inquired about her weariness: "My feets is tired, but my soul is at rest." They will be the young high school and college students, the young ministers of the gospel and a host of their elders, courageously and nonviolently sitting in at lunch counters and willingly going to jail for conscience' sake. One day the South will know that when these disinherited children of God sat down at lunch counters, they were in reality standing up for what is best in the American dream and for the most sacred values in our Judaeo-Christian heritage, thereby bringing our nation back to those great wells of democracy which were dug deep by the founding fathers in their formulation of the Constitution and the Declaration of Independence.

Never before have I written so long a letter. I'm afraid it is much too long to take your precious time. I can assure you that it would have been much shorter if I had been writing from a comfortable desk, but what else can one do when he is alone in a narrow jail cell, other than write long letters, think long thoughts and pray long prayers?

If I have said anything in this letter that overstates the truth and indicates an unreasonable impatience, I beg you to forgive me. If I have said anything that understates the truth and indicates my having a patience that allows me to settle for anything less than brotherhood, I beg God to forgive me.

I hope this letter finds you strong in the faith. I also hope that circumstances will soon make it possible for me to meet each of you, not as an integrationist or a civil-rights leader but as a fellow clergyman and a Christian brother. Let us all hope that the dark clouds of racial prejudice will soon pass away and the deep fog of misunderstanding will be lifted from our fear-drenched communities, and in some not too distant tomorrow the radiant stars of love and brotherhood will shine over our great nation with all their scintillating beauty.

Yours for the cause of Peace and Brotherhood,

Martin Luther King, Jr.[2]

NOTES

1. This response to a published statement by eight fellow clergymen from Alabama (Bishop C. C. J. Carpenter, Bishop Joseph A. Durick, Rabbi Hilton L. Grafman, Bishop Paul Hardin, Bishop Holan B. Harmon, the Reverend George M. Murray, the Reverend Edward V. Ramage and the Reverend Earl Stallings) was composed under somewhat constricting circumstances. Begun on the margins of the newspaper in which the statement appeared while I was in jail, the letter was continued on scraps of writing paper supplied by a friendly Negro trusty, and concluded on a pad my attorneys were eventually permitted to leave me. Although the text remains in substance unaltered, I have indulged in the author's prerogative of polishing it for publication.

2. [Martin Luther King Jr., "Letter from Birmingham Jail," in *Why We Can't Wait* (New York: Harper & Row, 1964), 77–100.]

{CHAPTER 14}

William Stringfellow (1928–1985)

SELECTED AND EDITED BY FRANK S. ALEXANDER

William Stringfellow came of age in the aftermath of World War II and Hiroshima, completing law school and going to work for a East Harlem Protestant parish in 1956. For the next three decades, until his death in 1985, he sought to interpret the American experiences of the 1950s, the 1960s, and the 1970s in light of the Incarnation, the Crucifixion, and the Resurrection. He was present in the poverty and racism of Harlem; his voice was raised in protest against the McCarthy hearings; he was active in the civil rights movement; he was charged with harboring Daniel Berrigan, a fugitive during the antiwar movement; he represented the Episcopal priests charged with the illegal ordination of women; and he served as a warden in the local government of his community. Though he happened to be a lawyer, an active Episcopalian, and was certainly an advocate, he recoiled from the common label given to him of being a prophet. Stringfellow's response to scripture was a sense of calling to a vocation as a Christian, no more and no less.

A SIMPLICITY OF FAITH: MY EXPERIENCE IN MOURNING

A LAWYER'S WORK

IF POLITICS, FROM time to time, has spawned for me prosaic temptation to mistake career for vocation, being a lawyer has not bothered me in any comparable way. I was spared that before I even entered Harvard Law School because of my disposition of the substantive issue of career versus vocation while I was a graduate fellow at the London School of Economics and Political Science. As I have remarked heretofore, I had elected then to pursue *no* career. To put it theologically, I died to the idea of career and to the whole typical array of mundane calculations, grandiose goals and appropriate schemes to reach them. I renounced, simultaneously, the embellishments—like money, power, success—associated with careers in American culture, along with the ethics requisite to obtaining such condiments. I do not say this haughtily; this was an aspect of my conversion to the gospel, so, in fact, I say it humbly.

... I believed then, as I do now, that I am called in the Word of God—as is *everyone* else—to the vocation of being human, nothing more and nothing less. I confessed then, as I do now, that to be a Christian means to be called to be an exemplary human being. And, to be a Christian *categorically* does not mean being religious. Indeed, all religious versions of the gospel are profanities. Within the scope of the calling to be merely, but truly, human, any work, including that of any profession, can be rendered a sacrament of that vocation. On the other hand, no profession, discipline or employment, as such, is a vocation.

Law students, along with those in medicine, engineering, architecture, the military, among others, are subjected to indoctrinations, the effort of such being to make the students conform quickly and thoroughly to that prevailing stereotype deemed most beneficial to the profession and to its survival as an institution, its influence in society, and its general prosperity. At the Harvard Law School, this process is heavy, intensive, and unrelenting, though I imagine that such indoctrinations are all the more so in pseudo-professional institutions, like those training insurance agents, stockbrokers, or realtors. Over and over again, while I was in the law school, I was astonished at how eagerly many of my peers surrendered to this regimen of professionalistic conditioning, often squelching their own most intelligent opinions or creative impulses in order to conform or to appear to be conforming.

... I understand in hindsight that the vocational attitude I had formed in London, and later, the experience I had as law student, apprehended the legal profession specifically, and the professions, disciplines and occupations in general, in their status among the fallen principalities and powers engaged (regardless of apparently benign guises and pretenses) in coercing, stifling, captivating, intimidating, and otherwise victimizing human beings. The demand for conformity in a profession commonly signifies a threat of death.

In that connection, my commitment to vocation instead of career began, while I was still in law school, to sponsor far-reaching implications for how I could spend the rest of my life. Anyway, I suffered the overkill ethos of the Harvard Law School—I think—with enough poise as a human being to quietly, patiently, vigilantly resist being conformed to this world.

The upshot of that resistance was that I emerged from the law school as someone virtually opposite of what a Harvard Law School graduate is projected by the prevailing system to be. I do say *that* proudly, and gladly.

Do not misunderstand me: I enjoyed the law school, but I did not take it with the literally dead earnestness of those of my peers who had great careers at stake. I respected the intellectual vigor of its environment, but I was appalled by the overwhelming subservience of legal education to the commercial powers and the principalities of property. I thought that a law school should devote at least as much attention in its curriculum to the rights and causes of people as it does to vested property interests of one kind or another. I also thought, while I was in law school, that *justice* is a suitable topic for consideration in practically every course or specialization. Alas, it was seldom mentioned, and the term itself evoked ridicule, as if justice were a subject beneath the sophistication of lawyers.

ADVOCACY AS A PASTORAL GIFT

When I first arrived in 1956 in East Harlem, I supposed that the rudimentary problem respecting the law was a failure to fully implement the existing American legal system among citizens who were economically dispossessed and who were victimized by racism. My supposition was, I soon enough discovered, mistaken. The issue, so far as the law was concerned, in the ghetto was the existence of another ruling system, distinct and apart from the constitutional and legal system pertaining elsewhere in the nation, based on coercion and the threat of coercion by those institutions and people who had commandeered the capabilities of coercion. It was a system of lawless authority, of official violence, a primitive substitution for the law. I wrote then that if such an extraordinary condition were allowed to continue and to fester, it would, sooner or later, infect and afflict the whole of this society. It has. There is a connection—direct and terrible and coherent—between the kind of regime to be found in the ghettoes in the Fifties and the way lawless authority and official violence dominate the life of most of this society today. . . .

... A critical dimension of this tension occasioned by being a biblical person who works as a lawyer is that the role of legal advocate at once coincides with and interferes with the pastoral calling to which I am disposed charismatically. In that calling, advocacy expresses the freedom in Christ to undertake the cause of another—including causes deemed "hopeless," to intercede for the need of another—without evaluating it, but just because the need is apparent, to become vulnerable—even unto death—in the place of another. By contrast, advocacy in the law is contained within the bounds of the adversary system, with all its implications of competitiveness, aggression, facetious games, debater's craft, and winning *per se*. There have been circumstances in my experience when the advocacy of the Christian in the world coincides with the advocacy of the lawyer (as in cases concerning the ordination of women), but there seem to be far more instances when the one interferes with the other (as in war resister cases). In part, here, of course, I am pleading within the legal profession for a more holistic approach to clients and cases than that afforded by the adversary system. Yet, more than that, I continue to be haunted with the ironic impression that I may have to renounce being a lawyer the better to be an advocate.[1]

THE CHRISTIAN LAWYER AS A CHURCHMAN

THE PROCLAMATION OF THE GOSPEL

The Church as the congregation is the event in which reconciliation between God and men accomplished in Jesus Christ is already known and celebrated and thereby the message of reconciliation is entrusted for proclamation in all the world and to the whole world. . . .

The most lucid and cogent witness of God's love for men is that through Jesus Christ He gives men a new life now, in the very midst of the old life, that the new life begins in history in His Church and in the faith of His Church, that men are born anew in His Church, that in His Church the new life is celebrated. The message of reconciliation for the world is entrusted to the Church by the event of reconciliation which constitutes the Church and which the Church celebrates. The Gospel is entrusted to the Church, the Church possesses the Gospel, but the Church is not possessive about the Gospel, for the Gospel does not mean that God loves the Church, the Gospel means that God loves the world and therefore elects the Church. Hence nothing is more demonstrative of the Gospel in the world and to the world than the concrete life of the Church in history. That is why it is always a very great tragedy for the world when the actual life of the Church is not a celebration of the Gospel but a conformation to the world. Where apostasy or heresy or sorcery are celebrated, the Gospel is not proclaimed. But where the celebration has integrity in the Gospel, it is integral to the Gospel, and celebration is proclamation.

THE OBVIATION OF A CHRISTIAN JURISPRUDENCE

What is before implicit, must now be put directly. The tension between law and grace is such that there is no Christian jurisprudence. There is not a particular philosophy of law which has special integrity in the Gospel. Nor is that a way really to make the positive law or the ethics of law, the purposes of law which men offer as a measure for positive legislation, compatible with the Gospel.

This does not at all mean that Christians disregard the law, rather they regard it for exactly and only what it is: law and justice are the manner in which men maintain themselves in history. Law is a condition of historical existence, a circumstance of the fall. Christians, both in congregation and in dispersion, are in the world, living in history, under the sanctions of secular law, and this is the locus of their proclamation of the Gospel for the world. For law, the proclamation of the Gospel means, in the first instance, the comprehension that law, though sometimes it can name sin, originates itself in sin and cannot overcome the power of sin.

This obviates, of course, a Christian jurisprudence, but poses—for Christians and for the world—just what any jurisprudence does not—the tension between grace and law. The Christian sees that the striving of law is for justice, but knows that the justice men achieve has no saving power; it does not justify them, for justification of man is alone in Jesus Christ. The grace of God is the only true justice any man may ever receive.

To have no special Christian jurisprudence does not mean that Christians are indifferent, or wholly negativist, toward law. Rather their concern is primarily an issue of vocation, not of jurisprudence.[2]

FREE IN OBEDIENCE

A RADICAL LIFE

The style of life, this ethics of witness, means that the essential and consistent task of Christians is to expose the transience of death's power in the world. That is a task which will not be exhausted until God's mercy brings this history to an end and fulfillment on the Last Day. Thus, the Christian in secular society is always in the position of a radical—not in the conventional political sense of that word, but in the sense that nothing which is achieved in secular life can ever satisfy the insight which the Christian is given as to what the true consummation of life in society is. The Christian always complains of *status quo*, whatever that happens to be; he always seeks more than that which satisfies even the best ideals of other men. Or, to put it differently, the Christian knows that no change, reform, or accomplishment of secular society can modify, threaten, or diminish the active reign of death in the world. Only Christ can do that, and now his reign is acknowledged and enjoyed in the society which bears his name and has the task of proclamation in all the world for the sake of that part of the world still consigned to the power of death.

At the same time the witness of Christians in the world is always both repentant and penitential. It is repentant in that Christians acknowledge the fallenness of life and the reality of sin and then confess—as much in and through their action in the world as in their worship—their own sins: shortcomings, omissions, failings, infidelities, profanities, weaknesses, vanities, angers, indulgences, errors, and corruptions. By intercession (as representatives before God, in behalf of and in the place of other men) they also confess the sins of the world, in which they share, and which they call upon other men to confess for themselves. This confession and intercession is repentance. But it is also penitential: recognition and realization of sorrow, regret, remorse, grief, mourning, and contrition for the offense of their own sins and the sins of others against God's own person and to his creation.

The penitential act, the authentication of true repentance, which invariably follows repentance and is the sacramental expression of repentance, is not an act of recrimination by which a man indulges in judging and punishing himself. Nor is it some form of restitution as if what has been done could be undone or as if there could be a return to the situation prior to the sin. Both recrimination and restitution are ways in which men attempt, even after acknowledging their sins specifically, to justify themselves by allaying God's judgment or earning his forgiveness. Such tactics may work between a child and a parent, between a criminal and society, or in the moralistic and legalistic religions, but they have nothing to do with the event of repentance and the penitential act characteristic of Christian witness in action and worship in the world. . . .

That *this* is the accusation should, by the way, dispose of the legend, so popular in modern treatments of the trial of Christ both in Good Friday sermons and popular secular versions of the event, that Christ is innocent of any offense and tried and condemned because of some corruption or failure or miscarriage of justice. Of the charge against him, Christ is guilty beyond any doubt.

In any case, the significant aspect of the trial is that it is not just an encounter between Christ and some men who were his enemies. The most decisive clash in all history is this one between Christ and the principalities and powers of this world, represented by and symbolized in Israel and Rome.

... It appears, in other words, to be widely believed in the churches in the United States that the history of redemption is encompassed merely in the saga of relationships between God and men. What there is of contemporary Protestant moral theology typically ignores any attempt to account for, identify, explicate, and relate the self to the principalities, although empirically the principalities seem to have an aggressive, in fact possessive, ascendancy in American life. Because of the biblical references to principalities and angelic powers are so prominent, and because the powers themselves enjoy such dominance in everyday life, their meaning and significance cannot be left unexamined.

What are the principalities and powers? What is their significance in the creation and in the fall? What is their relationship to human sin? How are these powers related to the presence and power of death in history? What is the meaning of the confrontation between Christ and the principalities? Does a Christian have any freedom from their dominion? There can be no serious, realistic, or biblical comprehension of the witness of the Church in the world unless such questions as they are raised and pondered.

WHAT ARE PRINCIPALITIES?

There is nothing particularly mysterious, superstitious, or imaginary about principalities, despite the contemporary failure to discuss them theologically. The realities to which the biblical terms "principalities and powers" refer are quite familiar to modern society, though they may be called by different names. What the Bible calls "principalities and powers" are called in contemporary language "ideologies," "institutions," and "images."

A principality, whatever its particular form and variety, is a living reality, distinguishable from human and other organic life. It is not made or instituted by men, but, as with men and all creation, made by God for his own pleasure.

In the biblical understanding of creation, the principalities or angelic powers, together with all other forms of life, are given by God into the dominion of men and are means through which men rejoice in the gift of life by acknowledging and honoring God, who gives life to all men and to the whole of creation. The dominion of men over the rest of creation, including the angelic powers, means the engagement of men in the worship of God as the true, realized, and fulfilled human life and, at the same time and as part of the same event, the commitment by men of all things within their dominion to the very same worship of God, to the very same actualization of true life for all things. All men, all angels, and all things in creation have origination, integrity, and wholeness of life in the worship of God. . . .

THE MEANING OF DEMONIC

Like all men and all things, the angelic powers and principalities are fallen and are become demonic powers. "Demonic" does not mean evil; the word refers to death, to fallenness. An angelic power in its fallen estate is called a demonic power, because it is a principality existing in the present age in a state of alienation from God, cut off from the life originating in his life, separated from its own true life and, thus, being in a state of death. In the fall, every man, every principality, every thing exists in a condition of estrangement from his or its own life, as well as from the lives of all other men, powers, and things. In the fall, the whole of creation is consigned to death.

The separation from life, the bondage to death, the alienation from God which the fall designates is not simply to be accounted for by human sin. The fall is not just the estate in which men reject God and exalt themselves, as if men were like God. The term does not merely mean the pretensions of human pride. It is all that and something more. The fall is also the awareness of men of their estrangement from God, themselves, each other, and all things, and their pathetic search for God or some substitute for God within and outside themselves and each other in the principalities and in the rest of creation. So men, in their fallenness, are found sometimes idolizing themselves, sometimes idolizing snakes, bugs, other creatures, or natural phenomena, or sometimes idolizing nation, ideology, race, or one of the other principalities. It is to such as these that men look to justify their existence, to find and define the lost meaning of their lives, and to fill the place of God himself. . . .

. . . All this is not for the sake of the Christians, not for their justification either individually or as the Church, but for the sake of the world, for other men. A Christian is free in his knowledge and experience of the love of God for the world to love the world himself. A Christian does not love another man for himself—else how would one love his own enemy?—but for his sake, that is, because of what God has done for him. A Christian loves another man in a way that affirms his true humanity, vouchsafed for him and for all men in the resurrection.

The life of the Christian both within and outside the gathered congregation is sacramental. But of what practical significance is that for a Christian in his daily decisions and actions? The witness which is obedience to God's freedom is one which celebrates the gospel, but of what guidance is that in choosing a job, casting a ballot, raising a child, facing illness, spending money, or any of the other ordinary issues of daily existence?

The short answer to such questions is that the witness which is truly obedience to the freedom of God means freedom without measure for men. That means that the Christian is free to take the world and every aspect of its existence, every person and every principality, seriously. Out of respect, as it were, for God's creation and for both the incarnation and the Holy Spirit, the Christian deals with history in this world just as it is and makes decisions in terms of the actual events in which he is involved as they happen. In doing so he knows that there is no place in which his presence is forbidden, no person whom he may not welcome, no work in which he may not engage, no situation into which he may not enter, without first of all finding that he has been preceded, so to speak, by the Word of God.

The Christian does not need to construct any hypothetical presuppositions, any theoretics of decision, after the manner of the Greeks, the Hebrews in the early Church, or the later pietists of one sort or another. To do that denigrates the freedom of God in judging the world and all the decisions and actions of men and nations in the way that it pleases him to do, by enthroning some principles of decision in the place of God. Such ethics, in any of their varieties, are no armor against the realities of the world, the temptations of the flesh, or the power of death; they are only means of hiding from all of these.

There are, to be sure, certain marks of the ministry and witness of the Church and of Christians in the world: radicality, penitence, intercession for the outcast, and the like; but that is not the same thing as some legalistic ethics. Such ethics have no saving power for the world for they invariably are the expression of the self-interest of the very persons and principalities which adhere to them and attempt to implement and enforce them. Nor do they have any efficacy in justifying those beholden to them.

Nor will any such scheme of ethics save any man from God's judgment. All men and nations are judged in all their ethics, motives, decisions, and actions by God himself. No one aids him in this office, and no one can take another's place, nor can one be spared God's judgment by any other means, though that be the intention of all ethics. That being so, the freedom of the Christian consists of his acceptance of the fact that his own justification by the working of God's freedom relieves him even of the anxiety over how he is judged by God.

The Christian goes about—wherever he be, which may be anywhere, whomever he is with, which may be anyone—edified and upheld by the sacramental community which is the church in the congregation. He is ready to face whatever is to be faced knowing that the only enemy is the power of death, whatever form or appearance death may take. He is confident that the Word of God has already gone before him. Therefore he can live and act, whatever the circumstances, without fear of or bondage to either his own death or the works of death in the world. He is enabled and authorized by the gift of the Holy Spirit to the Church and to himself in baptism to expose all that death has done and can do, rejoicing in the freedom of God which liberates all men, all principalities, all things from bondage to death.

That being so, the Christian is free to give his own life to the world, to anybody at all, even to one who does not know about or acknowledge the gift, even to one whom the world would regard as unworthy of the gift. He does so without reserve, compromise, hesitation, or prudence, but with modesty, assurance, truth, and serenity. That being so, the Christian is free, within the freedom of God, to be obedient unto his own death.[3]

AN ETHIC FOR CHRISTIANS AND OTHER ALIENS IN A STRANGE LAND

REVELATION AS ETHICS

It is a pity that Americans have been so recalcitrant toward the Bible, for all the contrary pretenses in the country's public rituals and despite the grandiose religiosity in America concerning the familiar fictions about the nation's destiny. It is specifically a misfortune, it seems to me, that most Americans, whether or not they keep a church connection, are either ignorant or obtuse about Revelation and the issues which the Book raises in its Babylon passages. Had the American inheritance been different, had Americans been far less religious and much more biblical, had the American experience as a nation not been so Babylonian, we might have been edified—in a fearful and marvelous and timely way—by this biblical witness, and Americans might be in more hopeful and more happy circumstances today.

Instead, Americans for the most part have dismissed the Bible as apolitical—a private witness shrouded in holy neutrality so far as politics is concerned, having nothing beyond vague and innocuous exhortation to do with the nation as such, relegated to the peripheries of social conflict. Thereby Americans have actually suppressed the Bible, since the Bible is *essentially* political, having to do with the fulfillment of humanity in society or, in traditional words, with the saga of salvation.

The treatment of the particular book of the Bible which I cite here, the Revelation to John, is the striking illustration at point. We have deemed it esoteric poetry, to be put aside as inherently obscure and impractical by definition; or we have regarded it, somewhat apprehensively, as a diary of psychedelic visions inappropriately appended to the rest of Scripture; or else we have suffered the arrogant pietism of itinerant evangelists preaching a quaint damnation from fragments of the book and acquiesced to their boast that *that* is what Revelation is about. Some have demeaned the whole of the Bible by distorting this book as a predestinarian chronicle. Seldom is the specific political use to which the book was put in its original context in the first century even mentioned in church or known to contemporary church folk. Most often, I observe, Americans, including the professed Christians and the habituated churchgoers, have just been wholly indifferent to Revelation.

Whatever reasons can be assigned for it, Americans fail to comprehend Revelation as an ethical literature concerning the character and timeliness of God's judgment, not only of persons, but over nations and, in truth, over all principalities and powers—which is to say, all authorities, corporations, institutions, traditions, processes, structures, bureaucracies, ideologies, systems, sciences, and the like. As such—except for the accounts of the Crucifixion of Jesus Christ in the Gospels—Revelation is manifestly the most political part of the New Testament. . . .

... The ethics of biblical politics offer no basis for divining specific, unambiguous, narrow, or ordained solutions for any social issue. Biblical theology does not deduce "the will of God" for political involvement or social action. The Bible—if it is esteemed for it own genius—does not yield "right" or "good" or "true" or "ultimate" answers. The Bible does not do that in seemingly private or personal matters; even less can it be said to do so in politics or institutional life. . . .

Yet human wickedness in this sense is so peripheral in the biblical version of the Fall that the pietistic interpretation that it represents the heart of the matter must be accounted gravely misleading. The biblical description of *the Fall concerns the alienation of the whole of Creation from God*, and, thus, the rupture and profound disorientation of all relationships within the whole of Creation. Human beings are fallen, indeed! But all other creatures suffer fallenness, too. And the other creatures include, as it were, not only cows, but corporations; the other creatures are, among others, the nations, the institutions, the principalities and powers. The biblical doctrine of the Fall means the brokenness of relationships among human beings and the other creatures, and the rest of Creation, and the spoiled or confused identity of each human being within herself or himself and each principality within itself. . . .

Biblical living honors the life-style of the people of God set out for us in the Bible. A spontaneous, intimate, and incessant involvement in the biblical Word as such—that is, Bible study—is the most essential nurture of contemporary biblical people while they are involved, patiently and resiliently, in the common affairs of the world. Biblical living means, concretely, practicing the powers of discernment, variously perceiving and exposing the moral presence of death incarnate in the principalities and powers and otherwise. And biblical living means, moreover, utilizing the diverse and particular charismatic gifts as the ethics and tactics of resistance to the power of death in the assurance that these gifts are in their use profoundly, radically, triumphantly humanizing.

Biblical living discloses that the ethical is sacramental, not moralistic or pietistic or religious. The identify of the ethical in the sacramental is, perhaps, most obvious in liturgy, where liturgy retains biblical style and scope and content, where liturgy has Eucharistic integrity and is not an absurd theatrical charade disguising the idolatry of death. But the sacramental reality of the ethics is, also, enacted empirically, day by day, transfiguring mundane politics by appealing to the presence of the Word of God in all events.[4]

THE POLITICS OF SPIRITUALITY

... The problem of America as a nation, in biblical perspective, remains this elementary issue of repentance. The United States is, as all nations are, called in the Word of God to repentance. That, in truth, is what the church calls for, whether knowingly or not, every time the church prays *Thy Kingdom Come.*

America needs to repent. Every episode in the common experience of America as a nation betells that need. If such be manifest in times of trauma and trouble—such as now—it is as much the need in triumphal or grandiose circumstances.

The nation needs to repent. If I put the matter so baldly, I hope no one will mistake my meaning for the rhetoric of those electronic celebrity preachers who sometimes use similar language to deplore the mundane lusts of the streets or the ordinary vices of people or to berate the Constitutional bar to prayer, so-called, in public schools while practicing quietism about the genocidal implications of the Pentagon's war commerce or extolling indifference toward the plight of the swelling urban underclasses.

Topically, repentance is *not* about forswearing wickedness as such; repentance concerns the confession of vanity. For America—for any nation at any time—*repentance means confessing blasphemy.*

Blasphemy occurs in the existence and conduct of a nation whenever there is such profound and sustained confusion as to the nation's character, place, capabilities, and destiny that the vocation of the Word of God is preempted or usurped. Thus the very presumption of the righteousness of the American cause as a nation *is* blasphemy.

Americans, for some time now, have been assured, again and again, that the United States will prevail in history because the American cause is righteous. Anyone who believes that has, to say the very least, learned noting from the American adventurism in Vietnam. Then, a succession

of presidents made similar pronouncements, but America suffered igno-
minious defeat nonetheless. And if in the last few years some sense of guilt
about Vietnam has begun to surface, this has been, for the most part, a
strange and perverted sentiment because it has attached not to the crimes
of American intervention in Southeast Asia—to massacre, despoilment,
and genocide—but to the event of American defeat. To feel guilty because
America lost, rather than because of what America did, is another, if ma-
cabre, instance of false righteousness. That is only the more underscored
when the unlawful invasion of Grenada is examined as an attempt to fanta-
size the victory for American superpower which was missed in Vietnam.

Furthermore, the confusion of a nation's destiny, and of a nation's capabilities, with the vocation of the Word of God in history—which is the *esse*
of blasphemy—sponsors the delusion that America exercises domination
over creation as well as history and that it can and should control events in
the life of creation. Other nations, ancient and modern, as has been mentioned, suffered similar delusions, but if there ever been a nation which
should know better (that is, which should repent), it is America, if only
because of the American experience as a nation and a society in these past
few decades.

After all, it is only in the period since, say, Hiroshima, in which American power, rampant most conspicuously in the immense, redundant, overkill nuclear-weapons arsenal, has been proven impotent, because if it is
deployed, it portends self-destruction, and if it is not, it amounts to profli-
gate, grotesque waste. In either instance, American nuclear arms are rendered practically ineffectual in dominating events, but they still mock the
sovereignty of the Word of God in history.

Much of the same must, of course, be said of the nation's society and
culture, which has become, as I have earlier remarked, overdependent
upon the consumption ethic, with its doctrines of indiscriminate growth,
gross development, greedy exploitation of basic resources, uncritical and
often stupid reliance upon technological capabilities and incredible naiveté about technological competence, and crude, relentless manipulation of
human beings as consumers. Increasingly, now, people can glimpse that
this is no progress, no enhancement of human life, but wanton plunder of
creation itself. People begin to apprehend that the penultimate implemen-
tation of the American consumption ethic is, bluntly, self-consumption.
In the process, it has become evident as well that the commerce engen-
dered by the American consumption ethic, together with the commerce of
weapons proliferation, relates consequentially to virtually every injustice
of which human beings are victims in this nation and in much of the rest
of the world.

And so I say the United States needs to repent; the nation needs to be freed of blasphemy. There are, admittedly, theological statements. Yet I think they are also truly practical statements. America will remain frustrated, literally demoralized, incapable of coping with its concrete problems as a nation and society until it knows that realism concerning the nation's vocation which only repentance can bring.

One hopes repentance will be forthcoming. If not, it *will* happen: in the good time of the Judgment of the Word of God.

Meanwhile, in this same context, persons repent and all persons are called to repentance. The confession and repentance of an individual does not take place, as some preachers and the like aver, in a great void, abstracted from the everyday existence of this world. The experience of each penitent is peculiar to that person, but that does not mean it is separated from the rest of created life.

This is the reason why the foisting of any stereotype of the experience upon people is coercive and false and, indeed, self-contradictory. It must be recognized, however, that this is quite what is involved where, for an example, a so-called born-again Christian stereotype is asserted. I can testify personally that I have been "born again"—my account constitutes the book aptly titled *A Second Birthday*—but that appears to mean something substantively different from sudden, momentary trauma. I do not thus imply that the latter is invalid or necessarily incomplete or otherwise questionable, but I do question the composition of *any* stereotype of the experience and the insinuation that it is normative, much less mandatory.

What is implicated in confession and repentance, which inaugurates the practice of a biblical spirituality whatever the style or detail of what happens to a particular person, is the establishment or restoral by the Word of God of that person's identity in the Word of God in a which in which the query *Who am I?* merges with the question *Where is God?* The transaction comprehends, as has been said, the risk that there is no one or nothing to affirm a person's existence and identity. As I have put it before, the confession of utter helplessness, the repentance which is requisite and efficacious, always involves the empirical risk of death. At the very same time, this repentance foreshadows and anticipates the perfection of each person's and each principality's vocation in the Kingdom of God.

JUSTIFICATION AND HOPE

Since the disillusionment and defection of Judas, a recurrent issue for people of biblical faith has been the confusion between justification and justice. It is, in fact, out of contemporary manifestations of that very confusion, especially during the decade of the sixties, that many Christian activists (as the media style them) have become more curious about spirituality and have begun to explore the significance of biblical spirituality for political decisions and actions. The widespread posthumous interest in the witness and ministry of Thomas Merton is one significant sign of that, as I have said.

I do not venture to unravel the confusion regarding justification and justice in terms of its prolonged and agitated annals in Christendom. I speak of the matter only theologically, not historically and analytically. As I understand it, justice is the accomplishment of the Judgment of the Word of God in the consummation of this age and embodies all the specifications, all the particular details of the Judgment with respect to all things whatsoever. Justice, as it is articulate in the Judgment, is essentially an expression of the faithfulness of the Word of God to the creation of the Word of God.

There is no capability in human effort or in the enterprise of nations or other principalities to approximate the justice of the Judgment. The decisions and actions of persons and powers may, in a sense, aspire to or render tribute to the justice of the Judgment, but they cannot fabricate it or duplicate it or preempt it. And, as has been mentioned, when they suppose that they have in given circumstances imitated or second-guessed the Judgment and its justice, they are most in jeopardy so far as the integrity of their respective vocations is concerned. Persons and principalities can neither play God nor displace God without risking self-destruction. This does not denigrate at all the struggle for justice in merely human and institutional terms; in fact, it upholds that struggle even in recognizing how fragile, transient, and ambiguous it is—and dynamic—how open it is to amendment, how vulnerable to change.

Within the scene of this world, now, where the struggle for justice in merely human and institutional translations is happening, and in the midst of the turmoil that stirs, the Word of God, as a matter of God's own prerogative, freedom, and grace, offers the assurance of redemption, the promise of wholeness and integrity and communication, the message of hope in the Kingdom which is to come together with the Judgment of the Word of God and the justice which that Judgment works.

This justification is both credible and accessible, not because any person, or any society, is worthy but because the Word of God is extravagant or, if you will, because the *Word of God is godly.* So the grace of the Word of God transcends the injustice of the present age, agitates the resilience of those who struggle now to expose and rebuke injustice, informs those who resist the rulers of the prevailing darkness, and overflows in eagerness for the coming of One who is the Judge of this world and whose justice reigns forevermore. By virtue of justification, we are freed now to live in hope.[5]

NOTES

1. [William Stringfellow, *Simplicity of Faith: My Experience in Mourning* (Nashville, Tenn.: Abingdon, 1982), 125–128, 131–133.]

2. [William Stringfellow, "The Christian Lawyer as Churchman," *Vanderbilt Law Review* 10 (August 1957): 953, 964.]

3. [William Stringfellow, *Free in Obedience* (New York: Seabury, 1964), 44–45, 50–53, 62–63, 126–128.]

4. [William Stringfellow, *An Ethic for Christians and Other Aliens in a Strange Land* (Waco, Tex: Word Books, 1973), 26–27, 54, 76, 151–152.]

5. [William Stringfellow, *The Politics of Spirituality* (Philadelphia: Westminster, 1984), 62–68.]

[CHAPTER 15]

John Howard Yoder (1927–1997)

SELECTED AND EDITED BY DUNCAN B. FORRESTER

John Howard Yoder was a Mennonite theologian who studied with Karl Barth and taught for much of his career at the University of Notre Dame. He brought Mennonite theological insights and emphases into the mainstream of theological discussion, and he communicated extensively with law scholars, military professionals, and theologians from the majority traditions, both Roman Catholic and Protestant. He conducted a prolonged, sympathetic, and penetrating critique of the tradition of natural law thinking, and emphasized the role of the church as having a responsibility for carrying through a consistent critique of the values and ethics of the broader community, offering in its own life an alternative "working model" of community and an alternative set of ethical emphases, particularly on peace, service, and forgiveness. Although he was in many ways theologically conservative and orthodox, on social and legal issues Yoder was consistently radical. His work emphasizes the importance of the Bible as containing a challenge to the values and assumptions of every age and culture.

The first extract is a sustained examination of the strengths and weaknesses of the idea of nature in ethics and law. The second extract is a brief discussion of the paradigmatic role of the church in ethical and legal thinking. This is followed by a discussion of the significance of Jesus and discipleship for moral action today. The fourth extract examines the implications for Christian thinking on ethics and the law of Christianity becoming the official and established religion, expected to validate power. Yoder's critical and perceptive treatment of the tradition of just war thinking is revealed in the fifth extract. The sixth, "Trial Balance," shows the challenging distinctiveness of Yoder's position over against mainstream views of the proper Christian attitude to the law and morality. The final extract, "Patience as a Method in Moral Reasoning: Is an Ethic of Discipleship Absolute?" briefly outlines an ethic of discipleship that is utterly relevant to issues of law and society today.

REGARDING NATURE

WHY IS THE PARTICULAR NO LONGER RESPECTABLE?

WE CALL "MODERNITY" the notion that there has been a normative historical development which has left its origins behind and become self-authen-
ticating. We call "secularity" the world view which claims to make sense
of present meaning without reference to the transcendent dimensions of
cultural origins. We may call "cosmopolitan" or "pluralistic" a culture in
which you may only participate if you outgrow the "provincial" or "ghetto"
qualities of your cultural background. This is partly because there are people out there who do not respect your scriptures or your rabbis; it is even
more so because the liberal political settlement forbids the shared polity to
deal with religion. We are further embarrassed by the memories of empire,
whereby one particular culture, namely that of a European elite, was imposed by force of arms and commerce on other peoples.

HOW THIS FORMULATION MAKES REASONABLE DIALOGUE
MORE DIFFICULT

The distinction between truths which are particular and truths which are
for all assumes that the line between them is clear. Yet when Roman Catholics are told by "pro-choice" advocates that they should not impose their
denominational convictions on the whole society, they respond that "the
sacredness of the life of the fetus is not a Catholic truth but a natural one."
To say that to kill a fetus is homicide is not a religious statement. It is true
for everyone. But how do you get the others to accept your vision of truth
as true for them? To call that truth claim "natural" identifies the kind of
claim you are making but it does not help to convince.

The matter becomes not only complex but paradoxical when we add the
claim, which is historically credible ... that the appeal to nature is itself a
Catholic doctrine. A second dimension of paradox is that the very notion
of "natural law" posits the access of all people of good will to these truths,
yet in fact most people do not see them, so that after all they need to be
told them by the Catholic magisterium.

SORTING OUT THE VARIETIES OF "NATURE" CLAIMS

A much fuller catalog of the varieties of usage of the appeal to "nature"
would be imperative, but to begin with we can say that they fall into two

families. For the first large family, "nature" is the way things obviously are. The epistemology is simple, descriptive. Socially it is positivistic; the institutions of slavery, of patriarchy, of monarchy are obviously the way it is. Biologically it is also positivistic: contraception and artificial insemination interfere with the "natural" functioning of the body. Its first ethical impact is usually conservative, since the nation, the class structure, the marketplace, the repertory of roles or vocations is the way it is. The system will seem convincing as long as all parties have been educated under the same customs, so that they really think "everyone knows ..." whatever they know, and as long as no skeptic draws attention to the is/ought equation. The appeal to nature in this sense works when there is no context.

This kind of argument can however be turned around and used against the consensus, when one chunk of the historical consensus can be read differently. The claim that homosexuality is "counter to nature" can be turned around by claiming that one's sexual capacities or inclinations are inborn.

The other large family of notions of "nature" is things as they ought to be, the essence of things as different from appearance, the "true nature" as contrast with the empirical one, the "real me" as better than the me you see. This normative non-empirical or "ideal" nature can be rooted in an ideal past (Eden, the Founding Fathers) or in the command of God, or perhaps in the future toward which one holds that we are moving or should move. Obviously the epistemology here is more complex than with the other family. This view is capable of being ethically critical, since its criteria are not drawn from the way things are. It is congenial with claiming that "an unjust law is no law," which enables civil disobedience (Martin Luther King Jr.) or the rejection of extant positive law.... Yet where does it get the knowledge by which it judges the present?

Other examples: social critics from the Czech Brethren of the 15th century to the English Diggers and Levellers of the 17th rejected social class distinctions on the basis of the equality of Eden:

When Adam delved
and Eve span
where was then the gentleman?

Thus both the ideal and the real, both the given and the critical, can and do claim to be "nature," the appeals are intrinsically contradictory, and can only be held together if a particular magisterium rules on which form fits where, and/or if the society is homogeneous so that awareness of the intrinsic logical contradictions does not arise.

The appeal to nature is mostly apt when it does not need to adjudicate in a setting of debate, and when it provides leverage or a safeguard over against some specific pitfall:

- against provincialism or the reproach of being in a ghetto
- against "heteronomous" or "alien" expectations
- against asking the impossible
- against exporting particular standards to another culture
- against hasty readings of "what everyone thinks"
- against interpreting Christian loyalty so as not to include everyone.

TRIAL BALANCE: WHAT THE "NATURE" APPEAL CANNOT DO

- It cannot resolve the tension between the given and the critical;
- It cannot adjudicate debates between different definitions of the given.
- It cannot resolve the paradox of someone with a particular position telling others what they are supposed already naturally to know but in fact do not.
- It cannot ultimately keep the promise of offering security or validation through ontology i.e., resolving "ought" conflicts by an "is" claim.

The formal description of why "nature" arguments are needed does not deliver the specific ethical substance claims which we need for the purposes of social ethics:

- slavery is a given institution;
- the nation is a morally binding identity definition, which determines whom I may/should kill.
- a national enemy is to be killed;
- the role of a prince is to dominate and to kill.

All of these elements are traditionally at stake. Thus the "Just War Tradition" is one of the primary instances of "natural argument." Yet the people who today argue for "nature" language do not support them all.

Yet the fact that it cannot ultimately convince does not make it useless. The territory which the "nature" debate names, and the kinds of arguments it uses, still are usable, as long as one does not attempt:

- to give this wisdom normative weight over against Jesus;
- to use it to resolve a debate between incompatible worlds.

There are arguments appealing to general lessons of experience; e.g.:

A. Revolutionary tyranny cannot last, even though the US establishment and the CIA from Dulles to Reagan made "the evil empire" larger than life. Central dictatorship abandons via coercion and centralization its capacity to build a healthy society. A tyranny which lasts more than a few years becomes less able to terrorize and coerce, thanks to some honest human values, the corruption and selfishness of cadres, the post-ideological skepticism of the next generation of youth, the survival of ethnicity. . . .

B. *Noblesse oblige*; if you claim to be of superior moral stature, that entitles us to hold you to a higher standard.

C. Turn about is fair play; I can check whether you should have done (x) to me by asking whether you want me to do (x) to you; trading places is a moral epistemology. This is one naive lay form of what Kant escalates into the "categorical imperative."

Each of these modes of argument is in some sense "natural"; yet they do not fall into the pitfalls identified above. They cannot be used to adjudicate deep debates, and they do not claim to set Jesus aside.[1]

THE PRIESTLY KINGDOM

THE KINGDOM AS SOCIAL ETHIC

The alternative community discharges a modeling mission. The church is called to be now what the world is called to be ultimately. To describe their own community Jews and Christians have classically used terms like those claimed by the structures of the wider world: "people," "nation," "kingdom," even "army." These are not simply poetic figures of speech. They imply the calling to see oneself as doing already on behalf of the wider world what the world is destined for in God's creative purpose. The church is thus not chaplain or priest to the powers running the world: she is called to be a microcosm of the wider society, not only as an idea, but also in her function. Let us look at some examples:

1. The church undertakes pilot programs to meet previously unmet needs or to restore ministries which have collapsed. The church is more able to experiment because not all ministries need to pay off. She can take the risk of losing or failing, more than can those who are in charge of the state. Popular education, institutionalized medicine, and the very concept of dialogical democracy in the Anglo-Saxon world generalize patterns which were first of all experimented with and made sense of in free-church Christianity.

408 ◆ DUNCAN B. FORRESTER

2. The church represents a pedestal or a subculture in which some truths are more evidently meaningful and some lines of logic can be more clearly spelled out than in society as a whole. The credibility and the comprehensibility of an alternative vision which does not always convince on the part of an individual original or "prophetic" person, is enormously more credible and comprehensible if it is tested, confirmed, and practiced by a community. This theme will be treated under another heading later.

3. The church exemplifies what has come to be called "sacramentality," which means that meanings which make sense on an ordinary level make more of the same kind of sense when they are embedded in the particular history of the witness of faith. Catholics now talk about the existence of the church as itself a "sacrament," in the sense that the church represents the kind of society that all of society ought to be. The church is able to be that because of the presence in her midst of witness and empowerment which are not in the same way accessible to the wider society. Sometimes this sacramental quality is read in the direction of saying about the church what one says about the rest of society. For instance, if in society we believe in the rights of employees, then the church should be the first employer to deal with workers fairly. If in the wider society we call for the overcoming of racism or sexism or materialism, then the church should be the place where that possibility first becomes real.

More striking and more concrete cases of "sacramentality" can be developed if we look at those specific activities which the church has more traditionally called "sacraments." Here the logic flows the other way; from what the sacrament means to what the world should be.

a. The Eucharist originally was and could again become an expression not only of the death of Christ for our sins but also of the sharing of bread between those who have and those who have not.

b. Baptism could again come to be, as it was in the New Testament, the basis of Christian egalitarianism, in the face of which male and female, barbarian and cultured, slave and free, etc., are all ascribed the same dignity.

c. The process of binding and loosing—i.e., deliberative morally accountable dialogue, dealing with offense and forgiveness (and thereby dealing with moral discernment)-may recover the connection with forgiveness and with decision-making which "church discipline" lost when it came to be tied with formal excommunication and the sanctions of hierarchical authority.

4. The church can be a foretaste of the peace for which the world was made. It is the function of minority communities to remember and to create utopian visions. There is no hope for society without an awareness of

transcendence. Transcendence [is] kept alive not on the grounds of logical proof to the effect that there is a cosmos with a hereafter, but by the vitality of communities in which a different way of being keeps breaking in here and now. That we can really be led on a different way is the real proof of the transcendent power which offers hope of peace to the world as well. Nonconformity is the warrant for the promise of another world. Although immersed in this world, the church by her way of being represents the promise of an- other world, which is not somewhere else but which is to come here. That promissory quality of the church's present distinctiveness is the making of peace, as the refusal to make war is her indispensable negative transcendence.[2]

THE FORMS OF ETHICAL DISCOURSE

What are the axioms of radical reformation ethics? Which of these matters the most will depend on the perspective of the interlocutor. The primary substantial criterion of Christian ethical decisions for the radical reformers is the humanity of Jesus of Nazareth. What he did is the primordial definition of the human obedience which God desires. There are issues concerning which his example gives us no guidance and for which other kinds of wisdom will be indispensable, but at those points where his example is relevant it is also revelatory and is not to be set aside in favor of other criteria.

Jesus was not only a model actor, but he was also a foundational teacher. He thereby incorporated into the body of guidance of which his disciples dispose an accumulation of wisdom which not only is predominantly Jewish in idiom and origin, but also no less Jewish at the points where he differed from some other Jewish traditions. That body of moral wisdom includes notions about nature and human nature, God and God's law, which can of course be classified in several types. General rules such as the love commandment, specific rules such as the prohibition of the oath or adultery, and parabolic examples combine to provide a rich repertory of tools for illuminating moral decision. This excludes any single-issue system whereby once one key theme is struck (law and gospel, or nature and grace, or love and justice, or providence, or creation, or vocation) the rest of ethics will unfold simply, almost deductively.

There would be no memory of Jesus if it had not been for the early communities' recording and interpreting his words in the ongoing process of defining the meaning of obedience in the first-century Mediterranean world. We have in the New Testament canon the ground floor of a few decades' experience. Stretching from then to the present we possess an additional nearly infinite accumulation of applications and interpretation. The extent to which various strata of these traditions can be fruitful for our guidance is a question too complex to unfold here. The radical reformation was with Protestantism in general in claiming that the canonical witness remains the baseline for judging subsequent evolution. Yet it would be a misinterpretation to be led at this point into a simple repetition of the naive sixteenth-century debate about Scripture versus the church.

The knowledge of the meaning for today of participation in the work of Christ is mediated ecclesiastically. The bridge between the words of Jesus or of the apostolic writings and obedience in the present is not a strictly conceptual operation, which could be carried out by a single scholar at his desk, needing only an adequate dictionary and an adequate description of the available action options. The promise of the presence of Christ to actualize a definition of his will in a given future circumstance (i.e., future to Jesus or to the apostolic writers) was given not to professional exegetes but to the community which would be gathered in his name (Matt. 18:19) with the specific purpose of "binding and loosing" (Matt. 18:18). Classical Protestantism tended to deny the place of this conversational process in favor of its insistence on the perspicuity and objectivity of the words of Scripture. Catholicism before that had provoked that extreme Protestant answer by making of this hermeneutical mandate a blank check which the holders of ecclesiastical office could use with relative independence. The free-church alternative to both recognizes the inadequacies of the text of Scripture standing alone uninterpreted, and appropriates the promise of the guidance of the Spirit throughout the ages, but locates the fulfillment of that promise in the assembly of those who gather around Scripture in the face of a given real moral challenge. Any description of the substance of ethical decision-making criteria is incomplete if this aspect of its communitarian and contemporary form is omitted.

A popular slogan which has become operative in the contemporary search to recapture the validity of the radical reformation tradition is the notion of the "hermeneutic community" ... The Spirit, the gathering, and the Scripture are indispensable elements of the process. A technical exegete alone in his office could not replace the actual conversational process in empirical communities where the working of the Spirit is discerned in the fact that believers are brought to unity around this Scripture. This "hermeneutic" process of conversation will often not be done with much explicit self-awareness in terms of the styles of ethical discourse or meta-ethical self-criticism. It is thus not possible, as it is in some of the other traditions, to distill out of the body of ethical teachings a few very broad axioms from which the total system is derived. One could as an ethicist try to formulate such a distillate, but it would be the observer's own concoction and would not be recognized as representative of what really happens when two or three gather and find Christ speaking in their midst.

This gathering process is in one sense a situational ethic. It does not seek advance wisdom on problems not being faced. It takes off immediately from a problem or an offense.[3]

THE CONSTANTINIAN SOURCES OF WESTERN SOCIAL ETHICS

From Genesis to Apocalypse, the meaning of history had been carried by the people of God as people, as community. Leadership *within* the people was dispersed (Moses, prophets, priests, judges). When kingship was introduced in order to be "like the other nations" it did not work long or well, and the king was not elevated above common humanity. Other rulers (Nebuchadnezzar, Cyrus, Caesar) were historically significant only as they have an incidental part in the history of the people of God. But the fact that with Constantine the civil sovereign becomes God's privileged agent is thus not merely a shift of accent but a change of direction.

A NEW UNIVERSALITY

After Constantine not only is the ruler the bearer of history; the nonsovereign ethical agent has changed as well. The "Christian" used to be a minority figure, with numerous resources not generally available to all people: personal commitment, regeneration, the guidance of the Holy Spirit, the consolation and encouragement of the brotherhood, training in a discipleship life-style. But now that Christianity is dominant, the bearer of history is Everyman—baptized but not necessarily thereby possessed of the resources of faith. Ethical discourse must now meet two more tests:

1. Can you ask such behavior of everyone? Are not servanthood and the love of enemy, or even contentment and monogamy, more than we have the right to expect of everyone? Is not the love ethic of the New Testament unrealistic, too heroic? The pressure builds rapidly for a duality in ethics. The "evangelical counsels" will be commended to the religious and the highly motivated. The "precepts," less demanding, will suffice for catechesis and the confessional. Two levels, two kinds of motivations and sanctions will be discerned, entailing different specific duties (contradictory ones, in fact, at points such as power, property, marriage, bloodshed, which were morally proper for the laity but not for the religious). Then the Reforma-

tion polemic against works righteousness and monasticism removed the upper, more demanding, level.

2. What would happen if everyone did it? If everyone gave their wealth away what would we do for capital? If everyone loved their enemies who would ward off the Communists? This argument could be met on other levels, but here our only point is to observe that such reasoning would have been preposterous in the early church and remains ludicrous wherever committed Christians accept realistically their minority status. For more fitting than "What if everybody did it" would be its inverse, "What if nobody else acted like a Christian, but we did?"

A New Value for Effectiveness

A third dimension of the great reversal is the transformation of moral deliberation into utilitarianism. Minorities and the weak have numerous languages for moral discourse:

- conscience, intention, inspiration, and other similar "subjective" measures of right action;
- revelation, "nature," "wisdom," and other "received" standards;
- covenant, tradition, "style," reputation, training, and other "community-maintenance" criteria.

Each of these ways of moral reasoning has its logical and psychological strengths and limits. We cannot evaluate them here. Yet it is important that each can, in given circumstances, lead persons to act sacrificially, for the sake of others, or for the sake of a "cause" more important than the individual. Each can lift decision and action above immediate cost/benefit calculation. But once the evident course of history is held to be empirically discernible, and the prosperity of our regime is the measure of good, all morality boils down to efficacy. Right action is what works; what does not promise results can hardly be right.

Perhaps the most evident example of the dominion of this axiom is today's debate about revolution, liberation, and violence. Any ethic, any tactic, is, in the minds of many, self-evidently to be tested by its promised results. To them, the rejection of violence is morally sustainable only if nonviolent techniques are available which are able to promise an equally rapid "revolution." Again it would be petitionary to argue that the utilitarian world view is "wrong" or that an ethic of "principles" would be "right." For the present our concern is only to report that the dominance of the engineering approach to ethics, reducing all values to the calculation of pressures promising to bring about imperative results, is itself a long-range echo of the Constantinian wedding of piety with power; it is an approach foreign to the biblical thought world and makes no sense in a missionary situation where believers are few and powerless.

A New Metaphysic

A fourth, more doctrinal implication of the Constantinian reversal must be named: it is the victory of metaphysical dualism. Historically the source of this view is predominantly Neoplatonism. But naming its source does not explain its success. Certainly one reason it took over was the usefulness of dualism to justify the new social arrangement and resolve the problems it raised. The church we see is not the believing community; the visible/invisible duality names, and thereby justifies, the tension. The dominant ethic is different from the New Testament in content (Lordship is glorified rather than servanthood) as in source (reason and the "orders of creation" are normative, rather than the particularity of Jesus' and the apostles' guidance). What could be easier than to reserve the ethics of love for the inward or for the personal, while the ethics of power are for the outward world of structures? Interiorization and individualization, like the developments of the special worlds of cult and meditation, were not purely philosophical invasions which took over because they were intellectually convincing. They did so also because they were functional. They explained and justified the growing distance from Jesus and his replacement by other authorities and another political vision than that of the Kingdom of God. [4]

WHEN WAR IS UNJUST

MAKING THE TRADITION CREDIBLE

Are there people who affirm that their own uncoerced allegiance as believers gives them strength and motivation to honor the restraints of the just-war tradition and to help one another to do so? This might be the only angle from which the development of the needed institutions could be fostered. Would believers commit themselves, and commit themselves to press each other, to be willing to enter the political opposition, or to resign public office, or to espouse selective objection? Does any church teach future soldiers and citizens in such a way that they will know beyond what point they cannot support an unjust war or use an unjust weapon?

Since the capacity to reach an independent judgment concerning the legality and morality of what is being done by one's rulers depends on information, which by the nature of the case must be contested, does the religious community provide alternative resources for gathering and evaluating information concerning the political causes for which their governments demand their violent support? What are the preparations being made to obtain and verify an adequately independent and reliable source of facts and of analytical expertise, enabling honest dissent to be so solidly founded as to be morally convincing? Is every independent thinker on his or her own, or will the churches support agencies to foster dissent when called for?

Neither the pacifist nor the crusader needs to study in depth the facts of politics in order to make a coherent decision. The person claiming to respect just-war rationality must do so, however, and therefore must have a reliable independent source of information. I have stated this as a question about the church, but it also applies to the society. Is there free debate? Are the information media free? Is opposition legitimate? Does the right of conscientious objection have legal recognition?

Are soldiers when assigned a mission given sufficient information to determine whether this is an order they should obey? If a person under orders is convinced he or she must disobey, will the command structure, the society, and the church honor that dissent? It is reported that in the case of the obliteration bombing of Dresden the pilots were not informed that it could hardly be considered a military target. For most of the rest of the just-war criteria factual knowledge is similarly indispensable.

Until today church agencies on any level have invested little effort in literature or other educational means to teach the just-war limitations. The few such efforts one sees are in no way comparable to the way in which the churches teach their young people about other matters concerning which they believe morality is important, such as sexuality. The understanding of the just-war logic that led American young men to refuse to serve in Vietnam came to them not primarily from the ecclesiastical or academic interpreters of the tradition but rather from the notions of fair play presupposed in our popular culture.

A FAIR TEST

Those who conclude, either deliberately or rapidly, that in a given situation of injustice there are no nonviolent options available, often do so in a way that avoids responsibility for any intensive search for such options. The military option for which they so quickly reach has involved a long lead time in training and equipping the forces. It demands the preparation of a special class of leadership, for which most societies have special schools and learning experiences. It demands costly special resources dependent on abundant government funding, and it demands broad alliances. It includes the willingness to lose lives and to take lives, to sacrifice other cultural values for a generation or more, and the willingness of families to be divided.

Yet the decision that nonviolent means will not work for comparable ends is made without any comparable investment of time or creativity, without comparable readiness to sacrifice, and without serious projection of comparable costs. The American military forces would not "work" if we did not invest billions of dollars in equipping, planning, and training. Why should it be fair to measure the moral claims of an alternative strategy by setting up the debate in such a way that that other strategy should have to promise equivalent results with far less financial investment and less planning on every level? The epigram of the 1960s—People give nonviolence two weeks to solve their problems and then say it has failed; they've gone on with violence for centuries, and it seems never to have failed-is not a pacifist argument. It is a sober self-corrective within just-war reasoning.

In sum, the challenge should be clear. If the tradition which claims that war may be justified does not also admit that in particular cases it may *not* be justified, the affirmation is not morally serious. A Christian who prepares the case for a justifiable war without being equally prepared for the negative case has not soberly weighed the *prima facie* presumption that any violence is wrong until the case for the exception has been made. We honor the moral seriousness of the nonpacifist Christian when we spell out the criteria by which the credibility of that commitment, shaped in the form of the just-war system, must be judged.[5]

THE POLITICS OF JESUS: VICIT AGNUS NOSTER

TRIAL BALANCE

... Relevance must be redefined. If it is not enough to say with the Reformation traditions that Jesus purges our will and dampens our pride, sending us back to follow the dictates of our "office" or "station" with greater modesty and thoroughness; if it is not enough to say with the Puritan traditions that we derive from Josiah and Theodosius the vision of a holy commonwealth constantly being reformed to approach increasingly the theocratic ideal; if it is not enough with the "natural law" to find our instructions in the givenness of the fallen world; if it is not enough with the quietist and sectarian traditions to let someone else take care of the world out there what can then be the shape of a reformulated social responsibility illuminated by the confession that it is Jesus who is Messiah who is Lord? Where are we called to an ethicist's repentance, i.e. to a reformulation of the thought patterns that underlie moral choice? I suggest that this reformulation must take five lines:

1. Recent systematic tradition tells us that we must *choose between the Jesus of history and the Jesus of dogma.*

If Jesus is the divine Word incarnate, then what we will be concerned about is the metaphysical transactions by means of which he saved humanity by entering into it. We will then leap like the creed from the birth of Jesus to the cross. His teachings and his social and political involvement will be of little interest and not binding for us.

If, on the other hand, we seek to understand the "Jesus of history" in his human context, as this is reconstructed by the historical disciplines, this will be in order to find a man like any other, a reforming rabbi fully within the limits attainable by our human explanations, who is sometimes mistaken, especially about the future, and whose authority over us will depend on what we ourselves can consent to grant to his teachings.

The nineteenth century chose the Jesus of history, until Albert Schweitzer showed us that Jesus "as he really was" really did take himself to be an apocalyptic figure and his age to be the one just before the New Order begins. Then the systematic tradition veered back to metaphysics, using literary criticism to demonstrate how the Gospel documents project onto Jesus the existential self-awareness of the young church-an awareness closely tied to the name of Jesus but not to his historical reality, so that if he hadn't really been who he was it wouldn't jeopardize anything of his "meaning for us."

If we confess Jesus as Messiah we must refuse this choice.

The Jesus of history is the Christ of faith. It is in hearing the revolutionary rabbi that we understand the existential freedom which is asked of the church. As we look closer at the Jesus whom Albert Schweitzer rediscovered, in all his eschatological realism, we find an utterly precise and practicable ethical instruction, practicable because in him the kingdom has actually come within reach. In him the sovereignty of Yahweh has become human history.

2. The systematic tradition tells us that we are obligated to *choose between the prophet and the institution.*

The prophet condemns and crushes us under his demand for perfection. He is right, ultimately, both in convincing us of our sinfulness and in pointing us toward the ideal which, although unattainable, must remain our goal. But as far as that social order is concerned which it is up to us to administer today and tomorrow, his demands are without immediate relevance. Love, self-sacrifice, and nonviolence provide no basis for taking responsibility in this world. Dependent upon the grace of God alone, one cannot act in history. Those who are called to assure the survival and the administration of institutions will therefore accept violence in order, one day, to diminish or eliminate it. They will accept inequality and exploitation with the goal of progressively combating them. This is a very modest task and one in which one dirties oneself, but an indispensable task if something worse is to be prevented. While respecting the prophet, the rest of us will choose the institution.

The new regime instituted by Jesus as Messiah forbids us to make this choice.

The jubilee which Jesus proclaims is not the end of time, pure event without duration, unconnected to either yesterday or tomorrow. The jubilee is precisely an *institution* whose functioning within history will have a precise practicable, limited impact. It is not a perpetual social earthquake rendering impossible any continuity of temporal effort, but a periodic revision permitting new beginnings.

3. The systematic tradition tells us to *choose between the catastrophic kingdom and the inner kingdom.*

Jesus announced the imminent certain end of history as an event which could happen tomorrow or which was, at the latest, sure to come soon after his death. The apostles maintained this intensity of expectation for a few decades but finally it had to be admitted that there had been a mistake about the date, or perhaps about what they were looking for so soon.

The other option begins by assuming that Jesus could not have been wrong. It must then be concluded that he was speaking of the kingdom of God and its coming only in order to teach, by means of the mythical language which was current in his time, about an inner, spiritual, existential kingdom, whose reality properly will always remain hidden to the eyes of the unbeliever and of the historian.

Once again if Jesus is the Christ we must refuse this choice.

The kingdom of God is a social order and not a hidden one. It is not a universal catastrophe independent of the will of men; it is that concrete jubilary obedience, in pardon and repentance, the possibility of which is proclaimed beginning right now, opening up the real accessibility of a new order in which grace and justice are linked, which men have only to accept. It does not assume time will end tomorrow; it reveals why it is meaningful that history should go on at all.

That men would refuse this offer and promise, pushing away the kingdom that had come close to them, this Jesus had also predicted. He was not mistaken.

4. The systematic tradition tells us we must *choose between the political and the sectarian.*

In the tradition of Ernst Troeltsch, Western theological ethics assumes that the choice of options is fixed in logic and for all times and places by the way the Constantinian heritage dealt with the question. Either one accepts, without serious qualification, the responsibility of politics, i.e. of governing, with whatever means that takes, or one chooses a withdrawn position of either personal-monastic, vocational or sectarian character, which is "apolitical." If you choose to share fully in the duties and the guilt of government, you are exercising responsibility and are politically relevant; if you choose not to, it is because you think politics is either unimportant or impure, and are more concerned for other matters, such as your salvation. In so doing you would have Jesus on your side, but having Jesus on your side is not enough, for there are issues to which Jesus does not speak. . . . We must therefore supplement and in effect correct what we learn from him, by adding information on the nature and the goodness of the specifically "political" which we gain from other sources.

If Jesus is confessed as Messiah this disjunction is illegitimate. To say that any position is "apolitical" is to deny the powerful (sometimes conservative, sometimes revolutionary) impact on society of the creation of an alternative social group, and to overrate both the power and the manageability of those particular social structures identified as "political." To assume that "being politically relevant" is itself a univocal option, so that in saying "yes" to it one knows where one is going, is to overestimate the capacity of "the nature of politics" to dictate its own direction.

Because Jesus' particular way of rejecting the sword and at the same time condemning those who wielded it *was* politically relevant, both the Sanhedrin and the Procurator had to deny him the right to live, in the name of both their forms of political responsibility. His alternative was so relevant, so much a threat, that Pilate could afford to free, in exchange for Jesus, the ordinary Guevara-type insurrectionist Barabbas. Jesus' way is not less but more relevant to the question of how society moves than is the struggle for possession of the levers of command; to this Pilate and Caiaphas testify by their judgment on him. . . .

5. The tradition tells us we must *choose between the individual and the social.*

The "ethics of the Sermon on the Mount" is for face-to-face personal encounters; for social structures an ethic of the "secular vocation" is needed. Faith will restore the individual's soul, and Jesus' strong language about love for neighbor will help with this; but then how a restored man should act will be decided on grounds to which the radical personalism of Jesus does not speak.

But Jesus doesn't know anything about radical personalism. The person-hood which he proclaims as a healing, forgiving call to all is integrated into the social novelty of the healing community. . . .

We could extend the list of traditional antinomies of which we must re-pent if we are to understand. Tradition tells us to choose between respect for persons and participation in the movement of history; Jesus refuses because the movement of history is personal. Between the absolute *agape* which lets itself be crucified, and effectiveness (which it is assumed will usually need to be violent), the resurrection forbids us to choose, for in the light of resurrection crucified agape is not folly (as it seems to the Hellen-izers to be) and weakness (as the Judaizers believe) but the wisdom and power of God (I Cor. 1:22–25).[6]

"PATIENCE" AS A METHOD IN MORAL REASONING: IS AN ETHIC OF DISCIPLESHIP ABSOLUTE?

What I do deny is (1) that such hard cases should be made, as they tend to be, the *center* of ethical deliberation, as if the fundamental moral question were ever simply either (a) whether in an imperfect world we can't have everything we want or (b) in case of collision which values take priority.

What I do deny is (2) that such crunch decisions are prototypical: i.e., that they represent the essential nature of ethical deliberation, so that it is by lining up crunch cases that one can prove a point, with regard, for instance, to the morality of war or abortion or lying, or that it is by list-ing hard cases that one can best teach and learn ethics. As has been said more fully by a roster of colleagues (Stanley Hauerwas, James McClendon, Alasdair MacIntyre ...) in the fields of philosophical and Christian ethics recently, such "quandarism," or "decisionism," or "punctualism" sets aside precisely those elements of moral discourse which are the most fundamen-tal, those where the specificity of a Christian perspective counts the most, and those where there is the most room for improvement.

What I do deny is (3) that such casuistic crunch decisions are typical: i.e., that most people most of the time are making decisions of that kind, which test at their outer edges the applicability of basic rules. Most of the time the basic rules do suffice, once one has identified an issue honestly. To concentrate only on where the basic rules do not quite reach, or on hard cases where two basic rules are in inevitable collision, is precisely to concentrate on the atypical. "Hard cases make bad law." Preoccupation with looking for loopholes is one of the most insidious ways to undermine the claims of ordinary moral obligation, and the viability of ordinary com-munity relationships.

What I do deny is (4) that powerful people have more crunch decisions than weak people or victimized people or middle-level people do. It is usually such questions as "what would you do if you were the president?" which people use to test how far general rules about love of the enemy can reach. Making the ruler the prototypic moral decider in that way is part of the Constantinian legacy to which our culture is heir. But the person in a position of much power is less torn between conflicting pressures and obligations than is the subordinate: the middle-level bureaucrat, the lieutenant or noncommissioned officer, the member of a team who shares equally in discussion but not in decision, the member of a minority whose priority wishes are never heard. Such middle-level people, who know enough to dissent but have less authority, are in the worse moral bind.

What I do deny is (5) that such casuistic crunch decisions are the definition of tragedy. Since Reinhold Niebuhr, the notion of "tragedy" has been cheapened by appealing to it as a way of self-justification when a person in political responsibility decides he must hurt someone (regularly an adversary; not himself) in order to serve someone else or some cause. Those are hard choices, although it is because of his desire to be able to make them his way (this usually is a masculine stance), rather than letting someone else make them otherwise, that the person in political responsibility got himself into that difficult position: to call them "tragedy" (or sometimes "courage") domesticates and exploits the concept. Its basic assumption, that moral obligation usually takes the form of a prohibition, in such a way that moral courage most of the time is a question of justifying exceptions, is itself anti-Judaic and unevangelical. To claim the label of "tragedy" for regularized and justified arrangements, whereby the defense of one's own interests is favored over the dignity or life of others, and further to claim, tacitly or overtly, that being "tragic" is itself a mark of being true, is a self-righteous abuse of language. It adds blasphemy to injury. It too is part of what has given "casuistry" a bad name. . . .

What I do deny is (6) that my critics are any more temperate or moderate, any less "absolute" than I, in what they consider decisive for obedience. They challenge my values because they prefer other values; but those other values are no less determining for them. After all, what they want to convince me of is that in the crunch case their values should overrule mine. They are willing to kill for their other values, as I am not. In the light of this fact about the lay of the land in the debate, the very popular use of terms like "ambiguity" or "ambivalence" to describe their view is misleading. Such terms seem to suggest fine differences of shading, debatable readings in complicated situations—but in fact the real choices usually being talked about are something very decisive and simple like bombing or not bombing a city.

What I do deny is (7) that these borderline cases are so probable, so frequent, and so predictable that we ought institutionally to honor them by planning ahead of time to be ready to respond to a worst-case projection of how bad it might be. To institutionalize readiness for war is already to deny that it is, as the theorists claim, an extreme last resort. One does not prepare ahead of time to be able to inflict overkill in a situation of last resort. Especially one does not delegate the decision about the cases which meet the logical requirements for the extreme case to professional Pentagon people running through the provisions of their briefing books.

Thus the very fact of institutionalizing the readiness to do something extreme means that it is no longer truly being considered extreme. It has been brought into the realm of the thinkable and therefore of the likely. Not only has it been built into a hypothetical scenario; it has been written up as an authorized "standard operating procedure" in the officers' manuals. This can be demonstrated by the fact that the real historical cases in which cities and populations have been destroyed in war have not been like the extreme imaginable borderline crunch cases with which the speculative debate of ethicists seeks to demonstrate that not all killing can be avoided. They are worse, less justifiable, and could have been more avoidable, but they were not avoided, because readiness for them was institutionalized, as the restraints were not.

What I do deny is (8) that an ethic responding to the Gospel of Jesus Christ is any more open to be strained, tested, challenged, or called into doubt, by facing "hard cases," than is an ethic claiming to possess as a warrant a nondialogical knowledge derived from "nature" or "reason" or even realistic self-interest. In fact, an ethic claiming to be founded in "nature" or "reason" is by definition less able to be "patient" in the sense I am talking about. It must *by the nature of its argument* claim that those values are defined self-evidently i.e., nondialogically.

What I do deny is (9) … that the question "can there be an exception?" ought to be one of the primary ways to test and exposit a rule. This is the methodological error of "quandarism." To look for exceptions, especially to be driven, before the hard case and as a general exercise in method, by the concern that there must be an exception to every rule, is the mirror image of the legalism it rejects. To use the general formal statement that "there may be exceptions" as a basis to institutionalize the infractions … is ultimately dishonest, since it clothes as an exception to one rule what is in fact a commitment to the greater authority of a different rule.

What I do deny is (10) ... the appropriateness of the special tilt toward permissiveness which once gave to the adjective "jesuitical" (not to Ignatius of Loyola himself) a bad name. Casuistry is not wrong, but essential. The same is true for exception making, an indispensable part of casuistry. But when the analysis, either in the actual practice of the sacrament of absolution or in the intellectual ground laid in manuals of moral theology for the exercise of that ministry, is tilted toward the individual convenience of the penitent and away from the values borne by (or in modern parlance the "rights of") the other parties to the case, with the result that one invests more ingenuity in authorizing exceptions than in helping to keep the rules, then the discipline has gone wrong.

What I do deny is (11) that, in holding to the priority of the prima facie duty more strongly than others do, I am thereby either in thought or in action more "pure" than others. . . . It is the Catholic casuistry which by cleanly distinguishing between physical and moral evils fosters the notion that moral purity is possible. The Niebuhrian or the Sartrian has no corner on dirty hands. The question is not whether one can have clean hands but which kind of complicity in which kind of inevitable evil is preferable.[7]

NOTES

1. [John Howard Yoder, unpublished text, 1994. Drafted and circulated, January 1994, in connection with a Notre Dame course on the tradition of just war (http://www.nd.edu/-theo/jhy/writings/philsystheo/nature.htm).]

2. [John Howard Yoder, "The Kingdom as Social Ethic," in *The Priestly Kingdom: Social Ethics as Gospel* (South Bend, Ind.: University of Notre Dame Press, 1984), 92–94.]

3. [John Howard Yoder, "The Forms of Ethical Discourse," in *The Priestly Kingdom*, 116–118.]

4. [John Howard Yoder, "The Constantinian Sources of Western Social Ethics," in *The Priestly Kingdom*, 138–141.]

5. [John Howard Yoder, "Making the Tradition Credible," in *When War Is Unjust*, rev. ed. (Maryknoll, N.Y.: Orbis Books, 1996), 77–80.]

6. [John Howard Yoder, "Trial Balance," in *The Politics of Jesus: Vicit Agnus Noster* (Grand Rapids, Mich.: Eerdmans, 1972), 105–114.]

7. [John Howard Yoder, "'Patience' as a Method in Moral Reasoning: Is an Ethic of Discipleship Absolute," in *The Wisdom of the Cross: Essays in Honour of John Howard Yoder*, ed. Stanley Hauerwas et al. (Grand Rapids, Mich.: Eerdmans, 1999), 37–40.]

PART III

The Orthodox Tradition

[CHAPTER 16]

Vladimir Soloviev (1853–1900)

SELECTED AND EDITED BY PAUL VALLIERE

Vladimir Soloviev was the first modern Orthodox thinker to give systematic attention to the problem of religion and law. Philosophy of law in Russia predated Soloviev, but its pioneers did not deal directly with religion. Russian Orthodox lay theologians before Soloviev, such as the Slavophiles Khomiakov and Kireevsky, were diverted from attention to law by their romantic, conservative bias against "juridicalism" in religion and culture. Clerical theologians, on the other hand, faced insuperable political barriers to open discussion of Orthodoxy and the legal order, and their preparedness for such a discussion was questionable in any case. The same can be said of church leaders in other parts of the Orthodox world, which for the most part lagged behind Russia in education and other measures of development. As a lay theologian with a superb modern education, Soloviev had the freedom and intellectual resources to think about the problem of Orthodoxy and law, even if state censorship withheld many of his writings from the public.

Soloviev was born in Moscow in 1853 to a prominent academic family. After graduation from Moscow University and a postgraduate year at the Moscow Theological Academy, the young philosopher embarked on an academic career but soon opted for the life of a freelance intellectual. He was extraordinarily productive. From 1874, the year of his first book, to his premature death in 1900, an unbroken stream of philosophical, historiosophical, and theological books and articles issued from his pen. In scope and originality of thought, no Russian thinker ranks ahead of him.

Soloviev's career can be divided into three periods corresponding to the three decades of his adult life. He devoted the 1870s mainly to writing projects including the masterpiece of his early career, The Critique of Abstract Principles (1880). In the 1880s, while continuing to publish, Soloviev also pursued an activist agenda, promoting a number of causes that he saw as integrally related: the advocacy of cultural and religious liberty in the Russian Empire, the reconciliation of Russia and the West, the reunion of the divided churches of Christendom (ecumenism), and the criticism of anti-Semitism. In the 1890s he once again spent most of his time on writing projects in philosophy and religion culminating in The Justification of the Good (1897).

Without question Soloviev's thought was the most important philosophical influence on Russian intellectual culture during the Silver Age (1900–17), a period of exceptional creativity in many areas including religious philosophy and theology. Sergei Bulgakov, Nikolai Berdiaev, Pavel Florensky, Evgeny Trubetskoi, Nikolai Lossky, Lev Karsavin, Semyon Frank, A. F. Losev, and many others all drew directly on Soloviev. Soloviev's works, like those of most creative Russian thinkers, were suppressed in Russia during the Soviet decades, although they were preserved in the emigration. The emergence of a subculture of Orthodox dissent in Russia in the 1960s and 1970s led to the recovery of Soloviev's legacy even before the glasnost reforms opened the way to republication of his writings. A complete critical edition of Soloviev's works in twenty volumes is currently being prepared by the Institute of Philosophy of the Russian Academy of Sciences.

Meanwhile, a new challenge to Soloviev's legacy has arisen from Orthodox neotraditionalism. Neotraditionalist theologians regard Soloviev as an aberrant thinker "infected" by German idealism, sophiology, religious universalism, ecumenism, and other tendencies that they reject as contrary to the teachings of the church fathers. Thus the debate about Soloviev continues.

AUTHOR'S PREFACE TO *THE SPIRITUAL FOUNDATIONS OF LIFE* (1882–84)

THE WICKEDNESS AND futility of the way our mortal life is lived is recognized by human reason and conscience, which clamour for its improvement; but man, immersed in this life, has to find some foothold outside of it before he can begin any process of correction. The believer finds this foothold in religion, whose function it is to renew and sanctify our life and make it one with the life of God. This is in the first place a work of God himself, but it cannot be carried through without our co-operation, our life cannot be regenerated without personal action on our own part: religion is a *theandric*, that is to say a divine-human, activity.

With religion, as with everything else, it is first of all necessary to master certain fundamental methods and activities without whose practical background no progress can be made, and these things must not be chosen haphazard and arbitrarily but must be determined by the essence and object of religion itself.

Generally speaking, we live unworthily, inhumanly, enslaved by temporal things; we are in rebellion against God, we quarrel amongst ourselves, we are self-indulgent—the very opposites of the essentials of what life ought to be, a free submission to God, a unity with our neighbours, a control of our natural inclinations. The task then with which we are faced is the correction of our perverted life.

It is quite within our ability to begin to live justly. The beginning of a free submission to God, of harmony with him, is prayer; the beginning of human concord is kindness and charity; the beginning of the conquest of unsupernaturalized nature is an effort towards control of our bodily appetites: personal religion may be said to consist in prayer, alms-deeds, and fasting.[1]

But man lives a social as well as a personal or private life. He lives in an inhabited world, and he has got to live *in peace* with his fellows.[2] But how can we live in peace amid so much discord, when "the whole world lieth in wickedness" [1 John 5:19]? It is imperative not to regard this wickedness as something *unchangeable*, for wickedness is deceptive and constantly changing, and the essential purpose of the world is not evil but peace, concord, unanimity. The common good, the supreme good and truth of the world, resides in the union of all into one will directed towards the same objects; there is no truth in disagreement and separation, and it is only by co-operation, conscious or unconscious, that the universe is kept in being and carried on. No being can subsist in a state of complete isolation, for such isolation is a falsity, in no degree conformed to the truth of universal unity and peace. This unity is acknowledged, in one way or another, willingly or not, by all who seek for truth. Ask a scientist, and he will tell you that the truth of the world is the unity of its universal mechanism; the philosopher, concerned with abstractions, will say that it is manifested in the unity of logical relations that hold it all together. Fully to understand what the world is, it must be seen as a living unity, a body that is endowed with a soul and that is a vehicle of the Godhead: there is the truth of the world, and there too its beauty; when the different forms of sensible phenomena are properly related to one another the resulting harmony is seen as "the beautiful" (*kosmos*, universe, harmony, beauty).

The governing idea of the world as the expression of peace contains everything that we seek, goodness and truth and beauty. But it is impossible that the world's essential purpose should be found only in the mind; the unity that sustains, carries on, and co-ordinates everything in the universe must be more than an abstract idea. It is, in fact, a living personal power of God, and the unifying essence of this power is manifested in the divine-human person of Christ, "for in him dwelleth all the fulness of the Godhead bodily" (*Col.* ii, 9). Were it not for Christ, God would hardly be a living reality to us; all personal religion tends towards Jesus as towards its centre, and it is on him that universal religion is based.

But even Christ, the God-man, cannot be real to us if we see him as nothing more than a figure of history. He must be revealed in the present as well as in the past, and this contemporary revelation is not, cannot be, dependent on us mediocre individuals: Jesus Christ is shown to us as a living reality, independent of our limited personality, by the Church. Those who think they can dispense with any intermediary and obtain personally a full and definite revelation of Christ are certainly *not yet ripe* for that revelation; what they take to be Christ are the fantasies of their own imagination. We have to look for the fullness of Christ, not within our own limited life, but in his universal sphere, the Church.

The Church as such and in her essence holds out to us here on earth the *divine* reality of Christ. Now in this person of Christ the Godhead has united with his substance the created principle of nature and a human nature properly so called,[3] and this union of natures accomplished in the "spiritual man" Jesus Christ as an *individual personality* ought equally to be represented *collectively* in the mankind whom he has spiritualized: the state, the purely human element in social life, and the individual people, the natural element in that life, ought to be in close union and harmony with the divine element, that is, with the Church. It is the office of the Church to sanctify and, with the help of the Christian state, to transfigure the earthly life of man and of society.

It is in this work of social religion that personal religion reaches its fullness: private prayer is shaped and completed by the Holy Mysteries; private philanthropy finds a support in the institutions of a Christian state and through them joins hands with social justice; and it is only where there is a Christian system of economic life that individuals can have a fundamentally right relation with the things of this world and exercise a perfecting influence over that whole creation which "groaneth and travaileth in pain together" [Rom. 8:22] through our fault. Just as by the deflection of our own will we are made partners in the sin that surrounds us, so our amendment lessens that sin; the proper activity of man's will is to carry out, with God's help, those things which conscience presents to him as right in inward and outward, private and public affairs.

Personal religion and social religion are in complete agreement in calling on every man *to pray to God, to do good to his fellows, to restrain his impulses.* They urge him *to unite himself inwardly with Christ, the living God-man; to recognize Christ's active presence in the Church; to make it his aim to bring Christ's spirit to bear upon every aspect and detail of natural human life, that so mankind may forward the Creator's theandric aim, that earth may be oned with Heaven.*[4]

LAW AND MORALITY: ESSAYS IN APPLIED ETHICS (1897)

ON THE DEATH PENALTY

1. The institution of the death penalty[5] is the last important position which *barbaric* criminal law (the direct transformation of *uncivilized* custom) still tries to vindicate in contemporary life. The matter can be considered closed. The densely numbered crowd of its defenders is gradually thinning more and more; the ancient half-rotten idol has gathered around itself what is left of them. But the idol is barely supported by two makeshift clay legs: on the theory of retribution and on the theory of deterrence.

2. . . . In the realm of biblical ideas, a mystical bond shines through between the two grounds for "sanctification": primogeniture and crime, insofar as the firstborn of the human species, Adam, and his firstborn, Cain, were both also the first criminals—one directly against God, the second—against man.[6] Without regard to the theological aspect of the question, we note, however, that precisely the Bible, examined in its entirety, raises human consciousness high above the dark and bloody soil of savage religion and religious savagery, which pagan nations broke loose from only partially in their higher classes, thanks to the development of Greek philosophy and Roman jurisprudence.

Three major moments relative to our question are marked in the Bible:

(1) *The proclamation of a norm* after the first murder: a criminal, even a fratricide, is not subject to human execution: "And the Lord put a mark on Cain, so that no one would kill him."

(2) *Adaptation of the norm* to the "hard-heartedness of people" after the Flood, which was called forth by extreme displays of evil in human nature: "He who spills the blood of a man—a man will spill his blood." This accommodating statute is developed at great length and made more complex in the Mosaic law.

(3) *A return to the norm* in the prophets and in the Gospels: "Vengeance is mine, says the Lord; I will repay." With what will he repay? "Mercy I desire, and not sacrifice." "I came to recover and save the lost."[7]

The Bible is a complex spiritual organism which developed over a thousand years. It is completely free of external monotony and unilinearity but amazing in its internal unity and in the harmony of the whole. To snatch out arbitrarily from this whole only intermediate parts without a beginning and an end is an insincere and frivolous business; and to rely on the

Bible in general in favor of the death penalty—attests either to a hopeless incomprehension or a boundless insolence. Those who, like Joseph de Maistre, draw together the concept of the death penalty with the concept of a sin offering, forget that a sin offering has already been brought for all by Christ, that it has abolished all other blood sacrifices, and itself continues only in the bloodless Eucharist—an amazing lapse in consciousness on the part of persons who confess the Christian faith.[8] Indeed, to permit any kind of sin offerings still—means to deny that which was accomplished by Christ, which means—to betray Christianity. . . .

4. "No one," says a noted scholar who is an expert on this question, "even among the most fiery advocates of the death penalty, could in the defense of its necessity muster even the smallest fact, which would demonstrate that its repeal in the aforementioned States (in Tuscany and others) involved an increase in crime; that it made the social order, life and property of citizens less secure. The aforementioned repeal naturally brought the study of the death penalty down from the clouds of theory to the soil of healthy and honest experience" (Kistiakovsky, p. 11). Thanks to this experience, the personal opinion of individual leading minds *about the uselessness* of the death penalty for the defense of society has now become a positive, experimentally demonstrated truth, and only either ignorance, unscrupulousness, or prejudice can argue against this truth.

But while the death penalty is materially useless for society, it is also spiritually harmful as an immoral action of society itself.

It is a profane, inhumane, and shameful act.

First, the death penalty is profane because in its absoluteness and finality it is an adaptation by human justice of an absolute character, which can belong only to the judgment of God as an expression of divine *omniscience.* After the deliberately and carefully considered expunging of this man from the ranks of the living, society announces: *I know* that this man is absolutely guilty in what took place, that he is absolutely worthless at present, and that he is absolutely irreformable in the future. In fact, nothing fully trustworthy is known to society and its adjudicating organs not only about the future irreformability of this man but also of his past guilt, even regarding the fact itself. Since this has been sufficiently demonstrated by the many judicial errors which have come to light, isn't this a glaringly profane infringement on eternal boundaries and a blind folly of human pride, which puts its relative knowledge and conditional justice in place of omniscient Divine truth? Either the death penalty makes absolutely no sense, or it makes profane sense.

Second, the death penalty is *inhumane*—not from the aspect of sensitivity, but from the aspect of moral principle. The question is completely one of principle: *should* there be any boundary recognized in the human individual regarding external action upon it, something inviolable and not subject to annulment from without? The horror which murder instills sufficiently demonstrates that *there is* such a boundary and that it is connected with the life of man. . . .

The special evil and horror of murder consist, of course, not in the actual taking of life but in the intrinsic renunciation of a basic moral norm, to sever decisively by one's own resolution and action the connection of common human solidarity regarding the actual fellow creature standing before me, who is the same as I am, a bearer of the image and likeness of God. But this *resolution to put an end* to a man more clearly and completely than in simple murder is expressed in the death penalty, where there is absolutely nothing apart from this resolution and carrying it out. Society only has left an *animus interficiendi* in absolutely pure form with respect to the executed criminal, completely free from all those physiological and psychological conditions and motives which darkened and obscured the essence of the matter in the eyes of the criminal himself, whether he committed the murder from calculation of gain or under the influence of a less shameful passion.[9] There can be no such complexities of motivation in the death penalty; the entire business is exposed here: its single goal—to put an end to this man in order that he not be in the world at all. The death penalty is murder, as such, absolute murder that is in principle the denial of a fundamental moral attitude toward man. . . .

While the death penalty is profane and inhumane, it also has a *shameful* nature, which was long ago secured for it by societal sensibility, as is seen in universal contempt for the *executioner*. . . . Here, a man who is unarmed and bound is in advance and wittingly killed by an armed man, risking absolutely nothing and acting exclusively out of lower self-interest. Hence the specifically shameful character of the death penalty and the limitless universal scorn for the executioner.

The direct moral consciousness and feeling so brilliantly expressed in Khomiakov's superb poem *Ritterspruch-Richterspruch* speaks here better than any abstract arguments:

You fly—a whirlwind, on a warhorse,
With your daring princely retinue,—
And the defeated enemy has fallen under horse,
And as a prisoner lies before you.
Will you dismount, will you raise your sword?
Will you tear off the powerless head from its shoulders?
So, he fought with savage fury of battle.
And laid waste cities and villages with fire—

Now he will raise prayerful hands:
Will you kill? O, shame and disgrace!
And if there are many of you, will you kill
The one who is caught in chains,
Who is trampled in the dust, and head bowed in prayer,
Not daring to raise it before you?
So, his soul is black, like the gloom of the grave,
So, the heart in him is ignoble, like a maggot in pus,
So, he is all covered in blood and brigandage,
Now he is powerless, the fire in his gaze is gone,
He is tied by authority, constrained by fear …
Will you kill? O shame and disgrace![10]

… Being contrary to the first principles of morality, the death penalty is at the same time a negation of law at its very essence. We know (see chapter 2) that this essence consists in the balance of two moral interests: of personal freedom and the common good, from which the direct conclusion is that the latter interest (the common good) can only *restrict* the former (personal freedom of each), but in no case can have the intention of its complete abolition, for then obviously any balance would be violated. Therefore, measures against any person whatsoever, inspired by the interest of the common good, in no way can reach as far as the elimination of this person, as such, through the deprivation of his life or through the taking away of his freedom for life. Thus, laws which allow the death penalty, life in exile with hard labor, or life imprisonment cannot be justified from the juridical point of view, as annulling finally a given lawful relationship through the abolition of one of its subjects. And besides, the assertion that the common good in certain cases requires the ultimate abolition of a given person also represents an internal logical contradiction. The common good is *common* only because it contains in itself the good of all individual persons without exception—otherwise it would be only the good of the majority. From this, it does not follow that the common good consist in the simple arithmetic sum of all particular interests separately taken, or include in itself the sphere of freedom of each person in all its infiniteness—this would be another contradiction since these spheres of personal freedom in themselves can negate one another and really do so. But from the concept of the *common* good follows with logical necessity that, while limiting particular interests and aspirations precisely as common (by common boundaries), it in no way can abolish even one bearer of personal freedom, or subject of rights, taking from him life and the very possibility of free action. The common good, according to its very idea, should be the good *of this man too*; but when it deprives him of existence and the possibility of free actions and hence the possibility of any good whatsoever—by the same token this supposed-common good ceases being a good for him too and thus loses its common character, itself becomes only a particular interest and therefore also loses its right to restrict personal freedom.

And in this point we see that the moral ideal fully conforms with the true essence of law. In general, law in its particular character of coercion toward a minimal good, although it does differ from morality in a narrow sense, in no case can contradict it, but even in its coercive character serves the real interest of that same morality. Therefore, if any positive law is found in contradiction of principle with a moral consciousness of the Good, then we can be certain in advance that it does not answer the essential requirements of rights either, and the interest of the law relative to such statutes can in no way consist in their preservation, but only in their *lawful* repeal.[11]

RUSSIA AND THE UNIVERSAL CHURCH (1889)

INTRODUCTION

A hundred years ago France, the vanguard of humanity, set out to inaugurate a new era with the proclamation of the Rights of Man. Christianity had indeed many centuries earlier conferred upon men not only the right but the power to become the sons of God (*edōken autois exousian tekna Theou genesthai*) (John i.12). But the new proclamation made by France was far from superfluous, for this supreme power of mankind was almost entirely ignored in the social life of Christendom. I am not referring so much to particular acts of injustice as to the principles which were recognised by the public conscience, expressed in the laws of the time, and embodied in its social institutions. It was by legal statute that Christian America robbed the Christian Negroes of all their human rights and ruthlessly abandoned them to the tyranny of their masters who themselves professed the Christian religion. In God-fearing England it was the law which condemned to the gallows the man who stole food from his rich neighbour to save himself from starvation. Lastly, it was the laws and institutions of Poland and of "Holy" Russia which allowed the feudal lord to sell his serfs like cattle.[12] I do not presume to pass judgment on the special circumstances of France, nor to decide whether, as distinguished writers more competent than myself declare,[13] the Revolution did this country more harm than good. But let us not forget that if each nation in history works more or less for the whole world, France has the distinction of having taken a step of universal significance in the political and social sphere.

Though the revolutionary movement destroyed many things that needed to be destroyed, though it swept away many an injustice and swept it away for ever, it nevertheless failed lamentably in the attempt to create a social order founded upon justice. Justice is simply the practical expression and application of truth; and the starting-point of the revolutionary movement was false. The declaration of the Rights of Man could only provide a positive principle for social reconstruction if it was based upon a true conception of Man himself. That of the revolutionaries is well-known: they perceived in Man nothing but abstract individuality, a rational being destitute of all positive content.

I do not propose to unmask the internal contradictions of this revolutionary individualism nor to show how this abstract "Man" was suddenly transformed into the no less abstract "Citizen", how the free sovereign individual found himself doomed to be the defenseless slave and victim of the absolute State or "Nation", that is to say, of a group of obscure persons borne to the surface of public life by the eddies of revolution and rendered the more ferocious by the consciousness of their own intrinsic nonentity. No doubt it would be highly interesting and instructive to follow the thread of logic which connects the doctrines of 1789 with the events of 1793. But I believe it to be still more important to recognise that the *prōton pseudos*, the basic falsehood, of the Revolution—the conception of the individual man as a being complete in and for himself—that this false notion of individualism was not the invention of the revolutionaries or of their spiritual forbears, the Encyclopaedists, but was the logical, though unforeseen, issue of an earlier pseudo-Christian or semi-Christian doctrine which has been the root cause of all the anomalies in the past history and present state of Christendom.

Men have imagined that the acknowledgment of the divinity of Christ relieves them of the obligation of taking His words seriously. They have twisted certain texts of the Gospel so as to get out of them the meaning they want, while they have conspired to pass over in silence other texts which do not lend themselves to such treatment. The precept "Render to Caesar the things that are Caesar's, and to God the things that are God's" [Matt. 22:21, Mark 12:17, Luke 20:25] is constantly quoted to sanction an order of things which gives Caesar all and God nothing. The saying "My Kingdom is not of this world" [John 18:36] is always being used to justify and confirm the paganism of our social and political life, as though Christian society were destined to belong to this world and not to the Kingdom of Christ. On the other hand the saying "All power is given Me in heaven and earth" [Matt. 28:18] is never quoted. Men are ready to accept Christ as sacrificing Priest and atoning Victim; but they do not want Christ the King. His royal dignity has been ousted by every kind of pagan despotism, and Christian peoples have taken up the cry of the Jewish rabble: "We have no king but Caesar!" [John 19:15]. Thus history has witnessed, and we are still witnessing, the curious phenomenon of a society which professes Christianity as its religion but remains pagan not merely in its life but in the very basis of that life.

This dichotomy is not so much a logical *non sequitur* as a moral failure. That is obvious from the hypocrisy and sophism which are characteristic of the arguments commonly used to justify this state of affairs. "Slavery and severe hardship," said a bishop renowned in Russia thirty years ago, "are not contrary to the spirit of Christianity; for physical suffering is not a hindrance to the salvation of the soul, which is the one and only end of our religion." As though the infliction of physical suffering by a man on his fellow-men did not imply in him a moral depravity and an act of injustice and cruelty which were certainly imperilling the salvation of *his* soul! Granted even—though the supposition is absurd—that a Christian society can be insensible to the sufferings of the oppressed, the question remains whether it can be indifferent to the sin of the oppressors.

Economic slavery, even more than slavery properly so called, has found its champions in the Christian world. Society and the State, they maintain, are in no way bound to take general and regular measures against pauperism; voluntary almsgiving is enough; did not Christ say that there would always be the poor on earth? Yes, there will always be the poor; there will also always be the sick, but does that prove the uselessness of health services? Poverty in itself is no more an evil than sickness; the evil consists in remaining indifferent to the sufferings of one's neighbour. And it is not a question only of the poor; the rich also have a claim on our compassion. These poor rich! We do everything to develop their bump of acquisitiveness, and then we expect them to enter the Kingdom of God through the imperceptible opening of individual charity. Besides, it is well known that authoritative scholars see in the phrase "the eye of a needle" simply a literal translation of the Hebrew name given to one of the gates of Jerusalem (*negeb-ha-khammath* or *khur-ha-khammath*) which it was difficult for camels to pass through. Surely then it is not the infinitesimal contribution of personal philanthropy which the Gospel enjoins upon the rich, but rather the narrow and difficult, but nevertheless practicable, way of social reform

This desire to limit the social action of Christianity to individual charity, this attempt to deprive the Christian moral code of its binding character and its positive legal sanction is a modern version of that ancient Gnostic antithesis (the system of Marcion in particular) so often anathematised by the Church. That all human relationships should be governed by charity and brotherly love is undoubtedly the express will of God and the end of His creation; but in historic reality, as in the Lord's Prayer, the fulfillment of the divine will on earth is only realised after the hallowing of God's Name and the coming of His Kingdom. The Name of God is Truth; His Kingdom is Justice. It follows that the knowledge of the truth and the practice of justice are necessary conditions for the triumph of evangelical charity in human society.

In truth all are one; and God, the absolute Unity, is all in all. But this divine Unity is hidden from our view by the world of evil and illusion, the result of universal human sin. The basic condition of this world is the division and isolation of the parts of the Great Whole; and even Man, who should have been the unifying rationale of the material universe, finds himself split up and scattered over the earth, and has been unable by his own efforts to achieve more than a partial and unstable unity, the universal monarchy of paganism. This monarchy, first represented by Tiberius and Nero, received its true unifying principle when "grace and truth" were manifested in Jesus Christ [John 1:17]. Once united to God, the human race recovered its own unity. But this unity had to be threefold to be complete; it had to realise its ideal perfection on the basis of a divine fact and in the midst of the life of mankind. Since mankind is objectively separated from the divine unity, this unity must in the first place be given to us as an objective reality independent of ourselves—the Kingdom of God coming amongst us, the external, objective Church. But once reunited to this external unity, men must translate it into action, they must assimilate it by their own efforts—the Kingdom of God is to be taken by force, and the men of violence possess it [Matt. 11:12]. At first manifested *for* us and then *by* us, the Kingdom of God must finally be revealed *in* us in all its intrinsic, absolute perfection as love, peace and joy in the Holy Spirit.

Thus the Church Universal (in the broad sense of the word) develops as a threefold union of the divine and the human: there is the priestly union, in which the divine element, absolute and unchangeable, predominates and forms the Church properly so called (the Temple of God); there is the kingly union, in which the human element predominates and which forms the Christian State (the Church as the living Body of God); and there is lastly the prophetic union, in which the divine and the human must penetrate one another in free mutual interaction and so form the perfect Christian society (the Church as the Spouse of God).

The moral basis of the priestly union, or of the Church in the strict sense of the word, is faith and religious devotion; the kingly union of the Christian State is based on law and justice; while the element proper to the prophetic union or the perfect society is freedom and love.

The Church, in the narrower sense, represented by the hierarchy, reunites mankind to God by the profession of the true faith and the grace of the sacraments. But if the faith communicated by the Church to Christian humanity is a living faith, and if the grace of the sacraments is an effectual grace, the resultant union of the divine and the human cannot be limited to the special domain of religion, but must extend to all Man's common relationships and must regenerate and transform his social and political life. Here opens up a field of action which is man's own proper sphere. The divine-human action is no longer an accomplished fact as in the priestly Church, but a task awaiting fulfilment, the task of making the divine Truth a reality in human society, of putting Truth into practice; and Truth, expressed in practice, is called Justice.

Truth is the absolute existence of all in unity; it is the universal solidarity which exists eternally in God, but which has been lost by the natural man and recovered in principle by Christ, the spiritual Man. It remains for human activity to continue the unifying work of the God-Man by contesting the world with the contrary principle of egoism and division. Each single being, whether nation, class, or individual, in so far as it asserts its own individuality in isolation from the divine-human sum of things, is acting against Truth; and Truth, if it is alive in us, must react and manifest itself as Justice. Thus having recognised the universal solidarity, the All-in-One, as Truth, and having put it into practice as Justice, regenerate Man will be able to perceive it as his inmost essence and to enjoy it fully in the spirit of freedom and love.[14]

THE JUSTIFICATION OF THE GOOD (1897)

THE ECONOMIC QUESTION FROM THE MORAL POINT OF VIEW

V

In opposition to the alleged economic harmony, facts compel us to admit that starting with private material interest as the purpose of labour we arrive at universal discord and destruction instead of universal happiness. If, however, the principle and the purpose of labour is found in the idea of the common good, understood in the true moral sense—i.e. as the good of all and each and not of the majority only—that idea will also contain the satisfaction of every private interest within proper limits.

From the moral point of view every man, whether he be an agricultural labourer, a writer, or a banker, ought to work with a feeling that his work is useful to all, and with a desire for it to be so; he ought to regard it as a duty, as a fulfilment of the law of God and a service to the universal welfare of his fellow-men. But just because this duty is universal, it presupposes that every one else must regard the person in question in the same way, *i.e.* to treat him not as a means only but as an end or purpose of the activity of all. The duty of society is to recognise and to secure to each of its members the *right* to enjoy unmolested *worthy* human existence both for himself and his family. Worthy existence is compatible with voluntary poverty, such as St. Francis preached and as is practised by our wandering pilgrims; but it is incompatible with work which reduces all the significance of man to being simply a means for producing or transferring material wealth. Here are some instances.

"We watch the *kriuchniks* [stevedores] at work: the poor half-naked Ta-tars strain every nerve. It is painful to see the bent back flatten out all of a sudden under a weight of eight to eighteen puds (the last figure is not exaggerated). This terrible work is paid at the rate of five roubles per thou-sand puds.[15] The most a *kriuchnik* can earn in the twenty-four hours is one rouble, and that if he works like an ox and overstrains himself. Few can en-dure more than ten years of such labour, and the two-legged beasts of bur-den become deformed or paralytic" (*Novoe Vremya*, N. 7356). Those who have not seen the Volga *kriuchniks* are sure to have seen the porters in big hotels who, breathless and exhausted, drag to the fourth or fifth floor boxes weighing several hundredweight. And this in our age of machines and all sorts of contrivances! No one seems to be struck by the obvious absurdity. A visitor arrives at an hotel with luggage. To walk up the stairs would be a useful exercise for him, but instead he gets into a lift, while his things, for which, one would have thought, the lift was expressly meant, are loaded on the back of the porter, who thus proves to be not even an instrument of another man but an instrument of his things—the means of a means!

Labour which is exclusively and crudely mechanical and involves too great a strain of the muscular force is incompatible with human digni-ty. But equally incompatible with it and equally immoral is work which, though in itself not heavy or degrading, lasts all day long and takes up *all* the time and *all* the forces of the person, so that the few hours of lei-sure are necessarily devoted to physical rest, and neither time nor energy is left for thoughts and interests of the ideal or spiritual order.[16] In addi-tion to hours of leisure, there are, of course, entire days of rest—Sundays and other holidays. But the exhausting and stupefying physical work of the week produces in holiday time a natural reaction—a craving to plunge into dissipation and to forget oneself, and the days of rest are devoted to the satisfaction of that craving.

"Let us not, however, dwell on the impression which individual facts susceptible of observation produce upon us, even though such facts be numerous. Let us turn to statistics and inquire as to how far wages satisfy the necessary wants of the workers. Leaving aside the rate of wages in the different industries, the quality of food, the size of the dwelling, etc., we will only ask of statistics the question as to the relation between the length of human life and the occupation pursued. The answer is as follows: Shoemakers live on the average to the age of 49; printers, 48.3; tailors, 46.6; joiners, 44.7; blacksmiths, 41.8; turners, 41.6; masons, 33. And the average length of life of civil servants, capitalists, clergymen, wholesale merchants, is 60–69 years.[17] Now take the figures referring to the death-rate in relation to the size of the dwellings and the amount of rent in the different parts of town. It will be seen that in parts of the town with a poor population, belonging chiefly to the working class and paying low rents, mortality is far higher than in the neighbourhood with a relatively larger number of rich people. For Paris this relation was established by Villarmé as early as the 'twenties of the present century. He calculated that during the five years from 1822 to 1826, in the II. arrondissement of Paris, where the average rent per flat was 605 francs, there was one death per 71 inhabitants, while in the arrondissement XII., where the average rent was 148 francs, there was one death per 44 inhabitants. Similar data are at hand for many other towns, Petersburg among them."[18] Hence the following true conclusion is deduced: "If a workman is not regarded as a means of production, but is recognised, like every other human being, to be a free agent and an end in himself, the average forty years of life cannot be regarded as normal, while men belonging to richer classes live on the average till sixty or seventy years. This life, the longest possible under the social conditions of the present day, must be regarded as normal. All deviation below this average, unless it can be ascribed to the peculiarities of the particular work in question, must be entirely put down to excessive labour and insufficient income which does not allow to satisfy the most essential needs and the minimum demands of hygiene with regard to food, clothing, and housing."[19]

The absolute value of man is based, as we know, upon the *possibility* inherent in his reason and his will of infinitely approaching perfection or, according to the patristic expression, the possibility of becoming divine (*theōsis*). This possibility does not pass into actuality completely and immediately, for if it did man would be already equal to God—which is not the case. The inner potentiality *becomes* more and more actual, and can only do so under definite real conditions. If an ordinary man is left for many years on an uninhabited island or in strict solitary confinement he cannot improve morally or intellectually, and indeed, exhibits rapid and obvious regress towards the brutal stage. Strictly speaking, the same is true of a man wholly absorbed in physical labour. Even if he does not deteriorate he is certainly unable to think of actively realising his highest significance as man. The moral point of view demands, then, that everyone should have the means of existence (*e.g.* clothes and a warm and airy dwelling) and sufficient physical *rest* secured to him, and that he should also be able to enjoy *leisure* for the sake of his spiritual development. This and *this alone* is *absolutely* essential for every peasant and workman; *anything above this is from the evil one.*[20]

MORALITY AND LEGAL JUSTICE

I

The *absolute* moral principle, the *demand*, namely, or the *commandment* to be perfect as our Father in heaven is perfect, or to realise in ourselves the image and likeness of God, already contains in its very nature the recognition of the *relative* element in morality. For it is clear that the demand for perfection can only be addressed to a being who is imperfect; urging him to *become* like the higher being, the commandment presupposes the lower stages and the relative degrees of advance. Thus, the absolute moral principle or the perfect good is for us, to use Hegel's language, a unity of itself and its other, a synthesis of the absolute and the relative. The existence of the relative or the imperfect, as distinct from the absolute good, is a fact not to be got over, and to deny it, to *confuse* the two terms, or, with the help of dialectical tricks and on the strength of mystical emotions, to affirm them as identical, would be false. Equally false, however, is the opposite course—the *separation*, namely, of the relative from the absolute, as of two wholly distinct spheres which have nothing in common. From this dualistic point of view man himself, whose striving towards the absolute is inseparably connected with relative conditions, proves to be the incarnation of absurdity. The only rational point of view, which both reason and conscience compel us to adopt, consists in recognising that the actual duality between the relative and the absolute resolves itself for us into a free and complete unity (but not by any means into an empty identity of indifference) through the real and moral process of approaching perfection—a process ranging from the rigid stone to the glory and freedom of the sons of God.

At each stage the relative is connected with the absolute as a means for *concretely* bringing about the perfection of all; and this connection justifies the lesser good as a condition of the greater. At the same time it justifies the absolute good itself, which would not be absolute if it could not connect with itself or include in one way or another all concrete relations. And indeed, nowhere in the world accessible to us do we find the two terms in separation or in their bare form. Everywhere the absolute principle is clothed with relative forms, and the relative is inwardly connected with the absolute and held together by it. The difference lies simply in the comparative predominance of one or the other aspect. . . .

V

The fact that we speak of *moral right* and moral duty, on the one hand proves the absence of any fundamental opposition or incompatibility of the moral and the juridical principles, and, on the other, indicates an essential difference between them. In designating a given right (*e.g.* the right of my enemy to my love) as *moral* only, we imply that in addition to the moral there exists other rights, *i.e.* rights in a more restricted sense, or that there exists *right as such*, which is not directly and immediately characterised as moral. Take, on the one hand, the duty of loving our enemies and their corresponding right to our love, and on the other, take the duty to pay one's debts, or the duty not to rob and murder one's neighbours and their corresponding right not to be robbed, murdered, or deceived by us. It is obvious that there is an essential difference between the two kinds of relation, and that only the second of them falls within the scope of justice in the narrow sense of the term.

The difference can be reduced to three main points:

(1) A purely moral demand, such, *e.g.*, as the love for one's enemies, is unlimited or all-embracing in nature; it presupposes moral perfection, or, at any rate, an unlimited striving towards perfection. Every limitation admitted as a matter of *principle* is opposed to the nature of the moral commandment and undermines its dignity and significance. If a person gives up the absolute moral ideal as a principle, he gives up morality itself and leaves the moral ground. Juridical law, on the contrary, is essentially limited, as is clearly seen in all cases of its application. In the pace of perfection it demands the lowest, the minimum degree of morality, that is, simply, actual restraint of certain manifestations of the immoral will. This distinction, however, is not an opposition leading to real conflict. From the moral point of view it cannot be denied that the demand conscientiously to fulfil monetary obligations, to abstain from murder, robbery, etc., is a demand for what is good—though extremely elementary—and not for what is evil. It is clear that if we ought to love our enemies, it goes without saying that we ought to respect the life and property of all fellow-men. The higher

commandments cannot be fulfilled without observing the lower. As to the juridical side of the matter, though the civil or the penal law does not demand the supreme moral perfection, it is not opposed to it. Forbidding every one to murder or be fraudulent, it cannot, and indeed has no need to, prevent any one from loving his enemies. Thus with regard to this point (which in certain moral theories is erroneously taken to be the only important one), the relation between the principles of the practical life may be only expressed by saying that *legal justice is the lowest limit or the minimum degree of morality.*

(2) The unlimited character of the purely moral demands leads to another point of difference. The way in which such demands are to be fulfilled is not definitely prescribed, nor is it limited to any concrete external manifestations or material actions. The commandment to love one's enemies does not indicate, except as an example, what precisely we ought to do in virtue of that love, *i.e.* which particular actions we ought to perform and from which to abstain. At the same time, if love is expressed by means of definite actions, the moral commandment cannot be regarded as already fulfilled by these actions and as demanding nothing further. The task of fulfilling the commandment, which is an expression of the absolute perfection, remains infinite. Juridical laws, on the contrary, prescribe or prohibit perfectly definite external actions, with the performance or non-performance of which the law is satisfied and demands nothing further. If I produce in due time the money I am owing, and pass it to my creditor, if I do not murder or rob any one, etc., the law is satisfied and wants nothing more from me. This difference between the moral and the juridical law once more involves no contradiction. The demand for the moral inner disposition, so far from excluding actions, directly presupposes them as its own proof or justification. No one would believe in the inward goodness of a man if it never showed itself in any works of mercy. On the other hand, the request to perform definite actions is in no way opposed to the inner states corresponding to them, though it does not demand them. Both the moral and the juridical laws are concerned with the inner being of man, with his will; but while the first takes this will in its universality and entirety, the second has only to do with particular expressions of it in respect of certain external facts, which fall within the province of justice in the narrow sense,— such as the inviolability of the life and property of each person, etc. What is of importance from the juridical point of view is precisely the objective expression of our will in committing or in refraining from certain actions. This is another essential characteristic of legal justice, and, in addition to the original definition of it as a certain minimum of morality, we may now say that legal justice is the demand for the *realisation* of this minimum, *i.e.*

for *carrying out a certain minimum of the good*, or, what is the same thing, for doing away with a certain amount of evil. Morality in the strict sense is immediately concerned, not with the external realisation of the good, but with its inner existence in the heart of man.

(3) This second distinction involves a third one. The demand for moral perfection as an inner state presupposes free or voluntary fulfilment. Not only physical but even psychological compulsion is here, from the nature of the case, both undesirable and impossible. External realisation of a certain uniform order, on the contrary, admits of direct or indirect *compulsion*. And in so far as the direct and immediate purpose of legal justice is precisely the realisation or the external embodiment of a certain good—*e.g.* of public safety—in so far the compelling character of the law is a necessity; for no genuine person could seriously maintain that by means of verbal persuasion alone all murders, frauds, etc., could be immediately stopped.

VI

Combining the three characteristics indicated we obtain the following definition of legal justice in its relation to morality: *legal justice is a compulsory demand for the realisation of a definite minimum of the good, or for a social order which excludes certain manifestations of evil.*

The question has now to be asked, what is the ground for such a demand, and in what way is this compulsory order compatible with the purely moral order, which apparently by its very nature excludes all compulsion. . . .

The moral law has been given to man "that he might live thereby"; and if human society did not exist, morality would remain merely an abstract idea. The existence of society, however, depends not on the perfection of some, but on the security of all. This security is not guaranteed by the moral law, which is non-existent for persons in whom anti-social instincts predominate, but it is safeguarded by the compulsory law which has actual power over every one. To appeal to the gracious power of Providence to restrain and exhort lunatics and criminals is sheer blasphemy. It is impious to lay upon the Deity that which can be successfully performed by a good legal system.

The moral principle demands, then, that men should freely seek perfection. To this end the existence of society is necessary. Society cannot exist if each person wishing to do so may, without let or hindrance, rob and murder his neighbours. Hence the compulsory law, which actually prevents these extreme expressions of the evil will, is a *necessary condition of moral perfection*; as such it is demanded by the moral principle itself, though it is not a direct expression of it.[21]

THE MORAL ORGANISATION OF HUMANITY AS A WHOLE

XIII

... Just as the Church is collectively organised piety, so the state is collectively organised pity. To affirm, therefore, that from its very nature the Christian religion is opposed to the state is to affirm that the Christian religion is opposed to pity. In truth, however, the Gospel not merely insists upon the morally binding character of pity or altruism, but decidedly confirms the view, expressed already in the Old Testament, that there can be no true piety apart from pity: "I will have mercy and not sacrifice" [Matt. 9:13, 12:7; cf. Hos. 6:6].

If, however, pity be admitted in principle, it is logically inevitable to admit also the historical organisation of social forces and activities, which raises pity from the stage of a powerless and limited feeling and gives it actuality, wide application, and means of development. From the point of view of pity it is impossible to reject the institution owing to which one can *practically pity*, i.e. *give help and protection* to tens and hundreds of millions of men instead of dozens or at most hundreds of people.

The definition of the state (so far as its moral significance is concerned) as organised pity can only be rejected through misconception. Some of these misconceptions must be considered before we go on to deal with the conception of the Christian state.

XIV

It is urged that the stern and often cruel character of the state obviously contradicts the definition of it as organised pity. But this objection is based on a confusion between the necessary and sensible severity and useless and arbitrary cruelty. The first is not opposed to pity, and the second, being an abuse, *is opposed to the very meaning of the state*, and therefore does not contradict the definition of the state—of the normal state, of course—as organised pity. The supposed contradiction is based upon grounds as superficial as the argument that the senseless cruelty of an unsuccessful surgical operation and the sufferings of the patient in the case even of a successful operation are in obvious contradiction to the idea of surgery as a beneficent art helpful to man in certain bodily sufferings. It is obvious that such representatives of state authority as Ivan the Terrible are as little evidence against the altruistic basis of the state, as bad surgeons are against the usefulness of surgery. I am aware that an educated reader may well feel insulted at being reminded of such elementary truths, but if he is acquainted with the recent movement of thought in Russia he will not hold me responsible for the insult.[22]

But, it will be maintained, even the most normal state is inevitably pitiless. In pitying peaceful people whom it defends against men of violence, it is bound to treat the latter without pity. Such *one-sided* pity is out of keeping with the moral ideal. This is indisputable, but again it says nothing against our definition of the state, for, in the first place, even one-sided pity is pity and not anything else; and secondly, even the normal state is not by any means an expression of the moral ideal already attained, but only one of the *chief means* necessary for its attainment. The ideal condition of mankind, or the Kingdom of God, when *attained*, is obviously incompatible with the state, but it is also incompatible with pity. When everything will once more be good there will be no one to pity. And so long as there are men to be pitied, there are men to be defended; and the moral demand for organising such protection efficiently and on a wide scale—*i.e.* the moral significance of the state—remains in force. As for the pitilessness of the state to those from whom or against whom it has to defend the peaceful society, it is not anything fatal or inevitable; and although it undoubtedly is a fact, it is not an unchangeable fact. In point of history there is no doubt that the relation of the state towards its enemies is becoming less cruel, and consequently more merciful. In old days they used to be put to painful death together with their family and relatives (as is still the case in China). Later, everyone had to answer for himself, and subsequently the very character of the responsibility has changed. Criminals have ceased to be tormented solely for the sake of inflicting pain; and at the present time the positive task of helping them morally is recognised. What can be the ultimate reason of such a change? When the state limits or abolishes the penalty of death, abolishes torture and corporal punishment, is concerned with improving prisons and places of exile, it is obvious that in pitying and protecting peaceful citizens who suffer from crimes, it begins to extend its pity to the opposite side also—to the criminals themselves. The reference, therefore, to the one-sided pity is beginning to lose force as a fact. And it is through the state alone that the organisation of pity ceases to be one-sided, since the human crowd is still for the most part guided in its relation to the enemies of society by the old pitiless maxims, "to the dog, a dog's death" ; "the thief deserves all he gets"; "as a warning to others," etc. Such maxims are losing their practical force precisely owing to the state, which is in this case more free from partiality either to the one side or the other. Restraining with an authoritative hand the vindictive instincts of the crowd, ready to tear the criminal to pieces, the state at the same time never renounces the humane duty to oppose crimes,—as the strange moralists, who in truth pity only the aggressive, violent, and rapacious, and are utterly indifferent to their victims, would have it do. This indeed is a case of one-sided pity!

XV

Our definition of state may lead to a less crude misconception on the part of the jurists, who regard the state as the embodiment of legality as an absolutely independent principle, distinct from morality in general and from motives of pity in particular. The true distinction between legal justice and morality has already been indicated. It does not destroy the connection between them; on the contrary, it is due to that connection. If this distinction is to be replaced by separation and opposition, an unconditional principle must be found which shall ultimately determine every legal relation as such and be altogether outside of, and as far as possible removed from, the moral sphere.

Such an a-moral and even anti-moral principle is to be found in the first place in *might* or force: *Macht geht vor Recht*. That in the order of history relations based upon right follow those based upon force is as unquestionable as the fact that in the history of our planet the organic life appeared after the inorganic and on the basis of it—which does not prove, of course, that inorganic matter is the specific principle of the organic forms as such. The play of natural forces in humanity is simply the *material* for relations determined by the conception of right and not the principle of such relations, since otherwise there could be no distinction between right and rightlessness. Right means the *limitation* of might, and the whole point is the *nature* of the limitation. Similarly, morality might be defined as *the overcoming of evil*, which does not imply that evil is the principle of morality.

We shall not advance any further in the definition of right if we replace the conception of might, derived from the physical sphere, by the more human conception of freedom. That individual freedom lies at the basis of all relations determined by law there can be no doubt, but is it really the unconditional principle of legality? There are two reasons why this cannot be the case. In the first place, because in reality it is *not unconditional*, and, secondly, because it is not the determining principle of *legality*. With regard to the first point, I mean not that human freedom is never unconditional, but that it is not unconditional in that sphere of concrete relations in which and for the sake of which law exists. Suppose that some man living in the flesh on earth actually possessed absolute freedom, that is, that he could by the act of his will alone, independently of any external circumstances and necessary intermediate processes, accomplish everything he wished. It is obvious that such a man would stand outside the sphere of relations determined by legality. If his unconditionally free will determined itself on the side of evil, no external action could limit it; it would be inaccessible to law and authority. And if it were determined on the side of the good it would make all law and all authority superfluous.

It is then irrelevant to speak of unconditional freedom in this connection, since it belongs to quite a different sphere of relations. Legality is concerned only with limited and conditional freedom, and the question is precisely as to what limitations or conditions are lawful. The liberty of one person is limited by the liberty of another, but not every such limitation is consistent with the principle of legality. If the freedom of one man is limited by the freedom of his neighbour who is free to wring his neck or chain him up at his pleasure, there can be no question of legality at all, and in any case such a limitation of freedom shows no specific characteristics of the principle of legality as such. These characteristics must be sought not in the mere fact of the limitation of freedom, but in the equal and universal character of the limitation. If the freedom of one is limited to the same extent as the freedom of the other, or if the free activity of each meets with a restriction that is common to all, then only is the limitation of freedom determined by the conception of law.

The principle of legality is then freedom within the limits of equality, or freedom conditioned by equality—consequently a conditional freedom. But the equality which determines it is not an absolutely independent principle either. The essential characteristic of the legal norms is that, in addition to equality, they should necessarily answer, too, the demand for *justice*. Although these two ideas are akin, they are far from being identical. When the Pharaoh issued a law commanding to put to death all the Jewish new-born babes, this law was certainly not unjust on account of the unequal treatment of the Jewish and the Egyptian babes. And if the Pharaoh subsequently gave orders to put to death all new-born infants and not only the Jewish ones, no one would venture to call this new law just, although it would satisfy the demand for equality. Justice is not mere equality, but *equality in fulfilling that which is right*. A just debtor is not one who equally refuses to pay all his creditors but who equally pays them all. A just father is not one who is equally indifferent to all his children but who shows equal love for all of them.

Equality, then, can be just or unjust, and it is the just equality or, in the last resort, justice that determines the legal norms. The conception of justice at once introduces us into the moral sphere. And in that sphere we know that each virtue is not in a cage by itself, but all of them, justice among them, are different modifications of one or, rather, of the threefold principle which determines our rightful relation to everything. And since justice is concerned with man's moral interaction with his fellow-beings, it is merely a species of the moral motive which lies at the basis of inter-human relations, namely of pity: *justice is pity equally applied*.

In so far then as legality is determined by justice it is essentially related to the moral sphere. All definitions of law which try to separate it from

morality leave its real nature untouched. Thus, in addition to the definition already mentioned, Jering's famous definition declares that "law is a
protected or safeguarded interest."[23] There can be no doubt that law does
defend interest, but not every interest. It obviously defends only the just
interests or, in other words, it defends every interest in so far as it is just.
What, however, is meant by justice in this connection? To say that a just
interest is an interest safe-guarded by law is to be guilty of the crudest possible logical circle which can only be avoided if justice be once more taken
in its essential, *i.e.* in its moral, sense. This does not prevent us from recognising that the moral principle itself, so far as the inevitable conditions of
its existence are concerned, is realised in different ways, and to a greater
or lesser degree. For instance there is the distinction between the external,
formal, or strictly-legal justice and the inner, essential, or purely-moral justice, the supreme and ultimate standard of right and wrong being one and
the same—namely, the moral principle. Possible conflict between "outer"
and "inner" justice in particular cases is in itself no argument against their
being essentially one, since similar conflict may arise in the carrying out
of the simplest and most fundamental moral demands. Thus, for instance,
pity may demand that I should save two men who are drowning, but being unable to save both, I have to choose between the two. The cases of
difficult choice between complex applications of legal justice and morality
in the strict sense are no proof of there being any essential and irreducible
opposition between the two. The argument that the conceptions of justice
and morality alter in the course of history is equally unconvincing. It might
carry some weight if the rights and laws remained meanwhile unchanged.
In truth, however, they change even more according to place and time.
What conclusion, then, are we to adopt? There is change in the particular
conceptions of justice, there is change in the rights and laws, but one thing
remains unchangeable: the demand that the rights and laws should be just.
The inner dependence of legal forms upon morality—independently of all
external conditions—remains a fact. To avoid this conclusion one would
have to go very far—to the country, seen by the pilgrim women in Ostrovsky's play, where lawful requests to Mahmut of Persia and Mahmut of
Turkey were to begin by the phrase "Judge me, O thou *unjust* judge." [24]

XVI

The connection of right with morality makes it possible to speak of the
Christian state. It would be unjust to maintain that in pre-Christian times
the state had no moral foundation. In the kingdoms of Judaea and of Israel, the prophets directly put moral demands to the state, and reproached
it for not fulfilling these demands. In the pagan world it is sufficient to

mention Theseus, for instance, who at the risk of his life freed his subjects from the cannibalistic tribute to Crete, in order to recognise that here too the fundamental moral motive of the state was pity, demanding active help to the injured and the suffering. The difference between the Christian and the pagan state is not then in their natural basis but in something else. From the Christian point of view the state is only a part in the organisation of the collective man—a part conditioned by another higher part, the Church, which consecrates the state in its work of serving indirectly in its own worldly sphere and by its own means the unconditional purpose which the Church directly puts before it—to prepare humanity and the whole earth for the Kingdom of God. From this follow the two chief tasks of the state—the conservative and the progressive: to *preserve the foundations of social life apart from which humanity could not exist*, and *to improve the conditions of its existence* by furthering the free development of all human powers which are to be the instrument of the future perfection, and apart from which the Kingdom of God could not be realised in humanity. It is clear that just as without the conservative activity of the state humanity would fall apart and there would be *no one left* to enter the fulness of life, so without its progressive activity mankind would always remain at the same stage of the historical process, would never attain the power finally to receive or to reject the Kingdom of God, and therefore there would be *nothing to live for.*

In paganism it was the conservative task of the state that was exclusively predominant. Although the state furthered historical progress, it did so involuntarily and unconsciously. The supreme purpose of action was not put by the agents themselves, it was not *their* purpose since they had not yet heard "the gospel of the kingdom." The progress itself, therefore, although it formally differed from the gradual perfecting of the kingdoms of the physical nature did not really have a purely-human character: it is unworthy of man to move in spite of himself to a purpose he does not know. God's word gives a beautiful image of the great heathen kingdoms as powerful and wonderful *beasts* which rapidly appear and disappear. The natural, earthly men have no final significance, and cannot have it; and the state, created by such men, is their collective embodiment. But the pagan state, conditional and transitory in nature, affirmed itself as unconditional. Pagans began by deifying individual *bodies* (astral, vegetable, animal, and especially human) in the multitude of their various gods, and they ended by deifying the collective body—the state (cult of the kings in the Eastern kingdoms, the apotheosis of the Roman emperors).

The pagans erred not in ascribing positive significance to the state, but only in thinking that it possessed that significance *on its own account.* This was obviously untrue. Neither the individual nor the collective body of man has life on its own account but receives it from the spirit that inhabits it. This is clearly proved by the fact of the decomposition both of the individual and of the collective bodies. The perfect body is that in which dwells the spirit of God. Christianity, therefore, demands not that we should reject or limit the power of the state, but that we should fully recognise the principle which alone may render the significance of the state actually complete—namely, its moral solidarity with the cause of the Kingdom of God on earth, all worldly purposes being inwardly subordinated to the one spirit of Christ.

XVII

The question as to the relation of the Church to the state, which has arisen in Christian times, can be solved in principle from the point of view here indicated. The Church is, as we know, a divinely-human organisation, morally determined by piety. From the nature of the case the Divine principle decidedly predominates in the Church over the human. In the relation between them the first is pre-eminently active and the second preeminently passive. This obviously must be the case when the human will is in direct correlation with the Divine. The active manifestation of the human will, demanded by the Deity itself, is only possible in the worldly sphere collectively represented by the state, which had reality previously to the revelation of the Divine principle, and is in no direct dependence upon it. The *Christian* state is related to the Deity, as the Church is; it too is in a certain sense an organisation of the God-in-man, but in it the human element predominates. This is only possible because the Divine principle is realised not *in* the state, but *for* it in the Church. So that in the state the Divine principle gives *full play* to the human and allows it *independently* to serve the supreme end. From the moral point of view both the independent activity of man and his absolute submission to the Deity as such are equally necessary. This antinomy can only be solved and the two positions united by distinguishing the two spheres of life (the religious and the political), and their two immediate motives (piety and pity), corresponding to the difference in the immediate object of action, the final purpose being one and the same. Pious attitude towards a perfect God demands pity for men. The Christian church demands a Christian state. Here as elsewhere *separation* instead of *distinction* leads to *confusion*, and confusion to dissension and perdition. Complete separation of the Church from the state compels the Church to do one of two things. It either has to renounce all active service of the good and to give itself up to quietism and indifference—which is contrary to the spirit of Christ; or, zealous actively to prepare the world for the coming of God's kingdom, but, in its separation and alienation from the state, having no means at its command for carrying out its spiritual activity, the Church, in the person of its authoritative representatives has itself to seize the concrete instruments of worldly activity, to interfere in all earthly affairs and, absorbed in the question of means, forget its original purpose—an unquestionably pure and high one—more and more. Were such confusion allowed to become permanent, the Church would lose the very ground of its existence. The separation proves to be no less harmful to the other side. The state separated from the Church either gives up spiritual interests altogether, loses its supreme consecration and dignity, as well as the moral respect and the material submission of its subjects, or, conscious of the importance of the spiritual interests for the life of man, but, in its separation from the Church, having no competent and independent institution to which it could entrust the supreme care of the spiritual good of its subjects,—the task of preparing the nations for the Kingdom of God,—it decides to take that task upon itself. To do so consistently the state would have to assume *ex officio* the supreme spiritual authority—which would be a mad and dangerous usurpation recalling the "man of lawlessness" [2 Thess. 2:3] of the last days. It is clear that in forgetting its filial attitude towards the Church, the state would be acting in its own name, and not in the name of the Father.

The normal relation, then, between the state and the Church is this. *The state recognises the supreme spiritual authority of the universal Church, which indicates the general direction of the goodwill of mankind and the final purpose of its historical activity. The Church leaves to the state full power to bring lawful worldly interests into conformity with this supreme will and to harmonise political relations and actions with the requirements of this supreme purpose. The Church must have no power of compulsion, and the power of compulsion exercised by the state must have nothing to do with the domain of religion.*

The state is the intermediary social sphere between the Church on the one hand and the material society on the other. The absolute aims of religious and moral order which the Church puts before humanity and which it represents, cannot be realised in the given human material without the formal mediation of the lawful authority of the state (in the worldly aspect of its activity), which restrains the forces of evil within certain relative bounds until the time comes when all human wills are ready to make the decisive choice between the absolute good and the unconditional evil. The direct and fundamental motive of such restraint is pity, which determines the whole progress of legal justice and of the state. The progress is not in the principle, but in its application. Compulsion exercised by the state draws back before individual freedom and comes forward to help in the case of public distress. *The rule of true progress is this, that the state should interfere as little as possible with the inner moral life of man, and at the same time should as securely and as widely as possible ensure the external conditions of his worthy existence and moral development.* The state which chose on its own authority to teach its subjects true theology and sound philosophy, and at the same time allowed them to remain illiterate, to be murdered on the high-roads, or to die of famine and of infection, would lose its *raison d'être.* The voice of the true Church might well say to such a state: "It is I that am entrusted with the spiritual salvation of these men. All that thou are required to do is to have pity on their worldly difficulties and frailties. It is written that man does not live by bread *alone*, but it is not written that he lives without bread. Pity is binding upon all, and upon me also. If, therefore, thou wilt not be the collective organ of my pity, and wilt not, by rightly dividing our labour, make it morally possible for me to devote myself to the work of piety, I will once more have to set myself to do the work of pity, as I have done in the old days when thou, the state, was not yet called Christian. I will myself have to see that there should be no famine and excessive labour, no sick uncared for, that the injured should receive reparation, and injurers be corrected. But will not then all men say: What need have we of the state, which has no pity for us, since we have a Church which took pity on our bodies as well as on our souls?" The Christian state, worthy of this name, is one which, without interfering in ecclesiastical affairs, acts within its own domain in the *kingly* spirit of Christ, who pitied the sick and the hungry, taught the ignorant, forcibly restrained abuses (driving out the money-changers), was kind to the Samaritans and the Gentiles, and forbade his disciples to use violence against unbelievers.[25]

NOTES

1. It was natural to Soloviev, as an Eastern Christian, to equate bodily asceticism particularly with fasting. All three things must be understood in a representative sense: prayer as all worship, alms-deeds as neighbourly love, fasting as all "self-denial." But *cf.*, Tobit xii, 8; Matt. xvii, 21; Mark ix, 28. [Donald Attwater, the translator of Vladimir Soloviev, *God, Man and the Church* (London: James Clarke & Co., n.d. [1938]).]

2. [The sentence in Russian is simply: *Zhivia v miru, on dolzhen zhit'* v mire; "Living *in the world*, [a human being] should live *in peace*" (emphasis Soloviev's). *Mir* means both "world" and "peace" in Russian, a concept not unlike *kosmos*, which means both "world" and "thing of beauty" in Greek.]

3. The traditional theology both of East and West teaches that by the hypostatic union two natures, divine and human, were united in the person of the Word. Soloviev here subdivides the human nature, as stated. [Attwater.]

4. [Soloviev, *God, Man and the Church*, xi–xvi. Although the English title obscures it, this book is a translation of *The Spiritual Foundations of Life*. The Russian text of this selection may be found in *Sobranie sochinenii Vladimira Sergeevicha Solov'eva*, ed. S. M. Solov'ev and E. L. Radlov, 2d ed., 10 vols. (St. Petersburg, 1911–14), 3:301–304. *The Spiritual Foundations of Life* (*Dukhovnye osnovy zhizni*) is a good primer of Soloviev's religious thought. A work of edification rather than systematic philosophy, the book lacks the complexity of Soloviev's masterworks but nicely epitomizes his basic values, especially his ecclesiastical and social understanding of the gospel. Like all Orthodox Christians, Soloviev believed that the fullness of Christ is found not in the spirituality of isolated individuals but in the church. Unlike some of his Orthodox compatriots, he also emphasized the church's prophetic social ministry and the responsibility to collaborate with other social agencies in making the world a better place. In the translation, theandric renders the Russian *bogochelovecheskii* (divine-human), from *Bogochelovek*, God-man, that is, the incarnate Christ.]

5. [Soloviev was a lifelong opponent of the death penalty. His debut as an activist on the issue came after the assassination of Tsar Alexander II by populist revolutionaries in 1881, when Soloviev called on the new tsar, Alexander III, to manifest a Christian spirit by refusing to impose capital punishment on his father's murderers. The philosopher's unsolicited appeal led to dismissal from his teaching position at St. Petersburg University. Soloviev's opposition to capital punishment reflected both the influence of modern humanitarianism and long-standing unease about judicial killing in Russia itself. One of the first policies that Grand Prince Vladimir of Kiev instituted after his conversion to Orthodox Christianity in 988 was abolition of the death penalty (subsequently rescinded). Capital punishment was less frequently applied in Russia than in Europe. The greatest writers of nineteenth-century Russia, Dostoevsky and Tolstoy, were united in their revulsion at capital punishment despite vast differences of opinion on other issues of social and political ethics. Abolished by the Provisional Government in 1917, the death penalty was restored by the new Soviet state and is still allowed in Russian law. An episcopal council of the Russian Orthodox Church addressed the issue inconclusively in 2000.]

6. The descendants of Cain, who were destroyed by the Flood, represented a third type of crime—that against nature, which was repeated afterward on a small scale in Sodom and Gomorrah. ["Sanctification" in this passage means retributive justice, as in the Latin phrase *Sacer esto*, "let it be sacred," i.e., forfeit, demanded by the gods as the penalty for an offense.]

7. Genesis 4:15; Leviticus 24:17; Romans 12:19; Deuteronomy 32:35; Hosea 6:6; Luke 19:10. [Wozniuk.]

8. Joseph Marie Maistre, Comte de (1753–1821) was a French diplomat and, at one time, the Sardinian envoy to Russia; he wrote prolifically on constitutions (*Essai sur le principe générateur des constitutions politiques et des autres institutions humaines*), social contract theory (*De la souveraineté du peuple: un anti-contrat social*), and punishment as sacrifice (*Eclaircissements sur les sacrifices*).

Soloviev claimed that de Maistre was the intellectual source of Russian nation-alists' cynical egoism and the degeneration of positive Russian national aspira-tions. See, for example, "Slavianofil'stvo i ego vyrozhdenie," *Vestnik Evropy* 11 and 12 (1889), also reprinted as a chapter in *Natsional'nyi vopros v Rossii* II, as found in *Sobranie sochinenii* 5:181–244. [Wozniuk.]

9. *Animus interficiendi*: "intent to kill." [Wozniuk.]

10. Because *Ritterspruch* is roughly "a knight's decree," and *Richterspruch*, "a judge's decree" [or "judgment"], the sense is that of the usurpation of *de jure* authority. Aleksei S. Khomiakov (1804–60) was a leading Slavophile who, along with oth-ers (e.g., Konstantin Aksakov), while being absolutely opposed to the ideas of Western liberalism for Russia, supported political and social reforms, including the emancipation of the serfs and freedom of speech. [Wozniuk.] [The translit-erated Russian text of Khomiakov's lines has been omitted.]

11. [Vladimir Soloviev, *Politics, Law, and Morality: Essays by V. S. Soloviev*, ed. and trans. Vladimir Wozniuk (New Haven, Conn.: Yale University Press, 2000), 171, 175–176, 179–184. The Russian text of this selection from *Pravo i nravstvennost'* may be found in *Sobranie sochinenii V. S. Solov'eva*, 8: 572, 577-578, 582-588.]

12. I am not forgetting that in 1861 Russia made amends by freeing the serfs.

13. See, among recent publications, the remarkable work of G. de Pascal, *Révolu-tion ou Evolution: Centenaire de 1789* (Paris, Saudax).

14. [Vladimir Soloviev, *Russia and the Universal Church*, trans. Herbert Rees (London: Geoffrey Bles, 1948), 7–11. Soloviev composed this work in French. For the original text of this selection see Vladimir Soloviev, *La Russie et l'Eglise universelle*, 4th ed. (Paris: Librairie Stock, 1922), ix–xviii. *Russia and the Uni-versal Church* is an exposition of Soloviev's ideal of theocracy. By theocracy Soloviev meant the reformation of social and political reality after the image of the Kingdom of God, to be realized through the collaboration of priestly (ecclesiastical), royal (political), and prophetic forces in society. Soloviev always distinguished between "false theocracy" and "free theocracy." By the former he meant traditional clericalism, the domination of society by religious institu-tions. By free theocracy he meant the remaking of a nominally Christian but essentially pagan social order into a just and caritative society. In *Russia and the Universal Church* Soloviev argues against religious and national isolationism to promote the twin ideals of European union and ecclesiastical reunion. An early prophet of ecumenism, Soloviev did not think that a just and caritative society was realizable without the reunion of the churches.]

15. [A *pud* is approximately 36.11 pounds.]

16. Tram conductors in Petersburg work more than eighteen hours a day for twen-ty-five or thirty roubles a month (see *Novoe Vremya*, N. 7357).

17. The author quoted refers here to Hanshofer's book, *Lehrbuch der Statistik*. All the figures quoted are apparently for the countries of Western Europe.

18. A. A. Isaev, *Natchala politicheskoi ekonomii* (*Principles of Political Economy*), 2nd ed., pp. 254–55.

19. Ibid., p. 226.

20. [Chapter 16 in the original Russian text; Part III, Chapter 7 in Duddington trans.]

21. [Chapter 17 in the original Russian text; Part III, Chapter 8 in Duddington trans.]

22. [Soloviev is referring to Tolstoyan anarchism.]

23. [Rudolf von Jhering (1818–1892), German historian and philosopher of law.]

24. [A. N. Ostrovsky, *The Storm*, Act 2, Scene 1.]

25. [Chapter 19 in the original Russian text; Part III, Chapter 10 in Duddington trans.] [Vladimir Soloviev, *The Justification of the Good: An Essay on Moral Philosophy*, trans. Nathalie A. Duddington (New York: Macmillan, 1918), 340–343, 362–363, 369–373, 448–460. For the Russian text see *Sobranie sochinenii V. S. Solov'eva*, 8: 376-380, 399, 406-411, 488-494, 496-500. *The Justification of the Good* (*Opravdanie dobra*) is arguably the most masterful work of moral philosophy in the Russian Orthodox tradition. Soloviev's conception of moral philosophy was very broad. It included not just the basic principles of ethics but philosophical anthropology, social and political philosophy, and the theological dimension of all of these disciplines. The wide range of subject matter treated in *The Justification of the Good* makes the book a summa of Solovievian practical reason.

    While the systematic power of *The Justification of the Good* lends it the status of an enduring masterwork, the book also served a specific purpose in its historical context. Intellectual culture in nineteenth-century Russia was polarized in matters of ethics, politics, and religion. Slavophiles battled Westernizers, custodians of tsarism battled revolutionaries, Orthodox traditionalists battled Tolstoyan anarchists and other purveyors of novel religious doctrines. In *The Justification of the Good* Soloviev approached these divisions in a manner which, for the Russian tradition, was exceptional: he summoned all sides to consider the advantages of a middle way based on faith in the wholeness of the divine-human Good.

    Soloviev's opposition to revolutionism did not betoken apathy about social and economic injustice. Criticism of unregulated capitalism and an economic ethic resembling that of the democratic welfare state of later times are conspicuous features of *The Justification of the Good*. It is interesting to note that Soloviev deploys the Orthodox Christian concept of theosis in this context. Theosis means the eschatological deification of human beings through the full actualization of the image of God in them. Soloviev utilizes the concept to criticize contemporary economic and social conditions, arguing that creatures called to theosis should not live in squalor but in an environment that reflects their divine nature and destiny.]

{CHAPTER 17}

Nicholas Berdyaev (1874–1948)

SELECTED AND EDITED BY VIGEN GUROIAN

Nicholas (Nicholai Aleksandrovich) Berdyaev was born in 1874 in the province of Kiev to a wealthy and highly privileged family. Like so many young men of aristocratic upbringing in nineteenth-century Russia, he was sent to military academy, which he intensely disliked. Eventually, he found his way to the University of Kiev, where he took up philosophy, despite the fact that he was supposed to study the natural sciences, which he also disliked. There Berdyaev began to associate with socialists and Marxists and, because of his radical views and activities, was sent into exile to the Volgoda region of north Russia in 1898. He was released after two and a half years. The experience, however, seemed only to intensify and deepen his radicalism.

During the late 1890s and early 1900s, Berdyaev pursued a goal of wedding Marxist social and economic analysis with Kantianism and Christianity. Berdyaev never was an orthodox Marxist, however, for he was quick to recognize Marxism's totalitarian impulse. Even in the most radical circles, Berdyaev staunchly defended the reality and priority of freedom, goodness, and truth against every form of determinism, relativism, and nihilism. As his discontent with Marxism increased, he moved increasingly to a personalist religious philosophy and defended the eternal value of the human being, personal freedom, and the transcendence of spirit.

Berdyaev entered the University of Heidelberg in 1901 to study with the acclaimed neo-Kantian Wilhelm Windelband. Yet, even at this time, he was growing disenchanted with Kantianism. While attracted to Kant's rule that the person should never be made the mere means to an end, he concluded that this personalist emphasis was undercut by Kant's ethical formalism ensconced in the principle of universalizability (that is, that a moral judgment, if it applies to one case, must also apply to any exactly or relevantly similar cases).

As Berdyaev distanced himself from Kantianism and Marxism, he drew nearer to Orthodox Christianity. The period between his move to St. Petersburg in 1905 and the outbreak of the Bolshevik Revolution is crucial to understanding Berdyaev's mature thought. During these years, Berdyaev became associated with a rich variety of Christian intellectuals, including Dimitri Merezhkovsky, Vassil Rozanov, Vyacheslav Ivanov, Pavel Florensky, and Leo Shestov, many of whom were either imprisoned or sent into exile by the Communists. Berdyaev also began to write as a Christian philosopher. He joined with Sergius Bulgakov in a joint editorship of the journals The New Way *and* Questions of Life. *In the pages of these journals, Berdyaev and Bulgakov espoused their special blend of social and economic radicalism and Christian spirituality.*

In 1907, Berdyaev and his wife moved to Moscow, where he became active in the Religious-Philosophical Society, founded in memory of Vladimir Soloviev. At the same time, he was reading heavily in the great nineteenth-century Russian Christian writers: Aleksei Khomyakov and Nicholas Fyodorov, Fyodor Dostoevsky and Leo Tolstoy. Berdyaev was disappointed, however, with the Russian secular intelligentsia of both the right and left, and also with the Russian Orthodox Church. He accused the former of being shallow and backward and the latter of a conservatism that ignored the material and spiritual needs of the Russian people. He initially supported the revolution of 1917 but did not favor its leaders or its immediate outcome.

In 1921, Berdyaev was arrested for his critical views and exiled from the Soviet Union. He and his wife first settled in Berlin and in 1924 moved permanently to Paris. Berdyaev became active in the rich ferment of philosophical and religious thought that stirred in that city at that time. He established ties with Russian figures such as George Fedotov and Mother Maria Skobtsova and made lasting friendships with the Roman Catholic religious philosophers Jacques Maritain and Gabriel Marcel.

Meanwhile, as mistaken as Berdyaev thought the Bolsheviks and Communists had been, he also was openly critical of the truculent anti-Sovietism of many of the Russian émigrés and their easy embrace of bourgeois capitalism. He judged that the bourgeois mindset was hardly less materialistic than Marxism and Communism and that it was almost as destructive of freedom and personality. The atheism of Communism was self-confessed, the atheism of the bourgeoisie was not, and yet a denial of Christianity was entailed in the bourgeois way of life.

Over the remaining years of his life, Berdyaev continued to oppose antihuman and anti-Christian forces on both the left and the right, within the church and in the secular culture, inside of the Soviet Union and in the Western democracies. He produced a massive corpus in which he elaborated a philosophy of history, a theosophical spirituality, aesthetics, and an ethics. One must look to Berdyaev's ethics especially, however, to find his theological anthropology and interpretation of the origin and meaning of law. In The Destiny of Man,

Berdyaev introduced his famous threefold typology of ethics: the ethics of law, the ethics of redemption, and the ethics of creativity. Other writings that are especially significant in this regard include Freedom and the Spirit *(1926),* Slavery and Freedom *(1939), and* The Beginning and the End *(1946).*

ON THE NATURE AND VALUE OF PERSONALITY

OUR CONCEPTION OF man must be founded upon the conception of personality. True anthropology is bound to be personalistic. Consequently it is essential to understand the relation between personality and individuality. Individuality is a naturalistic and biological category, while personality is a religious and spiritual one. . . . Personality is spiritual and presupposes the existence of a spiritual world. The value of personality is the highest hierarchical value in the world, a value of the spiritual order. . . .

The value and unity of personality does not exist apart from the spiritual principle. The spirit forms personality, enlightens and transfigures the biological individual and makes him independent of the natural order. Personality is certainly not an abstract norm or idea suppressing and enslaving the concrete, individual living being. The idea or ideal value of personality is the concrete fullness of life. . . . Conflict between good and evil or between any values can only exist for a person. Tragedy is always connected with the personality—with its awakening and its struggles. A personality is created by the Divine idea and human freedom. The life of personality is not self-preservation as that of the individual but self-development and self-determination. The very existence of personality presupposes sacrifice, and sacrifice cannot be impersonal. . . .

... Personality from its very nature presupposes another—not the "not-self" which is a negative limit, but another person. Personality is impossible without love and sacrifice, without passing over to the other, to the friend, to the loved one. A self-contained personality becomes disintegrated. Personality is not the absolute, and God as the Absolute is not a Person. God as a Person presupposes His other, another Person, and is love and sacrifice. The Person of the Father presupposes the Persons of the Son and of the Holy Spirit. The Holy Trinity is a Trinity of Persons just because they presuppose one another and imply mutual love and inter-communion.

On another plane the personality of God and of man presuppose each other. Personality exists in the relation of love and sacrifice. It is impossible to conceive of a personal God in an abstract monotheistic way. A person cannot exist as a self-contained and self-sufficient Absolute. Personalistic metaphysics and ethics are based upon the Christian doctrine of the Holy

Trinity. The moral life of every individual person must be interpreted after the image of the Divine Tri-unity, reversed and reflected in the world.
A person presupposes the existence of other persons and communion
between them. Personality is the highest hierarchical value and never is
merely a means. But it does not exist as a value apart from its relation to
God, to other persons and to human society. Personality must come out of
itself, must transcend itself—this is the task set to it by God. Narrow self-
centeredness ruins personality.

... The complexity of man lies in the fact that he is both an individual,
a part of the genus, and a person, a spiritual being. The individual in his
biological self-assertion and self-centredness may sever himself from the
life of the genus, but this alone never leads to the affirmation of personality, its growth and expansion. Hence Christian ethics is personalistic, but
not individualistic. The narrow isolation of personality in modern individualism is the destruction and not the triumph of personality. Hardened
selfhood—the result of original sin—is not personality. It is only when the
hardened selfhood melts away and is transcended that personality manifests itself.[1]

PERSONALISM V. EGOISM

Personalism transfers the centre of gravity of personality from the value of
objective communities—society, nation, state, to the value of personality,
but it understands personality in a sense which is profoundly antithetic
to egoism. Egoism destroys personality. Egocentric self-containment and
concentration upon the self, and the inability to issue forth from the self is
original sin, which prevents the realization of the full life of personality and
hinders its strength from becoming effective. . . . Personality presupposes
a going out from self to an other and to others, it lacks air and is suffocated
when left shut up in itself. Personalism cannot but have some sort of community in view.

At the same time this going out of the personality from itself to an other
does not by any means denote exteriorization and objectivization. Personality is I and Thou, another I. But the Thou to whom the I goes out and
with whom it enters into communion is not an object, it is another I, it is
personality. With an object, indeed, no communion is possible, no state
of community can be shared with it, there can be only mutual obligation.
The personal needs an other, but that other is not external and alien: the
relation of the personal to it is by no means exteriorization. Personality
is to be found in a series of external relations with other people and in

acts of communion with them. External relations mean objectivization, whereas communion is existential. External relations, being in the world of objectivization, are to be classed as determination and therefore do not liberate man from slavery. Communion on the other hand, being in the existential world, and having no cognizance of objects, belongs to the realm of freedom, and means liberation from slavery. Egoism denotes a double slavery of man—slavery to himself, his own hardened selfhood, and slavery to the world, which is transformed exclusively into an object which exercises constraint from without. The egocentric man is a slave, his attitude to everything which is non-I is a servile attitude. He is aware of non-I only, he has no knowledge of another I, he does not know a Thou, he knows nothing of the freedom of going out from the I. The egocentric man usually defines his relation to the world and to people in a way that is not personalistic, he very readily adopts the point of view of the objective scale of values. There is something lacking in the humanity of the egocentric man. He loves abstractions which nourish his egoism. He does not love living concrete people.[2]

PERSONALITY AND THEANDRIC EXISTENCE

... Human personality is theandric existence. Theologians will reply in alarm that Jesus Christ alone was God-man, and that man is a created being and cannot be God-Man. But this way of arguing remains within the confines of theological rationalism. Granted man is not God-man in the sense in which Christ is God-man, the Unique One; yet there is a divine element in man. There are, so to speak, two natures in him. There is within him the intersection of two worlds. He bears within himself the image which is both the image of man and the image of God and is the image of man in so far as the image of God is actualized.

This truth about man lies beyond the dogmatic formulas and is not completely covered by them. It is a truth of existential spiritual experience which can be expressed only in symbols, not in intellectual concepts. That man bears within himself the image of God and in virtue of that becomes man, is a symbol. One cannot work out an intellectual concept about it. Divine-humanity is a contradiction for the line of thought which inclines towards monism or dualism. Humanistic philosophy never rose to such a height as to understand the paradoxical truth about divine-humanity. Theological philosophy, however, has endeavoured to rationalize this truth. All theological doctrines of grace have been but the formulations of the truth about the divine- humanity of man, and about the inward action of the divine upon the human. But it is absolutely impossible to understand this mystery of divine-humanity in the light of the philosophy of identity, monism, immanentism. The expression of this mystery presupposes a dualistic moment, an experience of the process of transcendence, of falling into an abyss and of escaping from that abyss. The divine is that which transcends man, and the divine is mysteriously united with the human in the divine-human image. It is for this reason only that the appearance in the world of personality which is not a slave to the world is possible. Personality is humane and it surpasses the human, which is dependent upon the world. Man is a manifold being; he bears within him the image of the world, but he is not only the image of the world, he is also the image of God. Within him conflict between the world and God takes place. He is a being both dependent and free. The image of God is a symbolic expression and if it is turned into a concept it meets with insuperable difficulties. Man is a symbol, for in him is a sign of something different, and he is a sign of something different. With this alone the possibility of liberating man from slavery is connected. This is the religious foundation of the doctrine of personality—not the theological foundation but the religious, that is to say, the spiritually empirical, the existential. The truth about God-humanity is not a dogmatic formula, not a theological doctrine, but an empirical truth, the expression of spiritual experience.[3]

PERSONALITY AND COMMUNION

This same truth of the twofold nature of man, twofold and at the same time integral, has its reflection in the relation of human personality to society and to history. But here it is turned upside down, as it were. Personality is independent of the determination of society, it has its own world, it is an exception, it is unique and unrepeatable. And at the same time personality is social, in it there are traces of the collective unconscious. It is man's way out from isolation. It belongs to history, it realizes itself in society and in history. Personality is communal; it presupposes communion with others, and community with others. The profound contradiction and difficulty of human life is due to this communality. Slavery is on the watch to waylay man on the path of his self realization and man must constantly return to his divine image.

Man is subjected to forcible socialization during the very time that his human personality must be in free communion, in free community, in communality which is based upon freedom and love. And the greatest danger to which a man is exposed on the paths of objectivization is the danger of mechanization, the danger of automatism. Everything mechanical, everything automatic in man is not personal, it is impersonal, it is antithetic to the image of personality. The image of God, and the image of mechanism and the automaton clash against each other, the choice is either God-man or automatic humanity, machine-humanity. Man's difficulty is rooted in the fact that there is no correlation and identity between the inward and the outward, no direct and adequate expression of the one in the other. This is indeed the problem of objectivization. When he objectivizes himself in the external man enslaves himself to the world of objects; and at the same time, man cannot but express himself in the external, cannot dispense with his body, cannot but enter actively into society and history.

Even the religious life of humanity is subject to this objectivization. In a certain sense it may be said that religion in general is social; that it is a social link. But this social character of religion distorts the spirit, subordinates the infinite to the finite, makes the relative absolute, and leads away from the sources of revelation, from living spiritual experience. In the interior world, personality discovers its image through the image of God, through the penetration of the human by the divine. In the exterior world the actualization of truth denotes the subordination of the world, of society, and of history to the image of personality, it signifies permeation by personality. And that is personalism.[4]

CHRISTIANITY AND REDEMPTION

Christianity is the religion of Redemption and therefore presupposes the existence of evil and suffering. It is therefore idle to invoke them as evidence against the Christian faith. The very reason why Christ came into the world is because of its sin, and Christianity teaches us that the world and man must bear the Cross. If suffering is the result of evil it is also the path by which we are to be freed from it. For Christian thought suffering is not necessarily an evil, for God Himself, that is God the Son, suffers. The whole creation groaneth and travaileth together waiting for its deliverance. But the opponents of Christianity constantly base their attacks upon the fact that the coming of the Saviour has not delivered the world from suffering and evil. Almost two thousand years have passed since the coming of the Redeemer and the world is still full of bloodshed, while humanity is racked with pain and the amount of evil and suffering has actually increased. The old Jewish argument seems to have won the day. The true Messiah will be he who will finally deliver humanity from evil and suffering here below.

But we forget that Christianity recognizes the positive value of the sufferings which mankind endures on earth, and that it has never promised us happiness or blessedness here. Besides which Christian prophecy as to the fate of humanity has been fairly pessimistic in character. Christianity has never upheld the view that universal peace and the Kingdom of God upon earth would be achieved by the intervention of some overwhelming power. On the contrary, it recognizes the freedom of the human spirit in a very high degree, and it regards the realization of the Kingdom of God without its participation as an impossibility. If the justice of Christ is not realized in the world, that is due rather to human injustice. The religion of love is not responsible for the fact that hate predominates in our natural world. . . .

It is impossible for us to conceive the mystery of Redemption rationally any more than any other mystery of the divine life. The juridical theory of redemption, which from the days of St. Anselm of Canterbury has played such a big part in Catholic theology and from which Orthodox theology is not entirely free, is a rationalization of this mystery, which is thus interpreted according to a scheme of relationships existing in the natural world. This juridical conception was simply an attempt to adapt celestial truth to the level of the natural man. It is not a spiritual conception at all. To regard the universal tragedy as a judicial process initiated by an angry Deity against offending man is quite unworthy. To think in this fashion is to adapt the divine life which is always mysterious and unfathomable to pagan conceptions and the spirit of tribal vengeance. God, according to pagan-Jewish thought, is regarded as a fearful tyrant Who punishes and takes vengeance for every act of disobedience, Who demands a ransom, a propitiatory victim, and the shedding of blood. . . . Upon the juridical theory of redemption the stamp of Roman and feudal conceptions regarding the rehabilitation of man was irrevocably set. The transgression of the Divine Will leads to a judicial process and God demands repayment; He must receive compensation in order to pacify His wrath. No human sacrifice will satisfy Him or make Him yield. Only the sacrifice of the Son is proportionate to the crime committed and the offence it has caused. . . .

The Redemption achieved by the Son of God is not a judicial verdict, but a means of salvation; it is not a judgment, but a transfiguration and illumination of nature—in a word, its sanctification. Salvation is not justification, but the acquiring of perfection. The conception of God as judge is that of the natural man and not the spiritual, to whom a quite different aspect of the divine nature is revealed. It is impossible to attribute to God the kind of sentiments which even men themselves regard as blameworthy, as, for instance, pride, egoism, rancour, vengeance, and cruelty. The natural man has given to the world a monstrous idea of God. According to the juridical conception of Redemption the religion of Christ is still a legal religion in which grace is not conceived ontologically.

In Christianity Redemption is the work of love and not that of justice, the sacrifice of a divine and infinite love, not a propitiatory sacrifice, nor the settlement of accounts. "For God so loved the world that He gave His only-begotten Son that whosoever believeth in Him should not perish, but have everlasting life." Bukharev, on the theory that the Lamb was slain from the foundation of the world, puts forward the remarkable idea that the voluntary sacrifice of the Son of God was part of the initial plan of creation. God Himself longs to suffer with the world. The juridical interpretation of the evolution of the universe transforms Redemption into a judicial process....

The meaning of Redemption lies in the coming of the Second Adam, the new spiritual man, in the coming of that love of which the Old Adam was ignorant, in the transformation of the lower nature into the higher. It certainly does not lie in the mere regulation of the external relationships between the Old Adam and God, nor in the pardon and satisfaction granted to one party by the other. The meaning of the coming of Christ into the world lies in a real transfiguration of human nature, in the formation of a new type of spiritual man, and not in the institution of laws, by the carrying out of which the spiritual life may be acquired. ... Man hungers for a new and higher kind of life which is in accordance with his dignity and is eternal. It is this which really constitutes the revelation of the New Covenant. In Christianity the central idea is that of transfiguration, not justification. The latter has occupied too prominent a place in Western Christianity. In Eastern Christianity and in the Greek Fathers, on the other hand, the idea is modified in human nature. But the idea of transfiguration and of divinization was fundamental.

The coming of Christ and Redemption can be spiritually understood only as a continuation of the creation of the world, as the eighth day of this creation, that is to say, as a cosmogonic and anthropogonic process, as a manifestation of divine love in creation, as a new stage in the freedom of man. The advent of the new spiritual man cannot merely be the result of the evolution of human nature. On the contrary it presupposes an entry of the eternal and spiritual into this natural time-world of ours. The natural evolution of humanity leaves us shut up within the restraints and limits of natural reality. Original sin, the evil which lies at the root of this world, continues to isolate the terrestrial world and hold it in bondage. Deliverance can only come from above. The power of the spiritual and divine world has to come into our fallen natural reality, and by transfiguring our nature, break down the barriers dividing the two worlds. Thus the history of Heaven becomes that of earth. The human race which is that of the Old Adam had to be prepared historically to receive the new spiritual man who comes from another world; a preparatory spiritual development had to take place first. Within the sphere of humanity and in the natural world there had to be a pure and spotless being capable of receiving the divine element, a feminine principle enlightened by grace. The Virgin Mary, the Mother of God, was simply the manifestation of this principle, through which the human race was to receive the Son of God and the Son of Man. In Christ, the God-Man, the infinite divine love met the answering love of man. The mystery of Redemption is that of love and liberty. If Christ is not only God but also man (which is what the dogma of the Two Natures teaches us) then in Redemption not only the divine Nature played its part but also human nature, that is, the heavenly spiritual nature of mankind. Christ as God-Man reveals the fact not only that we belong to an earthly race but that the spiritual man, thanks to Him, abides in the very depths of divine reality.

In Christ, as Man in the absolute sense, summing up in Himself the whole of spiritual humanity, man makes a heroic effort to overcome by sacrifice and suffering both sin and death, which is the consequence of sin. And this he does in order to respond to the love of God. In Christ human nature co-operates with the work of Redemption. Sacrifice is the law of spiritual ascent and with the birth of Christ a new era in the life of creation begins. Adam underwent the trial of his freedom and failed to respond to the divine call by an expression of free and creative love. Christ, the New Adam, makes this response to the love of God and thereby points out the way to this response to all who are spiritually His.

Redemption is a dual process in which both God and man share; yet it is but one process, not two. Without human nature and the exercise of human freedom it would be impossible. Here, as everywhere else in Christianity, the mystery of the theandric humanity of Christ is the key to any true understanding. There is no final solution to this mystery except in the Trinity, for it is in the Spirit that the relations between the Father and the Son are resolved. Evil cannot be overcome except by the participation of human freedom in the process. But evil undermines and alters the character of this freedom which alone permits of its defeat.

Here we have the fundamental antinomy which finds its solution in the dual mystery of Christ's nature. The Son of God, the Second Hypostasis of the Divine Trinity, overcomes the opposition between human freedom and divine necessity by the suffering of the Cross. In the passion of the Son of God and the Son of Man on Calvary freedom becomes the power of divine love, which enlightens and transfigures human freedom in the saving of the world. Truth in the guise of suffering and love makes us free without constraint; in fact it creates a new and higher kind of freedom. The freedom which the truth of Christ gives us is not the result of necessity. Redemption cannot be understood as a return of human nature to its primitive state before the fall of Adam. Such a conception would indeed make nonsense of the whole process of the universe. But the new spiritual man is superior not only to fallen Adam, but to Adam before the Fall, and his advent marks a new stage in the creation of the world. The Old Adam gives us no clue to the mystery of infinite love and the new type of freedom, for that mystery is only revealed in Christ. . . .

The appearance of Christ marks a new era in the destiny of the world, a new moment in the creation both of the world and of man. Not only human nature but the whole universe and the whole of cosmic life was transformed after the coming of Christ. When the Blood of Christ shed upon Calvary touched the earth, earth became a new thing, and it is only the limitations of our receptive faculties which prevent us from seeing it with our very eyes.[5]

THE FALL. THE ORIGIN OF GOOD AND EVIL

Christianity has adopted the myth of the Fall and of the Garden of Eden; thinkers who have given up Christianity and do not want a religious basis for ethics reject it. But the problem of ethics cannot even be formulated unless it be admitted that the distinction between good and evil had an origin in time and had been preceded by a state of being "beyond" or "prior to" good and evil. "Good" and "evil" are correlative and in a sense it may be said that good comes into being at the same time as evil and disappears together with it. This is the fundamental paradox of ethics. Paradise is the state of being in which there is no valuation or distinction. It might be said that the world proceeds from an original absence of discrimination between good and evil to a sharp distinction between them and then, enriched by that experience, ends by not distinguishing them any more. . . .

The origin of the knowledge of good and evil has two essentially different aspects, and this leads to a paradox. It is possible to interpret the knowledge of good and evil as the Fall. When I know good and evil, when I make distinctions and valuations, I lose my innocence and wholeness, fall away from God and am exiled from paradise. Knowledge is the loss of paradise. Sin is the attempt to know good and evil. But another interpretation is possible. Knowledge in itself is not a sin and does not mean falling away from God. Knowledge is good and means discovery of meaning. But plucking the fruit of the tree of knowledge indicates an evil and godless experience of life, an attempt on the part of man to return to the darkness of non-being, a refusal to give a creative answer to God's call and resistance to the act of creation. Yet knowledge connected with this act is a manifestation of the principle of wisdom in man, a transition to a higher consciousness and a higher state of existence. It is equally wrong and contradictory to say that the knowledge of good and evil is good and to say that it is evil. Our terms and categories are inapplicable to that which lies beyond the state of being which has given rise to those terms and categories.

Is it a good thing that the distinction between good and evil has arisen? Is good-good, and evil-evil? We are bound to give a paradoxical answer to this question: it is bad that the distinction between good and evil has arisen, but it is good to make the distinction, once it has arisen; it is bad to have gone through the experience of evil, but it is good to know good and evil as a result of that experience. When Nietzsche substituted for the distinction between good and evil the distinction between the fine and the low, he thought he was replacing moral and cognitive categories by natural and elemental; i.e., by paradisiacal categories. But it was an Eden after the Fall. Nietzsche cannot find his way to paradise. "Beyond good and evil," i.e. in paradise, there ought to be neither good nor evil in our sense of these terms, but with Nietzsche evil remains. Man has chosen the knowledge of good and evil through experience, and he must follow that painful path to the end; he cannot expect to find Paradise half-way. The myth of the lost paradise symbolizes the genesis of consciousness in the development of the spirit. . . .

The origin of good and evil is expressed by a myth, and ethics is bound to have a mythological basis. Both at the beginning and the end ethics comes upon a realm which lies beyond good and evil: the life of paradise and the life of the Kingdom of God, the preconscious and the superconscious state. It is only the "unhappy" consciousness with its dividedness, reflection, pain and suffering that is on "this side" of good and evil. And the most difficult question of all is what is the nature of the "good" before the distinction between good and evil has arisen and after it has ceased to be? Is there "good" in paradise and in the Kingdom of God? This is the essential metaphysical problem of ethics which is seldom considered.[6]

GOD IS BEYOND GOOD AND EVIL

It is obvious that God is "beyond good and evil," for on "this side" of it is our fallen world and certainly not God. God is above good. And there cannot be in Him any evil that is on this side of the distinction. When we ask whether God is free to will evil we apply to Him the categories of our fallen world. One can only think of the subject in terms of negative theology. God certainly is not bound by the moral good and is not dependent upon it. He *is* the Good as an absolute force. But we have at once to add that He is above good, for the category of goodness is not applicable to Him. It is impossible to pass judgment on God, for He is the source of all the values by reference to which we judge. God reveals Himself to us as the source of values, as infinite love. Theodicy can judge God only in the light of what God has revealed to us about Himself. It defends God against human conceptions of Him, against human slander.[7]

FREEDOM, FREE WILL, AND VALUES

The problem of the relation between freedom and values is even more troublesome. It may be said that man in his freedom is confronted with ideal norms or values which he has to realize; his failure to do so is an evil. This is the usual point of view. Man is free to realize the good or the values which stand above him as for ever laid down by God, forming an ideal normative world, but he is not free to create the good, to produce values. The scholastic conception of free will comes precisely to this, that man can and must fulfil the law of goodness, and if he fails to do so, it is his own fault and he is punished. This choice between good and evil is forced upon him from without. Freedom of will is not a source of creativeness, but of responsibility and possible punishment. This purely normative conception has been specially worked out for legal purposes. True freedom, however, consists not in fulfilling the law, but in creating new realities and values. As a free being man is not merely a servant of the moral law, but a creator of new values. Man is called upon to create the good and not only to fulfil it. Creative freedom gives rise to values. As a free being, a free spirit, man is called to be the creator of new values. The world of values is not a changeless ideal realm rising above man and freedom; it is constantly undergoing change and being created afresh. Man is free in relation to moral values, not merely in the sense that he is free to realize or not to realize them. Similarly, in relation to God man is free not merely in the sense that he can turn towards God or away from Him, can fulfil or not fulfil His will. Man is free in the sense of being able to co-operate with God, to create the good and produce new values.[8]

THREE TYPES OF ETHICS

There exist three types of ethics—the ethics of law, of redemption and of creativeness. Ethics in the profound sense of the term must teach of the awakening of the human spirit and not of consciousness, of creative spiritual power and not of laws and norms. The ethics of law, the ethics of consciousness which represses subconsciousness and knows nothing of superconsciousness, is the result of the primitive emotion of fear, and we,

Christians, see in it the result of original sin. Fear warns man of danger, and therein lies its ontological significance.

The awakening of spirit in man is very painful. At the early stages the spirit divides and fetters man's vital energy, and only later does it manifest itself as creative energy. The spiritual superconscious principle separates man out of nature, and, as it were, dementalizes nature, depriving it of its daemonic power. In man too there is a struggle between spirit and nature. Consciousness becomes the arena of that struggle. The awakening of the spirit may be inspired by the idea of redemption or by creativeness. The idea of redemption subjects the soul to new dangers. The thought of perdition and salvation may become a morbid obsession. In that case salvation of the soul from being possessed by the idea of salvation comes from creative spiritual energy, from the shock of creative inspiration. Redemption is only completed through creativeness. This is the fundamental conception of the new ethics.[9]

THE ETHICS OF LAW

The ethics of law is the pre-Christian morality; it is to be found not only in the Old Testament but in paganism, in primitive communities, in Aristotle and the Stoics, and within Christianity in Pelagius and to a considerable extent in St. Thomas Aquinas. At the same time the ethics of law contains an eternal principle which must be recognized by the Christian world as well, for sin and evil are not conquered in it. The ethics of law cannot be interpreted chronologically only, for it co-exists with the ethics of redemption and of creativeness. Its history in the Christian world is extremely complicated. Christianity is the revelation of grace, and Christian ethics is the ethics of redemption and not of law. But Christianity was weighed down by extraneous elements and underwent changes in the course of time. It has often been interpreted in a legalistic sense. Thus, the official Roman Catholic theology is to a considerable extent legalistic. The Gospel itself has been constantly distorted by legalistic interpretations. Legalism, rationalism and formalism have actually introduced an element of law into the truth of the Christian revelation. Even grace received a legalistic interpretation. Theologians were alarmed by St. Paul's doctrine and did their best to limit and modify it. An element of rationalistic, almost Pelagian legalism penetrated into the very consciousness of the church. Luther protested ardently against the law in Christianity, against legalistic ethics, and attempted to take his stand beyond good and evil. But Luther's own followers were alarmed by him; they tried to render harmless his passionate protests and modify and rationalize his irrationalism. Only the school of K. Barth, following Kierkegaard, has returned to Luther's paradoxality. Throughout the history of Christianity there has always been a struggle between the principles of grace and spiritual regeneration and the formal, juridical and rationalistic principles.

Legalistic morality is deeply rooted in human society and goes back to the primitive clans with their totems and taboos. The ethics of law is essentially social as distinct from the personal ethics of redemption and creativeness. The Fall subordinated human conscience to society. Society became the bearer and the guardian of the moral law. Sociologists who maintain that morality has a social origin have unquestionably got hold of a certain truth. But they do not see the origin of this truth or the depth of its meaning. The ethics of law means, first and foremost, that the subject of moral valuation is society and not the individual, that society lays down moral prohibitions, taboos, laws and norms to which the individual must submit under penalty of moral excommunication and retribution. The ethics of law can never be personal and individual, it never penetrates into the intimate depths of personal moral life, experience and struggle. It exaggerates evil in personal life, punishing and prohibiting it, but does not attach sufficient importance to evil in the life of the world and society. It takes an optimistic view of the power of the moral law, of the freedom of will and of the punishment of the wicked, which is supposed to prove that the world is ruled by justice. The ethics of law is both very human and well adapted to human needs and standards, and extremely inhuman and pitiless towards the human personality, its individual destiny and intimate life. . . .

The primitive moral consciousness is communal and social. Its moral subject is the group united by kinship and not the individual. Vengeance as a moral act is also communal: it is carried out by one group of kinsmen against another, and not by one individual against another. Blood vengeance is the most characteristic moral phenomenon of antiquity and persists in the Christian world in so far as human nature in it is not transfigured and enlightened. . . .

In antiquity vengeance was not at all connected with personal guilt. Vengeance and punishment were not primarily directed against the person who was personally guilty and responsible. The conception of personal guilt and responsibility was formed much later. Blood vengeance was impersonal. When the state took upon itself the duty of avenging and punishing crime, the idea of personal guilt and responsibility began to develop. The law, which always has a social character, demands that the primeval chaos of instincts should be suppressed; but it merely drives that chaos inwards and does not conquer it or regenerate it. Chaotic primeval instincts have been preserved in the civilized man of the twentieth century. The world-war and the communistic revolution have shown this.

After the Christian revelation vengeance, which was at first a moral and religious duty, became an immoral unruly instinct that man had to overcome through the new law. The ancient awe-inspiring tyranny of the clan and kin with its endless taboos and prohibitions ceased to be a moral law as it was in antiquity, and became a part of atavistic instincts against which a higher moral consciousness must struggle. This is one of the important truths of social ethics. To begin with, society subdues and disciplines man's instincts, but afterwards, at the higher stages of moral development, ideas and emotions which had been instilled into man for the sake of disciplining him become, in their turn, unruly instincts. This happened in the first instance with vengeance. Society deprived the individual of freedom because he was possessed by sinful passions; but social restraint of freedom became an instinct of tyranny and love of power. Superstitions, tyranny and caste privileges had once served the purpose of bringing order into chaos and establishing a social cosmos; but they degenerated into instincts which stand in the way of a free social organization. Law plays a double part in the moral life of humanity: it restrains unruly instincts and creates order, but it also calls forth instincts which prevent the creation of a new order. This shows the impotence of the law. . . .

The fatal consequence of the legalistic discrimination between good and evil is tyranny of the law which means tyranny of society over the person and of the universally binding idea over the personal, the particular, unique and individual. The hard-set crystallized forms of herd life in which the creative fire is almost extinct oppress like a nightmare the creative life of personality. The law thwarts life and does violence to it. And the real tragedy of ethics lies in the fact that the law has its own positive mission in the world. It cannot be simply rejected and denied. If this were possible there would be no conflict of principles. The ethics of law must be transcended, the creative life of personality must be vindicated. But the law has a positive value of its own. It warps the individual life, but it also preserves it. It is a paradox, but the exclusive predominance of the ethics of grace in a sinful world would endanger the freedom and, indeed, the very existence of personality. A person's fate cannot be made to rest solely upon other people's spiritual condition. This is where the significance of law comes in. No one can be made to depend upon his neighbours' moral qualities and inward perfection. In our sinful world personality is doomed to share to some extent the herd life which both thwarts it and preserves it by means of law and justice. Justice is righteousness refracted in the common life of every day. The realm of the herd-man, *das Man*, is the result of the Fall; indeed, it *is* the fallen world. The life of personality is inevitably warped in it, and even Christian revelation becomes distorted. The primary evil is not in the law as such which makes sin manifest, but in the sin which gives rise to the law. But the law which denounces sin and puts a limit to the manifestations of it has a way of degenerating into evil. . . .

From its very nature law inevitably inspires fear. It does not regenerate human nature, does not destroy sin, but by means of fear, both external and inward, holds sin within certain bounds. Moral order in the world is maintained in the first place through religious fear, which later on assumes the forms of the moral law. Such are the direct consequences of the Fall. In the life of the state and the community we find at this stage cruel punishments and executions to which moral significance is attached. The characteristic feature of the ethics of law is that it is concerned with the abstract norm of the good but does not care about man, the unique and individual human personality and its intimate inner life. This is its limitation. It is interested not in man as a living being with his joys and sufferings, but in the abstract norm of the good which is set for man. This is the case even when it becomes philosophic and idealistic and proclaims the principle of the intrinsic value of human personality. Thus in Kant the conception of personality is purely abstract and normative, and has no relation to the concrete and irreplaceable human individuality in which Kant never took any interest. . . .

The law neither cares about the individual's life nor gives him strength to fulfil the good which it requires of him. This is the essential contradiction of the ethics of law, which inevitably leads to the ethics of grace or redemption. Dried up formal virtue deprived of beneficent, gracious and life-giving energy is frequently met with in Christian asceticism, which may prove to be an instance of legalistic morality within Christianity. A monastically ascetic attitude to life, a kind of resentment towards it, is the expression of the ethics of law within the religion of grace and redemption; it is powerless to raise life to a higher level. Only when asceticism is combined with mysticism it acquires a different character. The moral law, the law of the state, of the church, of the family, of civilization, of technics and economics, organizes life, preserves it and passes judgment upon it; sometimes it warps life but never sustains it with a gracious power, never illuminates or transfigures it. The law is necessary for the sinful world and cannot be simply cancelled. But it must be overcome by a higher force; the world and man must be freed from the impersonal power of the law. . . .

The ethics of law is not only religious and social; it is also philosophical and claims to be based upon freedom and autonomy. But even then its Old Testament character makes itself manifest. Philosophical ethics of law is normative and idealistic; it is not based upon any external authority but is autonomous. This is pre-eminently true of the Kantian system, which is the most remarkable attempt of constructing a philosophical ethics of law. Though Kant's ethics is autonomous, it is based on the conception of law, as the very term autonomy indicates. It is legalistic because it is concerned with the universally binding moral law, with man's moral and rational nature which is the same in all; it is not in the least interested in the concrete living man as such, in his destiny, in his moral experience and spiritual conflicts. The moral law, which man must freely discover for himself, automatically gives directions to all, and is the same for all men and in all cases of life. Kant's moral maxim that every man must be regarded not only as a means but also as an end in himself is undermined by the legalistic character of his ethics, because every man proves to be a means and an instrument for the realization of an abstract, impersonal, universally binding law. Morality is free in so far as it is autonomous; man, however, is not free or autonomous at all, but is entirely subject to law. Consequently Kant completely denied the emotional side of the moral life, provoking Schiller's famous epigram. Human personality has really no value for Kant and is merely a formal and universally binding principle. Individuality does not exist for Kantian ethics, any more than do unique and individual moral problems which demand unique and individual, i.e. creative, moral solutions. . . .

The moral philosophy of Tolstoy is as legalistic as that of Kant. It is not based on any external authority. Tolstoy regards the Gospel as an expression of the moral law and norm, and the realization of the Kingdom of God is for him on a par with abstention from tobacco and alcohol. Christ's teaching consists for him of a number of moral precepts which man can easily carry out, once he recognizes their rationality. Tolstoy was a severe critic of Christian falsity and hypocrisy, but he wanted to subordinate life to the tyrannical power of legalistic morality. There is something almost daemonic in Tolstoy's moralism which would destroy all the richness and fullness of life. Both Kant and Tolstoy had grown up against a Christian background, but in spite of their love of freedom their teaching is a legalistic distortion of Christianity. They preach righteousness achieved through fulfilling the law, i.e. they return to a philosophically refined form of pharisaism and Pelagianism, which also upheld moralism and had no need of grace.

It was against Pelagian moralism and rationalism, i.e. against legalism in the Catholic church, that Luther rebelled; but in its further development Lutheranism, too, became legalistic. The legalistic element was strong in Christianity at all times, and even the doctrine of grace was interpreted in that sense. Pharisaism was by no means overcome. Moralism in all its forms was essentially pharisaical. Asceticism assumed a legalistic character. A moralist as a type is a stickler for the law who does not want to know anything about the concrete, living individual. Amoralism is a legitimate reaction against this. The imperatives of legalistic ethics are applicable only to very crude, elementary instances—one must not indulge in vice, steal, commit murder, tell lies—but they are of no help in the more subtle and complex cases which demand an individual, creative solution. The law has been made for the Old Adam, vindictive, tyrannical, greedy, lustful and envious. But the real problem of ethics lies deeper; it is bound up with the individual complexity of life, which is due to conflicts between the higher values and to the presence of the tragic element in life. And yet it is generally supposed that the business of ethics is to teach that one ought not to be a pick-pocket! ...

The complexity and paradoxality of the Christian attitude to the law is due to the fact that although Christ denounced pharisaism, He said that He came to fulfil the law and not to destroy it. The Gospel transcends and cancels the ethics of law, replacing it by a different and higher ethics of love and freedom. But at the same time it does not allow us simply to reject the law. Christianity opens the way to the Kingdom of God where there is no more law, but meanwhile the law denounces sin and must be fulfilled by the world which remains in sin. Sinners need salvation, and salvation comes not from the law but from the Saviour; salvation is attained through redemption and not through law. But the lower sphere of the law exists all the time, and law remains in force in its own domain. The social life of Christendom is still under the power of the law almost to the same extent as the life of the primitive clans and totems. The law is improved and perfected while remaining the same in principle. There is an eternal element in it. . . . .

We are thus faced with the following paradox: the law does not know the concrete, unique, living personality or penetrate into its inner life, but it preserves that personality from interference and violence on the part of others, whatever their spiritual condition may be. Therein lies the great and eternal value of law and justice. Christianity is bound to recognize it. It is impossible to wait for a gracious regeneration of society to make human life intolerable. Such is the correlation of law and grace. I must love my neighbour in Christ, this is the way to the Kingdom of Heaven. But if I have no love for my neighbour I must in any case fulfil the law in relation to him and treat him justly and honourably. It is impossible to cancel the law and wait for the realization of love. That, too, would be sheer hypocrisy. Even if I have no love I must not steal, must not commit murder, must not be a bully. That which comes from grace is never lower but always higher than that which comes from the law. The higher does not cancel the lower, but includes it in a sublimated form. A legalistic misinterpretation of love and grace is an evil and leads to violence, denial of freedom and complete rejection of the law. This then is the relation between the ethics of law and the ethics of redemption. The latter cannot take the place of the former: if it does, it becomes despotic and denies freedom. The two orders co-exist, and the order of grace stands for regeneration and enlightenment, and not for tyranny. The highest achievement of the ethics of law is justice.[10]

THE ETHICS OF REDEMPTION

To every sensitive mind it is clear that it is impossible to be content with the law and that legalistic good does not solve the problem of life. Once the distinction between good and evil has arisen, it is beyond the power of man to annul it, i.e. to conquer evil. And man thirsts for redemption, for deliverance not only from evil but from the legalistic distinction between good and evil. The longing for redemption was present in the pre-Christian world. We find it in the ancient mysteries of the suffering gods. In an embryonic form it is present in totemism and the totemic eucharist. The thirst for redemption means an earnest hope that God and the gods will take part in solving the painful problem of good and evil and in human suffering. God will come down to earth like fire, and sin and evil will be burnt up, the distinction between good and evil will disappear, and so will the impotent legalistic good which does nothing but torture man. The thirst for redemption is the longing to be reconciled to God, and it is the only way to conquer atheism inspired by the presence of pain and evil in the world. Redemption is the meeting with the suffering and sacrificial God, with a God, i.e., who shares the bitter destiny of the world and of man. Man is a free being and there is in him an element of primeval, uncreated, pre-cosmic freedom. But he is powerless to master his own irrational freedom and its abysmal darkness. This is his perennial tragedy. It is necessary that God Himself should descend into the depths of that freedom and take upon Himself the consequences of pain and evil to which it gives rise. . . .

Everyone knows that the Gospel morality is totally different from the morality of law. But the Christian world has managed to live and to formulate its doctrine as though there had never been any conflict between them. No one can deny that there is an opposition between the Christian and the legalistic ethics. The Gospel morality is based upon the power of grace, unknown to the law, so that it is no longer morality in the old sense. Christianity means the acquisition of power in and through Christ, of power that truly regenerates man and does not fear life or death, darkness or pain. The real opposition is between power and law, between something ontologically real and something purely ideal and normative. This is why abstract moralism, so natural to all legalistic and normative theories, is not at all typical of Christianity. We touch here upon the central point of Christian ethics and of ethics in general. The fundamental question of ethics may be formulated as follows: can the idea of the good be the aim of human life and the source of all practical valuations? Moralists are only too ready to base their systems upon the idea of the supreme good and think it, indeed, indispensable to ethics. But as soon as the idea of the supreme good is put at the basis of ethics, ethics becomes normative and legalistic. . . .

The ethics of the Gospel is based upon existence and not upon norm, it prefers life to law. A concrete existent, a living being, is higher than any abstract idea, even if it be the idea of the good. The good of the Gospel consists in regarding not the good but man as the supreme principle of life. The Gospel shows that men, out of love for the good, may be vile and hypocritical, that out of love for the good they may torture their fellows or forget about them. The Sabbath is for man and not man for the Sabbath—this is the essence of the great moral revolution made by Christianity, in which man for the first time recovered from the fatal consequences of distinguishing between good and evil and from the power of the law. "The Sabbath" stands for the abstract good, for the idea, the norm, the law, the fear of defilement. But "the Son of man is the lord of the Sabbath." Christianity knows no abstract moral norms, binding upon all men and at all times. Therefore for a Christian every moral problem demands its own individual solution, and is not to be solved mechanically by applying a norm set once for all. It must be so, if man is higher than "the Sabbath," the abstract idea of the good. Every moral act must be based upon the greatest possible consideration for the man from whom it proceeds and for the man upon whom it is directed. The Gospel morality of grace and redemption is the direct opposite of Kant's formula: you must not act so that the principle of your action could become a universal law; you must always act individually, and everyone must act differently. The universal law is that every moral action should be unique and individual, i.e. that it should have in view a concrete living person and not the abstract good.

Such is the ethics of love. Love can only be directed upon a person, a living being and not upon the abstract good. To be guided in one's moral actions by the love for the good and not for men means to be a Scribe and a Pharisee and to practise the reverse of the Christian moral teaching. The only thing higher than the love for man is the love for God, Who is also a concrete Being, a Person and not an abstract idea. The love of God and the love of man sum up the Gospel morality; all the rest is not characteristically Christian and merely confirms the law. Christianity preaches love for one's neighbour and not for "those far off." This is a very important distinction. Love for "the far off," for man and humanity in general, is love for an abstract idea, for the abstract good, and not love for man. And for the sake of this abstract love men are ready to sacrifice concrete, living beings. We find this love for "the far off" in humanistic revolutionary morality. But there is a great difference between humanistic and Christian love. Christian love is concrete and personal, while humanistic love is abstract and impersonal; Christian love cares above all for the individual, and humanistic for "the idea," even though it be the idea of humanity and its happiness. There is, of course, a strong Christian element in humanism, for humanism is of Christian origin. Christianity affirmed the supreme value of man through the words of Christ that man is higher than Sabbath and His commandment of love for one's neighbour. But just as in Christianity the Scribes and Pharisees began to gain the upper hand, and "the Sabbath," the abstract idea of the good, was set above man, so in humanism its Scribes and Pharisees put the idea of human welfare or progress above man as a concrete living being. . . .

We have already seen that the Gospel morality is opposed to the legalistic morality of salvation by one's own efforts through carrying out the moral law. Since it is based not upon the abstract good but upon the relation to man as a concrete living person, it is highly dynamic in character. Christianity does not recognize the fixed types of "the wicked" and of "the righteous." An evil-doer may turn into a righteous man, and *vice versa.* St. John of the Ladder says: "You will be careful not to condemn sinners if you remember that Judas was one of the Apostles and the thief was one of a band of murderers; but in one moment the miracle of regeneration took place in him." This is why Christ teaches us "judge not, that ye be not judged." Up to the hour of death no one knows what may happen to a man and what a complete change he may undergo, nor does anyone know what happens to him at the hour of death, on a plane inaccessible to us. This is why Christianity regards "the wicked" differently than this world does; it does not allow a sharp division of mankind into two halves; "the good" and "the wicked"—a division by which moral theories set much store. . . .

The Gospel makes a complete change in our moral valuations, but we are not conscious of its full significance because we have grown used to it and adapted it too well to our everyday needs. "I am come to send fire on the earth." In this fire are burnt up all the old, habitual moral valuations, and new ones are formed. The first shall be last, and the last first. This means a revolution more radical than any other. Christianity was born in this revolution, it has sprung from it. But Christian humanity was unable to introduce it into life, for that would have meant rising "beyond good and evil" by which the world lives. When the mysterious words of the Gospel were made into a norm, "the last" became the new "first". It was just as it is in social revolutions when the oppressed class comes into power and begins to oppress others. This is the fate of all the Gospel words in so far as they are turned into a norm. The paradox is that the oppressed never can be masters, for as soon as they obtain mastery they become the oppressors. The poor never can be masters, for as soon as they obtain mastery they become rich. Therefore no external revolutions can correspond to the radical change proclaimed in the Gospel. The Gospel does not preach laws and norms, and cannot be interpreted in that sense.

The gospel is the good news of the coming of the Kingdom of God. Christ's call to us is the call to His Kingdom and can only be interpreted in that sense. The morality of the Kingdom of God proves to be unlike the morality of the fallen world, which is on this side of good and evil. The Gospel morality lies beyond the familiar distinction between good and evil according to which the first are first and the last are last. The ethics of redemption is in every way opposed to the ideas of this world. Most of what Christ says takes the form of "it hath been said, but I say unto you." Tareyev is right when he insists that the Gospel is absolute in character and incommensurable with the relative naturally historical life. "But I say unto you that ye resist not evil." The ordinary moral life is based upon resisting evil. "Love your enemies, bless them that curse you, do good to them that hate you, and pray for them which despitefully use you, and persecute you." If this call of the Gospel be understood as a law, it is impracticable; it is senseless from the point of view of the ethics of law, it presupposes a different and a gracious order of being. "Seek ye first the Kingdom of God and His righteousness, and all these things shall be added unto you." Herein lies the essence of the Gospel and of Christianity. . . .

It is impossible to understand the Gospel as a norm or law. If it is understood in that sense it becomes hostile to life and incompatible with it. The absolute character of the Gospel teaching about life then becomes unintelligible and impracticable. The chief argument that the world has always brought against the gospel is that it is impracticable and opposed to the very laws of life. And indeed the morality of the Gospel is paradoxical and contrary to the morality of our world even at its highest. The Gospel is opposed not only to evil but to what men consider good. Usually people have tried to make the Gospel fit the requirements of this world and so make it acceptable. But this has always meant a distortion of Christianity. How then are we to understand the absolute, transcendental and uncompromising character of the truth proclaimed in the Gospel? The Gospel is the good news of the coming of the Kingdom of God. This is the essence both of the Gospel and of Christianity as a whole. "Seek ye first the Kingdom of God and all these things will be added unto you." The Gospel reveals the absolute life of the Kingdom, and everything in it proves to be unlike the relative life of the world. The Gospel morality is not a norm or a law because it is the morality of paradise and is beyond our good and evil, beyond our legalistic distinctions between good and evil. . . .

Christ came to bring down fire on earth, and everything that men regard as valuable, all the kingdoms built up by them, are consumed in that fire. Be perfect as your Father in heaven is perfect. Is that a norm and a rule of life? Of course not. The perfection of the Heavenly Father cannot be the norm for a sinful world; it is absolute, while a law or rule is always relative to sin. It is a revelation of an absolute, divine life, different from the sinful life of the world. Thou shalt do no murder, thou shalt not steal, thou shalt not commit adultery—all this can be a norm or a rule for the sinful life of the world and is relative to it. But the perfection of the Heavenly Father and the Kingdom of God are not relative to anything and cannot be made into a rule. The Gospel appeals to the inner, spiritual man and not to the outer man, a member of society. It calls not for external works in the social world but for the awakening and regeneration of the spiritual life, for a new birth that is to bring us into the Kingdom of God. The Gospel is addressed to the eternal principle in the human soul independent of historical epochs and social changes, and in a certain sense it is not social. Everything in the Gospel is connected with the person of Christ and is incomprehensible apart from that connection. The injunctions of the Gospel are utterly unrealizable and impossible as rules of action. But what is impossible for man, is possible for God. Only in and through Christ is the perfection similar to the perfection of the Heavenly Father realized, and the Kingdom of God actually comes. The Gospel is based not upon law, even if it be a new law, but upon Christ Himself, upon His personality. Such is the new ethics of grace and redemption.[11]

THE ETHICS OF CREATIVENESS

The Gospel constantly speaks of the fruit which the seed must bring forth if it falls on good soil and of talents given to man which must be returned with profit. Under cover of parable Christ refers in these words to man's creative activity, to his creative vocation. Burying one's talents in the ground, i.e. absence of creativeness, is condemned by Christ. The whole of St. Paul's teaching about various gifts is concerned with man's creative vocation. The gifts are from God and they indicate that man is intended to do creative work. These gifts are various, and everyone is called to creative service in accordance with the special gift bestowed upon him. It is therefore a mistake to assert, as people often do, that the Holy Writ contains no reference to creativeness. It does—but we must be able to read it, we must guess what it is God wants and expects of man.

Creativeness is always a growth, an addition, the making of something new that had not existed in the world before. The problem of creativeness is the problem as to whether something completely new is really possible. Creativeness from its very meaning is bringing forth out of nothing. Nothing becomes something, non-being becomes being. Creativeness presupposes non-being, just as Hegel's "becoming" does. Like Plato's Eros, creativeness is the child of poverty and plenty, of want and abundance of power. Creativeness is connected with sin and at the same time it is sacrificial. True creativeness always involves catharsis, purification, liberation of the spirit from psycho-physical elements and victory over them. Creation is different in principle from generation and emanation. In emanation particles of matter radiate from a centre and are separated off. Nor is creation a redistribution of force and energy, as evolution is. So far from being identical with evolution, creation is the very opposite of it. In evolution nothing new is made, but the old is redistributed. Evolution is necessity, creation is freedom. Creation is the greatest mystery of life, the mystery of the appearance of something new that had never existed before and is not deduced from, or generated by, anything. Creativeness presupposes non-being μή όν (and not ούκ όν) which is the source of the primeval, pre-cosmic, preexistent freedom in man. The mystery of creativeness is the mystery of freedom. Creativeness can only spring from fathomless freedom, for such freedom alone can give rise to the new, to what had never existed before. Out of being, out of something that exists, it is impossible to create that which is completely new; there can only be emanation, generation, redistribution. But creativeness means breaking through from non-being, from freedom, to the world of being. The mystery of creativeness is revealed in the biblical myth of the creation. God created the world out of nothing, i.e., freely and out of freedom. The world was not an emanation from God, it was not evolved or born from Him, but created, i.e. it was absolutely new, it was something that had never been before. Creativeness is only possible because the world is created, because there is a Creator. Man, made by God in His own image and likeness, is also a creator and is called to creative work. . . .

Man cannot produce the material for creation out of himself, out of nothing, out of the depths of his own being. The creative act is of the nature of marriage, it always implies a meeting between different elements. The material for human creativeness is borrowed from the world created by God. We find this in all art and in all inventions and discoveries. We find this in the creativeness of knowledge and in philosophy which presupposes the existence of the world created by God—objective realities without which thought would be left in a void. God has granted man the creative gift, the talent, the genius and also the world in and through which the creative activity is to be carried out. God calls man to perform the creative act and realize his vocation, and He is expecting an answer to His call. Man's answer to God's call cannot entirely consist of elements that are given by and proceed from God. Something must come from man also, and that something is the very essence of creativeness, which brings forth new realities. It is, indeed, not "something" but "nothing"—in other words it is freedom, without which there can be no creative activity. Freedom not determined by anything answers God's call to creative work, but in doing so it makes use of the gift or genius received from God and of materials present in the created world. When man is said to create out of nothing it means that he creates out of freedom. In every creative conception there is an element of primeval freedom, fathomless, undetermined by anything, not proceeding from God but ascending towards God. God's call is address to that abyss of freedom, and the answer must come from it. Fathomless freedom is present in all creativeness, but the creative process is so complex that it is not easy to detect this primary element in it. It is a process of interaction between grace and freedom, between forces going from God to man and from man to God. . . .

Man's creative activity alone bears witness to his vocation and show what he has been destined for in the world. The law says nothing about vocation, nor does the ethics of redemption as such. The Gospel and St. Paul's Epistles speak of man's gifts and vocation only because they go beyond the mystery of redemption. True creativeness is always in the Holy Spirit, for only in the Spirit can there be that union of grace and freedom which we find in creativeness. Its meaning for ethics is twofold. To begin with, ethics must inquire into the moral significance of all creative work, even if it has no direct relation to the moral life. Art and knowledge have a moral significance, like all activities which create higher values. Secondly, ethics must inquire into the creative significance of moral activity. Moral life itself, moral actions and valuations have a creative character. The ethics of law and norm does not as yet recognize this, and it is therefore inevitable that we should pass to the ethics of creativeness, which deals with man's true vocation and destiny.

Creativeness and a creative attitude to life as a whole is not man's right, it is his duty. It is a moral imperative that applies in every department of life. Creative effort in artistic and cognitive activity has a moral value. Realization of truth and goodness is a moral good. There may, however, be a conflict between the creation of perfect cultural values and the creation of a perfect human personality. The path of creativeness is also a path to moral and religious perfection, a way of realizing the fullness of life. The frequently quoted words of Goethe, "All theory is grey but the tree of life is eternally green," may be turned the other way round: "All life is grey but the tree of theory is eternally green." "Theory" will then mean creativeness, the thought of a Plato or a Hegel, while "life" will stand for a mere struggle for existence, dull and commonplace, family dissensions, disappointments and so on. In that sense "theory" means rising to a higher moral level. . . .

The ethics of creativeness differs from the ethics of law first of all because every moral task is for it absolutely individual and creative. The moral problems of life cannot be solved by an automatic application of universally binding rules. It is impossible to say that in the same circumstances one ought always and everywhere to act in the same way. It is impossible if only because circumstances never are quite the same. Indeed, the very opposite rule might be formulated. One ought always to act individually and solve every moral problem for oneself, showing creativeness in one's moral activity, and not for a single moment become a moral automaton. A man ought to make moral inventions with regard to the problems that life sets him. Hence, for the ethics of creativeness freedom means something very different from what it does for the ethics of law. For the latter the so-called freedom of will has no creative character and means merely acceptance or rejection of the law of the good and responsibility for doing one or the other. For the ethics of creativeness freedom means not the acceptance of the law but individual creation of values. Freedom is creative energy, the possibility of building up new realities. The ethics of law knows nothing of that freedom. It does not know that the good is being created, that in every individual and unrepeatable moral act new good that had never existed before is brought into being by the moral agent whose invention it is. There exists no fixed, static moral order subordinated to a single universally binding moral law. Man is not a passive executor of the laws of that world-order. Man is a creator and an inventor. His moral conscience must at every moment of his life be creative and inventive. The ethics of creativeness is one of dynamics and energy. Life is based upon energy and not upon law. It may be said, indeed, that energy is the source of law. The ethics of creativeness takes a very different view of the struggle against evil than does the ethics of law. According to it, that struggle consists in the creative realization of the good and the transformation of evil into good, rather than in the mere destruction of evil. The ethics of law is concerned with the finite: the world is for it a self-contained system and there is no way out of it. The ethics of creativeness is concerned with the infinite: the world is for it open and plastic, with boundless horizons and possibilities of breaking through to other worlds. It overcomes the nightmare of the finite from which there is no escape.

The ethics of creativeness is different from the ethics of redemption: it is concerned in the first place with values and not with salvation. The moral end of life is for it not the salvation of one's soul or the redemption of guilt but creative realization of righteousness and of values which need not belong to the moral order. The ethics of creativeness springs from personality but is concerned with the world, while the ethics of law springs from the world and society but is concerned with the personality. The ethics of creativeness alone overcomes the negative fixation of the spirit upon struggle with sin and evil and replaces it by the positive, i.e. by the creation of the valuable contents of life. It overcomes not only the earthly but the heavenly, transcendental selfishness with which even the ethics of redemption is infected. Fear of punishment and of eternal torments in hell can play no part in the ethics of creativeness. It opens a way to a pure, disinterested morality, since every kind of fear distorts moral experience and activity. It may indeed be said that nothing which is done out of fear, whether it be of temporal or of eternal torments, has any moral value. The truly moral motive is not fear of punishment and of hell, but selfless and disinterested love of God and of the divine in life, of truth and perfection and all positive values. This is the basis of the ethics of creativeness.[12]

CREATIVENESS AND IMAGINATION

The ethics of creativeness presupposes that the task which confronts man is infinite and the world is not completed. But the tragedy is that the realization of every infinite task is finite. Creative imagination is of fundamental importance to the ethics of creativeness. Without imagination there can be no creative activity. Creativeness means in the first instance imagining something different, better, and higher. Imagination calls up before us something better than the reality around us. Creativeness always rises above reality. Imagination plays this part not only in art and in myth making, but also in scientific discoveries, technical inventions and moral life, creating a better type of relations between human beings. There is such a thing as moral imagination which creates the image of a better life; it is absent only from legalistic ethics. No imagination is needed for automatically carrying out a law or norm. In moral life the power of creative imagination plays the part of talent. By the side of the self-contained moral world of laws and rules to which nothing can be added, man builds up in imagination a higher, free and beautiful world lying beyond ordinary good and evil.

And this is what gives beauty to life. As a matter of fact life can never be determined solely by law; men always imagine for themselves a different and better life, freer and more beautiful, and they realize those images. The Kingdom of God is the image of a full, perfect, beautiful, free and divine life. Only law has nothing to do with imagination, or, rather, it is limited to imagining compliance with, or violation of, its behests. But the most perfect fulfillment of the law is not the same as the perfect life.

Imagination may also be a source of evil; there may be bad imagination and phantasms. Evil thoughts are an instance of bad imagination. Crimes are conceived in imagination. But imagination also brings about a better life. A man devoid of imagination is incapable of creative moral activity and of building up a better life. The very conception of a better life towards which we ought to strive is the result of creative imagination. Those who have no imagination think that there is no better life at all and there ought not to be. All that exists for them is the unalterable order of existence in which unalterable law ought to be realized. Jacob Boehme ascribed enormous importance to imagination. The world is created by God through imagination, through images which arise in God in eternity.[13]

CREATIVENESS AND BEAUTY

... From the ontological and cosmological point of view, the final end of being must be thought of as beauty and not as goodness. Plato defined beauty as the magnificence of the good. Complete, perfect and harmonious being is beauty. Teleological ethics is normative and legalistic. It regards the good as the purpose of life, i.e. as a norm or a law which must be fulfilled. Teleological ethics always implies absence of moral imagination, for it conceives the end as a norm and not as an image, not as a product of the creative energy of life. Moral life must be determined not by a purpose or a norm but by imagery and the exercise of creative activity. Beauty is the image of creative energy radiating over the whole world and transforming it. Teleological ethics based upon the idea of the good as an absolute purpose is hostile to freedom, but creative ethics is based upon freedom. Beauty means a transfigured creation, the good means creation fettered by the law which denounces sin. The paradox is that the law fetters the energy of the good, it does not want the good to be interpreted as a force, for in that case the world would escape from the power of the law. To transcend the morality of law means to put infinite creative energy in the place of commands, prohibitions, and taboos.[14]

CREATIVENESS AND THE KINGDOM OF HEAVEN

... All efforts to create new life, whether in historical Christianity, by social revolutions, or by the information of sects and so forth, alike end in objectivization, and adaptation to dull, everyday normality. The old rises in new forms, the old inequality, love of power, luxury, schisms and the rest. Life in our aeon is only a testing and a pathway, but the testing has a meaning and the path leads to a consummating end. It would become easier for man if he were aware of the fact that a further revelation of the unknown is at hand, a revelation not only of the Holy Spirit but of a new man and a new cosmos... .

The greatest religious and moral truth to which man must grow, is that we cannot be saved individually. My salvation presupposes the salvation of others also, the salvation of my neighbour, it presupposes universal salvation, the salvation of the whole world, the transfiguration of the world. The very idea of salvation arises from the oppressed condition of man; and it is associated with a forensic conception of Christianity. This ought to be replaced by the idea of creative transformation and enlightenment, by the idea of perfecting all life. 'Behold I make all things new'. It is not only God Who makes all things new, it is man too. The period of the end is not only a period of destruction, but also a period of divine-human creativeness, a new life and a new world. The Church of the New Testament was a symbolic image of the eternal Church of the Spirit. In the Church of the Spirit the eternal Gospel will be read. When we draw near to the eternal Kingdom of the Spirit the torturing contradictions of life will be overcome and sufferings which towards the end will be increased, will pass into their antithesis, into joy. And this will be the case not only for the future but also for the past, for there will be a reversal of time and all living things will share in the end.[15]

NOTES

1. [Nicholas Berdyaev, *The Destiny of Man* (New York: Charles Scribner's Sons, 1937), 71–75.]
2. [Nicholas Berdyaev, *Slavery and Freedom* (New York: Charles Scribner's Sons, 1944), 42–43]
3. [Ibid., 45–46.]
4. [Ibid., 46–47.]
5. [Nicholas Berdyaev, *Freedom and the Spirit* (London: Geoffrey Bles, 1935), 171–174, 176–179.]

6. [Berdyaev, *Destiny of Man*, 47, 49–50, 52.]

7. [Ibid., 56–57.]

8. [Ibid., 57.]

9. [Ibid., 100–101.]

10. [Ibid., 111–112, 115–116, 119–120, 122–126, 128–131.]

11. [Ibid., 133–142, 157–159.]

12. [Ibid., 162–165, 169–171.]

13. [Ibid., 182–184.]

14. [Ibid., 185.]

15. [Nicholas Berdyaev, *The Divine and the Human* (London: Geoffrey Bles, 1949), 199–202.]

[CHAPTER 18]

Vladimir Nikolaievich Lossky (1903–1958)

SELECTED AND EDITED BY MIKHAIL KULAKOV

Vladimir Lossky is probably the best known and most widely followed modern Orthodox theologian. His classic work The Mystical Theology of the Eastern Church, *first published in Paris in 1944, is a milestone in the ongoing dialogue between Eastern and Western Christianity. Lossky's brilliant critique of "Catholic essentialism" and "Protestant existentialism" has had a profound impact on both Western European and Eastern theology, and his portrayal of Orthodoxy as that which mediates between the two Western traditions continues to attract attention in both camps. Pope John Paul II expressed his admiration of the "courageous research" of Vladimir Lossky and compared his work in its speculative value and spiritual significance to the contributions of Jacque Maritain and Étienne Gilson in the West and Vladimir Soloviev and Pavel Florensky in the East.[1] Lossky's "originality and imagination in interpreting the Eastern fathers," wrote the Anglican theologian Rowan Williams, "should secure him a firm place among twentieth century theologians, and practically all Eastern Orthodox ecclesiology in the past few decades has taken his scheme as a starting-point."[2] Emphasizing the principal "dogmatic dissimilarity between the Christian East and the Christian West,"[3] he focused on the apophatic (negative) foundations of theology understood as a "personal encounter with God in silence." Building on this contemplative foundation Lossky called for a radical deconceptualization of personhood both in Trinitarian theology and in anthropology. He incorporated into his creative synthesis the insights of the Cappadocian fathers, Symeon the New Theologian, Maximus the Confessor, the spiritual masters of the Greek Philokalia, and Gregory Palamas. Lossky insisted that a person cannot be reduced to his nature or expressed in concepts. Nature can only be described as the "content of the person and not as the person."[4] There is an ethical depth in Lossky's ascetic teaching on personhood. The drive for self-transcendence and kenotic "self-forgetting" is the primordial foundation and the nerve of authentic personhood.*

Vladimir Nikolaievich Lossky was born in 1903 in St. Petersburg into the family of a well-known Russian intuitionist philosopher Nikolay Onufriyevich Lossky. He studied briefly at the universities of Petrograd and Prague; he graduated from the Sorbonne with a degree in medieval studies (1927). In 1922 Vladimir was exiled from Russia and left Petrograd on the famous "philosophical ship" together with all the members of his father's family and other notable intellectuals who refused to cooperate with the new Soviet government. After a two-year stay in Prague, the family eventually settled in Paris. There young Lossky immersed himself into the study of Western theology and spirituality, under the guidance of the influential Thomist scholar, Etienne Gilson. Except for the highly influential Mystical Theology of the Eastern Church, the Sofia Controversy, and several other essays, most of Lossky's theological works were published after his death in 1958. His pioneering study of Meister Eckhart was published in 1960, and collections of essays such as The Vision of God *and* In the Image and Likeness of God *appeared in the original French in 1962 and 1967 respectively. Lossky stimulated a fruitful ecumenical exchange not only in France, but he also led in the Anglican-Orthodox dialogue at the annual conferences of the Anglo-Russian Fellowship of St. Alban and St. Sergius in Abingdon, England. He had many followers among younger Anglican theologians associated with the Fellowship of St. Alban.[5] Lossky played an active part in the French resistance movement during the Nazi occupation of France in his own creative way.*

Lossky's diary Sept Jours sur les Routes de France *(which he wrote in June 1940) contains his reflections on divine and human justice, "holy wars," and "just wars." As the reader will observe from the following selections, Lossky's commitment to active resistance to aggression was not unqualified. He denounced the "spiritualist heresy" of infusing a war with an artificial soul and drew a distinction between absolute reality and relative or secondary concepts and values.*

Lossky's theology has had a profound influence on almost all notable Eastern Orthodox theologians of the twentieth century (such as Christos Yannaras,[6] Nikolai Afanasiev, Pavel Evdokimov, and Olivier Clément) as well as Western European Catholic and Anglican theologians (such as Lois Bouyer, Yves Congar, and Rowan Williams).

Lossky was not a philosopher of law like Vladimir Soloviev, and in his theological writings he certainly did not address political, social, and ethical issues with the directness and extensiveness that one finds in the works of Berdyaev or Soloviev. Lossky recognized Soloviev's genius, yet his strong emphasis on political neutrality and independence of the Church would not allow him to accept Soloviev's idea of a "Christian state" and Soloviev's notion of "theocracy" understood as a "harmonious cooperation" of prophet, priest, and king. In the Eastern Orthodox theological world of today, Lossky is indisputably more influential than Soloviev and Berdyaev. While he is primarily appreciated for his theological vision, his critique of nationalist and deterministic tendencies in Russian religious philosophy, his analysis of the pitfalls of Western conceptualism and juridicalism, and his holistic vision of human freedom contain profound implications for contemporary discussions of law and social ethics.

Lossky did not share the Western understanding of the eternal law of God, the lex aeterna as an objective body of norms outside the will of God to which He conforms his will. Lossky contrasted the dynamic personalist concept of direct divine economy, which entails risk on the part of God to the Western rationalist view which he described as a fixed "divine plan" of "immutable preordinations."⁷ This personalist stance shaped Lossky's understanding of the divine law and legal order. Citing St. Paul's qualification of the law as that "which was added because of transgressions" (Gal. 3:19), Lossky insists that the "divine Law is proper to the catastrophic state of created being in subjection to the law of sin and death." As one will observe from the following selections, the Eastern Orthodox and particularly Lossky's understanding of divine order in the universe is expressly personalist, apophatic, and experiential in contrast to the Catholic rational notion of natural law. Discursive reason is incapable of direct apprehension of dynamic divine economy. Truth is also understood experientially, rather than rationally.⁸ Thus, if at the foundation of Catholic legal consciousness and Catholic ethics lie the rational notion of natural law and the key role of human reason in the apprehension of this natural law, Lossky's ethics, by contrast, could be described as the internalized and experiential ethics of transfiguration through participation in the divine nature. Theosis or deification is at the heart of Lossky's ethics.

SEPT JOURS SUR LES ROUTES DE FRANCE

... I HAD THE IMPRESSION that the State—that indispensable convention so necessary to human societies, that great fictitious reality, anchored in our consciousness to the point of being part of ourselves—was ceasing to exist. But order, the State's function, carried on nevertheless, through a sort of inertia, an innate discipline, or—more likely—through the mute solidarity of French people suffering the same fate.

Did the Third Republic really exist anymore, with its Government, civil servants, courts, bailiffs, stamped papers, and with all its administrative symbolism? Or, going back in time ten centuries, would we find ourselves suddenly transported back to the era of the Norman invasions, the time when the kingship of the last Carolingians was disappearing; the royal feeling withdrawing into peoples' consciousness to be replaced by other instincts and other ties, more concrete and more personal—the instinct for companionship, the man-to-man ties that were the basis of feudal society, with its manly and solid virtues? ...

I was following my conscience when I made the decision to leave. Three days earlier, on Monday night, the TSF (radio) had communicated the order from the military governor of the Seine for all eligible men who had not yet been called up. Potential conscripts were to leave the Paris region within six days, starting Thursday June 13, and retreat to the provinces, to the destinations that would be assigned to them by the mobile guards at the main exit points on the south side of the capital. Above all else, my friend and I wanted to sign up to participate in the defense of Paris (we still expected the city to be defended). At the recruitment center on rue St. Dominique, our fate was resolved in an unexpected way: my friend—a Russian refugee—could not be accepted into the Foreign Legion due to his poor health. But I—French and eligible for mobilization—was told to wait until I was called up, and could not speed things up with a voluntary enlistment. "But I want to help defend Paris." The lieutenant shrugged, with a bitter smile. "Try to sign up with the territorial guards, at the police station." Same shrug and unhappy smile at the police station... The only thing left to do was to leave, "retreat to the provinces." My friend, who wanted to follow me, not obtaining in time the permit foreigners need, finally had to resign himself to staying behind. I prepared to leave.

At the Chevrot farm we were met by a sergeant's coarse kindness. They made room for us on the straw in a very large barn, next to other "eligible recruits." The other half of the barn sheltered refugee families. We each received a pack of 'troop' cigarettes—the Army's first welcome. Tomorrow I will finally be a soldier. I will have my place—modest, but clear and well defined—among those who would resist. I will have my nameless regimental number, one "unknown soldier" among so many others. I will no longer be on the sidelines of the communal job to be done. I will no longer be an intellectual set apart from the national destiny—a fragile and sensitive instrument that constantly turned in on itself to meditate, a being for whom life stops to make room for a thought. I will finally simply do my duty: no thoughts, no anguish—just gritting my teeth and staring straight at this monstrous reality that was still impossible to take in: the Germans are in Paris. . . .

But then [during the Hundred Years War] the enemy was "driven out of the Kingdom of France." The miracle of Joan of Arc took place at the limits of all human hope, where the resources—of valiant captains with prowess at arms, of wise counselors adept in political matters—reached their end. The miracle of Joan of Arc, this act of God, took place at the limit where all the prelates' magisteria and all the philosophy doctors' theology were nothing more than useless verbiage, incapable of reanimating the faith of the Christian people—vain words, like the insane comments made by Job's rational friends. . . .

Every day since the war started, we had heard words light in judgment but heavy in consequences, because it is always words that condemn, that deliver us to our destiny. They told us, "We will win this war because we are stronger, because we are richer. We will win because we want to." As if weapons were enough in themselves to secure the victory. As if the war were just a huge industrial endeavor, a question of capital. Military *maté-riel* war—inhuman war—materialistic war. Yet without a doubt we lost that war. We must have the courage to say it. And there's more: France could not have won that war, as it was presented to us. Otherwise France would no longer be France, a humane place par excellence. Otherwise, having won the war of military *matériel* (as it was presented to us), the country would have lost perhaps the most precious thing it possesses: the foundation of its being. France would have lost that which is France, that which differen-tiates it from every other country on Earth, if it had won that war without a human face. Everywhere where we resisted the enemy, that was an act of human courage; the French courage that gave up the battle to enemy *matériel*, superior in number and strength. Despite the laws of "*matériel* war," we defended the soil, the land. Without a doubt we lost the *matériel* war. But the human war, the French war, was not lost. The Germans are in Paris; they may already be on the Loire, on the Garonne, everywhere. But France is not yet conquered: the human war has just begun. It may last a century, like that other great time of trouble; the era that gave rise to a new France—the era we call the Hundred Years' War.

There was another heresy—spiritualist this time—that tried to superim-pose itself on the "*matériel* war," to infuse that war with an artificial soul. This was the ideology of a "holy war," of a "crusade." The ideology had sev-eral nuances: the struggle for the democracies, for freedom, for human dignity, for Western culture, for Christian civilization, and finally for divine justice. I say 'heresy' because these ideas—while often just in themselves—were not based on a living experience. They did not spring from a deep and healthy source that alone could have transformed them into "idea-forces." And these words rang false, as all abstractions do. They especially rang false because they tried to present secondary, relative concepts and values as *absolutes*. Even Christian civilization, as a civilization, is no more than a product, a creation, an external manifestation of an absolute reality, which is the faith of the Christian peoples. Holy war is not waged for cathedrals, for theological works, for missals. These are merely the trappings of the Church—Christ's clothes divided up by the soldiers at the foot of the Cross. As for the Church, source of all these secondary goods, it needs neither our material defense nor our childish swords. It is pointless to repeat Peter's naive gesture of slashing the slave's ear in the garden of Gethsemane... War is not fought for absolute values. This was the great error of the so-called "religious" wars and the main cause of their inhuman atrocities. War is equally not waged for relative values that we attempt to render absolute, for abstract concepts we cloak in religion. If we oppose the idol of the "pure race" with the more humane idols of law, liberty and humanity, they would not be any the less idols for it, ideas rendered hypostasized and absolute; the war would still be a war of idols, and not a human war. Human war, the only just war (inasmuch as any war may be called just) is a war for relative values, for values that we know to be relative. It is a war where man—a being called for an absolute goal—dedicates himself spontaneously and without hesitation for a relative value that he knows to be relative: the soil, the land, the Homeland. And this sacrifice acquires an absolute value, imperishable and eternal for the human person. Joan of Arc's divine mission had a relative value as its goal: taking the Dauphin to Reims to return France's king to her. Joan had no animosity toward the English she would "drive out of France." This is one of the primary characteristics of the human war she waged. It is also characteristic of France's soul, of which Joan of Arc is the most perfect image. . . .

We also talked about Justice, and even the justice of God, in the name of which we should fight so that justice (which is an attribute of God) would triumph in the face of our adversaries' iniquity. "Our cause is just. This is why God will grant us victory." This is how the prelates spoke, the people's spiritual leaders. The just cause often triumphed in "God's judgment," those judicial duels waged between two parties in conflict. But those two parties abandoned their justice, abandoned their just cause, to give place to divine justice alone—without possibility of appeal—which would manifest through their feat of arms. And again, the Church was obliged to oppose this practice eight hundred years ago. . . . I had heard a great prelate at Notre Dame speak before thousands of faithful about our just cause, call upon God that He would grant us victory in the name of this just cause. If we followed his thought to its logical end, God would find Himself obliged to help us because He is just, and we are defending justice. He could not act nor wish otherwise without contradicting Himself, without renouncing

His attribute of Justice, immutable (as is everything about God written in religious works and theological guides). So if we lost this war after all, after calling on God to give us victory in the name of His justice, what would there be left to say? It came down to this: either our cause was not the just cause, or God is unjust. Yes, He is unjust, if we wish to put it that way, because He is greater than justice, because His justice is not our justice, because His ways are not our ways. Because before His justice, which will one day shake the foundations of the universe, our poor justice is nothing less than injustice. . . . We should have prayed for victory with tears and great contrition, bearing in mind this fearsome Justice, before which we are all unjust. We should not have called on Justice, which is beyond our measure, which we could not bear, but on the infinite mercy which made the Son of God descend from Heaven.

"Lord, we are all unjust before You, and our justice is vain; yet come to our aid, because we are unjust and blind, and cannot find Your way. Stay Your sword of justice, and grant us the victory over our enemy, whom You have allowed to invade France. For nothing is done that is not Your will, and You are the Master of the peoples of the Earth, whom you punish for their own greater good."

But the blindness of an 'autonomous' lay morality hardened hearts, even among people of the Church. We have long since forgotten what Philippe de Commines, wise counselor to Louis XI and an historian well-versed in politics, knew: "Thus it seems that God tries to show us the way and give us many signs, and also strikes us with many rods for our bestial nature and our evil, which I think is better. Who can remedy this if God does not?"

At the crossroad, in the center of Arpajon, a sergeant—a Moroccan with a complacent smile—was acting the policeman. With a triumphant gesture he kept pointing out the same direction to all those who had the bad luck of turning toward his lights. Military convoys, troupes, refugee families were all heading toward La Ferté-Allais, instead of taking the Estampes route just a little below. I naively relied on him as well, and it cost me a detour of a few kilometers. Finally, having reached the right road by taking paths across fields, I headed once again toward Estampes, the ultimate goal of my long trip and certain refuge, where I will at last stop being an "individual" to become a member of the collective group, which carried out the huge task of national defense.

Strange failure awaited those great "trips abroad,"—the Crusades, that mysterious push toward the East. In spite of what is usually said, it was not just the cupidity of the noblemen, greedy for booty, nor the taste for war adventures peculiar of the feudal world, which made the Western Christians leave their families and worldly goods, in order to take the Cross and head out toward the unknown lands of the Middle East, overtaken by an irresistible impulse. It was above all an enormous pilgrimage, an armed pilgrimage, a movement of religious nature, to which other motives, other interests, were soon added on. At times, the legends which arise around an existing event, the poetry which it inspires, reveal to us the depth hidden in an historic act, while remaining unnoticed by historians who base themselves on "positive data." They traveled toward the East to deliver the Saint Sepulcher. They went also to find the mysterious country where the apostle St. John lived eternally, reigning over a Christian people. They went there above all pushed by a vague religious uneasiness, which will later find its expression in the mystical poem on "The Search of the Holy Grail," where the chalice of the Last Supper would symbolize the plenitude of the Gifts of the Holy Spirit, the Christian plenitude. But the Crusades became a war of pillage and destruction, relentless against the Orthodox Christian. In place of the spiritual kingdom of St. John, they founded an ephemeral kingdom, "the Latin Empire"; in place of the Holy Grail, the knights brought to the West the Manichean heresy of the Bulgarians. It is then that a new Crusade stirred the French people of the North against those of the South. The first "religious war" bloodied the French soil. The Languedoc would be bound to know others, three centuries later.[9]

THE MYSTICAL THEOLOGY OF THE EASTERN CHURCH

IMAGE AND LIKENESS

Men have therefore a common nature, one single nature in many human persons. This distinction of nature and person in man is no less difficult to grasp than the analogous distinction of the one nature and three persons in God. Above all, we must remember that we do not know the person, the human hypostasis in its true condition, free from alloy. We commonly use the words "persons" or "personal" to mean individuals, or individual. We are in the habit of thinking of these two terms, person and individual, almost as though they were synonyms. We employ them indifferently to express the same thing. But, in a certain sense, individual and person mean opposite things, the word individual expressing a certain mixture of the person with elements which belong to the common nature, while person, on the other hand, means that which distinguishes it from nature. In our present condition we know persons only through individuals, and as individuals. When we wish to define, "to characterize" a person, we gather together individual characteristics, "traits of character" which are to be met with elsewhere in other individuals, and which because they belong to nature are never absolutely "personal." Finally, we admit that what is most dear to us in someone, what makes him himself, remains indefinable, for there is nothing in nature which properly pertains to the person, which is always unique and incomparable. The man who is governed by his nature and acts in the strength of his natural qualities, of his "character", is the least personal. He sets himself up as an individual, proprietor of his own nature, which he pits against the natures of others and regards as his "me," thereby confusing person and nature. This confusion, proper to fallen humanity, has a special name in the ascetic writings of the Eastern Church—αυτότης, φιλαυτία or, in Russian, *samost,* which can perhaps be best translated by the word egoism, or rather if we may create a Latin barbarism "ipseity."

A difficulty is met with in reference to the Christological dogma which would see the will as a function of the nature; for us it is easier to envisage the person as willing, asserting and imposing himself through his will. However, the idea of the person implies freedom *vis-à-vis* the nature. The person is free from its nature, is not determined by it. The human hypostasis can only realize itself by the renunciation of its own will, of all that governs us, and makes us subject to natural necessity.

Made in the image of God, man is a personal being confronted with a personal God. God speaks to him as to a person, and man responds. Man, according to St. Basil, is a creature who has received a commandment to become God.[10] But this commandment is addressed to human freedom, and does not overrule it. As a personal being man can accept the will of God; he can also reject it. Even when he removes himself as far as possible from God, and becomes unlike Him in His nature, he remains a person. The image of God in man is indestructible. In the same way, he remains a personal being when he fulfills the will of God and in his nature realizes perfect likeness with Him. For according to St. Gregory Nazianzen, "God honoured man in giving him freedom, in order that goodness should properly belong to him who chooses it, no less than to Him who placed the first fruits of goodness in his nature."[11] Thus, whether he chooses good or evil, whether he tends to likeness or unlikeness, man possesses his nature freely, because he is a person created in the image of God. All the same, since the person cannot be separated from the nature which exists in it, every imperfection, every "unlikeness" in the nature limits the person, and obscures "the image of God." Indeed, if freedom belongs to us as persons, the will by which we act is a faculty of our nature. According to St. Maximus, the will is "a natural force which tends towards that which is conformed to nature, a power which embraces all the essential properties of nature."[12] St. Maximus distinguishes this natural will (θέλημα φυσικόν) which is the desire for good to which every reasonable nature tends, from the choosing will (θέλημα γνωμικόν) which is a characteristic of the person.[13] The nature wills and acts, the person chooses, accepting or rejecting that which the nature wills. However, according to St. Maximus, this freedom of choice is already a sign of imperfection, a limitation of our true freedom. A perfect nature has no need of choice, for it knows naturally what is good. Its freedom is based on this knowledge. Our free choice (γνωμή) indicates the imperfection of fallen human nature, the loss of the divine likeness.[14]

THE WAY OF UNION

Source of all intellectual and spiritual activity, the heart, according to St. Macarius of Egypt, is "a workshop of justice and injustice."[15] It is a vessel which contains all the vices, but where at the same time, "God, the angels, life and the Kingdom, light and the apostles, and the treasures of grace are to be found."[16] "Where grace fills the pastures of the heart, it reigns over all the parts and the thoughts: for there inhabit the intelligence (νομς) and all the thoughts of the soul."[17] In this way grace passes by way of the heart into the whole of man's nature. The spirit (νομς, πνεμμα), the highest part of the human creature, is that contemplative faculty by which man is able to seek God. The most personal part of man, the principle of his conscience and of his freedom, the spirit (νομς) in human nature corresponds most nearly to the person; it might be said that it is the seat of the person, of the human hypostasis which contains in itself the whole of man's nature—spirit, soul and body. This is why the Greek Fathers are often ready to identify the νους with the image of God in man.[18] Man must live according to the spirit; the whole human complex must become "spiritual" (πνευματικός), must acquire the "likeness." It is in fact the spirit which becomes united with baptismal grace, and through which grace enters into the heart, the centre of that total human nature which is to be deified. "The uniting of the spirit with the heart," "the descent of the spirit into the heart," "the guarding of the heart by the spirit"—these expressions constantly recur in the ascetic writings of the Eastern Church. Without the heart, which is the centre of all activity, the spirit is powerless. Without the spirit, the heart remains blind, destitute of direction. It is therefore necessary to attain to a harmonious relationship between the spirit and the heart, in order to develop and build up the personality in the life of grace-for the way of union is not a mere unconscious process, and it presupposes an unceasing vigilance of spirit and a constant effort of the will.

Love is inseparable from knowledge—"gnosis." There is an element of personal awareness necessary, without which the way towards union would be blind, and without any certain object, "an illusory discipline" (ἄσκησις φαινομένη), according to St. Macarius of Egypt.[19] The ascetic life, "apart from gnosis (ομκ εν τή γνώσει), has no value, according to St. Dorotheos;[20] only a spiritual life that is fully aware—ἐν γνώσει—a life in constant communion with God, is able to transfigure our nature by making it like the divine nature, by making it participate in the uncreated light of grace, after the example of the humanity of Christ who appeared to the disciples on Mount Tabor clothed in uncreated glory.[21]

REDEMPTION AND DEIFICATION

... When the dogma of the redemption is treated in isolation from the general body of Christian teaching, there is always a risk of limiting the tradition by interpreting it exclusively in terms of the work of the Redeemer. Then theological thought develops along three lines: original sin, its reparation on the cross, and the appropriation of the saving results of the work of Christ to Christians. In these constricting perspectives of a theology dominated by the idea of redemption, the patristic sentence, "God made Himself man that man might become God," seems to be strange and abnormal. The thought of union with God is forgotten because of our preoccupation solely with our own salvation; or, rather, union with God is seen only negatively, in contrast with our present wretchedness. . . .

It was Anselm of Canterbury, with his treatise *Cur Deus Homo*, who undoubtedly made the first attempt to develop the dogma of redemption apart from the rest of Christian teaching. In his work Christian horizons are limited by the drama played between God, who is infinitely offended by sin, and man, who is unable to satisfy the impossible demands of vindictive justice. The drama finds its resolution in the death of Christ, the Son of God who has become man in order to substitute Himself for us and to pay our debt to divine justice. What becomes of the dispensation of the Holy Spirit here? His part is reduced to that of an auxiliary, an assistant in redemption, causing us to receive Christ's expiating merit. The final goal of our union with God is, if not excluded altogether, at least shut out from our sight by the stern vault of a theological conception built on the ideas of original guilt and its reparation. The price of our redemption having been paid in the death of Christ, the resurrection and the ascension are only a glorious happy end of His work, a kind of apotheosis without direct relationship to our human destiny. This redemptionist theology, placing all the emphasis on the passion, seems to take no interest in the triumph of Christ over death. The very work of the Christ-Redeemer, to which this theology is confined, seems to be truncated, impoverished, reduced to a change of the divine attitude toward fallen men, unrelated to the nature of humanity.

We find an entirely different conception of the redeeming work of Christ in the thought of St. Athanasius.[22] "Christ," he says, "having delivered the temple of His body to death, offered one sacrifice for all men to make them innocent and free from original guilt, and also to show Himself victorious over death and to create the first fruits of the General Resurrection with His own incorruptible body." Here the juridical image of the Redemption is completed by another image, the physical—or rather biological—image of the triumph of life over death, of incorruptibility triumphing in the nature which had been corrupted by sin.

In the Fathers generally, as well as in the Scriptures, we find many images expressing the mystery of our salvation accomplished by Christ. Thus, in the Gospel, the Good Shepherd is a "bucolic" image of the work of Christ.[23] The strong man overcome by the "stronger than he, who taketh away his arms and destroys his power," is a "military" image,[24] which is often found again in the Fathers and in the Liturgy: Christ victorious over Satan, trampling upon the gates of hell, making the Cross his standard of triumph.[25] There is also a "medical" image, that of a sickly nature cured by salvation as the antidote to a poison.[26] There is an image which could be termed "diplomatic," the divine stratagem which deceives the devil in his cunning.[27] And so it goes. At last we come to the image used most often, taken by St. Paul from the Old Testament, where it was borrowed from the sphere of juridical relations.[28] Taken in this sense, redemption is a juridical image of the work of Christ, found side by side with many other images.[29] When we use the word "redemption," as we do nowadays, as a generic term designating the saving work of Christ in all its fullness, we should not forget that this juridical expression has the character of an image or simile: Christ is the Redeemer in the same sense that He is the Warrior victorious over death, the perfect Sacrificer, *etc.*

Anselm's mistake was not just that he developed a juridical view of the redemption, but rather that he wanted to see an adequate expression of the mystery of our redemption accomplished by Christ in the juridical relations implied by the word "redemption." Rejecting other expressions of this mystery as inadequate images, *quasi quaedam picturae*, he believed that he had found in the juridical image—that of the redemption—the very body of the truth, its "rational solidity," *veritatis rationabilis soliditas*, the reason why it was necessary for God to die for our salvation.[30]

The impossibility of proving rationally that the work of redemption was necessary, by making use of the juridical meaning of the term "redemption," was demonstrated by St. Gregory of Nazianzus in a magisterial *reductio ad absurdum*. . . . [31] For St. Gregory of Nazianzus, the idea of redemption, far from implying the idea of a necessity imposed by vindictive justice, is rather an expression of the dispensation, whose mystery cannot be adequately clarified in a series of rational concepts. He says, in later passage, that "it was necessary for us that God should be incarnate and die that we might live again" (c. 28). "Nothing can be compared with the miracle of my salvation: a few drops of blood re-make the whole universe" (c. 29).

After the constricted horizons of an exclusively juridical theology, we find in the Fathers an extremely rich idea of redemption which includes victory over death, the first fruits of the general resurrection, the liberation of human nature from captivity under the devil, and not only the justification, but also the restoration of creation in Christ. . . .

... Thus each person is an absolutely original and unique aspect of the nature common to all. The mystery of a human person, which makes it absolutely unique and irreplaceable, cannot be grasped in a rational concept and defined in words. [32]

THE TEMPTATIONS OF ECCLESIAL CONSCIOUSNESS

The Church is not of the world, but She is in the world and exists for the world in the same manner as Christ is not of the world, yet He came into the world for the sake of the world. Just as Christ, being free of the world, kept silence before the court of Pilate, the Church often standing silent before the powers of this world, preserves her transcendental freedom. Although it is at times difficult for us to recognize this freedom of hers under the external appearance of humiliation. "The scandal for the Jews"—the cross is also insurmountable for many Christians. Many would prefer to see in the Church one of the forces of history, comparable to other worldly factors and the "inferiority complex" before the powerful administration of Roman Catholicism is a temptation from which many Orthodox are not free.

Each of us, being of the earth, belongs to a definite political structure, a definite social class; each is in part the product of and at the same time a creator of modern culture, and so on—but each of us, participating in the unity of the Church, can and must become more than his political interests, more than his class, more than his culture, because the Church affords us the opportunity of being *free* of our limited nature. It is inevitable that there will be among Christians a variety of opinions and of political, ethnic, social, cultural, and other interests. To protest against these opinions and interests would be as absurd (and heretical) as to wish to suppress life with all its richness and complexity. The Church has never prescribed for her members any political views, social doctrines, or cultural peculiarities. This is why She cannot tolerate the interests or arrangements of individuals or groups being passed off as "the Church's interests," because her first concern must be the observance of unity, outside of which there is no catholicity, no certitude, no distinctions between the Church and the world.[33]

TRADITION AND TRADITIONS

One can say that Tradition represents the critical spirit of the Church. But, contrary to the "critical spirit" of human science, the critical judgment of the Church is made acute by the Holy Spirit. It has then quite a different principle: that of the undiminished fullness of Revelation. Thus the Church, which will have to correct the inevitable alterations of the sacred texts (that certain "traditionalists" wish to preserve at any price, sometimes attributing a mystical meaning to stupid mistakes of copyists), will be able at the same time to recognize in some late interpolations (for example, in the *comma* of the "three that bear record in heaven" in the first epistle of St. John) an authentic expression of the revealed Truth. Naturally authenticity here has a meaning quite other than it has in the historical disciplines.[34]

DOMINION AND KINGSHIP: AN ESCHATOLOGICAL STUDY

We need first of all to examine the terms which we are using here, in speaking of God's "dominion" and of its "fulfillment." Dominion is a relative concept implying, as its counterpart, submission to some dominant thing or person. But to speak of submission means necessarily to admit a possibility of "insubmissiveness" and rebellion against the dominion which is exerted. Only that which offers or is capable of offering resistance is dominated. The God of Aristotle is not lord over his eternal world: he is only the unconditioned first condition for the necessary operation of the machine of the universe, from which all contingency is excluded. Aristotle would have been astounded indeed if anyone had sought to give his God—the first unmoved Mover, the Thought which thinks itself—the name of Κύριος, Lord.

Now, the God of the Bible is the Lord, the Lord of the celestial hosts, of all spirits and of all flesh. His dominion is "from generation to generation";

it is exerted "in every place." Although it is impossible to escape from this universal dominion (which is made all the more absolute by the fact that the God of the Jews and Christians is the *Creator* of all things), one can, nevertheless, *resist* it; and the uttered curses of a man seeking to reach God in order to contend with Him face to face are not, in the Bible, what they are in ancient tragedy: the desperate outcry of a liberty falling back on itself and recognizing its absurd and illusory quality in face of a Destiny equally inexorable for gods and mortals.

We see, indeed, that God justifies Job, who contended with him, while his wrath is kindled against Eliphaz and his friends, who have spoken in favor of the irresistible and necessary absolutism of his dominion: "You have not spoken of me what is right, as my servant Job has" (Job 42 :7). For Job's protest, his refusal to accept a dominion which allowed of no dialogue between God and man, was a negative witness to the true nature of God's dominion. Job's complaint is a praise which exalts God higher, which enters more profoundly into His mystery, by refusing to halt at the abstract idea of His dominion which others make for themselves. This is a theology which aims higher than all clumsy theodicies, of which the speeches of Job's comforters are the prototype. While it is true that the absolute dominion of God is attested by many passages of the Old Testament, yet the Book of Job compels us to see in it something more than the anthropomorphic expression of a divine determinism.

It is true that in extension the dominion of the Creator includes all that exists, and even, according to St. Paul, reaches beyond existence, as a necessity to exist because of the creative word by which everything is maintained in being and can no more return into non-existence. Nevertheless this dominion, in its intensive aspect, is never uniform and invariable, but changing and dynamic. . . .

If the God of the philosophers and the learned is only a First Necessity who ordains the chain of cause and effect and corrects automatically every chance deviation which introduces itself, taking no more notice of human freedom than of a grinding noise in the machinery, the God of the Bible reveals Himself by His very wrath as He who undertook the risk of creating a universe whose perfection is continually jeopardized by the freedom of those in whom that perfection ought to reach its highest level. This divine risk, inherent in the decision to create beings in the image and likeness of God, is the summit of almighty power, or rather a surpassing of that summit in voluntarily undertaken powerlessness. For "the weakness of God is stronger than men" (I Cor. 1:25): it surpasses to an infinite degree all the attributes of majesty and dominion which the theologians enumerate in their treatises *De deo uno*. This category of divine risk, which is proper to a personal God freely creating personal beings endowed with freedom, is foreign to all abstract conceptions of the divine dominion—to the rationalist theology which thinks it exalts the omnipotence of the living God in attributing to him the perfections of a lifeless God who is *incapable* of being subject to risk. But he who takes no risks does not love: the God of the theology manuals can love only himself, and it is his own perfection which he loves even in his creatures. He does not love any *person:* for personal love is love for another than oneself. . . .

Since the fulfillment of God's dominion coincides with the final deification of created being, and since this ultimate vocation of the creation cannot be realized automatically, without the free cooperation of the person, both in angels and men, it is necessary for each stage of the way which leads to this end to include an agreement of the two wills: the will of God and the will of creatures. From the time of the First Adam's sin, which rendered man (and through him the whole of the earthly cosmos) incapable of progress in the way of his vocation, until the moment when Christ "the last Adam" (ο εσχατος ᾿Αδάμ, I Cor. 15:45) "will re-capitulate" (according to St. Irenaeus) fallen humanity—the harmony of the two wills can be only external. The successive covenants of the Old Testament are precisely of this kind: that made with Noah, with Abraham, and finally with Moses, imposing God's dominion as *Law* on the people whom He had chosen for Himself to realize the redemptive work which He alone could accomplish. The Law which convicted man of sin, making sin "exceeding sinful" according to St. Paul, manifested the slavery of man to a dominion *other* than that of God. This is a "third will," to which the First Adam submitted himself freely, seduced by the promise of a false deification outside the love of God. Along with this perverse will of a spiritual power at enmity with God, the dominion of sin and death entered the world, through man's sin. The Law of Moses, given by the mediation of angels (Gal. 3: 19) showed to those who received it the helplessness of man in face of the "law of sin" through which is exerted the dominion of the angels of Satan, now prince of this world. Harmony with the will of God is henceforth expressed by confession of sin, by recognition that it is impossible to be saved from the present situation except by God's own intervention, and finally by faith in the Promise which accompanies the Law, the Promise without which the Law could not be an expression of the divine economy, a "school-master to bring us unto Christ" (Gal. 3: 24). . . .

"Why then the law? It was added because of transgressions, till the offspring should come to whom the promise had been made: and it was ordained (διαταγείς) by angels" (Gal. 3:19). There is a close connection between the dominion of the Law and the law of sin and death, between the revealed Law and the law of sin which it makes manifest, between the legal order imposed by the agency of the angels of the Lord and the power exerted over the world since the Fall by the angels of Satan. There is no difficulty at all in recognizing that the divine Law is proper to the catastrophic state of created being in subjection to the law of sin and death. But we must also distinguish, in this miserable state imposed on the earthly creation by the sin of man, in that very law which St. Paul calls the "law of sin and death," the existence of an infallible order by means of which the dominion of God rules amid the disorders of the fallen world, preserving it from total destruction, setting bounds to the dominion of the powers of darkness. And there is more: even the dominion of the rebellious Angel over the fallen creature is not outside the scope of the will of God, who gives this captivity a certain legal character. God is sole Lord, and the spirits in revolt against him could not exercise their usurped dominion if in the last resort they did not remain subject, despite themselves, to his unique dominion. Though wishing to frustrate God's plan, the evil one finds himself finally compelled to serve it. . . .

The divine economy makes use of the rebel will to fulfill the design of the Creator, in spite of all the obstacles set up by human or angelic free will. If this is so, God's design, which is fixed as to the end in view (the deification of all created beings), must be likened, as to its execution, to a strategy of ever-changing tactics, infinitely rich in possibilities, to a multiform (πολυποίκιλος) Wisdom of God in action. But it is not so for the rationalist theologians. The devitalized theology of the Christian descendants of Job's comforters has accustomed us to think of the divine plan *sub specie aeternitatis,* lending to the eternal Will of God the only characteristic of eternity which they know: that of necessary and immutable preordinations, in the likeness of the miserable fixed eternity which is usually attributed to the truths of mathematics.

The magnitude of Satan's spiritual power, shown to Job, demonstrates the vastness of the cosmic catastrophe brought about by man's sin, the blindness and helplessness of his perverted freedom. All this is to show the beneficent character of the law of mortal existence, which rules by necessity over the new state established by God's will for His creation, enslaved by sin. The repentance of Job (whose "words without knowledge" had "darkened counsel") consists in recognizing, besides the necessary and ineluctable character of the dominion which he had refused to accept, the contingency of the divine economy, which always directs the terrestrial world towards the realization of its supreme vocation, that realization in which fallen man has become incapable of cooperating.

Job's attitude in accusing God is opposite to that of his friends, who, in assuming the hypocritical role of defenders of God, defended, without knowing it, Satan's right to an unlimited dominion. Like most defenders of the *status quo*, in wishing to justify the legitimate character of the present condition of humanity, they gave an absolute value to the legal situation, projecting it on to the very nature of God. In this wrong perspective, the different levels of human, demonic, angelic, and divine reality, bound up in the complex and shifting economy of salvation, are telescoped together, welded together and crystallized in a single vision of a God-Necessity, comparable to the inexorable and impersonal Fate ('Ανάγκη) of Greek paganism. They speak solely of the God of the Law, but not of the God of the Promise; God dominates their creation but does not become involved in it, does not run the risk of being frustrated in His love. This God is only a dictator, not a King. But Job aimed higher than his friends, for he believed the Promise, without which the Law would have been a monstrous absurdity and the God of the Old Testament could not have been the God of Christians. That is why the Book of Job is the first of the books of the Old Testament, in the traditional order, to open up the eschatological horizon, by placing the dominion of God and the condition of man in their true perspective—something which we must take into account in speaking of the fulfillment of the dominion.

St. Paul tells us that the creation awaits with impatience the revelation of the sons of God, which will set it free from the bondage of corruption, from the fixed law of birth and death, from the round of seasons, and the repeated cycles of existence. For the whole of terrestrial nature, of creation dependent on man, did not submit voluntarily to this universal necessity which Ecclesiastes and St. Paul call "vanity." The terrestrial universe, which was corrupted by man's sin, must also participate in the liberty of the glory of the sons of God (Rom. 8:19–22). When the cyclical law of repetition suddenly stops its rotating movement, creation, freed from vanity, will not be absorbed into the impersonal Absolute of a Nirvana but will see the beginning of an eternal springtime, in which all the forces of life, triumphant over death, will come to the fullness of their unfolding, since God will be the only principle of life in all things. Then the deified will shine like stars around the only Star, Christ, with whom they will reign in the same glory of the Holy Trinity, communicated to each without measure by the Holy Spirit.

... "We are not contending against flesh and blood" but against the "spiritual hosts of wickedness in the heavenly places" (Eph. 6:12). This struggle which began in the spiritual spheres of the angelic heavens is continued in the earthly cosmos, and in the struggle human freedom is at stake. The spiritual level where this war for the inheritance of the sons of God is waged is more profound than any of the superficial layers of reality which are accessible to analysis by the human sciences. None of the sciences—not psychology, nor sociology, nor economics, nor the political sciences—can detect the true origin of the different evils which they observe and attempt to define, in their efforts to exorcise them or at least to restrict the damage they do. Even philosophy, though it speaks of the human spirit and uses the terms "person" and "nature," cannot reach the level at which the problem of human destiny is posed. The terms which it uses are, for the most part, the result of the decadence and secularization of theological ideas. Philosophy is never eschatological: its speculation never goes to the furthest extremes, it inevitably transposes into ontology truths which are metaontological. Its field of vision remains on this side of the two abysses which theology alone can name, with fear and trembling: the uncreated abyss of the Life of the Trinity and the abyss of hell which opens within the freedom of created persons. . . .

We know that the gates of hell shall never prevail against the Church, and that hell's power, shattered by Christ, remains unreal so long as our will does not make common cause with that of the enemy of our final vocation. The Church strives only for the realization of this final goal set before all creation. All other conflicts in which we are obliged to take part in this world are restricted to the interests of a group, a party, a country, a human ideology: they inevitably exclude and sacrifice our enemies. Here, however, no one is excluded or sacrificed: even when the Church takes action against men, it is still for the salvation of these men that she continues to strive.

This is the guiding principle of her struggle, and its field extends ever wider as our eschatological involvement becomes more intense. But what is this intense involvement if not sanctity realized?[35]

THE THEOLOGICAL NOTION OF THE HUMAN PERSON

Thus, in the light of Christological dogma, Boethius' definition, *substantia individua rationalis naturae*, appears insufficient for establishing the concept of human person. It can only be applied to the "enhypostasized nature" (to use the expression created by Leontius of Byzantium) and not to the human hypostasis or person itself. We understand why Richard of Saint-Victor rejected Boethius' definition, remarking with finesse that substance answers the question *quid*, person answers the question *quis*. Now, to the question *quis* one answers with a proper noun which alone can designate the person.[36] Hence the new definition (for the divine persons): *persona est divinae naturae incommunicabilis existentia.*

... "Person signifies the irreducibility of man to his nature—"irreducibility" and not "something irreducible" or "something which makes man irreducible to his nature" precisely because it cannot be a question here of "something" distinct from "another nature" but of *someone* who is distinct from his own nature, of someone who goes beyond his nature while still containing it, who makes it exist as human nature by this overstepping and yet does not exist in himself beyond the nature which he "enhypostasizes" and which he constantly exceeds. I would have said "which he ecstacizes," if I did not fear being reproached for introducing an expression too reminiscent of "the ecstatic character" of the *Dasein* of Heidegger, after having criticized others who allowed themselves to make such comparisons.[37]

CATHOLIC CONSCIOUSNESS

No differences of created nature—sex, race, social class, language, or culture—can affect the unity of the Church; no divisive reality can enter into the bosom of the *Catholica.* Therefore it is necessary to regard the expression "national Church"—so often used in our day—as erroneous and even heretical, according to the terms of the condemnation of phyletism pronounced by the Council of Constantinople in 1872. There is no Church of the Jews or of the Greeks, of the Barbarians or of the Scythians, just as there is no Church of slaves or of free men, of men or of women. There is only the one and total Christ, the celestial Head of the new creation which is being realized here below, the Head to which the members of the one Body are intimately linked. At this point any private consciousness which could link us with any ethnic or political, social or cultural group must disappear in order to make way for consciousness "as a whole" (καθ᾽ ολον), a consciousness greater than the consciousness which links us to humanity at large. In fact, our unity in Christ is not only the primordial unity of the human race, which has only one origin, but the final realization of this unity of human nature, which is "recapitulated" by the last Adam—ο εσχατος ᾽Αδάμ. This eschatological reality is not some kind of ideal "beyond" but the very condition of the existence of the Church, without which the Church would not be a sacramental organism: her sacraments would have only a figurative sense, instead of being a real participation in the incorruptible life of the Body of Christ.

If we wish to apply the notion of consciousness to ecclesial reality, we must understand that in this reality there are many personal consciousnesses but only one subject of consciousness, only one "self-consciousness" (*Selbstbewusstsein*), which is the Church. In this sense the Fathers of the Church—and all those who, freed from their individual limitations, follow in their steps—are the fathers of the consciousness of the Church, those by whom Truth could be expressed in the councils in the form of dogmas, not as the "supra-conscious" constraint of a *deus ex machina*, but in full personal consciousness, engaging human responsibility. It is precisely this which permits us to make judgments in questions of faith and to say with catholic audacity: "It has seemed good to the Holy Spirit and to us" (Acts 15:28).[38]

ORTHODOX THEOLOGY: AN INTRODUCTION

THE CREATION

We are ... responsible for the world. We are the word, the logos, through which it bespeaks itself, and it depends solely on us whether it blasphemes or prays. Only through us can the cosmos, like the body that it prolongs, receive grace. For not only the soul, but the body of man is created in the image of God.

ORIGINAL SIN

Evil certainly has no place among the essences, but it is not only a lack: there is an activity in it. Evil is not a nature, but a state of nature, as the Fathers would say most profoundly. It thus appears as an illness, as a parasite existing only by virtue of the nature he lives off. More precisely, it is a state of the will of this nature; it is a fallen will with regard to God. Evil is revolt against God, that is to say, a personal attitude. The exact vision of evil is thus not essentialist but personalist.

The Old Testament did not know the intimate sanctification by grace, yet it knew saintliness, for grace, from outside, aroused it in the soul as an effect. The man who submitted to God in faith and lived in all righteousness could become the instrument of His will. As is proved by the vocation of prophets, it is not a question of agreement between two wills, but of lordly utilization of the human will by that of God: The Spirit of God swoops upon the seer, God takes possession of man by imposing Himself from outside on his person. God, invisible, speaks: His servant listens. The darkness of Sinai is opposed to the light of Tabor like a veiled mystery to an unveiled mystery. Man prepares himself to serve in the obscurity of faith, by obedience and purity. Obedience and purity are negative concepts: they imply the exteriority of God and the instrumental submission of man who, even when just, cannot free himself from his state of sin and death. Saintliness, as active sanctification of all being and the free assimilation of human nature to that of God, can only manifest itself after the work of Christ, by the conscious grasping of this work. That is why the Law is essential to the Old Testament, and the relationship of man and God is not union but alliance, guaranteed by loyalty to the Law.

Thus the history of the Old Testament is not only that of the foreshadowings of salvation but that of man's refusals and acceptances. Salvation approaches or withdraws as man prepares or not to receive it. The καιρὸς of Christ, His moment, will depend on human will. The entire meaning of the Old Testament lies in these fluctuations underlining the double aspect of Providence. The latter is not unilateral. It takes into account the human waiting and call. Divine pedagogy scrutinizes man, tests his dispositions.

This testing is sometimes a struggle, for God wishes that human liberty should not only resist Him but force Him, if not to reveal His name, at least to bless: thus Jacob becomes Israel "for you have wrestled with God and with man and you have won" (Gen. 32:29). And the patriarch *becomes* the people, and when this people is captive in Egypt, God raises up Moses to deliver it. On Sinai, God passes in His glory before Moses but prevents him seeing His Face "for man cannot see Me and live": divine nature remains hidden. But the election of Israel, the decisive stage, is affirmed in a new alliance: that of the Law. A written obligation to which the chosen people must submit, the Law is accompanied by divine promises that the Prophets will continue to make precise. Thus the Law and the Prophets complement each other; and Christ will always evoke them together to underline their completeness. The Prophets are the men whom God chose to announce the profound meaning of His Law. In contrast to the Pharisees, who gradually turned the Law into a static reality and the means of justification, the Prophets explain its spirit, its historical dynamism, the eschatological call that it contains in making man take cognizance of his sin and his helplessness before it.[39]

NOTES

1. [Pope John Paul II, *Fides Et Ratio*, VI, 74.]
2. [Rowan Williams, "Eastern Orthodox Theology," in *The Modern Theologians: An Introduction to Christian Theology in the Twentieth Century*, ed. David F. Ford (Oxford: Basil Blackwell, 1989), 2:163. See also the excellent pioneering study by Rowan D. Williams (to which I am greatly indebted for the lucid exposition of the essence of Lossky's personalism), "The Theology of Vladimir Nikolaievich Lossky: An Exposition and Critique," unpublished D.Phil. thesis (Oxford, 1976).]
3. [Vladimir Lossky, *The Mystical Theology of the Eastern Church*, trans. members of the Fellowship of St. Albans and St. Sergius (1957; reprint, Cambridge: James Clarke, 1991), 22; see also 12–14, 21–22.]
4. [In Lossky the person is the existence of nature: "There is nothing in nature which properly pertains to the person, who is always unique and incomparable." Ibid., 121. The human person is not to be controlled by nature but is rather called to control nature and continually transcend himself in grace. See Ibid., 241.]
5. [The English translation of his *Essai sur la Theologie Mystique*, published in 1958, was the work of these Anglican friends and disciples of Lossky.]
6. [Christos Yannaras, a Greek Orthodox theologian, created an original synthesis of Lossky's theology and Heidegger's metaphysics, building considerably on Lossky's ecclesiology and his notion of the human person.]
7. [Vladimir Lossky, "Dominion and Kingship," in *In the Image and Likeness of God*, ed. John H. Erickson and Thomas E. Bird, trans. Thomas E. Bird (1974; reprint, New York: St. Vladimir's Seminary Press, 2001), 218.]
8. [Following Khomiakov, Lossky insists on two specific attributes of the Truth. First, the "Truth can have no external criteria." (See Lossky, *Mystical Theology*, 128.) It stands on the basis of its own internal evidence. Second, "gnosis" (authentic knowledge) is inseparable from love. Thus, by connecting gnosis with love Lossky highlights the ethical and communitarian dimensions of the Eastern Orthodox epistemology. He follows Khomiakov, who insisted that the "Truth can only be apprehended in brotherly love."]
9. [Vladimir Lossky, *Sept Jours sur les Routes de France*, (Paris: Les Editions du Cerf, 1998), 16–17, 19–20, 20–24 , 26–27, 64–65. Eng. trans. for chapter: Heather Jones and Elizabeth Icks, "Superior Translations." Despite the fact that Lossky's diary (which he wrote in June of 1940) was first published forty years after his death in 1998, it seemed justifiable to make an exception and to place the following excerpts from it at the beginning of our selection. All the other selections in this chapter follow a chronological order on the basis of the date of first publication.]
10. Words of St. Basil reported by St. Gregory Nazianzen in "In laudem Basilli Magni, or. XLIII, 48", *P.G.*, t. 36, 560 A.

11. "In sanctum Pascha, or. XLV, 8", *P.G.*, t. 36, 632 C.

12. "Opuscula theological et polemica, Ad Marinum", *P.G.*, t. 19, 45 D–48 A.

13. *Ibid.*, 48 A—49 A, 192 BC. In St. John Damascene, "De fide orth, III, 14", *P.G.*, t. 94, 1036–7; 1044–5.

14. [Vladimir Lossky, "Image and Likeness," *The Mystical Theology of the Eastern Church*, 121–122, 124–125.]

15. "Hom. Spirit., XV, 32", *P.G.*, XXXIV, 597 B.

16. *Ibid.*, XLIII, 7, 776 D.

17. *Ibid.*, XV, 20, 589 B.

18. See above, the chapter "Image and Likeness." [In the 1991 English edition of *The Mystical Theology of the Eastern Church*, the chapter referred to is found on pages 114–134.]

19. "Spiritual homilies, XL, I", *P.G.*, XXXIV, 761.

20. "Doctrina, XIV, 3", *P.G.*, LXXXVIII, 1776–80.

21. ["The Way of the Union," *The Mystical Theology of the Eastern Church*, 201–202, 215.]

22. *De incarnatione verbi* 20; *P.G.* 25, col. 129D-132A.

23. Matt. 18:12–14, Luke 15:4–7, John 10:1–16.

24. Matt. 12:29, Mark 3:27, Luke 11:21–22.

25. St. Athanasius, *De incarnatione verbi* 30; *P.G.*, 25, col. 148.

26. St. John of Damascus, *De imaginibus* III, 9; *P.G.*, 94, col. 1332D. The image of Christ as the physician of human nature, wounded by sin, is often found in connection with the parable of the Good Samaritan, which was interpreted in this way for the first time by Origen, Homily 34 on St. Luke, *P.G.*, 13, cols. 1886–1888; *Commentary on St. John* 20, 28; P.G. 14, col. 656A.

27. St. Gregory of Nyssa, *Oratio catechetica magna* 22–24; *P.G.*, 45, cols. 60–65.

28. Rom. 3:24, 8:23; I Cor. 1:30; Eph. 1:7, 14:30; Col. 1:14; Hebr. 9:15, 11:35, with the sense of deliverance. I Tim. 2:6; I Cor. 6:20, 7:22; Gal. 3:13, with the sense of a ransom paid.

29. For St. Paul, the sacrificial or sacerdotal image of the work of Christ is basically identical to the juridical image—that of purchase or redemption properly so called—but it also completes and deepens it. In effect, the idea of propitiation in blood (Rom. 3:26) ties together the two images—the juridical and the sacrificial—in the notion of the expiatory death of the just man, a notion characteristic of the messianic prophecies (Isaiah 53).

30. *Cur Deus homo* I, 4; *P.L.*, 158, col. 365.

31. [*Or.* 45, 22; *P.G.* 36, col. 653.]

32. [Vladimir Lossky, "Redemption and Deification," trans. Edward Every, in *In the Image and Likeness of God*, 98–102, 107.]

33. [Vladimir Lossky, "The Temptations of Ecclesial Consciousness," trans. Thomas E. Bird, in *St. Vladimir's Theological Quarterly* 32, no. 3 (1988): 247, 248. Translation revised.]

34. [Vladimir Lossky, "Tradition and Traditions," trans. G. E. H. Palmer and E. Kadloubovsky, in *In the Image and Likeness of God*, 156.] Origen, in his homilies

on the Epistle to the Hebrews, after having expressed his views on the source of this epistle, of which the teaching is Pauline but the style and composition denote an author other than St. Paul, adds this: "If, then, some church considers this epistle as written by St. Paul, let it be honored also for that. For it is not by chance that the ancients have transmitted it under the name of Paul. But who wrote the epistle? God knows the truth." Fragment quoted by Eusebius, *Historia Ecclesiastica* VI, 25; P.G. 20, col. 584C.

35. [Vladimir Lossky, "Dominion and Kingship: An Eschatological Study," trans. Thomas E. Bird, in *In the Image and Likeness of God*, 212–218, 220, 225, 226–227. It is hardly accidental that Lossky published this powerful essay on divine dominion of love and freedom in 1953—the year in which the Soviet dictator Josef Stalin died.]

36. *De Trinitate* IV, 7; P.L. 196, cols. 934–935.

37. [Vladimir Lossky, "The Theological Notion of the Human Person," in *In the Image and Likeness of God*, 118–120.]

38. [Vladimir Lossky, "Catholic Consciousness: Anthropological Implications of the Dogma of the Church," trans. Thomas E. Bird, in *In the Image and Likeness of God*, 184, 194.]

39. [*Orthodox Theology: An Introduction*, 71, 80, 85–86, 88–89.]

{CHAPTER 19}

Mother Maria Skobtsova (1891–1945)

SELECTED AND EDITED BY MICHAEL PLEKON

*Mother Maria Skobtsova, born Elisabeth Pilenko, is one of the greatest trea-
sures of creativity, compassion, and sacrifice that the Eastern Orthodox Church
offers to the world. Trained in literature and the fine arts, a gifted poet and es-
sayist, she was among the first women to study theology in the St. Petersburg
Academy. She was a member of the circle of the poet Alexander Blok. During
the civil war she was almost executed by both the Bolsheviks and the White
Army. She was the first woman mayor of her childhood hometown of Anapa,
on the Black Sea. Married twice, divorced twice, the mother of three children,
a son and two daughters who were to die young, she would never have guessed
that she would spend the last decades of her life as a nun, running hostels for
the homeless, the troubled and ill in Paris and its suburbs.*

*Despite the demands of feeding and sheltering the residents of her hostels,
she managed to keep up a productive life as a writer, participating in the Religious-Philosophical Society led by Nicholas Berdyaev, contributing essays to
the famous journal he edited,* Put' *(The Way), and other publications. She em-
broidered vestments and painted icons for the chapels in her hostels, continued
to participate in the Russian Christian Students' Movement she helped found,
began Orthodox Action, yet another organization for serving those in need, and
engaged in the theological debates of her era. She had perhaps the greatest
theologian of the twentieth century and a mystic as her spiritual father, Sergius Bulgakov. Her close friends included many of the leading intellectuals of
the Russian emigration in Paris. During the Nazi occupation her efforts multi-
plied. Many fearing arrest were given shelter and new identities in her hostels.
She saved several children from the Jewish population herded into the Paris
cycling stadium Vélodrome d'Hiver on July 16–17, 1942, smuggling them out in
trashcans. With her chaplain, she devised ways to hide and protect both Jews
and others whom the Nazis sought to exterminate. In February of 1943 both
Mother Maria and Father Dimitri were arrested, along with her son Yuri. All*

were eventually sent to concentration camps. Mother Maria was the last to die there, surviving until March 31, 1945, when she reportedly took the place of another inmate scheduled to be gassed that day.

Many have called her a martyr, a model of holiness in our time. Yet the petition for her formal recognition as a saint in the Orthodox Church was not acted on for almost twenty years. However, suddenly, in January, 2004, the synod of the Ecumenical Patriarchate of Constantinople at the Phanar, in Istanbul, approved the petition. On May 8 and 9, 2004, in the St. Alexander Nevsky Cathedral in Paris, Mother Maria became Saint Maria Skobtsova. Canonized along with her were her son, Yuri, her chaplain, Father Dimitri Klepinin, and her financial secretary, Ilya Fundaminsky, all of whom perished, as she did, in the camps. Finally, the witness of her entire life, not only its heroic end, was recognized by her home diocese and the churches at large.

THE SECOND GOSPEL COMMANDMENT

... AN ABSOLUTE MAJORITY of them [daily morning and evening prayers] are addressed to God from *us* and not from *me*. ...

... What is most personal ... most intimate in an Orthodox person's life, is thoroughly pervaded by this sense of being united with everyone ... the principle of *sobornost'*,[1] characteristic of the Orthodox Church. ...

If this is so in a person's private prayer, there is no need to speak of prayer in the church. A priest cannot even celebrate the liturgy if he is alone; for that he must have at least one person who symbolizes the people. And the eucharistic mystery itself is precisely the common work of the Church, accomplished on behalf of all and for all.

... In the Orthodox Church man is not alone and his path to salvation is not solitary; he is a member of the Body of Christ, he shares the fate of his brothers in Christ, he is justified by the righteous and bears responsibility for the sins of the sinners. ... And that is not something invented by theologians and philosophers, but a precise teaching of the Gospel, brought to life through the centuries of existence of the Church's body. ...

... For the fulfillment of love for one's neighbor, Christ demanded that we lay down our soul for our friends. Here there is no sense in paraphrasing this demand and saying that it has to do not with the soul but with life. ...

Equally irrefutable is Christ's teaching about how we should deal with our neighbor, in His words about the Last Judgment [Mt 25:31–45], when man will be asked not how he saved his soul by solitary endeavor but precisely how he dealt with his neighbor, whether he visited him in prison, whether he fed him when he was hungry, comforted him—in short, whether he loved his fellow man, whether this love stood before him as an immutable commandment of Christ. And here we cannot excuse ourselves from active love, from the selfless giving of our soul for our friends.

But even if we set aside the separate and particular Gospel teachings in this regard and turn to the whole activity of Christ on earth, it is here that we find the highest degree of the laying down of one's soul for others, the highest measure of sacrificial love and self-giving that mankind has known. "For God so loved the world that He gave His only-begotten Son" [Jn 3:16], calling us, too, to the same love. There is not and there cannot be any following in the steps of Christ without taking upon ourselves a certain share, small as it may be, of participation in this sacrificial deed of love. Anyone who loves the world, anyone who lays down his soul for others, anyone who is ready, at the price of being separated from Christ, to gain salvation for his brothers—is a disciple and follower of Christ. . . .

. . . Here we cannot reason like this: Christ gave us the firm and true teaching that we meet Him in every poor and unhappy man. Let us take that into consideration and give this poor and unhappy man our love, because he only seems poor and unhappy to us, but in fact he is the King of Heaven, and with Him our gifts will not go for nothing, but will return to us a hundredfold. No, the poor and unhappy man is indeed poor and unhappy, and in him Christ is indeed present in a humiliated way, and we receive him in the name of the love of Christ, not because we will be rewarded, but because we are aflame with this sacrificial love of Christ and in it we are united with Him, with His suffering on the Cross, and we suffer not for the sake of our purification and salvation, but for the sake of this poor and unhappy man whose suffering is alleviated by ours. One cannot love sacrificially in one's own name, but only in the name of Christ, in the name of the image of God that is revealed to us in man.

A person should have a more attentive attitude toward his brother's flesh than toward his own. Christian love teaches us to give our brother not only material but also spiritual gifts. We must give him our last shirt and our last crust of bread. Here personal charity is as necessary and justified as the broadest social work. In this sense there is no doubt that the Christian is called to social work. He is called to organize a better life for the workers, to provide for the old, to build hospitals, care for children, fight against exploitation, injustice, want, lawlessness. In principle the value is completely the same, whether he acts on an individual or a social level; what matters is that his social work be based on love for his neighbor and not have any latent career or material purposes. For the rest it is always justified—from personal aid to working on a national scale, from concrete attention to an individual person to an understanding of abstract systems for the correct organization of social life. . . .

... In turning his spiritual world toward the spiritual world of another, a man encounters the terrible, inspiring mystery of the authentic knowledge of God, because what he encounters is not flesh and blood, not feelings and moods, but the authentic image of God in man, the very incarnate icon of God in the world, a glimmer of the mystery of the Incarnation and Godmanhood. . . . [2]

ON THE IMITATION OF THE MOTHER OF GOD

... We must be convinced that the question of an authentic and profound religious attitude toward man is precisely the meeting point of all questions of the Christian and the godless world, and that even this godless world is waiting for a word from Christianity, the only word capable of healing and restoring all, and perhaps sometimes even of raising what is dead.

If we decide responsibly and seriously to make the Gospel truth the ultimate standard for our human souls, we will have no doubts about how to act in any particular case of our lives: we should renounce everything we have, take up our cross, and follow Him. . . .

... That is the exhaustive meaning of all Christian morality. And however differently various peoples in various ages understand the meaning of this imitation, all ascetic teachings in Christianity finally boil down to it. . . .

The meaning and significance of the cross are inexhaustible. The cross of Christ is the eternal tree of life, the invincible force, the union of heaven and earth, the instrument of a shameful death. But what is the cross in our path of the imitation of Christ; how should our crosses resemble the one cross of the Son of Man? For even on Golgotha there stood not one but three crosses: the cross of the God-man and the crosses of the two thieves. Are these two crosses not symbols, as it were, of all human crosses, and does it not depend on us which one we choose? ...

What is most essential, most determining in the image of the cross is the necessity of freely and voluntarily accepting it and taking it up. Christ freely, voluntarily took upon Himself the sins of the world, and raised them up on the cross, and thereby redeemed them and defeated hell and death. . . .

In taking the cross on his shoulders, man renounces everything—and that means that he ceases to be part of this whole natural world. . . . Natural laws not only free one from responsibility, they also deprive one of freedom. . . .

And so the Son of Man showed his brothers in the flesh a supra-natural—and in this sense not a human but a God-manly—path of freedom and responsibility. He told them that the image of God in them also makes them into God-men beings and calls them to be deified, to indeed become Sons of God, freely and responsibly taking their crosses on their shoulders.

The free path to Golgotha—that is the true imitation of Christ.

... According to the Gospel, the sword is a symbol of suffering endured passively, not voluntarily chosen but inevitable—a weapon that pierces the soul. The cross of the Son of Man, accepted voluntarily, becomes a two-edged sword that pierces the soul of the Mother, not because she voluntarily chooses it, but because she cannot help suffering the sufferings of her Son.

And this two-edged sword is not uniquely and unrepeatably bound up with the destiny of the Mother of God[3] alone—it teaches all of us something and obliges us to something. To understand that, we need to feel the Mother of God's earthly path, to see all that is both exceptional and universal in it.

... She is not only the suffering Mother at the cross of her crucified Son, she is also the Queen of Heaven, "more honorable than the cherubim and more glorious beyond compare than the seraphim." Orthodox conscious-ness understands her, the Virgin of the tribe of Judah, the daughter of Da-vid, as the Mother of all that lives, as the living and personal incarnation of the Church, as the human Body of Christ. The veil of the Mother of God protects the world, and she is also the "moist mother earth."[4] This last im-age acquires new strength in connection with thoughts of the cross that becomes a two-edged sword. The earth of Golgotha with the cross set up on it, piercing it, the earth of Golgotha red with blood—is it not a mother's heart pierced by a sword? The cross of Golgotha, like a sword, pierces the soul of Mother-earth.

And if we turn away from what is revealed to us in the glorified image of the Mother of God, if we take her only in her earthly path, that is, where it is possible to speak of "imitating" her, that is quite enough to enable a Christian soul to understand some of the special possibilities opened up to it. It is precisely on this path of God-motherhood that we must seek the justification and substantiation of our hopes, and find the religious and mystical meaning of true human communion, which otherwise somehow escapes us.

And here the most important thing is to feel what the Son's Golgotha is for the Mother.

He endures His voluntary suffering on the cross—she involuntarily *co*-suffers with Him. He bears the sins of the world—she *co*llaborates with him, she *co*-participates, she *co*-feels, *co*-experiences. His flesh is cruci-fied—she is *co*-crucified.

... On Golgotha she is the handmaid of her suffering God-Son, the hand-maid of His sufferings. It is the same obedience as on the day of the Good News, the same *co*-participation in the Divine economy, but then it was the path toward the Nativity, toward *co*-participation in the angelic song:

"Glory to God in the highest, and on earth peace, good will toward men" (Lk 2:14), while now it is participation in the suffering of Golgotha, the *kenosis* of God, inevitable from all eternity. . . .

There is much in this maternal suffering that we can perceive and learn today, drawing conclusions with regard to our own human suffering.

First and foremost, we see Christ's humanity, the Church of Christ, the Body of Christ, of which the Mother of God is also the Mother. . . . And if so, then what she felt in relation to her Son is as eternally alive in relation to the Church. As the Mother of Godmanhood—the Church—she is pierced even now by the suffering of this Body of Christ, the suffering of each member of this Body. In other words, all the countless crosses that mankind takes on its shoulders to follow Christ also become countless swords eternally piercing her maternal heart. She continues to *co*-participate, *co*-feel, *co*-suffer with each human soul, as then on Golgotha.

... She always walks with us on our own way of the cross, she is always there beside us, each of our crosses is a sword for her.

But there is another thing, no less essential. Every man is not only the image of God, the icon of the Divinity, not only a brother in the flesh of the God-man, deified by Him, and honored by His cross, and in this sense a son of the Mother of God. Every man is also the image of the Mother of God, who bears Christ in herself through the Holy Spirit. In this sense, every man deep inside is this bi-une icon of the Mother of God with the Child, the revelation of this bi-une mystery of Godmanhood. . . . In this sense we can speak of the physical participation of mankind—and therefore of every separate man—in the birth of the Son of God. But of this we can and must speak at the deepest, most mystical level of human souls. And, finally, an analysis of the verbal equation "Son of God—Son of Man" gives proof of the God-bearing of man.

Thus the human soul unites in itself two images—the image of the Son of God and the image of the Mother of God—and thereby should participate not only in the destiny of the Son, but also in her destiny. Both the Son of God and His Mother are age-old archetypes, symbols by which the soul orients itself on its religious paths. In this sense it should imitate not only Christ but also the Mother of God. This means it should accept and take up not only its freely chosen cross; it should also know the mystery of the cross that becomes a sword. First of all, the cross of the Son of Man on Golgotha should pierce every Christian soul like a sword, should be experienced by it as a co-participation, a co-suffering with Him. Besides that, it should also accept the swords of its brothers' crosses.

If a man is not only the image of God but also the image of the Mother of God, then he should also be able to see the image of God and the image of the Mother of God in every other man. . . . The God-motherly part of the human soul begins to see other people as its children; it adopts them for itself. . . . So we must also perceive God and the Son in every man. God, because he is the image and likeness of God; the Son, because as it gives birth to Christ within itself, the human soul thereby adopts the whole Body of Christ for itself, the whole of Godmanhood, and every man individually.

The first founder of the deed of love teaches us the humble acceptance of these other crosses. She calls every Christian soul to repeat tirelessly after her: "Behold the handmaid of the Lord," even to shedding one's blood, even to feeling as if a sword has pierced one's heart.

This is the measure of love, this is the limit to which the human soul should aspire. We can even say that this is the only proper relation of one person to another. Only when one's soul takes up another person's cross, his doubts, his grief, his temptations, falls, sins—only then is it possible to speak of a proper relation to another.

THE MYSTICISM OF HUMAN COMMUNION

... All the trends of social Christianity known to us are based on a certain rationalistic humanism, apply only the principle of Christian morality to "this world," and do not seek a spiritual and mystical basis for their constructions.[5]

To make social Christianity not only more Christian-like but truly Christian, it is necessary to find one more dimension for it, to bring it out of flat soulfulness and two-dimensional moralism into the depths of multi-dimensional spirituality. . . .

... Worldly people are essentially separated from the world by an impenetrable wall. However much they give themselves to the joys of the world, whatever bustle they live in, there is always an impassable abyss in their consciousness: "I" and the world, which serves me, amuses me, grieves me, wearies me, and so on. The more egoistic a man is, that is, the more he belongs to the world, the more alienated he is from the authentic life of the world, the more the world is some sort of an inanimate comfort for him, or ... inanimate torture, to which his uniquely animate "I" is opposed. If he loves the world, science, art, nature, family, friends, politics, it is with what may be called lustful love—"my family," "my art," "my nature," "my politics." ... In this relation to the world there exist insuperable, high walls that separate man from man, nature, and God.

... In Christianity, where two God-given commandments—about the love of God and the love of man—should resound, we often run into the same separation from man and from the world. . . .

... When hermits wove mats and fashioned clay pots, it was a job. When we peel potatoes, mend underwear, do the accounts, ride the subway, that is also a job. But when the monks of old, by way of obedience, buried the dead, looked after lepers, preached to fallen women, denounced the unrighteous life, gave alms—that was not a job. And when we act in our modern life, visiting the sick, feeding the unemployed, teaching children, keeping company with all kinds of human grief and failure, dealing with drunkards, criminals, madmen, the dejected, the gone-to-seed, with all the spiritual leprosy of our life, it is not a job and not only a tribute to obedience that has its limits within our chief endeavor—it is that very inner endeavor itself, an inseparable part of our main task. The more we go out into the world, the more we give ourselves to the world, the less we are of the world, because what is of the world does not give itself to the world.

... The great and only first founder of worldly endeavor was Christ, the Son of God, who descended into the world, became incarnate in the world, totally, entirely, without holding any reserve, as it were, for His Divinity. . . .

In His worldly obedience He emptied Himself, and His emptying is the only example for our path ... when and at what moment did His example teach us about inner walls that separate us from the world? He was in the world with all His Godmanhood, not with some secondary properties. . . . In the sacrament of the eucharist, Christ gave Himself, His God-man's Body, to the world, or rather, He united the world with Himself in the communion with his God-man's Body. He made it into Godmanhood. . . . Christ's love does not know how to measure and divide, does not know how to spare itself. Neither did Christ teach the apostles to be sparing and cautious in love. . . . Here we need only learn and draw conclusions. . . .

I think that the fullest understanding of Christ's giving Himself to the world, creating the one Body of Christ, Godmanhood, is contained in the Orthodox idea of *sobornost'*.[6] And *sobornost'* is not only some abstraction, on the one hand, nor is it ... a higher reality having no inner connection with the individual human persons who constitute it: it is a higher reality because each of its members is a member of the Body of Christ, full-grown and full-fledged, because he is that "soul" which is worth the whole world. . . . He is indeed the image of God, the image of Christ, the icon of Christ. Who, after that, can differentiate the worldly from the heavenly in the human soul, who can tell where the image of God ends and the heaviness of human flesh begins! In communing with the world in the person of each individual human being, we know that we are communing with the image of God, and, contemplating that image, we touch the Archetype—we commune with God.

There is an authentic, and truly Orthodox, mysticism not only of communion with God, but also of communion with man. And communion with man in this sense is simply another form of communion with God. In communing with people we commune not only with like-minded people, friends, co-religionists, subordinates, superiors—not only, finally, with material for our exercises in obedience and love; we commune with Christ Himself, and only a peculiar materialism with regard to Christ's appearing and abiding in the world can explain our inability to meet Him within the bustle, in the very depth of the human fall. . . . He foresaw our rationalistic and proud lack of faith when He prophesied that, to his accusation, people would ask in perplexity: "Lord, when did we not visit you in the hospital or in prison, when did we refuse you a cup of water?" If they could believe that in every beggar and in every criminal Christ Himself addresses us, they would treat people differently. . . .

And it seems to me that this mysticism of human communion is the only authentic basis for any external Christian activity, for social Christianity, which in this sense has not been born yet. . . . Everything in the world can be Christian, but only if it is pervaded by the authentic awe of communion with God, which is also possible on the path of authentic communion with man. But outside this chief thing, there is no authentic Christianity.

THE CROSS AND THE HAMMER-AND-SICKLE

... The world now needs, and needs urgently, an authentic idea of the hammer and the sickle purified of communist perversion.[7] What's more, not only the world but also the cross needs that this authentic idea of the hammer and sickle be realized. . . .

... Only in Christ's name can we do the one thing that needs to be done to the world—lead it out of the dead end of contemporary godless fruitlessness and giftlessness. By the name of Christ, by the cross of Christ, the hammer-and-sickle can be given their authentic meaning; by the cross labor can be sanctified and blessed. . . .

Christ is freedom: the face of Christ is the affirmation in every person of his own free and God-like face; the Church is a free and organic union of the faithful with Christ, with Christ's freedom; and Christ calls those who labor and are heavy laden to take up His burden, which is light because it is taken up freely. Thus Christ and coercion are incompatible. . . .

How easy and simple it is to prove with very convincing arguments the possibility of free labor and of the free construction of society on the principle of labor! In fact, mankind has enough experience of the two opposite systems of coercion and violence. The old coercion of the capitalist regime, which destroys the right to life and leaves one only with the right to labor, has recently begun to deprive people of that right as well. Forced crisis, forced unemployment, forced labor, joyless and with no inner justification—enough of all that. But try going to the opposite system. It turns out to be the system of communist enforcement: the same joyless labor under the rod, well-organized slavery, violence, hunger—enough of that, too. It is clear to everybody that we must seek a path to free, purposeful, and expedient labor, that we must take the world as a sort of garden that it is incumbent upon us to cultivate. Who doubts that?

Christ, in giving us His free path and His freely chosen burden, thereby confirmed, as it were, the possibility of a belief in human freedom and in the divine dignity of the human face.

… Do we believe in that freedom? Do we believe in that dignity? Not only in someone else, but in ourselves, each in himself? …

What am I talking about? About the most terrible thing that exists in earthly life, in the historical process, in the throbbing of modernity: that no one, no one wants in a voluntary and friendly, free and brotherly fashion to build an authentic, laboring, free, and loving Christian life. If they do build, they build something different, and if there is something that is not different, it is not in the building of life, but always in words and theories, sometimes quite remarkable, but only words and theories.

As a pianist or singer must play or sing the simplest scales every day as exercise [and otherwise will be unable to do anything complicated], as a craftsman needs certain muscular habits, as a wrestler needs training—so in the Christian deed of transfiguring the world a small everyday life should be freely created.

Why speak of the brotherhood of the people, if we do not live with our roommate in brotherly fashion?

Why speak of freedom, if we are unable to freely combine our creative efforts?

Why speak of a Christian attitude toward labor, if we work under the rod or do not work at all?

Free laboring—that is the basis of our path in Christ. And this basis should pervade our everyday and routine life. . . .

… Our efforts should make of every common deed a sort of monastery, a sort of spiritual organism, a sort of minor order, a sort of brotherhood. . . .

Great is the joy of those who do not doubt that free laboring can be realized in people's lives. And woe to those who shake that faith.

TOWARDS A NEW MONASTICISM

One often hears mention of "the new monasticism."[8] Some people endow these words with a positive meaning: it's about time, they say. Others think that "new monasticism" means all but "no monasticism," and that there is a lie and a temptation hidden here. And yet I do think that even granted this negative attitude, everyone understands that the new monasticism is something that really exists.

... But there are other ways for the "new" to emerge.

For instance, there existed an ancient tradition, based on a Gospel text, of standing in church at the Palm Sunday vigil holding palm branches. This tradition was observed in Byzantium, and that without any difficulty, since it was easy for them to find palm branches. But imagine a Palm Sunday vigil in Moscow or even in Kiev. Where will they get palm branches? The tradition has to be changed. People start cutting pussywillow branches.[9] Probably warily at first, afraid of leading people into temptation—it's a matter of a clear deviation from the Gospel text. Later nothing was left of the temptation, the new thing became a tradition, and so much so that many would probably be tempted now if they were offered fir or birch branches instead of pussywillows. Now there are probably Russian people in Africa, where palm branches are easily obtained, who think: "How's that? 'Pussywillow Sunday' without pussywillows?" In the same way, probably, Byzantine dried figs and olives during the Great Lent were replaced in the Russian north by pickled cabbage. No Greek Typikon[10] makes any mention of this pickled cabbage, but imagine Russian lenten tradition without it! These are all little everyday things, you may say. Let them be little; they show the essence of the matter more easily, because the same things happen on a serious level as well.

There is thus a "new" that is not invented by the idle human mind, but that follows inevitably from the conditions of life. Every attempt to preserve the old on such occasions is either impossible (like palm branches in the north), or does not correspond to the spirit of the old tradition: in Constantinople the simplest food was olives, and so they were prescribed during Lent, while in Moscow an insistence on olives would not be the simplest thing—olives are a rarity there, a delicacy. The simple thing would be cabbage. . . .

It is undoubtedly not monasticism but only the monastic life that has been going through a crisis for a long time now, perhaps more than a century. . . .

... The old tradition (now corresponding infinitely less to the needs of life) was still being lived out, though no directive for it came from the surrounding life. . . . A tradition remains, if it does remain, only as such, as a certain petrified rite, whose performers gradually forget the reason for it. Even with the sharpest hatred of novelty and the most ardent striving to preserve the old, it is simply physically impossible to remain outside the new conditions. There are only two possible attitudes toward them, as it actually happens: either to deny the new needs of the time without understanding them—as purposeless, unthinking, unwitting innovations—or, taking this new life into consideration, to innovate according to a plan, in a creative way—more than that, to innovate so as to create a new tradition. In this alone lies the difference between contemporary traditionalists and innovators.

Traditionalists, having no physical possibility of preserving the old, also do not create a new life. Innovators, not trying to preserve the unpreservable, organically create a new life and a new tradition. Thus the roles here are essentially changed.

What are the new conditions of life to which this slowly created future tradition should correspond?

... We can put it like this: innovation is determined by the fact that the modern monk, *whether he likes it or not*, finds himself not behind strong monastery walls, within defined, ossified traditions, but on all the roads and crossroads of the world, with no opportunity of orienting himself by old traditions, with no hint of new traditions. And woe to him who dislikes these worldly roads and crossroads: he will neither preserve the old, nor create the new. In other words: today's monasticism must fight for its very core, for its very soul, disregarding all external forms, creating new forms.

Let us imagine a person who not only strives toward the core, toward the soul of monasticism, but who also does not want to embody his monasticism in the forms of the old tradition. . . . There is no monastery, no skete, no seclusion. Instead, there are the wide roads of life, a parish, maybe even in some backwater, and in the parish all the pains, all the wounds, all the sins of life, with drunkenness, depravity, thoughts of suicide. And, on the other hand, there is the longing for a little material well-being, there is competition, there is peaceful and quiet "everyday" godlessness—all that he saw in the world and that he wanted to leave behind, and did not leave behind, because he had *nowhere to go.* Nowhere, because as a monk he is not needed, or perhaps monasticism is not needed?

Absolutely wrong. He is both needed and not needed, precisely he, as a monk, because monasticism in general is needed, but it is needed mainly on the roads of life, in the very thick of it. Today there is only one monastery for a monk—the whole world. This he must inevitably understand very soon, and in this lies the force of his *innovation*. Here many must become innovators against their will. This is the meaning, the cause, and the justification of the new monasticism!

The new here is not characterized mainly by its newness, but by its being *inevitable*. . . .

. . . It would be incorrect to think that monasticism cannot exist outside this historical framework, and that we are now called at all costs to recreate what existed earlier—and, if the life conditions for it are not there, to create at least an external stage set, to restore the historically accurate costumes, so to speak, of the old monasticism.

Monasticism is determined not by a way of life, not by the monastery, not by the desert; monasticism is determined by the vows made during the rite of tonsuring. The rest is a historical covering, which can and must change, and which has only relative value: it is valuable as long as it contributes to the fulfillment of the vows.

[These vows are three:] obedience, chastity, and nonpossession. . . .

The vow of chastity has always been understood with perfect clarity, and historical conditions, of course, cannot introduce any changes in it. . . .

. . . The vow of nonpossession, meanwhile, was simplified to an elementary renunciation of the love of money or, at best, of one's own material property. . . .

Obedience as such remains unchanged, but its meaning becomes different. A monk should be obedient to the work of the Church to which he is assigned; he should give his will and all his creative powers entirely to this work. Obedience becomes service. . . . The Church herself becomes his *starets*, and also judges him, while the obedience requested is the responsible fulfillment of what the Church has charged him to do.

Is this an innovation? Perhaps so, but here life itself is the innovator. It does not ask us whether we want to understand the vow of obedience we have made in this or some other way. It tells us that in contemporary conditions it cannot be understood in any other way. . . .

The question here is simple: we need not to restore the old but to try responsibly to accept the new, to comprehend it, to make out precisely what it demands of us.

And, finally, the third vow: nonpossession . . . is in need of greater comprehension and deepening.

. . . It cannot be limited to a material understanding. . . .

. . . The principle of nonpossession can be expressed in any relationship. The subtler the egocentrism, the higher the limits of the human spirit it reaches, the more repulsive it is. . . .

Poverty of spirit is not, of course, the renunciation of any intellectual interests; it is not a sort of spiritual idiocy. It is the renunciation of one's spiritual exclusiveness, it is the giving of one's spirit to the service of God's work on earth, and it is the only path for common life in the one *sobornal* organism of the Church.

A monk should find the strength in himself to say together with Christ: "Into thy hands I commend my spirit" (Lk 23:46). He should consciously want to become the fulfiller of God's work on earth—and nothing else. He should be a conductor of divine love and a co-participant in divine sacrifice.

Nonpossession should not be merely passive—they don't ask, so I don't give. Nonpossession should be active: a monk should seek where to place the gifts given him by God precisely for that end.

It goes without saying that this point of view implies the necessity of monastic activity in the outside world. But it should be remembered that all its forms—social work, charity, spiritual aid—are the result of an intense desire to give one's strength to the activity of Christ, to the humanity of Christ, not to possess but to spend it for the glory of God.

It seems to me that this new understanding of the vow of nonpossession should determine the path of the modern monk. In practice, he may acquire some new and unaccustomed appearance because of it, but that is an external thing. In reality, he will stand on the foundation of the ancient vows that determine the very essence of his monastic effort.

THE POOR IN SPIRIT

... We know that Christ taught us to lay down our soul for our friends. This laying down of the soul, this giving of oneself, is what makes a person poor in spirit. It is the opposite in everyday life; even with the most negative attitude toward material possession, we are used to regarding the spiritual holding back of ourselves as something positive. . . .

Christ did not know measure in His love for people. And in this love He reduced His Divinity to the point of incarnation and took upon Himself the suffering of the universe. In this sense His example teaches us not measure in love but the absolute and boundless giving of ourselves, determined by the laying down of our soul for our friends.

Without striving for such giving of oneself, there is no following the path of Christ.

... People's care for their spiritual peace, their locking themselves away, leads before our eyes to self-poisoning, demoralization, loss of joy; they become unbearable to themselves, turn neurasthenic. In a most paradoxical way, they become poor from holding on to themselves, because their eternal self-attention and self-admiration transform them. The poor hold on to their rags and do not know that the only way not only to preserve them but also to make them precious is to give them with joy and love to those who need them.

And why?

These rags are the corruptible riches of the kingdom of this world. By giving them away, by giving himself away entirely, with his whole inner world, laying down his soul, a man becomes poor in spirit, one of the blessed, because his is the Kingdom of Heaven, according to our Savior's promise, because he becomes the owner of the incorruptible and eternal riches of that Kingdom, becomes it at once, here on earth, acquiring the joy of unmeasured, self-giving, and sacrificial love, the lightness and freedom of nonpossession.

... We know that in the time of the Russian civil war, choice implied death, imprisonment, exile, the total crippling of one's life. . . . And still more we know what it means to confess one's faith where it is persecuted, where the whole force of the state is raised against it ... how people would be deprived of their crust of bread for the baptismal cross on their neck, how they would be sent to the camps for a book of religious content, and so on.

Now we've become émigrés. What does that mean? First of all it means freedom. . . .

... We should understand the providential meaning of the freedom given us. We must receive it as a weighty gift, and not only relate to it externally, but let it penetrate to the very depths of our spirit, rethink and test in its light all our usual and habitual opinions and bases. . . .

... While we have lost our earthly motherland, we have not lost our heavenly motherland, that the Church is with us, in our midst—the whole Orthodox Church in her entirety, not divided into any sub-churches. . . .

Let us look at the Church's work from the point of view of our freedom. . . . Not long ago I happened to speak on this subject in a certain magazine. My article provoked a response that came as a total surprise to me. The mere observation of the fact of our extraordinary freedom, compared with the situation of the Church in all the time of her existence, made certain people suppose for some reason that I consider only the life of our émigré Church authentic, and that I throw away, cross out, count as nothing the two thousand years of Church history. Beyond that, the conclusion was drawn that I deny the righteousness and holiness of the Church in the time of her state captivity. It is hard to refute such arbitrary and totally unfounded conclusions drawn from one's own precise words. Perhaps the thing to do is not refute them, but simply repeat the same thoughts in different words until they finally become comprehensible. The history of the Church in all times contains pages devoted to authentic holiness. Privation of freedom in no case diminishes the possibility of holiness; what's more, it may be precisely in periods of the maximum privation of freedom that the most obvious, most unquestionable holiness blossoms. . . .

But the Church's destiny need not only be considered from the point of view of the increase of holiness. . . . And no one who says that the Church was not free is thereby saying that there was no holiness in her, or that she was torn apart by heresies, or anything else except one thing—that she was not free. . . .

Freedom obliges, freedom calls for sacrificial self-giving, freedom determines one's honesty and strictness with oneself and one's path. And if we want to be strict and honest, worthy of the freedom given us, we must first of all test our own attitude toward our spiritual world. We have no right to wax tenderhearted over all our past indiscriminately—much of that past is far loftier and purer than we are, but much of it is sinful and criminal. . . . We cannot stylize everything as some sweet ringing of Moscow bells—religion dies of stylization. We cannot cultivate dead customs—only authentic spiritual fire has weight in religious life. We cannot freeze a living soul with rules and orders—once, in their own time, they were the expression of other living souls, but new souls demand a corresponding expression. We cannot see the Church as a sort of aesthetic perfection and limit ourselves to aesthetic swooning—our God-given freedom calls us to activity and struggle. And it would be a great lie to tell searching souls: "Go to church, because there you will find peace." The opposite is true. She tells those who are at peace and asleep: "Go to church, because there you will feel real alarm about your sins, about your perdition, about the world's sins and perdition. There you will feel an unappeasable hunger for Christ's truth. There, instead of lukewarm you will become ardent, instead of pacified you will become alarmed, instead of learning the wisdom of this world you will become foolish in Christ."

It is to this foolishness, this folly in Christ that our freedom calls us. Freedom calls us, contrary to the whole world, contrary not only to the pagans but to many who style themselves Christians, to undertake the Church's work in what is precisely the most difficult way.

And we will become fools in Christ, because we know not only the difficulty of this path but also the immense happiness of feeling God's hand upon what we do.[11]

A JUSTIFICATION OF PHARASAISM

Long ages go by when the scribes, doctors of the law, and pharisees safeguard the law bequeathed them by their fathers, when everything is calm in this eternal, universal Israel, the prophets are silent, sacrifices are offered in the temple, the pharisee beats his breast and thanks God that he is not like this publican.[12] Then fire breaks out in the world. Again and again comes the Forerunner's call to repentance, again and again settled life is broken up, and the fishermen abandon their nets, and people leave their dead unburied to follow Him. And the eternal prophecy is fulfilled: the house is left empty, the sun goes out, the earth is shattered—and man has no refuge.

Golgotha grows, becomes the whole world. There is nothing left but the Cross.

Amidst the people of God ... the guardians of their truth, of their election, the keepers of the law, of every letter of the law, the scribes, the doctors of the law, the pharisees towered up like sturdy oaks, like invincible fortresses. Man betrays, but the law will not betray. Man's soul is perverse, but the letter is fixed. And therefore the letter is higher than the soul, the sabbath is higher than man.

... These are the rules for the whole nation; these are also the commandments for each separate human soul. Fulfill what is written, offer the prescribed sacrifice, give to the temple what you ought to give. Keep the fasts. Do not defile yourself by communing with the unclean—and you will get your reward, or if not you then your son will get it, but you already have it, too, because you have observed the law, every letter of it, because you are righteous, because you are not like this publican.

No doubt everyone feels this stiff-necked pharisaic truth, and can make no objection to it before the time comes. And no doubt even the contemporary human soul, every human soul, passes through this pharisaic truth, through the parched and fruitless desert of waiting, perhaps saving a last sip of water: I won't drink it, because there will be no new water.

Yes, in the desert of the spirit, in a time of terrible spiritual drought, the pharisee is justified; he alone is reasonable and thrifty, watchful and sober.

And it is not for the spendthrift, not for the one who, in the time of the great exodus, stuffs himself with manna and game, and drinks too much pure water, and dances before golden calves—it is not for him to denounce the stern thriftiness of the doctor of the law, who fasts even amidst universal famine and fulfills everything as he should. He will preserve the tables of the Covenant in the tabernacle; he will lead the souls of the people into the promised land.

How many times does the stern guardian of traditions and laws in each of our souls curse the unfaithful crowd of seducers, the violators of the law! The struggle goes on in each of us for the purity of the prescribed, for the Typikon,[13] for the letter of the law, for that which is connected with what is to come—only what is to come—the not yet incarnate promise.

When prophecy is silent in us, when our spirit is not molten, who will keep it from being dispersed and wasted if not the guardian of the law, who always stands on watch. He, too, is justified in our soul.

... There is something that displaces these laws of the natural world, that annihilates all the righteousness of the pharisees and all the faithfulness of the doctors of the law and all the wisdom of the scribes. And this something is fire.

Fire came down into the world. The word of God became flesh. God became man. Not for nothing and not by chance was this wonder, this fulfillment of the promised and the looked-for, opposed precisely by those who were guardians of the promised, looked-for covenant. A struggle began between the doctors of the law and that which was higher than the law of the sabbath, with the Son of Man. He who ate and drank with publicans and sinners, He who healed on the sabbath, He who spoke of rebuilding the destroyed temple in three days—was He not bound to appear to them as the most terrible violator of the prescribed, of the traditional, of the habitually saving? And they rose against Him in the name of their age-old truth. . . .

Fire came down into the world. Human hearts melted. The cross of Golgotha stood on the path of the Resurrection. It would seem that those who crucified Him, those who betrayed Him, remained on the other side, in the old, decrepit, yielding, and receding covenant. And on this side, with Him, remained those of the new covenant, the fiery ones, who took the cross on their shoulders, sanctified and transfigured by the mystery of the Resurrection—forever, until the end of the world, the members of His Church, which Hell cannot prevail against, participants in eternal life here in their earthly days.

But in fact Christianity preserved all the forces that were active in the Old Testament. The same stiff-necked, indifferent, inconstant crowd, the same guardians of the law (now His new law), Christian scribes, pharisees, doctors of the law—and also the same prophets to be stoned, the same holy fools, bearers of grace who do not fit into the framework of the law, lawless for those who are under the law.

Properly speaking, the entire history of Christianity is the history of the extinguishing and new igniting of the fire. History develops that way in each separate soul, and it has developed that way in the world. We know the coldness and deadness of whole epochs of Christianity, we know the flaring up and spreading of the flames of authentic Christian evangelization, we know how scribes and pharisees alternate with the initiators of new paths, and their time with broad waves of suffering, asceticism, witness, repentance, and purification.

And once again we must say in all fairness that the role of the pharisees in Christianity is not exhausted only with the extinguishing of the fire, the freezing and killing of all that is alive and ardent. They do actually and authentically watch over, keep, preserve, and bear the coffer of Christian treasures through the narrow passes of dead and self-satisfied epochs. . . . They faithfully defend Christianity against the paganism that abides eternally in the world, against the cult of petty passions, prejudices, the cult of various idols, calves made of various metals—the iron calf of state power, the golden calf of economic prosperity, and so on.

But along with that they try to protect the Church against authentic Christian fervor, against all fire in general; they only preserve what is sacred to them and keep others from being nourished by it. The evaluation of pharisaism's significance and usefulness for the Church depends largely on the epoch in which the pharisees live. That evaluation therefore varies greatly and is subject to very marked fluctuations.

We stand now at the beginning of a new epoch in the Church. Much in its character is already clear. From this clarity we may judge what the Church needs at the given moment, what will contribute to her growth and ardor, and what, on the contrary, is harmful for her.

... This gives us the possibility of seeing what new things the Church now demands of us and what we must now free ourselves from so as not to harm her with what is old and even antiquated.

INSIGHT IN WARTIME

... War.

Do we accept it? Do we not accept it? Is war heroic? Is war organized crime? Is a warrior a martyr, a "passion-bearer"? Was the warrior in ancient times denied communion? Are there wars that are just, that are almost righteous? So many questions, questions which show all the contradictoriness in the very nature of war. . . . [14]

I think that, in our notions of war, the definitions of attacking and defending sides are not sufficiently detailed. These notions are put in place at the beginning of a conflict with the aim of using them at the end for diplomatic, political, and economic purposes. But in fact the real moral or even religious distinction has not been made. If a robber breaks into a house and the one who lives in it defends himself, then later on, when the trial takes place, regardless of whether or not the robber carried out his crime, or even if the attacked one overcame him, it is still the robber who will be in the dock. And it is not that, while the robber was actually the first to attack, everything then became confused in the general fight, and it no longer even matters who began it, but what matters is who won. . . .

I think that Christian consciousness can never be guided by the motivation of the robber; that is, to take an aggressive part in war is never acceptable for it. Much more complicated is the question of enduring war, of passive participation, of war in defense. And here I am approaching the main thing that defines the Christian attitude toward war. The strength is not in war, but in what is beyond it.

There is something in war that makes people listen—not all, but many—and suddenly, amidst the roar of cannons, the rattle of machine guns, the groaning of the wounded, they hear something else, they hear the distant, warning trumpet of the archangel.

There is also, in a sense, a more terrible phenomenon, which cannot be accounted for by statistics: it is the brutalization of nations, the lowering of the cultural level, the loss of creative ability—the decadence of souls. Every war throws the whole of mankind back. . . .

The war demands of us, more than ever, that we mobilize absolutely all our spiritual powers and abilities. . . . In our time Christ and the life-giving Holy Spirit demand the whole person. The only difference from state mobilization is that the state enforces mobilization, while our faith waits for volunteers. And, in my view, the destiny of mankind depends on whether these volunteers exist and, if they do, how great their energy is, how ready they are for sacrifice.

And, finally ... I know with all my being, with all my faith, with all the spiritual force granted to the human soul, that at this moment God is visiting His world. And the world can receive that visit, open its heart—"ready, ready is my heart"—and then in an instant our temporary and fallen life will unite with the depths of eternity, then our human cross will become the likeness of the God-man's cross, then within our deathly affliction itself we will see the white garments of the angel who will announce to us: "He who was dead is no longer in the tomb." Then mankind will enter into the paschal joy of the Resurrection.

Or else ... Maybe it will not even be worse than before, but merely the same as before. Once again—and how often has it been?—we will have fallen, we will not have accepted, we will not have found the path to transfiguration.

TYPES OF RELIGIOUS LIFE

I will now move on to characterize the evangelical type of spiritual life, which is as eternal as is the proclamation of the Good News, always alive within the bosom of the Church, shining for us in the faces of saints and at times lighting with the reflection of its fire even righteous people outside the Church. . . . [15]

Christ gave us two commandments: to love God and to love our fellow man. Everything else, even the commandments contained in the Beatitudes, is merely an elaboration of these two commandments, which contain within themselves the totality of Christ's "Good News." Furthermore, Christ's earthly life is nothing other than the revelation of the mystery of love of God and love of man. These are, in sum, not only the true but the only measure of all things. And it is remarkable that their truth is found only in their conjunction. Love for man alone leads us into the blind alley of an anti-Christian humanism, out of which the only exit is, at times, the rejection of the individual human being and love for him in the name of all mankind. Love for God without love for human beings, however, is condemned: "You hypocrite, how can you love God whom you have not seen, if you hate your brother whom you have seen" (1 Jn. 4:20). Their conjunction is not simply a conjunction of two great truths taken from two spiritual worlds. It is the conjunction of two parts of a single whole.

... In fact, if you take away love for man then you destroy man (because by not loving him you reject him, you reduce him to nonbeing) and no longer have a path toward the knowledge of God. God then becomes truly apophatic, having only negative attributes, and even these can be expressed only in the human language that you have rejected. God becomes inaccessible to your human soul because, in rejecting man, you have also rejected humanity, you have also rejected what is human in your own soul, though your humanity was the image of God within you and your only way to see the Prototype as well. This is to say nothing of the fact that a human being taught you in his own human language, describing God's truth in human words, nor of the fact that God reveals Himself through human concepts. By not loving, by not having contact with humanity we condemn ourselves to a kind of a deaf-mute blindness with respect to the divine as well. In this sense, not only did the Logos-Word-Son of God assume human nature to complete His work of redemption and by this sanctified it once and for all, destining it for deification, but the Word of God, as the "Good News," as the Gospel, as revelation and enlightenment likewise needed to become incarnate in the flesh of insignificant human words. For it is with words that people express their feelings, their doubts, their thoughts, their good deeds and their sins. . . .

On the other hand, one cannot truly love man without loving God. As a matter of fact, what can we love in a man if we do not discern God's image in him? Without that image, on what is such love based? It becomes some kind of peculiar, monstrous, towering egoism in which every "other" becomes only a particular facet of my own self. I love that in the other which is compatible with me, which enriches me, which explains me—and at times simply entertains and charms me. If, however, this is not the case, if indeed there is desire for a selfless but nonreligious love for man, then it will move inevitably from a specific person of flesh and blood and turn toward the abstract man, toward humanity, even to the idea of humanity, and will almost always result in the sacrifice of the concrete individual upon the altar of this abstract idea—the common good, an earthly paradise, etc.

In this world there are two kinds of love: one that takes and one that gives. This is common to all types of love—not only love for man. One can love a friend, one's family, children, scholarship, art, the motherland, one's own ideas, oneself—and even God—from either of these two points of view. Even those forms of love that by common consent are the highest can exhibit this dual character.

What was Christ's love like? Did it withhold anything? ... Christ's divinity was incarnate fully and to the end in his spit-upon, battered, humiliated, and crucified humanity. The cross—an instrument of shameful death—has become for the world a symbol of self-denying love. . . .

We are not speaking here about good deeds, nor about that love which measures and parcels out its various possibilities, which gives away the interest but keeps hold of the capital. Here we are speaking about a genuine emptying, in partial imitation of Christ's self-emptying when He became incarnate in mankind. In the same way we must empty ourselves completely, becoming incarnate, so to speak, in another human soul, offering to it the full strength of the divine image which is contained within ourselves.

... There is not, nor can there be, any doubt but that in giving ourselves to another in love—to the poor, the sick, the prisoner—we will encounter in that person Christ Himself, face to face. He told us about this Himself when He spoke of the Last Judgment: how He will call some to eternal life because they showed Him love in the person of each unfortunate and miserable individual, while others He will send away from Himself because their hearts were without love, because they did not help Him in the person of his suffering human brethren in whom He revealed Himself to them. If we harbor doubts about this on the basis of our unsuccessful everyday experience, then we ourselves are the only reason for these doubts: our loveless hearts, our stingy souls, our ineffective will, our lack of faith in Christ's help. One must really be a fool for Christ in order to travel this path to its end—and at its end, again and again, encounter Christ. . . .

And this, I believe, is the evangelical way of piety. It would be incorrect, however, to think that this has been revealed to us once and for all in the four Gospels and clarified in the Epistles. It is continually being revealed and is a constant presence in the world. It is also continually being accomplished in the world, and the form of its accomplishment is the Eucharist, the Church's most valuable treasure, its primary activity in the world. The Eucharist is the mystery of sacrificial love. Therein lies its whole meaning, all its symbolism, all its power. . . . Again and again the sins of the world are raised by Him upon the cross. And He gives Himself—his Body and Blood—for the salvation of the world. By offering Himself as food for the world, by giving to the world communion in His Body and Blood, Christ not only saves the world by His sacrifice, but makes each person a "christ," and unites him to His own self-sacrificing love for the world. He takes flesh from the world, He deifies this human flesh, He gives it up for the salvation of the world and then unites the world again to this sacrificed flesh—both for its salvation and for its participation in this sacrificial offering. . . . He raises the world as well upon the cross, making it a participant in His death and in His glory.

... The Eucharist here is the Gospel in action ... the eternally existing and eternally accomplished sacrifice of Christ and of Christlike human beings for the sins of the world. . . . The Eucharist is true communion with the divine. And is it not strange that in it the path to communion with the divine is so closely bound up with our communion with each other? It assumes consent to the exclamation: "Let us love one another, that with one mind we may confess Father, Son, and Holy Spirit: the Trinity, one in essence and undivided."

The Eucharist needs the flesh of this world as the "matter" of the mystery. It reveals to us Christ's sacrifice as a sacrifice on behalf of mankind, that is, as His union with mankind. It makes us into "christs," repeating again and again the great mystery of God meeting man, again and again making God incarnate in human flesh. And all this is accomplished in the name of sacrificial love for mankind.

... It is possible to speak of the whole of Christianity as an eternal offering of the divine liturgy beyond church walls. . . . It means that we must offer the bloodless sacrifice, the sacrifice of self-surrendering love not only in a specific place, upon the altar of a particular temple; the whole world becomes the single altar of a single temple, and for this universal Liturgy we must offer our hearts, like bread and wine, in order that they may be transformed into Christ's love, that He may be born in them, that they may become "God-manly" hearts, and that He may give these hearts of ours as food for the world, that He may bring the whole world into communion with these hearts of ours that have been offered up, so that in this way we may be one with Him, not so that we should live anew but so that Christ should live in us. . . . Then truly in all ways Christ will be in all.[16]

NOTES

1. [*Sobornost'* is derived from the Russian word *sobor*, "council," which also became the word for "cathedral." It means "conciliarity" or "catholicity," the coming together of many to form a whole, a communion among free persons.]

2. [Translators' note:] Soloviev coined this description of the Incarnation, God's taking on humanity (*Bogocheloveschestvo*), and it has been commonly translated as "Godmanhood." Paul Valliere has argued that a better rendering is "the humanity of God" (*Modern Russian Theology* [Grand Rapids, Mich.: Eerdmans, 2001]). Nevertheless the more familiar expression is used here.

3. [The Mother of God is the image of our suffering with our neighbor in love. We learn more about how to give of ourselves and to love the neighbor from this essay.]

4. [Translator's note:] *Mat' syra zemlia*, literally "mother moist earth" in Russian, is a name given to the bountiful, nourishing earth in Russian folk tales. It was sometimes extended in the folk imagination to the Virgin Mary. An old peasant woman in Dostoevsky's *Demons*, when asked who the Mother of God is, replies: "The Mother of God is our great mother the moist earth, and therein lies a great joy for man."

5. [There is only one basis for loving the neighbor, for Christian social work in the world: teaching, providing shelter, food, clothing, medical care and other necessities. It is God's love for us and God's desire that we love God in return—in the sister or brother, the neighbor before us.]

6. [See note 2.]

7. [Mother Maria reflects on the deeper meaning of revolution. She never lost her revolutionary fervor. She found once more its real source: the freedom of Christ and his gospel.]

8. [Metropolitan Evlogy said Mother Maria's monastery would be in the desert of suffering people's hearts. Her following the gospel would not be in the traditional monasteries of the past but in the heart of the world, in the center of the city. And this is precisely where she lived out her monastic profession, at several different locations in Paris and its suburbs. In this essay she examines what this means.]

9. [Translator's note:] Russians traditionally use pussywillow branches in place of palms on Palm Sunday, which is popularly known as "Pussywillow Sunday." In Europe, boxwood branches are commonly used.

10. [Translator's note:] The Typikon is the collection of rules and canons governing the liturgical and ascetic life of the Church.

11. [Mother Maria cared for all kinds of needy people in her hostels, many being refugees, émigrés like herself, uprooted by a brutal revolution in Russia. Mother Maria nevertheless recognized God's hand in this as the gift of freedom as the following passages indicate.]

12. [This essay is a debate on the past and the present Church and world.]

13. [See note 10.]

14. [Mother Maria deals with many aspects of armed conflict. Preemptive or unilateral attack is unequivocally condemned by Christianity in her view. But in our time, the individual Christian or even the churches and other faith traditions often cannot stop states from war. Then spiritual mobilization is essential.]

15. [Mother Maria evaluates forms of piety in the recent history of her own Russian Church. While culturally specific and very particularly Orthodox, nonetheless those of other traditions can find the analogies to their own pieties. These selections are from the last form, for her that which most authentically conforms to the New Testament and Christ's preaching, what she called "evangelical" or Gospel Christianity.]

16. [All selections in this chapter come from *Mother Maria Skobtsova: Essential Writings*, trans. Richard Revear and Larissa Volokhonsky (Maryknoll, N.Y.: Orbis Books, 2003), 46, 47–49, 54, 57, 62, 63, 64–65, 67, 68, 69–70, 71, 75–76, 77–80, 82, 85, 86, 87, 88, 89, 91–95, 97–98, 100–101, 102–103, 105–106, 108–109, 112, 113–115, 117, 121–124, 135–137, 138, 139, 173, 175–177, 179, 183–185.]

[CHAPTER 20]

Dumitru Stăniloae (1903–1993)

SELECTED AND EDITED BY LUCIAN TURCESCU

Dumitru Stăniloae was born in the Romanian province of Transylvania. He was the youngest of five children. From 1922 to 1927 Stăniloae studied theology at the Faculty of Theology in Cernauti (now in the Ukraine). Young Dumitru, however, did not like the westernized style of academic theology, marked by scholasticism and nineteenth-century religious rationalism, that prevailed throughout the Orthodox world at the time. In 1927, he went to Athens for a few months of research. In 1928, back in Cernauti, he completed and defended a brief doctoral dissertation in church history entitled "The Life and Work of Patriarch Dositheos of Jerusalem and his Relations with the Romanian Lands." For almost another year after obtaining his doctorate in theology, Stăniloae traveled for additional study and research to Munich, Berlin, and Paris. During these trips, he became sensitive to the dialogical theology of Martin Buber and the French personalists, as well as that of Gregory Palamas (1296–1359), the main promoter of Hesychasm, a doctrine and practice of prayer of the heart and contemplation of God. Stăniloae's own theology is a deeply personalistic theology in which he successfully weaves together modern personalism with patristic views, Hesychasm, and Orthodox spirituality.

Stăniloae first taught theology at the Theological Academy in Sibiu (1929–46) and then at the Faculty of Orthodox Theology in Bucharest (1947–58, 1965–73). He became a married priest in the Romanian Orthodox Church and had three children. Some of Stăniloae's first books were collected articles he had previously published in theological and cultural journals and diocesan newspapers. Yet books such as The Life and Teaching of St. Gregory Palamas *(1938) and* Jesus Christ or the Restoration of Man *(1943) signaled a very original theological thinker. The former is considered a groundbreaking study in Palamite scholarship at a time when Palamism was presented in the West from a hostile perspective by the Roman Catholic scholar Martin Jugie. Nowadays, due to Orthodox scholars such as Stăniloae, Basil Krivocheine, Vladimir Lossky, and*

John Meyendorff, Palamism has been revived and has transformed Orthodoxy, while its presentation in a scholarly, more objective manner by Roman Catholic scholars such as Andre de Halleux, Jacques Lison, and Robert Sinkewicz has made it an important theological alternative to Westerners.

Between 1946 and 1991, Stăniloe published translations of twelve volumes of the Philokalia. Although based on the Philokalia of the Holy Ascetics (Venice, 1782), a collection of texts compiled by Nikodimos of the Holy Mountain and Makarios Notaras, Stăniloae's Philokalia differs from it in several important ways. Stăniloae not only substantially supplemented the texts of the original Philokalia, including among many other sections an appendix entitled "Hesychasm and the Jesus Prayer in the Romanian Orthodox Tradition" in volume 8, but also provided his own introductions for the modern reader and accompanied the texts with very rich commentaries and footnotes.[1]

From Stăniloae's Sibiu period also date his articles on the relationship between Orthodoxy and Romanianism, a theme he retrieved even after the fall of Communism in his Reflections on the Spirituality of the Romanian People *(Craiova, 1992). Greater Romania was the state formed in 1918 by the three formerly independent principalities of Wallachia, Moldova, and Transylvania, as well as several other smaller regions (the first two had become one unit in 1859). "Romanianism" has been an imagined shared identity allegedly superseding Moldovan, Wallachian, and Transylvanian allegiances.*

Stăniloae's magnum opus is his three-volume Orthodox Dogmatic Theology (1,347 pages in total), which appeared in 1978, when he was seventy-five years old. Like all of his works, the Dogmatics was written in Romanian, but it is partly available in French and English translations, and entirely available in German translation. The English translation came out as The Experience of God. There are two volumes published to date; they represent only the first volume of the Romanian edition. In his Dogmatics, Stăniloae tried to blend together in a very creative fashion patristic insights with contemporary theology, both Western and Eastern. Several other significant works by Stăniloae published in Romanian include Spirituality and Communion in the Orthodox Liturgy *(1986),* The Eternal Image of God *(1987),* Studies in Orthodox Dogmatic Theology *(1991),* The Evangelical Image of Jesus Christ *(1992), and* Commentary on the Gospel According to John *(1993). To these one should add numerous other Romanian translations from various church fathers and hundreds of journal and newspaper articles.*

The selections presented herein attempt to provide the reader with a taste of Stăniloae's theology on law and human nature, as well as some of his reflections on nationalism and more contemporary politico-religious issues in Romanian society. The subheadings follow some of the main subheadings in the analytic chapter on Stăniloae in volume 1. Stăniloae's reflections on the revelations (natural and supernatural) as well as on the meaning of the fallen human nature paves the way for his understanding of the role of the law.

Unlike other theologians presented in this volume, Stăniloae did not write directly and extensively on law. He saw law being introduced as a result of the Fall into sin of the first humans, Adam and Eve. The law given to Moses on Mount Sinai expresses the concentrated form of the will of God; it is God's supernatural revelation, but it is meant only as a transitory step toward something higher that comes through Christ. In line with Apostle Paul and the Book of Revelation, Stăniloae opposes the "newness of the spirit" to the "oldness of the law" and contends that as long as there is law there is sin and the law was given to remove humanity's sinful state. But eventually love has to take the place of the law.

In regard to politics, nobody was allowed to engage in any type of political activity other than in support of the Romanian Communist Party between 1947 and 1989. That period covered almost half of Stăniloae's life and, as a result, he refused to engage in communist politics. Indeed, he had to suffer five years of political imprisonment during that time for his political convictions, which bordered in some cases on the extreme right. Stăniloae's views on Romanian nationalism were set out in pre–World War II and postcommunist publications. Lacking long political experience or reflection, the elderly Stăniloae appeared incapable of dealing with some real issues facing postcommunist Romania—such as popular and clerical collaboration with the secret police (the Securitate) and the healing of Romanian society following the collapse of Communism in Eastern Europe and the Soviet Union.

NATURAL REVELATION

THE ORTHODOX CHURCH makes no separation between natural and supernatural revelation. Natural revelation is known and understood fully in the light of supernatural revelation, or we might say that natural revelation is given and maintained by God continuously through his own divine act which is above nature. That is why Saint Maximos the Confessor does not posit an essential distinction between natural revelation and the supernatural or biblical one. According to him, this latter is only the embodying of the former in historical persons and actions.[2]

This affirmation of Maximos must probably be taken more in the sense that the two revelations are not divorced from one another. Supernatural revelation unfolds and brings forth its fruit within the framework of natural revelation, like a kind of casting of the work of God into bolder relief, a guiding of the physical and historical world toward that goal for which it was created in accordance with a plan laid down from all ages. Supernatural revelation merely restores direction to and provides a more determined support for that inner movement maintained within the world by God through natural revelation. At the beginning, moreover, in that state of the world which was fully normal, natural revelation was not separated from a revelation that was supernatural. Consequently, supernatural revelation places natural revelation itself in a clearer light.

It is possible, however, to speak both of a natural revelation and of a supernatural one, since, within the framework of natural revelation, the work of God is not emphasized in the same way nor is it as evident as it is in supernatural revelation.

Speaking more concretely and in accordance with our faith, the content of natural revelation is the cosmos and man who is endowed with reason, with conscience, and with freedom. But man is not only an object that can be known within this revelation; he is also one who is a subject of the knowledge of revelation. Both man and the cosmos are equally the product of a creative act of God which is above nature, and both are maintained in existence by God through an act of conservation which has, likewise, a supernatural character. To the acts of conserving and leading the world towards its own proper end, there corresponds within the cosmos and within man both a power and a tendency of self-conservation and of right development. From this point of view, man and the cosmos can themselves be taken as a kind of natural revelation.

But man and the cosmos constitute a natural revelation also from the point of view of knowledge. The cosmos is organized in a way that corresponds to our capacity for knowing. The cosmos—and human nature as intimately connected with the cosmos—are stamped with rationality, while man (God's creature) is further endowed with a reason capable of knowing consciously the rationality of the cosmos and of his own nature. Nevertheless, according to Christian doctrine, this rationality of the cosmos and this human reason of ours which enables us to know are, on the other hand, the product of the creative act of God. Thus, natural revelation is not something purely natural from this point of view either.

We consider that the rationality of the cosmos attests to the fact that the cosmos is the product of a rational being, since rationality, as an aspect of a reality which is destined to be known, has no explanation apart from a conscious Reason which knows it from the time it creates it or even before that time, and knows it continually so long as that same Reason preserves its being. On the other hand, the cosmos itself would be meaningless along with its rationality if there were no human reason that might come to know the cosmos because of its rational character. In our faith, the rationality of the cosmos has a meaning only if it is known in the thought of an intelligent creative being before its creation and in the whole time of its continuing in being, having been first brought into existence precisely that it might be known by a being for whom it was created, and that a dialogue between itself and this created rational being might thus be brought about through its mediation. This fact constitutes the content of natural revelation.

Christian supernatural revelation asserts the same thing when it teaches that, to God's original creative and conserving position vis-à-vis the world, there corresponds, on a lower plane which is by nature dependent, our own position as a being made in the image of God and able to know and to transform nature. In this position of man, it can be seen that the world must have its origin in a Being which intended through the creation of the world—and through its preservation continues to intend—that man should come to a knowledge of the world through itself and to a knowledge of that Being.

We appear as the only being which, while belonging to the visible world and stamped with rationality, is conscious both of the rationality it possesses and, simultaneously, of itself. As the only being in the world conscious of itself, we are, at the same time, the consciousness of the world; we are also that factor able to assert the rationality of the world, and to transform the world consciously to our own advantage, and able, through this very act, to transform ourselves consciously by our own act. We cannot be aware of ourselves without being conscious of the world and of the things in it. The better we know the world, or the more aware we are of it, the more conscious we are of ourselves. But the world, by contributing in this passive manner to our formation and to the deepening of our self-consciousness, does not itself become—through this contribution—conscious of itself. This means that we are not for the sake of the world, but the world is for us, although man does also need the world. The point of the world is to be found in man, not vice versa. Even the fact that we are aware that we need the world shows man's superior position vis-à-vis the world. For the world is not able to feel our need for it. The world, existing as an unconscious object, exists for man. It is subordinated to man, even though he did not create it.[3]

THE ORTHODOX DOCTRINE OF SALVATION

Christ did not bring us salvation so that we might continue to live in isolation, but that we might strive towards a greater and ever more profound unity which has as its culmination the eternal Kingdom of God.

We see this reflected in the fact that we cannot gain salvation if we remain in isolation, caring only for ourselves. There is no doubt that each man must personally accept salvation and make it his own, but he cannot do so nor can he persevere and progress in the way of salvation unless he is helped by others and helps them himself in return, that is, unless the manner of our salvation is communal. To be saved means to be pulled out of our isolation and to be united with Christ and the rest of men. "Let us commend ourselves and each other and our whole life to Christ our God," sing the faithful at the Orthodox liturgy. Salvation is communion in Christ (*koinonia*) and therefore the obligation of Christians to strive to maintain and develop their ecclesial unity through love is plain: "For the love of Christ gathers us together." (2 Cor 5:14)

Inasmuch however as Christ has accomplished the work of salvation and continuously offers its fruits in order to bring all men together into the Kingdom of God, Christians, as servants of Christ obliged to strive for the union of all men in that Kingdom of perfect love, also have certain obligations towards those who are not Christians. In what follows a brief attempt will be made to set forth these obligations, or, more precisely, the motives which lie behind them... .

6. Reconciliation therefore does not consist of a purely formal peace, a mere coexistence and lack of aggression, covering over profound disagreements. Lasting reconciliation is inseparable from the kind of love which strives to secure equality and justice among men and nations, and to promote continuous mutual exchange animated by love. It is the result of a true understanding of the meaning of reconciliation with God who unites himself to man and causes him to partake of all good things in Christ. Through such a reconciliation God adopts us as his sons and divinizes us according to his grace.

7. Christians can make no fruitful contribution to this profound reconciliation between men and nations if they are concerned solely with service to individual men and therefore neglect to promote just and equitable relations on a broader social and international scale. If Christians in the past often limited their acts of service to needy individuals because social structures tended to remain static, today, when social structures are more elastic because of the powerful influence of those who are aware of their own solidarity as victims of injustice and who confidently believe that they can produce more satisfactory forms of social life, Christians must make the kind of contribution which will favour the continuous adaptation of these structures to meet contemporary aspirations for greater justice, equality, and fraternity in man's relation to man. It has become more obvious today that the whole world is being moved to seek more just and fraternal human relations, and it is our belief as Christians that we can see in this movement the effect of Christ's activity guiding the world towards the Kingdom of

Heaven, in spite of the fact that this is a goal which in its final form cannot be reached in this world, given the corruptible nature of matter and all its attendant ills.

Any reconciliation not founded on true universal justice and equality among men will always be threatened with collapse, and the absence of a lasting peace will threaten the life of every human being. Christians therefore must labour on behalf of such a lasting peace in order to assure to every man the chance to prepare for his own resurrection. Seen in this light, war presents as many risks to those who are killed as it does to those who do the killing. Though it may seem that the same risk sometimes attaches to a premature natural death, we can be sure that this happens according to the will of God and that God has his reasons. The Christian has a duty, therefore, to fight on behalf of justice because the presence of injustice can appear to provide a justification for eternal death, while the removal of injustice deprives eternal death of any such justification. One who struggles to end injustice follows in the path of Christ who was the first to use justice as a means to deprive death of its justification. Moreover, Christ gives us the power to do the same because our own struggle for justice depends on his power.[4]

8. Justice, equality, brotherhood and lasting peace cannot be realized if we have no interest in the material universe. The material universe, like mankind itself, is destined for transfiguration through the power of the risen body of Christ, and through the spiritual power of his love which urges us to restore the material universe to its original role of manifesting our mutual love, not, as is now the case, of serving as a means of separation and strife. We must demonstrate increasingly in practice the meaning of material goods as gifts, as the means of mutual exchange between men. The universe belongs to Christ; it is mysteriously attached to his crucified and risen body. Yet it also belongs to men, to Christians and non-Christians alike who suffer and advance towards salvation. Nicholas Cabasilas says: "That blood flowing from his wounds has extinguished the light of the sun and caused the earth to quake. It has made holy the air and cleansed the whole cosmos from the stain of sin."[5]

Only if all men are united can they transform the world and respond to the call to treat the world as a gift, as the means of mutual exchange. When we share in the material goods of the universe we must be conscious that we are moving in the sphere of Christ, and that it is by making use of these material things as gifts for the benefit of one another that we progress in our union with Christ and with our neighbour. We must also be aware that when the material world becomes the means whereby we communicate in love, then we are communicating in Christ. Thus, the universe is called to become the eschatological paradise through the agency of fraternal love. It is our duty to free the universe from the vanity of the blind and selfish use we make of it as sinners, and to see that it shares in the glory of the sons of God (Rom 8:21), the glory which is an inseparable part of our union as brothers.[6]

THE TREE OF THE KNOWLEDGE OF GOOD AND EVIL

We do not know how long the human being remained in the primordial state. In any case, he did not undertake to consolidate his own obedience to God or to grow in the knowledge of him, for had he done so, the Fall would not have come about so easily, or it would not have come about at all. St. Maximus the Confessor said:

> Perhaps the creation of visible things was called the tree of the knowledge of good and evil because it has both spiritual reasons that nourish the mind and a natural power that charms the senses and yet perverts the mind. Therefore, when spiritually contemplated, it offers the knowledge of the good, while when received bodily it offers the knowledge of evil. For to those who partake of it in the body, it becomes a teacher of passions, leading them to forget about divine things. Maybe that is why God had forbidden man the knowledge of good and evil, postponing for a while the partaking of it so that first of all, as was right—man knowing his own cause by communing with it in grace, and through this communion, changing the immortality given him by grace into freedom from passions and unchangeability, like one already becomes a god through deification—he, together with God, should gaze harmlessly and fearlessly on God's creatures and receive knowledge of them as God, not as man, possessing by grace and with wisdom the same understanding of things as God, thanks to the transfiguring of the mind and senses through deification.[7]

Likewise, Nicetas Stethatos, developing this idea, declared that the tree of the knowledge of good and evil is sensation applied to the sensible world or to the body. The human being was able to contemplate sensible things without danger by means of the sense faculties under the guidance of the mind. To behold sensible things through sense faculties not yet under the guidance of such a strengthened mind was, however, dangerous. Thus, the human being needed to grow first until he was capable of beholding the world with his sense faculties under direction from a mind that had become spiritual.[8]

The same opinion was expressed by St. Gregory Palamas, who is even more precise:

> Therefore, while they lived in that sacred land, it was to the profit of our ancestors and it was incumbent upon them never to have forgotten God, to have become still more practiced and, as it were, schooled in the simple, true realities of goodness and to have become accomplished in the habit of contemplation. But experience of things pleasant to the sense is of no profit to those who are still imperfect, those who are in mid-course and who, compared with the strength of the experienced, are easily displaced toward good or its opposite.[9]

We might infer that the primordial state lasted only a very short while, for in this state halfway between obedience and disobedience, our first parents were obliged from the very beginning to show themselves either as obedient or as disobedient. Had they shown themselves obedient over a period of time, they would have begun to be habituated to good, and so the Fall would have become a more difficult thing. It would seem, therefore, that they let themselves be overcome at once by the temptation to disobedience.

The expression "primordial state" thus points to that condition of our first parents when they came into existence through the creative act of God, and in which, as in their normal state, they were called to remain and to grow. St. Basil the Great spoke directly of the "rapidity" with which Adam decided in favour of disobedience, but he, too, affirmed the real existence of a short period of time prior to this decision for evil. He helps us to understand that, strictly speaking, the primordial state means that the human being did not come forth as intrinsically evil from the creative act of God, but that evil was chosen by the human being. Hence he had a short period of time in which to make up his mind before choosing. God could not create the human being evil, but he wanted man to strengthen himself in the good through his own cooperation as well. St. Basil even spoke of a certain complacency in the human being that came from his having everything. For the human being, all things lay too much ready at hand before he had grown spiritually by his efforts to win these things for himself. Instead of deciding to expend that effort required if he was to persist and advance in his participation in things that were good but less sensible, he preferred rather to choose enjoyment, without effort, of those good things more easily grasped. The fact that nature, too, was beautiful and rich in a way corresponding to the beauty of the intelligible meanings and realities constituted a further temptation for man to enjoy what was at hand rather than what demanded effort if he was to know and enjoy it.

> Adam was above, not spatially, but by the will, when, recently given (*arti*) soul and looking towards heaven, he rejoiced at what he had seen, loving the Benefactor who granted him the enjoyment of eternal life, rested upon him the pleasures of paradise, gave him mastery like that of the angels, and an existence like that of the archangels, and made him a hearer of the heavenly voice. Protected in all these matters by God and enjoying His good things, he was soon (*tachu*) satiated with everything and became somehow insolent in his repletion, preferring the delight appearing before the eyes of the flesh to intelligible beauty and placing a full belly above spiritual enjoyments. At once he was outside paradise, outside that happy way of life, not evil from necessity, but from lack of wisdom (*aboulia*). Thus he sinned because of a wicked choice and died because of sin.[10]

The *aboulia* of which St. Basil spoke partly means imprudence and partly lack of will, or laziness of the will. The human being had fallen because of imprudence and laziness in expending the effort to make use of his freedom. God wanted man to grow in freedom through his own effort. Freedom, as a sign of spiritual power, is more than just a gift; it is also a result of effort. From the beginning man refused that effort and so has fallen into the slavery of the easy pleasure afforded by the senses. God breathed spirit into man, but the spirit breathed into him was in great part a potency that man needed to make pass into act. By commanding man not to eat from the tree of consciousness before he was guided by freedom of the spirit, God, in fact, commanded him to be strong, to remain free, and to grow in spirit, that is, in freedom. This very commandment made appeal to man's freedom.

The human fall away from God consisted formally in an act of disobedience. Through that very act the human being detached himself interiorly from God and from positive dialogue with him. He no longer responded to God, believing that he was thereby affirming his freedom, and autonomy. In fact, it was this act that marked the beginning of the human's selfish confinement within himself. This was how he enslaved himself to himself. Reckoning on becoming his own lord, he became his own slave. The human person is free only if he is free also from himself for the sake of others, in love, and if he is free for God who is the source of freedom because he is the source of love. But disobedience used as an occasion the commandment not to taste from the tree of the knowledge of good and evil.

The fathers cited above imply that by the two trees we are to understand one and the same world: viewed through a mind moved by spirit, that world is the tree of life that puts us in relationship with God; but viewed and made use of through a consciousness that has been detached from the mind moved by spirit, it represents the tree of the knowledge of good and evil which severs man from God.

St. Gregory of Nyssa asserted this in his own way when he analyzed the ambiguous character of the tree of the knowledge of good and evil. The permitted tree of life is everything, or rather every instance of knowledge and experience, through which man advances in real goodness. The forbidden tree of the knowledge of good and evil is likewise every thing, or every instance of knowledge and experience of which man partakes, but in this case when he is led astray by the idea that it is good, when in reality it is evil "...for surely it is clear to all who are at all keen-sighted what that 'every' tree is whose fruit is life, and what again that mixed tree is whose end is death: for he who presents ungrudgingly the enjoyment of 'every' tree, surely by same reason and forethought keeps man from participating in those which are of doubtful kind."[11]

Like the fathers mentioned above, St. Gregory of Nyssa saw the tree of the knowledge especially in the sensible aspect of the world, but he put particular stress on the fact that this aspect may give rise to evil in the human person because it is grasped in an exclusive manner through his senses. In itself the sensible aspect of the world is by no means evil but can become quite dangerous for the human person because the senses, before they are spiritually strengthened, can be easily inflamed by the sensible beauty of the world. Accordingly, it is better for the human person to concentrate his attention on the spiritual meanings of the world until he himself is strengthened in spirit.[12] The danger in concentrating the powers of sensation on the sensible aspect of things comes, according to St. Gregory of Nyssa, from the possibility that due to the human bodily kinship with animal nature, the passions will be brought to birth in him.[13] Hence, the sensible aspect of the world acquires its characterization as the tree of the knowledge of good and evil, and through its encounter with the human powers of sensation, is mixed together with the sensible aspect of things, apart from any guidance by a mind moved by spirit. To this Satan, too, in the form of the serpent, symbol of all cunning insinuations, makes his contribution. "... and that fruit is combined of opposite qualities, which has the serpent to commend it, it may be for this reason that the evil is not exposed in its nakedness, itself appearing in its own proper nature..."[14] Evil would be ineffective if it did not deck itself in the colors of some good by which it lures those who are deceived into desiring it, but now the nature of evil is in a manner mixed; keeping destruction like some snare concealed in its depths and displaying some phantom of good in the deceitfulness of its exterior. The beauty of the substance [silver] seems good to those who love money: yet "the love of money is a root of all evil" ... so, too, [with] the other sins. . . . It speaks of it [the fruit] ... not as a thing absolutely evil (because it is decked with good), nor as a thing purely good (because evil is latent in it) ... [Thus] the serpent points out the evil fruit of sin, not showing the evil manifestly in its own nature (for man would not have been deceived by manifest evil), but giving to what the woman beheld the glamour of a certain beauty ... he appeared to speak to her convincingly ... "and she took of the fruit thereof and did eat," and that eating became the mother of death to men.[15]

Evil cannot captivate by itself but decks itself with flowers taken from the good. The human person preserves an indelible remnant of the good within himself and must deceive himself by thinking that the sin he is committing has some justification through good. In its inability to stand on its own, evil is ambiguous, hence the perversity—presenting evil as good—to which any tempter must resort if he is to persuade someone to commit the evil he puts forward. Certainly, one who allows himself to be deceived retains in his deception a certain amount of insincerity. He consents to being deceived and is aware that he is deceived. Yet even this need to deceive himself represents a minimum of good left in him like a flimsy bridge by which evil gets in. Without this, evil cannot enter into him.

Evil offers an initial sweetness or good but in the end shows its destructive effect. In regard to the beginning of evil, the devil has no great need of deceiving man, for evil captivates on its own. It is from the human being's fear of the end, that is, of the consequences of an evil deed, that the devil must calm the human soul. As long as the voice of God, which resounded in the depths of the woman's sincere conscience, was telling her: "If you eat from the, tree, you shall die" (Gen 2: 17), it set this fear over against the tempting whisper of the serpent who was deceiving her with the words: "Of course you will not die, but you will be like God" (Gen 3: 4–5). Afterwards, however, this reassurance regarding the end of her evil deed grew stronger in the display of its initial sweetness.

St. Basil the Great interpreted the good and the evil connected with the fruit of this tree in a different way. His interpretation opened up an optimistic perspective toward the future and completed rather than contradicted that of St. Gregory of Nyssa. For St. Basil, the good and the evil committed by Adam are to be seen in the fact that by eating from the tree, Adam committed an act of disobedience on the one hand, while on the other hand, he was led to the knowledge of his own nakedness and hence to the knowledge of shame. Thus—and here St. Basil's approach is the reverse of St. Gregory's—if the beginning is evil, the end is good; or rather, after the evil end, or as he comes to encounter evil, repentance is born in man. In Adam's case, it was through his eating that the idea came to him of making clothes for himself so as to curb his fleshly impulses. In general, the temptation of the serpent served to alert the first humans to the battle to protect themselves against his temptations and to the struggle necessary to vanquish Satan. It was God himself who placed in man this impulse to fight against Satan, and in the Son of Man, Christ, this impulse led to the breaking of Satan's power. In Christ the ultimate end of the battle is found. "I will put enmity between you and the woman, and between your seed and her seed; he shall bruise your head, and you shall bruise his heel" (Gen 3:15). Even the beauty of the tree has served for the human person as an occasion to fight against temptations. By himself the human person will certainly not be able to conquer the evil that was introduced within him, but neither will the evil do away entirely with the good in the human person. The human person will remain in an ambivalent state. Emphasizing this struggle on behalf of the good in the human person and against the evil likewise present within him, St. Basil the Great said: "That is why there was planted a tree bearing beautiful fruits, so that by abstaining from its sweetness and displaying the good of abstinence, we might justly be deemed worthy of the crown of patience. For not only disobedience followed upon the eating, but also the knowledge of nakedness."[16]

According to the interpretations of the fathers, the knowledge of good and evil, acquired when the activity of the senses unites with the sensible aspect of the world, consists in a knowledge of the passions born in the human person, while according to the special interpretation of St. Basil, it consists also in the fight against these passions. From the patristic interpretations we see that on account of the Fall, the human person was left with the knowledge of evil in himself but overwhelmed by it. He continued to be opposed to evil but could not succeed in bringing his struggle to a victorious conclusion.

From the fact that the state of disobedience as estrangement from God is reciprocally involved with the passionate impulse that takes its birth from the weaving together of sensuality and the sensible aspect of the world, a more complex understanding of this sad knowledge of good and evil results, that is, of the fall of man.

Disobedience, pride, and our own selfish appetite arise as a weakening of the spirit. These, moreover, produce a restriction on the knowledge of God's creation; the human person looks to what he can dominate and to what can satisfy his bodily needs and pleasures, now become passions. The bodily passions, in turn, will feed the pride in the human person that satisfies them. His exclusively material needs and passions will be a source of pride justified by his proud claim to be autonomous.

We should note, that in our description of this restricted knowledge of creation, we have already passed on to the consequences of sin, inasmuch as this restricted image of the world in a particular way, but in part, too, this restricted knowledge (which both hold sway within man against his will) are no longer produced by an actual sin.

This restricted knowledge is adapted to an understanding of the world as ultimate reality, but as a reality characterized as object and destined to satisfy exclusively the bodily needs—now become passions—of rational creatures. It conforms to the human passions and pride under whose power it has fallen, and it sees creation as a vast, opaque, and ultimate object possessed of no transparence or mystery that transcends it. This knowledge took its origin from a spiritually undeveloped human person, and it has remained at his measure, arresting his spiritual growth in relation to the horizon that lies beyond the sensible world. It is a knowledge that veils what is most essential in creation, hence a knowledge in the ironic sense that God uses to speak of in Genesis 3:22. It is a knowledge that will never know the ultimate meaning and purpose of reality.

The difficulty of coming to know the transparent character of creation and of person itself, characters that open their infinite meanings, derives also from the fact that creation and the human person can no longer put a stop to the process of corruption that leads each human person toward death. Had Adam not sinned, the conscious creature would have advanced toward a kind of "stable" motion within a greater and greater convergence and unification of the parts of creation, of the human person in himself and of humans among themselves and with God, within a movement of universal love whereby creation is overwhelmed by the divine Spirit. Instead, through the Fall, a motion toward divergence and decomposition entered creation. It is only through Christ, as God incarnate, that the parts of creation have begun to recompose themselves so as to make possible its future transfiguration, for from Christ the unifying and eternally living Spirit is poured out over creation.

We note that in the Orthodox view, the world after the Fall did not take on a totally and fatally opaque image, nor was human knowledge wholly restricted to a knowledge that conformed to an opaque, untransparent image of the world. Humans can penetrate this opacity in part by means of another kind of knowledge, and indeed, they often manage to do this, but they cannot wholly overcome this opacity and the knowledge that conforms to it. These remain dominant structures.[17]

PROVIDENCE AND THE DEIFICATION OF THE WORLD

A good part of more recent theology puts the idea of hope in the forefront. "Any idea of God that cements the existing social order is abandoned. Today it makes sense to speak about God only if he opens a future and has a function of transforming the world."[18] That is, only if, as God leads the human being toward himself and toward salvation, he is leading him to higher levels.

This work of God is bound up *par excellence* with the category of the "new": "Behold, I make all things new" (Rev 21:5). This is the final perspective opened for us by God. But in the view of this final newness, humans must become new from now onwards (Eph 4:24; 2 Cor 5:17; Gal 6:15). Not at the end alone will all things be made new; it is true from the first coming of Christ (2 Cor 5:17). And this newness is not one that grows old, but one in which we must unceasingly be walking and growing: "[so that] ... we too might walk in newness of life ... so that we might serve not under the old written code but in the newness of spirit" (Rom 6:4, 7:6). To walk in "newness of life" or "newness of spirit" means to be always open to "the new." For the "spirit" is always alive, that is, spirit does not remain within the same things. This is that "stability" within the movement of ascent described by St. Gregory of Nyssa, a stability that is simultaneously motion and without which the human being no longer remains within continuous newness but as a consequence, falls.[19] Moreover, God is life. St. Gregory of Nyssa said: "True being is true life ... It is not in the nature of what is not life to be the cause of life. This truly is the vision of God: never to be satisfied in the desire to see him."[20]

St. Paul the apostle opposed the "newness of spirit" to the oldness of the letter or the law as he opposed the life of the resurrection to abiding in death. Now where the law is, there is found a sign that sin reigns. "The sting of death is sin, and the power of sin is the law" said St. Paul (1 Cor 15:56). When the law does not prepare men to go beyond the level it has helped them to attain, that is, when man does not draw the conclusion as a kind of constant newness, that Christ is "the end of the law" or that "love is the fulfilling of the law" (Rom 10:4, 13: 10), then the law is the power of sin that leads to death. Moreover, sin is the sign of the survival of the old man. To remain always within the identical forms is an expression of the survival of sin, of staying within the limits of the self. The genuinely "new" does not represent growth in self-centeredness, but rather continual surpassing of the self, advancement beyond the self; it is not the extension of one's own dominion in order to provide even greater security for the ego.

The law is repetition, according to an external norm, within the monotonously confined horizon of egoism and death. To walk in "newness of life" means to live beyond repetition as love or knowledge or the good passes by degrees from one stage to another, from *epektasis* to *epektasis*, as St. Gregory of Nyssa put it.[21] God makes any state already attained, any result already achieved, a relative thing only. Every such state only represents a step leading to another and higher one. The "reign of freedom" transcends any level that is attainable, and it is toward such liberty that we are advancing, always unhindered by any level we might have reached already.

God reveals himself in this way as the factor that forms a humanity that is being raised higher and higher, and as the force that is leading us toward a future that is never closed back in on itself. This factor shows itself in the form of a love for humans that is continuously bestowing more upon them and wanting them to be more and more loving toward one another. Thus, love for God, or more strictly, thought taken for God, represents a continuous contribution toward keeping the world in movement toward more and more authentically human relations among humans. God resists making any structure or condition humans have achieved among themselves into an absolute reality. He shows his effectiveness in two ways: first, by keeping the human person's spiritual horizon free when it is confronted with any degree or form of this kind of absolute structure or relationship; second, by bestowing upon our nature the impulse to find paths that lead toward ever more improved relations among humans and to the goal of a humanity elevated to the highest possible degree, a degree that cannot be defined beforehand. St. Maximus the Confessor expressed this vision through evaluating movement in time in a positive manner, that is, as movement toward the ultimate goal of rest in loving union with God who has no limits and who, at the same time, is not identical with our own "I." "For necessarily the free movement of all things in desire around anything else will cease when the ultimate goal, which is wished and participated in, appears, the goal that will fill to overflowing, so to speak, those who will participate in it according to their capacity. For it is toward it that every way of life and every thought of what is elevated tends and in it all desire rests and is by no means carried beyond it."[22]

SEVEN MORNINGS WITH FATHER STĂNILOAE

Sorin Dumitrescu [SD]: I would like to ask you whether it is not the time for the Church, out of respect for history and society, to make some distinctions to help renew the civil society or to bring about at least an imaginary consensus in [the Romanian] society? Today we [Romanians] have a country in which executioners and victims live side by side, mixed up deliberately to the point of being indistinguishable from each other.

Dumitru Stăniloae [Fr. DS]: As I said earlier, as social beings humans need other humans. Nevertheless, I cannot say that I exist up to this point and from thence there is someone else. I have to be in a relationship with both good and bad people, always having the consciousness of a [Christian] mission. I mean to say that churchmen—first bishops, priests, monks—and lay people should not separate themselves from the other members of the society. Churchmen should not imitate the others, but help them to improve themselves by personal example, help, and words of consolation. Churchmen should always be dynamic and efficacious examples in society. I do not get involved in politics and will not say, "I belong to such and such party, let's get rid of the other party, or I want such and such ministers. . . ."

SD: That is politics. However, do you not think the Church should deliver a speech on guilt? Should it not theologize a little on guilt also?

Fr. DS: Not on the guilt of certain persons, because the Church always preaches on how people ought to be. Churchmen—priests, monks, bishops—should be an example in realizing the behavior proposed by writings such as the *Philokalia*.[23] Yet we have to realize that they themselves are humans and that they cannot always be perfect examples. . . .

SD: My question is a little different though. The political leadership tries to use the Christian theme of forgiveness as an electoral slogan, imposing a homogenization of guilt. Today everybody says he or she is not guilty. Those who shot dead young people [protesting against the communist regime of Nicolae Ceausescu in December 1989] say they obeyed orders, while the others, of course, say they are right. The political leadership says, "Look, we are the real Christians, because we do not punish anybody." In this case, should not the Church intervene more decisively?

Fr. DS: The Church cannot publicly condemn anybody, because confession is an intimate matter. Where would hatred stop if one were to say, "This one is guilty, and that one too, and so on and so forth"? These are intimate issues. The Church teaches, it does not condemn publicly. If someone comes to confession saying, "I am wrong, I stole, I killed," the Church tells that person "You cannot have communion with the Lord." Do you think that is an easy thing?

SD: But I do not mean the condemnation of a certain person, but the Church should draw attention—if the matter is real—that God, nevertheless, has two arms: one for forgiveness and love, the other for justice. Can we live only with love? Because the political leadership says now "We love you, nobody is guilty; it's good we got rid of the demon Ceausescu; other than that, calm down because nobody is guilty."

Fr. DS: The Church lives through love, but also by certain goodness. When real believers come to the Church [to confess their sins], the Church tells them simply that they have to change. You are forgiven but you have to promise you will not sin again. When the adulterous woman was brought to Jesus, he said that those without sin should throw the first stone. All her accusers put their stones down and left, while Jesus said to her, "I forgive you, too, but sin no more." He cannot say, "I do not forgive you; I condemn you for what you did." So does the priest: I forgive you, but sin no more. There is goodness mixed with intransigence, as you see. I do not like the sin, but I do not condemn someone definitively either. . . . I repeat, the Church does not condemn. . . . The Church does not prevent the State from making its own laws required by history. State laws condemn the perpetrator if necessary. If an executioner ... comes to a priest, the latter cannot say, "I will hand you over and let you be killed." If you repent, stop doing what you have been doing, start leading a very different life, we shall see. For now, you do not receive communion for the next ten years. After ten years, if you changed, you receive communion. . . . I cannot hand him over to the police. Jesus forgave the repenting thief. I have to see real repentance, and this is one way of correcting people.

SD: Excuse me, but what you say refers to the personal relationship between the penitent and the confessing father. . . . Do you not think the Church, without naming names, should take a public stand and say that its teachings are misused? Because, you see, the Church does not want to homogenize guilt by [indiscriminate] forgiveness; the Church can be intransigent if it wants to.

Fr. DS: So, you suggest the Church should prevent the State from using its laws.

SD: No, to the contrary. The Church should tell the State to use its laws. We have set free all those who for 45 years have mocked the people. Everybody is now acquitted; the executioners ride with the victims on the same buses, applaud together at the same shows. Do you think that is normal?

Fr. DS: Can the Church say, "Kill the executioners"?

SD: No, it cannot say that. Nevertheless, it can say, "Justice is needed."

Fr. DS: Well, that is what it says all the time.

SD: Still, the Church did not say it loud enough, because the Church itself is culpable.

Fr. DS: What can we do? There is a long road from teaching to practice. Nobody is perfect in this world. Nor are the churchmen. We plead for the good, we seek to win the others to our cause, but few of us are perfect supporters of the Christian teachings in their own lives. That is how we are, as St. Apostle Paul said it, "we are sinners and I am the first among them." I could not punish. I was in jail myself and I do not even remember well those who tortured me. Nevertheless, if I knew them, I would not ask for their punishment.

SD: Yes, but you cannot ask the same from a whole nation, can you? You keep forgetting that there is a whole crowd of people out there who want to know who shot the young people dead in 1989. This crowd wants a trial, regardless of whether they end up forgiving or condemning the executioners. Yet, they want to discern truth from lie. Do you consider this an unchristian wish?

Fr. DS: I do not know if Christians, priests, the Church could ask for the punishment of those people.

SD: What about discerning who is guilty and who is not?

Fr. DS: Of course, the Church together with others [the State] can discern. If the others [the State] do not do it, should the Church be harsher and say "Kill them, punish them"? Did Jesus say this thing? Did he instigate the people against those who judged him, Pharisees and priests?

SD: Yet he entered the temple with a whip.

Fr. DS: That is true, but he did not ask for the death of the moneychangers. The Church does whip at times. There was a time until the fourth century when public confession was practiced—people confessed their sins in public. That was not a good idea. The Church cannot instigate the society to proceed with punishment... .

SD: ... According to the tradition of the church, penance always accompanies the confession of guilt, that is, so and so comes, confesses his or her sins, and then receives a penance. The Church should propose this model to the political leadership and the civil society. Do you agree with this?

Fr. DS: The Church would have to ask each government to recognize its guilt and thus it would meddle too much in politics.

SD: No, just to suggest it.

Fr. DS: The Church did suggest it, but it cannot do this publicly by saying, "This or that government or party is sinful." There is no perfect party. The Church has another method: it works with people, not with political forces. The Church wants to avoid becoming a force in history itself, in order to avoid critique such as, "Why do you say that, are you better?"

SD: Do you think that one of the Church's methods is to validate immediately a newly installed government who usurped the power? Would it not be wise for the Church to wait a little?

Fr. DS: That is something else. I should not show immediately that I am on their side.

SD: The Romanian Orthodox Church did the exact opposite.

Fr. DS: Well, just a minute. Did all of us do it? There are people and people in the Church. Such and such metropolitan gave opportunistic speeches, approving of the new political power. That was his business, but the Church did not do it. The Church is something else: it is the general consciousness of the Christians. The Church as such, I think, does not approve of what is happening. Orthodoxy, in fact, keeps itself at a distance from these kinds of things.[24]

THE MORAL ASPECT OF NATIONALISM

"Nationalism is the consciousness of belonging to a certain ethnic group, the love for that group and the enacting of that love for the well-being of the group."[25]

THE PERMANENT NATIONAL IDEAL

"The Romanian nation (*neam*) is a biological-spiritual synthesis of a number of elements. The most important of them are the Dacian element, the Latin element, and the Christian Orthodox element. . . . The synthesis is new, it has its own individuality, and a principle of unity which differs from the partial components. The highest law of our nation (*neam*), the law which expresses what the nation is in the most appropriate way, is the one that the whole experiences, not the ones experienced by the parts. The parts are stamped with a new, unifying, and individualizing stamp which is Romanianhood (*românitatea*). Therefore, we can say that the highest law for our nation (*neam*) is Romanianhood. Not Romanity, not Dacianism, but Romanianhood with all it includes is the highest law by which we live and fulfill our mission. . . . Which is the Romanian way of communion with the transcendental spiritual order? History and the current life of our people tell us that: it is Orthodoxy. Orthodoxy is the eye through which Romanians gaze at heavens and then, enlightened by the heavenly light, they turn their eye toward the world while continuing to attune their behavior to it. We also know that this is the only eye that is correct and healthy. . . . Certainly, in theory it is hard to understand how it is possible for Orthodoxy to interpenetrate with Romanianism without either of them to have to suffer. Yet, the bi-millennial life of our nation (*neam*) shows that in practice this is fully possible. . . . Orthodoxy is an essential and vital function of Romanianism. The permanent national ideal of our nation can only be conceived in relation with Orthodoxy."[26]

BRIEF THEOLOGICAL INTERPRETATION OF THE NATION

"Concerning man in particular, God created Adam and Eve in the beginning. In them were virtually present all nations. These are revelations in time of the images which have existed eternally in God. Every nation has an eternal divine archetype that it has to bring about more fully. . . . There is one instance when nations may not be from God and we would have to fight against them: when human diversification into nations would be a consequence of sin and a deviation from the way in which God wanted to develop humanity. In that case, the duty of every Christian would be to get humanity out of that sinful state and to fuse all nations into one.

Is diversification of humanity a sin or a consequence of sin? We could reject that presupposition by the mere universal law of fauna and flora. . . . Nevertheless, the answer can be given differently also: sin or evil is of a different order than unity or diversity. Sin means a deformity, a disfiguration of a given thing. . . . Is national specificity a deformity of humanity, a decay of the human being? This would be the case when national specificity would be something vicious, petty, and without heights of purity and thought. . . . The removal of humanity from the sinful state is being done not through the annulment of the national features, but by the straightening of human nature in general. If there were something sinful in national specificity, then one could not distinguish between good and evil people within a nation, but all would be evil. . . . We should note that there is no a-national person. Adam himself was not a-national, but he spoke a language, had a certain mentality, a certain psychic and bodily structure. A pure human, un-colored nationally, without national determinants, is an abstraction."[27]

NOTES

1. [For a fine presentation of Stăniloae's *Philokalia*, see Maciej Bielawski, "Dumitru Stăniloae and his Philokalia" in Lucian Turcescu, ed. *Dumitru Stăniloae: Tradition and Modernity in Theology* (Iasi, Romania: Center for Romanian Studies, 2002), 25–52, as well as Maciej Bielawski, *The Philocalical Vision of the World in the Theology of Dumitru Stăniloae* (Bydgoszcz, Poland: Homini, 1997).]

2. Cf. *The Ambigua*, PG 91.1128D–1133A, 1160B–D.

3. [Dumitru Stăniloae, *The Experience of God*, trans. Ioan Ioniță and Robert Barringer (Brookline, Mass.: Holy Cross Orthodox Press, 1994), 1:1–3.]

4. I have taken this idea from a work found in the Athanasian corpus, *Sermo in Sanctum Pascha*, *PG* 28,1077A–C.

5. *De Vita in Christo* 4, *PG* 150, 592A.

6. [Dumitru Stăniloae, "The Orthodox Doctrine of Salvation and its Implications for Christian Diakonia in the World," in *Theology and the Church*, trans. Robert Barringer (Crestwood, N.Y.: St. Vladimir Seminary Press, 1980), 204, 210–212.]

7. *To Thalassius: On Various Questions*, Introduction, PG 90.257C-260A.

8. *Vision of Paradise* 15–17, ed. Darrouzes, *SChr81*, pp. 170–172.

9. *The One Hundred and Fifty Chapters* 50.1–7, ed. Sinkewicz, 142; ET = Sinkewicz, 143.

10. *God is Not the Author of Evil* 7, PG 31.344C-345A.

11. *The Making of Man* 19.3, PG 44.197A; ET = Wilson, 409.

12. St. Basil the Great considered, however, that the tree of the knowledge of good and evil as a particular tree, but it was not evil in itself, even though it was tempting because of its beauty and the sweetness of its fruits, hence, as representing the beauty and sensible sweetness of creation. Cf. *God is Not the Author of Evil* 8, PG 31.348C–D.

13. Cf. *The Making of Man* 18.1–9, PG 44.192A–196B.

14. *The Making of Man* 20.2, PG 44.200A; ET = Wilson, 410.

15. *The Making of Man* 20.2–4, PG 44.200A–D; ET = Wilson, 410.

16. *God is Not the Author of Evil* 8, PG31.348D.

17. [Dumitru Stăniloae, *The Experience of God*, trans. Ioan Ioniţă and Robert Barringer (Brookline, Mass.: Holy Cross Orthodox Press, 2000), 2:163–172.]

18. Gotthold Hasenhüttl, "Die Gottesfrage heute," in *Gott, Mensch, Universum. Der Christ vor den Fragen der Zeit*, ed. I Hüttenbügel (Graz, 1974), 545–573, 563–564.

19. *The Life of Moses* 2.243–244, PG 44.405C-D; ET = Abraham J. Malherbe/Everett Ferguson, *Gregory of Nyssa. The Life of Moses*, NY etc. 1978, 117–118.

20. *The Life of Moses* 2.235 [233], 239, PG 44.40IB [A], D; ET = Malherbe/Ferguson, 115–116.

21. Cf. *Homilies on the Song of Songs* 6, PG. 44.888A; ET = McCambley, 128, and *The Life of Moses* 2.238–239, PG 44.404C–405A; ET = Malherbe/Ferguson, 116.

22. *The Ambigua*, PG 91.1076C–D. [Stăniloae, *The Experience of God*, 2:194–196.]

23. [*Philokalia* is a collection of Eastern Orthodox spiritual writings. Stăniloae single-handedly produced a monumental twelve-volume Romanian translation between 1946 and 1991.]

24. [Sorin Dumitrescu, *Seven Mornings with Fr. Stăniloae* (Bucharest, Romania: Anastasia, 1992), 53–60. Translated by Lucian Turcescu.]

25. [Dumitru Stăniloae, "The Moral Aspect of Nationalism," *Telegraful Roman* 85, no. 47 (1937): 1. Translated by Lucian Turcescu.]

26. [Dumitru Stăniloae, "The Permanent National Ideal," *Telegraful Roman* 88, no. 4 (1940): 1–2. Translated by Lucian Turcescu.]

27. [Dumitru Stăniloae, "Brief Theological Interpretations of the Nation," *Telegraful Roman* 82, no. 15 (1934): 2. Translated by Lucian Turcescu.]

Contributors

FRANK S. ALEXANDER, J.D. (Harvard University), M.T.S. (Harvard University), is Interim Dean and Professor of Law at the Emory School of Law. He is founder and co-director of the Center for the Study of Law and Religion at Emory University.

MILNER BALL, J.D. (University of Georgia), S.T.B. (Harvard University), holds the Harmon W. Caldwell Chair in Constitutional Law at the University of Georgia.

GERARD V. BRADLEY, J.D. (Cornell University), is Professor of Law at the University of Notre Dame.

PATRICK M. BRENNAN, J.D. (University of California, Berkeley), M.A. (University of Toronto), is Professor of Law at Arizona State University.

ANGELA CARMELLA, J.D. (Harvard University), M.T.S. (Harvard University), is Professor of Law at Seton Hall University.

DAVISON M. DOUGLAS, J.D. (Yale University), M.A.R. (Yale University), Ph.D. (Yale University), is the Arthur B. Hanson Professor of Law and Director of the Institute of Bill of Rights Law at the College of William and Mary.

DUNCAN B. FORRESTER, D.PHIL. (University of Sussex), M.A. (University of St. Andrews), B.D. (University of Edinburgh), is Professor of Theology and Public Issues, Emeritus, at New College, University of Edinburgh.

ROBERT P. GEORGE, D.PHIL. (Oxford University), J.D. (Harvard University), is McCormick Professor of Jurisprudence and Director of the James Madison Program of American Ideas and Institutions at Princeton University.

DAVID GREGORY, J.D. (University of Detroit), LL.M. (Yale University), J.S.D. (Yale University), is Professor of Law at St. John's University.

LESLIE GRIFFIN, J.D. (Stanford University), M.Phil. (Yale University), Ph.D. (Yale University), holds the Larry and Joanne Doherty Chair in Legal Ethics at the University of Houston.

VIGEN GUROIAN, PH.D. (Drew University), is Professor of Policy and Ethics at Loyola College and Adjunct Professor at St. Mary's Seminary and University.

RUSSELL HITTINGER, PH.D. (St. Louis University), is Research Professor of Law and Warren Professor of Catholic Studies at the University of Tulsa.

GEORGE HUNSINGER, PH.D. (Yale University), B.D. (Harvard University), is Hazel Thompson McCord Professor of Systematic Theology at Princeton Theological Seminary.

TIMOTHY P. JACKSON, PH.D. (Yale University), M.Phil. (Yale University), M.A. (Yale University), is Associate Professor of Christian Ethics at the Candler School of Theology, Emory University.

MIKHAIL KULAKOV, PH.D. (Christ Church, Oxford University), M.A. (University of St. Andrews), is Associate Professor of Political Studies and Philosophy at Columbia Union College.

MARY D. PELLAUER, PH.D. (University of Chicago), is a freelance writer in Chicago.

MICHAEL PLEKON, PH.D. (Rutgers University), M.A. (Rutgers University), is Professor of Sociology and Coordinator of the Religion and Culture Program at Baruch College, City University of New York.

PAUL E. SIGMUND, PH.D. (Harvard University), is Professor in the Department of Politics at Princeton University.

LUCIAN TURCESCU, PH.D. (University of St. Michael's), M.T. (Bucharest University), is Associate Professor in the Religious Studies Department and Director of the Centre for Post-Communist Studies at St. Francis Xavier University, Nova Scotia.

PAUL VALLIERE, PH.D. (Columbia University), M.A. (Columbia University), is Professor of Religion and McGregor Professor of the Humanities at Butler University.

JOHN WITTE JR., J.D. (Harvard University), is the Jonas Robitscher Professor of Law and director of the Center for the Study of Law and Religion at Emory University.

NICHOLAS P. WOLTERSTORFF, PH.D. (Harvard University), M.A. (Harvard University), is Noah Porter Professor of Philosophical Theology, Emeritus, at Yale University.

Copyright Information

We are grateful to the following individuals and publishers for their permission to reproduce copyright material in this volume as follows, listed as the authors appear in the book. Material not specifically cited is held in the public domain.

Pope Leo XIII

- *The Papal Encyclicals*, 5 vols., Claudia Carlen, ed. Copyright 1981. Reprinted with permission of Ayer Company Publishers.

Jacques Maritain

- Anson, D. C., *The Rights of Man and Natural Law, Jacques Maritain*. Copyright 1945. Reprinted with permission of Pearson Education, Inc., Upper Saddle River, NJ.
- *God and the Permission of Evil*. Copyright 1966 Bruce Publishing, Milwaukee. Reprinted with permission of the Jacques Maritain Center, 714 Hesburgh Library, University of Notre Dame, Notre Dame, IN 46556.
- "Inaugural Address to the Second International Conference of UNESCO," in *Human Rights: Comments and Interpretations* by Edward H Carr and Jacques Maritain, a symposium edited by UNESCO. Copyright 1949. Reproduced by permission of UNESCO.
- *An Introduction to the Basic Problems of Moral Philosophy*. Copyright 1990 Magi Books, Inc. Reprinted with permission of the Jacques Maritain Center, 714 Hesburgh Library, University of Notre Dame, Notre Dame, IN 46556.
- *Man and the State*. Copyright 1951. Reprinted by permission of the University of Chicago Press.
- *Moral Principles of Action*, Ruth Nanda Anshen, ed. Copyright 1952 by Harper & Row, Publishers, Inc. Copyright renewed 1980 by Ruth Nanda Anshen. Reprinted with permission of HarperCollins Publishers, Inc.
- *Scholasticism and Politics*. Copyright 1940 Macmillan Company. Reprinted with permission of the Jacques Maritain Center, 714 Hesburgh Library, University of Notre Dame, Notre Dame, IN 46556.

Dietrich Bonhoeffer

Reinhold Niebuhr

Nicholas Berdyaev

- *Slavery and Freedom*. Copyright 1977. Reprinted by permission of Pearson Education, Inc., Upper Saddle River, NJ.

Vladimir Nikolaievich Lossky

- *In the Image and Likeness of God*, ed. John H. Erickson and Thomas E. Bird, trans. Thomas E. Bird. Copyright 1974, reprint 2001. Reprinted by permission of St. Vladimir's Seminary Press, 575 Scarsdale Road, Crestwood, NY 10707.
- *The Mystical Theology of the Eastern Church*, trans. members of the Fellowship of St. Albans and St. Sergius. Copyright 1957, reprint 1991 by James Clarke. Reprinted by permission of St. Vladimir's Seminary Press, 575 Scarsdale Road, Crestwood, NY 10707.
- *Orthodox Theology: An Introduction*, trans. Ian and Ihita Kesarcodi-Watson. Copyright 2001. Reprinted by permission of St. Vladimir's Seminary Press, 575 Scarsdale Road, Crestwood, NY 10707.
- *Sept jours sur les routes de France*. Copyright 1998 Les Éditions du Cerf, Paris. Trans. Heather Jones and Elizabeth Icks, "Superior Translations," for this volume.
- "The Temptations of Ecclesial Consciousness," trans. Thomas E. Bird. Copyright 1988 St. Vladimir's Theological Quarterly. Reprinted with permission of St. Vladimir's Seminary Press, 575 Scarsdale Road, Crestwood, NY 10707.

Mother Maria Skobtsova

- *Mother Maria Skobtsova: Essential Writings*, trans. Richard Revear and Larissa Volokhonsky. Copyright 2003. Reprinted with permission of Orbis Books.

Dumitru Stăniloae

- *The Experience of God*, vols. 1 and 2, trans. Ioan Ioniță and Robert Barringer. Copyright 1994. Reprinted by permission of Holy Cross Orthodox Press.
- "The Orthodox Doctrine of Salvation and Its Implications for Christian Diakonia in the World," trans. Robert Barringer, in *Theology and the Church*. Copyright 1980. Reprinted by permission of St. Vladimir's Seminary Press, 575 Scarsdale Road, Crestwood, NY 10707.
- "Seven Mornings with Fr. Stăniloae," "The Moral Aspect of Nationalism," "The Permanent National Ideal," and "Brief Theological Interpretations of the Nation" were translated for this book by Lucian Turcescu.

Index

References to notes are indicated by "*n*" after the page number.

abolitionism. *See* Anthony, Susan B.; slavery
abortion, 199, 201–203, 206–208
Accademia di S. Tommaso, 3
actions, basis for, 476
activism. *See* civil disobedience; liberation theology
activism, social, Skobtsova on, 514, 519
Ad petri cathedram (1959), 96
Adler, Helen, 172
advocacy, Stringfellow on, 389–390
Afanasiev, Nicolas, 488
African American churches. *See* King, Martin Luther, Jr.
agape. *See* love, agapic
aggiornamento, 114*n*10
Alabama, 376
Alabama Christian Movement for Human Rights, 372, 373
America. *See* United States
American Colonization Society, 274
Ammon. *See* Hennacy, Ammon

Amos (prophet), 343, 380
Anabaptists. *See* Yoder, John Howard
Anselm of Canterbury, St., 497, 498
Anthony, Susan B., 249–278; "The Church and the Liquor Traffic," 251–256; on disenfranchisement's effects on women's economic and social status, 265–267, 269–276; on freedom of expression, 277–278; history of women's movement chronicled by, 250; importance, xiii–xiv; life and career, 249–251; "Make the Slave's Case Our Own," 257–260; parallels drawn between slavery and women's subjugation by, 274–275, 276; on prostitution, 269–272; *The Revolution*, 250, 263; slavery of African Americans resisted by, 256–261, 279*n*3; on social reform, 269–276; spiritualism and, 276–277; Stanton's relationship with, 249; on suffrage, 261–263, 265–266, 267–268, 272–273; on temperance,

251–256; "What is American Slavery?", 256–257; *Woman's Bible* controversy, 277–278, 279*n*8
anthropology. *See* human nature; persons and personhood
anti-Semitism. *See* Jews and Judaism; World War II
apocalyptic. *See* eschatology
apophatic theology, Lossky's, 487
Apostolate of the Sea, 155
apostolic youth movements, 122–123
Aquinas. *See* Thomas Aquinas, St.
Aristotle, 230, 500
asceticism, Berdyaev on, 472
associations: John XXII on, 97–99; Leo XIII on forming, 13–14, 164; *Pacem in terris* on, 104; of workers, 157–158. *See also* communion; labor and workers' rights; subsidiarity, principle of
Athanasius, St., 498
atheism, John Paul II on, 187, 196
Augustine, St., on freedom, 209
authority: as basis of law, 8; body politic and, 40;

Bonhoeffer on mandate of government, 335; governmental, Barth on, 283–285; Leo XIII on, 15–18, 19, 20; mechanical sovereignty of state, Kuyper on, 234; source of, 9–10; sphere sovereignty, Kuyper on, 232–237; Stringfellow on principalities and powers, 392–393. *See also* papal authority

autocratic regimes. *See* totalitarian regimes

Baptists, King's background and ministry with, 369, 370

barbarism, 74–75

Barth, Karl: Bonhoeffer and, 308, 323; Bonhoeffer on, 281, 318; on church-state relationship, 285–291; on civil disobedience, 291–293, 301; on faith and politics, relationship between, 294–296; on human righteousness, 303–305; on humanity of God, 293–294; importance, 280–281, xiii; life and career, 280–281; nuclear arms, opposition to, 301–303; on peace, 298–299; on prayer, 291; on revolution, 283–285; on social justice, 281–283, 296; on socialism, 281–282; theological achievements, 280; war theology, 296–301

Basil the Great, St. (Basil of Caesarea), 545, 548–549, 558n12

Batterham, Forster, 150

beauty, Berdyaev on creativeness and, 484

Belgium, 32n70

Berdyaev, Nicholas (Nicolai Aleksandrovich), 456–485; creativeness, ethics of, 479–483; on creativeness and beauty, 484; on creativeness and imagination, 483–484; eschatology of, 485; on ethics, threefold typology, 468–469; on free will, 468; on God's nature, 467–468; importance, xv; on law, ethics of, 469–475; life and career, 456–458; Lossky, comparison with, 488; on love, 476–477; on objectification, 459–460, 462; on original sin, 466–467; personalism, 459–460; on personality, 458–459; on personality and communion, 461–462; on redemption, 462–466, 475–479; on religion, 462; Skobtsova and, 512; Soloviev's influence on, 426; on theandric existence, 460–461; trinitarian theology, 458–459, 465

Bergson, Henri, 59

Berrigan, Daniel, 387

Besant, Annie, 276–277

Bethge, Eberhard, 308, 316–320, 321–329, 341n6, 342n7

Betowsky, Xagr, 154

Bible: Bonhoeffer's use of, 316–317; Stanton's *The Woman's Bible*, 277–278, 279n8; Stringfellow on Revelation, 396–398; women's rights movement and, 277–278. *See also* biblical references, New Testament; biblical references, Old Testament

biblical living, Stringfellow on, 397–398

biblical references, Old Testament

Genesis: 1:26–27, 190; 1:26–28, 198; 1:27, 190; 1:27–28, 256; 2:7, 190; 2:9, 190; 2:15, 190; 2:16–17, 190; 2:17, 548; 3:4–5, 548; 3:5, 186; 3:15, 549; 3:22, 550; 4:9–15, 198; 32:29, 508

Exodus: 1:17, 206; 20:15, 198

Deuteronomy 5:17, 198

Job: 7:11, 142; 42:7, 501

Psalms: 19:14, 198; 139:13–14, 210

Ecclesiastes 9:3, 187

Wisdom: 1:13, 198; 2:23, 190; 2:24, 198

Isaiah: 11:3, 293; 41:14, 198; 53, 327; 58:6, 250, 255; 61:1-2, 136–137

Jeremiah 50:34, 198

Daniel 11:31, 257

Hosea 6:6, 444

Amos 5:24, 293

biblical references, New Testament

—Matthew: 5:14, 253; 5:38–40, 200; 5:48, 209; 6:33, 304; 7:16, 255; 7:18, 253; 7:21, 255; 8:17, 327; 9:13, 444; 10:39, 358; 11:12, 436; 11:27, 177; 12:7, 444; 12:31–32, 257; 13:39–40, 243; 16:26, 192; 18:18, 410; 18:19, 410; 19:6, 257; 19:16, 197; 19:16–19, 199; 19:17, 197; 19:18, 198; 19:21, 69; 21:28–31, 256; 22:21, 287, 434; 22:36–40, 199; 22:39, 250, 258; 22:39–40, 251; 23:14, 255; 25:25, 305; 25:31–45, 513; 25:31–46, 251, 255; 25:40, 256; 28:18, 434–435; 28:18–20, 177

—Mark: 7:6, 255; 12:17, 434; 12:31, 200; 15:34, 327; 16:15–16, 176

—Luke: 2:14, 517; 6:31, 251, 258; 10:27, 209; 19:20, 305; 20:25, 434; 23:46, 525; 24:46–48, 177

—John: 1:2, 339; 1:12, 433; 1:14, 320; 1:17, 362, 436; 1:18, 177; 1:29, 327; 1:30, 334; 3:8, 210; 3:16, 514; 3:34, 177; 5:36, 177; 8:44, 198; 14:6, 177; 15:5, 45–46; 16:13, 286; 17:4, 177; 17:18, 20, 21, 177; 18:36, 434; 19:15, 435

—Acts of the Apostles: 1:8, 177; 5:29, 206, 287; 15:28, 507; 19:28,34, 261

—Romans: 1:5, 178; 2:6, 207; 3:24, 320; 6:4, 551; 7:6, 551; 8:21, 543; 8:22, 428; 10:4, 551; 13:1, 283–285; 13:1C, 340; 13:4, 287; 13:7, 207; 13:9, 199; 13:10, 551; 14:12, 207

—1 Corinthians: 1:22–25, 419; 1:25, 501; 8:6, 339; 15:27, 179; 15:45, 502; 15:56, 551

—2 Corinthians: 5:14, 542; 5:17, 551; 10:5–6, 178

—Galatians: 3:19, 489, 502; 3:24, 502; 4:19, 330–331; 5:14, 199; 6:15, 551

—Ephesians: 4:24, 551; 5:32, 335; 6:12, 504

—Philippians 2:10–11, 241

—Colossians: 1:1, 340; 1:16, 334, 340; 1:16–19, 241; 1:17, 340; 1:19, 191; 2:9, 427; 2:9–10, 177

—1 Timothy: 2:1–4, 291; 2:2, 205; 6:14, 178

—Titus 2:13, 178

—Hebrews: 1:2, 339; 13:3, 258

—1 Peter: 2:13–14, 207; 2:14, 340

—1 John: 3:16, 210; 4:20, 532; 5:19, 426

—Revelation: 13:10, 206; 21:5, 551; 21:22, 285

Birmingham, Alabama, 371–374, 384

bishops, nomination of, 4

black churches in U.S. See King, Martin Luther, Jr.

black nationalism, 379

blasphemy, Kuyper on, 237

Blok, Aleksandr (Alexander), 512

Bloy, Leon, 34

body politic (political society), Maritain on, 39–41

Boehme, Jacob, 484

Boethius, 505

bogochelovechestvo (God-manhood) and theosis. See God, humanity of

Bonhoeffer, Dietrich, 307–341; on action in the world, 309–310; on Barth, 281, 323; Barth and, 308; Bethge and, 341n6, 342n7; Bible as used by, 316–317; on changes in Christianity, 320–321; on Christian ethics, 329; on Christian life, 331–332; Christology and Christocentricity, 310–311; on Church, mandate of, 335; on church/state relationship, 339–341; on civil courage, 314; on commandment of God, 337–339; on confession of faith, 308–309; conspiracy against Hitler, role in, 307; Ethics, 342n20; on ethics, 329–341; on evil, 313–314; on faith, 328–329; on formation, 330–331; on freedom, 336–337; on God, 321–322, 327–328, 329–330; on grace, 311; on guilt, 336; on history and success, 314; on human nature and human life, 310, 314, 315; on inner life, 325–326; Jews championed by, 342n20; on knowledge's effect on God's place in human life, 322–323, 324–325; on labor, 334; legacy, 308; letters and papers from prison, 312–316; letters to Eberhard Bethge, 316–320, 321–329; life and career, 307–308; on love of God, 317; on Luther, 336; on marriage, 335, 338; on the natural, 332–333; on nature of reality, 333–334; on "others," 342n20; on redemption, 324; on religionless Christianity, 317–320; on sovereignty of God, 315; on the state, 335; on temptation, 311–312; on

tragedy, 336; on vocations, 337; on weakness of God, 326–327

Boniface VIII (Pope), 289

Borden Milk Company, 151–152, 161–162, 163–164

Boutwell, Albert, 374

Bouyer, Lois, 488

Bradlaugh, Charles, 277

Brant, Neil, 158–159

Bright, John, 263

Bright, Mrs. Jacob, 276

Brunner, Emil, 362–363

Buber, Martin, 376, 537

Bukharev, Alexander, 464

Bulgakov, Sergei N. (Sergius), 426, 457, 512

Bultmann, Rudolf, 320

Bunyan, John, 380

Cabasilas, Nicholas, 543

Callahan, Bill, 163

Calvin, John, 363

Calvinism, Kuyper on, 220–227

capital punishment. See death penalty

careers, Stringfellow on, 387–388

Catholic Church: Apostolate of the Sea, 155; Councils of (See entries at "Councils"); freedom of, Leo XIII on, 88–89; John Paul II on, 178–179; Kuyper on, 222; in Latin America, 122–123, 124; and liberation process, 130–131; as locus theologicus, 119, 120; religious freedom, late recognition of, 92; social doctrine, 193–195, 213n48. See also names of individual popes; papal authority

The Catholic Worker and The Catholic Worker movement, 151–156, 160–163; activities of, 161–163; founding of, 150; houses of hospitality, 150, 168–169; poor, concern for, 167; publication's circulation, 161, 162; publication's twenty-fifth anniversary issue, 165–173. *See also* Day, Dorothy; labor and workers' rights

Catholic Worker movement, 150

Catholicism, modern: on law and love, 362; natural law theory as emphasized by, 359, 366n7; Niebuhr on, 366. *See also* Catholic Church; papal authority

Cavour, Camillo Benso di, 345

cemetery workers' strike, New York, 153–154, 172

censorship, Murray on, 78–80

Centesimus annus (1991), 193–197

Che Guavera, Ernesto, 130

cheap grace, 311

Chicago, 275–276

child labor, 158–159, 161, 169

The Children of Light and the Children of Darkness (Niebuhr), 368n10

Christ: Barth on social justice and, 281–283; Bonhoeffer on formation and, 330–331; Jewish origins of teachings of, 409; King on, 380; Kuyper on, 241–242; Second Vatican Council on role of, 177; Skobtsova on teachings of, 532; Thomas Aquinas on, 24–25. *See also* Christology

Christian life: Bonhoeffer on, 331–332; Stringfellow on, 391–392, 394–396, 397–398

Christian love, 139–140, 146–147

Christian realism, 343

Christian teaching, 3–4, xi

Christianity: Berdyaev on Redemption and, 462–466; Bonhoeffer

on changes to, 320–321; Bonhoeffer on mandate of the Church, 335; early, power of, 382–383; equality and, 38–39; governments and, 60; influence of, ix; religionless, Bonhoeffer on, 317–320; Skobtsova on, 518–520; temperance and, 251–253; white churches' lack of action against segregation, 381–383

Christology: Bonhoeffer's, 310–311; John Paul II on, 177–178; Leo XIII on, 24–27; Lossky on, 498; Skobtsova on, 515–516, 519; Soloviev's, 427–428; Yoder on, 415–419

the church. *See* Catholic Church; ecclesiology

church and state, relationship of: attempts to restore alliance between, during nineteenth century, 4; Barth on, 285–291, 287–289; Bonhoeffer on, 339–341; Kuyper on, 230–240; Leo XIII on, 22–23; Lossky on, 506–507; Maritain on, 43–45; Murray on, 83; Soloviev on, 436–437, 444, 448–452; Stăniloae on, 552–556. *See also* separation of church and state

"The Church and the Liquor Traffic" (Anthony), 251–256

Church Councils. *See* First Vatican Council; Second Vatican Council

civil courage, 314

civil disobedience, 291–293, 301, 375–377

civil society, 8–9, 245. *See also* church and state, relationship of

civil unity, 81–83

civitas. See state

class, rights and, 14–15

class struggle: causes, 118; faith and, 144–147; liberation theology and Gutiérrez on, 132–133, 139; Pius XI on, 145. *See also* labor and workers' rights; poverty and the poor

Clément, Olivier, 488

coercion, 80, 521

collective will, 72

collectivism. *See* Marxism, communism, and socialism

commandment of God, Bonhoeffer on, 337–339

Commines, Philippe de, 493

common good: civil law and, 205, 206; Day on, 165; economics and, 437; Leo XIII on, 21–22; Maritain on, 40–41, 44–45, 61–63; *Pacem in terris* on, 107; society and, 61–62; Soloviev on death penalty and, 432–433; universal nature of, 109–110

common grace, Kuyper's doctrine of, 240–246

common law of civilization. *See ius gentium* (international law)

commonwealth. *See* state

communion (relationship) and community: families vs., 12; Skobtsova on, 520; Stăniloae on, 542. *See also sobornost;* society

communism. *See* Marxism, communism, and socialism

company unions, 164

Comstock Era, 77–78

Confessing Church, 307

confession in Orthodox tradition, 553–554

"Confidentially" (Kuyper), 219–220

Congar, Yves, 488

Congregation for the Doctrine of the Faith, 117

connatural knowledge, 48

Connecticut, 77–78

Connor, Eugene "Bull," 373, 374, 384
conscience, freedom of, 84
consciousness, Church and, 507
consent, law and, 80
Constantinianism, 413
Constitution (U.S.): First Amendment, 83–84, 377
consumerism, 399
conversation, 74–75
Cort, John, 163, 168
Councils: Vatican I, 4; Vatican II (*See* Second Vatican Council)
creation, Lossky on, 507
creativeness, Berdyaev and, 479–483, 483–484, 484, 485
the cross, 515–516, 518
cruelty, 444
Crusades, 493–494
customs (traditions), 522

Dawson, Christopher, 81
Day, Dorothy May, 149–173; activities, 165–166; on anti-sharecropper violence, 159–160; on Borden Milk Company, 151–152, 161–162, 163–164; *The Catholic Worker*, selections from, 151–154; on Catholic Worker movement, activities of, 161–163; on *The Catholic Worker*'s twenty-fifth anniversary, 165–173; on child labor, 158–159, 169; on common good, 165; on fair wages, 154; on Hennacy, 169–170, 171, 172–173; importance, xii; life and career, 149–152; Maurin's influence on, 167, 169, 173; personalism and subsidiarity espoused by, 167; poor, concern with, 167; on private property, 169–170; socialism, connection to, 149; Spellman, letter to, 153–154; on strikes, 152–153,

162–163; unemployed, unionizing activities for, 157–158; Wobblies (IWW), membership in, 150; on women and women's rights, 169; on workers' duties, 155–156. *See also Catholic Worker* and The Catholic Worker movement; labor and worker's rights
Day, Grace Satterlee, 149
Day, John I., 149
Day, Tamar Theresa, 150
de Maistre, Joseph. *See* Maistre, Joseph Marie, Comte de
death and sin, law of, 502–503
death penalty, 200–201, 429–433, 445, 453n5
Declaration of Religious Freedom (Vatican II). *See Dignitatis humanae* (1965)
democracy, 58–60, 354–360
demonic powers, 393–394
developing world, 120–121, 128–129
devil. *See* Satan
Didache (Doctrine of the Twelve Apostles), 199
Dignitatis humanae (1965), 89–91, 113
dignity of human person, 192–193. *See also* freedom of human person; life, sanctity of
direct action. *See* nonviolence
discipleship, 419–422
disenfranchisement, 263, 265–267, 269–276. *See also* Anthony, Susan B.
divine faith. *See* faith
dominion, God's, 500–502, 503
Dominus Iesus (2000), 176–179
Dorotheos, St., 497
drinking. *See* temperance movement

dualism, metaphysical, 413
Dumitrescu, Sorin, 552–556
duties. *See* rights theory

ecclesiology: Lossky on, 499–500; Stăniloae on, 552–556; Stringfellow on, 390; Yoder on, 407–409. *See also* church and state, relationship of; Constantinianism
Eckhart, Meister, 488
economic growth, 116
economic justice: Catholic position on (*See Mater et Magistra; Rerum novarum*); Soloviev on, 435, 437–440; women and, Anthony on, 269–276. *See also* class struggle; labor and workers' rights; liberation theology
economic rights, 103–104
ecumenism, 111–112, 245–246
education, 102
egoism, 459–460, 518
Eliot, T. S., 384
Eliot, William G., 270
encyclical letters, Leo XIII's use of, 3
Encyclopedia of Sacred Theology: Its Principles (Kuyper), 227–230
enfranchisement. *See* Anthony, Susan B.
equality, 37–39, 447. *See also* racial justice; women and women's rights
error, 110
eschatology, 417, 485, 500–505
eternal law, 50–52
ethics. *See* morals, morality, and moral theology
Ethics (Bonhoeffer), 342n20
Eucharist, 533–534
euthanasia, 201, 203, 206–208
Evangelium vitae (1995), 197–210
Evdokimov, Pavel, 488

evil: Berdyaev on good and, 466–467; Bonhoeffer on, 313–314; democracies and, 356–367; evil actions, cooperation in, 208–209; Lossky on, 507; Maritain on, 45–47; Satan, power of, 503; Stăniloae on, 545, 547–548. See also sin
existence, materialism vs., 188–193
Exodus (of Jews from Egypt), 131–132
extremism, 380

faith: Barth on relationship between politics and, 294–296; Bonhoeffer on, 328–329; confession of, 308–309; John Paul II's contrasting of theological faith with religious belief, 178; Leo XIII on, 5–7; morality and, 26–27
the Fall. See original sin; sin
family life, 12, 40. See also marriage
farms and farm workers, 163
Farnsworth, D., 168
Favre, Genevieve, 34
Favre, Jules, 34
Fedotov, George, 457
Fellowship of St. Alban and St. Sergius, 488
feminist theology. See women and women's rights
First Amendment (U.S. Constitution), 83–84, 377
First Vatican Council, 4
Florensky, Pavel, 426, 457, 487
formation, Bonhoeffer on, 330–331
Foundling Hospital (New York City), 270
four mandates, 334–335
France: Catholic unions, 155; Leo XIII's concerns regarding, 22–23; Lossky on, 489–491; religion, suppression of, 4; religious wars in, 494;

Soloviev on Revolution, 433–434
Frank, Semyon, 426
Frederick the Great, 345–346
freedom. See rights theory
freedom of expression, 277–278
freedom of human person: Anthony on women's rights and, 263–268; Berdyaev on, 468; Bonhoeffer on, 336–337; God and, 183; John Paul II on, 181–188; Leo XIII on natural liberty, 7–8; Lossky on, 495–496; Skobtsova on, 526. See also dignity of human person; slavery
freedom of religion. See religious liberty
free will, 468. See also freedom of human person
Fundaminsky, Ilya, 513
Furfey, Paul H., 151

Gallagher, Donald and Idella, 35
Gandhi, Mahatma, 370
Gaudium et spes (1965), 113
general welfare. See common good
Germany, 347, 349, 352–353. See also World War II
Gift and Mystery: On the Fiftieth Anniversary of My Priestly Ordination (John Paul II), 176
Gilson, Étienne, 487, 488
God: Berdyaev on, 467–468; Bonhoeffer on, 315, 317, 326–327, 337–339; divine mandates, 334–335; dominion of, 500–502; eternal law and, 50; freedom and, 183; God's will, 329–330; Gutiérrez on, 140–141; Lossky on justice and, 492–493. See also Christ
God, humanity of (Godmanhood (bogochelovechest-

vo)): Barth on, 293–294; Berdyaev on, 460–461; Skobtsova on, 515; Soloviev on, 427
the good, 466–467. See also common good
government. See political philosophy; state
grace: Bonhoeffer on, 311; common grace, Kuyper's doctrine of, 240–246; Leo XIII on, 8; Maritain on, 65–66; Niebuhr on, 362–364, 364; Stringfellow on law and, 391. See also sin
Greater Romania, 538
greed, 344
Greek Orthodox Church. See Orthodoxy, modern
Gregory of Nazianzus, St. (Gregory Nazianzen), 495, 499
Gregory of Nyssa, St., 547, 548–549, 551, 552
Gregory XVI (Pope), 3
Grenada, U.S. invasion of, 399
Grotius, Hugo, 326
group pride, 345
guilt, 336
Gutiérrez, Gustavo, 116–147; on Christian love, 139–140, 146–147; on Church's role in liberation process, 130–131; on class struggle, 132–133, 139, 144–147; on conflict in history, 139; on developing world, 120–121, 128–129; on economic growth, 116; on God, 140–141; importance, xii; On Job: God-Talk and the Suffering of the Innocent, 118, 140–142; on liberation, meaning of term, 121–122; on liberation movements, 129–130; life and career, 116–118; on Pius XI, 145; on poverty and the poor, 124–125, 133; The Power

of the Poor in History, 117, 134–137; on problem of theology in Latin America, 141–142; on salvation and liberation, 131–132; on signs of the times, 125–126; on theology, meaning of term, 119–120; *Theology and the Social Sciences*, 138–140; *A Theology of Liberation*, 116, 118–133; *A Theology of Liberation*, revised edition, 118, 142–147. See also liberation theology; Marxism, communism, and socialism

Hague, Frank, 163
Halleux, André de, 538
Hamilton, Alexander, 273
Hannan, Jerome, 152
Harper, Ida Husted, 279*n*5
Harvard Law School, 388
heart, spirit and, 496
Hennacy, Ammon, 169–170, 171, 172–173
Hergenhan, Steve, 169
hermeneutic community, 410–411
Hesychasm, 537
history: conflict in, 139; Lossky on legends and, 494; Murray's sense of, 75–77; Niebuhr on, 351–352; success and, 314
Hitler, Adolf, 307, xiii. See also World War II
Holocaust. See Jews and Judaism; World War II
holy wars, 491–492
houses of hospitality, 168–169
human development, 188–193
humanism, 477
humanity of God. See God, humanity of
human nature: Berdyaev on, 458–459, 460–461, 461–462; Bonhoeffer on, 310, 314, 315; inner life,

325–326; John Paul II on, 196; jurisprudence and political philosophy based on concepts of, 354–358; Kuyper on, 221–222; Lossky on personhood and, 487, 494–495, 505–506; Niebuhr on, 343–349; Soloviev on, 426–427; Stăniloae on the Fall and, 544–551. See also dignity of human person; freedom of human person; individuals and individualism; persons and personhood
human person. See dignity of human person; freedom of human person
human reason. See reason and rationalism
human righteousness, 303–305
human rights. See rights theory

ideology, theology vs., 127
idolatry, 186–187, 394
imagination, 483–484
individuals and individualism: Berdyaev on distinction between personhood and, 458–459; Kantian ethics and, 473; Lossky on, 494–495; Maritain on, 63–65; Soloviev's critique of, 426–427, 434; Yoder's rejection of Pietist tradition of, 418–419. See also personalism; society
infanticide, 270
inner life, 325–326
instincts, 11
intellectual agreement, 36
Irenaeus, St., 502
Islam, 222
ius gentium (international law), 53–56
Ivanov, Vyacheslav, 457

Jefferson, Thomas, 83, 264, 380
Jeremias, Joachim, 327

Jering, Rudolf von (Jhering), 448
Jews and Judaism, 112, 512
Jhering, Rudolf von (Jering), 448
Joan of Arc, 490–491, 492
Job, 141, 501, 503–504
John of the Ladder, St., 477
John XXIII (Pope): *aggiornamento* encouraged by, 114*n*10; on associations, 97–99; *Dignitatis humanae* (1965), 113; ecumenism encouraged by, 111–112; *Gaudium et spes* (1965), 113; importance, xii; life and career, 94–95; on moral order, 99–100; Murray on, 92; *Nostra aetate* (1965), 112–113; *Pacem in terris* (1963), 101–111, 206; religious liberty, espousal of, 113; rights theory, in *Pacem in terris*, 102–106; *Unitatis redintegratio* (1964), 111–112
John Paul II (Pope), 175–210; on abortion, 201–203, 206–208; on atheism, 187, 196; on Catholic Church, 178–179; on Catholic Church's social doctrine, 193–195; *Centesimus annus* (1991), 193–197; on Christology, 177–178; on class conflict, 145; on culture of life, 210; on death penalty, 200–201; *Dominus Iesus* (2000), 176–179; on euthanasia, 201, 203, 206–208; *Evangelium vitae* (1995), 197–210; on freedom, 181–188; on human development, 188–193; on human person, dignity of, 192–193; on idolatry, 186–187; importance, xii; on labor and worker's rights, 197; on law, 205–208; on legitimate defense, 200; on liberation theol-

ogy, 117, 179–181; on life, sanctity of, 197–210; life and career, 175–176; on Lossky, 487; Marxism, socialism, and communism, criticism of, 180–181, 195; on morality and moral theology, 205–210; on rights theory, 205–206; on salvation, 179; on sin, 186, 187, 188; on solidarity, 197; *Sollicitudo rei socialis* (1987), 188–193; on subsidiarity, 197; on superdevelopment, 188–189; theological faith contrasted with religious belief by, 178

Judaism. *See* Jews and Judaism

Jugie, Martin, 537

jurisprudence: Christian, lack of, 390–391; juridical systems, *Pacem in terris* on, 107–108; laws, responsibility to obey (*See* civil disobedience); moral standards and law, relationship between, 77–80; natural law theory influencing (*See* natural law); power and, 354; students' indoctrination in law schools, 388–389. *See also* law; positivist legal theory

just war theory, 492–493

justice: democracies and, 60; law and, 365; Stăniloae on, 543; Stringfellow on justification vs., 401–402. *See also* law

The Justification of the Good (Soloviev), 437–440, 455*n*25

Kaczorowska, Emilia, 175

Kant, Immanuel, 472–473; on love, 362

Karsavin, Lev, 426

Kelsey, George D., 369

kenosis (selflessness, renunciation), 513–515, 525–527

Kester, Howard, 159, 160

Khomiakov (Khomyakov), Aleksei S., 431–432, 509*n*8

King, Coretta Scott, 370

King, Martin Luther, Jr., 369–385; activism, 371–372; assassination, 371; Baptist background and ministry, 369, 370, 371; on black nationalism, 379; on blacks in U.S. history, 383–384; on civil disobedience, 375–377; on early Christian church's power, 382–383; on extremist label, 380; Gandhi's influence on, 370; importance, xiv; influence, 371; on just vs. unjust laws, 375–377; life and career, 369–371; Niebuhr and, 370, 374; on nonviolent resistance, 372, 373–374, 379; optimism, 370, 383–384; personalism, 370; Rauschenbusch's influence on, 370; on slavery, 384; on Southern Christian Leadership Conference, 371–372; on time, 378–379; on white moderates' resistance to racial justice, 377–378, 381–383

King, Martin Luther, Sr., 369

King, Mrs. (Martin Luther Jr.'s mother), 369

King, Yolanda, 370

Klepinine, Dimitri, 513

knowledge: effect on God's place in human life, 322–323, 324–325; Leo XIII on, 5–7; nature of, 466–467; Stăniloae on human nature and the Fall, 544–551. *See also* sciences (theoretical knowledge)

Knox, John, 291

Kovalak, Michael, 172

Krivocheine, Basil, 537

Kulturkampf, 4

Kuyper, Abraham, 219–246; on blasphemy, 237; on Calvinism, 220–227; Calvinist tradition, *Weltanschauung* (world view) construal of, 221–223; on Christ, 241–242; on church and state, 230–240; common grace, doctrine of, 240–246; "Confidentially," 219–220; *Encyclopedia of Sacred Theology: Its Principles,* 227–230; on human nature, theoretical knowledge, and pluralism, 221–222; importance, xiii; life and career, 219, 246*n*1; on mechanical sovereignty of state, 234; on natural law, 226; on paganism, 222, 226; on religion, 247*n*6; on religious liberty, 238, 239; on science, 227–229; on science and sin, 229–230; on secularization of the state, 245–246; on sin, 226, 230–231; on slavery, 222; on society, organic development of, 231; sphere sovereignty, 232–237

Kuzmina-Karavaeva, Elisabeth. *See* Skobtsova, Maria

labor and workers' rights: anti-sharecropper violence, 159–160; Bonhoeffer on mandate of labor, 334; Borden Milk Company, boycott of, 152–153, 161–162, 163–164; Catholic Worker movement, 150, 161–163; Catholics in unions, 163–165; child labor laws, 158–159; company unions, 164; Day's labor activism, 150–151; Day's theory of labor, 154, 158–159, 169; Day's views on unions and, 157–158; enfranchisement of workers, 263–264; fair wages, 154; farms and farm workers, 163; John Paul II on, 197; Leo XIII on, 11; Lowell Textile strike, 162–163; open shops, 164–165; religions and unions, 155; sit-down strikes in Michigan, 152–153; Soloviev on economic justice for workers, 437–440; strikes of 1936 and 1937, 162; unemployed, Day's unionizing activities for, 157–158; women workers, 265–267, 272, 273; workers' duties, 155–156; workers' life expectancy, 439; workers' suspicion of unions, 164. *See also Mater et Magistra; Rerum novarum*

Larrowe, Dwight, 170

Las Casas, Bartolomé de, 143, 148n19

Latin America: Catholic Church in, 122–123, 124; John Paul II on, 181; liberation theology and, 122, 129–130, 134; problem of theology in, 141–142; racism in, 143; women's rights, 143. *See also* Gutiérrez, Gustavo; liberation theology

law: Berdyaev on ethics of, 469–475; death penalty, 200–201, 429–433, 445, 453n5; human law, St. Thomas Aquinas on, 30n43, 206; *ius gentium* (law of nations), 53–56; John Paul II on, 205–208; King on just vs. unjust, 375–377; Kuyper on, 234; Leo XIII on, 8–10; Lossky on, 508; Maritain on, 47–57; moral standards and, 77–80; Murray on legal and moral order, 77–78; of sin and death, Lossky

on, 502–503; Soloviev on morals and, 441–443, 447–448; Stăniloae on, 539, 551–552; unjust law, 375–377; use as term, 67n19. *See also ius gentium;* jurisprudence; natural law; positivist legal theory; Soloviev, Vladimir; Stringfellow, William

law schools, 388–389

Lecky, William Edward Hartpole, 271

legal questions and legal philosophy. *See* jurisprudence

legends, 494

Legitimism, 284

Lehmann, Karl, 140

Leo XIII (Pope), 3–27; on associations, right to form, 13–14, 164; on authority, 15–18, 19, 20; on Catholic Church, freedom of, 88–89; Christological teachings, 24–27; on church/state relationship, 22–23; on civil society, 8–9; on common good, 21–22; on faith, 5–7; on form of government, 18–21; on France, 22–23; on grace, 8; on instincts, 11; on knowledge, 5–7; on labor, 11; on law, 8–10; on life and career, 3–5; on marriage, 10–11; Murray's reinterpretation of, 88–89; neo-Thomism, xi–xii; on philosophy, 5–6; private property, right of possessing and using, 11–12; on reason, 5–7, 7–8, 11; on religious communities, 13–14; on St. Thomas Aquinas, 6–7; on socialism, 11; on society, 13; on the state, 14; on subsidiarity, principle of, 12–13; teaching letters and encyclicals, 3–4; on United States, 23–24, 32n76

Leontius of Byzantium, 505

lex indita, concept of, 27n3

liberation, 121–122, 128–129

liberation theology: Catholic Church, tensions with, 122–123, 124, 130–131; class struggle's link to, 118, 132–133, 139, 144–147; Congregation for the Doctrine of the Faith and, 117; John Paul II on, 117, 179–181; Latin America and, 122, 129–130, 134; Marxism and, 126; politics and the political and, 135–136; poor, preferential option for, 124–125, 133, 147; sexism and racism as issues for, 143–144. *See also* Gutiérrez, Gustavo; Marxism, communism, and socialism

liberty. *See* freedom of human person

life: right to, 102; sanctity of, 197–210 (*See also* war); will to live, 357–358

The Life and Teaching of St. Gregory Palamas (Stăniloae), 537

life expectancy of workers, 439

Lincoln, Abraham, 266, 380

Lison, Jacques, 538

Locke, John, 354

Losev, A. F., 426

Lossky, Nicolas (Nikolai), son of Vladimir, 426

Lossky, Nikolay Onufriyevich (father of Vladimir), 488

Lossky, Vladimir Nikolaievich, 487–508; apophatic theology, 487; on church-state relationship, 506–507; on creation, culture, and cosmology, 507; ecclesiology, 499–500; ecumenism, 488; eschatology, 500–505; on evil, 507; on freedom of human person, 495–496; on

God, 492–493, 500–502, 503; on grace and the spirit, 496–497; on holy wars, 491–492; on human nature and personhood, 487, 494–495, 505–506; importance, xv; involvement in French resistance during WWII, 491, 493; on Job, 501, 503–504; on law, 508; on law of sin and death, 502–503; legacy, 487, 489; life and career, 488–489; mentioned, 537; military service, 490; *The Mystical Theology of the Eastern Church,* 494–496; neopatristic theology, 487; on Old Testament, 508; on original sin, 507–508; *Orthodox Theology: An Introduction,* 507–508; on prophets and prophecy, 507–508, 508; on redemption, 497–499; *Sept Jours sur les Routes de France,* 488, 489–494; on sin, 502; on tradition and traditions, 500; on war, 491–494

love, agapic: Berdyaev on, 476–477; Christian love, 139–140, 146–147; class struggle and, 132–133; Niebuhr on law and, 361–366, 368n11; Niebuhr on law of, 352, 354, 363, 364; Skobtsova on, 513–515, 518, 532–533; Stringfellow on, 394; Yoder on, 419

Lowell Textile strike, 162–163

Luther, Martin, 336, 362, 363, 380

Macarius of Egypt, St., 496, 497

Machiavelli, Niccolo, 326

Maistre, Joseph Marie, Comte de, 430, 453n8– 454n8

"Make the Slave's Case Our Own" (Anthony), 257–260

Marcel, Gabriel, 457

Maria, Mother. *See* Skobtsova, Maria

Maritain, Jacques, 34–66; Berdyaev and, 457; on the body politic, 39–41; on church and state, 43–45; on common good, 40–41, 44–45, 61–63; connatural knowledge, concept of, 48; on democracy, 58–60; on equality, 37–39; on eternal law, 50–52; on evil, 45–47; on faith and reason, unity of, 35; on grace, 65–66; importance, xii; individuality and personhood distinguished by, 63–65; on intellectual agreement, 36; on *ius gentium,* 53–56; on law, 47–57; life and career, 34–35; natural law theories, 47–50, 51, 52–53, 366n7; neo-Thomism of, 34; positivist legal theory, 52, 56–57; rights theory, 43, 52–53, 57–58; on society, 61–62; on the state, 41–43

Maritain, Raissa (née Oumansoff), 34

marriage: Anthony on, 274; authority over marriage, 29n31; Bonhoeffer on, 335, 338; Leo XIII on, 10–11. *See also* family life

martyrdoms: King's assassination, 371; modern Russian Orthodox canonizations, 513; Skobtsova's imprisonment and death, 512–513

Marxism, communism, and socialism: Barth on, 281–282; Berdyaev and, 456; communists in unions, 153–154; Day's relationship to, 149; Gutiérrez on, 116; John Paul II's criticism of, 180–181, 195; Leo XIII on, 11; liberation theology's use of, 126, 130; Maurin's beliefs about, 167; Romanian communist regime and Orthodox Church, 553–556; Skobtsova on, 520–521; socialism as cure for problems of private property, 131

Mary (mother of God), 465, 516–518

Mater et Magistra (1961), 96–100

materialism, 188–193, 543

Maurin, Peter: Day and, 150; Hennacy, comparison with, 172; on houses of hospitality, 168–169; on men and women, 173; mentioned, 153; religiosity, 166; teachings and beliefs of, 167, 171, 172; on unions, religious support for, 155

Maximus (Maximos) the Confessor, St.: on the Fall, 544; Lossky and, 487; Lossky on, 495; on movement toward God, 552; Stăniloae on, 539; on will, 495–496

McGuire, John M., 152–153

Memorial Day massacre (anti-labor violence, 1937), 162

Merezhkovsky, Dimitri, 457

Merton, Thomas, 401

Meyendorff, John, 538

MIA (Montgomery Improvement Association), 370

Michigan, 152–153

modern, use of term, x–xi

modernism, 221–222

Moise, Lionel, 149–150

monasticism, Orthodox, 522–525

Montgomery, Alabama, 370–371

Montgomery Improvement Association (MIA), 370

Montini, Giovanni Battista. *See* Paul VI (Pope)

morals, morality, and moral theology: Berdyaev on vengeance, 470–471; Berdyaev's ethics of creativeness, 479–483; Berdyaev's ethics of redemption, 475–479; Berdyaev's threefold typology of ethics, 468–469; Bonhoeffer on ethics, 329–341; cruelty vs. severity, 444; faith and morality, 26–27; John Paul II on, 205–210; John XXIII on moral order, 99–100; law and, 77–80; Murray on, 77–78; private vs. public, 77–78; Skobtsova on, 515; Soloviev on law and, 441–443, 447–448; Stringfellow on, 398; Yoder on forms of discourse in, 409–413; Yoder on natural law and, 404–407

mortality rates, 439

Mother Maria. See Skobtsova, Maria

Mott, Lucretia, 278

movement, rights of, 104

Mowrer, Dean, 166

Muhammad, Elijah, 379

Murphy, Frank, 152, 153

Murray, John Courtney, 68–92; on censorship statutes, 78–80; on church-state separation, 83; on the Church's late recognition of religious freedom, 92; on civil unity, 81–83; on conscience, freedom of, 84; on conversation, 74–75; on *Dignitatis humanae*, 89–91; on First Amendment, 83–84; on historical consciousness, 75–77; importance, xii; on legal and moral order, 77–78; Leo XIII reinterpreted by, 88–89; life and career, 68–69; on natural law, 69–73; on public con-

sensus, 75; on religious liberty, 84–88; on Second Vatican Council, 92; on society and state, 91–92; on subsidiarity, 72; on United States, 73–74

The Mystical Theology of the Eastern Church (Lossky), 494–496

National American Woman Suffrage Association (NAWSA), 277–278, 279n8

National Biscuit Company strike, 161

nationalism, 556, 557

nations. *See* state

nations, law of. *See ius gentium*

the natural, 332–333

natural law: *ius gentium* and, 54–55; Kuyper on, 226; Leo XIII on, 7–8; Maritain on, 47–50, 51, 52–53, 366n7; Murray on, 69–73; Niebuhr on, 359–360, 365; *Pacem in terris* on, 105; positive law and, 56; rights theory and, 57–58; Thomas Aquinas on, 28n17, 50; Yoder on, 404–407

natural reason. *See* reason and rationalism

natural revelation, 539–541

natural rights. *See* rights theory

Naughton, Irene Mary, 172

NAWSA (National American Woman Suffrage Association), 277–278, 279n8

Nazism, 349, 377. *See also* Jews and Judaism; World War II

neo-Thomism, 34, xi–xii

the new, 551–552

New York City, 153–154, 166, 172, 173

Niebuhr, Reinhold, 343–366; biblical prophets influencing, 343; *The*

Children of Light and the Children of Darkness, 368n10; Christian realist theology, 343, 366n6; on democracy, 354–360; Gifford Lectures, 366n5; on history, 351–352; on human nature, 343–349; importance, xiii; King and, 370, 374; on law of love, 352, 354, 363, 364, 368n11; life and career, 343; on love's relationship to law, 361–366; on natural law, 359–360, 365; on pacifism, 349–354; on pride, 343–349, 366n5–367n5; rejection of pacifism, 366n6; Stanford University lectures, 368n10; on the state, 346–349; on World War II, 353; Yoder on, 420

Nietzsche, Friedrich, 467

nihilation, 45–46

Nikodimos of the Holy Mountain, 538

Nolasco, Peter, 157

non-Christian religions, *Nostra aetate* on, 112–113

nonpossession, principle of, 524, 525

nonviolence, 369, 372, 373–374, 379. *See also* pacifism

Nostra aetate (1965), 112–113

Notaras, Makarios (Makarios of Corinth), 538

nuclear weapons, 301–303, 399

objectification, 459–460, 462

Old Testament: Lossky on, 508. *See also* biblical references, Old Testament

omania, 552–556. *See also* Stăniloae, Dumitru

On Job: God-Talk and the Suffering of the Innocent (Gutiérrez), 118, 140–142

open shops (nonunion workplaces), 164–165

Origen, 510*n*25, 510*n*34–511*n*34

original sin: Berdyaev on, 466–467; Lossky on, 507–508; personality and, 459; Stăniloae on fallen human nature, 544–551; Stringfellow on the Fall, 394, 397. *See also* evil; sin

Orthodox Action group, 512

Orthodox Church, spiritual resources, xiv

Orthodox Dogmatic Theology (Stăniloae), 538

Orthodox Theology: An Introduction (Lossky), 507–508

Orthodoxy, modern: legal, social, and political concerns, avoidance of, 425; neotraditionalist criticism of Soloviev, 426; philokalic and philosophic areas of thought in, 538; Romanian communist regime and Orthodox Church, 553–556

"others," 342*n*20

Oumansoff, Raissa (*later* Raissa Maritain), 34

ownership. *See* private property rights

Pacem in terris (1963), 101–111, 206

pacifism, 296–301, 307, 349–354, xiii. *See also* nonviolence

paganism, 222, 226, 449–450

Palamas, Gregory, St., 487, 537, 545

Palamism, 537–538

Palm Sunday vigil, 522

papal authority, 4

Papal States, 4

Paris, France, 439

Parks, Rosa, 371, 385

Paul, St.: on death and law, 551; King on, 380; Niebuhr on, 350, 351, 365; on society, basis for, 105

Paul VI (Pope), 191

peace, 146, 298–299, 351

Pecci, Gioacchino Vincenzo. *See* Leo XIII (Pope)

penitence, 392

the penultimate, 331–332

personalism: Berdyaev's belief in, 459–460; Day's practice of, 167; King's practice of, 370; Maurin's belief in, 63–64. *See also* individuals and individualism

persons and personhood, 494–495. *See also* dignity of human person; human nature; individuals and individualism

pharasaism, Skobtsova on, 527–530

Philokalia and philokalic school of thought in modern Orthodoxy, 538

philosophy, 5–6, 505. *See also* political philosophy

Pilenko, Elisaveta Iurevna. *See* Skobtsova, Maria

Pillsbury, Parker, 250

pity, 444, 445, 447, 452

Pius VII (Pope), 3

Pius IX (Pope), 3

Pius XI (Pope), 145

Pius XII (Pope), 90, 103

Plato, 484

political philosophy: Barth on revolution, 283–285; government, forms of, 18–21; human nature and, 339. *See also* state

political society (body politic), 39–41. *See also* state

politics and the political, 135–136, 418. *See also* church and state, relationship of; state

the poor. *See* poverty and the poor

Popes. *See* papal authority; *specific Popes, e.g. John Paul II*

positivist legal theory, 52, 56–57

possessions. *See* private property rights

poverty and the poor: Barth on Church and, 296; Day and Catholic Worker Movement's concern with, 167; death rates, 439; Gutiérrez on, 124–125; Kuyper on, 222; liberation theology and, 124–125, 133, 147; poor, preferential option for, 147; *The Power of the Poor in History* (Gutiérrez), 117, 134–137; Soloviev on, 435

power: democracy and, 355; injustice and, 355; jurisprudence and, 354; morality and force, 446; Niebuhr on pride and, 344–345; will to live and, 358

The Power of the Poor in History (Gutiérrez), 117, 134–137

praxis, 125–127

prayer, Barth on, 291

prelatura (Papal States bureaucracy), 3

pride, Niebuhr on, 343–349, 366*n*5–367*n*5

Priest, Eddie, 163

priests, political activities, 123

primordial state, 544–545. *See also* original sin

principalities, 393. *See also* state

Pritchett, Laurie, 384

private property rights: Day on, 169–170; Leo XIII on, 11–12; Skobtsova on possessions, giving of, 525–526; social good and, 131. *See also* rights theory

private society, 13

professions, indoctrination to, 388

property. *See* private property rights

prophets and prophecy, 343, 507–508, 508

prostitution, 269–272

Protestant Reformation, separation from Catholicism, 350–351

Protestantism, modern: on law and love, 362. *See also* specific denominations, e.g. Lutherans

Protestants, political preoccupations, xiii

prudence, 31*n*60

public consensus, 75

Quadragesimo anno (1934), 145

racial justice: American blacks' movement toward, 380; Catholic Church and, 213*n*48; racism in Latin America, 143; rule of law and, 389; white churches' lack of action supporting, 381–383; white moderates' resistance to, 377–378, 381. *See also* King, Martin Luther, Jr.; slavery

rationalism and rationality. *See* reason and rationalism

Ratti, Abrogio Damiano Achille. *See* Pius XI (Pope)

Rauschenbusch, Walter, 370

reality, Bonhoeffer on nature of, 333–334

reason and rationalism: civil unity and reason, 82–83; Leo XIII on, 5–7, 7–8, 11; Maritain on, 47, 49, 50; natural law, role in concept of, 360; Stăniloae on, 540–541

reconciliation, 542–543

redemption: Berdyaev on, 462–466, 485; Berdyaev's ethics of, 475–479; Bonhoeffer on, 324; John Paul II on salvation, 179; Lossky on, 497–499; salvation and liberation, 131–132; Stăniloae on salvation, 541–544

Reformation. *See* Protestant Reformation

religion: Berdyaev on, 462; Bonhoeffer on basis for, 317–319; changing place in human life, 322–323; Kuyper on, 223–226, 247*n*6; Soloviev on, 426. *See also* Catholic Church; Christianity; church and state, relationship of; God; grace; liberation theology; religious liberty; sin; theology

religiosity, actions vs., 254–255

religious communities, 13–14

religious liberty: Catholic Church's late recognition of, 92; John XXIII's support for, 102, 113; Kuyper on, 238, 239; Murray on, 84–88. *See also Dignitatis humanae*

Religious-Philosophical Society, 512

renunciation. *See* kenosis

repentance, 392, 398–400, 400

repressive regimes. *See* totalitarian regimes

Rerum novarum (1891), 114*n*9, 194, 196

respublica. See state

The Return of Nathan Becker (movie), 156

revelation, 539–541

Reville, Jean, 34

revolution, 283–285, 520–521

The Revolution (Anthony), 250, 263

Richard of Saint-Victor, 505

righteousness, human, 303–305

rights theory: Barth on right to resist tyranny, 291–293; Bonhoeffer's, 333; class and, 14–15; duties and rights, 104–106; John Paul II on, 205–206; John XXIII and *Pacem in terris*

on, 102–106; Kuyper on, 236; legitimate defense, 200; Maritain on, 43, 52–53, 57–58; natural law and, 359; Soloviev on, 433, 441, 446–447. *See also* labor and worker's rights

Ritterspruch-Richterspruch (Khomiakov), 431–432

Rogers, Beth, 165

Romanianism, 538

Roncalli, Angelo. *See* John XXIII (Pope)

Rose, Ernestine L., 277

Rozanov, Vassil, 457

Russell, Bertrand, 344

Russia and the Universal Church (Soloviev), 433–437

Russia/Soviet Union, 455*n*25

Russian Christian Students Movement, 512

sacramentality of the church, Yoder on, 408

Saints. *See* specific names, e.g. Augustine, St.

salvation. *See* redemption

Sapieha, Adam Stefan, 175

Satan, 503. *See also* evil

scholasticism, Thomistic. *See* neo-Thomism; Thomas Aquinas, St.

Schweitzer, Albert, 416

sciences (theoretical knowledge): Bonhoeffer on God and, 321–322; John Paul II on, 185; Kuyper on, 227–229; sin and, 229–230. *See also* knowledge

SCLC (Southern Christian Leadership Conference), 371

scripture. *See* Bible

seamen's strike of 1936, 162

Second Vatican Council, 95–113; announcement of, 95; on Christ's role, 177; Murray on, 92; opening address to, 100–101. *See also* specific documents, e.g. *Dignitatis humanae*

sectarianism, 418

secularism and secularization, 245–246
Seeley, John, 346–347
segregation. *See* King, Martin Luther, Jr.; racial justice; slavery
Selden, Henry R., 262
self-consciousness, 541
self-interest, 356
self-realization, 357
selflessness. *See kenosis*
senses, 544, 547
separation of church and state, 22–23, 83, 88, 450–451. *See also* church and state, relationship of
Sept Jours sur les Routes de France (Lossky), 488, 489–494
sexism. *See* women and women's rights
sharecroppers, 159–160
Shestov, Leo, 457
Shoah. *See* Jews and Judaism; World War II
Shoemaker, Joseph, 159
Shuttlesworth, Fred, 373
signs of the times, 119, 125–126
Silver Age (Russia), 426
sin: Berdyaev on, 466; Christ and, 325; and death, law of, 502–503; John Paul II on, 186, 187, 188; Kuyper on, 226, 230–231; Lossky on, 502; science and, 229–230; Stringfellow on law and, 391. *See also* grace; original sin
sin offerings, 430
Sinkewicz, Robert, 538
Skobtsov, Yuri (Iouri), 512
Skobtsova, Maria, 512–534; on agapic love, 513–515, 518, 532–533; Berdyaev's association with, 457, 512; Bulgakov's influence on, 512; canonization and sainthood, 513; on "Christification," 534; Christology, 515–516, 519; on coercion, 521; on communism, 520–521; on

the cross, 515–516, 518; on the Eucharist, 533–534; on freedom, 526; hostels run by, 512; on humanity of God, 515; importance, xv; imprisonment and death, 513; life and career, 512–513; on monasticism, 522–525; on Mother of God, 516–518; on pharasaism, 527–530; on revolution, 520–521; on *sobornost,* 519–520; on social Christianity, 518–520; on traditions, 522–523; on types of religious lives, 531–534; on war, 530–531
slavery: Anthony on, 256–261; Anthony's parallels between women's subjugation and, 274–275, 276; Berdyaev on egoism as, 460; King on, 384; Kuyper on, 222
sobornost, 513, 519–520, 535n1
social activism. *See* activism
social conflict. *See* class struggle; poverty and the poor
social conversation, 74–75. *See also* associations
Social Gospel Movement, 370
social justice, 30n38, 281–283, 296. *See also The Catholic Worker* and The Catholic Worker movement
social sciences, 138–140
socialism. *See* Marxism, communism, and socialism
society: Berdyaev on personality and, 461–462; ethics of law and, 470, 471; Kuyper on organic development of, 231; Leo XIII on, 13; Maritain on, 61–62, 65; Maritain on body politic, 39–41; *Pacem in terris* on, 105–106;

purpose of, 438; Soloviev on nature of, 434–436, 443; Yoder on individualism vs., 418–419. *See also* communion (relationship) and community; individuals and individualism
solidarity, 197
Sollicitudo rei socialis (1987), 188–193
Soloviev, Vladimir Sergeevich, 425–452; Christology, 427–428; on church-state relationship, 436–437, 444, 448–452; on criminal justice and death penalty, 429–433, 445; death penalty, activities against, 453n5; on economic justice, 435, 437–440; on the good and the law, 443; on human nature, 426–427; importance, xv; on individualism, 426–427, 434; *The Justification of the Good,* 437–440, 455n25; life and career, 425–426; Lossky, comparison with, 487, 488; on morality and force, 446; on morality and law, 441–443, 447–448; neotraditionalist criticism of, 426; on the pagan state, 449–450; on religion; rights theory, 441, 446–447; *Russia and the Universal Church,* 433–437; on separation of church and state, 450–451; on society, 434–436, 443; *The Spiritual Foundations of Life,* 426–428, 453n4; on theocracy, 454n14; *theosis,* 455n25; on truth, 437
South America. *See* Latin America
Southern Christian Leadership Conference (SCLC), 371–372
Southern Tenant Farmers' Union, 159–160

Soviet Union. *See* Russia/Soviet Union
Spain, 4
Spellman, Francis, 153–154
sphere sovereignty, 232–237
the spirit, 496–497
The Spiritual Foundations of Life (Soloviev), 426–428, 453n4
spiritualism, 276–277, 279n7
Spring Hill College, Alabama, 381
Stallings, Earl, 381
Stăniloae, Dumitru, 537–557; on church-state relationship in Romania, 552–556; on community, 542; on confession in Orthodox tradition, 553–554; Dumitrescu's interview with, 552–556; on evil, 545, 547–548; on human nature and the Fall, 544–551; importance, xv; on law, 539, 551–552; life and career, 537–539; *The Life and Teaching of St. Gregory Palamas*, 537; on nations and nationalism, 556, 557; on the new, 551–552; *Orthodox Dogmatic Theology*, 538; political naiveté, 539; on reconciliation, 542–543; on revelation, 539–541; on Romania, 556; on salvation, 541–544
Stanton, Elizabeth Cady, 249, 250, 277, 278
Stanton, Henry, 249
state: American vs. Jacobin traditions of, 73–74; Barth on war and, 296–301; Bonhoeffer on, 335; common good and, 109–110; forms of government, *Pacem in terris* on, 107; ideal Catholic, 87–88; Kuyper on, 230–240; Leo XIII on, 14, 18–21, 89; Leo XIII's use of term, 29n37; limited state, Murray's reinterpretation of Leo

XIII's concept of, 88–89; Maritain on, 41–43; Maurin on, 167; Murray on, 91–92; Niebuhr on, 346–349; Orthodox concepts of, 557; pity and, 444, 445, 452; Pius XII on, 90; purpose of, 14; *Rerum novarum* on, 196; rights and duties of, 109. *See also* authority; church and state, relationship of; democracy; Marxism, communism, and socialism; separation of church and state
Steed, Bob, 165
Stethatos, Nicetas, 544
strikes. *See* labor and worker's rights
Stringfellow, William, 387–402; on advocacy, 389–390; on agapic love, 394; on Christian life, 391–392, 394–396; on consumerism, 399; on ecclesiology, 390; on ethics, 398; on the Fall, 394, 397; on grace and law, 391; on idolatry, 394; importance, xiv; on indoctrination to professions, 388; on justice vs. justification, 401–402; on law schools, 388–389; life and career, 387; on nuclear arms, 399; on penitence, 392; on principalities and powers, 392–393; on repentance, 392; on Revelation, 396–398; on sin and law, 391; on United States, 398–400; on vocation, 388
subsidiarity, principle of, 12–13, 72, 197
subways, New York City, 166, 173
suffering, 462
suffering of God, 327–328
suffrage. *See* Anthony, Susan B.
superdevelopment, 188–189

supernatural revelation: Stăniloae on, 539–541
Symeon the New Theologian, 487

teaching, Christian. *See* Christian teaching
teaching letters, Leo XIII's use of, 3–4
temperance movement, 251–256
temptation, 311–312
tension, nonviolent, 373–374, 378
theocracy, Soloviev on, 454n14
theology: Berdyaev on suffering of God, 464; Gutiérrez on meaning of term, 119–120; John Paul II's contrasting of theological faith with religious belief, 178; problem of, in Latin America, 141–142; Stringfellow on biblical, 397. *See also* liberation theology; morals, morality, and moral theology; trinitarian theology; *specific types and topics*
Theology and the Social Sciences (Gutiérrez), 138–140
A Theology of Liberation (Gutiérrez), 116, 118–133; revised edition, 118, 142–147
theosis, 455n25
Thomas Aquinas, St.: on Christ, rule of, 24–25; on eternal law, 50; on grace, 65; on human law, 30n43; King and, 376; on law, 50, 361; on law and morality, 206; Leo XIII on, 6–7; on *lex indita*, concept of, 27n3; on love and old law, 362; on natural law, 28n17, 50, 364; on private society, 13; on prudence, 31n60; revival of thought of (*See* neo-Thomism)
Tillich, Paul, 376

time, 378–379
Tobey, Barkeley, 150
Tolstoy, Leo, 473
Torrance, James B., 280
totalitarian regimes, 349, 377
Toynbee, Arnold, 81
trade unions. *See* labor and
  worker's rights
traditions, 500, 522–523
tragedy, 336, 420
tree of the knowledge of
  good and evil. *See* original sin
trinitarian theology,
  458–459. *See also* Lossky,
  Vladimir Nikolaievich
Trubetskoi, Evgeny, 426
Trueltsch, Ernst, 418
truth, 96, 404, 437

Unam sanctam (1302), 289
underdevelopment, 121–122,
  128
unemployed, 157–158
UNESCO, 35–36
unions. *See* labor and
  worker's rights
Unitatis redintegratio (1964),
  111–112
United States: King on
  blacks in history of,
  383–384; lack of biblical
  knowledge in, 396–397;
  Leo XIII's views on,
  23–24, 32*n*76; Murray
  on, 73–74; slavery and
  abolitionism in, 256–261
  (*See also* Anthony, Susan
  B.; slavery); Stringfellow
  on, 398–400. *See also*
  Constitution (U.S.)
Universal Declaration of Human Rights (1948), xii
unjust law, 375–377. *See also*
  civil disobedience
unjust war, 413–415. *See also*
  nonviolence; pacifism

U.S.S.R. *See* Russia/Soviet
  Union
utopianism, 408–409

Van Buren, Martin, 264
Vatican I. *See* First Vatican
  Council
Vatican II. *See* Second Vati-
  can Council
vengeance, 470–471
Vietnam War, 398–399
Villarmé, Louis René, 439
violence, 130–131, 268
Vishnewski, Stanley, 163
Vladimir of Kiev, 453*n*5
vocations, 337, 388
voting rights, 376

war: Barth on nuclear weap-
  ons, 301–303; Barth on
  the state and, 296–301;
  Lossky on war, 491–493;
  Skobtsova on, 530–531;
  Stăniloae on, 543; Yoder
  on, 413–415, 420. *See also*
  pacifism; Vietnam War;
  World War II
We Hold These Truths (Mur-
  ray), 68
wealthy nations, 99
Weizsäcker, Carl Friedrich
  von, 321
Weston, Dorothy, 161
"What is American Slavery?"
  (Anthony), 256–257
Whitehead, Alfred, 360
Wilhelm II (Kaiser), 280
will of God and man, 502
Williams, Roger, 83
Williams, Rowan D., 487,
  488
Windelband, Wilhelm, 456
Wojtyla, Karol, 175
Wojtyla, Karol Józef. *See*
  John Paul II (Pope)
The Woman's Bible, 277–278,
  279*n*8

women and women's rights,
  143, 169, 173. *See also*
  Anthony, Susan B.
work and workers. *See* labor
  and workers' rights
workers' rights. *See* labor
  and workers' rights
World War II: Bonhoeffer
  during, 307, xiii; Lossky's
  involvement in French
  resistance during, 491,
  493; Niebuhr on, 353;
  Skobtsova's activities during, 512–513
Wylie, Philip, 79–80

Yannaras, Christos, 488
Yoder, John Howard,
  403–422; Bible as used by,
  403; breadth of theological achievements of, 403;
  Christology, 415–419; on
  discipleship, 419–422;
  ecclesiology, 407–409;
  on eschatology, 417; on
  forms of ethical discourse,
  409–413; on hermeneutic
  community, 410–411; im-
  portance, xiv; on individualism vs. society, 418–419;
  life and career, 403; on
  love, 419; Mennonite tradition influencing thought
  of, 403; on metaphysical
  dualism, 413; on moral
  discernment, 408; on
  natural law and morality,
  404–407; on Niebuhr, 420;
  on pacifism and peace witness, 413–415; on politics
  and sectarianism, 418;
  rejection of Constantinianism, 413; on sacra-
  mentality of the church,
  408; on tragedy, 420; on
  truth, 404; on utopianism,
  408–409; on war, 420